June 2006

To

Brenda

With admiration & affection

from

Timothy

The God of Metaphysics

The God of Metaphysics

Being a Study of the Metaphysics and Religious Doctrines of Spinoza, Hegel, Kierkegaard, T. H. Green, Bernard Bosanquet, Josiah Royce, A. N. Whitehead, Charles Hartshorne, and Concluding with a Defence of Pantheistic Idealism

T. L. S. Sprigge

CLARENDON PRESS · OXFORD

OXFORD
UNIVERSITY PRESS

Great Clarendon Street, Oxford OX2 6DP

Oxford University Press is a department of the University of Oxford.
It furthers the University's objective of excellence in research, scholarship,
and education by publishing worldwide in

Oxford New York

Auckland Cape Town Dar es Salaam Hong Kong Karachi
Kuala Lumpur Madrid Melbourne Mexico City Nairobi
New Delhi Shanghai Taipei Toronto

With offices in

Argentina Austria Brazil Chile Czech Republic France Greece
Guatemala Hungary Italy Japan Poland Portugal Singapore
South Korea Switzerland Thailand Turkey Ukraine Vietnam

Oxford is a registered trade mark of Oxford University Press
in the UK and in certain other countries

Published in the United States
by Oxford University Press Inc., New York

British Library Cataloguing in Publication Data

Data available

Library of Congress Cataloging in Publication Data

Data available

Typeset by SPI Publisher Services, Pondicherry, India
Printed in Great Britain
on acid-free paper by
Biddles Ltd,
King's Lynn, Norfolk

ISBN 0–19–928304–4   978–0–19–928304–0
1 3 5 7 9 10 8 6 4 2

This book is dedicated to
St Mark's Unitarian Church, Edinburgh

Preface

In this book a number of metaphysical systems are examined in such detail as is practicable. There are probably only a few of my hoped for readers who are at home with each and all of them, and so most readers should learn something about a significant philosophical system not very familiar to them. However, the book is intended also as a contribution to the continuing debate about these thinkers among the *cognoscenti*.

What links these systems together is that each provides a case for a religious view of the world based on rational or would-be rational argument. That a seriously religious perspective on things can derive, or win important support, from metaphysics is denied by many thinkers—for example, by Blaise Pascal (criticizing especially René Descartes), by Søren Kierkegaard (criticizing especially Hegel and Hegelians), and by William James, John Macmurray, and others. According to such thinkers, a God whose existence is supposed to be demonstrated in a philosophical treatise is not the God of 'Abraham, Isaac and the Christians' or (so those not thinking exclusively from the point of view of Judaeo-Christianity may add) of any actual or possible living religious faith at all. In the light of this, the present book examines some of the metaphysical systems which their authors did think of as offering some kind of demonstration of (or at least a philosophical locus for) religious truth, whether Christian or otherwise. Thus it sets out to test the objections to what might be called 'metaphysical religion' by investigating the works, and even to a limited extent the lives, of some of those who may be thought to have advanced something of that sort (as well as probably the best critique of such efforts by Kierkegaard in his attack on 'Hegelian Christianity'). However, the investigation of the metaphysical systems is also for its own philosophical sake. I do not engage in the kind of lofty evaluation, as from a higher authority, of these metaphysical systems and the arguments in support of them, that, as I fear, some commentators do today. My more difficult aim has been to promote understanding of, and interest in, the systems and their relation to religious issues, and to criticize only for the sake of advancing this aim. My own views on metaphysics and religion are given in Chapter 9.

The reader should realize that I am aware that it may be thought cheek to investigate, and even propound, general views of reality and say little about how they relate to the scientific conceptions of today, which may be thought to be the most important clues we have as to the nature of things. This is a reasonable charge. From this point of view, I think that the ideal thinker on such general matters is someone scientifically well equipped but also aware of the way in which metaphysicians have grappled with these issues. Of all the thinkers studied here, Whitehead was the best equipped to do this, though Spinoza was well equipped in relation to the science of his day. Einstein's general theory of relativity would have appealed, I think, to Spinoza, while Whitehead's philosophy fits well, I believe, with quantum physics. More generally, one can only work at what one is capable of, and this is what I have done, believing that the product is not entirely worthless.

My main helpers in writing this book have been the philosophers themselves and some commentators. I have had some help, for which I am most grateful, with several chapters from John Llewelyn especially on Hegel; from Alastair Hannay on Kierkegaard; from William Sweet on Bosanquet; from John Clendenning on Royce; from John Cobb, Pierfrancesco Basile and Michel Weber on process thought and over the years from Leemon McHenry on process thought and much else. Most of these have not seen my text and are not to blame for it, but they have helped me much, either in discussion or in answers to my e-mail questions. I should also say how valuable it has been to be able to meet and talk with fellow idealists, or idealist scholars, from around the world in a series of conferences at Harris Manchester College, mostly organized by Bill Mander (himself a notable contributor to idealist philosophy), on current and historical idealist trends in philosophy. I am afraid that I am not a great reader of philosophical articles (as opposed to books) just as I avoid reading short stories. Neither of these forms allows one to immerse oneself in another's world, but acts only so as to jerk one out of one's own. So I apologize to all those who have written on the philosophers studied here in that medium for any apparent failure to take account of their work. I may well have read their articles, but they tend to float away from my conscious mind, though probably exerting some influence on my conscious thought. This is not the case (I think) with books. I am also grateful to all those with whom I have discussed philosophical and religious issues over the years, but it would be invidious to pick out any of them especially, with the exception of my late brother Robert, from whom I have learnt so much on philosophical and religious matters. I am also deeply appreciative for all the help of very various kinds which I have had from my wife, Giglia.

There is a separate bibliography for each chapter which gives abbreviations in square brackets for books used in the text. These abbreviations are in small capitals. Sometimes when an author's name does not appear in the text, it is used for the reference. Some repetition across chapters should make them independently intelligible.

T. L. S. SPRIGGE

Acknowledgements

Quotations from Spinoza, Complete Works, with translations by Samuel Shirley (Indianapolis: Hackett Publishing Company, 2002), appear here by kind permission of Hackett Publishing Company, Inc.

Quotations from Spinoza, *Tractatus Theologico-Politicus*, translated by Samuel Shirley (Leiden: E. J. Brill, 1991), appear here by kind permission of E. J. Brill.

Quotations from G. F. W. Hegel, *Early Theological Writings*, translated by T. M. Knox (Philadelphia: University of Pennsylvania Press, 1948), appear by kind permission of the University of Pennsylvania Press.

Quotations from Søren Kierkegaard, *Concluding Unscientific Postscript to Philosophical Fragments*, translated by H. V. Hong and E. H. Hong. © 1992 Princeton University Press. Reprinted by permission of Princeton University Press.

Quotations from Charles Hartshorne, *Creative Synthesis and Philosophic Method* (London: SCM Press Ltd, 1970), appear here by kind permission of SCM Press, Canterbury.

I am extremely grateful to OUP for accepting this book, and to the two anonymous readers for some good advice.

Summary Contents

Detailed Contents

Chapter 1

Introductory

I Metaphysical Religion and its Critics

The philosophers discussed in this book (apart from Kierkegaard) each thought that they could establish, by metaphysical argument, the existence and something of the character of an (in some sense) *infinite* individual, suitably called either 'God' or 'the Absolute' or both, and whom or which they thought a suitable focus for some kind of religious emotion. Such an attempt to support a religious view of the world on the basis of metaphysical arguments has been much criticized by such thinkers as Pascal, Søren Kierkegaard, William James, John Macmurray, and others. The main purpose of this book is to consider how far the work of certain thinkers who produced metaphysical systems in which God or the Absolute figures fall foul of this criticism. However, it is not so much the relation of their metaphysics to *Christianity* (even though that was the main concern of the critics mentioned, James excepted) which is my concern as their relation to any form of *religious belief*.[1]

It was Pascal who most notoriously criticized the God of the philosophers for his (or its?) irrelevance to religion. He was thinking primarily of Descartes and said:

The God of Christians does not consist of a God who is simply the author of mathematical truths and the order of the elements: that is the job of the pagans and Epicureans. He does not consist simply of a God who exerts his providence over the lives and property of people in order to grant a happy span of years to those who worship him: that is the allocation of the Jews. But the God of Abraham, the God of Isaac, the God of Jacob, the God of the Christians is a God of love and consolation; he is a God who fills the souls and hearts of those he possesses; he is a God who makes them inwardly aware of their wretchedness and his infinite mercy, who unites with them in the depths of their soul, who makes them incapable of any other end but himself. (PENSÉES, 172)

Around two centuries later, Søren Kierkegaard similarly contrasted the God of Christian faith with the God of the philosophers: in particular, that of Hegel and some of his Danish followers. The latter at best provides a solution to a purely abstract problem, whereas the former is discovered as the only adequate resolution of the problems of personal life.

William James was another who thought that philosophical (and theological) argument could not be the origin of any significant religious belief. At best it could provide some logical clarification of knowledge or belief gained from religious experience.

All these intellectual operations [of theology and philosophy] presuppose immediate [religious] experience as their subject matter. They are interpretative and inductive operations, operations after the fact, consequent upon religious feeling, not coordinate with it, not independent of what it ascertains.

The intellectualism in religion which I wish to discredit pretends to be something altogether different from this. It assumes to construct religious objects out of the resources of logical reason alone, or of logical reason drawing rigorous inference from non-subjective facts. It calls its conclusions dogmatic theology, or philosophy of the absolute, as the case may be. (VRE, 433)

But its conclusions are largely meaningless except as edifying verbiage. John Macmurray explained Kierkegaard's position well, as follows:

The Danish eccentric, Kierkegaard, discovered that the Hegelian philosophy was ludicrously incapable of solving—even, indeed, of formulating, the problem of 'the existing individual'. If we apply the Hegelian logic to the data of personal reality, we produce, he showed, 'a dialectic without a synthesis'; for the process of the personal life generates a tension of opposites which can be resolved, not by reconciliation but only by a choice between them, and for this choice no rational ground can be discovered. He concluded that we must abandon philosophy for religion. (THE SELF, 36)

And on his own account Macmurray insisted that a God whose existence is supposed to be proved by reasoning has little real religious significance. Thus he maintained that

the traditional proofs [of God's existence], even if they were logically unassailable, could only conclude to some infinite or absolute being which lacks any quality deserving of reverence or worship. The God of the traditional proofs is not the God of religion.

Particular targets of such criticism have been certain post-Hegelian absolute idealists who claimed to have arrived rationally at the existence of the Absolute, which many of them identified with God. Such a supposed reality contrasts sadly, it is said, with the living God of Judaeo-Christianity.

Edward Caird, for example, in his *The Evolution of Religion*, where he described God as 'a principle of unity in the whole, akin to that which gives unity to our own existence as self-conscious beings' (EVOLUTION, 33) is said to have made religious faith into a matter of mere intellectual assent to a philosophical theory.

More seriously objectionable still is said to be 'Caird's tendency to leave out of his primary definitions of God everything that makes God lovable, adorable, worthy of being worshipped.' (SELL, 114–15)[2]

As against such objections this book will take up the cudgels on behalf of the God of some philosophers who elaborated metaphysical systems in which what they called either 'God' or 'the Absolute' played an intellectually essential role. I shall consider their reasons for claiming that God or the Absolute exists and possesses certain attributes, and then consider whether the existence of such a Being is, or would be, of any relevance to the theism which is central to most of the world religions, and, if not, whether it would be religiously significant in some other way. It is not to be expected that the answer will be the same with each philosopher; but in some cases, at least, I shall claim, not only that the reasonings of the philosophers deserve to be taken seriously, but that the God or Absolute whose existence they purport to establish is, or would be, a Being who mattered religiously (though not necessarily in the Judaeo-Christian or Muslim way).

Whether the God of one philosopher is the same individual as the God of some other philosopher, or of some theology, or some sacred book or other form of revelation, is a tricky question for the theory of identity. If God does not exist in any relevant sense, then the question whether it is the same not really existing God who is postulated by various different thinkers or a different God is like the question as to whether Poseidon was really the same person as Neptune, which, since neither of these expressions names a real individual, can only concern the likeness of two concepts (a Greek and a Roman one), which will be a matter of degree. But if there is a single, genuine God, the question should have a precise answer.

One aspect of Pascal's critique of the God of the philosophers, is that the philosophers, by the very fact of putting forward such a demonstration, show themselves quite alienated from the proper Christian recognition of the feebleness of human reasoning.

We desire truth, but find in ourselves nothing but uncertainty. We seek happiness, but find only wretchedness and death. We are incapable of not desiring truth and happiness and incapable of either certainty or happiness. We have been left with this desire as much as a punishment as to make us feel how far we have fallen. (PENSÉES, 199)

And Pascal himself sees our desire for certainty and happiness as showing that the human race has fallen from a perfection it still longs for but lacks.[3]

We shall see that our metaphysicians, especially Spinoza and Hegel, are as opposed to this point of view as could be. Each thinks he can rationally establish his view of things as an absolute certainty. Moreover, while claiming to be theists (or at least believers in the Absolute) and some of them even Christians, they object to the kind of theistic ethic, represented by Pascal and Kierkegaard, according to which men must foreswear all hope of happiness in this world as a quite unjustified pessimistic block on human development.

II Descartes

The philosopher whom Pascal was particularly objecting to was Descartes. For Descartes offers a (supposed) proof, or rather proofs, of God's existence in the course of finding a solution to the problem of scepticism and for the source of mathematical and scientific truth. Not that there is any reason to doubt (though it has been doubted) that Descartes seriously believed in God and was a genuine Christian. But for Pascal this was not a proper context in which to argue for God's existence; in fact, it was hardly proper to argue for God's existence at all.

Let us briefly consider what Descartes's arguments were for God's existence. A brief summary of what is most relevant for our purposes in his *Meditations* should suffice for our purposes.

1. I currently think of myself as knowing many things without any adequate investigation of whether I have good reason to believe them.

2. I shall temporarily discard all beliefs which are open to any possible doubt and not re-adopt them as cases of knowledge until I find good reason so to do.

3. I therefore temporarily discard all my beliefs about the existence and character of a real physical world in which I exist as a conscious being. For I can conceive the possibility that it is all an illusion.

4. However, I cannot discard my belief in my own existence as a conscious individual mind with certain thoughts. The very fact that I am doubting so much proves that I exist as a thinking being who has certain ideas (whether these ideas are true or not).

5. Among the ideas which I find within myself is the idea of a perfect being (which I call 'God') who created whatever exists, including myself (and apart from God himself, who exists necessarily).

6. But the idea of this perfect being, which I find in my mind, could not have been caused by anything other than an actually existing perfect being. Nothing else could have caused such a magnificent idea.

7. So God exists. What is more, there is an additional reason for believing in his existence: namely, that just as I cannot separate the idea of a valley from that of a mountain, so I cannot separate the idea of this perfect being from the idea of his actually and necessarily existing.

8. But, granted that God exists, he would not have given me the power to think if I could not use it to discover various truths about the world. If I make mistakes, it must be my own fault, because I have not thought hard enough, thereby misusing my free will.

9. Therefore I can trust my senses and my intellect whenever it would be my own fault if they mislead me. So my belief that I have certain sense experiences caused by a real physical world such as they seem to portray must be true.

10. But I am not merely returning to my starting-point, for my practice of methodical doubt has revealed two things.
    (a) The absolute certainty of God's existence.
    (b) That my mind is a distinct reality or substance from my body. For when I was doubting all I could, I could not doubt my existence as a thinking mind. But if I can doubt the existence of my body and not doubt the existence of my mind, they must be quite distinct things.

11. I know that other people are conscious, because the thoughts expressed in their speech can only be explained as coming from a genuinely conscious mind. But I have no reason to believe that animals are conscious, since their behaviour is in principle explicable mechanically. This is shown by the fact that they cannot speak.

There are of course other philosophical arguments for God's existence, besides those to which Descartes appealed, and the ones which I find most interesting were developed after his time. Particularly interesting in relation to the claim, common to Pascal, Kierkegaard, William James, and John Macmurray, that a God whose existence is supposed to be proved philosophically must be religiously irrelevant are those promoted by independent metaphysicians rather than by religious apologists. At any rate, it is the purpose of this book to investigate several metaphysical systems in which the existence of God, or something pretty like him, emerges as an essential part of the general account of reality which they present, and to ask whether such a God is 'religiously available'.[4]

Pascal and Kierkegaard were of course concerned with the relevance of a philosopher's God to the God of Christianity as they conceived him. However, my enquiry will be broader than that, inasmuch as I shall be asking whether the God of each metaphysical system is religiously relevant at all, whether in a Christian context or otherwise.

The metaphysicians whom I shall study most thoroughly in relation to this question are Spinoza, Hegel, T. H. Green, Bernard Bosanquet, Josiah Royce, Whitehead, and Hartshorne. After the chapter on Hegel there is a chapter examining Kierkegaard's critique of the Hegelian approach to religion.

Although I am not considering any thinkers before the seventeenth century, it would certainly be important in a more thorough survey to include discussion of some earlier thinkers, more especially Plato and the Stoics. But there are several reasons for not going earlier than Spinoza—a sufficient one is that I doubt that I have much of interest to say about any previous thinkers, and that if I wrote on them, it would be only as a copyist of the work of other commentators. As for the great theologians of the Middle Ages, I must emphasize that my interest is in thinkers who cannot be described as Christian apologists, or indeed as apologists on behalf of any standard religion.

My exposition and discussion of the work of my chosen metaphysicians, I might add, does not confine itself to their explicit dealing with religious issues. I shall consider their systems in the round, both because this is worth doing in itself and because it is the religious implications of their systems as a whole which are in question, not isolated claims about God. In fact, so far as can be done in single but long chapters I aim to provide a commentary on these metaphysical systems which should be of interest to anyone concerned with metaphysical issues, whether for the implications for religion or otherwise.

III The Meaning of 'God' and the Idea of the Absolute

But what does the word 'God' mean? The traditional Judaeo-Christian and, I think, Muslim idea of God is as the uniquely almighty, all-good, and all-knowing creator of the universe. But I shall take the expression more broadly than that.

Roughly put, I shall regard as 'God' anything which a metaphysician in a not unreasonable way refers to by this word. But I shall also allow the expression for something which (even if they do not call it 'God') plays a role in their thought, feeling, and life significantly akin to what God does for others.

A word is in order here as to the relation between the word 'God' and the expression 'the Absolute' (Bernard Bosanquet and Josiah Royce) and 'the Eternal Consciousness' (T. H. Green) on the part of the three Anglo-American absolute idealists to whom chapters are devoted. I reserve my comments on Hegel himself till my chapter on him.

For Green *the Eternal Consciousness* was properly called 'God', though clearly his conception of God differs from that of standard Christianity. The basic difference is that each of us is in some sense identical with God, or the Eternal Consciousness; that is, *the Eternal Consciousness* is somehow operating through us in all that we do. Royce likewise identifies God and the Absolute. But for him we are each *part of God* in a sense which Christian orthodoxy would deny. Still, in the case of both Green and Royce, their God is expected to play a part in our religious life not very different from that which he plays in Christian orthodoxy.

The case of Bosanquet is somewhat different. For him, as for F. H. Bradley, it is inappropriate to call the Absolute 'God', and they may well be right in this. Bosanquet in fact seldom speaks of anything which he calls 'God'. So far as he has a use for the word at all, it is to refer to the main forces of good acting within the Absolute, rather than the Absolute itself, the latter being more the scene for the struggle between good and evil than good itself. None the less, it is the Absolute which plays the role in his thought and feeling most similar to that of God for others. For it is the perfection ascribed to the Absolute which is foundational to his sense that in the last resort all is well with the world. He did, indeed, once say that neither Bradley nor he thought of worshipping the Absolute; but it is clear that he thinks it an eternal reality whose perfection gives point to the world. So I think it appropriate to consider each of these absolute idealists as presenting something suitably called a philosophical version of theism, and therefore as each a target for all those who think that a 'philosophical God' is bound, whatever is claimed for such, to be in the end a religious dead end.

We might be more precise if we accepted the following use of the expression 'God'[5] and say that something is appropriately called 'God' if and only if he, she, or it (a) satisfies (or is believed to satisfy) at least one of the fourteen conditions below (understood in some not too far-fetched sense) and (b) satisfies more of them than does anything else:

1. is creator of the universe (the totality of everything not himself, herself, or itself);
2. is uniquely all-knowing;
3. is uniquely all-experiencing (that is, feels the experiences of all beings);
4. is either uniquely real or real to a degree which nothing else is;
5. exists with a unique kind of necessity;
6. is omni-present;
7. is the explanation for the existence of everything else;
8. is uniquely all-powerful;
9. is morally perfect to a degree which nothing else is;
10. is uniquely perfect in some possibly non-moral sense;
11. is the one proper object of worship;
12. is the one proper object towards which certain specifically religious emotions should be felt;
13. is the one thing through appropriate relation to which a human being can be 'saved';
14. is an all-knowing and, so far as he or she wants to be, all-controlling person.

I suggest that Green's eternal consciousness answers at least to (2)–(4), (11), (12), and perhaps (13); that Bosanquet's Absolute answers at least to conditions (2)–(7), and perhaps (12); and that Royce's God answers to at least (2)–(4), (7)–(10), and perhaps to (11) and (12). Moreover, for each philosopher there is nothing which satisfies more of them.

I ask the reader at this point to note that henceforth in this book pronouns referring back to 'God' will mostly be grammatically masculine. Most of the philosophers discussed in the book think of God neither as father-like nor as mother-like, but 'he or she' might suggest that God was both, and 'it' could be misleading in another way (while 'she' alone looks as though a point is being made). I shall also occasionally capitalize 'He' with reference to God, partly for clarity. Incidentally, in speaking of an indefinite person, I shall use 'he' rather than 'he or she' in order not to make my prose more tortuous than it has to be, while alternative uses of 'he' and 'she' would be unhelpfully distracting in a book of this kind.

IV What Religion Is and what it may Do for Us

One way of asking how far these metaphysical systems ground a genuinely religious outlook is to consider what it is that religion, or religion at its best, is said to have done for people. One can then consider whether these metaphysical systems have this value. There are, of course, two distinct questions: (1) Do they lend support to any kind of genuinely religious outlook at all? (2) Do they lend support to any form of Christianity, this being the religion to which Pascal and Kierkegaard thought that they were irrelevant? However, both these questions concern me in this study, though more the first, than the second.

Perhaps I should start by offering a definition of religion. As is often pointed out, a religion need not be theistic in character, since no one denies that Buddhism is a religion. John Stuart Mill, among others, has argued that a religion of humanity for which 'a sense of unity with mankind and a deep feeling for the general good, may be cultivated into a sentiment and a principle capable of fulfilling every important function of religion and [is] justly entitled to the name' (MILL, 110 ff.).

Taking all such things into account, I suggest initially that religion is best understood as 'a truth to live by' typically satisfying the following conditions. (In this phrase 'truth' means 'something believed to be a truth'.) This may be made more precise by saying that a religion properly so called must meet the following four conditions. It must be:

1. A belief system, held to be true by its adherents, which affects the whole way in which those who seriously believe in it live their lives.

2. A belief system intrinsically associated with emotions which can be called 'religious'. (It is hard to say precisely which emotions count as such. However, they must be in some way 'cosmic': that is, directed at the nature of things in general, envisaged somehow as forming a spiritual whole not exhaustively describable in terms of purely empirical or scientific terms.)

3. A system of moral precepts which the belief system and the cosmic emotion encourage and help people to live by.

4. Furthermore, a life suffused by these beliefs, emotions, and moral precepts must offer some kind of salvation, whether this be expressed secularly as happiness of an enduring kind, or as some general sense of well-being—or some reward in terms of happiness in the life to come. More generally, it offers a way of being saved from something bad, whether this be despair or sin or whatever.

This list of conditions for what a religion is will seem inadequate to some who belong to an organized religion.

5. Some would hold that a religion must, in addition to the foregoing, be held in common by a larger or smaller number of people, normally with

some ceremonies expressive of their beliefs and feelings, or even for its supposed supernatural effects. In short, some people think that the only real religions are community religions.

In the light of this I suggest that we call an outlook and practice a community religion only if it meets conditions (1)–(5), while we call a religion personal if it meets only the first four. Outlooks which arise from, or are closely associated with, a metaphysical system are likely to be personal religions. However, something may be called a personal religion if it operates as a special form or, as one might put it, a personal interpretation of a community religion with no independent community aspect of its own.

Thus there have been followers of Whitehead and Hartshorne who felt at home with Methodism, while conceiving God and other religious realities in terms of process philosophy. Bosanquet and Hartshorne each had some association with Unitarianism, as do I myself. Thus a religious outlook especially associated with process philosophy (the philosophy of Whitehead and Hartshorne and their followers) might be called a personal form of Christianity, or some denomination thereof. Moreover, perhaps each of the metaphysical systems could enter into some kind of synthesis with commitment to a particular faith community, more especially a Christian church. But our concern here is primarily with the religious implications of these metaphysical systems as possible personal religions, as they stand. A personal religion may of course have many adherents, but inasmuch as it has no organizational aspect, it counts as a personal religion. (Spinozism, I shall claim, is a personal religion for an unknown number of persons.)

To this I add a sixth condition which must be satisfied by a religion, community or personal, if it is to be a good one.

6. A religion is a *good* religion if and only if it promotes ethically desirable behaviour. This does not require that the belief system be true. (So far as sheer logic goes, it could be true but bad, though whether a bad religion could really be true, I doubt.)

Thus a religion can be a good one without the belief system being true. And there is nothing inconsistent in an adherent to a religion thinking that other religions are less true, contain less of the truth than the adherent's religion, and may yet be good religions. This point is the essential basis for religious tolerance. Everyone has a right to their own religion, and can exercise that right provided there is some belief system of the relevant kind which they believe to be true. We should never judge adversely someone whose belief system we think false. However, we are entitled to object to a religion which promotes bad behaviour. Society must do something to protect itself against the ill effects of such a religion.

Turning to the question of whether the God postulated in some metaphysical system is religiously relevant or not, we may now take this as the question of whether belief in this God could be an essential ingredient of a religion in the sense just indicated.

More generally, it is worth mentioning that some of the things which religion is thought to do for people are as follows:

1. provide an eternal object of love, which also provides a kind of ultimate safety;
2. give the encouraging news that ultimately the good is more powerful than the bad or evil;
3. provide a degree of comfort when the world looks bleak;
4. rid us of the sense of cosmic loneliness, which some feel;
5. promise (or threaten) a life after death, and perhaps reunion with one's loved ones;
6. promote ethically desirable behaviour, giving it a stronger motivation than a moral outlook abstracted from any system of beliefs about the world can do;
7. make moral demands upon us, not all of which are easy;
8. give practical guidance as to how to behave.

V Worship and Prayer

Worship and prayer are likely to be the things which a Pascal or a Kierkegaard finds most lacking in a religion based on metaphysics.

As a public act, prayer can hold as an element only in a community religion. But could a belief in God based upon metaphysical reasoning promote private prayer? If it means a period of fresh commitment to one's highest ideals, with the aid of feelings directed at God, however conceived, I see no reason why it should not be practised by someone whose personal religion derived much of its force for him from metaphysics. If it is petitionary prayer, asking for certain things to happen not within the individual's power in any ordinary way, I suspect that it would be rejected by the philosophical religionist as inappropriate. But if it was a similar commitment to one's own self-improvement, it might well be recommended and practised. It is also worth remembering the saying: 'Prayer changes people and people change things.'

Worship, again, is most naturally thought of as a public act on the part of a community. The whole concept of worship has been associated with the idea of God requiring it of us. It seems to many of us that a God who longs to be praised is not a very ethically compelling one. But if it is a way of opening oneself to a sense of the glory of God, however conceived, that is rather different.

VI The Religious Relevance of a Metaphysical God

So I now turn to our metaphysicians to decide, in the light of the three numbered lists above, how far the God they postulate is religiously relevant, and, more generally, whether their philosophy can play the part of a religion for one who adopts it. However, I have found it impractical to apply these conditions one by one to each philosopher, so they will just lie in the background. Anyone who wishes may of course test my claims in relation to each philosopher by using these three lists. I shall also try to say a little as to how far these philosophers seem to have lived lives genuinely inspired by their philosophy, apart, that is, from in philosophical writing and discussion.

I should perhaps say here that I do not intend to offer a discussion of the standard arguments for God's existence. The main traditional ones are:

1. The First Mover argument. Things cannot move unless set in motion. Therefore, there must have been something which set them in motion without itself needing to be set in motion. And this is what we call God.
2. The First Cause argument. There must be a first cause of anything occurring or existing at all. And this we call God.
3. The Cosmological Argument. The ordinary natural world being something which might not have existed, but which does exist, must have been brought into existence by something that did not need to be brought into existence because it eternally existed of necessity. And this we call God.
4. The Perfection Argument. Things are of various degrees of perfection. But there must be something which sets the standard for degrees of perfection, and this being must be perfect. And this we call God.
5. The Teleological Argument. Many or all things in the world have a purpose or function. Therefore they must have been made by something which made them for that purpose. And this we call God.

These are the five proofs of God's existence promoted by St Thomas Aquinas (somewhat adapted), none of which has enjoyed a very good press in recent times, though all except the first still have defenders.

It was a version of the fifth argument, commonly called the Argument from Design which for a long time held the field as the most persuasive. It seemed so obvious that an enormous number of things are there for a purpose, most obviously the various organs of human and animal bodies, which seem to be there to perform some specific function. Unless there is a designer, it is difficult to see how they could be so precisely suited for this purpose. And the only possible designer seems to be a rational being who created the world, in short, God.

This argument as it used to be mainly understood (most famously by William Paley) suffers from Darwin's evolutionary explanation of design in living nature as occurring through natural selection, almost universally accepted in the educated world (though not by American Christian fundamentalists).[6] However, there are versions of it in the form of the 'anthropic principle' that the universe appears to have been geared, from the Big Bang on, as eventually propitious for the emergence of life, even intelligent life. (See, for example, BARROW AND TIPLER.) Important as this issue is, I shall not concern myself with it here.

To these six arguments must be added the 'Ontological Argument' first formulated by St Anselm (1033–1109), archbishop of Canterbury, and less effectively advanced again by Descartes among others. According to this argument (which Aquinas rejected), an adequate understanding of the meaning of the word 'God' (or equivalent expression), as the serious believer in God uses it, is enough to show that God must necessarily exist. Otherwise put, the proposition that God does not exist is self-contradictory. There are a number of variants upon this argument. When first heard, it is liable to sound ridiculous, but properly reflected on, it is arguably the most forceful. This argument will be examined quite thoroughly in the chapters on Spinoza and on Whitehead and Hartshorne.

Finally, there is what I myself think the best argument: namely, the idealist argument (or rather a set of slightly different idealist arguments). These turn on the claim that the idea of anything existing without being experienced, however obviously *coherent* and even *true* it seems at first sight, is, in fact, evidently *false*. The only satisfactory way of explaining why things evidently do exist even when *not experienced by any finite being* is to postulate an *infinite being who experiences them*, and granted that it experiences what we finite beings do not, it is reasonable to infer that it also experiences what we do experience. This infinite being is God.

13

This argument is put forward only vaguely here, as a gesture in the relevant direction. It certainly is not a complete argument as it stands (even apart from the fact that a good deal of effort must be expended to support the claim that nothing exists unexperienced). But some argument of this sort will figure largely in our discussion of Green, Bosanquet, and Royce, and to some extent of Whitehead and Hartshorne, and then finally in my own positive position. Spinoza's case is somewhat different.

The main argument *against* the existence of God is that there is so much evil which God, conceived of as both omnipotent and all-good, would have prevented if he existed, from which it follows that he does not exist. This will receive a good deal of discussion in what follows.

It seems to me that the position of each of the metaphysicians discussed in this book (not Kierkegaard, whom I do not count as a metaphysician) is capable of providing an individual, who thinks it largely true, with a personal religion which may further serve him, if such is his wish or need, as a personal interpretation of some liberal form of community religion. However, it has seemed rather unnecessarily laborious explicitly to check out how the God or Absolute of each philosopher (and the general tone of their metaphysics) relates to the criteria set out here. But it should be clear enough how they do, at least on my account of them.

VII Texts

Most of the philosophers studied here wrote in English. However, three of them did not: Spinoza wrote in Latin, Hegel in German, and Kierkegaard in Danish. In the case of Spinoza's Latin I know enough of the language to take some account of his original text, but I have mostly relied on English translations. As regards Hegel, I do know some German, but I would not trust myself to be sure of understanding him in his own language, so here again I have mostly relied on translations; I have also made substantial use of commentaries (in English) on his so deeply problematic work, as is not true with the other thinkers studied here, though of course I have not ignored what others have said about them. As regards Kierkegaard, I know no Danish at all, so my study of him is based entirely on translations, with an occasional question to an expert. Since that is my own basis, I have included only English-language books in my bibliography.

Some of those with appropriate skills (or perhaps some Germans or Danes) will approach my work with the thought that Hegel and Kierke-gaard, can never be understood by reading them only in English. To this I say that reading them in the original would certainly be better. But we all approach philosophical writings with different skills, and I hope that I have sufficient philosophical skills to compensate somewhat. I have even received some praise for my clarification of the work of some philosophers whom I approached almost wholly through translations.

On another point I should remark that in the case of each of these philosophers, more especially Hegel and Kierkegaard, there are experts whose main intellectual avocation has been the study of their work. But unless books which study a number of disparate philosophers are not to be written, the author (a few authors of outstanding learning excepted) of such a book is bound to be less expert on many of them than are those who specialize in understanding them. I can claim, at any rate, that my study of each of these thinkers has been quite long and earnest, and it is my hope that I have something worth saying about them. I hope too that most readers will actually learn something about the thinkers in the book about whom they know least. For they are all worth knowing about.

So in spite of the main purpose of this book, which is to insist on the religious relevance of many metaphysical systems, I hope that it may for some people be useful simply as a way of learning something new about thinkers on whose work they do not claim to be experts. There must be many, for example, who, while knowing the work of Hegel well, are not too familiar with the philosophers sometimes called the English or Anglo-American Hegelians.

I can say, at any rate, that for the most part I am stressing aspects of the thinkers which tend to be neglected today. This comes partly from the fact that many commentators of recent times attempt to make them more respectable (in their eyes and by their criteria) than they really are, and that my own views, currently (but I am confident not for ever) thought rather weird, may make me more willing to allow that these philosophers really meant what they said, not some sanitized version of it.

VIII Good and Bad Religion

In his book *Religion in the Making* A. N. Whitehead remarks that in seeking to understand the phenomenon of religion, we should do so without presupposing that religion is always a good thing. For him, as for me, some forms of religion are good, others bad. We are especially aware of this in the opening of the twenty-first century, when the most terrible deeds and irrational restrictions, and unwise responses thereto, are made in the name of religion, usually from what is called a fundamentalist perspective of extreme intolerance. Without wishing to play down the horrific forms which religion can take, I shall be concerned with more beneficent forms of religion.

So I now begin my investigation of our metaphysicians with Spinoza.

Notes

1. That most of the thinkers studied are idealists is not just a matter of my own interests. For it is difficult to think of any important metaphysician since the seventeenth century who elaborates a metaphysic with religious implications who was not an idealist, the exceptions being Spinoza and Whitehead (and these are only partial exceptions). Those with the best claim to be doing this today are too much Christian apologists for my purposes (the two Canadian philosophers Leslie Armour and John Leslie are the exceptions, and I have learnt quite a bit from their writings). Incidentally, I have not discussed Leibniz, because his religious outlook is much less of an option for us today, as I see it, than are the positions of the thinkers examined here.
2. On the matter of worship, Bosanquet said in a letter to C. C. J. Webb with reference to Bradley and himself, 'we do not think it possible to worship the Absolute. What is worshipped, at once must become less than the whole' (SELL, 119). But other absolute idealists, such as C. C. J. Webb and Henry Jones, held that the Absolute was God, and appropriately worshipped (ibid. 119). See also ibid. 123 and *passim* for other thinkers who have protested against any attempt to assimilate the God of religion to the Absolute of absolute idealists.
3. That we are thus fallen is not, however, something which can be proved, and can be known only by revelation to those who accept this by faith. Still, once possessed of this belief, one can recognize this human limitation as the product of the original fall of man (in the persons of Adam and Eve). (This remark is indebted to Susan James, PASSIONS, 238–9.)
4. I borrow this fine expression from *The Religious Availability of Whitehead's God*, by S. E. Ely.
5. This is taken from my article 'Pantheism', *The Monist*, 80/2 (April 1997), 191–217.
6. For an important critique of it, see DAWKINS.

Chapter 2

The God of Spinoza

PART ONE: LIFE OF THE PHILOSOPHER

Spinoza (1632–77) held the following view on the importance or otherwise of knowing something about the author of a work in order to understand and evaluate it. In the case of matters of a historical kind, it was important to know something about him and his cultural background. In the case of a work dealing with non-historical necessary truths, however, it was not. Thus, in order to grasp the work of Herodotus or the authors of the various books of the Bible, one needs to know something about them and their times. In the case of Euclid, such things are quite irrelevant.

Spinoza evidently thought that his great work, the *Ethics*, was of the latter kind. But we are free to doubt his opinion on this, and, in fact, it is difficult to come to grips with it adequately without knowing something about Spinoza himself and his background. Indeed, this is more true of Spinoza than of most of the other thinkers studied in this work. So I shall begin this chapter with a sketch of his life and background.

Baruch, (later Benedictus) Spinoza was born in 1632 in Amsterdam. Both his parents were Marrano immigrants from Portugal, who, like many others, had fled the increasing persecution of Jews there. (Marranos were Spanish or Portuguese Jews who had been forcibly converted to Roman Catholic Christianity, but many of whom practised Judaism secretly. If they were discovered, there would be dire consequences.)

Spinoza's father, Michael Spinoza, or d'Espinoza, born about 1600, emigrated to Amsterdam at some time before 1620, when he married his first wife there. After her death, he married his second wife, Hannah Deborah, probably also a Marrano, who died in 1638, when their first-born son, the philosopher, was 6. Michael Spinoza had established himself as a successful merchant and respected member of the Jewish community.

Spinoza was given a good education in Hebrew and in the Scriptures and Jewish learning. Indeed, he became a considerable Hebrew scholar; one of his last works was a Hebrew grammar.

Our philosopher's mother tongue must have been Portuguese, the language of the Marranos from Portugal. Presumably he later spoke Dutch for his ordinary affairs and with his Dutch friends, while in adulthood he spoke Latin to the various distinguished scholars from other countries who visited him on occasion; certainly all his philosophical works and most of his correspondence were written in Latin.[1]

Among those under whom he studied were Saul Morteira, the senior rabbi of Amsterdam, who later presided over the court of rabbis that excommunicated him from the synagogue. Morteira is reported to have marvelled at the 15-year-old Spinoza's 'intelligence and predicted a great future for him'. A more important influence among his teachers was Rabbi Manasseh ben Israel, rabbi of the second Amsterdam synagogue and a teacher at the Jewish school. He was the author of numerous philosophical and theological works, and a man of wide culture who may inadvertently have encouraged Spinoza to read outside Jewish literature, in books which sewed the seeds of his heterodoxy. (When Spinoza was excommunicated, ben Israel was away negotiating with Oliver Cromwell for the readmission of Jews to England. It has been suggested that, if he had been present, he might have influenced the court towards a happier outcome.) Spinoza also studied Latin with Frances van Ende, an ex-Jesuit physician, who had a stormy life and was eventually executed in Paris for involvement in a plot against Louis XIV. He probably played a more provocative part in alienating Spinoza from Jewish orthodoxy. It may be that Spinoza first encountered the Cartesian philosophy, by which he was so much influenced, through van Ende.

Spinoza's father died when he, the philosopher, was 22. For a shortish time thereafter, Spinoza and his brother Gabriel ran the family fruit import and export business together. Meanwhile he continued as a respectable member of the synagogue, paying his dues properly. However, it became known that he had expressed highly heretical views, and on 27 July, 1656, when he was 24 (after his failure to comply with a request for public repentance), he was formally cursed and excommunicated from the synagogue. The excommunication, or *cherem*, includes the following words: 'By the decree of the Angels and the word of the Saints we ban, cut off, curse and anathematize Baruch d'Espinoza ... We warn that none may contact him orally or in writing, nor do him any favour, nor stay under the same roof with him, nor read any paper he wrote.' Spinoza wrote a defence of his views, which has not survived, though it doubtless included anticipations of those famous doctrines which soon reached a fairly stable form in his mind.

There have been periodic attempts in modern times to have the ban posthumously lifted. In the 1950s David Ben-Gurion, for one, campaigned for this. This has not yet happened, but in 1953 there was a formal judgement by the Chief Rabbi of Israel, Yizhak Herzog, that the prohibition on reading Spinoza's books should be deemed only to have held during his lifetime, and was thus no longer in force.

What were the heretical opinions of Spinoza which led to the ban? They may have included the denial of the immortality of the human soul and the identification of God with Nature. The second is certainly a main feature of Spinoza's mature philosophy, while the first was not, though the precise nature of the human immortality, or rather eternity, which he definitely postulated, is somewhat problematic.

There is much controversy among scholars as to the circumstances which led up to the excommunication, or *cherem*.[2] Why was such strong action taken against him? One view is that the Jewish community needed to show the Christian authorities that they shared the same basic form of theism, and were as down on scepticism as they were. Another view is that so many of the Jews in Amsterdam were Marrano immigrants that the rabbis had difficulty in maintaining a cohesive Jewish practice, since all sorts of irregularities had grown up when Judaism could only be practised in secret.

It is significant, at any rate, that there were several other such excommunications during this period. The most famous case occurred in 1640, when Spinoza was 8. Uriel da Costa had been a (perhaps genuine) Marrano convert to Catholicism in Spain; indeed, he had even been a church treasurer. However, he turned against Catholicism, and believed that he could find the word of God in its original purity in the Hebrew scriptures, returning thus to Judaism. This inspired him to leave Portugal for Amsterdam, where he could practise his ancestral faith. However, he was very dissatisfied with the Judaism he found there, believing that it, as much as Christianity, had betrayed the truths revealed by God. This led to his being excommunicated, after which he lived in Amsterdam in unhappy isolation. Finally he repented and recanted, at least outwardly. However, he again voiced his heretical opinions, and was excommunicated a second time, in 1640. Seven years later he recanted again, but was required to confess his sin and receive thirty-nine lashes 'and to prostrate himself on the doorstep of the synagogue while the members of the congregation trod over his body'.[3] Shortly after this he shot himself, after writing an account of his life and reflections on religion.

Although da Costa died when Spinoza was only 8, some historians think that his life and ideas (which included the denial of human immortality) had an influence on Spinoza, though the extent of this is controversial.

Another significant ban was that of Juan de Prado, who suffered a *cherem* about the same time as Spinoza. Prado was another Marrano who fled persecution in Spain but, after settling in Amsterdam in 1655, rebelled against many features of Judaism as he found it practised there.[4]

After the *cherem*, Spinoza stayed in Amsterdam for four years, though the family business was soon sold up. At this time he became associated with an undogmatic Christian sect called Collegiants, who are said to have been somewhat similar to Quakers (with whom Spinoza also seems to have had contact). It was presumably during this period that he trained as an optical lens grinder (preparing lenses for spectacles, microscopes, and telescopes) as a source of income. It is thought that it was around this period that Spinoza worked on his unfinished *Treatise on the Emendation of the Intellect* (first published in the *Opera Posthuma* of 1677), the famous opening of which tells us that he was in search of a true good which, unlike 'honour and wealth', could afford him 'a continuous and supreme joy to all eternity'.

In early 1660 Spinoza moved to lodgings in Rijnsburg near Leiden, a centre of the Collegiants. By this time he had a circle of intimate friends, almost disciples, many of them merchants with strong religious and philosophical interests, who met regularly to discuss Spinoza's ideas. (This says a lot for the intellectual culture of the Dutch bourgeoisie.)

They included the merchants Pieter Balling, who in his *Light of the Candlestick* 'gave expression to the simple and somewhat mystic piety of the [collegiants]' (ROTH, 7); Jarigh Jelles, the principal editor after Spinoza's death of his *Opera Postuma* in Latin, and who himself wrote a book on theology and Cartesianism; Jan Hendrikszen Glazemaker, translator of the collected works into Dutch; and Simon Joosten De Vries, a particularly close friend and disciple. Besides these intellectual merchants, there was Lodewijk Meyer, a physician of wide intellectual interests, and Jan Rieuwertsz, 'a bookseller in Amsterdam, who published the writings of Spinoza, as well as of many other unorthodox authors'.[5]

Among Spinoza's followers, mention must be made of Count Ehrenfried Walther von Tschirnhaus (1651–1708), a German count who had spent much time in the Netherlands. They became acquainted only towards the end of Spinoza's life, but von Tschirnhaus is important as the most philosophically insightful of Spinoza's friends, and their correspondence is of considerable philosophical significance. It may have been Tschirnhaus who first communicated something of Spinoza's philosophy to Leibniz.

Four years later Spinoza moved to Voorburg and then to The Hague, living in modest lodgings, associating particularly with his group of devoted friends and followers. (The houses at Rijnsburg and The Hague now contain the library and offices of the Dutch Spinoza Society, the *Vereniging Het Spinozahuis*.) His income was derived partly from his lens grinding, partly perhaps from some small financial support provided by his followers. In fact, Simon de Vries, just before his own premature death in 1667, failed to persuade Spinoza that he, rather than de Vries's own brother, should be his primary heir, though Spinoza did accept something much smaller.

Spinoza lived very humbly, but was renowned for his courteous manners, and he had many distinguished philosophical, scientific, and artistic friends. He carried on an extensive correspondence on scientific and philosophical matters with a varied range of people, perhaps most notably Henry Oldenburg, secretary to the Royal Society in London, who had become his friend on a visit to the Netherlands in 1661. He was also somewhat involved in Dutch politics as a supporter of the De Witt brothers (important political figures), though it is unclear whether he knew them personally or not. The De Witt brothers represented republicanism as against Calvinist domination and the aspirations to royalty of the House of Orange. At any rate, though he sought long periods of solitude, Spinoza was by no means detached from social and public life. He also painted portraits, including a self-portrait, but none is known to have survived.

The only book which Spinoza published in his lifetime under his own name was *The Principles of Descartes' Philosophy*, with an appendix called *Metaphysical Thoughts* (*Cogitata Metaphysica*). This was written, when he was in Rijnsburg (initially for a private pupil who studied with him there), and was only published on the persuasion of his friends. It is an account of Descartes's philosophy, presented in the geometrical mode, which Spinoza later used for the exposition of his own philosophy in the *Ethics*. Lodewick Meyer wrote an introduction to it, emphasizing that it was not an account of Spinoza's own philosophical views, which only corresponded to Descartes's in part. Commentators on Spinoza's philosophy tend to divide into those who see his philosophy as essentially a more logical development of aspects of Cartesianism and others who prefer to emphasize the Jewish background to his thought.

That Spinoza had gone a long way to developing the essentials of his own final viewpoint during the Rijnsburg period is shown by his correspondence and by a work which he left unpublished called *A Short Treatise on Man and his Well-Being*, in which the main themes of his final philosophy are adumbrated. The only book besides the Cartesian treatise that he published in his lifetime was his *Tractatus Theologico-Politicus* (standardly abbreviated *TTP*). This often puzzling work, part biblical study, part political treatise, was published anonymously in Amsterdam in 1670. It was deemed so explosive that the publishers only issued it under a false cover and frontis-piece, giving the title and author of different works and the place of publication as Hamburg, though it seems that Spinoza himself was not out to shock but to persuade. It combines an examination of the Bible (speculating on the circumstances in which its various books were written and their true purport) with the development of a political philosophy.

Thus the primary aim of the book is to argue that a proper understand-ing of the Bible cannot justify religious intolerance. He does this by a mixture of considerations, chief of which is a firm attempt to distinguish the permanent moral message of the biblical prophets from a mass of outdated beliefs (and no longer relevant precepts) in which they were embedded, and which neither Jews nor Christians need see as binding on a modern community.

The work was partly motivated by the political situation in the Nether-lands at the time. The De Witt republican government was in difficulties, more especially as a result of failures in the current war with Sweden and England, and the Calvinist clergy were taking the opportunity to chal-lenge its policy of religious toleration.

According to Spinoza, the prophets were men who combined great moral wisdom with peculiarly vivid imaginations, but with only the sci-entific and metaphysical ideas of their day. Thus their ethical message was associated with all sorts of imaginative adjuncts, regarding such things as angels, in which there was no longer call to believe. But it was not so much that they were talking down to the people as that God-or-Nature 'talked' down to them. That is, God taught them ethics via their imaginations rather than their intellects. It is therefore their moral teaching to which we should attend today, not their views on more factual matters.

Clearly relevant to the issue of religious freedom, the most important theme of the *TTP*, is the relation that should hold between church and state. And Spinoza thinks that the history of the Jewish people casts a good deal of light on this. This leads him on to the development of a political theory of the state which owes a good deal to Hobbes, utilizing similarly the idea of a social contract, but deriving a more liberal and democratic lesson from it.

Spinoza's examination of the Bible (mostly the Hebrew Bible, or Old Testament, though Spinoza touches on the life of Jesus) is often regarded as the first truly historical enquiry into its genesis as a natural historical phenomenon, rather than as an infallibly inspired work. As such it pointed the way to the 'higher criticism' of the nineteenth century.

Though Spinoza unobtrusively identifies God and Nature, one of the major themes of his *magnum opus*, the *Ethics*, he writes in a seemingly more orthodox vein, even while denying the genuinely supernatural character of reported miracles. It is much debated whether this shows that those who now read the *Ethics* in too unreligious a way are misunderstanding it, or whether Spinoza was adapting his presentation, not indeed to the masses, but to conventionally religious intellectuals of his time, among whom he wished to promote tolerant liberal ideals. However, not surprisingly, most readers recognized that Spinoza rejected almost everything supernatural in the Bible and regarded it, therefore, as an outrageous attack on both Christianity and Judaism. The anonymous author was reviled as an agent of the devil, and this boded no good for Spinoza when his authorship became known. It led him to be cautious about the publication of his *Ethics*, which was published only after his death.

Spinoza's support for the De Witt brothers took a dramatic form some years after the publication of the *TTP*. In 1672 Johan De Witt was forced to resign his post as Grand Pensionary of Holland, while his brother Cornelius had been arrested on a charge of conspiring against the Prince of Orange, who was planning to re-establish the House of Orange as in effect a monarchy. When Johan visited his brother in prison, a mob broke in, seized on the two brothers, and tore them to pieces. When Spinoza heard of this, he prepared a placard on which he wrote 'the very lowest of the barbarians' and planned to parade the streets with it. To save him from likely death at the hands of an irate mob, his landlord, a painter, Van Der Spyck, managed to lock Spinoza up till the riots were over.

Spinoza was again in some personal danger the next year, in 1673, when the Dutch and French were at war. The French army at that time was occupying Utrecht, under the leadership of the Prince of Condé. One of his officers, a Colonel Stouppe, told him that Spinoza lived nearby, and the Prince invited Spinoza to visit him. Spinoza, perhaps through a misunderstanding, thought that he was being given a chance to act as a peace mediator, and with the permission of the Dutch authorities crossed enemy lines. At all events, nothing much came of Spinoza's visit, as the Prince had had to leave by the time Spinoza arrived. Its only upshot was that Spinoza was offered a pension from the French if he would dedicate a book to Louis XIV, an offer which not surprisingly he refused. However, on his return to Amsterdam, word got around among some of the populace that he was a spy, and a mob surrounded his lodging, threatening to kill him. Apparently they were dispersed by a speech he made on his doorstep explaining his innocence.

Earlier in the same year Spinoza was invited by the Elector Palatine, Karl Ludwig, to hold the chair of philosophy in Heidelberg. However, Spinoza declined, because although promised complete freedom of expression (provided he did not attempt to subvert the public religion), he felt that in fact he would be pushed into insincerity about his beliefs.

In 1676, when Spinoza was near to death, Leibniz visited him in The Hague, and apparently held long conversations with him. The character of the discussion between the two greatest philosophers of the century has been the subject of much speculation. A rather intriguing dramatization of it was recently broadcast on Dutch radio in a play about Spinoza, with Leibniz becoming more and more upset at the daringness of Spinoza's thought and Spinoza having to conclude the meeting through shortage of breath.

Spinoza died in 1677 (on 21 February) at the age of 44, from tuberculosis, partly due to the inhalation of glass dust from his lens grinding. After his death, his friends published a volume called *Opera Postuma*, in which the *Ethics* was published for the first time. The author's name is only given as B.D.S., partly out of respect for Spinoza's own expressed wish, partly probably from caution, as his name had become quite notorious. No details were given of the place of publication. Besides the *Ethics* it included an unfinished second political treatise, called *Tractatus Politicus*, the Hebrew grammar, and other works which I have not mentioned. Another work of Spinoza's, which was not included here, was a treatise on the nature of the rainbow.

PART TWO: THOUGHT OF THE PHILOSOPHER (THE *ETHICS*)

I The Aim of Part 1 of the *Ethics*

Spinoza's great work, the *Ethics*, has five parts: 1. Concerning God; 2. Of the Nature and Origin of the Mind; 3. Concerning the Origin and Nature of the Emotions; 4. Of Human Bondage, or the Strength of the Emotions; 5. Of the Power of the Intellect or of Human Freedom. Each part opens with definitions and axioms in the style of Euclid. There follow propositions supposed to be proved on the basis of the axioms and definitions of that part (together with those of previous parts in the case of 2, 3, 4, and 5). These propositions often have scholia, or notes which express what Spinoza is getting at more informally, and each part also has an informal introduction.

In referring to these propositions etc., I shall use the following quite common conventions:

'E3p11' means proposition 11 of Part 3 of the *Ethics*.
'E3p11dem' means demonstration or proof of E3p11.
'E3p11cor' means corollary of E3p11.
'E3p11s' means scholium to E3p11.
'E3a1' means first axiom of Part 3.
'E3d1' means first definition of Part 3.

The translation from the Latin which I shall be using is that of Samuel Shirley.[6] Shirley does not, however, use the conventions just described, but I shall change his references to this form.

I shall try to provide the gist of some of the reasoning and conclusions of each part in an informal way.

The aim of Part 1 is to show that there is just one substance, that this substance is appropriately called 'God', and that every other existing thing is a mode of God, sometimes called God-or-Nature (my hyphens).

II There is Just One Substance

The most fundamental metaphysical claim made in the *Ethics* is that there is only one *substance*, and that everything else which in any manner exists is a *mode* of it. The one substance is referred to by Spinoza as 'God', and less often as 'God or Nature' (Deus sive Natura). In book 5 he claims that the highest human good is 'the intellectual love of God' (see below).

Even so, much suggests that Spinoza's God is intended to be the fitting object of religious emotion, and that Spinoza was not the hidden atheist he has sometimes been thought to be. According to this charge, Spinoza simply referred to the Universe as 'God' in order to provide a veneer of religious language in setting forth a view of things which is really atheistic. For, after all, the veriest atheist believes in the existence of Nature: that is, of the Universe. You don't avoid atheism merely by referring to the Universe as 'God'.

This interpretation is well expressed in the course of an eighteenth-century poem called 'The Creation' by Richard Blackmore:

> Spinoza, next, to hide his black design
> And to his side the unwary to incline,
> For heaven his ensigns treacherous displays:
> Declares for God, while he that God betrays:
> For whom he's pleased such evidence to bring,
> As saves the name, while it subverts the thing.

This view of Spinoza was quite common until the nineteenth century, when the German Romantic poet Novalis described Spinoza as a God-intoxicated man. In more recent years, enthusiasts for conceiving human beings as natural robots with advanced computers for brains have sometimes claimed him as their own, while many, such as James Thomas and I, still continue to think of him as essentially a pantheist not miles away from absolute idealism. The idea of him as a proto-materialist seems to me quite wrong,

In fact, in calling Nature 'God', Spinoza was doing so because it had some of the main characteristics standardly taken as God's unique attributes in all (or almost all) developed forms of monotheism. Most obviously, God is conceived of by Spinoza as *knowing everything*.

It is sometimes debated whether Spinoza identified God with the totality of all things or only with that which is permanent in it: namely, the one and only substance, but not including its modes—that is, all finite things. But it does not make much difference, it seems to me, whether you say that for Spinoza reality consisted in God *and* his modes, or in God, *including* of course his modes.

III How Finite Things are Related to the One Substance

But how does Spinoza conceive of ordinary finite things as related to the one substance? The quick answer is that all ordinary finite things are 'finite modes' of God.

To explain this, I must offer some account of Spinoza's terminology, not only his use of the expressions 'substance' and 'mode', but also of 'essence' and 'attribute'.

The word 'substance' has a long and complicated history in philosophy. The traditional meaning which Spinoza is drawing on is best explained as follows.

Things which in any sense exist may be divided into two kinds:

1. Those whose existence consists in the fact that something more fundamental is in a certain state, is doing something, or undergoing something. Such things have been referred to by various expressions, such as attributes, properties, states, modes, etc. Spinoza uses the expression 'modes'. (He gives a quite different meaning to 'attribute'; see below.)

2. Those whose existence does not consist in the fact that something more fundamental is in a certain state, doing something, or undergoing something. Such things are called 'substances'.

The traditional view is that there are a lot of substances. Examples are individual persons, organisms of any sort, and such inanimate physical things as have a certain unity.

On this *traditional* view, an individual person, like John Robinson, is a *substance*. When he is in a bad temper, the bad temper is a temporary *mode* of his. More generally, all his thoughts, deeds, and feelings, and all the physical states he is in from time to time (such as a disease), are modes of his. In the case of a tree or a stone, its modes include such things as its weight and its shape (and anything it can be said to *do*, such as grow).

Spinoza's initial terminology is in line with this, allowing for there being many *substances*. But early on he professes to prove that there is only one *substance*, God-or-Nature (see E1p4). Everything else, in particular all those things which on the traditional view are substances, are all really *modes* of the one unique *substance*. Every person, every rock, is a *finite mode of the one substance, God-or-Nature*.

Spinoza distinguishes between two types of *mode*: those which are necessarily permanent modes of the one substance, and those which are temporary modes of it. The first are *infinite modes* (they include 'motion and rest' as following from the attribute of extension); the second are *finite modes*. Infinite modes are permanent features of the universe derived from the ultimate divine essence (while finite modes are individual mortal things). It would take me too long to consider just how the attributes relate to their infinite modes.

Axiom 1 of Part 1 says: 'All things that are, are either in themselves or in something else.' (Note that he is not as yet claiming that there is only one thing of the first type, the one substance.)

This is because his way of referring to the relation of a *mode* to its *substance* is to speak of it as IN the *substance*. As for a *substance* itself, it is described as IN itself. (See definition 3 of Part 1.)

This terminology complicates what conversationally is the best way of explaining a *finite mode*. Conversationally, one might say that finite modes are states that the universe (= God-or-Nature) is temporarily IN, just as conversationally one speaks of someone being IN a bad temper, although, in accordance with Spinoza's terminology, one should speak of the bad temper as IN him.[7]

Finally, finite modes are not only IN the one substance; they must be conceived 'through it', that is, by reference to it—either as particular formations in the one substance *qua physical* or as particular formations in the one substance *qua mental*.

IV How a Thing Relates to its Essence

I shall now try to explain the relation between something and its essence. Modes have essences, and so do substances (for Spinoza, the one substance).

An *essence* is a possible form of being which, if it is not merely possible, but actual, is a *substance* or a *mode*. I, Timothy Sprigge, might not have existed, but I could not have been impossible. If I had not existed, then I would have been an unactualized *essence*. But since I do exist, I am an actualized essence, in fact, an existing *finite mode* of the one *substance*. So to speak of a thing's *essence* is to speak of the possible form of being which would still have been there as a possibility even if it had not existed, and which is eternally there before and after its period of existence.[8]

However, in the case of God (as we shall see), his *essence* has the peculiarity that it could not have failed to be actualized as an existent thing. None the less, in so far as we speak of the *divine essence*, we are not presupposing that he, she, or it really does exist, though if we think about it adequately, we shall see that it must be actualized as the existing *divine substance*.

Thus the essence of a thing is not something in it, in the sense in which a mode of something is in it. Rather, it is the thing itself. Thus, since substance is in itself, it follows also that the essence of substance is in itself.

It is important to understand how this bears on the notions of substance, essence, and mode. Many philosophers understand by a thing's 'essence' a set of properties which the thing must possess if it is to be itself, so to speak. That is, they think that if a sufficient change happens to a thing X, then it may no longer be proper to regard it as the same thing, because it now lacks some of its essential properties.

If, for example, something happens which one is inclined to describe as a lady changing into a fox, then, presuming that the fox lacks some of the properties which are appropriately regarded as pertaining to the essence of the original lady, then we should say, not that the lady has changed into a fox, but that the lady has been replaced by a fox.

In this sense of essence, it would seem that it would be 'in' the original lady, in the sense in which everything which is not in itself is in another thing.

This is not Spinoza's use of 'essence'. A thing's essence is not something in the thing. Rather, is it the thing itself in so far as it is an actualized rather than an unactualized essence.

For one of the most significant differences between God and 'his'[9] modes is that God is the explanation of his own existence, whereas finite things exist only in virtue of a causal process which brought them into existence. In short, the essence of God is such that anyone who grasps it can see that it must be actualized in an existing God, while the essence of each finite thing is such that one can only know that it exists either through having directly confronted it or through being aware of a causal process which is bound to have produced it. Spinoza expresses this by saying that God is uniquely self-caused.

V God-or-Nature is through and through both Physical and Mental; thus it is Mentally Aware of Everything which it is Doing Physically

On the face of it, there are two main types of thing in the universe: physical things and mental things, such as minds, thoughts, emotions, ideas, and so forth.

That these were utterly distinct substances was one of the main doctrines of Descartes. His essential argument was that (1) we can conceive any sort of mind existing without anything physical existing at all, and (2) that we can conceive physical things as existing without any sort of mind at all (God, who is an infinite non-physical mind, excepted). For this reason, my mind and my body, as things which could exist apart, are distinct substances somehow linked together so that they can act on each other.

How does this relate to Spinoza's view that all ordinary things are finite modes of the one substance, God? Surely if God is a mind, he cannot have bodies among his modes.

Spinoza's answer is that God is through and through both physical and mental. He is both an infinite cosmic mind and an infinitely extended physical world. Spinoza's way of saying this is to ascribe two distinct attributes to God: thought and extension. (God also has an infinite number of other attributes, but we do not know what they are.)

To explain Spinoza's conception, so far as we can, we must turn to another terminological matter, Spinoza's use of the word 'attribute'. However, there are considerable differences of opinion as to how we should understand Spinoza's, as always, somewhat laconic way of explaining his meaning.

It is time to look at Spinoza's actual definition of God.

E1d6 By God I mean an absolutely infinite being; that is, substance consisting of infinite attributes, each of which expresses eternal and infinite essence.

This must be related to Part 1, Defn 4, according to which

E1d4 By attribute I mean that which the intellect perceives of substance as constituting its essence.

Taken together with Spinoza's later assertion that infinite extension and infinite thought are the two attributes of God known to us, this means that one way of conceiving the essence of substance is as an infinitely extended physical reality, and another way of conceiving it is as an infinitely knowledgeable mind.

So Spinoza holds that, although God has just one *essence*, there are many different ways of conceiving this essence, all of which reveal it in a distinct manner. Actually, human beings can access only two *attributes*, infinite physical reality and infinite mind, but Spinoza thinks that there must be an infinite number of other *attributes*, or ways of conceiving the divine essence, perhaps available to minds of other types. What we call physical things (including ourselves as physical organisms) are finite modes of the one substance conceived as physical, whereas what we call minds or their mental contents (including our own minds) are finite modes of the one substance conceived as mental. It is vital to grasp that an attribute is not IN the one substance, like a mode, but that each of them is its very essence (that is, the substance itself) conceived in a particular way. So they are things which are 'in themselves' in the sense of axiom 1. Spinoza's later proof that there is only one substance cannot be understood unless this is realized.

VI The Attributes of Substance: Different Interpretations

It is time to remark that there is a good deal of argument as to how Spinoza meant us to conceive the relation between the essence 'expressed' by two or more so-called attributes and the attributes themselves.

First, there is the so-called subjective interpretation of the attributes. According to this, the real essence of the one substance is hidden from us; all we have access to are attributes, which are a kind of subjective representation of this essence, but which hide it from us rather than display it.

In contrast, we have the so-called objective interpretation of the attributes. According to this, an attribute is simply a constituent of the essence of its substance, so that the essence is really a compound of many quite distinct attributes.

I believe that both these views are wrong. The subjective interpretation runs counter to what seems a clear aspect of Spinoza's outlook: namely, that we can have genuine insight into ultimate truth (not indeed of the totality of such truth, but truth absolute so far as it goes). But if the essence of the one substance were hidden from us, then we would be ignorant of ultimate truth in the most basic way possible. So those who proffer the objective interpretation on the ground that the subjective interpretation cannot be right, are making a good point. But the objective interpretation does not seem right either. One reason for saying this is that Spinoza's proof, which we shall be considering shortly, that there is only one substance, becomes invalid on this interpretation, while it is valid on the subjective interpretation. And apart from this, Spinoza's frequent insistence that the divine idea of something is identical with the thing itself makes better sense on the subjective interpretation.

It seems that an intermediate interpretation is called for. This is the one which I have just been expressing. On this intermediate interpretation, an attribute is a particular way in which the essence of the one substance (and of its finite modes) can be revealed to the intellect. The essence is not hidden behind its attributes, but revealed through them. They are alternative ways of conceiving the essence, each of which does justice to that essence in one particular way. Whether this makes Spinoza's view finally a coherent or intelligible one may be questioned, but this is surely what he is meaning to convey.

But, it may be asked, when Spinoza says that an attribute is 'that which the intellect perceives of substance as constituting its essence', which is the intellect of which he is speaking, the divine one or the human? My belief is that he means that each attribute is a manner in which in principle the essence of substance could be revealed to a suitable intellect. God's intellect is obviously a suitable intellect in all cases, so God must conceive himself in the infinite number of different ways which are his infinite attributes. Human beings can have a revelation of his essence through just two of these attributes, thought and extension. Whether there are other finite intellects similarly served by others among the infinite attributes is left open.

It may be objected to Spinoza that we cannot in practice make a sharp distinction between the mental and physical aspects of human beings (likewise animals) and of their activities. Is the stock market, for example, something purely mental or purely physical? As against this, Spinoza could reply that this is *either* because we do not bother to distinguish things which normally go together *or* because we eke out our ignorance about their physical aspect by referring to their mental aspect, and vice versa, but that none the less, if we were careful enough, we could divide what we know or think about, the one from the other.[10] To me, at any rate, it seems that Spinoza is on the right lines here.

VII God's Infinity

Let us look again at Spinoza's definition of God.

E1d6 By God I mean an absolutely infinite being; that is, substance consisting of infinite attributes, each of which expresses eternal and infinite essence.

There are thus two senses in which God is infinite. First, under whichever attribute we conceive him, God, and his essence, must be conceived as infinite. I shall call each of these attributes 'an infinite attribute'.

What does that mean? Spatially it means that God is stretched out infinitely in every direction. He is an infinite plenum. Any ordinary physical thing is simply a (moveable) bit of this plenum, though one (as we shall see) with a certain *conatus*, or endeavour, to keep itself in existence as best it can in changing circumstances). (The Latin word *conatus* is a semi-technical term in Spinoza's *Ethics*, so I shall use it rather than 'endeavour'.) Mentally, it means that he is an infinite consciousness, and that a finite mind is a bit (though not in a physical sense) of this infinite consciousness possessed of a similar *conatus*, or endeavour, to go on existing if this is at all possible.

I say 'plenum' because Spinoza, like Descartes, denied that there was such a thing as a vacuum, holding that there was no real distinction between space and the matter which filled it. I don't know that Spinoza's main thought really turns on the outmoded denial of a vacuum. Could he not even now say that 'empty space' is one form which the infinitely extended world assumes in certain parts of itself at certain times?

It is worth noting that both Descartes and Spinoza took the conception of the infinite as more basic than that of the finite. A finite thing is something which can be picked out within the infinite. This conception is in contrast with the view of Locke, Berkeley, and I think Hume, that the idea of infinite extension is a kind of limiting conception reached when we try to think of larger and larger finite spaces. For Descartes and Spinoza our very notion of the physical world turns on our having an intuitive sense of sheer, infinite, stretched-out three-dimensionality. They also thought this true of finite mind—we recognize that our mind is finite by noting its deficiencies: that is, the way in which it fails to be an infinite mind, this latter being in truth the more positive conception.

But God is infinite not merely in the sense that each of his attributes is so, but infinite also in the quite different sense that he possesses or includes every conceivable attribute which a substance could possess. And since an attribute is the essence of a substance conceived in a particular way, this means that for every possible coherent way of conceiving the essence of a substance, you must assume that God can properly be conceived in that way. Let us call infinitude in the first sense attribute infinitude, and infinitude in the second sense essence infinitude.

VIII Proofs of the Uniqueness and Necessary Existence of God

The Basic Outline

We must now consider why, according to Spinoza, this doubly infinite substance is the only substance which there could be, and, what is more, that it exists.

The following sketch of Spinoza's main line of thought may be helpful before we consider his own three formal proofs of the existence and uniqueness of God or the one infinite substance. Call this the *Outline*.

1. First premiss: two substances could not have an attribute in common.
2. Second premiss: the divine substance exists of necessity as having all possible attributes. For its nonexistence is inconceivable.
3. Conclusion: therefore the divine substance exists of necessity, and is the only substance that could exist at all.

Valid enough, but we must consider the justification of the two premisses so as to make of this valid argument one which may be sound. Spinoza's justification for the second premiss is simply his first proof of God's existence, which I shall consider shortly. But what of the first premiss? Spinoza's line of thought here is somewhat as follows.

Justification of the First Premiss of the Outline

(A) TWO SUBSTANCES COULD NOT BE DISTINGUISHED MERELY BY THEIR MODES

Two things would need to be distinct already, in order that they should have different modes. A mode is a state which a substance is in, in the popular sense of 'in' (at some particular time), and substances could not be in different states unless they were distinct, so to speak, already.

An analogy may help. Could two men be distinguished simply because one was in a bad temper and the other in a good temper? Or could they be distinguished by the fact that they had different beliefs? Surely not. They would have to be different people in order that they should be in different moods or have different beliefs. The identity and distinctiveness of a substance must turn on what it essentially is, rather than in virtue of some temporary, or even permanent, state that it is in.

(B) NOTHING ELSE COULD DISTINGUISH THEM EXCEPT THEIR ESSENCE AND ATTRIBUTES

There simply is nothing in reality other than substances, their essences, their attributes, and their modes. See the second of my two comments below.

(C) TWO SUBSTANCES COULD NOT HAVE THE SAME ESSENCE

Why not? Simply because a substance just is its essence, and therefore two substances require two essences.

(D) CONCLUSION: TWO SUBSTANCES COULD NOT HAVE AN ATTRIBUTE IN COMMON

An attribute is the essence of a substance conceived in a particular way. It follows that substances could share an attribute only if they had the same essence. For an attribute could not be a correct way of conceiving two different essences.

It has sometimes been objected, most notably by Leibniz, that Spinoza ignores the possibility that two substances could have some attributes in common, but not all of them. (See E1pp4–5.) For example, X might have attributes a, b, and c, and Y attributes b, c, and d. They would then both be distinguished by their attributes (as opposed to their modes), and yet share an attribute.

Spinoza, however, is taking it for granted that two substances could not have one attribute in common without having all attributes in common. Though he does not spell this out sufficiently, he is surely right. For an attribute is a way of conceiving an essence, and could not be a way of conceiving two different essences. From this it follows that if two substances X and Y had the same attribute, call it F, they would have to have the same essence: namely, that essence which could be conceived by way of F. It follows further that they must have all attributes in common. For it could not be the case that the very same essence *qua* pertaining to X could be conceived in a certain way, while *qua* pertaining to Y it could not be conceived in that way. For how an essence can be conceived must turn on the character of that essence itself, and not on anything else, such as who is conceiving it and in what situation.[11]

From this it can be seen that Spinoza is right, granted the basic concepts with which he is operating, that one attribute in common implies all attributes in common. So the suggestion mooted by Leibniz is ruled out.

It is worth insisting that this argument works only if an attribute is indeed a *way of conceiving an essence*. This shows that the purely objective interpretation of the attributes explained above is wrong. For if each attribute of a substance is simply a constituent of its essence, so that the essence is simply a compound of many quite distinct attributes, it would seem that there might be two essences, one compounded of one set of attributes, the other of another set, but with some overlapping in membership of each set. To me this seems sufficient ground for rejecting the 'objective' interpretation of the attributes.

The subjective interpretation makes much better sense of this argument. For if an attribute is a way in which the essence appears to us, it is hard to see how there could be two substances with an attribute in common but with a different essence. And if they share the same essence, this would surely mean that they have all attributes in common; for presumably that shared essence must also be able to appear in all the same ways.

However, I have not quite accepted the subjective interpretation, substituting what might be called the 'revelatory' interpretation. But that, even more than the subjective interpretation, supports the view that one attribute in common implies all attributes in common.

For if an attribute is a way of conceiving an essence, because revelatory of its nature, it could not be a way of also revealing a quite different essence. From this it follows that if a substance X had the same attribute, call it F, as another substance Y, they would have to have the same essence: namely, that essence which could be conceived by way of F. It follows further that they must have all attributes in common. For the very same essence could hardly serve as a way of conceiving one and the same essence in some cases but not in others. For what is in question is not whether this or that particular mind could conceive a substance in a certain way, but the manner in which the substance could be conceived in principle.

From this it can be seen that Spinoza is right, granted the basic concepts with which he is operating, that one attribute in common implies all attributes in common.

Maybe he is not spelling it out altogether clearly, but I think that the idea that two substances could have an attribute in common only if they had the same essence, and for that reason would have all attributes in common, just seemed obvious to him.

Justification of the Second Premiss of the Outline

This is essentially E1p11, to which, and the three proofs of it offered there, I now turn.

SPINOZA'S FIRST PROOF OF GOD'S NECESSARY EXISTENCE

E1p11 God, or substance consisting of infinite attributes, each of which expresses eternal and infinite essence, necessarily exists.

(a) Spinoza's proof of this is very abrupt. He says that it is absurd to suppose that God's essence does not involve his existence, and refers us back to E1p7, and it is this proposition which is the crucial one.[12] This proposition argues that since a substance cannot be produced by another substance (or by anything else), it must therefore be produced by itself—that is, it must exist of its own nature or essence. (That one substance cannot be caused by another substance follows from the fact that different substances must have totally different attributes, and therefore can have nothing in common, while cause and effect can hold only between items which do have something in common. See E1p6.)

(b) This may look specious. It seems just to say that if a substance X does exist, then it must somehow exist of its own essence. But how does this tell you that any substance, such as X, in fact, exists? God, for example. What I think Spinoza means here is that every coherently conceivable substance must exist, and that the concept of a substance which has every conceivable attribute—that is, which can in principle be conceived in every possible way in which a substance might be conceived—is coherent.

(c) However, that this concept is coherent is not as obvious as Spinoza evidently thinks it is. Nor indeed is it so obvious that every coherently conceived substance must exist. Spinoza's line of thought may be more persuasive when we realize that, as he claims in Part 2, the two infinite attributes of which the human mind can conceive are infinite extension (that is, an infinitely extended physical world, of which finite physical things are modes) and infinite thought (that is to say, an infinite mind of which all ideas of individual physical things are the finite modes). Now it is easy to see how someone could believe that infinite space necessarily exists.[13] It may be less easy to see how someone could believe that infinite mind necessarily exists. However, Spinoza thought it evident that of everything which exists there must be an idea. Thus there must be an idea of every physical object and, more importantly, an idea of the infinite physical world as a whole, and this is equivalent to an infinite mind. Spinoza, as I understand him, would claim further that the infinite mind and the infinite extension must be the same substance conceived differently. For the only way we can conceive of an infinite mind knowing an infinitely extended world is as the same substance knowing itself in one particular way. For the attributes would otherwise be too cut off from each other for such knowledge to be possible.

(d) Many commentators deny that the attribute of thought is an infinite mind. Yet this was intended to resolve the mind–body problem as it arose from the work of Descartes. But that which has our minds among its finite modes must surely be mental—that is to say, a mind. Certainly it must be very different from a finite mind, but a mind, none the less.[14]

(e) But what of all the other infinity of attributes of which the human mind does not know? Well, Spinoza takes it for granted that there must be an idea of each of these and that each of them will be an infinite attribute. But is it the same infinite attribute as that which is the mind which knows the physical? Is it even an infinite attribute of the same substance? Perhaps Spinoza would hold that if there are N attributes (whether N be an infinite number or not) of a possible substance, an idea of this fact must exist, and that such an idea could exist only in a mind which has trans-attribute knowledge of all of them, and that this requires in turn that it is the same substance as each of them.[15] Actually, in so far as it includes the idea of itself, it has trans-attribute knowledge anyway, though this of course is a special case.

(f) Spinoza, at any rate, is satisfied that he has a coherent conception of a substance which answers to every intelligible conception which could be formed of a possible substance.

So the divine substance, having all possible attributes, exists, and from this it follows that no other substance can exist because it would have to have an attribute in common with God or Nature.

Besides this proof, Spinoza has two others (also in E1p11).

SPINOZA'S SECOND PROOF OF GOD'S NECESSARY EXISTENCE

Spinoza's next two proofs of God's existence (as further demonstrations of E1p11) rest on the idea that every essence—that is, every possible form of being—has a kind of *nisus*, or thrust, towards being actualized as an actually existing thing. The second proof claims that for anything you can conceive, there must be a reason either why it exists or why it does not exist. Some things don't exist because their essence is self-contradictory. So they keep themselves out of existence. Other things don't exist because the processes needed to produce them never take place. But there is nothing like this which could explain the nonexistence of the divine substance. Only another similar substance could do this, but there can't be two similar substances. (See E1p5.)

SPINOZA'S THIRD PROOF OF GOD'S NECESSARY EXISTENCE

The third proof is not so dissimilar. It rests on the supposition that there is a kind of battle between all the essences as to which shall exist. All of them would exist unless other essences kept them out. But no other essence could be potent enough to prevent such a potent essence as that of the divine substance from actualizing itself. He calls this an a posteriori proof, because it turns on the actual existence of finite things (which shows that the battle to exist between essences is actually on).

These proofs may seem quite strange. But it is instructive (at the very least) to know that very clever people have accepted them or something very like them. Among quite recent philosophers who think something like these proofs is correct are J. N. Findlay (fairly recently dead), Norman Malcolm (fairly recently dead), Alvin Plantinga (alive), and John Leslie (alive).[16]

TWO COMMENTS

First comment   A last struggle against the argument might challenge the assumption that there cannot be a substance without any attributes at all. For if this assumption is false, there might, on the face of it, be a substance other than God which does not share any of his attributes. However, to reject this assumption is to suppose that there might be a substance either with no essence at all or an essence which in principle no mind could have a way of grasping. But a substance without an essence would not be the actualization of any possibility, and therefore impossible, while a substance with an essence but no attributes would be one in principle absolutely closed to any possible mind. Some might think this a possibility, but certainly not Spinoza. For some further light on this, see my discussion of bare particulars in what follows.

Second comment   A crucial step in Spinoza's reasoning is the claim that if there were to be two substances, something would have to distinguish them and that this, since it cannot be their modes, must be their essence and attributes. (See E1pp4 and 5.)

An objector might ask whether there might not be two substances which were merely numerically different, even though they had the same basic character. Or again he might ask whether they might not be distinguished simply by their different positions in the universe (as some mass-produced objects or some sub-atomic particles may be thought to be).

(a) Spinoza would reply to the second question, I am sure, by reminding us that

E1p8 Every substance is necessarily infinite.

The reason for this is that something which was finite would have to have boundaries cutting it off from other things. But whatever is on either side of a boundary must be of essentially the same sort, e.g. spatial. But as being of essentially the same sort, they would share an essence, and this would be impossible if they were distinct substances.

From this it follows that Spinoza would not regard things which could be identified only by their position within reality (spatial position or some mental analogue) as substances. For it is only finite things which can have a position in something larger; substances cannot be said to be in a position at all.

(b) As for the first suggestion, that things might be different merely numerically without there being anything which could be called the ground of their difference, this would seem absurd to Spinoza. It depends on the notion of what, since Spinoza's day, have been called 'bare particulars', things which have a character but which are not to be identified with, or by, that character. But since, for Spinoza, a thing is its character, then if by that, one means its essence, it makes no sense to attempt to think of things as having some sort of being apart from their characters.

So grounds for rejecting Spinoza's line of thought here would have to turn on some radical critique of his whole conceptual apparatus, rather than from objections to the moves he makes within it. Such a critique may be in order, but it should not be made while we are still attempting to understand him.

The notion of a number of distinct infinite minds and infinite spaces in no relation to other such minds or spaces might play a part in such a critique, but this may never have occurred to Spinoza.[17] Nor should we feel too comfortable with the idea inasmuch as we, who are confined to just one of them, would have no way of referring to anything belonging to another.

IX Alternative Proof of God's Necessary Existence

Spinoza implicitly offers another proof which may be found more persuasive. (See E2p8.) This turns on the meaning of questions as to whether some specified thing exists or not, and on the meaning of a negative answer.

For what can it mean to say that something, or some things, do not exist? For Spinoza (so I understand him) it must always mean that something else more fundamental fails to be in a certain state which, *on the face of it*, it might have been in.[18] To say that unicorns don't exist is to say that the earth or, better, the physical universe lacks unicorns. But one cannot say that the physical universe might not have existed, because there is nothing more basic which might have lacked it.

The same thing applies in the case of minds which do not exist (say, minds which have thought that the *Odyssey* was written by a committee of exactly twenty-one women). It is to say that the universal mind lacks a content which it might *on the face of it* have had. But one cannot say that the universal mind might not have existed, since there is nothing more basic which might have lacked it.

It follows that an infinite physical universe and an infinite mind necessarily exist, since there is no conceivable alternative to their existence. However, it does not immediately follow from this that they are in truth one and the same thing.

This, I believe, is best achieved by a more idealistic argument than Spinoza actually gives at this point. It must turn on the fact, I suggest, that we cannot really form any conception of a physical world which is not somehow experienced by, or displayed to, a mind. The nearest Spinoza comes to saying this is at E2p7s where he speaks of some of the Hebrews having seen darkly that God's ideas and the things of which they are the ideas are the same thing understood in terms of different attributes:

[From E2p7s] So, too, a mode of Extension and the idea of that mode are one and the same thing, expressed in two ways. This truth seems to have been glimpsed by some of the Hebrews, who hold that God, God's intellect and the things understood by God are one and the same. For example, a circle existing in Nature and the idea of the existing circle—which is also in God—are one and the same thing explicated through different attributes.

To sum up this line of argument: all conceivable finite physical things might or might not have existed. This is because they are possible but not necessary ways in which some more ultimate physical thing might have been modified in a certain way. This can only be an infinite physical plenum. All conceivable finite mental things might or might not have existed. This is because they are possible ways in which some more ultimate mental thing might or might not have been modified in a certain way. This can only be an infinite mind. The best explanation of this is that the infinite physical world and the infinite mind are, in fact, the same thing. For the physical can exist only as the object of a mind, while a mind can exist only as aware of something. And in the case where a physical infinite is in question, it can only be an infinite mind which is aware of it, while an infinite mind must be aware of everything, and this must include what is physically infinite. Thus they are really the same thing, which we may now call the infinite substance, conceived in different ways. There are doubtless infinitely other ways in which the infinite substance could be conceived by a mind other than ours, but we do not know what they are.

X Further Remarks on Essences

Both the one substance and each of its individual modes have their essences. As I have suggested above, a thing and its essence are not two distinct things; rather, the thing is simply its essence in a state of actualization. If the thing ceases to exist, its essence continues merely as an unactualized essence. The case of God-or-Nature is only different inasmuch as it is the actualization of an essence of which the non-actualization is inconceivable.

We can now say that one's mind is one's mental essence in so far as one means by one's mind something relatively permanent. For it seems to be part of Spinoza's viewpoint that each mind must have its own slightly distinct way of conceiving things (corresponding to something distinctive about its body), and that its continued existence as a mind turns on this remaining the same. The same goes for my body, the essence of which Spinoza equates with a distinctive ratio of motion and rest within it.

However, we need to distinguish between the essence as the core of the thing which exists as long as the thing exists, and its passing states or affections. You and I do not pertain to the divine essence, since that can exist without us, but we are finite modes of it—that is, states which it is in for a certain time or, more philosophically, are 'in it'. Similarly, my essence is the core of my being, which remains the same as long as I exist, whereas my passing thoughts, feelings, and, on the physical side, my ever shifting bodily states are temporary only. In effect, they are therefore related to my mind or body as that is related to God's mind or body, and are therefore modes of modes. However, Spinoza does not put it like that, but always speaks of them as the mode's *affections*.

But cannot the character of my mind and body (as displayed in behaviour) so change that my distinctive essence is no longer actualized? Spinoza holds that in that case my mind and body have changed into another individual. (He is a bit cagey over the fact that this will typically happen gradually.)

E4p39s In Part V I shall explain to what extent these things can hinder or be of service to the mind. But here it should be noted that I understand a body to die when its parts are so disposed as to maintain a different proportion of motion-and-rest to one another. For I do not venture to deny that the human body, while retaining blood circulation and whatever else is regarded as essential to life, can nevertheless assume another nature quite different from its own. I have no reason to hold that a body does not die unless it turns into a corpse; indeed, experience seems to teach otherwise. It sometimes happens that a man undergoes such changes that I would not be prepared to say that he is the same person. I have heard tell of a certain Spanish poet who was seized with sickness, and although he recovered, he remained so unconscious of his past life that he did not believe that the stories and tragedies he had written were his own. Indeed, he might have been taken for a child in adult form if he had also forgotten his native tongue. And if this seems incredible, what are we to say about babies? A man of advanced years believes their nature to be so different from his own that he could not be persuaded that he had ever been a baby if he did not draw a parallel from other cases. But I prefer to leave these matters unresolved, so as not to afford material for the superstitious to raise new problems.

It has been suggested that one's DNA quite closely corresponds to what Spinoza had in mind as the essence of one's body, determining not only one's more grossly physical aspects, but one's character and how it led one to behave in any given situation. Up to a point this seems right. However, the Spanish poet presumably did not change his DNA, while for Spinoza he was replaced by another individual with a different essence. And of course a modern Spinozist would need to postulate a divine idea of one's DNA which would be the same thing conceived under the attribute of thought. In any case, I suggest that one's essence, as Spinoza understands it, includes features due to infantile experiences as well as what is determined before birth, like DNA. Another objection is that this suggestion would imply that identical twins (or clones and cloned) would have to be called the same individual.

XI The *conatus*

Every finite thing, so Spinoza claims, constantly endeavours to continue to exist (i.e. its essence struggles to keep itself actualized). What is more, it endeavours to continue to exist in as perfect a form as possible. But what makes one form of existence more perfect than another? It must mean something like possessing a greater degree of individuality: that is, with having more precise contours which distinguish it from other things. Thus an essence can be more or less fully actualized, sometimes only in a rather attenuated form, at other times in a more robust form.

So a thing and its essence can change from time to time in two different ways. (1) It can exist in a more or less robust form, or in a more or less attenuated form. It is its constant endeavour, or *conatus*, to be in the former state which explains all its more specific actions. (2) Its affections can change: that is, it can be in varying states or do varying things, without necessarily this strengthening or attenuating its essence.

Does the divine substance have its own *conatus*? In a certain sense it does. For everything which it does is what is necessary, in present circumstances (i.e. in its present overall state), to keep itself going with its own essence.

Spinoza says that the endeavour to continue in existence is the very essence of the thing itself, not something distinct from the essence. There is a certain awkwardness in this way of putting it, for surely we need to specify the essence as what the *conatus* is an endeavour to preserve. However, the essential point is clear enough: namely, that every actualized essence is always doing its best to keep itself actualized in as robust a form as possible.

It will be seen from this that there are two aspects to the causation of any human action. On the one hand, there is the *conatus* of the individual, its perpetual endeavour to continue to exist in as full and robust a form as possible; on the other hand, there are the *external circumstances* impinging on it, and to which it is reacting. This contrast is the key to Spinoza's account of freedom, to which I now turn.

XII The Divine Freedom

One of the biggest contrasts between God-or-Nature and its finite modes is that God is completely free, in the only coherent sense in which anything can be free, whereas individual things such as ourselves are at best partially free.

This requires that we attend to Spinoza's notion of freedom.

Actually, Spinoza operates with two concepts of freedom which he thinks are commonly confused. Nothing at all is free in the sense of the first concept, while things are free to various degrees in the sense of the second. In this latter sense God alone is absolutely free, but other things, more especially human beings, can be, and are, free in different degrees.

According to the first conception of freedom, an individual acts freely provided only that it is a contingent, not a necessary, truth that it thus acts, so that in the same circumstances it is quite possible that it might have acted otherwise. This is what is sometimes called the freedom of indifference, or contra-causal freedom. For Spinoza the idea of such a freedom is absurd, because it is absurd to think that anything can occur which does not have a fully determining cause.

E1p32 Will cannot be called a free cause, but only a necessary cause.
[From *E1 Appendix*] It will suffice at this point if I take as my basis what must be universally admitted, that all men are born ignorant of the causes of things, that they all have a desire to seek their own advantage, a desire of which they are conscious. From this it follows, firstly, that men believe that they are free, precisely because they are conscious of their volitions and desires; yet concerning the causes that have determined them to desire and will, they have not the faintest idea because they are ignorant of them. Secondly men act always with an end in view, to wit, the advantage that they seek. Hence it happens that they are always looking only for the final causes of things done, and are satisfied when they find them, having, of course, no reason for further doubt.

In the other sense a thing is completely free if and only if its acting in a certain way has no necessitating cause outside itself.

E1d7 That thing is said to be free (liber) which exists solely from the necessity of its own nature, and is determined to action by itself alone. A thing is said to be necessary (necessarius) or rather, constrained (coactus), if it is determined by another thing to exist and to act in a definite and determinate way.

In this respectable sense only the Divine Substance is completely free. (See E1p17 and cor.) That is, everything which it does (or which happens to it, except that nothing does *just* happen to it) follows from its essence together with its present modal state (how things are with its modes), and this follows necessarily, but not under compulsion from anything external to it, since there is nothing external to it.

But though nothing else can be completely free, finite individuals can be free to some degree. Such an individual is acting more freely the more what it does is the result of its own essence, and the less the result of things outside it.

Compare the basis on which a stone moves from one place to another and that on which a human being does. Basically, a stone just lies where it is until a human being picks it up, or some other external factor acts on it. Certainly the way the stone moves has something to do with its own *conatus* to persist in its essence. The fact that if I pick it up and leave go of it, it falls to the ground has a good deal to do with its essence as a physical thing with a certain mass subject to attraction by other bodies.[19] Still, this is just an instance of a rather pervasive fact about all physical things. But how a human being moves about turns far more on its own essence. True, a human being is continually responding to external stimuli, but what it will do in response to these stimuli is due to complicated facts about his own internal nature (whether we conceive this in mental or physical terms). So when the image of another person is produced in me, what I do will depend to a great extent on how well I know them and how, if so, I feel about them. And these will be a matter of my essence as presently modified. For Spinoza, then, an individual is free to the extent that it can respond to external stimuli in a flexible manner according to its internal state.

XIII Freedom as Determination by Adequate Ideas, i.e. by Rational Thought

However, Spinoza often operates with a notion of freedom which, on the face of it, is rather different from the notion of it as determination by one's own essence. According to this account, an individual is free the more what they do is the result of what Spinoza, following Descartes and others, calls 'clear and distinct ideas' on their part, and the less free the more what they do is the result of confused ideas. Thus, in so far as I act on the basis of a clear grasp of my present situation and my own needs and know what I am doing and why, the more free I am, whereas if I act, say, on a sudden burst of anger, without grasping what it is that has made me angry, or conception of what my anger is likely to lead to, the less free I am. To be free in this sense is to be active as that is specified in E3p1.

E3p1 Our mind is in some instances active, and in other instances passive. In so far as it has adequate ideas it is necessarily active; and in so far as it has inadequate ideas, it is necessarily passive.

This also seems a promising account of freedom, but is it the same as the previous one?

The identification evidently turns on Spinoza's assumption that the most significant element in a human being's essence is rationality (with a certain individuality of tone which distinguishes him from other human beings), and that I am therefore the more free the greater part reason plays in determining my actions.

But is it proper so to privilege the rational aspect of a human mind? Spinoza did not think of animals as very rational, yet there are so many similarities between humans, and at least the higher animals, that he could hardly deny some partial affinity in their essences. Indeed, his whole philosophy implies that, physically considered, we are just a specially complex arrangement of physical components of the same kind as make up any physical object, so that our essence has a good deal in common even with that of a stone.

An answer to this problem is to be found in Spinoza, but it is somewhat abstruse.

XIV Rational and Irrational Minds

The existence of an individual mind over time, like the existence of anything else, on its mental side, consists in the fact that the Divine Substance is having certain thoughts over that time. In fact, the thing, as it is at any moment and on its mental side, is a part of the current divine thinking. The contents of this divine thinking are innumerable adequate ideas—that is, true ideas. But not every part of an adequate idea is itself an adequate idea. This allows for the possibility that the articulation of the physical world into individual physical objects does not correspond precisely to the articulation of the Divine Mind into adequate ideas. Every physical individual has a mind, and this mind is God's idea of it. But some of these minds will be very far from being adequate ideas, inasmuch as they are only parts of adequate ideas in God; while others will be much closer to being so, inasmuch as they are closer to being the whole of adequate ideas in God. And in so far as an individual's mind is the whole of an adequate idea in God, the succession of his thoughts (the changing 'affections' of his essence) will be the more rational, since they will include more of that in God which is determinative of them.

Thus the divine idea which constitutes a creature's mind will approximate to rationality the less supplementation it needs from other ideas in the divine mind to constitute an adequate idea. And since adequate ideas are the real motors of the world (*qua* mental), in so far as my mind is rational in this sense, it will be a substantial part of the cause of what I do; whereas in so far as my mind is irrational in this sense, it will indeed be part of the real cause of what I do, but it will be a much smaller part thereof. It will be seen that rationality is a matter of degree on this account, but the more rational an individual is, the more substantial a part he plays in the determination of his behaviour, and in Spinoza's sense, therefore, the more free.

So the universe moves on through God's *adequate ideas*. What, at any moment, is to happen next is due to the divine ratiocination in the coinage of adequate ideas. Or rather, that is what happens next in the mental world, while what happens next in the physical world is some kind of analogue of this. Inadequate ideas are causes only inasmuch as they are necessary parts of adequate ideas.

Thus the mind of a rational human being is nearer to being the whole of an adequate idea in God than is the mind of an irrational human being, and both again are probably nearer to being so than is the 'mind', the mental aspect, of this cup from which I am drinking coffee.

One might illustrate this point by pretending that the divine thinking is an entirely linguistic affair. Then the more my mind is like a complete sentence, the more rational it is. And the more it is like a complete, well-argued paragraph, the more rational still is it. But the more it is like a few words in a sentence which make little or no sense in isolation, the less rational will it be. And if it is rather like a sentence which is false taken on its own, though it is a clause in a complete sentence in the divine mind which is true, the more that mind will be thinking falsely. (See E2p35.)

Thus it is only the rational part of my mind which approximates to being the complete determinant of my behaviour. When I do things which are not determined by this rational part of my mind, outer influences play a much larger part in determining what I shall do. That is, my own essence plays only a rather limited part, in so far as I am irrational, in determining what I shall do.

So the difference between a more rational and a less rational man is that the mind of the former approximates to being a complete (= adequate) idea in the Divine Mind, as the mind of the latter does not. Therefore the essence of the former plays a larger part than the essence of the latter in determining what he will do. So we now see how it is that degree of freedom can be described either as the extent to which one's essence determines what one does, or as the extent to which adequate ideas do so.

But when a rational man does something for a rational reason, it is more natural to say that the cause of his action was a present rational thought rather than his rational mind. The answer, of course, is that it was his rational mind as presently qualified by a rational idea. That is, from God's point of view, the man's mind approximates to being one of his (God's) adequate ideas, but this adequate idea causes behaviour only in so far as it is united moment by moment with adequate ideas of the man's changing states and circumstances. And this, I think, leaves open the possibility that even a somewhat irrational man, whose mind is far from being a complete divine idea, may still occasionally be affected by an idea of his present state and circumstances sufficiently adequate to cause rational behaviour, though this will happen less often than with a rational man.

So external circumstances act on us differently according to how rational we are. In a highly rational person the effect of external circumstances is usually to create within his mind an adequate idea (or something close to this) of his situation and needs, and it is this which is the main cause of his behaviour, while in an irrational person they usually create only a highly inadequate idea of all this, and most of the cause of his behaviour is outside him. Such inadequate ideas are just miserable fragments of ideas which are adequate in God. And since it is God's adequate ideas which are the real power which operates in the world (*qua* thought), the more rational a person is, the larger the role that his mind has in controlling the process of events.

To stick strictly to Spinoza's principles, the above must be understood as concerning only the mental states of all concerned. The mind of the rational man produces experiences of action which are rational in character, while the mind of the irrational man produces experiences of action which mostly are not. Brain events, and muscular contractions etc. which are analogues of what I have been describing, occur in God *qua* physical nature.

I cannot claim great precision in this account of the distinction between rational and irrational action and how it applies to each of mind and body. But I suggest finally that 'mind' covers not just thinking in a common or garden sense, but also what phenomenologists call the lived body. This is an impression of the state of our body as a whole, and does not include all the details known to God.

XV What Distinguishes One Finite Mind from Another as Ideas in the Divine Mind?

But a problem is lurking here. Granted that all finite minds are components in the one infinite Divine Mind, what marks them off as individual minds at all? The units do not consist simply of God's more adequate ideas, for then there could not be irrational creatures.

The obvious answer is that minds are individuated by the bodies of which they are the divine ideas. But that only raises the question of what individuates some part of infinite extension into an individual body. Presumably, that it has its own particular effort to continue in existence. But if so, why can we not apply this criterion directly to the mental? For the mental and the physical are meant to be independently intelligible.

Perhaps we need to revise the view that less rational minds are without adequate ideas. Perhaps at the core of every individual mind there is an adequate idea struggling to keep itself actualized (each corresponding to something physical about one which lasts one's whole life). What distinguishes it from a more rational mind may, then, be two things: (1) that it is a rather negligible adequate idea, and very simple in character; (2) that it is more mixed up with inadequate ideas than is the adequate idea at the core of a more rational mind. Thus the rational part of its essence plays a smaller part in determining behaviour than does that of a more rational individual. To be quite true to Spinoza's conceptual scheme, one would have to say that it is only in so far as the behaviour is caused by that active part of the essence that the individual can really be said to be acting at all; however, one needs some way of talking about so-called irrational action.

XVI Emotion and Perception

Now the ideal which prompts all one's activity is ultimately the wish to continue existing in as 'perfect' a form as possible. But in what does such perfection consist? Ultimately in that 'intellectual love of God' which consists in a joyful understanding of how the universe really works and the part one is oneself playing in it.

But all more ordinary pleasures which strengthen rather than weaken the life force within one contribute to this perfection.

E4p45cor Certainly nothing but grim and gloomy superstition forbids enjoyment. Why is it less fitting to drive away melancholy than to dispel hunger and thirst? The principle that guides me and shapes my attitude to life is this: no deity, nor anyone else but the envious, takes pleasure in my weakness and my misfortune, nor does he take to be a virtue our tears, sobs, fearfulness and other such things that are a mark of a weak spirit. On the contrary, the more we are affected with pleasure, the more we pass to a state of greater perfection; that is, the more we necessarily participate in the divine nature. Therefore it is the part of a wise man to make use of things and to take pleasure in them as far as he can (but not to the point of satiety, that is not taking pleasure). It is, I repeat, the part of a wise man to refresh and invigorate himself in moderation with good food and drink, as also with perfumes, with the beauty of blossoming plants, with dress, music, sporting activities, theatres and the like, in which every man can indulge without harm to another. For the human body is continually in need of fresh food of various kinds so that the entire body may be equally capable of all the functions that follow from its own nature, and consequently that the mind may be equally capable of simultaneously understanding many things. So this manner of life is in closest agreement both with our principles and with common practice. Therefore, of all ways of life, this is the best and is to be commended on all accounts. There is no need for me to deal more clearly or at greater length with this subject.

So all pleasure is good in itself, and only bad if it harms us more than it does us good. But what exactly is pleasure? Well, every individual is aiming to preserve itself—that is, to keep its essence actualized, in as robust a form as possible. And pleasure is what we feel when the vigour of our essence is increased, while pain is what we feel when it is decreased. And 'pleasure' and 'pain', together with 'desire' (which is simply our essence in action, that is, producing successful behaviour), are the three primary emotions in terms of which, together with 'idea', Spinoza sets out to explain the nature of all emotions.

E3p11s We see then that the mind can undergo considerable changes, and can pass now to a state of greater perfection, now to one of less perfection, and it is these passive transitions (passiones) that explicate for us the emotions of Pleasure (laetitia) and Pain (tristitia). So in what follows I shall understand by pleasure 'the passive transition of the mind to a state of greater perfection', and by pain 'the passive transition of the mind to a state of less perfection'. The emotion of pleasure when it is simultaneously related to mind and body I call Titillation (titillatio) or Cheerfulness (hilaritas); the emotion of pain when it is similarly related I call Anguish (dolor) or Melancholy (melancholia). But be it noted that titillation and anguish are related to man when one part of him is affected more than others, cheerfulness and melancholy when all parts are equally affected. As to Desire (cupiditas), I have explained what it is in E3p9s, and I acknowledge no primary emotion other than these three [i.e. pleasure, pain, and desire]; for I shall subsequently show that the others arise from these three.

Spinoza offers an analysis of a long list of emotions along these lines.[20] A few examples will give the general idea. The fuller account of each occurs *passim* in E3. The following definitions are from 'Definitions of the Emotions' at the end of E3.

1. Desire is the very essence of man in so far as his essence is conceived as determined to any action from any given affection of itself.
2. Pleasure [*laetitia*] is man's transition from a state of less perfection to a state of greater perfection.

3. Pain [*tristitia*] is man's transition from a state of greater perfection to a state of less perfection.[21]

6. Love is pleasure accompanied by the idea of an external cause.

7. Hatred is pain accompanied by the idea of an external cause.

16. Joy [*gaudia*] is pleasure accompanied by the idea of a past thing which has had an issue beyond our hope.

17. Disappointment is pain accompanied by the idea of a past thing whose outcome was contrary to our hope.

18. Pity is pain accompanied by the idea of ill that has happened to another whom we think of as like ourselves.

23. Envy is hatred, in so far as it so affects a man that he is pained at another's good fortune and rejoices at another's ill-fortune.

25. Self-contentment is pleasure arising from a man's contemplation of himself and his power of action.

26. Humility is pain arising from a man's contemplation of his own impotence or weakness.

27. Repentance is pain accompanied by the idea of some deed which we believe we have done from free decision of the mind.

34. Gratitude is the desire, or eagerness of love (*amoris studium*) whereby we endeavour to benefit one who, for a like emotion of love, has bestowed a benefit on us.

35. Benevolence is the desire of benefiting one whom we pity.

36. Anger is the desire, whereby we are urged from hatred to inflict injury on one whom we hate.

48. Lust is the desire and love of sexual intercourse.

A word should be said here about Spinoza's view of perception. An individual *perceives* an external object, according to Spinoza, when God has an idea of him as affected by it. This divine idea, however, is, from the individual's point of view, his sense that there is such an external object in the offing. Actually it seems that Spinoza takes much the same view of what it is for a finite individual merely to *think about* something external. The difference is simply the directness of the causation involved.

This certainly seems a strange view. It is sometimes said (by Pollock, for example, POLLOCK, 124–7) that Spinoza confuses two senses of 'idea': that in which a finite person has the idea of something which he is perceiving or thinking about, and that in which his mind and its passing states, are ideas in God's mind. However, this is not a confusion, but an essential element in Spinoza's position. For it turns on his belief that a finite mind can contain part of a divine idea, and that as such it does not possess the full truth pertaining to the divine idea of which it is a part. Suppose that God has the idea 'This body is being affected by object X'. Then, if it is *my* body, I just have a bit of the idea: namely, 'object X' (which for Spinoza is tantamount to 'X exists—in the vicinity' or in some context which the idea itself indicates). This is how Spinoza explains illusion. When I seem to see an object X which is not really there, God is having the idea 'This body is in a state very much as though object X was in its vicinity', while I just have a *bit* of the idea, namely, 'object X in the vicinity'.

XVII Spinoza's Determinism

It should be clear by now that Spinoza is a complete determinist. The essence of the divine substance includes or implies all the basic laws of nature, both in its physical and in its mental aspect. Everything which happens is completely determined by the previous state of the universe together with the laws of nature. Take any date you like far back in history or pre-history, and it will have already been settled by events on that date that you, dear reader, would be doing just what you are doing at this very moment. Similarly with myself and everyone and everything else. Propositions 26–29 of Part 1 make this abundantly clear.

Human thought and activity are no exception. The mental world changes from moment to moment according to mental laws, and the physical world changes from moment to moment according to physical laws, and these are such that mental and physical are continually isomorphic to one another. However, we should not complain that our actions are forced upon us, for when we are truly active, our essence, which is the core of ourselves, is producing (that is, according to the best lights available to us, which too often are harmful misconceptions) just what we both need and want to do.

There is a good deal here which is pretty problematic. What is the relation between the explanation of what a person does in terms of the activity of their essence and as following from the laws of nature? Are the laws of nature somehow logically derivative from the way in which all essences seek to actualize themselves, or is the way in which all essences seek to actualize themselves somehow derivative from the laws of nature?

I cannot provide a satisfactory answer to these questions. But one thing I will insist on in defence of Spinoza in this connection. He is remarkably often charged with having confused causation and logical entailment.

This is quite to misunderstand his position. As he uses 'cause', the laws of nature are themselves causes. Therefore, an event always has two causes: first, the relevant laws of nature, and secondly, antecedent conditions. (See E1pp21–9.) Today people analyse causation in terms of initial conditions and a covering law, but they use the word 'cause' only for the initial conditions. Spinoza uses 'cause' to cover both, and is quite right that causation in this sense is a form of logical necessitation.

XVIII Absolute and Relative Necessity

Spinoza did, however, distinguish between two types of necessity. First, there are things which follow from the essence of God, such as the nature of space and time and the laws of nature. Secondly, there are things which do not follow immediately from the essence of God, but only from that essence taken in conjunction with previous events. (See E1pp21–9.) Let us call the first of these cases of *absolute necessity* and the second cases of *relative necessity*. Events occurring in time are never absolutely necessary, but only relatively necessary.

Although he distinguishes between these clearly enough, Spinoza seems to think that absolute necessity and relative necessity, taken together, are sufficient grounds for saying that nothing whatever could have been different from how it is, whether it be the nature of space or the occurrence of historical events. On the basis of this he says, in effect, that this is the only possible world, rejecting in advance Leibniz's view that it is one among an infinity of possible worlds which God has chosen as being the best.

Some think Spinoza confused on this matter. If events in time are only relatively, and not absolutely, necessary, how does it follow that this is the only possible world? Surely a quite different chain of states of a world would have been quite compatible with the absolute nature of God, that is, with his essence. And is not this to say that this is not the only possible world?

One who holds that this is the only possible world has been called a necessitarian.

(1) Some believe that Spinoza was a strict necessitarian in his belief, but that this is not logically grounded in his basic viewpoint—indeed is inconsistent with it.

(2) Others believe that Spinoza says nothing that implies that this is the only possible world in the relevant sense, and that he was therefore not a strict necessitarian.

(3) Maybe there is a third group who believe that Spinoza was a necessitarian and that some not easily grasped character of his position does, in fact, imply this.[22]

I suggest that Spinoza's position may be this:

(4) Events in time are only *relatively necessary*, but they are so relative to an infinite series reaching back through an infinite past time with no beginning. Thus there was no moment at which a different series of events could have been set off in conformity with the actual and, on Spinoza's view, necessary laws of nature. And Spinoza may have thought (quite convincingly, as it seems to me) that being necessary relative to a past which extends infinitely backwards justifies the kind of things he says which suggest that this is the only possible world. For certainly this view implies that never, never, never was it not already settled what you or I or any other individual would be doing at this moment.

He could then, not unpersuasively, argue that recognizing that there has never been any alternative to what is happening today should help us adjust to the world and not complain too much at the less fortunate things which happen to us. We should have an attitude to their occurrence not so dissimilar from that which we have to such a truth as that the internal angles of a triangle add up to two right angles.

This requires that the series of moments of the world process which led up to this moment, and will do so to all subsequent moments (in an infinite series) had no beginning. For if there had been a first moment, it would have been neither relatively nor absolutely necessary. I am a bit doubtful myself as to whether it can be true that the world process had no beginning, but Spinoza's view is intellectually very respectable, as any number of clever people have believed it to be true. So I suggest that Spinoza was right, in his own terms, to hold that things could not have been otherwise than they are.[23]

Modern physics runs counter to this sort of absolute determinism, but I would not accept its present judgement on such matters as final. Besides, determinism qualified by sheer chance does not provide the free will in which people like to believe.

XIX Determinism does not Make Careful Decision Making Pointless

Determinism tends to be regarded as a pessimistic view of the world. Both those who believe it true and those who believe it false tend to think that it is a sad view of things, and that if it is true, so much the worse for us. Spinoza took just the opposite view. He thought that it was something to rejoice at, and that belief in it should be morally improving.

That everything happens necessarily does not make serious thought about what to do pointless. For whether you think carefully or not will affect what you do. You would not have acted thus if you had not thought seriously, though whether you were or were not going to think seriously was predetermined. Hence self-criticism and sensitive advice to others are of great importance.

Some people seem to think that if determinism is true, then one's fate is sealed and one can do nothing about it. Taken to its logical, or rather illogical conclusion, they think that if determinism is true, there's no point in being careful when you cross the road, for if it's already settled that you will die this day, such care is pointless, while if it's settled that no serious trouble will come to you this day, you may as well relax and act with spontaneous carelessness.

There is something wrong here. Determinism does not say, 'whether you cross the road carefully or not, if it's your death day, you will die today'. Rather, it says that if you cross the road carefully, you will probably not get hurt, while if you cross it carelessly (when there is much traffic about), you probably will suffer death or injury.

Counterfactual conditionals, of the form 'If you had done that, X would have happened', remain just as true (if they are true) on the determinist view as on any other. There are some problems about the nature of counterfactual conditionals, but they do not arise uniquely for determinism.

More importantly, it is a mistake to think that if determinism is true, there is no point in ever giving or taking advice, because it can never make a difference to what the advisee does. Spinoza has plenty of advice for us, as to how we should live our lives. His hope is that reflection upon what he says will join the determinants of his readers' behaviour, and make it better than it would have been otherwise. It is perfectly logical for him to hold this.

I am speaking here of determinism in a quite general sense, not of something specific, such as tends to worry us today, such as genetic determinism. If a virtually irresistible tendency to violent behaviour is determined by a certain genetic endowment, then moralizing and punishment are unlikely to stop the person acting violently. But if rational thought of which the individual is capable can be as truly a determinant of behaviour as genes can be, then attempts to induce rational thought in a potentially violent person may be effective and worthwhile. Of course, the problem may be solved, with the knowledge of genes which scientists are now gaining, by genetic modification of the genes of individuals who would otherwise have the 'wrong' ones. But that is a different matter. The point at present is that determinism in general does not necessarily imply that our more unfortunate genetically produced tendencies can never be checked by moral education or mild punishments.

XX Belief in Determinism should Make for Tolerance

Why did Spinoza think that belief in determinism should be morally improving? There are two main reasons. First, it should make us more tolerant of people whose behaviour annoys us. (See E2p49s towards the end.) This is because such emotions can only be felt towards something which we think is the free cause of what it does (in the bad sense of 'free'). If we believe that an individual was absolutely bound to act just as he did, in those circumstances at that time, our response is directed more towards a historical situation. And as we understand a historical situation as a whole, the activity and pleasure of understanding tends to dominate emotions directed at particular factors within it. One may be angry with the Nazis, but can we be angry with the whole history of Germany and Europe? Spinoza would think not. But surely we may regret it. I think Spinoza's answer, right or wrong, is that as our understanding increases, so we will see that the whole of human history must be wished away in order that we may wish that terrible episode away. (Many will feel that this is tough-minded to excess.) For more on determinism, see section XXXIII ('Determinism as a Religious Doctrine').

XXI Is the Universe Perfect, Properly Understood?

The second reason why Spinoza thinks determinism a morally improving doctrine is that it teaches us not to rail against fate. Everything is so connected with everything else that we cannot intelligibly wish anything away without wishing everything away, and that, for Spinoza, would be meaningless. And in any case, the whole system of the universe, could we understand it as a whole, would exhibit itself as somehow perfect.

Spinoza certainly thinks God-or-Nature—that is, the grand conscious totality of everything—'perfect', but in quite what sense of 'perfect' is somewhat problematic. (See E1 appendix at end.) But though he is not too clear on the matter, I think his position is that the divine mind, since it can experience no frustration (there being nothing outside it to frustrate it), must enjoy the whole thing (with an active rather than a passive joy) and that its judgement, being that associated with a grasp of the total nature of reality, must be final. (See E5p35.) Therefore, in so far as we can hope to come anywhere near the divine point of view, we must find the world good in its totality, and everything bad a necessary part of the perfect totality.

[F]or Nature's bounds are set not by the laws of human reason whose aim is only man's true interest and preservation, but by infinite other laws which have regard to the eternal order of the whole of Nature, of which man is but a tiny part. It is from the necessity of this order alone that all individual things are determined to exist and to act in a definite way. So if something in Nature appears to us as ridiculous, absurd, or evil, this is due to the fact that our knowledge is only partial, that we are for the most part ignorant of the order and coherence of Nature as a whole, and that we want all things to be directed as our reason prescribes. Yet that which our reason declares to be evil is not evil in respect of the order and laws of universal Nature, but only in respect of our own particular nature. (*TP* ch. 2, §8)

It should not be thought that Spinoza's deterministic optimism made him a quietist who thought that we should not seek to improve our own lot, or that of humanity in general. Indeed, there is no question of this, granted Spinoza's doctrine of the *conatus*. We can, and in so far as we are enlightened will, act as our clear ideas of things dictate we should do, to fulfil ourselves— that is, to keep our essence going in as robust a manner as possible. We simply cannot be complete quietists, since the more we understand things, the more we will form adequate ideas which energize us to improve things both for ourselves and for others. And this requires that we aim at certain sorts of relationship, rather than others, with our fellows. And this is my cue for a discussion of Spinoza's strictly ethical doctrines.

XXII Spinoza's Chief Ethical Doctrines

1. These are largely presented (mainly in E4) in the form of propositions about how the 'free man' will behave. And this amounts to showing us how a man will come to think and behave, the more he is guided by

'adequate ideas'. But such propositions are not bare statements of fact, for they have a prescriptive force inasmuch as they tell us how we may best achieve what is inevitably our main objective: namely, to keep ourselves going in as robust a form as possible.

2. Since pleasure is an emotion which occurs when the body and mind pass 'to a state of greater perfection', and pain is an emotion which occurs when they pass 'to a state of less perfection', it follows that we seek what gives us pleasure and what diminishes pain, for this is simply our *conatus* to continue in existence in as robust (which Spinoza calls as 'perfect') a state as possible. It follows further that all that anyone can sincerely mean when he calls something 'good' or 'bad' is that it is something he is or is not eager to experience or encounter.

3. Thus ethical precepts can only be expected to influence conduct if they give acceptable advice as to how we may best live so as to maximize our own perfection. (This does not have to be the language in which they are couched, but it must be their implicit message.) It is, therefore, pointless to advocate a morality which people cannot recognize as helping them to preserve and enhance their nature.

   Many people think that to base morality on its egotistical advantages, however lofty, for those who live by it, is misplaced, even immoral. But Spinoza was not unusual in doing this; indeed, it may have been almost the standard view among philosophers till Spinoza's own time (a view which certainly still has its supporters) that all motivation is in the end similarly egotistical. I understand that even Thomas Aquinas did so. For, according to him, all voluntary acts are performed only 'because they are beneficial to the agent himself'.[24] Spinoza, like others, is to be praised for basing such a noble ethic on this seemingly rather ignoble basis. In any case, Spinoza's norms are presented in the spirit of—'Look, what you ultimately want is to persist in as robust a form as possible and this requires that your behaviour conforms to them'. He does not simply declare that we should concern ourselves with the welfare of others, but seeks rather to show why the welfare of others should and, if we are clearly aware of what is involved, will matter to us. (See around E4p37.)

4. Even if Spinoza's form of psychological egoism is not wholly acceptable, he is surely right that there is no point in saying that people ought to do something unless you can tell them something which will actually induce them to do so. A limited amount of control over people's

behaviour may, indeed, arise from the way words with strong emotive meaning may affect their behaviour. Various other ways of encouraging them to picture certain sorts of behaviour in an unpleasing light may work to some extent. But in the long run it is pointless for a moralist to say that we ought to behave in a certain way unless he can provide some genuine motive for our doing so, and this is a main part of Spinoza's message.

This, it seems to me, is an important step towards an intelligent moral philosophy. For example, saying that we should accept a lower 'standard of living' in order to raise that of others is too often just an incantation; it is useless unless it can latch on to genuine human motives. Whether Spinoza had an adequate idea of the range of human motivation is another matter.

5. Thus much of his ethics is based on the fact that human beings have such a need of each other that the clear-sighted person will make good relations with others one of his primary purposes. This was the basis for him of the really significant precepts of Judaeo-Christian morality.

Most strikingly, the precept of returning good for evil can be derived from this. (See E3pp43–4, E4p46, and E4 appendix, §11.) For love engenders love, and hate engenders hate but can be destroyed by love. We should therefore attempt to act lovingly, or at least under-standingly, to those who hurt us (or hurt those whose welfare concerns us), thereby improving them and our relations with them.

6. So we must try to love rather than hate our neighbours. Spinoza's development of this theme shows him at his closest to Judaeo-Chris-tianity, and was the basis for a special reverence he held for Christ.

Moreover, hate is an unpleasant emotion, and this of itself gives us every ground for seeking to free ourselves of it. And the main cause of hate is that we think that someone has harmed us, or harmed someone we love, out of contra-causal free will. Once we grasp something of the elaborate concatenation of causes which necessitated his acting in this way, we will no longer feel towards him as though he was the sole cause of the harm done us. What is more, one can more effectively deal with another's malice (and effect some improvement in his character) by acting lovingly towards him rather than in a hostile manner.[25]

Thus for Spinoza

E4p45 Hatred can never be good.

Love, in contrast, is of itself good. It can, however, be excessive, more especially when it takes the form merely of enjoying pleasant sensations (*titillatio*) caused in one by another. (See E4pp43–4.) Moreover, misplaced love can do a great deal of harm. But love to all men, in the sense of a real desire for their welfare, is, I take it, always good, just as truly as hate is always bad. Spinoza should really have done more to distinguish the many sorts of love which there are. But he would think them all special cases of 'pleasure with the idea of an external cause'.

Thus Spinoza endorses and argues for the central Christian precept of loving one's neighbour (but perhaps not quite as one loves oneself) and returning good for evil. (See E4pp36, 37–40, 45, 46.)

7. But on some important matters his ethical teaching contrasts sharply with Judaeo-Christian teaching. This is because he thought that irrational emotions were among the main causes of human suffering. And he believed that, although one can never rid oneself of these entirely, their deleterious effects can be reduced by understanding their nature and causes, and many of his precepts are concerned with ways in which such emotions can be superseded and replaced by more positive ones.

8. For example, he is completely opposed to the tendency sometimes associated with Judaeo-Christianity to regard enjoying oneself as somehow bad; for Spinoza this is stupid and superstitious.

E4p44 Pleasure [*laetitia*] is not in itself bad, but good. On the other hand, pain [*tristitia*] is in itself bad.

Still, this requires some qualification. For we should heed Spinoza's distinction, in the passage quoted above (E3p11), between pleasure as a state of the whole person (*hilaritas*) and mere pleasant sensations (*titillatio*). (See E4pp42 and 43.) The latter satisfy the *conatus* of some mere part of the individual and may check that of the individual as a whole. (See also E3p11s, E3p36 dem, E3, and definitions 2 and 3 in DEFINITIONS OF THE EMOTIONS at the end of E3.) Such pleasures are not deeply satisfying and often lead one astray from pursuing the path of reason. It is a state of over all joyfulness which one should seek, not the mere satisfaction of physical or mental parts of us.

Another important distinction which Spinoza makes is between active pleasure and passive pleasure. (See E3p58 and, by implication, *passim*.) In both we are in the process of moving to a higher level of perfection, but in the first case this is due more to the action of outer things upon us, while in the latter it is due more to ourselves.

9. He was opposed also to some more fundamental features of the Judaeo-Christian tradition. These are the high value it sets upon humility and repentance, which he regards as negative emotions which move us in a direction away from perfection. These emotions are painful in themselves and do not improve our relations with others.

Thus Spinoza says:

E4p53 Humility is not a virtue, that is, it does not arise from reason.

Certainly we make ourselves ridiculous if we pride ourselves on qualities which we do not have, but we should raise our energies by reflecting on what is good about us, rather than on our deficiencies. For a mere deficiency is not a positive thing at all. And seeking to lower ourselves in our own esteem reduces the general vigour with which we can make the best of our lives.

So likewise does repining over what one has done amiss in the past. One should forgive oneself just as one should forgive others, and simply learn from experience to be more sensible in future. It follows that:

E4p55 Repentance is not a virtue, or does not arise from reason; but he who repents of an action is doubly wretched or infirm.

To see something of this negative side of Spinoza's attitude to Judaeo-Christianity, compare it with the call of John the Baptist to repent or with the following quotation from Luther:

If I, wretched and damnable sinner, through works or merits could have loved the Son of God, and so come to him, what needed he to deliver himself for me? If I, being a wretch and damned sinner, could be redeemed by any other price, what needed the Son of God to be given? (Quoted in William James's *Varieties of Religious Experience*, 245)

Spinoza's recommendation to avoid negative emotions is more troubling when it comes to what he has to say about compassion.

E4p50 In the man who lives by the guidance of reason, pity (commiseratio) is in itself bad and disadvantageous.

For, although (so argues Spinoza) one's reason should lead one to help others in their need, one should not spoil one's ability to make the best of one's own life by excessive sympathy with their troubles when one cannot do much about them. It is better to help others from the rational thought that we are all so bound up with each other that to do so is to help oneself through the promotion of good community life. Simply being made miserable by another's misfortune about which one can do nothing is useless on the part of a rational man. It lowers his own energies while doing no good at all.

However, in the case of irrational men, it is better that they should feel compassion, for this may be the only way in which they can be induced to do what the rational man does for a more positive reason. (See E4p50s.) All such negative emotions as humility, repentance, and even useless compassion, can be removed to some extent by recognizing the truth of determinism and its application to particular cases. In short, as we have already seen, the truth of determinism is good news, not bad news.

10. Action based on positive emotions is always better than action based on negative emotions.

In all walks of life we should seek to encourage both ourselves and others to be activated by the former rather than the latter. For negative emotions drag us down and enervate us. The same thing done as a result of a positive emotion will be done not only more cheerfully but more effectively.

11. Although many things are good, the greatest good for man is the intellectual love of God. For this is an emotion which will not disappoint as others do. (See E5pp14–20, E5p33–7.) This, as we have partly seen, is a kind of participation in the joy with which God-or-Nature experiences itself as a great system in which everything hangs together in a free necessity. It arises above all from such understanding as we gain of things in so far as our ideas are adequate.

This requires a kind of rationality in behaviour and emotion which one can most easily achieve when others are likewise directed towards it. Therefore, there is a very special bond between rational and free men (these come to the same) which will promote especially positive relations of mutual aid between them. (See E4p71.) Only free men are thoroughly grateful one to another. This being so, the free man will do his best to bring others to the same level as himself in this respect. (See E4pp37 and 71.)

But the rational man will recognize that he benefits from good relations even with irrational men. So even when the special bond between free or rational men is missing, there will still be a motive for establishing good positive relations with them. Moreover, no men are altogether beyond the capacity to live rationally. For at the basis of us all there is a struggle to see things clearly, and in virtue of this we may all have some small share in the intellectual love of God.

He did not extend the same generosity to animals, however. He rejects the view of Descartes that animals have no feelings. But since the friendship of animals does not help us to live well, as does friendship with other human beings, no basis can be found for claiming that we have any obligations to them. Or so Spinoza thought.

12. We shall see later that the intellectual love of God may even give one a kind of eternal being, so that one is not wholly destroyed at death. I shall consider how Spinoza reached this view and what he meant by it later. In any case, Spinoza emphasizes that the main reasons for living virtuously are quite independent of this. Whether we have any sort of eternal life or not, negative emotions are equally bad for us, and friendly relations with others good for us.

13. Finally we should note that for Spinoza, although the free and rational person will lead a good life because he sees that it is essential for his own personal fulfilment, many people are not sufficiently rational for this, and need to be taught to co-operate by less rational means of persuasion.

PART THREE: SPINOZA ON ORGANIZED RELIGION AND THE REDUCTION OF RELIGIOUS STRIFE

XXIII The Universal Religion

In considering Spinoza's position *vis-à-vis* religion, there are two main questions to be discussed. First, how did Spinoza view organized religion, or what in Chapter 1 I called community religions? And secondly, can Spinozism function as a personal religion for one who accepts it in large part? This section will be concerned with the first of these questions.

In his *Tractatus Theologico-Politicus* Spinoza makes some proposals for the reduction of religious strife within a nation-state.

For this purpose he said that in an ideal state there should be a minimal state religion with a minimal creed (to be invoked on official occasions, etc.) and that, in addition, with certain qualifications, any religions should be allowed to flourish which incorporated its basic principles, with whatever extra teachings suited them. (See *TTP* ch. 14; BRILL, 224–5; GEBHARDT, iii. 177–8.)[26]

This minimal creed consists of seven basic propositions, which may be abbreviated thus:

1. God exists.
2. God is unique.
3. God is omnipresent.
4. God has supreme right and dominion over all things.
5. The worship of God consists in 'obedience'; that is to say, in morally acceptable or admirable behaviour under two main heads, 'justice' and 'charity'.
6. All those, and only those, who obey God are saved.
7. God forgives repentant sinners.

Spinoza thought that all men of good will could join in accepting these doctrines, *in an ethically equivalent sense*, however much they might diverge in their precise understanding of them or in the ceremonies, if any, with which they were associated. On the basis of their universal acceptance in this fashion, people should welcome religious diversity in society, since different understandings of the doctrines, provided they come to the same at the ethical level, suit different sorts of mind. (See *TTP* Preface; GEBHARDT, iii. 11; BRILL, 55.) These different interpretations of the common core creed would then be 'personal interpretations' of the universal religion in the sense characterized in my first chapter.

No one can fail to realise that all these beliefs are essential if all men, without exception, are to be capable of obeying God as prescribed by the law explained above; for if any one of these beliefs is nullified, obedience is also nullified. But as to the question of what God, the exemplar of true life, really is, whether he is fire, or spirit, or light, or thought, or something else, this is irrelevant to faith. And so likewise is the question as to why he is the exemplar of true life, whether this is because he has a just and merciful disposition, or because all things exist and act through him and consequently we, too, understand through him, and through him we see what is true, just, and good. On these questions it matters not what beliefs a man holds. Nor, again, does it matter for faith whether one believes that God is omnipresent in essence or in potency, whether he directs everything from free will or from the necessity of his nature, whether he lays down laws as a ruler or teaches them as being eternal truths, whether man obeys God from free will or from the necessity of the divine decree, whether the rewarding of the good and the punishing of the wicked is natural or supernatural. The view one takes on these and similar questions has no bearing on faith, provided that such a belief does not lead to the assumption of greater license to sin, or hinders submission to God. Indeed, as we have already said, every man is in duty bound to adapt these religious dogmas to his own understanding and to interpret them for himself in whatever way makes him feel that he can the more readily accept them with full confidence and conviction. For, as we have already pointed out, just as in olden days faith was revealed and written down in a form which accorded with the understanding and beliefs of the prophets and people of that time, so, too, every man has now the duty to adapt it to his own beliefs, so as thus to accept it without any misgivings or doubts. For we have shown that faith demands piety rather than truth; faith is pious and saving only by reason of the obedience it inspires, and consequently nobody is faithful except by reason of his obedience. Therefore the best faith is not necessarily manifested by him who displays the best arguments, but by him who displays the best works of justice and charity. How salutary this doctrine is, how necessary in the state if men are to live in peace and harmony, and how many important causes of disturbance and crime are thereby aborted at source, I leave everyone to judge for himself. (*TTP* ch. 14, at BRILL, 225–6; GEBHARDT, iii. 178–9)

Clearly Spinoza saw his own philosophy as providing a 'personal interpretation' (see Chapter 1) of the universal religion for sufficiently rational persons which would allow them to understand the principles of that religion in a manner which they could accept as true. But note his remark that one's faith is not especially dependent on one's arguments, a touching remark from the great rationalist.

Alexandre Matheron has analysed with particular clarity, how each proposition in this universal creed could be given either a popular meaning or a philosophical one consonant with what Spinoza took to be the real truth of things. (MATHERON, 94–114).

Thus what 'God (i.e. a supreme being who is the model of the true life) exists' means for the simple man is that 'God (who may be a fire, a spirit, or a light) possesses a just and merciful heart', while for the Spinozistic philosopher it means that 'there is an absolute thought (or idea of God) through participation in which we conceive what is our true good': namely, a life of justice and charity (against the background of which one might develop one's own intellectual love of God). Or again, 'the worship of God consists solely in justice and charity' means for the plain man that 'God has ordered him as a prince might do to worship him only by living a life of justice and charity and the good man obeys this of his own free will', while for the philosopher it means that 'it follows from the nature of God and man as an eternal truth that one can only fulfil oneself properly through a life of justice and charity and he obeys this because it follows necessarily from his grasp of this'. (Quotations translated from the French with slight modification; MATHERON, 99.)

Thus, as Spinoza saw it, in an ideal society, each would be expected to acknowledge the propositions of the universal religion, interpreting them in whatever sense he can accept them as true, provided only that he derives from them a determination to act justly and charitably to his fellows. This accepted, all religious denominations or community religions would be tolerated as special forms of the universal religion. Thus while some might be Presbyterians, Roman Catholics, Jews, or Muslims, provided that their religion conformed to the universal religion, the most rational members of the society will be Spinozists or something akin to this, but many will belong to a more specific community religion. If the Spinozists have no such specific 'community religion' themselves, their Spinozism can only function as a personal religion, but maybe Spinoza once found a community religion on a small scale for himself among the collegiants who were quasi-disciples of his at least for a time. Of course, Spinoza does not talk of 'Spinozism', but clearly he thought that an outlook like his would eventually have the assent of the most rational members of such a society.

XXIV Spinoza on Jesus and on Salvation

It should be noted that while Spinoza never became a Christian, and spoke very explicitly of the doctrine of the Incarnation as unintelligible, he did conceive of Jesus as very different in his nature from the prophets or any other men of which he knew. The Hebrew prophets were (as we saw above in Part One) men with a highly developed moral sense and a vivid imagination, but otherwise subject to many delusions. God expressed himself to them, therefore, through their imagination, in teaching them the basic principles of morality.

Spinoza distinguished Jesus from the prophets in two ways. The first was that God talked to Jesus 'mind to mind' rather than through his imagination. This means, I believe, that Jesus participated in the wisdom of God through the intuitive insight which constitutes the third kind of knowledge. Thus he grasped the basic principles of ethics by his grasp of necessary truths about how individuals exemplifying the human essence[27] could find salvation—that is, true happiness. His intellectual intuition may even have extended to aspects of the nature of matter, as perhaps indicated by some of his miracles, some of which Spinoza seems to take seriously (as exploitation of facts about matter concealed from ordinary people).

The other main contrast between Jesus and the prophets was that they were concerned with rules and norms which should govern Jewish life, whereas Jesus universalized these teachings so that they applied to all men at all times and places.

Before the coming of Christ the prophets used to proclaim religion as the law of their own country by virtue of the covenant made in the time of Moses, whereas after the coming of Christ the Apostles preached religion to all men as a universal law solely by virtue of Christ's Passion. The books of the New Testament contained no different doctrine [from those of the Old Testament], nor were they written as documents of a covenant, nor was the universal religion—which is entirely in accord with Nature—anything new, except in relation to men who knew it not. (*TTP* ch. 12; GEBHARDT, iii. 163; BRILL, 209)

It must not be thought, of course, that men could discover the basic principles of the Universal Religion, only through Christ; Spinoza means only that he was a peculiarly qualified exponent of it. He says, for example, with reference to those pagans or Muslims who 'worship God by the exercise of justice and charity towards their neigbour, I believe that they have the Spirit of Christ and are saved, whatever convictions they may in their ignorance hold about Mahomet and the oracles' (LETTER 43).

But what exactly is salvation for Spinoza? Is it enough to say simply that it means 'true happiness'? The *TTP* hardly supplies an adequate answer, while what it means in the *Ethics* is open to much debate. I believe that it does mean 'true happiness', but that this is identified (at any rate in any complete form thereof) with the intellectual love of God. This may be enjoyed in this life, while to the extent that we do achieve it in the here and now, we may carry it into eternity, for it is only that part of us engaged in this love which is eternal.

In this connection Spinoza says that there is one important truth which we can know only on the basis of Jesus apparently having known it through his peculiarly intimate relation with the mind of God. For Jesus apparently knew, by intellectual intuition of a kind closed to us, that even those who did not achieve such love in this life would achieve it afterwards if they lived morally good lives. This information is of value rather to the philosopher than to the ordinary man, for he has the comfort that people whom he respects morally will not fail to gain eternal life. The ordinary person him or herself will probably have a simpler idea of the salvation which awaits them as a reward for their good behaviour. But Jesus's teaching is an additional motivator to the good life, on the part of both the ordinary man and of the philosopher, by the clarity it brings to such things.

This appeal to revelation may seem at odds with the general tenor of his metaphysical system; but revelation, as Spinoza effectively understands it, is any way in which natural processes operate so that men gain knowledge. The imagination is one way in which a particular class of minds acquire knowledge of a particular kind of truth. Such revelation through the imagination does not have the reliability of revelation through reason, but for many minds it is a chief and highly motivating way of grasping moral truth. (Compare Hegel.) But for Spinoza there seems to have been a third form of revelation: that special intuitive insight into the divine mind possessed by Jesus, and perhaps by him alone.

I should note that there is a school of thought which holds that what Spinoza says about Jesus was not meant sincerely. At best it was an attempt to mollify Christians whom he wanted to teach the virtues of tolerance; at worst it was, like, so it is claimed, much else in the *TTP*, a form of ironic discourse which was meant to exhibit the falsehood of what it said to the knowing. I cannot enter into this dispute beyond saying that I do not accept this deconstruction of the text. For one thing, there was so much that was inflammatory in the text—for example, on the topic or miracles, and in the case of Jesus, the denial of his resurrection—that it hardly seems to be designed to mollify anyone; nor do I believe that a man like Spinoza would have liked to play a game with the truth. (See STRAUSS and HARRIS 1 and 2.)

XXV Spinoza's Inter-faith Message for Today

Spinoza was proposing solutions to the particular forms of religious strife of his day, in particular between the Calvinists and the Remonstrants in the Netherlands, and was concerned, therefore, with rather different kinds of state from those of the here and now. But it seems to me that with some adaptation Spinoza's views could be made relevant to our own time.

For it would be an excellent thing, in my opinion, for us here and now (in European countries), if some kind of modern *universal religion* could be regarded as the religion of the state, to the extent at least of being taught at all state schools and sometimes affirmed on public occasions. In Spinoza's time the seven propositions of his universal religion might reasonably be put forward for this purpose. And perhaps even now, with a generous enough notion of 'God', the larger part of the population would be prepared to have their basic values associated with theistic language and this could form a basic inter-faith declaration. However, to bring in those who would reject theistic language, even interpreted in the least dogmatic of ways, some other formula would be needed. I have developed this theme more fully in an article called 'Is Spinozism a Religion?'

PART FOUR: SPINOZISM AS A PERSONAL RELIGION

I now turn to the question as to whether Spinozism is capable of constituting a personal religion or a personal interpretation of the Universal
Religion or some more specific community religion.

XXVI Could Spinozism Function for Some People as a Personal Religion?

It is obvious that if being a Spinozist means accepting every proposition of
the *Ethics*, there would be no Spinozists today, if only on account of
subsequent developments in natural science. So let us mean by 'Spinozism' any body of beliefs of which the core incorporates much of what is
most distinctive in Spinoza's philosophy. And let us consider whether
Spinozism as thus understood could be a personal religion for anyone
today, or even a personal interpretation of a community religion (or
indeed of some modern form of the universal religion should one arise).

One could hardly adopt Spinozism as a personal religion unless one
thought that

(a) it contained a great deal of truth;
(b) it encouraged certain emotions which are 'religious' in a broad sense;
(c) its ethical message was good, well grounded and practicable;
(d) it offered some kind of salvation, in however secular a sense.

More specifically, we may say that today's Spinozist would attempt to
live by the ethics which I have described above, to control his irrational
emotions by developing so far as he could clear and distinct ideas as to
their causes, and aspire to something like 'the intellectual love of God'.
Moreover, his belief in determinism would have a deep effect on his
attitudes, which I shall be discussing more fully shortly. On much of
this, sufficient has been said or implied already, but I finish with a few
matters which are relevant to the claim of Spinozism to offer a personal
religion.

XXVII The Intellectual Love of God

Though it is not the only good which the free man will recognize, the
supreme good for him is 'the intellectual love of God', and it is time to

examine what Spinoza means by this expression more closely than we have done as yet.[28] In trying to understand it, we must bear in mind that for Spinoza God is the universe, the reality of which we are a part, not something beyond it, and that the expression 'intellectual' covers almost any sort of consciousness. The whole expression is perhaps equivalent to 'conscious delight in the reality we are in the midst of'.

Both this and Spinoza's own formulation may seem so general as to be vacuous. We may surmise that for Spinoza a certain definite way of experiencing the unity of the universe, and of particular things as pertaining to that unity, were denoted by the expression, but he can hardly be said to have made it clear what this experience was. Is this because, in spite of Spinoza's extreme rationalism, it did, in fact, have an ineffable, mystical aspect to it?

Certainly part of what he has in mind is that one can come to know and love the most general characteristics of the universe, and to love particular things as specifications of these most general characteristics. This might suggest that what Spinoza really recognizes as the completest form of human fulfilment is the enjoyment of the scientific researcher (a rather different creature then from today).

Perhaps the truth is, rather, that it is the enjoyment given by any kind of understanding and discovery that he celebrates; for after all, any sort of knowledge is knowledge of reality, and can be seen as a partial revelation of the general character of the universe, whether it is the physicist's knowledge of the ultimate articulation of matter, the novelist's grasp of the possibilities of human nature, or perhaps the painter's knowledge of the intrinsic possibilities of form and of colour. And of course everyone else who gains something of this knowledge by his or her appreciation of their achievements will be sharing in this intellectual love of God.

One thing which may trouble us mildly is that if the intellectual love of God consists of the appreciative understanding of the nature of things, the status of the enjoyment of what purports to be understanding, but is really misunderstanding, is somewhat problematic.

Actually, Spinoza distinguishes three types of knowledge: knowledge gained by hearsay or rote learning, knowledge of an abstract kind, and knowledge consisting in an intuitive grasp of reality in the concrete, and he identifies the intellectual love of God with the third. (See E2p40s and E5p333.) But surely what seems to be an example of the third kind of knowledge may be infected with errors springing from what purports to be knowledge of the second kind (general scientific knowledge). Spinoza himself, it seems likely, sometimes thought that he had gained intuitive knowledge of some particular phenomenon, while this was in fact an error in the scientific knowledge of his time.[29] (I am not suggesting that this was always so.) And in so far as science may still contain mistakes, the same may be true of people today. Moreover, many of us lack much grasp at all of what even purports to be correct scientific knowledge. Does this mean that knowledge of the third kind, and hence the intellectual love of God, is closed to us?

Well, I believe that for Spinoza, however limited and even wrong our scientific 'knowledge' may be, whenever we enjoy what seems to us an immediate insight into how things hang together, we have in fact engaged with some aspect of the nature of reality in an understanding way, be it only the essential structure of a certain system of concepts, this system itself being, after all, part of the nature of things. Embedded as it may well be in misunderstandings generated outside our active thinking, that thinking itself, in so far as we experience it as a real achievement, has certainly homed in on the true nature of some aspect of reality. I am inclined to believe that this Spinozistic claim is correct.

Yet it does seem rather odd to call what is merely the enjoyment of one's own intellectual powers, such as they are, 'love of God', even though this is qualified by 'intellectual'. So I suspect that the expression really stands for an experience of a more mystical nature, some rapturous sense of one's oneness with the cosmos at large, and of its essential oneness in all phenomena. This is certainly suggested by the following passage in *The Emendation of the Intellect*. True, this is an early and unfinished work, but here it surely sets out his life purpose.

[For] Man conceives a human nature much stronger than his own, and sees no reason why he cannot acquire such a nature. Thus he is urged to seek the means that will bring him to such a perfection, and all that can be the means of his attaining this objective is called a true good, while the supreme good is to arrive at the enjoyment of such a nature, together with other individuals, if possible. What that nature is we shall show in its proper place; namely, the knowledge of the union which the mind has with the whole of Nature.

This, then, is the end for which I strive, to acquire the nature I have described and to endeavour that many should acquire it along with me. . . . To bring this about, it is necessary (1) to understand as much about Nature as suffices for acquiring such a nature, and (2) to establish such a social order as will enable as many as possible to reach this goal with the greatest possible ease and assurance. . . .

But our first consideration must be to devise a method of emending the intellect and of purifying it, as far as is feasible at the outset, so that it may succeed in understanding things without error and as well as possible. So now it will be evident to everyone that my purpose is to direct all the sciences to one end and goal, to wit (as we have said), the achievement of the highest human perfection. Thus everything in the sciences which does nothing to advance us towards our goal must be rejected as pointless—in short, all our activities and likewise our thoughts must be directed to this end. (EMENDATION, §§12–16; GEBHARDT, ii. 8–9; SHIRLEY, 5–6)

Here, it is plain, scientific knowledge need only be pursued so far as it helps us to perfect our nature, through our recognition of 'the union which the mind has with the whole of nature'. At that stage, then, Spinoza did not think of indefinite scientific enquiry as essential to achieve this true good.

The sense of oneness with the cosmos at large in some people takes the form of what may be called a meditation upon pure being. One brings home to oneself the fact that everything *is*, has *being*, and directs one's consciousness to this sheer *being* in which everything participates. In doing so one may realize that even what distinguishes one thing from another was always implicit in sheer *being* as such, inasmuch as it pertains eternally to the nature of *being* that the differentiating characteristics of each particular thing are among the ways in which being in general may become concrete. A Spinozist may think of *consciousness* and *extension* as built into *being* as such in this way, and think of every particular kind of consciousness, or type of extended thing, as a determination built into each of these as *they* are built into *being*.

There are, indeed, remarks in the *Ethics*, about the vacuousness of such a word as 'being', which appear to clash with suggestions such as these, yet I believe that in the end his intellectual love of God was, or at least included, a meditation of this kind.[30]

But however, precisely, we understand this adoration of the Universe, is it not in many respects so dreadful that it would be more appropriate to join Schopenhauer in hating it? Does it really merit the adoration which the ordinary theist feels for a transcendent God?

Spinoza's answer to this question is seldom thought quite satisfactory. He says in the first place that in so far as one understands sorrows, which the course of the universe brings one's way, one's sorrow gives way to joy in one's own understanding. Thus the sorrows for which the irrational man would blame God or the Universe are for the rational man simply further joys. Likewise, for any of the calamities of humankind of which one knows; they are all capable of giving the active mind the pleasure of understanding them as necessary episodes in the history of things, following of necessity from what preceded them, as that did from its predecessors back through infinite time, in virtue of the basic and necessary features of the world considered physically or psychologically.

E5p18 Nobody can hate God.
Proof. The idea of God which is in us is adequate and perfect. Therefore in so far as we contemplate God, we are active. Consequently there can be no pain accompanied by the idea of God; that is nobody can hate God.
E5p18c Love towards God cannot turn to hatred.
Scholium: It may be objected that in understanding God to be the cause of all things we thereby consider God to be the cause of pain. To this I reply that in so far as we understand the causes of pain, it ceases to be a passive emotion; that is to that extent it ceases to be pain [since pain is 'the passive transition of the mind to a state of less perfection', according to E3p11s]. So in so far as we understand God to be the cause of pain, to that extent we feel pleasure.

Here is another case where determinism plays an essential role in Spinoza's thought. To the extent that one understands the causation and present necessity of one's pain, it ceases to be pain. Is he going too far here? Myself, I grant that pain may sometimes be reduced in this manner, but always and reliably eliminated—hardly.

If one thinks of a vague feeling of distress when one wakes one morning, it sometimes helps to recognize its psychological cause. However, this depends on the kind of cause. If it is at someone having snubbed one in some way yesterday, it helps when one identifies this rather trivial cause, and also perhaps understands why it occurred. But can it be so when it is the death of a loved one? Perhaps to some extent, if one reflects on the fact that all must die, and perhaps that what one loved in them is still an eternal feature of the universe. (See below.) But Spinoza's claim for such a remedy seems exaggerated.

What if the pain is physical? Well, most of us have a pretty limited idea of the causes of physical pain. But it is true up to a point that thinking about its cause may help somewhat. (Physical suffering whose cause cannot be identified has its own special extra nastiness.) It sometimes helps also simply to attend to what pain precisely is, by a kind of phenomenological attention to it.

But whatever the extent to which this may work with one's own pain, it may strike one as an immoral way to deal with distress at the sorrows of others, especially those which arise from history's worst atrocities or natural disasters. Is it desirable to thank God-or-Nature for having provided these as objects of intellectual intuition?

Yet a somewhat modified claim may be more acceptable: namely, that if all its evils really are necessary features which the universe must possess if it is to exist at all, and if, taken on the whole, it is better that it should, rather than that it should not, exist, we may be able to delight in the universe as a whole and in general while not denying that it has elements which are foul. Personally I believe that the only possible solution to the problem of evil, either for a more orthodox theism or for a pantheistic position for which the universe itself is a divine unity, does lie in holding that in some way, largely beyond us, everything is so bound up with everything else that the evils are essential elements in a universe to which it is still proper to take a positive, even an adoring, attitude. (Saying that they are essential elements in the universe does not mean that they themselves are somehow good when understood in the light of the whole, as some absolute idealists proclaim.)

XXVIII God as the Infinite Physical Universe

The most basic of all Spinoza's beliefs is that there is just one substance, to be called 'God' or 'Nature', and that all finite things are modes of this one substance. Now although people do not naturally clothe their thoughts today in the language of substance and modes, the general message remains highly persuasive. It has two aspects: first, that we can form a legitimate conception of something we can call God-or-Nature, of which every finite thing is simply a passing state; and, secondly, that there is no need to postulate anything else more basic than itself as the explanation for its existence.

It seems to me that we can indeed form a conception of something we may call the universe or total reality. We can look up from the earth to the stars and form the conception of one single unitary physical universe of which both earth and stars and anything else we can perceive through our senses, or their artificial aids, belong. The most natural way of conceiving this is indeed to think of it as extending outwards infinitely in three dimensions from our bodies, in a manner which conforms to Euclidean geometry. Doubtless that way of conceiving it is not considered finally satisfactory by scientists today, for whom Euclidean geometry and a relatively simple dynamics are no longer an adequate description of the spatial aspect of the universe. All the same, the conception of the world as extending infinitely outwards from our own bodies in a three-dimensional manner *à la* Euclid seems to provide us with an initial sense of an infinite something which remains the object of our thought even when we move to more sophisticated accounts of its spatiality. The same is true of the temporality of the universe. We can form the conception (or it often seems to us that we can) of a temporal process extending back infinitely into the past and infinitely into the future of which what we call the present is just one phase.

These conceptions may be thought wrong in detail in the light of subsequent science, and even philosophy. The idea that the universe is infinite in space and time in the way Spinoza thought may no longer be acceptable, and the contrast between them is less sharp. But speculation about the nature of the universe as a whole is still concerned with the same total reality conceived in a manner which is a development, rather than a negation, of those earlier and still today more readily intelligible conceptions. In short, we can form the notion of the total physical world on the basis of concepts which may change somewhat, but which still target the same vast reality.

Actually, the notion of a universe which is self-bounding rather than infinite in the going-on-and-on-for-ever sense gives a stronger sense of the oneness of the physical universe than does one utilizing more traditional notions of the infinity of space and time (which in fact Spinoza had himself surpassed). (See LETTER 12.) The Spinozist notion that, as physical beings, we are components of a total individual which is in some sense infinite, and more of a genuine unit than we are ourselves, still stands unchallenged. And the reason for thinking it a more genuine unit than ourselves is much what Spinoza claimed. We think of something as more of a genuine individual the more we can form a conception of it in abstraction from anything else. And the conception of the physical universe as a whole is of something which is more individual in this sense than is anything else physical.

XXIX God as Infinite Mind

Now the sense of the universe as a single individual, of which we and our familiar world are simply little fragments, is of itself calculated to produce certain emotions of awe with some kinship to the Christian's response to God as he conceives him. It puts our own little worries, and perhaps even some of the more distressing human events, in the context of something so much vaster, that they may seem a little less important to us.[31] But the belief or recognition that the universe is an individual is hardly of itself a religious belief unless some kind of spiritual character is attributed to it. This condition is, however, met by Spinozism. For just as our bodies are little fragments of the one infinite individual *qua* physical universe, so are our mind fragments of it *qua* infinite individual mind. Thus our awe at the unimaginable infinite vastness and richness of the universe, *qua* physical, will be accompanied by awe at its unimaginable comprehensiveness *qua* infinite mind.

Yet, some present-day commentators decline to interpret Spinoza as holding that there is a single universal cosmic consciousness of which our minds are fragments. Nevertheless, attempts to understand him in a purely materialist sense do not convince me. (See CURLEY 1988, 74–82.) Surely the attribute of thought is meant to be a psychological reality.[32]

But certainly Spinoza's conception of the divine mind contrasts with traditional Judaeo-Christian conceptions of God, inasmuch as for Spinoza

(1) God's mind is somehow identical with the total physical universe;
(2) God is not conceived as a creator distinct from his creation;
(3) and, most strikingly, God does not simply exist of necessity but acts of necessity, without any special purposes for man or indeed any purposes at all. Things and processes simply follow from his nature, and his understanding of everything is identical with his willing of everything.

In spite of the equal reality of the attributes of extension and of thought, according to Spinoza's official view, commentators divide into those who most stress the one and those who most stress the other. The first assimilates Spinoza's position to materialism, the second to monistic idealism. One way in which Spinoza may be interpreted as close to materialism is by taking it that what corresponds in the attribute of thought to an occurrence in the attribute of extension is fully describable simply by the use of a certain logical operator which converts physical descriptions into mental ones. Thus the proper description of any mental event in an individual's life is to be found by the discovery of a physical description of the underlying bodily (presumably brain) state, call it B, and the attachment to this description of such an expression as 'idea of B'—let us write it 'IB'. In short, the conversion of a description of something on its physical side into a description of it on its mental side, and vice versa, is an entirely mechanical procedure of adding or removing the operator 'I'.

I recognize that this fits in with some aspects of how Spinoza presents his case and has, in effect, the support of such a distinguished commentator as Edwin Curley. (See CURLEY 1988.) But it tends to trivialize Spinoza's idea that there are two different ways of conceiving and explaining what goes on in the universe which should not be confused, and I cannot think that Spinoza would have been happy with it.

The alternative is to ascribe what one might call 'a language of thought' to God, in which there is a vocabulary of mental occurrences in which each symbol has its own inherent qualitative character, as do words in English or French whereby God describes what is going on in the physical world to himself.

It seems to me that Spinoza's own accounts are ambiguous between these two conceptions, but that it is only the second interpretation which gives him a chance of being right. One reason for this is that only thus can any sense be made of secondary and hedonic qualities.[33]

On this conception, my personal stream of consciousness occurs as a process in the divine mind, whereby God describes to himself the overall fate of my organism (or controlling core). Thus the sensations of different sounds and colours are a summary way in which he notes that certain gross physical processes are going on within me, while feelings of pleasure and pain (and all emotions derivative from these) will similarly be used by him to give an overall characterization of an increase or decrease in the perfection of my body. (God will also, of course, have ideas of the finer grain of the physical facts in question, but these will lie outside my personal consciousness). We must take it, too, that such sensory and hedonic ideas, while not providing us with scientific knowledge of the state of our bodies, still have a certain inherent intentionality whereby they are experienced as *of the body and of what is currently acting on it*. I do not see how else a would-be Spinozist can regard the matter, unless he takes on the more implausible side of materialism. If Spinoza did not mean his doctrine thus, a modern Spinozist needs to do so.

There are some indications that Spinoza did view the matter somewhat thus. For example, the contrast between the lusts of different creatures suggests a kind of summatory idea of the conditions of their flourishing which is not easy to square with the thesis that the articulation of the mental is precisely isomorphic with the articulation of the physical. (See E2p7.) On this matter I agree with Professor Parkinson's tentative suggestion that 'although Spinoza's physics are purely quantitative, his psychology admits of differences of quality' (PARKINSON, 109).

If one looks at Spinoza's psychological examination of the emotions in E3, it must be said that it is doubtful that he manages to stick to his own principle of keeping physical and mental explications and explicata sharply distinct.

The difficulty in interpreting Spinoza on this point is, indeed, an instance of a more widespread difficulty in grasping how seventeenth-century rationalists in general managed to conceive of our sensory and emotional experience as a confused awareness of physical facts. A satisfactory interpretation of Spinoza on this is important for our present theme, since (for me at least) it bears on the religious value of his conception of the world. If his system is assimilated to certain modern forms of materialism, which seek to deny the very existence of the qualitative aspect of our life, it would be hard for someone like me to see it as having religious significance. In contrast, I do see religious significance to Spinozism interpreted in the manner I am suggesting; moreover, thus taken, I think it justifies whatever religious sustenance it gives, by being, so far as the most relevant matters go, substantially true. But how much genuinely religious, as opposed to ethical, sustenance it provides must depend partly on the sense in which Spinoza thought of God as 'perfect'.

If the physical is to be described in purely quantitative terms, while a rich range of qualities enters into the attribute of thought, it is tempting to interpret the Spinozistic claim that the modes of both attributes are really the same thing as the thesis that physical descriptions give the structure of that of which mental descriptions specify the quality. It would then be claimed that physical explanation is a quantitative type of explanation, and psychological explanation a more qualitative type of explanation, and that these two types of explanation run in parallel. Something along these lines has seemed a promising account of the world to many, and I must declare myself among its partisans.

It is, indeed, doubtful that one can attribute precisely this view to Spinoza.[34] But there is a *via media* between saying that Spinoza explicitly held it and denying it any validity as an interpretation. For might not the following be the case?

Spinoza came to the conclusion on the basis of arguments which we have examined (and even more so, perhaps, as a result of more general reflections on the problematic dualist legacy of Descartes) that God or the Universe was at once an infinitely large physical system and an infinitely comprehensive mental system, and that to every physical thing or event there corresponded a mental thing or event which could be called the divine idea of it, and that these two were somehow really identical. (Whether these are the only mental things or events is more problematic.[35])

But although there is much that is persuasive in this claim, Spinoza left it problematic precisely how two such apparently different things as mind and body could really be the same thing. This gap in his thinking, I suggest, can best be filled by interpreting the relation between the physical and the mental as that between abstract structure and internal qualitative essence. Thereby the Spinozistic view of the world is rendered more intelligible with almost every positive claim of Spinoza's left standing. So people who hold this view are (I suggest) in the right to call themselves Spinozists. For, as they see it, they have found the missing piece necessary for the construction of a relatively unproblematic version of his philosophy.

This modern form of Spinozism claims that science knows only (and at best) the structural aspect of things. It is like a musical score as that might be intelligently studied by someone born deaf; he would not know what it depicts qualitatively, but he would know the structure of what it depicts.

Now is there anything in Spinoza to suggest that science deals only with structure? You may be inclined to say not. Indeed, you may say that Spinoza thought that we did know the quality of the physical world, for we know it as possessing the one quality of spatial spread-out-ness in three dimensions.

But, however exactly Spinoza conceived of space or extension, he certainly thought of it as properly characterized only by the traditional primary qualities (or qualities akin to these): that is, as fully conceivable in a purely geometrical or geometrico-dynamic way, devoid of 'secondary' and 'hedonic' character. And it seems essentially in line with this to say that our conception of the world as physical is a conception of it of a purely structural kind, and that everything of a more qualitative kind (colour, smell, pleasure, and pain) pertains to the attribute of thought or consciousness. So this modern form of Spinozism can claim at least some continuity with Spinoza's actual position.

My claim, then, is that the interpretation I am offering of Spinoza (following in the footsteps of several others) does indeed include certain additions to it, but that they are additions which are compatible with most of what Spinoza says, and that they add to it by supplying a necessary ingredient if the theory is to have a chance of being (in broad terms) true.[36]

XXX Human Immortality or Mortality

Belief in an afterlife is a main feature of most religions. Spinoza certainly believed in some kind of immortality, but it is quite problematic what this is.

E5p23 reads thus:

The human mind cannot be absolutely destroyed along with the body, but something of it remains, which is eternal.

Proof. In God there is necessarily a conception, or idea, which expresses the essence of the human body, and which therefore is necessarily something that pertains to the essence of the human mind. But we assign to the human mind the kind of duration that can be defined by time only in so far as the mind expresses the actual existence of the body, an existence that is explicated through duration and can be defined by time. That is, we do not assign duration to the mind except while the body endures. However, since that which is conceived by a certain eternal necessity through God's essence is nevertheless a something, this something, which pertains to the essence of mind, will necessarily be eternal.

Scholium. As we have said, this idea, which expresses the essence of the body under a form of eternity, is a definite mode of thinking which pertains to the essence of mind, and which is necessarily eternal. Yet it is impossible that we should remember that we existed before the body, since neither can there be any traces of this in the body nor can eternity be defined by time, or be in any way related to time. Nevertheless, we feel and experience that we are eternal. For the mind senses those things that it conceives by its understanding, just as much as those which it has in its memory. Logical proofs are the eyes of the mind, whereby it sees and observes things. So although we have no recollection of having existed before the body, we nevertheless sense that our mind, in so far as it involves the essence of the body under a form of eternity, is eternal and that this aspect of its existence cannot be defined by time, that is, cannot be explicated through duration. Therefore our mind can be said to endure, and its existence to be defined by a definite period of time, only to the extent that it involves the actual existence of the body, and it is only to that extent that it has the power to determine the existence of things by time and to conceive them from the point of view of duration.

This should be read in conjunction with:

E5p29s We conceive things as actual in two ways: either in so far as we conceive them as related to a fixed time and place or in so far as we conceive them to be contained in God and to follow from the necessity of the divine nature. Now the things that are conceived as true or real in this second way, we conceive under a form of eternity, and their ideas involve the eternal and infinite essence of God, as we demonstrated [above].

Spinoza is claiming[37] that:

1. An idea of each human body as a possible form of being exists eternally in the divine mind.

2. Just as God has an idea of my body as existing, when I do exist, and that idea is my mind, so when I do not exist, God has *an idea of my body as a*

possible form of being, and this is my eternal as opposed to temporal mind.

3. And we may add that this idea is adequate enough to stand out as a rational consciousness in contrast to ideas (of other possible bodies) which are not in the same way individual units.

4. Spinoza is clear that in the sense in which we have an eternal existence after death, so did we before our birth. And in fact that eternal existence goes on equally when we are alive, but is somehow blocked off from our day-to-day consciousness.

Some may feel that the body looms too large here for comfort. But Spinoza does not conceive the body as a mere lump of flesh and bones. Rather, does he mean the deep hidden essence of the body which, when it exists, determines what one does, physically conceived, and includes the physical basis of one's personality.

Spinoza's proof has bred so much suspicion that it has been thought a cowardly retreat from the main tenets of his philosophy. For example, Jonathan Bennett thinks that it expresses a pathetic failure of Spinoza to free himself from the fear of death. (See BENNETT, 374–5.)

One possible objection is this. The essence of one's body, after one's death, appears to pertain to God, *qua* physical, only in the sense in which a statue is in a block of stone waiting to be separated from what environs it by a Michelangelo.[38] On this analogy one might suppose that, when one is not alive, the idea of one's body, which is to say one's mind, only exists in the divine consciousness, as a possibility whose time for existence (as a distinct idea) is either not yet come or is over. Yet Spinoza evidently thinks that one's mind exists eternally as an actuality.

But how strong is this objection? God is supposed to have an idea of all things which are possible. (See E1p16.) And since one's body is possible, the idea of it must exist in God, not only the possibility of such an idea.

What seems more problematic is that somehow what exists eternally is only that part of us which constitutes a rational grasp of our own essence, and that therefore the more rational we are in understanding ourselves, the more there is in us which is eternal. (See E5p40cor.) Associated with this is the difficulty that the argument for the human mind's eternal existence may seem to carry over to everything whatever, since everything possible has an essence of which God always or eternally has an idea.

The solution to both these difficulties must lie in the distinction between rational and non-rational minds which we discussed in section XIV. The more rational one is, the larger the part of one's mind that constitutes a complete idea. And a complete idea, even when that of which it is the idea is no longer temporally existent (or has not been so yet), must exist as a unit in the divine mind as incomplete ideas do not (though they are parts of, or overlap with, complete ideas). Thus complete ideas are there in the divine mind with their own distinct consciousness, as incomplete ideas are not. And, as for, most, or all non-human things, the ideas of them are incomplete ideas in God even when the things exist, and one might suppose that such thin partitioning of them into distinct units as holds when the things exist—as things with their own little endeavour to survive—becomes thinner still when they do not.

But it is still rather puzzling how Spinoza explains the fact (which he affirms) that, as eternal, we know what our own essence is, as we never do as temporal beings. In the latter case we only know something of the interaction of our essence with other things, but at the eternal level we know it as it is in itself. (See E2p19, E5pp23, 30.) So what we know, as eternal beings, does not coincide even with our complete ideas when alive, since it concerns our own essence rather than its adventures in time. It must follow, I think, that there is always a divide between our consciousness as existing beings, which is a consciousness only of our interaction with other things, and our consciousness as eternal features of God's thought. For, as we have just seen, we possess this eternal existence as much during our temporal existence as before and afterwards. But strictly, that eternal existence is not in time at all, so it neither occurs before or after or during our life, or does so only in the sense in which $7 + 5 = 12$ is there as a fact at all times.

But though we do possess a kind of immortality, this is not what motivates the rational person to act virtuously. (See E5p41 with demonstration and scholium.) That is simply the fact that our life in the here and now can be satisfactory only to the extent that we do so.

XXXI Further Remarks on Time and Eternity

How one interprets Spinoza's view on immortality or eternal life must depend on precisely what view of time we attribute to him—time in the sense of 'duratio', that is. ('Tempus' for Spinoza is the measure of time in units, such as days, while 'duratio' refers rather to the passage of time, whether measured or not.) And if one is looking for an essentially Spinozistic view of things which one might endorse oneself, one must decide which view of time has one's own vote.

There are two contrary views of time, each of which would fit tolerably well with what Spinoza says on the matter. On the first view, duration is real in just the way it seems to be. Events lie first in the future, then have their moment of presentness, and then sink into the past. And this transition of events through states of futurity into, first, presentness and, then, pastness is the absolute truth of the matter.[39] If Spinoza is interpreted thus, then God himself really changes modally—that is, passes from being actualized in one system of modes to actualization in others—so that the essences of things are first contemplated by the divine mind as things to come, then as present existences, then as past. (We may bypass the status of essences, if there are such, never to be actualized.)

On the second view of time, there is an element of illusion in our ordinary conception of events as emerging from the future or from nothingness into the concrete existence of present reality and then passing on into the shadow land of the past. Rather, are all events (though each feels itself—at least if it is a conscious state—to be emerging from and passing on into other events) just eternally there, each in its own particular niche in the eternal *Nunc Stans* of the universe, and are arranged there in a manner isomorphic with the space and time of ordinary thought, but with no real coming into and passing out of existence.

This, as we shall be seeing in later chapters, is the position of many absolute idealists, and perhaps some orthodox theists. What is more, it coheres better with Einsteinian relativity theory than the theory of absolute becoming (although there are independent metaphysical arguments for it). If Spinoza had a conception of time like this, then his view must have been that God is aware of the whole of cosmic history in one eternal grasp, and we are eternally just there within God at each of the successive positions we occupy in our life, without any real process of becoming present and then past.

Which view of time is Spinoza's own? Different experts seem to interpret him in one way or other quite confidently. I am somewhat torn myself, because the second interpretation makes Spinoza more in tune with my own firm opinions, while a case can be made for his actual view being more the first. However that may be, I still think the better view for the Spinozist (and in the end the only coherent one—see later chapters) is that there is no real change for or in the eternal self-conscious unity of the world. Rather, are all things eternally there for God (*qua* mind or idea of the world) as elements in an eternal system of necessarily related modes.

Although many people think that this was Spinoza's view, the emphatic way in which Spinoza seems to distinguish between God's idea of something as currently existing and as simply an eternal form of possible being, rather suggests that he held the first view. (See article by Martha Kneale in GRENE.) On the other hand, the second view would fit better, I think, with the general emotional mood of Spinoza's philosophy. At any rate, he evidently conceived of God as eternally aware of total history, whether its events are always sliding from future, through presentness, to past, or as eternally just there each in its particular spatio- or psycho-temporal niche. Either way, we should seek to view things so far as possible *sub specie aeternitatis* rather than *sub specie temporis*.

We are still left with the question of whether anything like Spinoza's view of our place in eternity is acceptable. By my lights, the answer is positive. If one once accepts that we are all passing modes of an infinite mind, then it seems reasonable to think that something of us belongs eternally and unchangingly to that mind, whether as eternal essences with just a brief period of historical actualization or as permanent elements in a divine overview of the whole of history. In either of these cases, Spinoza would evidently think that there is more individuality to us, the greater the mental unity of what we are in time.

XXXII In What Sense is God Perfect?

One of the greatest problems for me is whether Spinoza's description of God as perfect has (in spite of the disclaimers in E4praef.) not some laudatory sense. Related to this is the question as to whether his identification of God with nature leaves any real distinction between his theism (or pantheism) and atheism.

Spinoza encourages us to be reconciled to fate, because everything follows of necessity from God's perfect nature together with the infinite course of past events. Does that mean that, understood as a whole, God or Nature is *good* in any at all sympathetic sense of the word? Or does it mean only that he (or it) is something the understanding of which could give complete intellectual satisfaction? A sample of the kind of statement in the *TTP* which might encourage the first view is as follows:

Finally, nearly all the prophets found considerable difficulty in reconciling the order of Nature and the vicissitudes of men with the conception they had formed of God's providence, whereas this has never afforded difficulty to philosophers, who endeavour to understand things not from miracles but from clear conceptions. For they place true happiness solely in virtue and peace of mind, and they strive to conform with Nature, not to make Nature conform with them; for they are assured that God directs nature in accordance with the requirements of her universal laws, and not in accordance with the requirements of the particular laws of human nature. Thus God takes account of the whole of nature, and not of the human race alone. (*TTP* ch. 6; GEBHARDT, iii. 87–8; BRILL, 130–1)

Spinoza certainly did not himself think that God chose, in any remotely ordinary sense, the system of laws which would maximize the extent to which the interests of all individuals are met. But he did perhaps think that if we could see things as a whole, we would say that they are for the best, when the needs of all finite creatures (or modes) are taken into consideration. If so, the universe is a more encouraging place than it might seem on a purely scientific (whether seventeenth- or twenty-first century) account. Such a conception seems implied in Letter 32 to Oldenburg. On the other hand, this may simply be a manner of speaking for the comfort of those lesser souls who require more of the universe than intellectual intelligibility if they are to be reconciled to it.

In a way, the problem with Spinoza is the converse of the problem with Leibniz. A simple reading of Leibniz makes one think that, on his account, the world is the best of all possible ones in an 'encouraging' sense, while a more sophisticated reading tends to reduce its maximal goodness to the purely logical conception of maximal variety of phenomena combined with maximal simplicity of laws.

Spinoza differs radically from Leibniz in believing that this is the only possible world, not the one which God has chosen as the best. But one may still ask in what sense this only possible world is perfect. The simpler reading of the *Ethics* is that there is no very humanly appealing aspect to the perfection of God, while a more thorough reading in the light of the *TTP* may lead one to think that, after all, there is something more than intelligibility to the perfection of the universe, which Spinoza often understresses in his anxiety to be free from any taint of anthropomorphism. The trouble is the apparently systematic ambiguity of Spinoza's language. Shortly after the passage just quoted, Spinoza (as translated by Shirley, somewhat altering the sentence structure) says: 'Miracles did not teach them that God cares equally for all; only philosophy can teach that' (*TTP* ch. 6; GEBHARDT, iii. 88; BRILL, 131).

In what sense does God care for all equally? Because of his equal lack of care (in any genuine sense) for any of us,[40] or in the sense that the goodness of existence is as good for each as is compatible with non-reduction of the good of others?

Spinoza speaks of two types of assistance that men can receive from God: the internal assistance being their own *conatus*, when functioning appropriately, the external assistance consisting in fortunate external circumstances. (See *TTP* ch. 3, 89–90; GEBHARDT, iii. 45–6; BRILL, 88–9.) But does God's internal assistance, and the associated caring, consist simply in the fact that each cares for himself (herself, itself), while the external consists simply of natural causes which have allowed the individual to exist for a time? In short, does Spinoza postulate some real feeling on the part of God-or-Nature as a whole, or does he mean simply that he, she, or it contains the self-love of every individual conscious creature, something which any atheist would allow? The atheistic reading of Spinoza is certainly encouraged by some statements in the *TTP*, as when Spinoza says that he will demonstrate:

[f]rom scripture that God's decrees and commandments, and consequently God's providence, are in truth nothing but nature's order; that is to say, when scripture tells us that this or that was accomplished by God or by God's will, nothing more is intended than that it came about in accordance with nature's law and order, and not, as the common people believe, that nature for that time suspended her action, or that her order was temporarily interrupted. (*TTP* ch. 6; GEBHARDT, iii. 88–9; BRILL, 131–2)

However, that is only atheistical if we are already given an entirely atheistical interpretation of nature and her laws:

However, I am confident that reflection will at once put an end to their outcry [at Spinoza's separating the wheat from the chaff in the Bible]. For not only reason itself, but the assertions of the prophets and the apostles clearly proclaim that God's eternal word and covenant and true religious faith are divinely inscribed in men's hearts—that is, in men's minds—and that this is the true handwriting of God which he has sealed with his own seal, this seal being the idea of himself, the image of his own divinity, as it were....

To the early Jews religion was transmitted in the form of written law because at that time they were just like children; but later on Moses and Jeremiah told them of a time to come when God would inscribe his law in their hearts.... Whoever reflects on this will find nothing in what I have said that is at variance with God's word or true religion and faith, or can weaken it; on the contrary, he will realize that I am strengthening it ... [So] I feel I must not abandon my task, and all the more so because religion stands in no need of the trappings of superstition. On the contrary, its glory is diminished when it is embellished with such fancies. (*TTP* ch. 12; GEBHARDT, iii. 158–9; BRILL, 205)

At any rate, I have already given reasons for rejecting attempts to reduce Spinoza's position to atheism. For it is surely evident that he postulates as genuinely unitary a divine consciousness, in which ours is somehow included, as he does a divine body, of which we are physical components. Thus, 'We are parts of a thinking thing whose thoughts—some in their entirety, others in part only—constitute our mind'.[41] Does not that imply that the divine mind is coloured and enriched by the human emotions which it contains, more especially those which signal our successes? As for the miseries, we must, if my approach is right, suppose that Spinoza, somewhat like F. H. Bradley, thought that that which on its own was suffering is literally present as an element in what is joyous in God's sense of his own creativity.[42]

Be that as it may, Spinoza certainly thought that God (on his mental side) finds real joy in the world of which he is the substance and the immanent cause, and that we, at our spiritual best, can relate to that joy in a manner which goes beyond the mere pleasure of a dry intellectual understanding. For at this spiritual best we are enriched and calmed by our awareness of ourselves as necessary elements in God's enjoyment of his own being, in a way which may sometimes culminate in a quasi-mystical experience.

XXXIII Determinism as a Religious Doctrine

Thus understood, Spinozism certainly poses something akin to the traditional problem of evil. How can God-or-Nature be perfect in any sense except that of being perfectly intelligible (in principle) with so much horrible evil in it? The Spinozistic answer, surely, should be that the universe is necessarily what it is, and that, taken as a whole, we can be pleased that it exists, just as the divine mind is pleased that it, and the other attributes of substance of which it is the awareness, all exist. This is quite compatible with its being dreadful in certain parts (and felt by God as being so), implying only that, could we see things as a whole (as God does), we would recognize that if there is to be a universe at all, these must exist as parts of it.

Yet we saw above (in section XVIII) that it is doubtful that Spinoza has given himself the right to suppose that this is the only possible universe. For while his axioms certainly imply that it was already settled at every moment of the past what would happen thereafter, they do not evidently imply that this is the only logically possible world. On the other hand, strict necessitarianism accords better with his ethical conclusions and the general mood of his thought. Still, he might reasonably claim that the necessitation of everything relative to everything else shows that all that is good in the world could only have been produced by processes which include much evil, and perhaps this is enough to justify the universe to man. It is, at any rate, a better approach to evil than to hold the view that evil is simply privation, as Spinoza argues in LETTER 23.

Certainly the necessity, in some sense, of everything which happens is not simply a factual thesis of Spinozism, but one on which frequent meditation must be regarded as essential to the way of life it recommends. Indeed, for Spinoza, it is almost one of the 'consolations' of the true religion, as well as a morally improving doctrine.

It is a consolation, because the more deeply we grasp the fact that something about which we are sad could not have been otherwise, the less will we feel sad about it, and the more we will find satisfaction in trying to understand why it was bound to happen. And it is, as we have seen, morally improving, because it will increase tolerance and reduce hatred (including self-hatred) if we see that those who have acted badly from our point of view were bound so to act, granted their nature and circumstances.

People often regret certain things they have done in their own lives; they may feel bad about the way in which they have harmed others, or they may feel bad because they have missed some opportunity themselves. Thus a politician might regret the harm a piece of legislation which he promoted has turned out to do, or he may regret some decision he made as a result of which he lost office. If he looks back and can understand that really he was bound to have behaved like that, granted the circumstances and shortcomings of his own of which he was not then conscious, he may come to see that the matter was never really open, and become more reconciled to it in consequence. Similarly, if you have been badly treated by someone else, you will feel less resentment if you realize that inescapable features of his character and circumstances of his upbringing made it impossible that he should have behaved otherwise. Though this will be more so if you understand these causes in some detail, even the mere knowledge that there must be such causes will have something of the same effect.

One reason why determinism has often seemed a dispiriting doctrine (whether it be true or false) is its seeming to provide an excuse for, and thus encouragement of, misconduct. But Spinozistic determinism encourages us to believe that, if people can be taught to understand the causes and effects of their undesirable conduct, this will be a fresh factor which will improve it in future, while those so irrational that they are incapable of such understanding must continue to be controlled, so far as possible, by threats and emotive language. As for our dissatisfaction with ourselves, here again self-understanding may to some considerable extent keep us from doing again what we now regret, and when it cannot, we can at least be more comfortable with ourselves through understanding how our reason was overwhelmed by passions beyond our control.

E4, Appendix, §32 But human power is very limited and is infinitely surpassed by the power of external causes, and so we do not have absolute power to adapt to our purposes things external to us. However, we shall patiently bear whatever happens to us that is contrary to what is required by consideration of our own advantage, if we are conscious that we have done our duty and that our power was not extensive enough for us to have avoided the said things, and that we are a part of the whole of Nature whose order we follow. If we clearly and distinctly understand this, that part of us which is defined by the understanding, that is, the better part of us, will be fully resigned and will endeavor to persevere in that resignation. For in so far as we understand, we can desire nothing but that which must be, nor, in an absolute sense, can we find contentment in anything but truth. And so in so far as we rightly understand these matters, the endeavor of the better part of us is in harmony with the order of the whole of Nature.

So a belief in the necessity with which events unroll answers to the description of a religious belief meditation on which can comfort and improve. But it may still be objected that a belief in the necessity of all that happens can help us cope only with the less extreme vicissitudes of life and not with its worst horrors.

There is no belief, presumably, which can make one happy and tranquil under all circumstances. Spinoza insists on this himself, in opposition to the Stoics. (See E5 Preface.) Yet it may still be thought that a simple belief in a conventional benign God can provide comforts and stimuli to moral behaviour in difficult circumstances unavailable to the Spinozist. It is said that it was those of a simple traditional faith who coped best in concentration camps; how would or do Spinozists fare in the worst of human situations? A belief in the necessity of all things can help in such circumstances, so it may reasonably be suggested, only if combined with the belief that all evils are somehow essential concomitants of an ultimate goodness of the universe which is more than mere rational intelligibility.

Such a belief would be a comfort in a more conventionally religious way than is the mere belief that everything is necessary. For it implies not just that it is necessary, but that each detail is necessary for some larger good. Spinozism would then be at one with Stoicism in holding that if we could understand it as a whole, we would rejoice that *it is as it is* rather than merely in our own grasp of *why it has to be as it is*.

> All discord, harmony not understood;
> All partial evil, universal good.
> (Alexander Pope, *Essay on Man*)

How far did Spinoza believe this? It seems to me at least a reasonable deduction from what he clearly did believe. For if one believes that the universe displays itself to its own mind as a totality, and that it is eternally satisfied with itself, must one not conclude that we ourselves would be satisfied with the universe if we saw more deeply into its workings?

Developed along these lines, Spinozism seems to me to have the potentiality to be a religion in an important sense. But how far this is how Spinoza himself saw things is not altogether clear.

Certainly he gives little impression of holding that every evil in the world is finally justified in a manner with much appeal to our moral sense. However, if he seriously believed that all those who behaved morally were somehow saved—perhaps in some future incarnation, as Alexandre Matheron has surprisingly, but not altogether unconvincingly, maintained—even our moral sense might be satisfied.[43] But I suspect that his position is more to the following effect: the more we understand the universe as a whole, the more magnificent it will seem, while the more inconceivable it will seem that any detail of it might have been different. Total understanding, I think Spinoza would maintain, would lead to delight in the whole infinitely vast system. And since this system could not exist without the evil in it, we would have to be reconciled to this.

So the Spinozist need not hold that everything we regard as evil (such as the many atrocities of our own time) itself contributes to the perfection of the universe. He need only claim that the existence of the universe, and our own existence as tiny fragments of it, is something to be glad of, and that this is so in spite of the horrors. This is a severe religion lacking many of religion's usual comforts (though also many of its usual discomforts), but I think it may reasonably be regarded as a religion in the sense for which we are considering Spinozism as a candidate.

PART FIVE: CONCLUSION

If there is any message which is unambiguously Spinoza's, it is the recommendation that we use our reason to think about the world and ourselves as clearly as we can. Granted our different human infirmities and our different cultural heritages, it is to be expected that few if any will take quite the same view of things. Therefore it would be most un-Spinozistic to try to adopt his views in their entirety. My claim is not that anyone today can be a Spinozist in the sense of accepting his every word, or even some substantial part of what he says without modification. Rather, I make the following two claims:

1. That if Spinozism were accepted almost *en bloc* by an honest enquirer, it would function as (in a good sense) a religion for him;
2. That there are good reasons for holding a view of things which, though often different in detail, is sufficiently like his doctrine to be called a form of Spinozism, and which, as such, may function either as a non-institutionalized religion or as a personal interpretation of such a religion.[44]

Notes

1. The *Short Treatise on God, Man and his Well-Being* has come down to us in Dutch, but is probably a translation of Spinoza's Latin by one of his followers. The manuscript, not in Spinoza's hand, was rediscovered in 1862. It seems to have been written as a basis for discussion with his followers. See LETTERS 8 and 9.
2. For a recent study of this, see NADLER LIFE. This is highly informative on the views about immortality held by Jewish thinkers. I cannot, however, quite accept his view that Spinoza denied any kind of personal immortality whatever. See below.
3. YOVEL HERETICS, 43–4. The best modern biography of Spinoza is NADLER LIFE. But many other books, such as Yovel's, contribute to a sense of the man and his world. There are two short seventeenth-century biographies of Spinoza, one by an unreliable follower, the other more interesting one by Johannes Colerus, a Lutheran minister who came to The Hague in 1693 and lodged in rooms where Spinoza had lived when he first moved to The Hague. Colerus, while regarding Spinoza's books as 'abominable' and 'the most pernicious Atheism that ever was seen in the world', set out to gather information and impressions from people who had known him, and ended up depicting him in a very appealing light, as almost a saint. See ROTH, ch. 1 and 'The Life of Spinoza by Colerus' included as an Appendix in POLLOCK.
4. Some think that Prado had a decisive influence on Spinoza, but others question this, suggesting that the influence was more probably the other way around. At any rate, they reacted to their excommunications very differently. Unlike Spinoza, who set about making a life for himself outside the Jewish community, Juan de Prado fought long and hard in a vain attempt to have it lifted.

   These cases show that the ban against Spinoza was not such an exceptional event, but must be understood as either part of a general process of preserving Jewish unity in the Netherlands or as a way of reassuring the city authorities about the nature of Jewish belief.

5. I can no longer identify the text from which I took this quotation.

6. The more scholarly translation may be that of Edwin Curley, who is a major commentator on Spinoza's philosophy. However, his translation sometimes implies interpretations concerning which some have their doubts. My text is supposed to be intelligible without reference to Spinoza's, but the references are there for the scholar.

7. One is inclined to say that if John Robinson is a mode of God, then his bad temper is a mode twice over, that is, *the mode of a mode*. Spinoza does not use this expression, but he does speak of modes as having 'affections', which comes to much the same thing.

8. I am unclear as to whether things which are impossible are also there as necessarily never actualized essences.

9. Please note the remark on pronouns referring back to 'God' in the previous chapter. Spinoza was of course forced by Latin grammar to say 'he' when referring to *Deus*.

10. Thus if I say that I went for a walk in the Botanical Gardens, it would be assumed *both* that my body moved across certain terrain in certain ways *and* that I had certain feelings of locomotion and sensory presentations of the changing flora etc. around me. And the claim that if we knew enough, we could describe the whole thing either in purely physical terms or purely mental terms has a lot to be said for it. Whether it is Descartes or Spinoza who is right on whether this implies that they are completely distinct things is another matter.

11. It is doubtful whether one should speak of the *character* of an essence, but it is a convenient way of putting the point in question.

12. He also refers us back to axiom 7 of Part 1, which contrasts that of which the existence follows from its essence with that of which this is not so.

13. I am not endorsing this as true, just as something which can readily be thought to be true. After all, 'nothing' is often identified with empty space. And Kant also thought that one could not think space away.

14. I am ignoring the distinction between the essence of substance and its infinite modes.

15. If it is through the same attribute of thought that God knows all the different attributes, then he is not precisely isomorphic with each of the other attributes. This was a point made by Tschirnhaus, and not adequately answered by Spinoza. At any rate, this allows me an interpretation which departs in a similar way from one of Spinoza's claims, though I doubt that the claim is essential for Spinoza. (See LETTER 70 and E2p7.)

16. Personally, I am inclined to agree with Schopenhauer and Bergson that the idea of *nothing at all* is incoherent, and that by 'nothing' is normally meant nothing of a certain sort. If so, something had to exist. And if something had to exist (so I would argue) there had to be some kind of unified experience of it, and this can be called God. So this is my own 'ontological proof'.

17. For an important treatment of this issue see LESLIE.

18. On the face of it in the sense that their existence or nonexistence is not absolutely necessary, but only relatively necessary. See below.

19. Spinoza wrote before Newton's *Philosophiae Naturalis principia mathematica* (1687), so I am not sure just how he would put it.

20. Spinoza's psychology is largely supported in a modern version by Antonio Damasio in his *Looking for Spinoza*.

21. Curley translates *laetitia* and *tristitia* by 'joy' and 'sadness' and *gaudia* by 'gladness'.

22. For the first view see CURLEY, 1969, ch. 3, esp. pp. 101–6, and for the first or third view see Don Garrett, 'Spinoza's Necessitarianism' in YOVEL 1991.

23. What might be more disturbing to Spinoza would be the idea, touched on above (at n. 15), that there may be other spatio-temporal and/or psychical-temporal universes out of all relation to ours, with a different total history from ours but the same laws of nature. But that would still leave everything necessary in our world, in the sense that there was never a time when it was not already settled what would be happening now (and at every other moment past or present), so it would not perhaps much alter Spinoza's basic viewpoint, though it is not a possibility which he seems ever to have considered.

24. I derive this information about Aquinas from HOSLER, 26. He is referring to Aquinas, *De veritate catholica fidei contra gentiles, seu summa philosophica* (Nemausi, 1853), iii. 3.

25. Even if we just know that determinism is true, and not much about the causation of any particular person's actions, we can find some sort of peace in the general idea that if we could understand those causes, we would feel more tolerant and accepting of that person.

26. Gebhardt III has two distinct numberings of the pages, one of the volume, the other just of the *TTP*; my reference is always to the higher number. Page references to *TTP* are to the Shirley single-volume trans.

27. Although he sometimes seems to deny it, Spinoza does seem to have thought that there was a generic human essence as well as an absolutely specific essence for each human individual.

28. Quite a bit of this section is borrowed from my *Theories of Existence*, 172–6.

29. In the EMENDATION Spinoza says that there are only a few things concerning which he has gained knowledge of the third kind.

30. Perhaps it was because in speaking thus dismissively of the notion of *being* he was concerned with *being* as a bare abstraction, while *being* in a more Hegelian sense as a concrete universal implying all its possible forms was, indeed, a proper object of contemplation.

31. It may be noted that its doing so was one of Kierkegaard's main complaints against Hegelianism. However, I am more of a Spinozist or Hegelian than a Kierkegaardian.

32. Or perhaps, rather, the infinite idea of God which derives from it as 'an infinite mode'. For the sake of simplicity I have glossed over some distinctions in Spinoza's conceptual scheme without, I think, distorting it significantly.

33. I realize that many materialists today try to dispense with these as the distinctive realities they seem obviously to be; but to me their efforts seem quite hopeless.

34. However, some diligent readers have found it natural to take this as his actual view. See, e.g., POLLOCK, 1899.

35. Partly on account of the supposed infinity of the attributes, but for other reasons too, such as the divine idea of the nonexistent.

36. Modern materialists such as D. M. Armstrong and Daniel D. C. Dennett would, of course, disagree with me on this, but I cannot argue the point further here. See bibliography for relevant works of these authors.

37. I have given the interpretation which seems to me correct. It is close to that of Alan Donagan (DONAGAN). For a survey of interpretations, and decision for one other than mine, see NADLER HERESY.

38. This is simpler than the example Spinoza uses to make what seems essentially the same point. See E2p8s.

39. This conception has been developed philosophically most carefully by C. D. Broad in his doctrine of Absolute Becoming. (See BROAD, 66–9.)

40. STRAUSS, 171 and 196. Errol Harris has, to my mind, refuted Strauss's views on such matters. [See HARRIS 1.]

41. 'quod pars sumus alicujus entis cogitantis, cujus quaedam cogitationes ex toto, quaedam ex parte tantum nostram mentem constituunt' (EMENDATION, §73; GEBHARDT, ii. 28. See also Letter 32, at SHIRLEY 849–50.)

42. See BRADLEY, ch. 17. Cf. E5pp17, 35.

43. MATHERON, 207–8; 226–48.

44. Any discussion of Spinozism as a possible religion for today should take note of the invocation of his philosophy as a rational basis for a radical environmentalist ethics. This use of Spinoza is associated especially with Arne Naess (see NAESS 1 and 2, also LLOYD 1 and 2, and MATTHEWS). This is an application of Spinozism, but Spinoza sounds no such note himself; nor could we expect him to have done so in the seventeenth century.

Chapter 3

Hegelian Christianity

PART ONE: INTERLUDE—IMMANUEL KANT

It may perhaps have struck the reader that a certain name which might be expected to be included in the chapter titles is missing. I speak of 'Kant'. For not only were all the philosophers to be studied in this and subsequent chapters in various ways influenced by, or reacting against, his thought, but he is clearly one of the most important philosophers who have written about religion and God.

However, my discussions are directed to the religious availability of a God (or an Absolute) supposedly proved to exist by metaphysical argument. Immanuel Kant (1724–1804), in contrast, thought that there could be no metaphysical or indeed other proof of the existence of God. Thus he criticized all the standard arguments for God's existence, such as the ontological, the cosmological, and physico-theological (argument from design), and would surely have criticized all those propounded by the thinkers to whom this book devotes extended discussion. (Kierkegaard, of course, takes the same line, but it seemed important to include him as a critic of Hegelian Christianity.)

For Kant, practical reason did indeed give decisive reasons for postulating the existence of a God, but this was no proof that he did actually exist. Indeed, he may have held that what was important was that one should, in one's moral life, think in terms of there being a God, without it much mattering whether he 'really' did so or not.

The purpose of this was so that one could live in accordance with the categorical imperative. This was the moral requirement that one should so act that the maxim of one's action could be universalized as a rule which everyone could live by. (Not everyone can be a burglar, without property and burglary jointly disappearing.[1]) This, according to Kant, requires that one treat 'humanity, whether in your own person or another, never merely as a means but also at the same time as an end in itself'. The point about the categorical imperative is that it is not a hypothetical imperative like 'If you want to achieve this, you ought to do that', but that it is incumbent upon everyone whatever they may or may not wish or feel.

Kant believed in the existence of a 'noumenal' reality, of which the world displayed to our senses and thoughts is the misleading appearance. And he thought it proper to have the faith that the universal causal determinism which applies to all human activity in the world as it appears is none the less somehow false of the world as it really is (the noumenal world), and that, as a noumenal reality, each of us has freely chosen to be the kind of person we are and to act as we do. Similarly, it was proper to believe in the existence of a God, by whose grace we could somehow be saved at the noumenal level, and that this fact would present itself in the phenomenal world as a life after death, in which we might continuously improve morally, never actually reaching perfection, but only approaching it asymptotically as a goal never actually to be reached. And the existence of God, as something to be believed in, though never known as a fact or satisfactorily grasped in our concepts, would also provide the promise of a just requital for each of us for our behaviour in terms of reward and punishment. But this is such a different position from that of any thinker who claims to prove the existence of God, or the Absolute, metaphysically, that it would need a quite different approach from that adopted here to such thinkers.

For this reason, and because the book cannot be swelled by an adventure into such a different territory, there will only be this very brief discussion of Kant here. For myself, I am no Kantian, but there are two things pertaining to his philosophy which I find extraordinarily powerful. First, that the human mind is unavoidably spatializing, so that everything in which we believe, even if we believe it to be non-spatial, is only with an effort thought of as such. This, I think, can be done, but one is continually falling back into a spatialization of what one believes in. And secondly, that a distinction should be made between the phenomenal world and the noumenal world, or the world as it really is. He thought, further, that space and time are features only of the phenomenal world, imposed on it by the forms of our intuition (roughly speaking, sensory perception) and inevitable ways of thinking.

As regards the first, when we speak of something as distorted by the spatial way in which we imagine or think about it, Henri Bergson comes immediately to mind, according to whom the human intellect distorts the nature of time by representing it to itself in spatial terms. With this I agree. But what is the real nature of time? Is it truly only a form of our intuition? I can only answer here that I think time is not completely real. For I hold by what I call eternalism, according to which each moment of experience seems to itself to be merely a transition point from a previous experience to a subsequent one, but that really these moments are all just eternally there in ultimate reality, or the Absolute—that is, are positioned within a great *Nunc Stans*.

As for space, I think that there is (1) the spatiality of the somatico-perceptual fields of each of us; (2) the conceived but impossible space of which these fields are each supposedly a fragment; and (3) the real or noumenal space which is an arrangement of all moments of experience within the Absolute, this having its own kind of geometry.

And as for noumenal reality, I think, like Schopenhauer, that we need not think of it as quite so unknowable as Kant supposed. But whereas Schopenhauer thought it consisted in *Will*, I think that it consists in a *System of Experiences* all of which are felt in union by the Absolute.

A word should be said about the relation between Kant and Hegel, to whom I now turn. Kant thought that the only reality which we know is a reality created by our minds, in accordance with our special type of intuition and the concepts which we bring to the world, a world which we can know only in so far as its impingements on us are interpreted (wrongly, in ultimate truth) in the terms of our special modes of perception and thought. For Hegel it was true that our world is structured in this way, more especially by certain key concepts, without which there could be no conceivable world at all. But, unlike Kant, he thought that it was the real world which was thus structured by thought, and perhaps even sensory perception (it's hard to say), and that this shows that it is somehow the realization of mind or spirit (*Geist*)—that is, not just by finite personal minds but by the mind which is the universe, and which eventually recognizes itself as such via the thoughts of human beings.

With this apology for such a slight engagement with Kant, I pass on to Hegel.

PART TWO: HEGEL AS A PERSON

Georg Wilhelm Friedrich Hegel was born in Stuttgart in 1770 and died in 1831.[2] His father was secretary to the Revenue office at the Würtemberg court, but many of his forebears were Lutheran ministers. Hegel's parents belonged to what was known as the *Ehrbarkeit*, the non-noble notables, which seems to have been the most influential class in the main developments of life in Würtemberg. (See PINKARD, 5.) He had a particularly affectionate relationship with his very well-educated mother, who even taught him Latin. After his schooling, he was a student at the University or Protestant Seminary of Tübingen, first in the Philosophy and then in the Theology faculty, notionally with a view to becoming a minister, though it is doubtful that this was ever his real intention. Among his friends at Tübingen were Friedrich Schelling and the poet Friedrich Hölderlin (PINKARD, 21). After graduating he became, in 1799, a *Hofmeister* (private tutor) to a family in Berne, where he was not very happy. After that, he took up a similar position with a wine merchant in Frankfurt, where things went better. He then moved to Jena, where in 1801 he published his first book, *The Difference between Fichte's and Schelling's Systems of Philosophy* (1801). He taught at the university there as a *Privatdozent*, which left him in considerable financial straits much of the time. He then completed his *Phenomenology of Spirit* (1806), with which he at last won the reputation as a major thinker which he so desired. In 1807 he moved to Bamberg, where he became editor of an intellectual newspaper. This was followed by a period of seven years as rector of the Gymnasium (secondary school for high-flyers). One is amazed at the difficulty of the philosophy which he seems to have taught the pupils there.

In 1812 he published *The Science of Logic*, and was married in the same year. In 1816 he became professor of philosophy in Heidelberg, thus reaching at the age of 46 the proper academic position so far denied him. Then in 1818 he became professor of philosophy at Berlin, and a leading light in the intellectual life of Prussia.

But what sort of man was he?

He seems to have been a rather pleasantly ordinary man, for a great philosopher. He clearly found satisfaction in writing philosophy and in reading it, but he neither did nor tried to move to a higher plane of living than the ordinary man. He was thoroughly sociable, an enthusiastic player of whist, and a regular opera-goer. He had the usual concerns, troubles, and satisfactions of a married man with children. He was often worried about his finances. He was ambitious, and wished to shine as a great philosopher. He was an efficient administrator. But he was also by and large a good man ready to help others in need, and a good husband and parent—though he may have unduly privileged his two legitimate sons over the illegitimate son (by an affair prior to his marriage) who lived with him and his wife. His philosophy provided the satisfaction of having an extraordinarily well informed and well thought out general vision of reality, more particularly of human life. It also seemed to have given him a rational basis for a kind of religious feeling of 'being at home in the world'. But it seems not to have inspired him to actually doing anything especially interesting other than that of being a brilliant philosopher.

He was an enthusiast for the modernization of German life. He thoroughly approved of the French Revolution in its main character, regarding the Terror of Robespierre as untrue to its real essence, even if a necessary stage in its development towards Napoleon, who was refashioning Europe in essential ways (see PINKARD, 200). Thus the conquest of most of the German states by the French was approved as leading to their modernization. This modernization was largely a matter of sweeping away the old system of social organization according to hereditary social class, and the creation of a meritocracy. For him, society should be led into better forms by the combined efforts of professors and civil servants, this being the ideal which he saw Prussia as on the way to when he, Hegel, became professor there. On the other hand, he recognized the reduction in social cohesion, and of a sense of belonging, which the decline of the old ways produced. He was concerned that modern societies should have something of the organic quality of the old ones. What really mattered most, however, was that the society should foster freedom of thought and high levels of culture.

Later in his life he seemed too conservative for some of his admirers. In his *The Philosophy of Right* (published in 1820) he gave the impression that he thought of the Prussia of his time as almost the ideal state. But this was because he thought that the revolution in France, and its effects on the countries thereby brought (briefly) under French control, had achieved all that required revolutionary action for its achievement. Progress should henceforth take the form of gradual improvement on the basis of rational deliberation.

Hegel always thought of himself as a Christian (apart from a brief period in his youth). And we shall see that his mature philosophy was conceived by him as the conceptual presentation of what Christianity expressed in poetic symbolism. But he seems primarily to have seen it as a ground for being essentially cheerful about the way the world went (and about his own role in society). On the whole, his extraordinarily rich learning and philosophical genius apart, he was just an ordinary, quite jolly person, who after a lot of struggle was finally extremely successful in his career.

So I do not see how becoming a Hegelian can offer much help to anyone who finds life difficult and is not content with the satisfactions of any successful and fairly decent person. But at least it would not add fresh torture to life, as in different ways acceptance of the thought of either Kierkegaard or Schopenhauer is likely to. Its message seems to be essentially that which Bradley characterized, and only partly endorsed, as that of the ethic of 'my station and its duties'.

What is important, however, is that for many of his followers (the so-called right-wing Hegelians) he provided a philosophical interpretation of Christian doctrine which allowed them to remain Christians, just as did Hegel himself.

We shall not be concerned with the left-wing Hegelians such as Paul Johann Feuerbach and Karl Marx. What should be said, however, is that Hegel may have been the most widely influential (in a variety of ways) philosopher who ever lived. His rivals in this would be Plato, Aristotle, and Kant, but even their influence may not have been so broad as his, in philosophy of all sorts, perhaps especially in political and social thought, and in actual political upheavals.

PART THREE: HEGEL'S EARLY THOUGHT

In various youthful writings on religion and Christianity (published only posthumously early in the twentieth century) Hegel had taken up a series of positions each of which is fairly, though decreasingly, remote from his mature philosophy.

Says T. M. Knox in his prefatory note to his translation of these early theological writings (henceforth ETW):

In reading these essays, it is essential to take account of their dates. The first two parts of *The Positivity of the Christian Religion* were written in 1795–96, when Hegel was twenty-five and living in Bern; *The Spirit of Christianity* was written in Frankfort, probably in 1798–99; Part III of *The Positivity of the Christian Religion* was also written in Frankfort, probably in 1800. (ETW, vii)

The mature philosophy—in particular, the interpretation of religion which it offered—can be understood without reference to these early (and only posthumously published) works of his youth. But something of its tone is likely to escape one unless one knows something of these. To some of us, and certainly to me, the treatment of religion in his early manuscripts is often more attractive than his final position. It is always a puzzle when one prefers a thinker's early thought to his later thought. For, after all, if its originator deserted it for something else, this suggests that there was something wrong with it. All the same, sometimes one cannot withhold such a judgement. Moreover, there is the possibility that at some level the thinker still held by much of the earlier view, but that it represented an aspect of things which was so internalized that its particular message no longer sought external expression.

a. The Tübingen Period (1788–1793)

In a fragmentary essay known as 'The Tübingen Essay of 1793',[3] written when he was a student at Tübingen, Hegel celebrated as the most desirable form of religion 'a folk religion' which could really unite a people and express and promote their highest ideals.

A folk religion, accordingly, must meet these three (not obviously compatible) criteria.

1. Its doctrine must be grounded on universal Reason.
2. Fancy, heart, and sensibility must not thereby go empty away.
3. It must be so constituted that all the needs of life—the public affairs of the state—are tied in with it. (HARRIS, 499; NOHL, 20)

These conditions were met by Greek religion, so Hegel oddly claimed—oddly because it is a strange claim that it meets the first condition. But be that as it may, Hegel contrasted the dead Christianity of his time and place (such as that of the teachers at his seminary) with the living religion of the ancient Greeks, which he thought did meet these three criteria. Contemporary Christianity was composed of rationally unfounded propositions to be believed and ceremonies to be performed, neither of which had any real emotional hold on its practitioners or serious influence on their conduct; moreover, it did not serve to bind them together in a fulfilling way of life. What every society needed was a true *Volksreligion* (folk religion) which underpinned a really satisfying form of communal life. It was doubtful how far Christianity could serve this role—it certainly was not doing so at present.

It is to be noted that Hegel was already contrasting *Verstand* (understanding) with *Vernunft* (reason). This, however, differs significantly from the distinction marked by these words in his mature philosophy.

In his earlier usage *Verstand* was an inferior kind of thought which deals in dead conceptual formulas, while *Vernunft* was thought which is deeply entrenched in our psyche as a whole, and is the product of (and contributor to) a full experience of life. Thus the former produces a passionless theoretical assent to certain ideas, while the latter produces assent of a genuinely living personal kind. In his mature philosophy these contrasting expressions acquire a somewhat different sense.

b. The Berne Period (1793–1796)

Later (during his period as a private tutor in Berne), he thought that it was only a debased version of Christianity which was dead in this way. As a first attempt to formulate a truly living form of Christianity, Hegel wrote 'A Life of Jesus' (NOHL, 73–186). (This appears to have been finished by 1795.)

Jesus is there depicted as essentially a Kantian moralist, and, as satisfying the doubtfully compatible desiderata (1) and (2) above, as close to founding a new *Volksreligion*. But he fell short of satisfying desideratum (3), something done better by Socrates, whose teachings were not, like those of Jesus, directed primarily to an élite twelve.

Hegel's picture of Jesus is somewhat revised in the first two parts of *The Positivity of the Christian Religion*.[4] In this work he tries to explain how the strictly ethical religion of Jesus became, after his death, a merely positive religion.

A positive faith is a system of religious propositions which are true for us because they have been presented to us by an authority which we cannot flout. In the first instance the concept implies a system of religious propositions or truths which must be held to be truths independently of our own opinions, and which even if no man had ever perceived them and even if no man has ever considered them to be truths, nevertheless remain truths. These truths are often said to be objective truths and what is required of them is that they should now become subjective truths, truths for us. ('The Positivity of the Christian Religion', in NOHL, 233)

It was only after his death that his followers lost sight of the essentially ethical religion of Jesus and turned it into a positive religion of which the central theme was a dubious doctrine about Jesus himself. Thus it developed all the faults which pertain to a positive religion of any sort. Instead of a truly living faith, it thus became an uninspiring system of lifeless formulas and ceremonies.

It is, as Harris says, ironic that Kierkegaard's later objection to Hegelian Christianity was precisely on the ground that it exchanged 'subjective truths for us' for dead objective truths. (See HARRIS 1, 38.) Still, there is nothing like Kierkegaard's non-rationality in Hegel's notion of 'a truth for us', since it is precisely because it is revealed to our own rational thought that it is a subjective truth for us, rather than an externally imposed dogma.

So Church or positive Christianity appealed neither to reason nor to our emotions. For it made of God himself an alien being, whose true nature was unknowable. Worse still, he was conceived as the source of unreasoned commands which negated human freedom. Christianity suffered from this diseased form of religion partly in virtue of becoming the official religion of the Roman Empire. Thus it conceived of God as though he were a mysterious emperor, hidden from the view of the general public, like Justinian, rewarding and punishing us as though he were simply a very powerful person, and morality consisted in obedience to his arbitrary commands. This contrasted sharply with any idea of God as immanent in us all and the source of all that is best in us.

c. The Frankfurt Period (1797–1800)

These ideas developed further while Hegel was at Frankfurt. Three concepts dominate his manuscripts at this period: love, life, and spirit.

Love, Hegel contends, in a fragment written in 1797 known as 'Love', is the one thing which can resolve the conflict of man with man. (See ETW, 302–8.) For love reveals the true unity in which all men, and indeed all things, are united, and such love, so Hegel seemed to think at this time, is God. As thus conceived, God is no longer a separate individual holding arbitrary sway over us, but our own inner essence grasped in its true unity with the essence of all others.

This is followed by a truly marvellous work called 'The Spirit of Christianity and its Fate' (ETW, 182–301), thought to have been written in Frankfurt in 1798–9, when he was around 28 years old. Hegel here develops a new account of Jesus, and examines with great subtlety both the strengths and limitations of Jesus as a man and the problems faced by the apostles when he died.

Now Jesus is no longer represented as a Kantian moralist teaching the categorical imperative in such manner as was then possible. Instead, he becomes the destroyer of Judaism, which was far too Kantian in character for its own good. Thus, in this work, Hegel presents Jesus as moving from an ethics of imperatives to an ethics of love.

Of course, an ethics of imperatives as commands from God (e.g. in the Ten Commandments) is, as Kant realized, a heteronomous form of ethics, for which right and wrong are determined by an external authority, God. Kant, of course, believed that an autonomous ethic could be found in those imperatives which conformed to certain formal criteria recognized as valid by reason. But a religion does not cease to be imperatival, and therefore heteronomous, by substituting the categorical imperative for a system of divine commands. For Kant did not overcome the problem of a division between that which gives the orders and that which ought to obey them simply by regarding reason as the lawgiver and the natural passions as its obedient or disobedient subjects. For this left the universal (reason) sharply distinct from the particular (the natural passions). If we move to an ethics of love, this is different. For love is a matter of particulars, particulars, however, which in virtue of the spread of relationships with others and with society acquire a universal character. Thus there is no diremption of the personality into two here.

This spirit of Jesus, a spirit raised above morality, is visible in the Sermon on the Mount, which is an attempt, elaborated in numerous examples, to strip the laws of legality, of their legal form. The Sermon does not teach reverence for the laws; on the contrary; it exhibits that which fulfils the law but annuls it as law and so is something higher than obedience to law and makes law superfluous. Since the commands of duty presuppose a cleavage [between reason and inclination] and since the domination of the concept declares itself in a 'thou shalt', that which is raised above this cleavage is by contrast an 'is', a modification of love, a modification which is exclusive and therefore restricted only if looked at in reference to the object, since the exclusiveness is given only through the restrictedness of the objects and only concerns the objects. When Jesus expresses in terms of commands what he sets against and above the laws ... this turn of phrase is a command in a sense quite different from that of the 'shalt' of a moral imperative. It is only the sequel to the fact that, when life is conceived in thought or given expression, it acquires a *form* alien to it, a conceptual form, while, on the other hand, the moral imperative is as a universal, in *essence* a concept.   ('The Spirit of Christianity', in ETW, 212–13)

It is remarkable among other things that Hegel here speaks as though 'life' stands in contrast to anything specifiable in concepts, a position which seems to be reversed in his later thought. Still, the aim to remove a cleavage between the universal and the particular, thought and life, remained a constant feature of his thought, though quite differently understood later.

The trouble with Kant was that he had not really thrown over the Judaic side of Christianity. For Judaism was essentially a slavish religion of lifeless subservience, for which duty consisted in obeying a God between whom and us there was no real sympathy of feeling. And Kant, however much he might insist that the categorical imperative was a rule which each imposed freely on himself, in fact, by setting duty and natural inclination in opposition to each other, demanded of the natural man that he act as the slave of something with no appeal to his natural feelings. Jesus, in contrast, taught that love should take the place of the ethico-divine law, and that God was not some alien dictator, but the spirit present in everything and which each human being may discover in himself.

Love, in contrast, cannot take the form of a command; rather, is it a spiritual condition, and will find a way of expressing itself in ever new situations which no prescriptions could specify in advance.

Kant had held that 'love' must not be conceived of as an emotion if we are to accept the Christian message of loving one's neighbour as oneself, for as an emotion it cannot be commanded, whether by an external or by an internal authority. But for Hegel this only shows how wrong it is to think of the content of ethics as appropriately expressed in imperatives.

For such an ethics, and the religion with which it is associated, tears the individual into two: a rational self and an affective ('pathological') self, and the latter has to accept its oppression by the former. This situation is essentially as heteronomous as the ethics of hypothetical imperatives derived from contingent emotion. It is no better than treating ethics as based on a God who can reward or punish. Thus both Kantian ethics and Judaic ethics are servile and inflexible.

Of course 'love cannot be commanded'; of course it is 'pathological, an inclination'; but it detracts nothing from its greatness, it does not degrade it, that its essence is not a domination of something alien to it. But this does not mean that it is something subordinate to duty and right; on the contrary, it is rather love's triumph over these that it lords it over nothing, is without any hostile power over another. 'Love has conquered' does not mean the same as 'duty has conquered,' i.e. subdued its enemies; it means that love has overcome hostility. It is a sort of dishonor to love when it is commanded, i.e. when love, something living, a spirit, is called by name. To name it is to reflect on it, and its name or the utterance of its name is not spirit, not its essence, but something opposed to that. Only in name or as a word, can it be commanded; it is only possible to *say*: Thou shalt love. Love itself pronounces no imperative. It is no universal opposed to a particular, no unity of the concept, but a unity of spirit, divinity. To love God is to feel one's self in the 'all' of life, with no restrictions, in the infinite. In this feeling of harmony there is no universality, since in a harmony the particular is not in discord but in concord, or otherwise there would be no harmony. 'Love thy neighbor as thyself' does not mean to love him as much as yourself, for self-love is a word without meaning. It means 'love him as the man whom thou art,' i.e. love is a sensing of a life similar to one's own, not a stronger or a weaker one. Only through love is the might of objectivity broken, for love upsets its whole sphere. The virtues, because of their limits, always put something objective beyond them, and the variety of virtues an all the greater and insurmountable multiplicity of objectivity. Love alone has no limits. What it has not united with itself is not objective to love; love has overlooked or not yet developed it; it is not confronted by it. ('The Spirit of Christianity', in ETW, 247)

To the extent that Jesus's actual language was not quite adequate to the expression of this truth, it was because he had to use language accessible to people of his day. This the bulk of the Jews could not grasp; hence they promoted his crucifixion. After Jesus's death his followers lost sight of his real message: namely, that what should bind them together was their love one for another. Rather than finding their unity in love, they manufactured the belief in Jesus's resurrection as the hope and belief in which they were united. Thus losing their sense of unity in God, they reverted to the Jewish conception of God as something alien. Thereby Christianity developed as a positive religion (a religion based upon the acceptance of certain propositions).

For Hegel, in any case, there were problems which dog Christianity, and which were present even in the teaching and life of Jesus. Jesus found the Jewish community, with its concern with spiritually impoverished ceremonies and laws governing every aspect of behaviour, deeply unsatisfactory.[5] His visionary ideal was that of a community acting under the non-prescriptive spirit of love for one another and sharing his own unique sense of unity with God. But in doing so he had to cut himself off from all the normal ties of human life, both those of sociality in the community and family ties, of which he spoke so scornfully. In doing so, he lost all that richness of life which can exist only in a community offering a wealth of different types of satisfaction. And the disciples in following him lost this also. (See especially ETW, 284–8.) Jesus even became harshly embittered as he experienced the contrast between his own solitude (for his disciples were scarcely his equals) and the corrupt (Jewish) society which was the only alternative, and which he had rejected.

The struggle of the pure against the impure is a sublime sight, but it soon changes into a horrible one when holiness itself is impaired by unholiness, and when an amalgamation of the two, with the pretension of being pure, rages against fate, because in these circumstances holiness itself is caught in the fate and subject to it. ('The Spirit of Christianity', in ETW, 286)

It is noteworthy that at this stage Hegel thought religion superior to philosophy, and continued to do so in what is now known as 'Fragment of a System', written in 1800. This was because, at that time, he saw philosophy as an affair of *Verstand* which distorts our sense of reality with its hard and sharp distinctions. It was only Love, which could counter this and grasp the unity of things.

At this time Hegel wrote a new introduction to his essay on 'Positivity'. Jesus, he argues as before, had not wanted to establish a positive religion; however, he could not simply present his true spiritual message, but had to associate it with Jewish messianic hopes. The unintended result was that Christianity became a matter of belief, rather than of a new form of consciousness of the unitary life binding all things together in the potentiality of mutual love.

d. The Jena Period (1801–1807)

When Hegel moved to Jena to practise as a *Privatdozent*, he renewed relations with his old friend Friedrich Schelling (1775–1854). And it was here that something like his final philosophy started to develop. The great philosophical issue of the day among German thinkers was whether it was J. G. Fichte (1762–1814) or Schelling who was making the more successful advance on Kant. Both thought that Kant's idealism was too half-hearted in leaving a system of unknowable things in themselves with an unknowable character disconnected from any knowledge available to the human mind. Fichte closed the gap by conceiving of us all as belonging to a universal Ego, and the external world as what it posited as a field for ethical endeavour. Schelling tried to remedy the excessive subjectivism of this account of nature by conceiving it as on a par with mind, the two, however, being identical at the level of absolute reality. Hegel expressed his agreement with Schelling in his *The Difference between Fichte's and Schelling's Philosophy*. Schelling's vision of an ultimate unity between mind and world, his conception of nature as the expression of spirit, and his dialectical treatment of this became the inspiration for the main themes of Hegel's final philosophy, in which, however, he gradually detached himself more and more from Schelling, above all because he thought Schelling's 'identity philosophy' operated with an essentially vacuous notion of identity.

It was in this connection that the Hegelian notion of dialectic (a series of concepts each of which corrects the inadequacies of its predecessors) first became explicit. Hegel's great concern, now, was to do away with the blank oppositions between mind and nature, and indeed all other such oppositions, while not simply identifying them (as Schelling was supposed to have done) in a manner which loses sight of all differences.

Whereas previously he had used the concept of an infinite 'life', expressing and externalizing itself in finite things, to understand this, he now moved to the belief that this dialectical nature of reality is best grasped when we conceive of *Geist* (= Spirit or Mind, according to translator's preference) as the fundamental reality. And to understand *Geist* is the task not of feeling but of thought.

It was now that his distinction between Understanding (*Verstand*) and Reason (*Vernunft*) was crystallizing into its final form. Both are activities of the intellect, and each has its proper place of operation. *Verstand* is a pre-dialectical form of reasoning which makes sharp distinctions between concepts, while *Vernunft* is a higher form of thought which grasps the way in which every concept needs to be qualified. It is only by *Vernunft* that *Geist* can be properly understood, and the deep truths about the world, which are grasped imaginatively in the higher forms of religion, laid bare by speculative philosophy. *Vernunft* shows us that all plurality is really the expression of a self-differentiating unity, whereas *Verstand*, which is the level of ordinary, day-to-day thought, blinds us to the unity of the world, through which it seeks to understand things for its own limited purposes.

Towards the end of his time at Jena, Hegel completed what some consider his greatest, though it is certainly not his most approachable, book, *The Phenomenology of Spirit* (1807). This is, indeed, the great work for those who are interested in Hegel as offering an examination of the concrete development and problems of human life. However, our concern with him is as a philosopher who elaborated a metaphysical system purporting to provide a rational grounding for religion, and more specifically for Christianity, and for this purpose I have found it better to look elsewhere.

Our look at Hegel's earlier thought puts his mature thought, which will be the topic of the rest of this chapter, in a fuller context of Hegel's ultimate concerns, especially his wish to relieve us of a constant tension between things we would like to unite, such as, above all, God as the infinite being and ourselves as finite beings, and faith and reason. Hegel certainly thought of himself as showing how man could feel at home in the world, though how much he can actually do this, for most of us, is doubtful. In my view, the early Hegel was nearer to doing this than the later one.

PART FOUR: THE FINAL SYSTEM

Introductory

What is the universe for Hegel, according to his final system? It is the self-realization in concrete reality of the Absolute Idea.[6] What is the Absolute Idea? It is the summatory concept or notion[7] in a line of concepts in which each concept so modifies the previous concept, or pair of concepts, that it removes contradictions within them. What is the general character of this line of concepts? It starts with the concept of Pure Being, and ends with the concept of the universe understanding itself as the self-realization of the Absolute Idea. What can this view of the universe do for a man? It teaches him that the universe in which he lives is not something alien to him, but his own creation, he being really the Absolute Idea become conscious of itself. Thereby it brings him peace, for all the pain in the universe, and in his own mind, is seen as a necessary step to his own consciousness of himself as the Lord of All, for he is, as just said, the Absolute Idea come to self-consciousness. What exactly are 'concepts' or 'notions'? They are 'moments', stages in the reality of what God was before the creation. That is, they are the ideas which must be true of all that actually exists. They have a kind of being apart from the world of concrete existence, and yet the world of concrete existence is nothing but their self-actualization.

How do mere concepts actualize themselves? They do so just as every concept in the line of concepts leading to the Absolute Idea corrects a certain abstractness and deficiency in what preceded it, so that finally the Absolute Idea itself, *qua* mere idea, must have its own abstractness corrected by something which exists as a concrete reality rather than as a mere concept. And, just as the line of concepts develops from its beginning till its end by its own inherent necessity, so it leads to an actually existing world which these concepts describe. And since the concept of anything leaves the details of what answers to it to some extent unsettled, the actually existing world must have all sorts of empirical details which give it a richer texture than its mere concept can describe.

What exactly is the sense in which one concept in the dialectic leads on to another? Perhaps the best way of putting it is to say that formulating the one concept in one's mind as clearly as one can will force one on to a formulation of the next concept, whether as correcting some incoherence in the first or as a necessary implication of it. The mind's passage from one concept to another is not according to psychological laws but to logical laws. What is more, the concepts do imply each other quite apart from this becoming clear to any mind, though eventually minds must arise which grasp this. Moreover, the earlier concepts do not just vanish as the line moves on beyond them; rather, are they 'sublated' in it, which is how Hegel's expression *aufgehoben* is usually translated. It is part of the genius of the German language, according to Hegel, that the single word *aufheben* has the double meaning of 'abolish' and 'preserve', and it is in this double way that earlier concepts are abolished by later ones in the dialectic process. That is, they are abolished as initially and unsatisfactorily understood, but are retained as elements in richer subsequent concepts.

This account requires some qualification when we move on from the Logical Idea to the second and third members of the overarching triad: namely, Nature and Spirit. For then we are concerned not solely with a series of concepts, but with concrete reality. For we are following something of the way in which the concepts, developed in the Logical Idea, are actualized in the concrete world, and may therefore help ourselves by taking some notice of things known empirically. It is not, however, less dialectical, and the same basic principles apply.

What is the relevance of all this for religion? Religion is a stage in the development of Spirit in which it comes in sight of understanding itself as the Lord of Creation. It, or rather religion at its highest level, is a pictorial grasp of its own nature as the actualization of the Absolute Idea. But it does not grasp this truth with full conceptual clarity. It grasps it, rather, by a kind of myth. And philosophy is the stage beyond religion in which the actualized Absolute Idea grasps what it is in clear, non-mythical, conceptual fashion.

Hegel is a thinker whose philosophy has received very various evaluations from his own day to this, and not only very different evaluations but very different interpretations.

There is a strong tendency today to dismiss Hegel's basic metaphysics as 'implausible' (Richard Rorty) or 'incredible' (Charles Taylor)—in fact, as 'bankrupt'—while regarding him as an outstandingly significant cultural critic. Charles Taylor goes so far as to say that, though for many reasons his thought is receiving increasing attention today, 'his actual synthesis is quite dead. That is, no one actually believes his central ontological thesis, that the universe is posited by a Spirit whose essence is rational necessity' (TAYLOR, 538).

Such judgements are as much prejudices of the present (or recent) day as any of those opinions held by Hegel which we may think belong only to a past phase of philosophy. Hegel himself might regard such judgements as a negative mode in which Spirit had to move before reaching discoveries about itself beyond those achieved in the nineteenth century. It is extraordinary how confident thinkers of our time are as to the unique reasonableness of standard contemporary assumptions. Personally, I see no more reason why a nineteenth-century thinker might not be right as against what seems undeniable common sense today.

Another approach to Hegel, by those who do not like the metaphysics usually ascribed to him, is to hold that he did not really have any such metaphysical views at all, and that passages which look metaphysical are just his rather strange way of making quite ordinary suggestions about politics, ethics, nationality, and so forth. Such an approach, I suggest, comes from some people's difficulty in believing that Hegel really could have held such apparently *outré* views. But this is to forget that what is *outré* at one time is not so at another, and that to be an idealist of a fairly extreme kind was not in the least strange in the intellectual context in which Fichte and Schelling were the chief voices of philosophy. Moreover, it seems impossible to square such a reductive interpretation of Hegel's thought with some of Hegel's clearest accounts of what he thought his philosophy established.

Philosophy is

the knowledge of the universe as in itself *one single* organic totality which develops itself out of its own conception, and which, returning into itself so as to form a whole in virtue of the necessity in which it is placed towards itself, binds itself together with itself into *one single* world of truth. (INTRODUCTORY AESTHETICS, XL)

On what I think is the right way of understanding Hegel I will quote a passage from Richard Kroner's introduction to the translation of Hegel's early theological writings previously cited.

Speaking of the 'Fragment of a System' of 1800, Kroner writes:

It shows that the deepest root of Hegel's system was a personal religious experience; living through this experience, he contended with all the influences of his time, especially with Fichte and Schelling. In an attempt to articulate his mystical certainty and embrace the contrasts of thought, he proposed as a formula the 'union of union and nonunion'—his future philosophic system in a nutshell. In this system a triumphant victory was won over the powers about to destroy the unity of Hegel as a person. (ETW, 13–14)

The great difference, however, as we have seen, was that, while as a young man in 1800 he thought that philosophy must give way to religion if we are to grasp how finite and infinite relate to each other, in his later thought he claimed that philosophy gave a more adequate grasp of how this was than religion, and marks a step beyond religion in the history of human advance. Any suggestion that Hegel was a mystic seems highly doubtful, but that he was in his own way intensely religious seems clear, even if his replacement of his earlier idea that it was love, cosmic and personal, which unified the world by the view that it was Reason (*Vernunft*) which does so, seems less religiously inspiring to many of us.

Hegel is so difficult a philosopher that I have managed to grasp his thought, to the extent that I have, only with the aid of many commentators.

Commentators whose work has been especially helpful include W. T. Stace,[8] H. S. Harris, Raymond Williamson, James Yerkes, H. A. Reyburn, Charles Taylor, and Peter Hodgson (in the apparatus of the edition and translation of Hegel's *Philosophy of Religion* which he edited).

One of the oddities of Hegel's philosophy is that, while to the modern analytical philosopher, much of his thought seems like a feast of unreason, his aim was to give a completely rational foundation to a viewpoint (that of the fundamental unity of the world, from which it follows that all sharp divisions between concepts are falsifications of reality) which previously had been supported primarily by those who rejected the supremacy of reason over feeling. (See again Kroner, at ETW, 22–4.)

In what follows I first present an attempt at a summary of Hegel's mature philosophy, following for the most part the three volumes of his *Encyclopaedia of the Philosophical Sciences*. After that, I consider how this relates to his views specifically about religion. Inevitably my account is an extreme simplification, but not, I hope, too much of a distortion.

It is notorious that the dialectical method consists in the construction of a series of triads which follow one upon another with a peculiar kind of necessity. This turns on the fact that each triad consists of a thesis which requires correction by an antithesis, and that the two together require a synthesis which retains the merits of each while moving beyond its limitations. (Hegel does not actually use these expressions, but they are useful as an expository device for explaining the most usual pattern of these trials.) Then the synthesis, or its close associate, becomes the thesis of a new triad of the same general pattern which similarly leads on to a further triad. Sometimes the thesis is a concept whose contradictions are supposed to be corrected by the antithesis, which, however, has its own problems, so that both need to be rescued from their deficiencies by the synthesis. Sometimes the thesis changes before our conceptual eyes into an antithesis which is, on the face of it, its opposite, while the synthesis combines them more harmoniously, but with its own deficiency, which calls for a fresh thesis.

Related to this, as Hegel sees it, is a tendency for the first moment of a triad to be a universal, the second moment to be a differentiation of this, and thus in Hegel's sense a particular, while the third is the synthesis of the universal and the particular in the singular individual, which means, in effect, in a more concrete conception than either universal or particular in isolation from one another. What is more, *universality* is usually associated with a mind at the level of mere feeling, *particularity* with a mind at the level where it thinks in terms of hard and fast distinctions and thus breaks up the unity of feeling ('we murder to dissect'), while *individuality* restores something of the immediacy of feeling but feeling as an aspect of rational thought. We will see more of this later. Hegel's use of all these ideas is often impressionistic rather than precise.

Many recent commentators suggest, not simply that the dialectical method is unimportant for understanding Hegel's philosophy, but that Hegel had no intention of establishing his conclusions by any such method. That this latter point is quite untrue has been shown to my satisfaction by Michael Forster in his contribution to the *Cambridge Companion to Hegel*, where he quotes massively from Hegel to show that he regarded this method as an essential part of his message. (See HEGEL COMPANION, 130–70.) For one thing, Hegel's peculiar interpretation of the Christian Trinity turns upon the conception of nature as the middle term between God as Creator and God the Holy Spirit.

Certainly the idea of a system of concepts, somehow all united in one master concept (the Absolute Idea), and such that they have some sort of *existence* or *being* logically (rather than temporally) prior to any concrete instantiation of any of them, but with the power to actualize themselves, puzzles many of us. One suggestion which may reduce the puzzlement is this. We need not try to think of them as existing without being actualized; but rather we may think of them as indeed actualized, but necessarily so. That is, we may think it a necessary truth that the universe exemplifies, or includes what exemplifies, those particularly basic concepts which constitute the Logical Idea. Thus, on this view, the universe must answer, or include what answers, to such concepts as Being, as including things with their Properties, Causality, Forces and their Manifestations, and individuals with various levels of Consciousness. This way we do not try to conceive what a world of mere concepts would be. Rather, we think of the actual concrete world, and conclude that at least some of its properties are ones which it could not have been without. I, at any rate, find this less puzzling than the idea of concepts so to speak existing on their own. However, I shall not stress this interpretation in my account of Hegel's system.

Outline of the Dialectic

A The Logical Idea

Reality as a whole has for Hegel three great stages: (1) THE LOGICAL IDEA, THE IDEA IN ITSELF; (2) THE IDEA OUTSIDE ITSELF, NATURE; (3) THE IDEA IN AND FOR ITSELF, SPIRIT.

So we start with THE LOGICAL IDEA. This is expounded in Volume 1 of the *Encyclopaedia* ('The Shorter Logic'), and more fully in *The Science of Logic* of

1812–1813 and 1832 ('The Greater Logic'). This is the system of concepts or notions which must be used in any kind of thinking whatever about any kind of subject-matter. Without going into excessive detail, I shall try to show how the dialectic forces us ever on from one concept to another until we reach the climactic concept of the Absolute Idea: that is, the concept of spirit as the experienced unity of all things.

What we may call the higher triads have as their more detailed structure a lower level triad. This mostly extends down to level 4, although a few level-4 triads have 5- or even 6-level triads below them. I shall indicate the levels thus. The names of the three great master triads will be in large boldface capitals, thus:

THE IDEA IN ITSELF, OR THE LOGICAL IDEA
THE IDEA OUTSIDE ITSELF, OR NATURE
THE IDEA IN AND FOR ITSELF, OR SPIRIT

Then the concepts falling within each of these are on four levels (occasionally five or six). There are, for example, three main concepts falling under THE IDEA IN ITSELF, or THE LOGICAL IDEA: namely, BEING*, ESSENCE*, and the NOTION*. The number of asterisks after the name for each concept will indicate the level to which it belongs (below one of the three master triads) in the unrolling of the dialectic. The reader has no need to take notice of the distinction between the levels except if and when he finds it helpful.

Note that there is sometimes reason to use one of the key words of Hegel's system without indicating a level. This is particularly true with Spirit, Idea, and Absolute Idea. This is because, though each of these figures as a particular stage in the development of the dialectic, each is, in fact, the reality behind everything which is, and the different categories which occur at each phase of the dialectic are simply a particular way in which they are more or less adequately conceived. So sometimes I need simply to use the words to refer to this reality as what is always there more or less behind the scenes. Actually Idea (*Idee*) is used more often like this than Absolute Idea, but I feel happier with the full expression.

It may be noted in this connection that I shall for the most part use 'spirit' for Hegel's *Geist*. Some translations use 'mind'. And there are a few occasions where I shall use 'mind' myself as being the more appropriate expression in a particular context.

So now we may get down to work.

BEING* is the concept of things as immediate, simply presented to our experience with either no, or minimal, inference. (Roughly speaking,

Hegel speaks of X as mediated when it or its character is inferred, and as mediated by Y when it is inferred from Y. However, 'mediation' has a somewhat wider, and vaguer, meaning, so that a thing is said to be mediated when it is approached only by way of rational thought.)

ESSENCE* is a region in which mediation is involved, but its distinctive character is that it consists of concepts or pairs of objects one of which is somehow in the foreground, while the other is in the background and somehow more 'real'.

NOTION* consists of concepts which characterize the world as an object of thought or characterize our ways of thinking of it.

A1 BEING

The three main phases of BEING* are Quality**, Quantity**, and Measure**. Quality** again has its own main three phases: Being***, Determinate Being***, and Being for Self***. Again, Being*** has its own three phases, and these are Pure Being****, Nothing****, and Becoming****.

Pure Being**** is the simplest conception we can have of the universe. It consists simply of what is just there, but about which there is no more to be said by a mind stuck at the level of this concept. However, Pure Being**** transforms itself, as we try to think about it, into mere Nothing****. For a thing which just *is* is as good, or as bad, as nothing. Thus the concept of Pure Being**** turns into the concept of Nothing****.

But Nothing**** is not a satisfactory concept on its own at all. We can hardly conceive the universe as just nothing, just nonentity. Somehow we must form an idea of it which combines Being and Nothing. There must be some concept, then, which shows how Being**** and Nothing**** can somehow be the same (as well as different). The concept which does this is Becoming****, for what becomes is Being****, which is perpetually in transition from and into Nothing****. Indeed, Being and Nothing keep changing into each other before our eyes, so to speak.

Thus the three phases of Being*** are Being****, Nothing****, and Becoming****. We now move on to the second phase of Quality**, which is Determinate Being***.

By Determinate Being*** is meant the concept of being something in particular. And it is quite easy to see this as a combination of Being and Nothing, for the only way in which something can genuinely be is by being something and not being something else. To be a bird, for instance, is to have certain definite features, but it is equally not to have (i.e. to lack) certain other features. Thus 'x is a bird' implies 'x is a creature with wings', but it also implies 'x is not a creature which suckles its young'. Of course, there is no reference to the idea of 'being a bird' at the level of the mere concept, but the example illustrates how Determinate Being synthesizes Being and Nothing.

The movement from Becoming**** to Determinate Being*** has troubled some commentators, because the former seems to refer to something temporal, whereas the latter does not.

The explanation, I believe, is something like this. Becoming***, at first, contains a tension between Being and Nothing. It is 'a union which can only be stated as an *unrest of incompatibles*, as a *movement*' (GREATER LOGIC, 91). But as its success in uniting being and becoming increases, it changes into a definite and unitary concept in its own right. As such it is a stable rather than an unstable unity of Being*** and Nothing***, and no longer an oscillation between the two. In doing so, it takes the form of Determinate Being***, in which Being and Nothing are combined in a more steady fashion, and the premature hint of temporality drops away.

Determinate Being*** is on a higher level than are Being****, Nothing****, and Becoming****, for it is the second phase of Quality**. Its own three phases are Quality****, Limit****, and the True Infinite****.

Quality**** comes first because it is simply what Determinate Being*** initially presents itself as being. For what makes something a determinate something is its quality, and at this stage there is no ground for distinguishing this quality from what has the quality. Now a quality is what it is by not being another quality, and this other quality is its Limit****. Thus *red* functions as a limit of *blue*. However, if it is to be itself a quality in its own right, the other quality must have its own other. And that will be equally true of this other other. So we have an infinite series. But the mind cannot really form any proper idea of an infinite series. It is not something which can be grasped. For that reason we must replace the idea of the infinite series by the idea of a system of qualities within which each quality can find its other. This is the True Infinite****, a system in which every item is determined to be what it is by its relation to the rest.

A complication of this, however, is that at the level of abstraction at which the dialectic is so far working, there is no way of distinguishing between one quality and another. So each is just a quality (*tout court*). Thus, as Hegel sees it, there are various contradictions in the concept of Determinate Being***: that is, of things conceived simply as qualities.

These contradictions require a more quantitative conception of what things are, and this is supplied (after some more detailed transitions, including Being for Self*** as the third triad of Quality**, which I shall ignore) by the concept of Measure** (the third triad of BEING*).[9] However, the notion of Quality** must not be lost sight of, so what we need to do is to grasp how Quality** and Quantity** are related to each other. And this is just what Measure** achieves. For it unifies the conceptions by showing how they relate to each other, inasmuch as a change of quantity can go on for a certain period without any change of quality, but at a certain stage quantitative change becomes qualitative change. An empirical example is the fact that increasing heat (quantitative change) changes the quality of water so that it becomes steam, while decreasing heat eventually changes its quality so that it becomes ice. Thus to grasp the concept of measure** is to recognize that quality and quantity are essentially two sides of one coin.

Yet, at least at a superficial level, they do not always change together. For some qualities seem to be independent of any quantitative magnitude. Yet their apparent independence may vanish at a deeper level.

We see, in the first place, existences in Nature, of which measure forms the essential structure. This is the case, for example, with the solar system, which may be described as the realm of free measures. As we next proceed to the study of inorganic nature, measure retires, as it were, into the background. At least we often find the qualitative and qualitative characteristics showing indifference to each other. Thus the quality of a rock or a river is not tied to a definite magnitude. But even these objects when closely inspected are found not to be quite measure-less; the water of a river, and the single constituents of a rock, when chemically anlaysed, are seen to be qualities conditioned by quantitative ratios between the matters they contain. In organic nature, however, measure again rises full into immediate perception. (ENCYCLOPAEDIA I, §107)

There is thus a struggle between Quality** and Quantity** as to whether they are identical or different, and this leads to a general contrast between a level within things, in which quality and quantity are identical, and another level, at which they are different, or, more conventionally put, how far they are or are not correlated.

The relation of Quantity to Quality points us towards the conception of a two-level world in which there is, in everything, a level which is highly obvious and changeable (quality) and another deeper level (quantity) at which it is the quantity of something constant and homogeneous which sustains or changes the former. But this is precisely the contrast we often make in thought between the deep Essence** of a thing (or of reality in general) and its changing states or appearances. And thus the dialectic process forces us on from Being*, the first of the main triads of THE LOGICAL IDEA, to its second main triad, ESSENCE*.

A2 ESSENCE

The category of ESSENCE* is primarily that with which natural science works. But it is to be noted that it also plays a role in one type of (ultimately inadequate) religious thought. For God, or the Absolute, is often conceived of as the ground or essence of the world, which latter has a more superficial kind of reality than the divine.

However, the level of thought which mainly uses the categories of ESSENCE*, is natural science rather than religion. For ESSENCE*, as remarked above, is the realm of hard and fast distinctions, where each thing is sharply distinguished from each other thing. That is to say that in Hegel's terms these are the categories of understanding (*Verstand*) rather than of reason (*Vernunft*), while the categories of BEING* were those by which we apprehend the sheerly immediate by intuition (*Anschauung*).

The first stage of ESSENCE* is Essence as Ground of Existence**. To explore this category is to investigate the way in which the ground of a reality must be conceived somehow as both identical with what it grounds and different from it. To do this is to engage with the first moment of Essence as Ground**, which, unsurprisingly, has three moments. First come the pure Categories of Reflection***, which consist of Identity****, Difference****, and the Ground****. The first of these, Identity****, attempts to treat the ground as identical with its phases, with what it grounds; the second, Difference****, attempts to treat them as simply different; while the third, Ground****, moves beyond these two attempts to a satisfactory notion of them as both the same and different, same as essence, different as ground and grounded. (Or so at least one feels the dialectic ought to go. In fact, Hegel's position is more problematic.)

The discussion of Identity**** and Difference**** is a locus for one of Hegel's more persuasive views: namely, that identity always involves difference, and difference always involves identity. It also provides an opportunity for some reflections on the nature of likeness and unlikeness (which are basically identity and difference when these are born from a comparison between them, rather than determined solely by what each is). Hegel's detailed treatment of all this, as of so much, proceeds by what seem highly specious reasonings, in which there is constant confusion between what must be true of things falling under certain concepts and what is true of the concepts themselves. Indeed, Hegel's dialectical progression sometimes seems the expression of a crazy stream of consciousness in which some often valuable insights somehow find expression in logically specious word-play.

Thus examination of the Categories of Reflection***** explains how ground and grounded easily change places. For the ground is meant to be that on which the grounded depends, yet it turns out that the ground requires something it grounds in order that it should *be* at all. So the distinction between the two breaks down, and they are no longer two but one. Yet, after all, they are two, for otherwise there would be nothing between which the distinction could break down. For it takes two to be the same, as also to be different. Thus for the first time in the dialectic we encounter relational concepts rather than what are essentially one-place predicates.

This multiplicity of mutually grounding things is the system of existents which constitutes the category of Existence***** (the second mode of Essence as Ground**). So far as BEING* is concerned, there might just be one thing in the world, and even if there are many things, the being of one tells us nothing about the being of anything else. But now, with the category of Existence*****, we come to the idea that every single thing is part of a system of things, a system within which they interact, and their place within which determines what they are.

The Existence****** which things possess as part of a system is more than the mere Being***** which supposedly pertains to a thing simply within its own bounds, so that it is not intrinsically connected with anything else.

The distinction can be expressed more epistemologically thus: Existence***** is something more than BEING (of any kind), for the assertion that something simply *is* expresses merely a dumb sensory acquaintance with it, while to conceive of it as existing is to conceive of it as an element in a world of interacting elements.

There is much to be said for Hegel's distinction here, weird as is the way in which he arrives at it.[10] This conception of reality as a system of interacting things has tacitly introduced us to the concept of the Thing*****. This category has the usual three subcategories, which are the Thing and its Properties******, the Thing and Matters******, and Matter and Form******.

In examining the concept of the Thing*****, Hegel starts using the expression 'reflection' in ways which, like so many of his expressions, is difficult to pin down as having any stable meaning. There is some connection with the reflection of light. So far as I can see, if X is said to reflect into or on to Y, it means that X somehow lights up Y, while if it reflects on to itself, it means that it lights up itself. There does not seem to be any particular reference to some more ultimate source of the light which is reflected on to something. So in Hegel's sense the moon reflects on to us as much as the sun does. Sometimes the word seems to mean little more than 'relates to'.

Thus 'X reflects on to Y' sometimes seems to mean simply that X is related to Y, and that grasp of its being so is essential to the grasp of what X is.

Existence^{***} is, from this point of view, the category of things which reflect on to each other, though also reflecting on to themselves. That is, existing things can only be understood in terms of their relation to other things, while still containing an element of self-intelligibility.

In this context Hegel plays around with the problem of how a thing is related to its properties. As he sees it, once we ask ourselves this question, we tend to conceive of the thing as somehow composed of its properties. When this is done, the properties become things, which Hegel calls *matters*, while so-called things are merely the product of their interaction. The Properties^{****}, in fact, become rather like the particularized qualities which some subsequent philosophers have called either 'tropes' or 'perfect particulars', ultimate elements out of which so-called things are made.

The category of Thing and Matters^{****} now passes into that of Form and Matter^{****}. This is because the *matters* tend to collapse into a kind of featureless stuff out of which *things* are made, while *things* are this featureless stuff somehow arranged in a certain way. This leads easily enough into the traditional or Aristotelian contrast between matter and form. But Hegel has no difficulty in finding this contrast problematic in various ways. This suggests that the world of things, as containing so many contradictions, cannot be real, and must only be the appearance of the real.

So we are led to the category of Appearance**, the second phase of ES-SENCE*. In the world of Appearance**, nothing is quite what it seems. Hegel associates this contrast with two others: those of Content and Form^{***}, and Relation and Correlation^{***}. Passing over this, we arrive, by steps which I shall not examine, at the third main category of ESSENCE*, which is Actuality**.

The general character of Actuality** is that it is an (in the end inadequate) attempt to resolve a tension between the categories of BEING* and the categories of ESSENCE*, of which it is the final stage. For BEING* each thing (if indeed there is more than one thing) is complete in itself, with nothing indicating relationship to anything else. It may be said, therefore, to be concerned with what a thing is in itself, within its own bounds. For ESSENCE*, by contrast, each thing is there only as a component in a larger system of things and seems to lose any independent character whatever. For Actuality**, which attempts a synthesis of these two, the supposed contrast between the inner independent being of something and its standing in relation to other things dwindles into almost nothing.

Actuality** has three subcategories: Substance and Accident***, Cause and Effect***, and Reciprocity***. But these cannot really ease the strain between conceiving things under the category of BEING* and conceiving them under the category of ESSENCE*.

APPEARANCE* terminated in the category of the Inner and the Outer****. The inner was the underlying reality of anything, while the outer was the face it turned to the world, so to speak. The problem was how these two items, the inner and the outer, are related.

Actuality** purports to solve the problem by regarding it as essential to the Inner**** that it should have an outer expression, and essential to the Outer that it should express something Inner****. In this way the stark contrast between inner and outer is overcome, and we see how they stand together.

Hegel regards Actuality** as bound up with necessity—which first enters our concept of the world here. This is because the Inner**** must be manifested in the Outer****, and contrariwise. So to conceive the world in terms of Actuality** is also to begin to see it as a necessary system.

The first subcategory of Actuality** is that of Substance and Accident***. This is a specific form of the relation of inner expressing itself in the outer. What something visibly does is a manifestation of its inner being; that is, it is an accident of an underlying substance.

But this contrast between Substance*** and its Accidents*** cannot be thought of for long without its turning into a relation of Cause and Effect***. Consider someone's cowardly behaviour on some occasion. This may be thought of as a manifestation of the nature of his inner being. But this is hardly distinguishable from saying that it was his cowardice which caused the behaviour. So the contrast between Substance and Accident*** melts into the contrast between Cause and Effect***.

But if we think seriously about the relation between cause and effect, we will see that they too are barely distinguishable. Is it not his habit of behaving in a particular way which constitutes him a coward? So the behaviour is really the cause of the cowardice as much as vice versa. More generally, a thing which is acted on causally by something else can only thus be acted on in virtue of being what it is. So it is the cause of what happens as much as what we initially regarded as the cause.

Certainly there are many historical cases where we are hard put to it to distinguish between what is cause and what effect. Is it the philosophical thought of such as Rousseau and the *philosophes* which caused the unrest which came to a climax in the French Revolution, or the unrest which produced the thought?

Thus, a better way of conceiving the world than as a series of cause and effect relations is as a system in which everything is in reciprocal relations to other things. Reciprocity*** then replaces the category of Cause and Effect*** as the finale of Actuality**.

But Reciprocity*** is really the end-point of Actuality**, for it can only be understood (according to Hegel) if the world is conceived as a system of thought. And this conception constitutes the category of the NOTION*, which is the third great phase of THE LOGICAL IDEA.

There are fairly obvious ways in which we can dub Hegel's reasoning here as flawed. For one thing, cause and effect is a relation between events, whereas reciprocity, as Hegel understands it, is a relation between things. Two things can mutually influence each other, but each case of influence is a case of causation between events.

But detailed criticism of Hegel's dialectic is not my main concern. What is important is Hegel's idea that all ordinary concepts of the world are inadequate, and that we try to resolve their inadequacy by moving to other concepts which, however, soon display their own fresh inadequacy. This is a grand idea, which may be true whatever the limitations of much of Hegel's attempt to show this in detail.

A3 THE NOTION

At any rate, we must now move to the category of the NOTION* and explain how this emerges from the inadequacy of the previous categories, culminating in Reciprocity***.

The problem about reciprocity was this. It wants to distinguish two (or more) items which are in reciprocal relations. But this it cannot do. For since cause and effect have turned out to be one and the same, there are not two items to interact! Rather is there just one item, which is both cause and effect, and which interacts with itself. But there is an evident tension here, which requires resolution in another category.

The oddity of this 'deduction' turns on the fact that each phase of the dialectic of the LOGICAL IDEA (as opposed to NATURE and SPIRIT) is the system of concepts as they exist independently of their exemplification in concrete reality. For this reason we cannot distinguish one item from another as we do empirically, and if things are to be distinguished, it can only be because they are different as concepts. Now at one stage of the development of the dialectic, cause and effect presented themselves as different. But once we see that these are not genuinely distinct concepts, cause and effect collapse into one, and there is only one term for Reciprocity*** to work on. Thus Reciprocity*** consists in a thing's causing itself. But, because there is a residual difference between the concepts of cause and effect, in causing itself, it causes what is different as well as identical with it! (This is really hopeless, logically, but don't blame me!)

Now the characteristic feature of Reciprocity, that of self-production in a state of difference, is in fact the distinguishing mark of Spirit (*Geist*), as we shall see more fully later. And since thinking is characteristic of Spirit, we now move into the realm of the NOTION*, which means essentially the realm of THOUGHT. It is not, indeed, thought itself as a mental phenomenon which is now reached. That will only come when we move to the third member of the great triad: namely, SPIRIT. Rather, since we are only at the level of the concepts which constitute God 'as he was before the creation of the world', it is the concept of Thought which we shall examine under the heading of the NOTION*, which is the last member of the great Triad called the LOGICAL IDEA. And in the conception of the world as thought, we may hope to find all the contradictions implicit in the categories of BEING* and of ESSENCE* reconciled.

A key feature of the categories of the NOTION is that they all ultimately turn on the identity of opposites. For Hegel, as already implied, the identity of a bare A with the same bare A is a vacuous conception. (See GREATER LOGIC, book 2, ch. 2, remark 2.)[11] I agree with him on this. Identity, so it seems to me, is a relation which holds between terms which are also other than each other. For example, in listening to a piece of music one may hear the identical theme appearing at different stages. However, it is the identical theme in a state of difference from itself inasmuch as it occurs at a different point in the piece, perhaps in a different key, or played by different instruments, and in any case coloured by what preceded or will succeed it. This is a real identity of what is also different. The same phrase heard at the same moment by the same person is not identical with itself, it just is.

The standard modern explanation of why 'A is identical with B' need not be vacuous is that the verbal expressions 'A' and 'B' may have different senses, different ways of identifying the thing in question, even though they refer to just one thing A. The trouble with this is that it makes identity something which is not so much a reality out there in the world as a mere consequence of our language. Hegel is concerned (odd as this may seem on the part of an idealist) with a real identity, not something created by language. And such a real identity does seem to require an account along Hegel's lines. Moreover, on the modern view, 'A is identical with A' is true, not vacuous, as Hegel, I think rightly, says that it is.

For this reason I think there is something to the Hegelian notion of identity-in-difference, though of course the supposed *unity of opposites* goes much further than this.

NOTION* consists itself, as usual, of three main triads. These are the Subjective Notion**, the Objective Notion**, and the Idea**. The Subjective Notion** is the concept of the world as consisting in conceptual thought; the Objective Notion** is the thought of the world as physical; the Idea** is the thought of the world as thought thinking itself.

I shall pass over more of the details in my discussion of the NOTION* than I did with BEING* and ESSENCE*. One reason for this is that so much of the content here is repeated when we come to the third member of the great triad, SPIRIT.

To conceive the world under the categories of the Subjective Notion** is to conceive it as consisting in conceptual thought. And the most obvious way to do this is in terms of the way in which it addresses itself to reality, first by way of concepts (category of The Notion as Notion***), then by way of judgements (category of The Judgment***), then by way of reasoning (category of The Syllogism***). Note that these are not so much increasingly sophisticated ways of thinking, as increasingly sophisticated concepts of what thinking is.

The most important thing to emerge in the discussion of the Notion as Notion*** is Hegel's distinction between the Universal Notion**** (*Der allgemeine Begriff*), the Particular or Specific Notion**** (*das besonderes Begriff*), and the Individual Notion**** (*das Einzelne*). The meaning of this triad may initially be indicated by the use of an empirical example. Thus we may conceive an individual as being of some universal type, such as human being, or as belonging to a particular differentiation or subset of this universal type, such as Italian male composer, or we may finally conceive of him as being this quite individual man, Giacomo Puccini.

As Hegel sees it, the universal is something which is identically the same in each of its instances: e.g. that which is identical in all men, and as such its nature is entirely positive. In contrast, the notion of some men puts them in a negative relation to many of the rest (e.g. Italian negates French, male negates female, and composer—well, let us say—negates tone-deaf stockbroker). As for the individual, or singular, concept, this shows how the negative character of the particular concept and the positive character of the universal concept are united in the notion of this one individual, who both belongs with all other human beings and contrasts with them in nationality, sex, and calling. However, these empirical examples are merely helpful illustrations. We are supposed to grasp such a very general triad of concepts in abstraction from any empirical instances of them, since the latter do not exist at the pure level of the LOGICAL IDEA. This triad is pervasive in Hegel's thought, and is by no means confined to this stage of the dialectic.

As applied to the notion as judgement, it produces the three standard types of judgement: universal judgement, 'all X's are Y's'; the particular judgement, 'some (but not all) X's are Y's'; and the singular judgement, 'this A is Y'. As Hegel sees it, the first says that the universal is the particular; the second says that the universal is not always the particular; and the third says that the singular individual is the universal. This is a rather peculiar interpretation of such judgements. But we must remember that Hegel is operating in a realm of pure concepts or thought forms, and their meaning must be culled only from what is available at this level of abstraction.

Hegel's treatment of the category of judgement contains further distinctions which I shall not examine. Nor shall I consider the category of The Syllogism*** except for one brief element within it. This is Hegel's view that every type of syllogism is an effort to use one of the three items: universal, particular, and singular, or individual, as a link which can join the other two together.

Consider the most familiar of all syllogisms (allowing it an empirical filling for clarity):

All men are mortal.
Socrates is a man.
Therefore, Socrates is mortal.

For Hegel, this is of the form S-P-U, since it serves to unite the singular individual (Socrates) with the universal (mortal) by way of the intervening link of the particular (man), man being just one type of mortal.

This, in traditional logic, is a universal syllogism of the first figure. Hegel holds that all forms of the syllogism can be represented in this way. In every form there is an attempt to link two of the three of S, P, and U together by the mediation of the third. Hegel's development of this in detail is often quite baffling, and, to the ordinary logician, he seems to commit many fallacies. But all we need to bear in mind is that, for Hegel, the whole dialectic which constitutes reality as he sees it is powered by a process which consists in the manner in which something singular or individual is brought into being by a process in which the universal divides itself into the particular.

This is why Hegel can say, so bizarrely, that everything is a syllogism. But we can distinguish his main point from this weird way of putting it. What he means is that every genuine thing combines a *universal* aspect, a *particular aspect*, and a *singular*, or *individual*, *aspect*.

Indeed universal, particular, and singular are three absolutely basic features of reality for Hegel, and are present in his thought about almost everything. However, so flexible is his use of the terms that it is none too easy to define them once and for all. What exactly, in their pervasive being, they are, must be grasped by throwing oneself, so far as one can, into a Hegelian mode of thought, without expecting to be able to explicate this mode of thought, in terms of more common concepts, such as, for Hegel, would belong to *Verstand* rather than *Vernunft*.

But their general feel may be expressed like this. The universal is some kind of undifferentiated unity; the particular is some sort of differentiation within this unity, which destroys it as a unity; while the singular, or individual, is something in which unity is restored without differentiation being lost. This it tends to do by showing the differentiation as issuing from the unity rather than negating it. Thus it is famously 'the negation of the negation'. For, as Hegel sees it, the universal is positive and immediate, the particular is negative, while the singular, or individual, negates the negativity of the particular and resumes the positivity of the universal, but enriched by the negativity of the particular.

More generally, the distinction between THE LOGICAL IDEA, THE IDEA OUT-SIDE ITSELF, or NATURE, and THE IDEA IN AND FOR ITSELF, or SPIRIT, illustrates this pervasive triad, since the LOGICAL IDEA is a unity (universal) which differentiates itself into NATURE (particulars) and is finally united in SPIRIT (the individual for which the Idea and Nature and Spirit itself are grasped as a necessarily self-differentiating One).

Most importantly for my purposes, we will see the distinction between universal, particular, and singular, or individual, playing a significant part in Hegel's religious ideas. For God the Father is figured as the universal; God the Son, or rather the realm of God the Son, in which he makes an empirical appearance, as the particular; and God the Holy Spirit as the singular individual within which there are many particular individuals united as one. (This will become clearer later.)

Thus, if our sights are on reality as a whole, on the 'ALL', it presents itself, according to Hegel, as initially just a largely uncharacterized something very general but at the same time unitary. As such it is immediate. Then, within this very general something, we lay out boundaries between one part of it and another. As such, it is a collection of particulars with no intimate relation between any of them or the whole to which they all belong. Then, eventually, we find a way in which the world is a real whole or unity, but differentiated of its own nature into particulars each playing its own part in constituting the whole, and only capable of existing as doing so.

But the distinction between these three aspects arises not only when we are thinking about reality in general but equally, if a little differently, when our thoughts are directed at what might normally be called particular parts of reality. It is here that the Hegelian doctrine of the so-called concrete, as opposed to abstract, universal comes into its own.

The abstract universal, which Hegel largely scorns, is what we find if we strip off all the richness of the particulars of a certain type and keep only what is present in them all without giving any hint of its relation to them. The concrete universal, however, which is the genuine universal, intrinsically implies what falls under it. (See especially ENCYCLOPAEDIA I, §163.) That is, it somehow implies the various more specific universals which fall under it. Thus the universal triangle is not a mere abstraction from the different sorts of triangles. Rather, it is of the nature of universal triangularity that it can take all the different forms of triangle: isosceles, scalene, and equilateral. Likewise, the universal man somehow implies all the specific sorts of men and types of human activity. (To grasp the nature of an individual triangle or man is to see it or him as one of the actualizations implied in the universal.) The supreme concrete universal is Spirit which determines and creates its own instances, namely everything which is. And the dialectic progression shows how the Idea becomes gradually conscious of itself as such.

I suggest that there is a certain vagueness as to whether a concrete universal implies the being of all its possible instances simply as possibilities or as existing things. Does the whole range of possible men follow from the concrete universal man? Or does the existence of every genuinely possible man do so? It is easier, on the face of it, to accept the first alternative; on the other hand, the second alternative suits best the idea of concepts as self-actualizing, which is certainly the Hegelian idea. So I am inclined to take it in the second sense, whatever we may think of this.

Another ambiguity is this. On the interpretation just given, a concrete universal is akin to a Platonic Idea, but one which generates its own instances. But individuals which are not normally thought of as universals also come under this heading. Thus for Hegel a nation-state in which particular men are all united so that each owes his being to his precise role in it is a concrete universal; and equally, indeed, mankind, so far as it is a living unity. In these cases the particulars which fall under the concrete universal are not instances of it—a citizen is not a state, a particular man is not the human species.

For Hegel, doubtless, the distinction between these two senses or kinds of concrete universal is vanishing, since, on the one hand, the fact that many things exemplify one Idea makes their totality into a distinct unit; while, on the other hand, the fact that many things are parts of a genuine Whole (not a mere assemblage of things) is reflected in the individual character of each.

The category of The Syllogism*** (which has prompted our discussion of universal, particular, and individual) is the third and final category of the Subjective Notion** which exhibits the different levels at which we can conceive Reality as consisting in conceptual thought. As such, it exhibits the breakdown of this conception of reality and pushes the dialectic on to the category of the Objective Notion**. This is the level at which the world is conceived as a physical system.

The transition from the Subjective Notion** to the Objective Notion** (via The Syllogism***) is among Hegel's weirdest. It runs somewhat as follows.

Hegel has managed to 'deduce' various forms of syllogism, one from another. The last main head of this is what he calls the Syllogism of Necessity**** (we need not trouble ourselves with the meaning of 'necessity' here), which has, as its three subcategories, the Categorical Syllogism*****, the Hypothetical Syllogism*****, and the Disjunctive Syllogism*****. In the last of these, for reasons into which I shall not enter, the syllogism turns against itself, inasmuch as the process of mediation between the terms gives way to an immediate identity between them. And in terminating its character as a process of mediation, the syllogism ceases to be a form of thought, and becomes rather 'a thought-object', in short, the Objective Notion**.

This consists of the categories under which we think of the physical world. But how can the physical world pertain to the NOTION*, since this is the stage at which the world is seen as thought? The answer is that the Objective Notion is the physical world, not *as an 'objective' reality*, but *as we think it*. The Subjective Notion** conceived the world in terms of conceptual thought; the Objective Notion** now conceives it as thought about certain sorts of object. And the objects which first present themselves to thought are physical objects, processes, or substances.

The categories which pertain to the Objective Notion** are initially concepts of Mechanism***, then of Chemistry***, and finally of Teleology***. That is to say, the most elementary way of thinking of the physical is to conceive it as a mechanism, a way of thinking the inadequacies of which show the need to advance to conceptions of a more 'chemical' nature. These conceptions reveal in turn the need for an advance to conceptions of a more teleological kind, though not the kind of teleology which belongs only to mind.

The teleological conception of things in its more primitive form sharply divides Means from Ends**** . What is more, it requires an intermediate term, that of the activity which leads from the one to the other. This is external teleology. However, this is an inadequate conception of teleology, which is only really intelligible when that to which it applies includes both means and end in unity. And this synthesis of means and end is the characteristic of an organism, whose total functioning is the end. In true teleology, then, the means is simply the whole regarded with emphasis on the parts, and the end is simply the parts with the emphasis upon the whole which they form.

Thus to conceive physical processes as teleological is virtually to conceive them as living, and life is, in fact, the humble, initial form in which the category of the Idea** (which culminates in the all-covering conception of the Absolute Idea) presents itself. For to conceive of the physical as living leads inevitably to conceiving of it as possessing cognition*** . And this is the second category of the Idea** (the third synthesizing category of the NOTION**).

It seems reasonable enough to think that life (at least of the higher sort) requires some kind of representation of the environment which it must take account of in its activity.

Cognition*** has two subcategories rather than the usual three: namely, Cognition Proper**** (thinking that something is the case) and Volition**** (desiring or willing that something shall or should be the case). Either way, it involves a contrast between subject and object.

However, the conception of cognition and volition as two distinct things is incoherent, since neither can be what it is without the other. (Pragmatists would agree with this.) But cognition and volition are, finally, unsatisfactory concepts. For one conceives of the object as determining the subject, and the other of the subject as determining the object. But these are contradictory conceptions, which cannot be true of the world. Thus the ultimate category in terms of which we think of reality should not be that of a subject confronting an object, whether as something thought or as something willed, but of a unitary reality from which subject and object are abstractions, without independent reality.[12] But to conceive reality in this way is to conceive it as THE ABSOLUTE IDEA, or as Spirit grasping itself, *qua* spirit, as what the universe really is. Otherwise put, it is the conception of the universe as a self-experiencing Whole in which all oppositions between its parts are sublated; that is to say, their opposition to each other remains as a kind of throb within the Whole without threatening its unity.

This is the final phase of the Idea**, and thus the climax of the whole realm of the first member of the master triad THE LOGICAL IDEA. As such, it is the all-comprehending concept under which reality must be thought. It is not, indeed, itself total reality, but only the climactic concept of such. At this point the dialectic leads on from THE LOGICAL IDEA, the world of concepts without reference to their actualization, to their initial actualization in THE IDEA OUTSIDE ITSELF, or NATURE.

B The Idea Outside Itself, or Nature

There is much argument as to just how Hegel conceives the alleged fact that the LOGICAL IDEA 'lets itself go' (and, what is more does so, 'freely') into Nature, where it exists in a state of alienation from itself. The answer which I have suggested above is that the LOGICAL IDEA is a series of concepts which are decreasingly abstract and increasingly concrete, and that this process can continue (when the final, merely logical category, that of the *Absolute Idea**** is reached) only if it is followed by something which throws off the abstractness of mere concepts and is, rather, the concrete instantiation of such.[13]

A slightly different approach is to take it that for Hegel, as for Spinoza and Leibniz, every possible form of being has a certain *nisus* to actualize itself in something actually existing, and does so unless prevented by a 'somehow' more powerful possibility. The following passage would seem to suggest this.

The concept is, however, the deepest and the highest thing; it is the nature of every concept to sublate its deficiency, its subjectivity, this difference from being; it is itself the action of bringing itself forth as having being objectively.[14]

So nature comes into being as the (initial) actualization of the LOGICAL IDEA. It is the IDEA, as Hegel puts it, OUTSIDE ITSELF, that is, as having a being which is not merely ideal or conceptual. And it is there, it would appear, in order to provide the background and material for the life of SPIRIT.

But how is Hegel's account of Nature supposed to relate to that of natural science? According to J. N. Findlay, whom I find the most helpful of commentators on this point, Hegel is unclear as to how his philosophical account of nature relates to the accounts given, or to be given, by scientists (see FINDLAY, 69–70). On the whole, however, according to Findlay, we should see Hegel as a philosopher who 'knew' that certain categories (discovered in the *Logic*) must be actualized in Nature, but recognized that which phenomena actualized which categories must be learnt by looking for them in the accounts of natural scientists. Moreover, natural science will discover details of the ways in which the categories are actualized which cannot be discovered by philosophy alone. (In Hegel's usage 'science' (*Wissenschaft*) applies properly only to speculative philosophy, but I am using 'natural science' in its ordinary modern sense.)

However that may be, certainly if the IDEA OUTSIDE ITSELF is to be the actualization of the LOGICAL IDEA, then it must actualize every phase of the latter, or rather every phase of BEING and of ESSENCE, leaving it to SPIRIT to actualize the NOTION. Thus nature must have a feature which answers to the concept of Pure Being****. This it does in the form of Space. For Space is the concrete reality which best actualizes mere Being. What is more, like Pure Being****, it is readily identified with Nothing****.

That space is three-dimensional arises for Hegel from the triadic nature of reality in general, more especially from the pervasive triad of universal, particular, and singular. That the three dimensions of space do not differ qualitatively from each other is because the resources for qualitative distinction are not present at the level of mere Being.

As for Time**, one might expect the Becoming**** which synthesized Pure Being**** and Nothing**** to come into play here. However, Hegel introduces it by arguing that space requires time so that it may have a structure; for its structure turns on the possibilities of moving about in it. Thereby it is shown that Space and Time point necessarily to Motion, and also to Matter, in order that there shall be something which moves.

The parts of matter seem to be outside each other. Yet there is a real identity between them, since each is in itself just extended matter. This identity expresses itself in their mutual attraction, or gravitation, while that they are also different is expressed by the repulsive force which they exert on each other (cf. FINDLAY, 276). Hegel interprets the behaviour of the solar system on the basis of these two forces (thus aligning himself with Kepler, rather than Newton).

After this treatment of the features of the physical world covered by mechanics, Hegel moves on to consider such physical phenomena as the traditional four elements, fire, air, earth, and water. Light, however, is taken along with these and given a particularly basic status as the binding force of the whole physical universe: that is, as the medium through which everything is related to everything. In this, indeed, it stands together with gravity, but gravity is a lower grade of reality, inasmuch as light is half-way to mind.

And so it goes on until, after a few more similarly strange deductions, we are led to the necessary presence in nature of organisms, both plant and animal, thus to the phenomenon of life. And from there only a small step remains before we see how nature must give birth to SPIRIT, initially in the natural souls of animals and humans.

It should be emphasized that Hegel did not regard the dialectical series of moments of nature as a chronological series. They were all as much just there once and for all as are the moments of the LOGICAL IDEA. Thus, in tracing the higher and higher levels of physical phenomena from space, gravitation, the solar system, etc., up to life, in which the character of every lower form of life points to the need for there to be a higher level of life correcting its deficiencies, Hegel had no idea that something somewhat similar might one day be established as a temporal process. Indeed, he dismissed such mootings of this view as were current in his day. The dialectical series is only temporal at the level of human history (not in the development of life forms).

None the less, when the theory of evolution came to be accepted by all serious thinkers, Hegelian philosophers thought that Hegelianism offered an ideal philosophical home for it, and were quite ready to embrace what for Hegel was only logical as also historical.

The question naturally arises as to how far Hegel believed in an independent physical reality arising initially (logically, if not temporally) from the LOGICAL IDEA, and giving birth to SPIRIT, but with its own independent reality. In short, was he essentially either a Berkeleyan or a Kantian? Or was his position rather that of a physical realist offering a special explanation for the existence of the physical but in no way denying that it existed of itself in its own right?

A possible answer is this. Hegel largely accepted from Kant the view that the physical world is specifiable only in terms which mark it as mind-dependent: that is, as existing only for mind. However, whereas for Kant the physical world existed only as an appearance for finite minds, all of which excogitated it similarly in virtue of their similar modes of experiencing and thinking, Hegel took it as showing that the physical world, while as real as anyone could wish, was the product of a system of ideas: namely, the LOGICAL IDEA.

If the LOGICAL IDEA is thought of as constituting or pertaining to a conscious God, then this would suggest that for Hegel the physical world is indeed only there for mind, but that in the first place this mind is a cosmic mind, and only in the second place a community of finite minds. (The result, even if not the reasoning, would not, then, have been so far from

Berkeley.) However, difficult as it is to be clear on the matter, it seems that we should not reduce the realm of the LOGICAL IDEA to the content of a conscious mind. Rather, both nature and mind (*Geist*) are the product of a system of Ideas which produce, rather than are, the product of mind (and of nature).

God reveals Himself in two different ways: as Nature and as Spirit. Both manifestations are temples of God which he fills, and in which he is present. God, as an abstraction, is not the true God, but only as the living process of positing His Other, the world, which comprehended in its divine form is His Son; and it is only in unity with His Other, in Spirit, that God is Subject. (ENCYCLOPAEDIA, ii § 246)

I conclude, therefore, that Hegel was an unusual kind of physical realist.[15] The physical world is not a system of representations either for infinite or finite mind. It is, however, totally accessible to any mind, because the logical ideas of which it is the necessary actualization are in their very nature addressed to mind, as ways in which it is bound to think.

But perhaps we can go a little further and say that God, *qua* ABSOLUTE IDEA ejecting itself from itself, does partially become the physical world, a world which, so to speak, professes to be other than him, but is not so really, and that at the level of Absolute Spirit*, He becomes aware of the physical world as indeed an aspect of himself.

The making or creation of the world is God's self-manifesting, self-revealing. In a further and later definition we will have this manifestation in the higher form that what God creates God himself is. (LECTURES 1827, 129)

For the notion is the universal, which preserves itself in its particularizations, dominates alike itself and its 'other', and so becomes the power and activity that consists in undoing the alienation which it had evolved. (INTRODUCTORY AESTHETICS, § XXI)

C Spirit or the Idea In and For Itself

SPIRIT, the third great triad of the whole dialectic, is eventually the medium through which the Idea understands itself consciously. But before it can do this, it must pass through a series of subordinate forms. Or rather, these subordinate forms must be perpetually present in reality as undergirding Spirit in its highest form (Absolute Spirit).

There are three levels of Spirit, constituting its great triad. These are SUBJECTIVE SPIRIT*, OBJECTIVE SPIRIT*, and ABSOLUTE SPIRIT*.

C1   SUBJECTIVE SPIRIT*

The categories of SUBJECTIVE SPIRIT* are the categories used by individual psychology, the subject-matter of a work like William James's *Principles of Psychology*.[16] The dialectic progression follows a series either of ways in which the individual mind may be conceived, or of ways in which individual minds of greater and greater sophistication exist in nature—it is hard sometimes to say which.

The three great phases of subjective spirit are the Soul** (discussed under the heading of Anthropology), Consciousness** (discussed under the heading of Phenomenology), and Mind** (*Geist*) (discussed under the heading of Psychology). Soul, consciousness, and mind here refer just to what they are at this level. The first of these is concerned with the animal soul. This is consciousness of the type possessed by animals, and subsisting as a basis on which all the more subtle aspects of human consciousness rest. Each category here is an aspect of the way in which an animal organism feels its own bodily existence.

After Soul** we move to Consciousness**. This has three phases: Consciousness Proper***, Self-consciousness***, and Reason***. The three grades of the first of these are Sensuous Consciousness****, Sense Perception****, and Reason or Intellect****.

Soul** and Consciousness** contrast like this. At the former level the soul lives through various different felt phases, but these bring it no information as to what lies outside itself. In contrast, at the level of Consciousness**, the internal states of soul or mind mediate awareness of an external world.

In the first form of this, Consciousness Proper***, we move from what seems an immediate confrontation with an object involving no thinking, properly speaking, to a more intellectual manner of grasping what is around us. (Compare PHENOMENOLOGY, A1.)

Thus we start with Sensuous Consciousness****, which is a kind of blank unconceptualizing confrontation with something. And since no concepts are applied, there is no awareness of what kind of something it is. We really have no idea at all of what it is or what distinguishes it from anything else. In effect, it is Being = Nothing, and corresponds to Sense-Certainty in the *Phenomenology*. (See PHENOMENOLOGY, A1.)

It may be suggested that we can at least mark out some object of special attention by the mental equivalent of referring to it as 'this'. But this does not tell us anything about it, or distinguish it from anything else, since everything in the world is as truly a 'this'. Sense Perception**** moves us on a little bit, because it includes the rudiments of conceptual thought. Thus at this level we see (or otherwise perceive) something as a such-and-such, say a hazel nut (if one were a squirrel) available as food. However, if we try to express this verbally, we would be distinguishing the object before us as something with certain properties. But in doing so we would be thrust into a maze of problems as to how a thing is related to its properties: that is, how a particular relates to the universals under which it falls.

Something towards a solution of this is discovered by Intellect[****]. Intellect achieves this by treating the universals (the properties) as the reality, and the particulars as mere appearances or illusions. To carry this out, moreover, it evokes universals of a deeper and more pervasive kind than those which merely classify the objects around us in a day-to-day fashion. In short, it moves on to the level of natural science, where universals like 'table', 'chair', and 'tree' give way to universals like 'force', 'gravity', and 'law'.

Intellect is the mind become scientific (in our, rather than Hegel's, sense of the word). It is in fact the understanding (*Verstand*) at work, a mode of thought which is of essential value for much of human life, but which, as a way of gaining a more final grasp of reality must give way to reason (*Vernunft*). Its main concepts are, in fact, those of Essence[*] rather than Self-Consciousness[****].

But Intellect[****] leaves us still with plenty of problems. And these can only be solved when we move towards the next grade of Consciousness[**]: namely, Self-Consciousness[***].

The transition to this from Intellect[****] turns on the idea that Intellect conceived its objects as universals, while Self-consciousness[****] twigs the fact that universals are modes of thought—are, that is, its own way of classifying and understanding things. As such, they no longer seem so alien. What is more, Intellect[****] distinguished between the multiplicity of the sense world and the unity of the laws which govern it, and took the second to be the fundamental reality. In doing so, however, it risked making the universals or laws quite blank, for in separating them from the phenomena which they govern, it made them quite characterless, seeing that their character is constituted by their manifestation in particular phenomena. Self-Consciousness[***] solves the problem by seeing the universals, or laws, as a unity which necessarily expresses itself as a multiplicity. In doing so, it recognizes that they are concrete universals rather than merely abstract or nominal ones; universals, that is, which (as we learnt from the category of the NOTION[*] in the LOGICAL IDEA) are fertile of the many, and thus are the work of creative mind. Such is an overall characterization of Self-Consciousness***, but Hegel develops it, as usual, through three phases, or 'moments': Appetite or Instinctive Desire****, Self-Consciousness Recognitive****, and Universal Self-Consciousness****.

Appetite or Instinctive Desire**** is characterized by Hegel in a curious manner. Self-Consciousness*** becomes troubled by the question of whether the object is or is not simply itself, does or does not have an independent being. In short, it does not know whether it is consciousness of itself or consciousness of another. Its solution is to deny that the other is something separate from itself. This denial of the object as something other than the subject to whom it appears is solved not by mere thinking but by eating the object!!!

This sounds rather ludicrous. But this is just Hegel's dramatic way of claiming that it is the goal of all desire and appetite to deny the independence of the other and reduce it to a process within oneself. This has some validity as an account of loveless lust.

Self-Consciousness**** thereby insists that everything apparently other than itself is really not so. It expresses this by satisfying its appetite at their expense. But with Self-Consciousness Recognitive**** the recognition of myself in the apparently other takes a higher form, realized when I take the other as another consciousness, or mind, in particular when I see another human organism as myself in a state of only apparent separateness from myself over here.[17]

One might complain that, presuming that Self-Consciousness Recognitive is an attitude directed only at human beings (and animals?), it has not been shown that self-consciousness, with its reductive view of the other, needs to be superseded in all cases (for what of inanimate objects?). But perhaps this is dialectically satisfactory since the earlier concepts in the dialectical sequence are not meant to replace the earlier ones in all contexts. Yet Hegel also thinks that the dialectic is leading us to a final concept of universal application. Obscurity on this point is endemic to Hegel's dialectic.

At any rate, dialectically speaking, Appetite**** becomes Self-Consciousness Recognitive****, because the destructive impulses expressive of the former meet an obstruction when its object resists it by showing signs of being itself a consciousness. It follows that the Appetitive Consciousness**** can only have its way by destroying the other, and this destruction allows it to triumph in its own success as the only real individual which there is. However, since this triumph is now what it most delights in, it must not finally destroy the other consciousness but must keep it going in sufficiently robust a form to be the object of this satisfying form of destruction.

It is not clear to me why Appetite**** in becoming Self-Consciousness Recognitive**** cannot destroy a series of others, even other consciousnesses, and renew its triumphant enjoyment thus. However, as so often with Hegel, plural and singular are barely distinguished, and perhaps we should think of there just being one other which insists on its own status as a consciousness. Thus the destruction of one other individual is seen as the destruction of them all.

We are now in the thick of Hegel's famous treatment of master and slave, (originally presented in PHENOMENOLOGY, B IV A) a celebrated *tour de force*. Here are two egos each attempting to establish its monopoly of reality by crushing the other, but not so finally that it loses its chance to enjoy such crushing. The most effective way in which one of the two can achieve this is by making the other his slave.

But the master's enjoyment of his triumph cannot last long, for in fact he becomes dependent on the slave. This is both because he needs him to triumph over and, more basically, because he needs his labour to satisfy his own physical needs. Meanwhile, the slave, through his labour on physical reality, becomes more and more aware of its products as himself realized outside himself. Thus he comes to enjoy a richer form of Self-Consciousness than the master, since the form of external things, the fields of crops or the domesticated animals, bear his stamp more than they do the master's.

Through this development, each of master and slave has to recognize the other as a self-conscious ego like himself; in fact, himself in a state of otherness from himself. Thus is born Universal Self-Consciousness****, in which all egos come to respect all others as identical, but with a difference, from themselves, so that eventually slavery ceases, and a more equal state of things develops.

Here, as in most of Hegel's account of Spirit, it is difficult to know whether the supposed ontological series is meant to be a logically necessary historical series too.

The third phase of Phenomenology, or Consciousness**, is Reason***. For in grasping the fact that another person is both oneself and not oneself (the same essential Spirit but actualized in a different historical role), Spirit is learning that the sharp distinctions made by Understanding (*Verstand*), in which everything is itself and not another thing, are inadequate to reality. In fact, everything is both different from and identical with everything else. This is a truth which it is the peculiar role of reason (*Vernunft*) to grasp and apply. Thus we have arrived at Reason*** as the final stage of Consciousness**.

From there we pass to Psychology**, which treats of Spirit** (in a much narrower sense than that in which the word refers to the whole third phase of the Master Triad).

Soul** was an immediate unity. Consciousness** distinguished between conscious subject and the external objects of which it is aware. Psychology/Spirit** restores the unity, but it is a unity enriched by the adventures in an apparently external world which constituted consciousness. Thus it is Spirit engaged with itself, rather than anything outward, but enriched by its apparent adventures with something other than itself. Spirit** (at the level of Psychology**) is therefore free—that is, self-determinative—as it has not been in its previous phases.

Psychology/Spirit** has three phases: Theoretical Spirit***, Practical Spirit***, and Free Spirit*** in which it fully realizes its own freedom. Theoretical Spirit*** divides into Intuition****, Representation****, and Thinking****. Intuition**** is the most elementary form of thought, in which an object somehow simply hovers before us without any explicit awareness of oneself as thinking of it.

A more adequate form of thinking is Representation****. Here Spirit** (at the level of Psychology**) is aware of the objects of its thought as having been brought within it from outside. They are therefore no longer external. A perceived rose is something external to Spirit** (at the level of Psychology**), but when the flower is thought of, it becomes internal to it, becomes in fact a Representation**** (*Vorstellung*). As usual, Hegel discusses this as though in being brought into thought the object ceases to exist outside.

Representation**** itself has three modes: Recollection*****, Imagination*****, and Memory*****. Recollection***** is simply the transforming of an external object into something thought of or imagined. In Imagination***** the mind becomes more fully aware of itself as creating its objects, since it can do so without assistance from anything outside. Memory***** seems to be an advance on Recollection***** and Imagination*****, since it requires no imagery, but can be conducted in words alone. Words, however, are not mere sensuous noises, but mental contents somehow essentially imbued with meaning. Denuded of meaning, they become mere noises.

Memory***** in this sense develops into Thinking Proper****. The most important feature of thinking is that it involves judgement. The previous types of mental activity established only a problematic relation between their objects considered as universals and as particulars. Thinking**** resolves the problem, since it consists in seeing the Universal in the Particular, and this is precisely what *judgement* is. As such, it ceases to employ concepts which are sharply distinct from each other in a manner untrue to their exemplification in fact. Instead, it moves fluidly from one concept to another in virtue of their dialectical relations.

Thinking**** (the third mode of Theoretical Spirit***) is aware that its objects are its own creations, and thereby assumes control of them! It thus becomes Practical Feeling***. As such, it moulds objects to its own wishes. It does so at first in an immediate fashion. This is a very unthought-out way of dealing with the world. However, it is an immediacy which hankers after something more rational. This leads on to the level of choice between different immediate objects: that is, the category of Impulses and Choice****. At this level Spirit has no clear way of making its choices, and is merely the chaotic scene of impulse struggling against impulse. For Hegel this means that it is a self-contradictory state of Spirit**. To resolve this contradiction Spirit passes into its next phase, which is Happiness****.

Impulses and Choice**** exhibited Spirit** as dividing into a multiplicity of particulars. To avoid this contradiction, Spirit** directs itself to the universal under which these particulars fall, and this universal is Happiness****, a state in which it hopes to find compatible satisfactions for all its impulses. But this poses a problem for Free Spirit***. For this grasping after happiness proves in vain, since satisfaction of all these warring impulses is impossible. And this is because Spirit is a universal, and cannot find satisfaction in any object which is not truly universal too. But this it can do only if it objectifies itself, and this means that it must fulfil itself in something objective. This will in one sense be external—it will not be mere subjectivity. Rather, will it be subjectivity actualized in the objective world. As such, it becomes Objective Spirit*, Spirit realizing itself in an external world, but consciously so, not unconsciously as in Nature. OBJECTIVE SPIRIT constitutes the third phase of Spirit (in the largest sense), coming between SUBJECTIVE SPIRIT* and ABSOLUTE SPIRIT*.

C2 OBJECTIVE SPIRIT*

Free Spirit*** was seeking satisfaction in something which, though universal, is not merely abstractly so. To do so, it had to remain free, but with a solid external expression of itself in something concrete. And it does this by creating a system of institutions as its objective habitation. As such, it is an 'objective' reality, but not a merely natural one.

Spirit as objective is a concrete universal, not the mere abstract universal which it was when it only existed lonesomely in its own being. A concrete universal, it will be recalled, is one which produces its own particular instances in order to be all that it has in it to be.

The concrete universal within which a group of human beings is unified by the categories of OBJECTIVE SPIRIT* is called by Hegel the 'Ethical Substance'. We cannot follow the dialectic of these categories in detail, but a general idea of it will suffice for our purposes. The transitions from one category to another are often quite perplexing. None the less, his account of OBJECTIVE SPIRIT* is one of the most impressive features of Hegel's thought.

The main triad of categories of OBJECTIVE SPIRIT* are Abstract Right**, Morality**, and Social Ethics**.

As in most of Hegel's treatment of human life, the series of categories is not primarily, if at all, chronological. What the categories pick out are the main features of human life in all societies (or all societies that are not barbaric). These features may be more dominant in some actual societies than in others, but each is present in at least an embryonic form in all even minimally civilized human life. And in true dialectic fashion, each of them makes up for the limitations inherent in the others.

Abstract Right** is the level at which persons recognize each other as ends in themselves, in Kant's sense, who should never be treated as mere means. In contrast to persons stand things which *are* mere means***. And as an end in himself, each person needs to have certain such means in his own single control. That is to say, there must be an institution of private Property*** and this, therefore, is the first moment of Abstract Right**.

However, a thing would not really be at the disposal of a person as his Means*** unless this disposal included the right to transfer it to another. Contract*** is, however, essentially free, and this inevitably includes the possibility of failing to treat the other as an end in himself***, by possessing oneself of his property other than by contract. Such an exercise of freedom constitutes Crime****.

By his behaviour, the criminal negates the system of Abstract Right**, as the rules governing property and contract. Hegel regards Crime**** as a self-contradictory or 'untrue' phase of Spirit, for it contradicts the essence of Spirit, which is freedom, by negating another's freedom. In order that Abstract Right can exist, it must include the power to negate this negation, and this is punishment. To regard punishment merely as a deterrent, or as aimed at the criminal's reform (though it may incidentally serve these purposes), is quite superficial. Its real nature is Spirit negating that which negates itself in order to establish the essential unreality of crime as a phase of Abstract Right.

The concept of crime, however, serves to move us on from Abstract Right** to Morality**. For in crime the Particular (person) asserts himself against the Universal, and thereby acts as he *ought* not to have done. And this moves us beyond the essentially external nature of the demands of Abstract Right to the inner demands of Morality. For while Abstract Right concerns only behaviour, Morality is concerned more with the motives and emotions behind it.

After two intermediate phases, Hegel reaches the category of Goodness and Wickedness***, and begins to develop the idea of a Universal Will, with which the Particular Will does or does not correspond.

Spirit, and, more specifically Spirit in the mode of Will, is present both in you and in me. As present in us both, it is a universal, but it is particularized within each of us. For Hegel the universal which is common to us both is the true nature of our particular wills, and as such its content is determined by the basic idea of Spirit and Will as Hegel sees them, and this basic idea is of it as something rational. When I act in a way which does not fall under this basic idea, then I am said to be acting against my true nature, the Universal Will, and this is Wickedness***, while when I act in accordance with this basic idea, my action exemplifies Goodness***. Wickedness***, like Crime***, is a contradiction, because there is a clash between what my particular Will does and what essentially it is. And since the clash is within the Universal Will or Reason, which is what I essentially am, I can become conscious of this clash and seek to avoid it. Such consciousness constitutes conscience.

Good behaviour for Hegel, as for Kant, is rational behaviour. But, unlike Kant, Hegel is not content to reduce Morality** to the categorical imperative conceived as the need to avoid inconsistency in one's behaviour and thoughts. Our duties are much more concrete than this, and call for explanation at the level of Social Ethics**.

Here Spirit expresses itself in the social institutions of the public human world. Social Ethics** meets a defect in Morality**, which was its extreme abstractness. Goodness*** and Wickedness*** were distinguished, but only as conformity or nonconformity of the particular with the universal Will. But this told us nothing definite as to what constitutes goodness and wickedness, or for that matter what the rights of Property*** and the rules of Contract*** should be. It is only in so far as our duties are determined by the concrete life of an existing society that they become definite enough to constitute a genuine *ought* or obligation. The claims of conscience would otherwise be merely formal, and therefore vacuous. The move to Social Ethics** from Morality** is akin to that from Being**** to

Nothing****, at the beginning of the LOGICAL IDEA, and then (ignoring Becoming) to Determinate Being***. For an *ought* cannot be of any use as a guide to conduct unless it has a definite content.

Hegel now moves through the categories of the Family*** and Civil Society*** to the category of the State***. And each of these gives rise to its own distinctive set of duties.

Family*** is the first immediate phase of 'the Ethical Substance', in which feeling is dominant, and its duties derive from natural love. But families do not endure as single individual units. For the children depart when they become adults, and spouses are separated through death.

Once the family is dissolved, its various members become independent persons, atomic particulars speciously complete in themselves. And their motivation, no longer rooted in family or fellow feeling, must be self-interest. Yet they need each other's aid and protection from too unpleasant forms of competition.

So Civil Society*** appears as a system in which self-interested individuals can live together to the advantage of each, with certain agreed rights and the means of enforcing their recognition. However, it is merely a kind of contract whereby each person can seek their own fortune with minimal conflict with others. As such, it inevitably comes into conflict with the purposes of the individual person. Thus it contradicts itself as both the means of, and the frustration of, its members' plans. The problem is dealt with by physical enforcement of its laws. But this achieves only a very external kind of relation between individuals, and the contradiction between their various purposes is never quite resolved.

In this form, or aspect, of life the ethical attachment of the individual to something larger than himself—namely, the family—is lost, and he is left concerned only with his own selfish needs. Thus Civil Society*** is (as it should be, as the second moment in the triad of Social Ethics**) concerned with the particular, while the family is an immediate and natural universal. However, it is too limited a universal to deal with the needs of a large human society.

This contradiction can only be resolved adequately if Civil Society*** passes into the State***, which combines both the universality of the Family*** and the particularity of the collection of self-interested agents which band together in civil society. The State***, as is usual with the third member of a triad, is a true concrete universal, which synthesizes the immediacy of the relations between members of a Family*** with the externality of the relations between persons in Civil Society*** (with the inadequate form of personal freedom which this provides).

So the State***, it would seem, has the warmth (through patriotism) of the Family***, but includes a much wider range of particulars than pertain to Civil Society***. Its existence is thus a rational necessity, and it is an end in itself, not merely a means to the advantage of particular persons. States may be bad, certainly, but so may men; this does not show that a man who really answers to the proper notion of man is bad, and no more does the existence of bad states show that the state, when it answers to its notion, is bad; rather, it is the highest good, at the level of Objective Spirit. In his treatment of the State***, Hegel elaborates his views on constitutional matters (concerning the relations between monarch, the executive, and the legislature.)

The state is as much an individual as are human persons; indeed, it is much more so. Therefore it must belong with other states in an analogue of Civil Society***. In this 'interstate civil society' each state is concerned simply with its own interests. And since it has a value over and above individual persons, these must be prepared to die for it in war. What correspond to Civil Society*** are essentially the treaties which states make with one another. But since each state is rightly concerned to perpetuate its own existence, war is bound to occur, and is not to be regretted, as it strengthens the tie between individual persons and their state. International law****, therefore, is a matter of treaties between individual states, and there is no higher individual to which they belong, as the members of Civil Society*** belong to the more genuine individual of the State***.

It is not clear that Hegel had any rational ground for rejecting the notion of an international community such as in our own day the United Nations may be in the slow process of becoming. The nearest to any such thing is, in fact, the World Spirit—that is, the ABSOLUTE IDEA, or *Geist*, as expressed in World History****, and its judgements consist in the successes or failures of each state. History is essentially the process by which each state gradually fulfils the goals determined by its own particular nature. At any one time there is a dominant state in which the World Spirit is developing itself most significantly. Thus philosophical history only bothers itself with a narrative of what each state contributes to the development of humanity in its phase of dominance, and how the torch of progress passes from it to the next state. This is the subject of one of Hegel's more accessible works, *The Philosophy of History*.

For Hegel, the supposed purpose of human history was the development of human freedom. It is an oddity of his philosophy that in his whole treatment, especially of the state and of world history, the freedom of the individual seems to become less and less important to him. His response would be that the individual person is only really free in so far as he can become a fully human person as a citizen of a state, with all its associated institutions. For the actions of state and institutions, corresponding as these do to his own more universal self, are, metaphysically considered, his own acts.

C3 ABSOLUTE SPIRIT*

ABSOLUTE SPIRIT* arises because *Geist* can completely fulfil itself neither in the mere individual person nor in Objective Spirit. The first is too subject-ive and internal, the second too objective and external. Moreover, each of these is a form of mere finite existence, while *Geist* is in essence infinite and can therefore only actualize itself in the infinite—an infinite, of course, which is pervasively present in the finite. As such, each form of ABSOLUTE SPIRIT* shows *Geist* trying to grasp its own essential nature; that is, each is an aspiration to become conscious of Absolute Reality, or the Divine Mind, in fact to become conscious of it as its own essential being or substance.

ABSOLUTE SPIRIT* is of course itself a triad—indeed, a master triad, with three great moments: Art**, Religion**, and Philosophy**.

C3.1   Absolute Spirit Revealing itself in Art**

Each of Art**, Religion**, and Philosophy** is a way of conceiving the Absolute, in the recognition, dim or lucid, that the Absolute is Spirit. However, they differ in the way in which they comprehend this. Art** sees the Absolute through sensory objects; Religion sees it through mental pictures; while Philosophy, finally grasps it conceptually in its true es-sence, without the distortion which the previous two involve.

Putting Art before Religion in the dialectic of Absolute Spirit may seem odd, and in the *Phenomenology* it comes as the second phase, the aesthetic phase, of religion, between natural and revealed religion. However, it comes before Religion in the *Encyclopaedia* because it is (for Hegel) a less sophisticated way in which the Absolute begins to reveal itself as Spirit (*Geist*).

Hegel treats the following types of Art** as increasingly adequate revela-tions of the Absolute, culminating in a form of art which is on the verge of becoming religion. The most elementary aesthetic manifestation of the Absolute is in the beauties of Nature. Thus the Beauty of Nature**** is, in effect, the first phase in the triad called ART, and its immediacy is what is typical of the opening thesis in any dialectical triad. (However, the triadic structure is a bit doubtful in Hegel's aesthetics here.)

Beauty in Nature*** is, for the un-romantic Hegel, an elementary and unsatisfactory form of beauty.[18] The beauty of art is far superior to it as a manifestation of the Absolute. For art is quite evidently the work of spirit or mind, while nature is only revealed as such to an adequate metaphysics. And this is all the more difficult because nature is Spirit, or *Geist*, in a state of alienation from itself. 'The hard rind of nature and the common world gives the mind more trouble in breaking through to the idea than do the products of art' (INTRODUCTORY AESTHETICS, XV).

However, it is similarly true that art, in turn, is inferior to religion and philosophy, because these manifest *Geist* still more adequately and obviously. For it is in thought rather than sensation that the highest truth is discovered. It follows that art can never be as important for the modern world as it was in its greatest days (especially those of the ancient Greeks), because man has moved beyond it to grasping reality by pure conceptual thought.

The peculiar mode to which artistic production and works of art belong no longer satisfies our supreme need. (INTRODUCTORY AESTHETICS, XVI; see also CIV)

The next two dialectical phases of Art** are the Types of Art*** and the Particular Arts*** (see INTRODUCTORY AESTHETICS, CII and ff.). The second of these consists simply in the primary examples of the types of art listed in the former. Thus we have Symbolic Art, of which, strangely, architecture is the prime example; Classical Art****, of which sculpture is the prime example; and Romantic Art****, of which painting, music, and poetry are the main examples. However, these prime examples are not the only instances of each type, for each art-form has instances which approximate more or less to each of the three types.

There are two aspects to every art-form or object: the spiritual content and the material embodiment, or form. Symbolic Art** is art in which these two sides are linked only in a rather external manner. Thus the Material Embodiment*** is, and is felt to be, an inadequate expression of the Spiritual Content*** which it strives to actualize. One thinks here especially of allegory, since the underlying meaning is conveyed by the story only in a rather mechanical fashion. But for Hegel, Architecture**** is the prime form of Symbolic Art****. This seems odd, but what he has chiefly in mind is temple architecture, where the building is not designed for practical purposes, or other such apparently useless constructions as the pyramids. Hegel's general idea is that the creators of such things tried desperately to wring a spiritual meaning out of massive physical structures which were not really subtle enough for this purpose. At a later stage the shapes become more complicated and contorted, as in Hindu art, where the inadequacy of the material form to spiritual content is experienced and dealt with by attempts at stranger and stranger constructions. And Hinduism is, above all, the religion in which Spirit finds itself incapable of expressing itself physically.

Next comes Classical Art****. Here the sensory form is much more adequate as an embodiment of the spiritual content. The highest form of classical art is sculpture. For, as the three-dimensional representation of the essentials of the human form, it exhibits both the Spirituality which lies behind matter and the variety of humanity, though only of that idealized humanity in which Spirit becomes most obviously present to itself. (See INTRODUCTORY AESTHETICS, CVI.)

The third main type of art is the Romantic****. *Qua* art, this is less perfect than the classical, but this is because it is a higher expression of Spirit, in which the impossibility of its adequate sensory manifestation is becoming clear. Such inadequacy of the material or sensory for the embodiment of Spirit is, indeed, a source of suffering, as the IDEA as SPIRIT seeks to find itself in the IDEA as physical.

Such suffering cannot be exhibited adequately in Sculpture****, still less in Architecture. But in the Romantic Arts**** of Painting****, Music****, and Poetry****, Spirit presents itself to itself in its phases of struggle and suffering, even ugliness. In painting solidity is there only as an illusion, while all forms of human behaviour in the world can be presented with a vividness impossible in sculpture. In Music**** the spatiality of the world is lost sight of, and we begin to experience Pure Spirit in a sensory world which has no substantial existence. Finally, in Poetry**** the physical medium is itself barely sensory or physical, and human life appears in something approaching its fullness. But in poetry we are moving into Religion**. For the physical has virtually dropped away, and we have spiritual phenomena presented to us in a form which is only residually sensory.

This inadequacy of the sensory to reveal the spiritual creates a tension which is more or less fully resolved by Religion**.[19]

C3.2   *Absolute Spirit Revealing itself in Religion***

We now move on from Art** to Religion**. The three 'moments' of this are Religion in General***, followed by Definite Religion*** and the Absolute Religion*** (= Christianity). I will consider these in turn.

C3.2a   *Religion in General*** Art**, Religion**, and eventually Philosophy**
are all ways of grasping the Absolute (that is, the Actualized Idea) in its true

character. Their difference is the medium through which this character is more or less fully grasped. The most adequate medium is the purely conceptual, which is provided by Philosophy**. Religion** lies between Art and Philosophy. It grasps the Absolute in the form of *Vorstellungen*, a *Vorstellung* being a kind of pictorial concept. It is not, indeed, a full sensory reality, like a sense presentation or a sensory image, but it is still pictorial in a manner which the concepts of philosophy have transcended. It is, it would seem, a sensory image which is so suffused with its meaning that it has no graspable independent sensory character.

We must continue to bear in mind that for Hegel, unlike many other philosophers, conceptual thought, when the concepts are those of Reason (*Vernunft*) rather than of Understanding (*Verstand*), grasps reality in a more full and concrete way than does any other form of consciousness. Many philosophers (e.g. Bergson, James, and in Hegel's own time Schopenhauer) have thought of conceptual thinking as necessarily giving us only a thin awareness of reality, in comparison with its character as revealed in some more sensory or immediate way. But for Hegel there is something too thin and abstract even about thinking in the form of religious *Vorstellungen*. It is only when we grasp all this in philosophical terms—that is, follow the dialectic of Hegelian philosophy, or at least something close to it—that we get at the full concreteness of reality.

*C3.2b   Definite Religion*** There are two basic forms of Definite Religion, the Religion of Nature**** and the Religion of Spiritual Individuality****. (The triad is effectively completed by The Absolute Religion, i.e. Christianity, but it serves more significantly as the third triad of Religion *tout court*.)

Under the heading of Definite Religion, Hegel characterizes a series of religions which present an increasingly adequate *Vorstellung* of the spirituality of God or the Absolute.

The first of the definite religions is the Religion of Nature****, which finds the Absolute in nature. Its most elementary form is Magic*****, where the status of Spirit as the highest actualization of the Absolute is vaguely and inappropriately pictured as the superiority in power of a man (the magician) to the powers of nature.

The next form of religion, moving up the scale, is the Religion of Substance*****. This appreciates that God or the Absolute is the universal, but it is the blankness of the abstract universal rather than the riches of the concrete universal which it pictures. Thus, for Hinduism****** the Absolute has no relation to particulars, and religious observance consists in trying to reproduce the blankness of the Absolute in the blankness of one's consciousness. (Chinese Religion[******] and Buddhism[******] are treated as other moments of the religion of substance.)

This is followed by a transitional triad of religions which forms the transition between Religions of Substance and Religions of Spiritual Individuality, of which the moments are Zoroastrianism, Syrian religion, and Egyptian religion. These are half-way between conceiving the Absolute as Substance and conceiving it as Spirit. This triad is followed by the Religions of Spiritual Individuality[****], in which the Absolute is grasped as Spirit, though not quite adequately. These are Jewish religion, Greek religion, and Roman religion. (However, in the 1827 lectures, Jewish religion comes after Greek religion.)

But what is the difference between conceiving the Absolute as Substance and conceiving it as Spirit? This is an important question, since Hegel regards the replacement of the conception of the Absolute as Substance by the conception of it as Spirit or Subject as a chief triumph of his philosophy.

To conceive the Absolute as substance is to conceive it as an essentially sterile lump of being, or mere abstract universal, from which all the rich differentiation of the world has been creamed off, leaving it as that low level of Being which is scarcely distinguishable from Nothing. This is much what Hegel very unfairly thought of Spinoza's substance as being.

In contrast, Hegel's Absolute 'is the universal, which preserves itself in its particularizations, dominates alike itself and its "other", and so becomes the power and activity that consists in undoing its [self-imposed] alienation [from itself]' (INTRODUCTORY AESTHETICS, XXI). For it had lost sight of its own true character when it alienated itself from itself in Nature, and for this to be recovered, Nature had to produce human beings as the medium through which it could grasp this again in a fuller form. For it is through human beings (exceptional ones, I should imagine) that it grasps itself self-consciously as the real source of everything that is.

I express this in quasi-temporal language, as seems so natural to us heirs of Darwin. But Hegel did not think, so I have suggested, that Nature existed before human beings did; nor perhaps that the Logical Idea did before Nature existed (though in the latter case he himself uses rather temporal language). Rather, it is an account somewhat like the traditional concept of the great chain of being, in which each thing plays its own particular role in the system of reality as an abiding whole.

The religions of Spiritual Individuality[****] came near to representing, in the pictorial manner of religion, the spirituality and personality of the Absolute or God. But each did so to some degree defectively. Judaism conceived God and Man as too remote from each other; Greek religion joyously celebrated all aspects of life through its multiplicity of gods, but lost anything but a dim sight of the unity of God; while Roman religion divided the divine into two ill-unified parts, that of private family life (the Lares and Penates) and trade (e.g. Jupiter Pistor, the baker) and that of the state, for which the aim was universal dominion as symbolized by Jupiter Capitolinus (LECTURES 1827, 318–88).

C3.2c   The Absolute (or Consummate) Religion (= Christianity)*** It is only with Christianity that a religion arose which expressed the real truth about the world in the imaginative mode peculiar to religion. Each of the main doctrines of Christianity in fact provides an image of the literal truth about the world (as finally discovered by Hegel).

For the difference between the final and absolute religion and the final and absolute philosophy—that is, between Christianity and Hegelianism—consists not in the truths about the world which each grasps, but in the manner of this grasp. Christianity understands the truth about reality in a quasi-pictorial or mythical manner, while speculative philosophy grasps it in a purely conceptual manner.

Thus each of the main doctrines of Christianity provides an image, or *Vorstellung*, of the literal truth about the world. The Christian doctrine of the Trinity is particularly significant from this point of view. And the literal truth behind this, which is grasped conceptually and adequately by philosophy, is that what is symbolized by God the Father, God the Son, and God the Holy Spirit are the three moments of the great triad of the dialectic: namely, the LOGICAL IDEA, the IDEA OUTSIDE ITSELF, or NATURE, and SPIRIT.

(1) The Absolute Idea necessarily actualizes itself in a concrete world. Thus God's creation of the world is not really a temporal event; rather, the concrete world eternally proceeds from him. However, the *Vorstellung* of a temporal event of creation is an appropriate expression of it. (2) This world which issues from the Absolute Idea (a.k.a. God the Father) is the kingdom of the Son, consisting in the natural world together with the world of human institutions and interacting persons.[20] (These are at an apparent distance from the LOGICAL IDEA, and their apparent otherness from it is what is signified by the doctrine of the Fall of man.) (3) Finally, the human mind becomes the home of Absolute Spirit (a.k.a. the Holy Spirit) and grasps in increasingly adequate ways (i.e. the various phases of Art, Religion, and Philosophy) its identity with the Absolute Idea of which it and the world are the necessary actualizations.[21]

Hegel is able to associate this interpretation with the fact that the first moment of a dialectical triad is universal, the second particular, and the third the individual. Thus:

The Logical Idea as the first, THE UNIVERSAL, moment of the triad necessarily differentiates itself into a world of particulars, and this is the creation of the world by GOD THE FATHER.

These PARTICULARS constitute the natural world, or THE IDEA OUTSIDE ITSELF. This is the habitation of humankind, and may be called THE KINGDOM OF THE SON in so far as it is here that the IDEA takes on the form of a man who through his sufferings allows humanity to move on to a higher plane.

On this higher plane, the true INDIVIDUAL emerges as SPIRIT coming to recognize, through the medium of the human mind, that through all the PARTICULAR vicissitudes, defeats, and triumphs of humanity, it is the one UNIVERSAL REALITY coming to fruition and to knowledge of itself as, in all its many manifestations, the one ultimate reality.[22]

How exactly does Jesus fit in here? The answer is that his life is the point at which the alienation from itself, which occurred when the Idea let itself go freely into Nature, is overcome. It has been very gradually escaping from this through the sequence of stages through which it has passed since it emerged, as Spirit, in Nature. And the crucifixion represents (or is?) the point at which Spirit is finally freed from its merely natural character, while the resurrection represents (or is?) the point at which it unites itself consciously with God the Father—that is to say, with the Absolute Idea. Henceforth men may soak themselves in spirituality and let their merely natural being fall away or (more realistically) become the mere background of their life. All this is well expressed by Peter C. Hodgson.

The association of resurrection and faith suggests that the resurrection-event constitutes a transition from the sensible presence of God in the community of faith. It can be treated under the figures of both 'Son' and 'Spirit,' and thus considerable overlap in content occurs... It is not possible to pinpoint a precise historical moment of transition from sensible to spiritual presence, since the resurrection is not a past spatio-temporal datum... but rather is an ongoing historic process. Hegel uses a revealing expression when he says that the 'sensible history' of Christ has been 'sublated to the right hand of God'... The *Auferstehung* (resurrection) of Jesus entails an *Aufhebung*—annulling of his sensible presence, yet a preservation of his real presence and its transfiguration into the modality of Spirit. The resurrection *means* the spiritual presence of Christ in the community, Christ's presence *as* Spirit, the universal actualization of the redemption accomplished definitively in him. (THE CHRISTIAN RELIGION, appendix, p. 339)

But perhaps this account centring on Jesus is still too much at the level of mere *Vorstellung* for philosophy, and the more fundamental metaphysical truth pictured in the life, death, passion, and resurrection of Jesus is a general truth about humanity, rather than about the significance of any historical event. In that case, the crucifixion represents the fact that in becoming the particular the Absolute has to reach for the extreme of finite particularity symbolized by violent death. Similarly, the resurrection represents the fact that in the end Spirit as alienated in particulated Nature is united with the Absolute Idea to constitute the 'saved' individual. Jesus, on this account, exemplifies a general truth rather than constituting a unique one.

Are we, then, to suppose that for Hegel everyone who rises to the spiritual heights is equally an incarnation of the Divinity? The answer would seem to be that we must not press this question in a manner which confuses religion and philosophy. For religion, the Incarnation in the person of Jesus was a fact, unlike any fact about other persons.[23] However, the metaphysical truth which it conveys is the fact that Spirit comes to consciousness of itself only in enlightened human minds.[24]

And this leaves us with the greatest problem of all in Hegel's philosophy of religion: namely, whether the Absolute Idea, which Hegel equates with God, has any consciousness of its own, besides the consciousness which it has through the multiple media of human minds. I shall touch on this matter shortly.

Digression: Some Problems of Interpretation I have taken Hegel's thought in a strong metaphysical sense. Thus I have taken his basic conception of the (Absolute) Idea as being that which is the source of everything, but which could only adequately grasp that it is so, and its own true character, by producing nature and life and finally human beings, so that it could know all this through, or with the help of, the human mind.

Now, as I remarked above, there are commentators on Hegel today for whom none of what Hegel says has any such metaphysical or ontological meaning, and who understand whatever looks like this in the text as simply Hegel's rather high-flown way of referring to, and evaluating, certain features of human life which we need no metaphysics to recognize as real.

If this interpretation is sustained then my exploration of Hegel's thought has set out on the wrong foot. But I cannot believe that these reductive interpretations are right. If they are, it was very wrong of Hegel to use such strange language to say something so un-strange. And it seems

unlikely that so many people have misunderstood him in such a fundamental way (for surely those who take him in a strong metaphysical way
have been in the majority). Moreover, the philosophical ambience in
which he wrote was one in which forms of idealism, shocking to many
less adventurous philosophers today, were the norm rather than some
personal extravagance.

Of course, anyone has the right to find Hegel inspiring as a commentator on human life, while rejecting the metaphysics. It may even be true
that Hegel was more interested in the problems and achievements of
humankind than in the usual philosophical questions to which idealists
have in general been addressing themselves. But this does not mean that
his viewpoint on these matters was not of the very strong absolute idealist
character which I have been sketching.

Terry Pinkard's is the most reductive account of Hegel's idea of the
Absolute Idea or God which I have come across. Thus, as he sees it,
Absolute Spirit consists simply in 'the practices in which humanity col-
lectively reflects on its "highest interests"'. In short, God becomes little
more than the human mind at its best, where this is essentially a matter of
abiding by norms in force in the most developed type of community. If
Hegel was really simply describing the climb of humanity upwards to an
increasing degree of rationality in its thought and social organization, he
certainly deceived many of his most careful readers to an extent which
I find too astonishing to credit. Consider, for example, T. H. Green, who,
while rejecting much of the detail of Hegel's thought, still saw him as the
exponent of the central message of absolute idealism.

That there is one spiritual self-conscious being, of which all that is real is the
activity or expression... and that this participation is the source of morality and
religion; this we take to be vital truth which Hegel had to teach. (Green, *Collected
Works*, iii. 146)[25]

And it seems to me that it is for the reductionists to justify themselves to
those who interpret Hegel in a strongly idealist fashion, since the substance of the texts is so evidently nearer to the latter's interpretation.

Can the writer of such a passage as the following really not have meant
anything more than the anti-metaphysician regards as intelligible?

If we ask our ordinary consciousness only, the idea of spirit that presses on us is
certainly that it stands over against nature, to which in that case we ascribe a like
dignity. But in thus putting nature and spirit alongside one another and relating
them to one another as equally essential realms, spirit is being considered only in
its finitude and restriction, not in its infinity and truth. That is to say, nature does

not stand over against spirit, either as possessing the same value or as spirit's limitation; on the contrary, it acquires the standing of having been posited by spirit, and this makes it a product, deprived of the power of limiting and restricting. At the same time, absolute spirit is to be understood only as absolute activity and therefore as absolutely self-differentiating within. Now this other, as spirit's self-differentiation, is precisely nature, and spirit is the bounty which gives to this opposite of itself the whole fullness of its own being. Nature, therefore, we have to conceive as itself carrying the Absolute Idea implicitly, but nature is the Idea in the form of having been posited by absolute spirit as the opposite of spirit. In this sense, we call nature a creation. But its truth is therefore the creator itself, spirit as ideality and negativity; as such spirit particularizes itself within and negates itself, yet this particularization and negation of itself, as having been brought about by itself, it nevertheless cancels, and instead of having a limitation and restriction therein it binds itself together with its opposite in free universality. This ideality and infinite negativity constitutes the profound concept of the subjectivity of spirit. (FINE ART, 92–3)

Someone convinced of the meaninglessness of speculative metaphysics might (from his own point of view, reasonably) suggest that, although Hegel thought that he was meaning more than anything merely naturalistic, *that more* is in truth meaningless, and that when it is removed, a kernel of important empirical ideas is left. But I would rather look for what Hegel took himself to be saying, especially as I am not a sceptic about metaphysics.

The most basic question about what Hegel really meant concerns whether Spirit, as it acts out its salvation through us, has any sort of more totalized consciousness of its own. Is Spirit, in short, basically a common essence present in us all, so that we are the only concrete actualizations of the Absolute Idea as Spirit, or is there a divine mind, with its own consciousness, in which we somehow participate?

It is worth hearing Josiah Royce (from lectures delivered in 1906) on this question:

With respect to the question as to whether the Absolute in its wholeness is a conscious being, the *Phaenomenologie* is distinctly ambiguous in its result. In the closing chapter of the book, where the results are outlined, it at once appears that the Absolute is a consciousness of the meaning of the entire human process, and that for the absolute consciousness, the various *Gestalten*, the various phases of life, are in a genuine meaning present, and present at once. But since in this closing chapter Hegel is especially describing the philosophical type of consciousness itself, there is at least a strong indication that the consciousness which he here attributes to the Absolute is identical merely with the consciousness expressed in philosophy. The prevailing indication of the text would be that the Absolute comes to its completest form of consciousness in rational individuals who, as seers or thinkers, become aware of the rational nature of the entire process of rational life. I do not myself believe that this view of the matter remained for Hegel finally. I believe that the sense of his later religious philosophy, as stated in his mature system, especially, one might add, in *The Lectures on Religion* demand the reality of a conscious Absolute, whose consciousness while inclusive of that of the rational human individuals, and in fact of all finite beings, is not identical with the mere sum-total of these individual consciousnesses. But it is true that this result is not made manifest in the *Phaenomenologie*. It is also true that Hegel always expressed himself so ambiguously upon the subject that a well-known difference of opinion as to his true meaning appeared among his followers. This difference led to the division and ultimately to the dissolution of the Hegelian school. (MODERN IDEALISM, 167–8)

One must grant at the least that Hegel thought that there was something one and the same thinking through all of us, and that this something is a more fundamental reality than is any of us personally. And that this is something which is the fundamental source of all reality (under the name of the Idea (Idee)) either enlarges its sense of what it is or first acquires its sense of what it is (under the name of Spirit, or *Geist*) through the medium of human minds as they grope for an adequate religion and philosophy.

A good expression for what I take to be the meaning of *Geist* in Hegel is 'collective human soul'. (I take this expression from R. B. Pippin; see HEGEL COMPANION, 60.) Then we may say that Hegel's philosophy is primarily an account of how the collective human soul, apparently existing in diverse persons, through the consciousness of the most developed of them, becomes aware of itself by the mutual recognition of itself as present both in itself (whoever is carrying the relevant thoughts) and in each of his fellow human beings.

However, that still leaves it open whether for Hegel there was also a totalized consciousness, or *Geist* as a whole, including all finite consciousnesses. But I can do no more than leave it open myself.

C3.3 Absolute Spirit Revealing itself in Philosophy

Be all that as it may, Christianity, for Hegel, has grasped the truth about reality more fully, in the quasi-pictorial manner of religion, than has any other religion, while Philosophy** (i.e. the dialectical philosophy of which he is the chief author and champion) has grasped it, in the more literal and conceptual manner of philosophy, more fully than has any other philosophy. And Hegel would seem to think that it is in the latter, self-understanding of itself through philosophy that the Absolute Idea reaches its peak embodiment or expression.

155

PART FIVE: CONCLUSION

The Anti-climactic Feature of Hegelianism

It is hard not to be disturbed by this account of philosophy as that to which religion at its highest still aspires. As a defence of Christianity, in a philosophical manner, it is certainly somewhat bizarre.

For it implies that the crucifixion and resurrection of Jesus occurred to symbolize the fact that after a good deal of intellectual toil, a philosophy would arrive which explicated the whole world system. If this is an exaggeration, since Hegel surely does recognize that other things are valuable too, it is still, above all, philosophical thinking—that is to say, Hegelian thinking—that constitutes the supreme value. All the blood and toil of history, all the religious wars, all physical suffering, seem to be there just so that Hegel, or to put it more charitably, men like Hegel, shall grasp the subtleties of the dialectic.

Hegel would retort that the philosopher goes through his own form of suffering in order to reach truth. For he can reach truth only by travelling through the valley of death of agonizing logical contradictions which he must overcome by a painful process of dialectical thinking. Without wishing to dismiss this answer as entirely absurd, I still think that the suffering of the dialectical philosopher is pretty small beer besides the suffering of all those non-philosophers who have been crucified or otherwise tortured whether by their fellow men or by natural causes.

In any case, even if Hegel's philosophy were as near to truth as humans will ever come, I would not want to put its value above that of great music, art, and poetry. Hegel thought that the time for expressing the Absolute through *Art* was over, but not, I think, very convincingly.

He did not, however, mean to deny the importance of *religion* for the modern world. For religion, and more specifically Christianity, is the only way in which the mass of human beings can grasp the truth of things. For what Christianity expresses through the medium of *Vorstellungen* is the very same truth as philosophy (the Hegelian system) expresses more literally through the concepts of *Vernunft*. It may even be that the philosopher needs the existence of religion as his initial guide over the common ground of both types of knowledge.

Moreover, Absolute Spirit (that is to say, philosophy, religion, and art) is not the only way in which *Geist* comes to itself in human life. For

Objective Spirit has its own importance too, especially as it develops dialectically in human history. Indeed, for Hegel, everything in history, and indeed in nature, is a partial and necessary feature of the Absolute, is, in fact, the Absolute doing or thinking something or other. Thus great men like Napoleon are, for Hegel, I suppose, almost as much the point of the universe as Hegel himself. Moreover, great human institutions, like the state, have their own value as embodiments of the IDEA. So we must not exaggerate the extent to which Hegel thinks that philosophy alone is the point of it all.

It remains true, I think, that philosophy is for Hegel the supreme achievement of *Geist* in human history. And religion, more specifically Christianity, for philosophically educated people, should be understood in terms of Hegelian philosophy. But personally, I doubt whether any religion thus interpreted could really satisfy. Napoleon, if he thought along these lines, could indeed regard himself as the World Spirit in one of its most significant phases. (Could Hitler, or Genghis Khan, do this likewise, and be right?) But can more ordinary and average mortals do likewise? At best, it might seem that they can enjoy playing their role in the state, which, a few accidents apart, is something essentially glorious.

Well, perhaps we can (if Hegel is right). Perhaps we should each of us see himself or herself as one essential moment in the actualization of the IDEA, at one level in NATURE, and on another level, as a component of OBJECTIVE SPIRIT, and at another level again, if we are artists or thinkers or worshippers, however good or poor, as an actualization of some aspect of ABSOLUTE SPIRIT. Each of us, in fact, in Spinoza's words, may, so far as we possess the 'intellectual love of God', understood as the appreciation of any aspect of the ultimate perfection of the world, be 'part of the infinite love with which God loves himself' (E5p36).

Still, whatever else he may have thought valuable, it remains true that for Hegel it is philosophical thought which is the coping stone of everything. Indeed, he even describes philosophy as itself a form (the highest form?) of worship. (See REARDON, 108.) It is far from me to regard philosophy as unimportant, but philosophical achievement is not, surely, that for the sake of which, more than for the sake of much else, humanity has toiled and suffered throughout the ages.

The dialectic takes us through the great comprehensive categories of the *Logic*, the ascending levels of physical phenomena in Nature, and finally the stages of Spirit, with all their turmoil and suffering, only to present its highest achievement as the thoughts of great philosophers. If the finale is something grander than this, it is not at all clear what it is. Even if the universe is to some large extent as Hegel thought it, I cannot think that his philosophical achievement is more what the point of the world is than the music of Beethoven or the art of Michelangelo, to whatever extent anything human is the world's main purpose. And it seems more likely that the vast physical universe has purposes other than human achievement, granted that it has purposes at all. The same is true, indeed, of Hegelian ethics, which tends to boil down to the life of civil servants in a well-organized state.

One just cannot find a satisfactory religion along these lines. If the history of humanity is a struggle to 'some far-off divine event to which the whole creation moves', it must surely be something fuller and better.

But even if we allow that other human achievements and satisfactions are as important as philosophy, there is something unsatisfactory about Hegel's vision of how the world is justified as leading to them.

For Hegelianism, thus qualified, would still find the justification of the world in the gradual triumph of *Geist*, conceived as the human Spirit. But the fact that *Geist* is on the way to triumph, and that all that it suffered on the way to this is justified as the necessary means to this triumph, offers small comfort to those finite individuals who are unhappy with their own personal lot, and unhappy very often in a manner in no way due to their own fault. Traditional religions, and in particular Christianity, have usually held out some personal comfort to such people, at least if they live good lives. But Hegelianism offers no such comfort, and probably does not include belief in personal immortality. (This was a feature of Hegel's thought which especially troubled J. M. E. McTaggart, who tended to think, at least till his own philosophy was fully developed, that Hegel had upon the whole been the discoverer of the truth of things.)

This trouble was well expressed by Andrew Seth:

The achievements of the world-Spirit do not move me to unqualified admiration, and I cannot accept the abstraction of the race in place of the living children of men. Even if the enormous spiral of human history is destined to wind itself at least to a point which may be called achievement, what, I ask, of the multitudes that perished by the way? 'These all die, not having received the promises.' What if there *are* no promises *to them*? To me the old idea of the world as the training-ground of individual characters seems to offer a much more human, and, I will add, a much more divine, solution than this pitiless procession of the car of progress. Happily, however, the one view does not necessarily exclude the other; we may rejoice in the progress of the race, and also believe in the future of the individual. (SETH, 61–2)

On the face of it, the only thing which could reconcile the advance of humanity and the salvation of individuals, as both features of the divine purpose, is reincarnation, for then we could all share in this triumph, marching towards it together through a succession of lives.

For without any hope that our troubles will ultimately serve a purpose for us personally, what is the use of being told that we are the Lord of All, when painful disease may cut us down at any moment or an earthquake shatter all the conveniences of our life?[26] What is the use of being Lord of All, for those who are starving? What is the use of being Lord of All for those who suffer from the wickedness of others? The idea that somehow the world is my creation, because I am somehow identical with the World Thought which made it, seems absurd. (It is very different to say that it is the creation of a Cosmic Thought of which I am just one little phase who must bear with the necessity of things, for this requires no glossing over the tragedy of many individual lives.)

At any rate, I agree with Andrew Seth that some eventual triumph of the World Spirit can hardly justify things to those who will not participate in it. Moreover, I cannot accept Hegel's conception of what that triumph is: namely, Spirit learning through philosophy what it essentially is.

Admittedly, Hegel says that the point of the world does not lie in the future but in what is eternally actualized at all times. So it may seem wrong to criticize him along these lines.

The consummation of the infinite End, therefore, consists merely in removing the illusion which makes it seem yet unaccomplished. The Good, the absolutely Good, is eternally accomplishing itself in the world: and the result is that it needs not wait upon us, but is already by implication, as well as in full actuality, accomplished. This is the illusion under which we live. (ENCYCLOPAEDIA I §212)

Kant said that the three great questions were:

What can I know?
What ought I to do?
What may I hope?

Hegel's answer to these questions seems to me rather empty. The answer to the first question is that I may know the truth of the Hegelian philosophy.

His answer to the second question is, at least if I am a top person, that I may enjoy the fact that I am identical with the source of the world and of humanity, while if my role in life is more humble, I can at least appreciate the glory of the state to which my best efforts contribute their mite.

His answer to the third question, as it seems to me, is, put in ordinary terms, that there is nothing especial to hope for, or for that matter to fear, which I learn from the Hegelian philosophy.

And to return to the second question, which is the most important, there seems to be little by way of philosophy of life at all offered by Hegel. The sole message for the ordinary person seems to be that one should be content with whatever place has been allotted to one by the Absolute Idea, and do one's best to fill it satisfactorily. Perhaps that is all that anyone can offer. But it is not really much of an advance on Voltaire's advice that one should 'cultivate one's garden'. At any rate, what troubles me is that, in spite of all its vast claims, Hegelianism seems to have little implication outside the study.

But am I not forgetting that Hegel led to Marx? Well, that is indeed one thing which his strange thought did lead to, and clearly that had an immense impact upon the world (though not entirely a good one). But if one is not to be a Hegelian Marxist, I think my point stands. I qualify it, however, by allowing that it did inspire other philosophers with a clearer and more practical message for what ordinary persons should actually do with their lives (T. H. Green, for example). I infer from this that something went wrong as Hegel moved towards his philosophical climax, and that his earlier thought (in ETW) pointed towards something more attractive.

Another matter on which Hegel's conclusions may seem rather inadequate to some of us is his attitude to evil.

Our mode of treating the subject is, in this aspect, a Theodicæ—a justification of the ways of God—which Leibnitz attempted metaphysically in his method, i.e. in indefinite abstract categories—so that the ill which is found in the World may be comprehended, and the thinking Spirit reconciled with the fact of the existence of evil. Indeed, nowhere, is such a harmonizing view more pressingly demanded than in Universal History; and it can be attained only by recognizing the *positive* existence, in which that negative element is a subordinate and vanquished nullity. On the one hand, the ultimate design of the World must be perceived; and, on the other hand, the fact that this design has been actually realized in it, and that evil has not been able permanently to assert a competing position. (HEGEL HISTORY, 15–16)

Such is my own rather negative response to Hegel as a religious thinker. So although I am myself perhaps even further from being a Kierkegaardian than from being a Hegelian, I sympathize a good deal with Kierkegaard's critique of Hegelian Christianity, which we will be examining in the next chapter.

James Yerkes on Hegel's Christianity

It may be said that my objection rests on too dry a concept of what philosophical thinking on religious matters can achieve. Perhaps it can lift our spirits to a more mystical intuition of the nature of the universe as essentially divine. But it is by no means as a general fact superior to other ways of approaching deity. As Bradley puts it:

All of us, I presume, more or less, are led beyond the region of ordinary facts. Some in one way and some in others, we seem to touch and have communion with what is beyond the visible world. In various manners we find something higher, which both supports and humbles, both chastens and transports us. And, with certain persons, the intellectual effort to understand the universe is a principal way of thus experiencing the Deity. (APPEARANCE AND REALITY, 5)

That there is an element of mystical feeling, rather than mere cognitive enquiry, in Hegel's philosophizing is emphasized by James Yerkes in his brilliant book *The Christology of Hegel*. For, according to Yerkes, something remains in Hegel's final philosophy of the almost mystical pantheistic enthusiasm sometimes expressed in his earlier unpublished papers, as in the passage from 'The Spirit of Christianity' which I quoted from above. 'To love God is to feel one's self in the "all" of life with no restriction, in the infinite' (ETW, 247; quoted in YERKES, 51; see also 116). Thus Yerkes conceives of Hegel as much more deeply religious than he is sometimes depicted as being. He participated, it is said, in the ordinary Christian believer's imaginative ideas of the Holy Trinity and the Incarnation. But he also gave himself the more austere task of grasping the same truth conceptually, as the fact that the whole world is the actualization and bringing to self-consciousness of the Absolute Idea.

If there is, indeed, an element of mysticism in Hegel's thought, it is mysticism of a highly intellectualist kind.[27] More so, I think, than Spinoza's philosophy, and less able to support true religious feeling. Or so I personally find it.[28]

It is not that Hegel's vision of the universe is without nobility. His view of the empirical world as the actualization of the logical idea which comes to know itself for what it is through *Geist* is a form of pantheism with much appeal. Were it a little less anthropocentric and more celebratory of the natural world, I could almost accept it myself. No, what jars is the idea that philosophical thinking is the finest way of participating in this great unity, and is even what makes the universe worthwhile. For surely the experience which reveals and justifies the world is much more the experience of love and beauty.

In fact, I might quote Hegel himself here:

[A]rt is what cheers and animates the dull and withered dryness of the idea, reconciles with reality its abstraction and its dissociation therefrom, and supplies out of the real world what is lacking to the notion. (INTRODUCTORY AESTHETICS, VIII)

Unfortunately Hegel is arguing against this opinion. If Hegel did, in fact, believe that *Geist* had its own unitary consciousness, of which our mental processes are fragments, as he has been understood more tradition- ally, he would be close to Spinoza, not so much as Hegel interpreted him, but as I suggest he should be understood. But if, as Hegel is most often interpreted nowadays, *Geist*'s only consciousness is through our mental processes, that effectively implies that it is the philosophical thoughts of humans which are what justifies the existence of everything else, and however excellent fellows we philosophers may be, I can hardly stomach that.

But my objection to the Hegelian view of things rests above all on his opinion that conceptual thought, purged of all imagery and sensory con- tent, is both the highest form of Spirit or Mind and that most revelatory of how things really are. I am at one with Bradley on this.

When in the reason's philosophy the rational appears dominant and sole possessor of the world, we can only wonder what place would be left to it, if the element excluded might break through the charm of the magic circle, and, without growing rational, could find expression. Such an idea may be senseless, and such a thought may contradict itself, but it serves to give voice to an obstinate instinct. Unless thought stands for something that falls beyond mere intelligence, if 'thinking' is not used with some strange implication that never was part of the meaning of the word, a lingering scruple still forbids us to believe that reality can never be purely rational. It may come from a failure in my metaphysics, or from a weakness of the flesh which continues to blind me, but the notion that existence could be the same as understanding strikes me as cold and ghost-like as the dreariest materialism. That the glory of this world in the end is appearance leaves the world more glorious if we feel it is a show of some fuller splendour; but the sensuous curtain is a deception and a cheat, if it hides some colourless movement of atoms, some spectral woof of impalpable abstractions, or unearthly ballet of bloodless categories. Though dragged to such conclusions, we cannot embrace them. Our principles may be true, but they are not reality. They no more make that Whole which commands our devotion, than some shredded dissection of human tatters is that warm and breathing beauty which our hearts found delightful. (BRADLEY LOGIC, 590–1)

Notes

1. F. H. Bradley said that this created a contradiction for morality, since if everyone lived by certain important moral principles, there would be no opportunity to apply them (ETHICAL STUDIES, 155).
2. Most of what I know of Hegel's life is from Terry Pinkard's invaluable biography of him (PINKARD) or from HARRIS.
3. NOHL, 1–29, trans. HARRIS, 481–507.
4. Among other things, this little work includes an extraordinarily wise discussion of the psychology of religious tolerance and intolerance.
5. For Hegel Judaism was a dismal religion of total subjection to an unappealing God, and hostility to the rest of humankind. In fact, the Jews lived a kindly life of feeling only when they temporarily abandoned Jehovah. See ETW, 195–6 and *passim*.
6. Hegel's use of the expression 'absolute' is, so far as I know, derived from Kant's use of it to refer to the ideal unity of all true thought, to which all thinking aspires but never reaches. See *The Critique of Pure Reason*, A323–7, B380–4.
7. I note here that 'concept' and 'notion' both translate the same German word '*Begriff*', but I shall oscillate between them, mostly using 'notion' in the names of moments of the dialectic and 'concept' in my own exposition. Incidentally, '*Begriff*' is used by Hegel in two distinct senses: first, simply to refer to any kind of concept, and secondly, to denote the third triad of the *Logical Idea*, in which case it will take a single asterisk.

   We must also grasp the contrast between '*Begriff*' and '*Idee*' (translated here as 'Idea'). The Idea is the concept taken together with its realization in the concrete. Michael Inwood explains it thus in introduction to INTRODUCTORY AESTHETICS, pp. xix–xx: 'He often illustrates this with the case of a man: his soul is the concept, his body is the reality, and the whole man is the Idea. Only certain types of entity are seen in this way. A man, unlike a stone, is first, an intimately unified, yet differentiated whole, and, secondly, has an inner and an outer aspect between which there is nevertheless a close correspondence, so that (ideally at least) every feature of his soul is expressed in the structure and attitudes of his body, and, conversely, every feature of his body expresses some feature of his soul.'
8. I have found Stace's *The Philosophy of Hegel* and his chart particularly helpful on the details of the dialectical transitions. His book, such is my impression, is not much respected by Hegelian scholars and commentators of the present day. But if it seems rather naïve, that is, I suspect because it often gives, in clearer words than Hegel's, just about precisely what he was saying, and what his arguments were. And Hegel's arguments, are often not so much naïve, as specious in the extreme. There is considerable wisdom, indeed outstanding genius, in Hegel, but it is wisdom which is somehow conveyed by way of all manner of logically hopeless arguments. Stace by and large accepts the arguments, and just because of that, does not turn them into something else deemed more respectable by modern commentators.

9. Hegel's discussion of the relation between quality and quantity is of great interest, but is so complicated that I shall deal with it only very lightly. It includes a discussion of the sense in which God is the measure of all things, and of the relation between science and ordinary experience.

10. The contrast is somewhat akin to C. S. Peirce's distinction between *firstness* and *secondness*, though Hegel does not specify anything quite corresponding to Peirce's *Thirdness*.

11. See my article 'Personal and Impersonal Identity', *Mind*, 97/385 (Jan., 1988), 29–49.

12. It should be borne in mind that these categories are meant to provide a characterization of reality as a whole. And Hegel is claiming that to see it under the category of the thought or the willed are both inadequate. McTaggart suggests that it is really the contrast between the good and the true which are integrated in this final stage of the dialectic. Still, this transition seems to have troubled many commentators (see McTaggart, §§ 284–9). It relates to Fichte's contrast between idealism and materialism.

13. In his exposition of the *Phenomenology*, J. N. Findlay very helpfully puts the matter thus: 'The eternal abstract Spirit must therefore create a World, the word "creation" being merely an imaginative symbol for the entailment holding between the being of an abstract notion and the being of cases in which it may be instantiated' (FINDLAY, 141).

14. Unfortunately I copied this out without recording its source.

15. Findlay says: 'The complete misunderstanding of Hegel's idealism by British philosophers, and its reduction to a refined form of subjectivism, are probably due to their ignoring of the *Naturphilosophie*' (FINDLAY, 267).

16. Sometimes in this section it seems more appropriate to translate *Geist* by 'mind' rather than 'spirit'. I follow Stace in this.

17. Had Hegel been a vegetarian, he might have deduced vegetarianism as a moment in the dialectic. The lion does not see itself in the antelope which it eats, nor does the thoughtless man do so when he eats a rabbit. But let him look deeper at the situation, and he will realize that the rabbit is really another consciousness, whose reality as such he has been denying in skinning it for the pot.

18. As Charles Taylor puts it: '[T]he work of art is incomparably higher than the works of mere nature however much we may have been misled by the theory of art as imitation to praise the works of nature as higher than those of man. It is true of course that nature is an embodiment of spirit in sensuous form. In particular a living being is such an embodiment, and at the summit, man is the highest. But this is still not the same as art. Even the most perfect human form still has much in it which is purely contingent, that is, not rigorously necessary to its vocation of embodying *Geist*. And even in regard to what is necessary, the necessity is not manifest, it is inner; that is, it is discovered by thought, but is not there on the surface of things. Before natural living beings, we come to a

"presentiment" (Ahnung) of the concept, but we have no clear manifestation of it' (TAYLOR, 472).

19. There is an interesting passage on beauty as a concrete universal at INTRODUC-TORY AESTHETICS, XXXVII. The true universal of beauty, like every other genuine concrete universal, is 'fertile out of its own resources, in contrast to the barrenness of one-sided reflection. For it has in accordance with its own conception to develop into a totality of attributes, while the conception itself as well as its detailed exposition contains the necessity of its particulars, as also of their progress and transition one into another. On the other hand, again, these particulars, to which the transition is made, carry in themselves the universality and essentiality of the conception as the particulars of which they appear' (ibid.).

20. Thus the kingdom of the Son actually includes the earlier stages of the realm of Spirit.

21. Consider the following: 'The concept that has determined itself, that has made itself into its own object, has thereby posited finitude in itself, but posited *itself* as the content of this finitude and in so doing sublated it—that is spirit.' I copied this quotation down, but have unfortunately lost the source.

22. On the Trinity, see ENCYCLOPAEDIA III, §§566–71. It is set out more elaborately in LECTURES 1827, *PASSIM* (see volume's index).

23. Incidentally, we are told by some informed commentators that Hegel did not deny—he may even have meant to affirm—the life, passion, and death of Jesus as a historical fact. Likewise, even the resurrection. But if it was a fact, it issued from the Absolute Idea as a pictorial representation of the more ultimate metaphysical truth.

24. For further useful commentary see Peter C. Hodgson in his appendix to *The Christian Religion*, 335.

25. The passage occurs in a review of John Caird's *Introduction to the Philosophy of Religion*.

26. 'Self-fulfillment is the attainment of that stage in which the self no longer regards the surrounding universe as something other, as a limitation; the human longing for integrity can only be frustrated so long as man sees himself as a finite being depending on other things in the surrounding world, but that longing finds fulfillment as man comes to recognize himself as the "other", as man undergoes "transformations which will raise him to a grasp of the universal"' (WILLIAMSON, 104–5). Unfortunately, the surrounding world puts us in all sorts of situations which we would rather not have been in, and would not have been in if the world had been our own creation.

27. On Yerkes's side it should be noted, however, that Hegel believed that the mystics Meister Eckhart and Jacob Boehme had possessed a special awareness of the true nature of God. See WILLIAMSON, 228 and 260.

28. In the next chapter I discuss what is perhaps the most interesting critique of Hegelian Christianity, that of Søren Kierkegaard. I might note here that since

this book went into production with the publishers, I have read *Kierkegaard's Relations to Hegel Reconsidered* by Jon Stewart, Cambridge University Press, 2003. In this book Stewart argues that Hegel was never much in the sight of Kierkegaard when he published his *Concluding Unscientific Postscript*, (which will be the main focus of my discussion) only Danish Hegelians, especially J. L. Heiberg and H. L. Martensen. This is a fascinating and very scholarly book. However, I think that he overstates his case. For a quite thorough discussion of his claims see my Review discussion of it in the *British Journal of Philosophy* 12(4) 771–778. Personally, as will be seen, however, I find Kierkegaard's own form of Christianity rather unattractive; though there is no doubt of his great importance in pointing the way to a more existentially involved Christianity than that of Hegel and Hegelians, I prefer Hegel's attempt to be rational to Kierkegaard's determination not to be.

Chapter 4
Kierkegaard and Hegelian Christianity

Can a historical point of departure be given for an eternal consciousness; how can such a point of departure be of more than historical
interest; can an eternal happiness be built on historical knowledge?

Lessing, quoted on the frontispiece of Kierkegaard's
Philosophical Fragments[1]

PART ONE: *PHILOSOPHICAL FRAGMENTS*

I On the Provenance and Pseudonymous Authorship of *Philosophical Fragments*

Including a chapter on the great Danish religious thinker Søren Kierkegaard (1813–55) in this book is somewhat rash. For Kierkegaard wrote an
extraordinarily large number of books, and left an enormous amount of
unpublished material, which it requires intense specialism to get on top
of. Even worse is the problem that most of the philosophically more
important works were published under pseudonyms. Not that this itself
is a problem, for a pseudonymous work may be as much an expression of
the true author's own point of view as one published under his own name.
However, Kierkegaard's pseudonyms stand for imaginary persons whose
views are not, or need not be, Kierkegaard's own. For example, Johannes,
imaginary author of 'Diary of the Seducer', which forms Part 3 of the *Either*
part of *Either/Or*, is an immoralist with whose opinions Kierkegaard
certainly did not concur, while Judge Williams, of the *Or* part of *Either/
Or*, though more approved of by Kierkegaard than Johannes the Seducer,
expresses a somewhat limited moralistic point of view which Kierkegaard
thinks in the end an inadequate form of life. As to the relation between the

various imaginary persons named by the pseudonyms and each other, and with Kierkegaard himself, there is an immense amount of scholarly discussion into which I neither can nor wish to enter.[2]

On the other hand, it is essential that I do discuss Kierkegaard, since he is the most important representative of the view that metaphysical conclusions are irrelevant to genuine religion. As a fervent Christian, he is, of course, mainly concerned with the irrelevance of metaphysics to Christianity, but an examination of his thought will have bearings on our larger concern with the relations between metaphysics and genuine religion of any sort.

Faced with this problem, I have decided to discuss the position presented in two related works by Kierkegaard: namely, *Philosophical Fragments* (1844) and the related *Concluding Unscientific Postscript* (1846). These two works were published under the pseudonym 'Johannes Climacus'.[3] If Climacus and Kierkegaard are not exactly the same in outlook, they are certainly closer than Kierkegaard is to many of his other imaginary persons, and, in any case, we can take Climacus on his own terms, however he is related to Kierkegaard. Actually at least one authority says that we can mostly take Climacus as Kierkegaard's own voice, and that the pseudonymity here is not the introduction of an imaginary person in the way that most of the others are.[4] However, since Climacus declares himself not so much a Christian as a sympathetic but neutral observer of Christianity, the identification could not be complete. The truth would seem to be that Climacus examines as a hypothesis or thought experiment what Kierkegaard passionately held for true.

Incidentally, the pseudonym (which means *Johannes the Climber*) is taken from the name of a monk in a Sinai monastery who died around 759, and was thus named on account of his book *The Ladder of Divine Ascent*. Kierkegaard apparently chose it to signify that the author was exhibiting the appropriate way of climbing away from idealist philosophy to Christian truth.

II The Socratic (and Hegelian) Perspective on Religious Knowledge and Experience

Kierkegaard or Climacus opens *Philosophical Fragments* by considering the problem raised by the Platonic Socrates as to how one can seek the truth about anything. Socrates sees this as problematic inasmuch as one must know what one is seeking, to seek it, yet if one knows it already, there is no need to seek it. This being so, there is a problem as to how one can hope to learn anything from a teacher, such as Socrates himself.

Socrates' solution to this problem, Kierkegaard reminds us, turns on his doctrine of recollection, according to which the acquisition of apparently new knowledge of genuine truth is really the recollection of what one knew pre-natally through direct awareness of the (Platonic) Forms, rather than through their inadequate 'copies' in the world of flux.[5]

For Kierkegaard, the essential thing here is not so much the theory of recollection as the theory which, though implied by it, can be held on other grounds, that all truth is really there already within one's own mind, or is at least inferable from what is there, and that what is called *discovering truth* is really simply making explicit what one's mind already contains. It is, in short, the proposition that all genuine knowledge is innate. And Kierkegaard holds that this is the doctrine of Hegel, even if somewhat differently expressed.

My own conventional aside here is that there is some plausibility in this as a theory about the knowledge of necessary truths, but that it is not so plausible as a theory about knowledge in general. Indeed, the Kantian association of the a priori with *the necessary* and the a posteriori with the *contingent* makes this very point. However, Hegel is often understood as regarding what others consider contingent truth as really necessary, and as therefore discoverable by thought left to itself without the aid of empirical experience (this being only a kind of second-best way of discovering such truth). This is perhaps a parody of Hegel. What is probably true, however, is that he thought that all the more basic and pervasive truths about the nature of reality were *necessary*, and discoverable a priori, by the dialectical process. If this is not quite the same as saying that they are innate, it is close enough for our purposes.

Be all that as it may, Kierkegaard's concern is not so much how we can know truths of any sort whatever (e.g. concerning how life was lived in Roman Britain) but how we can know, or be right about, the fundamental truths of religion.

The Socratic view, and perhaps the Hegelian one too, is that knowledge of the divine is really innate (or at least can be reached from each individual's own internal mental resources). Climacus points out various implications of this, implications which are quite explicit in what (the Platonic) Socrates says.[6] The most important implication is that a teacher only provides the occasion for the learner's implicit knowledge of a religious truth to become explicit. Another implication is that the particularity of the teacher as a person, and the particular time at which he 'instructed' the learner, are of no importance for the learner. Just as I may have learnt from some particular teacher at school, and on a particular day, what prime numbers are, and that seven is one of them, there is no need for me to keep the teacher and the time in mind when I reflect on, or make use, of this truth later.

The Socratic view, in short, provides negative answers to the first and third questions in the passage from Lessing which is quoted on the title-page of *Fragments*.

Is an historical point of departure possible for an eternal consciousness; how can such a point of departure have any other than a merely historical interest; is it possible to base an eternal happiness upon historical knowledge?

In short, how far can an adequate spiritual life be lived on the basis of the individual person's own mental resources (resources which another can prompt him to draw on but never actually provide)? And the main question in this connection is how we can know about God.

III Transition to an Alternative (the Christian) Point of View: The Incarnation

Climacus now suggests that we consider another point of view, examining its contrast with the Socratic and Hegelian one, without committing ourselves to either. According to this alternative view, a human person does not have the resources for knowing about God. He can learn about God only if God himself teaches him by somehow exhibiting himself to that person.

However, this requires that the finite individual acquire the resources for coming to know God, resources which, if we are looking for an alternative to the Socratic view, we must take it that he does not of himself possess. Thus God must provide what Climacus calls 'the condition': that is, a capacity to become aware of God. But even when this condition has been bestowed, God must take a positive step to reveal himself to the finite person.

This, however, he cannot, or at least will not, do by somehow appearing to the finite person in his full glorious reality. This is the same idea as lies behind such ancient stories as that of Semele (my example): that this would destroy the individual just as gazing at the sun can destroy sight. But more subtly, God's purposes, in his relations with mankind, do not allow this. For God wants finite persons to return God's love for them, without becoming infinitely depressed about their own unworthiness to be loved by God. Therefore God must appear to man as a very humble human, on an ontological par, so to speak, with a human being.

Kierkegaard illustrates this point by a story about a king who fell in love with a peasant girl and wished to make her his wife. He did not, however, want her to feel humbled and unworthy of him; therefore he courted her dressed as a beggar. There are, however, contrasts between this story and the story of the Incarnation: above all, that the king never really becomes a peasant as God really does become a man.

For it is not enough that God disguises himself as a humble human being; he must really become one. Clearly, however, he cannot become just any sort of human being. He must be an exceptional person, without any of the usual human ambitions for wealth and comfort or even self-preservation. Thus he must have no home, and must wander from place to place, belonging nowhere in particular.

Climacus's description of the form that God must take so that there be mutual love between him and human persons, and a love which does not degrade the latter, is clearly a description of Jesus (though it rather reminds me of Wotan in *The Ring*). However, Climacus is playing with an idea, so he says, and is not at this stage claiming that anything corresponding to it has happened.

In what sense will this God-become-man act as a teacher to those who respond to his love? Not as a Socratic teacher. For Socrates claimed only to draw out from the mind of his interlocutor what the latter implicitly knows already, and it is of no particular importance to the interlocutor that it was Socrates who drew it forth rather than someone else, or at one time rather than another. When the teacher is God-become-man, however, the situation is quite different, for the essential thing is not to learn some abstract proposition, but actually knowingly to encounter God himself. What the learner takes away, then, from an encounter with the God-become-man is awareness that that man is God, so that he has encountered God himself in encountering that man.

IV The Paradox of the Moment

There is, however, a mighty paradox in the whole idea of God becoming man, and in particular, of there being one particular moment in time ('moment' here covering the length of a human life) in which God revealed himself, and therefore one particular moment to which one must relate if one is going to know the eternal reality of God, and of the possibility of salvation through devotion to him. The paradox is that of a positive answer to Lessing's questions. More strikingly, the idea of a unique moment at which God reveals himself seems to be self-contradictory, for it suggests that the eternal (for God is certainly eternal, if he is at all) belongs to history. It is rather as though the number 4 appeared at one particular historical moment, and could only be known about by knowing what occurred just then. The Moment is, then, something paradoxical and absurd. Yet, according to the hypothesis being considered, this paradoxical occurrence is a real event at once historical and eternal.

The truth about this historical and eternal moment at which God appeared in human form, or rather did not just *appear* as such, but really became a historical individual, cannot be exactly *known*, or even *believed*; rather, there is a special way of *cognizing* it, that of *faith*. And faith is something which I choose, rather than am simply given. It is only God, indeed, who can give me the power and opportunity to make the choice of faith, but when he does so, I may either choose faith or respond with a fatal refusal.

V Where Hegelianism is Un-Christian

What can in no way substitute for the experience of God as appearing at the Moment is a dialectical process within the individual's mind, or even within human minds thinking together (this latter is surely implied). Moreover, it is essential to realize that the Moment did not occur necessarily. It was a free act on God's part, and it is a free act on the individual's part to respond to it either with faith or with rejection.

This is quite unlike the Hegelian view that in religion the Absolute Idea is becoming aware of itself at the precise historical moment which is necessitated by its nature. Still more is it contrasted with the view that the philosophical grasp of this necessity is a fuller grasp of it than can be gained through religious experience.

VI Necessity and Contingency

In an interlude (FRAGMENTS, 72–88) within the main discussion, Kierkegaard presents some philosophical views about necessity, possibility, and actuality. All possible beings have their own type of necessary being and necessary relations to one another. However, there is no necessity in the fact that any of these have entered into factual or actual existence.

Therefore necessity is something which belongs to the realm of possibility, while contingency and freedom belong to the realm of existence.

There is clearly some kinship here to Leibniz, whom Kierkegaard had carefully studied. Surprisingly, it reads very like George Santayana, who developed this as a variant on the Platonic scheme quite similarly to Leibniz and Kierkegaard himself.[7] It is perhaps Kierkegaard's best treatment of the kinds of question typically raised by philosophers.

Kierkegaard insists interestingly that although, on the one hand, when a possibility comes into existence, it cannot change its character, else it would not be that possibility, all the same it is importantly different as an actuality from what it was as a mere possibility. And the most important difference is that as actualized it can suffer as it could not as a possibility, or, otherwise put, as a necessity. (See FRAGMENTS, 74.)

The trouble with a Hegelian, or with a Spinozistic, approach to religion is that these philosophies profess to produce necessary conclusions. But necessary truth can concern only the eternal realm of the possibles, and therefore cannot tell us about what is actual. And we human beings are actual beings, who can and do suffer, not mere possibilities, and we cannot be saved by learning about the ideal necessary relations which hold in the realm of pure possibility.

This, incidentally, is one aspect of Kierkegaard's influence on subsequent existentialism, though actually it has, as I have mentioned, more in common with Santayana's contrast between the realm of essence and the realm of matter than with any other philosophical outlook of which I know.

Is the existence of God for Kierkegaard a pure possibility (and all truths about him necessary), or is he an actuality? Certainly Kierkegaard thinks attempts to prove God's existence altogether beside the point, since the existence of an actuality cannot be proved. (See POSTSCRIPT, 545–6.) And certainly God acts freely, for Kierkegaard. But to think of his existence as merely contingent would be odd. In fact, according to Kierkegaard, God's peculiar way of possessing both the necessity of a pure possibility (like a number) and the actuality of contingent beings is part of his (for our understanding) paradoxical nature and the reason why faith in him is a free act, not a necessary deduction.

VII Original Sin

What makes God's revelation of himself to man through his incarnation in human form so supremely good is that Man does not simply lack, but through sin has forfeited, the condition required for knowing God. Man may complain that he lacks this condition, but that is his own fault. In fact, Kierkegaard's text suggests that each of us has *personally* forfeited this condition. But (we may ask) if I have done so, and you, he, and she have done so, is it not probable that there are some, perhaps very few, who have not done so, if this is really an affair of freedom? Yet Kierkegaard obviously thinks the condition universal, and thereby surely commits himself to the doctrine of original sin.

This doctrine should surely be troubling for Kierkegaard. A certain type of metaphysical monist who thinks that we are all one may regard each of us as responsible for the sins of others. Also C. S. Lewis, I seem to remember, suggests that our relation to Adam and Eve (or perhaps to some demythologized version thereof) is one of a mysterious kind of identity, virtually identity-in-difference in the Hegelian sense. But surely this is not a doctrine which should appeal to the highly individualistic ontology of Kierkegaard, who indeed is adamant that I cannot owe my salvation to another man (except God-become-man), in which case surely I should not owe my sinful condition to another. However, we will see that he does seem to hold it when we turn to *Postscript*.

VIII The Disciple at Second Hand

It is an obvious enough objection to Kierkegaard's line of thought, as I have outlined it so far, that if one can only come to God through Jesus (let us throw off the pretence that the God-become-man has not yet been identified with that particular historical person), one must have been Jesus's contemporary and have lived in Palestine.

But here Kierkegaard elaborately argues that the person who knew Jesus, as one knows a personal friend, did not thereby know him as God, and did not therefore necessarily encounter God in encountering him. For that Jesus's life constituted the Moment at which history and eternity meet is not something which could be known in an ordinary empirical way, since it is somehow jointly an eternal and a historical truth or fact. To encounter Jesus as God requires both that I encounter him somehow empirically and that I grasp the special eternal nature of this empirical occurrence. But how can I encounter him as God? Answer: only through that special form of cognition properly called 'faith'. And this is as much a possibility for Kierkegaard in the nineteenth century or for us in the twenty-first century as it was for those living at the time of Jesus. For we do know him empirically, if not by seeing him.

Just as the historical becomes the occasion for the contemporary to become a disciple—by receiving the condition, please note, from the god himself, (for otherwise we speak Socratically)—so the report of the contemporaries becomes the occasion for everyone coming later to become a disciple by receiving the condition, please note from the god himself. (FRAGMENTS, 101)[8]

We do not, however, have to know very much about him. For it does not matter religiously how much of the Gospel narratives is true.[9] It is enough that they put us in touch with a real historical person whom we realize, through faith, to have been God incarnate. In fact, all we really need to know is that God was incarnated somewhere and somewhen.

The heart of the matter is the historical fact that the god has been in human form, and the other historical details are not even as important as they would be if the subject were a human being instead of the god. (FRAGMENTS, 103)

Thus we can be in touch with him simply by the faith that God was once incarnated as a human being who loved us and whom we can love.

IX Comment On All This

There is much that is disconcerting about all this. What is the value, anyway, of encountering God through Jesus? It is certainly not for Kierkegaard primarily Jesus's ethical teaching which matters.[10] He is not keen on the idea that God came to earth simply in order to teach us how to behave. Kierkegaard's concern seems to be that through encounter with Jesus as God, we can know that, in spite of all our sins, we can expect to enjoy an eternal happiness (an expression used only now and then in this work, but occurring pervasively in *Postscript*).

But does Kierkegaard hold that those who do not encounter God in this way are damned? Was his beloved Socrates damned?[11] And what of Africans and American Indians before missionaries reached them? What indeed of all the others, besides Socrates, who died before Jesus's birth? I shall consider later what Kierkegaard's view on this really was. But we shall see in *Postscript* that Kierkegaard's position is not better, and perhaps worse.

So how far should we sympathize with Kierkegaard's insistence that the abstractions of idealist philosophy, whether that of Hegel or Socrates (regarded as an idealist by Kierkegaard) or whoever, cannot work on us as real living persons as can the idea of the Eternal reaching out to us personally from a particular position in space and time? There is surely something in Lessing's suggestion that one's salvation (one's 'eternal happiness') cannot turn on one's being appropriately aware of certain historical events.[12] I myself feel that I could have spent my whole life in historical research as to the real truth about the Jesus of history, and yet had to admit at the end that I could find no certainty there. Finding a position which satisfies one in metaphysics may in principle be as difficult, but it does not require a lifetime's study of dusty documents and shreds of papyrus.

However, Kierkegaard does have something of an answer to this. For in playing down the need to decide on the historical truth of the Gospels, he goes so far as to say:

Even if the contemporary generation had not left anything behind except these words: 'We have believed that in such and such a year the god appeared in the humble form of a servant, lived and taught among us and then died'—this is more than enough. (FRAGMENTS, 104)

In this connection it is also worth noting that, at any rate according to Kierkegaard, Christianity is the only religion for which certain historical claims are of the essence, and that therefore if God was incarnated at all, it can only have been in Jesus, since there is no other claimant for this role.

As is well known, Christianity is the only historical phenomenon that despite the historical—indeed, precisely by means of the historical—has wanted to be the single individual's point of departure for his eternal consciousness, has wanted to interest him otherwise than merely historically, has wanted to base his happiness on his relation to something historical. (FRAGMENTS, 109)

And elsewhere he even says that anyone who has faith that God has incarnated himself in some bit of the historical world has faith enough to obtain his eternal happiness. (See FRAGMENTS, e.g. 201.)

PART TWO: *CONCLUDING UNSCIENTIFIC POSTSCRIPT*

X Outline of *Unscientific Postscript*

In *Philosophical Fragments* Climacus implies that it may be continued in a later work, in which the 'thought experiment' of that work will appear with its 'historical costume': that is, as Christianity. (See FRAGMENTS, 109.) For in *Fragments* Climacus, for the most part, merely tried out the idea of God incarnating himself in order to achieve mutual love with men, in spite of their fallen state, but did not specify Christianity as proclaiming the realization of this idea. Now, in *Concluding Unscientific Postscript* the focus is more explicitly on Christianity.

The first question to ask might seem to be: Is Christianity true? So Climacus examines two ways in which its truth has been argued for.

The first is the historical method. According to this, the truth of Christianity is to be learnt from the Scriptures: that is, mainly, the New Testament, and more particularly the Gospels. But immediately we attempt to establish Christianity in this way, we are involved in a historical enquiry which can never give more than an approximate truth, as Kierkegaard calls it. He seems to mean both that it can never be certain and that it can never be precise. Moreover, it constantly needs to take into account new historical evidence or argument, so it can never provide anything other than a belief which we accept as true pro tem. Historians can accept this characterization of their conclusions without minding about it. But the Christian cannot take up such an attitude to 'the evidences' of his religion. For Christianity requires a complete commitment of the whole personality, quite incompatible with holding the possibility of falsification constantly in reserve.

The contradiction [between the passionate longing for an eternal happiness and historical enquiry] first appears when the subjective individual at the peak of his subjective passion (in his concern for an eternal happiness) is to base this on historical knowledge, of which the maximum remains an approximation. The research scholar calmly goes on living. That which occupies him objectively and scientifically makes no difference one way or the other in his subjective being and existing. If it assumed that someone is in subjective passion in some way and then the task is to relinquish this, the contradiction will also disappear. But to require the greatest possible subjective passion, to the point of hating father and mother,[13] and then join this together with historical knowledge that at its maximum can become only an approximation—this is the contradiction. . . . Granted that the historicity of Christianity is true—if all the historiographers of the world united to do research and to establish certainty, it would still be impossible to establish more than an approximation. (POSTSCRIPT, 575–6)

Thus to base Christianity on the complete or partial historicity of the Gospel narratives is to leave one for ever subject to doubts as a result of fresh historical research.

The next method is that of philosophy: in particular, Hegelian speculative metaphysics, whether in its original form or as developed by the numerous Danish and other professors of Kierkegaard's time who sought to follow in his steps. (And though for Kierkegaard the main point is that it is a quite wrong approach to Christianity, a case could be made for saying that it is a wrong approach to *any* genuine religion.)

But this is no way to establish Christianity. For one thing, nobody is ever quite sure that speculative metaphysics has been brought to its final conclusion, since Hegelianism calls for developments. Its proponents always promise an eventual clinching conclusion, but they never reach it. And a dialectical system which has not reached a conclusion is a fraud. Moreover, the actual dialectical arguments put forward are generally admitted to be in want of a final tuning before they are quite satisfactory.

More importantly, the whole approach is faulty. Hegel tried to make logic move—that is, to show that logic is a moving train on to which we can jump and be carried on from one concept to another, like stations at which we never alight more than momentarily, until it enters a magically transformed landscape in which the stations are existing facts rather than concepts. But this is absolutely impossible, confusing two realms, the realm of pure possibilities or essences, with their intrinsic relations one to another, and the realm of fact, in which nothing is necessary.[14] In fact, existing things are never quite the actualization of static essences, since they possess a contingency and a freedom that pure essences must lack. 'A logical system is possible, but an existential system is not.'

These two attempts to exhibit the truth of Christianity, the one by historical research, the other by speculative metaphysics, are thus deeply flawed. Though different, they share a common fault: the attempt to show that Christianity possesses objective truth. But Christianity and our relation to it are subjective, not objective, matters. (What he means by this we shall see more fully below.)

In short, all attempts to prove the truth of Christianity, whether on the basis of history or on the basis of dialectical reasoning, are utterly mistaken, and to bother with them is to make faith impossible. For the belief of the religious man—that is, of the true Christian—must be a complete commitment of the will. It is, if you like, a venture, but it is a venture in which we engage with all doubt of its success set aside. This is a bit like Pascal's wager, but it is meant to be a far more passionate venture of our *all* (for the sake of the eventual eternal happiness which we crave) than the idea of a mere wager suggests. But that it has an aspect of a venture, rather than of an intellectual certainty, is vital to its calling forth the right subjective response from us.

If that of which I am to gain possession by venturing is certain, then I am not venturing, then I am *trading*. (POSTSCRIPT, 425; see also p. 427)

Without risk, no faith. Faith is the contradiction between the infinite passion of inwardness and the objective uncertainty. If I am able to apprehend God objectively, I do not have faith; but because I cannot do this, I must have faith. If I want to keep myself in faith. I must continually see to it that I hold fast to the objective uncertainty, see to it that in the objective uncertainty I am 'out on 70,000 fathoms of water' and still have faith. (POSTSCRIPT, 204)

XI Religiousness A and Religiousness B

Almost at the end of the *Unscientific Postscript* Climacus or Kierkegaard introduces a distinction between two types of religiousness: Religiousness A and Religiousness B. Each of these is distinct from the pseudo-religiousness of those living in a so-called Christian country who think that they are Christians simply because they have been baptized, go to church on Sunday, and live respectable bourgeois lives (a remark which was more relevant to Kierkegaard's time and place than to mine or those of my likely readers).

Religiousness in general, it is worth remarking or recalling here, is the third of three forms of life which for Kierkegaard form an existing dialectical series: (1) the aesthetic, a life lived for the pleasures it can provide; (2) the ethical, living according to universal principles; and (3) the religious, a life lived in felt relation to God. (The main development of this triad is in *Stages on Life's Way*, published about a year before *Postscript*, though the ground for it was prepared in *Either/Or* and *Fear and Trembling*.) But now we have to do with two distinct forms of religiousness.

The difference between these two sorts of religiousness is that Religiousness A is not distinctively Christian and is derived from the individual's own personal resources. Such religiousness was open to the pagans, and it is all that the religiousness of those Christians who have not really responded to what is distinctive in the Christian faith amounts to. (The merely bourgeois form of so-called Christianity is not of course a genuine form of religiousness at all.)

Climacus says, towards the end of *Postscript*, that so far he has been concerned only with Religiousness A. However, one cannot take this seriously, since throughout the work up till then, he has been discussing the nature of Christianity conceived entirely as a form of what he is now calling Religiousness B. Therefore, I shall ignore that statement as a false account, added later in the book, of what he has been doing, and regard the whole work as concerned with Christianity, in the sense of Religious-ness B, except where he clearly appeals to the distinction.

A few remarks on the two forms of religiousness are in order at this time. Religiousness A is the necessary background of Religiousness B. It can exist in paganism, but it prepares the ground for Religiousness B. (See POSTSCRIPT, 556.) Both forms of religiousness hold a faith which involves acceptance of something apparently logically absurd, but the apparently absurd content of the faith is greater in Religiousness B than in Religiousness A.

Thus the Religious A person has a sense of the contradiction between himself as an existing individual and himself as an eternal possibility, and he tries to bring the values of eternity into the realm of existence. He is thus fully sensitive to the paradoxical contradiction between eternity and existence in his own person, and suffers from this contrast, though he also finds it comic, inasmuch as he is ironically aware of the contrast between finite ends and infinite ones. The Religious B person, however, is aware of the still greater contradiction in the historical fact that the wholly infinite individual, God, entered the finite world at a particular moment in his-torical time.

Something eternal-historical is a playing with words and is a changing of the historical into myth, even if in the same paragraph one combats the mythologizing endeavor. Instead of being aware that there are two dialectical contradictions—first, basing one's eternal happiness on the relation to something historical, and then that this historical is constituted contrary to all thinking—one omits the former and volatizes the latter. A human being according to this possibility is eternal and becomes conscious of this in time: this is the contradiction within immanence. But that the by-nature eternal comes into existence in time, is born, grows up, and dies is a break with all thinking. If, however, the coming into existence of the eternal in time is supposed to be an eternal coming into existence, then Religiousness B is abolished, 'all theology is anthropology,' Christianity is changed from an existence communication into an ingenious metaphysical doctrine addressed to professors, and Religiousness A is prinked up with an esthetic-metaphysical ornamentation that in categorical respects neither adds nor detracts. (POSTSCRIPT, 579)

Moreover, Religiousness B is more dialectical, which seems to mean that it proceeds by a more explicit process of moving to its positive positions through a series of contradictions.

The distinction between the pathos-filled and the dialectical must, however, be qualified more specifically, because Religiousness A is by no means undialectical, but it is not paradoxically dialectical. Religiousness A is the dialectic of inward deepening; it is the relation to an eternal happiness that is not conditioned by a something but is the dialectical inward deepening of the relation, consequently conditioned only by the inward deepening, which is dialectical. On the other hand, Religiousness B, as it will be called from now on, or paradoxical religiousness, as it has been called, or the religiousness that has the dialectical in second place, makes conditions in such a way that the conditions are not the dialectical concentrations of inward deepening but a definite something that qualifies the eternal happiness more specifically (whereas in A the more specific qualification of inward deepening is the only more specific qualification), not by qualifying more specifically the individual's appropriation of it but by qualifying more specifically the eternal happiness, yet not as a task for thinking but as paradoxically repelling, and giving rise to new pathos. (POSTSCRIPT, 556)

Religiousness B, through its positive use of the self-contradictory, is in a sense more 'dialectical' than Religiousness A. Thus it may be called the paradoxical form of religiousness. (See POSTSCRIPT, 556.)

So much for the moment on Religiousness A and Religiousness B.

XII Why be Interested in Christianity?

What is the motive for concerning oneself with Christianity? Well, according to Climacus, his interest arose because he had heard that there was 'a highest good, called an eternal happiness' which it offered to those who embraced it. (See POSTSCRIPT, 15–16.[15]) Although he remains himself 'outside it', this, he opines, is its special attraction, and makes it an important matter how one relates to it. (See POSTSCRIPT, 14–15 and 617–18.) And this seems to be at least one motivation on the part of Kierkegaard for accepting all the risks associated with being a Christian.

But can we really accept Christianity? Are not its claims too logically absurd to be taken seriously? Moreover, when we look into it, it hardly holds out to us much by way of the pleasure which we are always seeking; in fact, it offers no escape from suffering, but rather its intensification.

Still, the suffering seems to be of a nobler kind, and, what is more, appears to be necessary if we are to find the eternal happiness we crave. Despair at the purely aesthetic or hedonistic approach, and a certain inadequacy in the purely ethical approach, point us on to something which through a *via dolorosa* may in the end be more satisfying.

But whether it is attractive or not, how can we possibly accept its strange claims as objectively true? Moreover, it seems to make a category mistake in confusing the mode of being of the eternal and the mode of being, which Kierkegaard calls 'existing', of finite contingent things like ourselves.

Yet we will never find happiness other than by becoming Christians. The simple uneducated man can turn to the Christian hope without intellectual scruples, but the over-educated modern person has scruples which true religious instruction may help him overcome. And his first lesson might be that truth is to be distinguished into two kinds, or at least aspects: objective truth and subjective truth.

XIII Objective and Subjective Truth

When the question about truth is asked objectively, truth is reflected upon objectively as an object to which the knower relates himself. What is reflected upon is not the relation but that what he relates himself to is the truth, the true. If only that to which he relates himself is the truth, the true, then the subject is in the truth. When the question about truth is asked subjectively the individual's relation is reflected upon subjectively. If only the how of this relation is in truth, the individual is in truth, even if he in this way were to relate himself to untruth. (POSTSCRIPT, 199)

An objective uncertainty, held fast through appropriation with the most passionate inwardness, is the truth, the highest truth there is for an existing person. (POST-SCRIPT, 203)

Faith is the objective uncertainty with the repulsion of the absurd, held fast in the passion of inwardness. (POSTSCRIPT, 611)

Thus we should distinguish between objective truth and subjective truth, and recognize that the second is of prime importance in religion. Kierkegaard might have put it better if he had said that truth has an objective and a subjective aspect. Hegelianism and other attempts to rationalize Christianity are concerned with the former, but in genuine Christianity it is the latter that matters.[16]

Kierkegaard's contrast between subjective and objective truth is somewhat notorious, and quite what he means by it is debatable. It certainly relates to the distinction which he makes between the *what* and the *how* of knowledge. Knowledge is something which occurs only as a feature of human thought (the divine thought apart), and in any case of knowledge we should distinguish what is grasped as being the case and how it is grasped as being the case. Suppose I am told (truly) that a friend of mine has just died—call him 'George Lopez'. This fact that he has died is the *what* of the truth which I thereby learn—we may call it the truth's content.

Now I may experience this content in various ways. One way is simply as a fact to be added to the sum of facts I have about my acquaintance. I may, for example, think that I had better cross his name off the list of people to whom I send Christmas cards. Or alternatively, I may feel an overpowering sense of loss, in which an image of him comes vividly into my mind and I am overcome with sadness. These, I take it, are two different 'hows' by which that content of this person's death may come to be known to me.

In Kierkegaard's terminology the fact (if it is a fact) that the person is dead is an objective truth, while my way of grasping the fact is a subjective truth. I should remark that Kierkegaard does not give any such example, as he is concerned solely with religious truth. I cannot vouch for the fact, therefore, that my example is really one of the contrast between the *how* and the *what*. It is, however, the best that I can do to clarify the distinction before we turn to religion.

There is some analogy here to Cardinal Newman's distinction between notional assent and real assent. I have not *really* assented to the death of my friend until it has been realized in a fully emotional way. But for Kierkegaard—I am not sure how it was for Newman—it is by assenting emotionally to the reality of God, the Incarnation, and so forth, that I come to know the objective truth. I cannot know this objective truth as a result of reasoning. And this is where Kierkegaard's famous leap of faith comes in. If I am to know this objective truth, if it is a truth, I must, *without evidence*, launch myself into *real*—that is, *personally transforming*—assent to it, and then I will realize that its objective truth is undeniable.

Let us now either agree or suppose that God does, indeed, exist. The truth that he does so can be realized only as a state or act of a finite mind. (I continue to ignore truth as it is for God, though I shall touch on this later.) And the truth possessed by this act will have its *what* and its *how*. The *what* is the existence of God, the *how* is my way of grasping this content. And, as with the death of George Lopez, the former constitutes an objective truth, and the latter a subjective truth. Now, according to Kierkegaard, what makes me religious is a matter of the subjective truth, the *how* of what I believe. For the appropriate way of grasping the fact of God's existence is that I love and fear him; and I am only 'in the truth', as Kierkegaard puts it, if I genuinely feel that. If I simply register it as an interesting fact about the universe, or as assisting the solution of a philosophical problem (e.g. as to how physical things can exist unperceived by finite minds), or as the consequence of an ontological argument, I am not 'in the truth', however much my belief possesses objective truth.

The same applies to the central Christian belief that God, the eternal and infinite, transformed himself into a historical human being for a period, so that he could meet human beings on a par and take on the punishment which was properly theirs. This may be registered in someone's mind as an article of the religion to which he is formally committed, or as a historical event which plays an intriguing role in the self-realization of the Absolute Idea. But however much someone may thereby grasp this content as an objective truth, he is not *in the truth* in the way that he must be in order to be a Christian, unless it fills his own being with wonder, gratitude, and devotion.

A third belief which must be subjectively true for someone if they are to be a Christian is belief in immortality and in the possibility of gaining, or failing to gain, an eternal happiness according to one's thoughts, feelings, and actions in this life. And immortality must not somehow be reinterpreted as the eternity pertaining to a possibility or essence. (See POSTSCRIPT, 171.)

We have not so far considered falsehood, but we must surely do so in order to enter into the logic of Kierkegaard's position. What makes the *how* of one's grasping a fact subjectively true or subjectively false? For Kierkegaard's view is not just that there always is a *how*, but that this *how* is either subjectively true or false. Actually, he does not speak of subjective falsehood, but he does speak of one's *how* of grasping an objective truth as either placing one *in the truth* or not. It seems fair to take this as a distinction between subjective truth and subjective falsehood. So what constitutes the difference? The answer must be, I think, that it is the emotional adequacy of one's response to the fact.

Consider again the example of the death of George Lopez. One is not to be condemned for keeping grief at bay for a time. But if one never feels grief, one has certainly not registered the fact with an adequate *how*. If the *how* of one's grasp is to possess subjective truth, it must involve a deep feeling of grief, and perhaps some emotionally charged reflection on death as a feature of human life.

But now we move to the real puzzle, which is that Kierkegaard sometimes seems to say that all that matters for the Christian is the subjective truth of his beliefs, and that the objective truth is largely irrelevant. Indeed, he says that to seek objective truth about God and Christ is altogether inappropriate.

Some commentators understand Kierkegaard to be saying that it does not matter whether God *really*, as most of us would put it, exists or not. What matters is that one has certain emotions and engages in certain activities which are appropriate to there being a God, and an incarnation, and so forth.

If this were Kierkegaard's view, most of us would probably think it pretty wrong-headed. What is the point of reacting appropriately to these supposed facts if they are not really facts at all? Shouldn't we respond to such facts as the best evidence suggests there really are, and respond to putative facts not thus supported, or perhaps quite contrary to the best available evidence, as we do to frank fictions.

Supposing that George Lopez really is dead, my grief seems appropriate. But if I discover that he is not dead, it will be inappropriate to continue in my grief (except as grief at an inevitable feature of human life, of which his death seemed to be an instance). And even if I do not discover it, there will be a sense in which my grief is inappropriate to things as they are. Should the appropriateness of a feeling to an event which did not take place, but which I thought had taken place, be called *true* at all? At any rate, it would surely be absurd simply to seek subjective truth about the lives of my friends and family without bothering myself as to whether they are objectively true or not?

Part of the answer is that Kierkegaard is not advocating a privileging of subjective over objective truth in general, but only in connection with religion. In so far as the death of Lopez is not a religious event (which is not to deny that we will regard it differently according to our own religion), what matters in the first place is objective truth, and only after that subjective truth.

But what makes religious belief so different? It is tempting to say that Kierkegaard's position is much the same as that of William James in 'The Will to Believe', and that his point is that, since the objective truth cannot be known in religious matters, we must go for what is emotionally most satisfactory. This, in the case of Kierkegaard, at any rate, would not mean the most pleasing, but that which somehow appealed most to the depths of our nature.

Or again, one might endorse 'non-realism' with regard to religion, and hold that there is no real truth of the matter in matters religious, and that the only possible truth or falsehood is conformity with our deepest feelings.

However, neither of these interpretations seems right. There are two other possibilities. One is that Kierkegaard is just taking for granted that the religious propositions are objectively true, and that the only thing of interest is what we need to do to make them subjectively true for us.

A more satisfactory interpretation, which Kierkegaard seems sometimes to affirm, is that, in the case of religion, having subjectively appropriate responses to ideas about God, Christ, and so forth is the one human way of grasping their objective truth. To ask for some other way of discovering that they are objectively true is radically misconceived. That it is misconceived, is, indeed, something that we can only expect those for whom these ideas are subjectively true to realize. But still, this possession of subjectively true ideas does carry with it absolute evidence of their objective truth. Just as we need eyes to see, so we need subjectively true ideas—that is, feelings adequate to the reality of God, the Incarnation, and suchlike—to grasp that their reality is an objective truth.

In the case of Lopez's death, the matter is different. I cannot know its objective truth via my subjectively true ideas about his death. And I do have another way of knowing the objective truth: that is, by ordinary empirical evidence. It is only then that the question of whether my ideas are subjectively true should come up.

This answer seems along the right lines, but requires some qualification. For in fact Kierkegaard does seem to think that there are cases where a religious belief is subjectively true but objectively false.

If someone who lives in the midst of Christianity enters, with knowledge of the true idea of God, the house of God, the house of the true God, and prays, but prays in untruth, and if someone lives in an idolatrous land but prays with all the passion of infinity, although his eyes are resting upon the image of an idol—where, then, is there more truth? The one prays in truth to God although he is worshiping an idol; the other prays in untruth to the true God and is therefore in truth worshiping an idol. (POSTSCRIPT, 201)

Still, the idea that a belief can be subjectively true, though objectively false, does seem rather odd. But what Kierkegaard is saying, I think, is that though a belief may be objectively false taken *au pied de la lettre*, as it would be expressed in words, it may still (at least in the religious case) be a way in which an individual gets in touch with a reality which he has misconceived.

Let me try now to express what I take to be the essence of Kierkegaard's view, even if he does not spell it out quite like this. I note first that I am avoiding speaking of the *proposition* that Lopez is dead, or that God exists, or that Jesus was God incarnate, or whatever, because Kierkegaard says that being a Christian is not a matter of accepting certain tenets (see POST-SCRIPT, 215), and in the light of this is very suspicious of terms like 'proposition', and even of 'idea'.

Related to this is a certain vagueness as to precisely what sort of thing an objective truth is. It seems to be, for Kierkegaard, not so much a true proposition as an object or state of affairs. The objective truth of my belief that there is a war between two nations is rather the war than a proposition about it. But what, then, is objectively false belief directed at? Perhaps at unreal objects, objects which do not exist. I don't find Kierkegaard very clear on this but it does not matter enormously.

Here, then, is my own formulation.

1. A belief in virtue of its inherent conceptual character is directed at a certain object, which may be real or unreal. In the former case, it is objectively true, and in the latter case objectively false. It will further have an emotional character which is or is not appropriate to the object at which it is directed. Should that object be real, and the emotion appropriate, then the belief is both objectively and subjectively true.

2. In the case of a non-religious belief, the appropriateness of its emotional character to its object (considered as real) does not of itself show whether that object is real or not. However, if the object is real, then the belief is subjectively as well as objectively true. If the object is not real, there is some doubt as to whether Kierkegaard would say that it was still subjectively true, but it would be best for him to classify it as not so, though perhaps avoiding the expression 'subjectively false'.

3. In the case of a religious belief, the appropriateness of its emotional character to its object does show that its object is real—indeed, this is the only thing which can show it to be real. The case, therefore, does not arise where such a belief can fail of objective truth, so that there is no need for any way of characterizing its truth-value, both of the objective and of the subjective kind, should its object be unreal.

4. What of a religious belief which is directed conceptually at a real object but where the emotional attitude to it is inappropriate (most typically by its feebleness)? One might at first suppose that it would be objectively true but subjectively false. However, Kierkegaard might say that this case was also impossible, since a religious belief has no real object at all in the absence of any appropriate emotional response.

5. What now of a belief which *is directed conceptually at an unreal object* but possesses an emotional attitude which it could not possess unless there *were a certain real object* to which it was appropriate? In that case Kierkegaard would say that it was subjectively true though objectively false. (This is the case described in the last quotation.)

6. The explanation for this difference between religious and non-religious beliefs is that the emotional character of a religious belief plays a role in

determining what its object is which it does not play in the case of a non-religious belief. Moreover, there are certain religious emotions which could occur only in a mind responding to a genuine divine reality.

We can sum all this up as follows: A religious belief is subjectively true if and only if it is an appropriate emotional response to something with which I am really engaged even if my belief as to what it is with which I am engaged is objectively all at sea.

A good story will illustrate much of this. A learned man has always been fairly content with his existence, as a respected thinker on religious and related matters. His wife dies, and his children go to the bad. He is wretched beyond belief, and he finds his religious faith failing, failing at any rate to help him personally in his distress. He goes out for a long walk and finds himself in a village which he has not visited previously. There is a church there, and he finds the minister within it. He pours out his heart to the minister, and asks whether he can help him. The minister is deeply saddened by the situation, but he cannot help him much. But he does say this. There is a book on how the Christian can cope with misfortune which has brought comfort and help to many. He tells his visitor its title and author. The learned man sighs, and says: 'The only trouble is that I wrote that book.'[17]

Clearly, whatever there was of objective truth in what the learned man had said in his book, he was not in the truth, for he had not acquired subjectively true ideas about troubles on life's way.

Since Kierkegaard's critique of Hegel and Hegelianism could be summed up by saying that it offered (at best) only objective truth, and could not become a subjective truth for its partisans, that is one with real existential import for them, it is rather remarkable, as we saw in the last chapter, that Hegel in his youthful writings, before his system was developed, objected to the Christianity of his time on precisely the same ground, arguing that the so-called objective truths of religion must become 'subjective truths, truths for us', if they are to have any religious value. (See Ch. 3 p. 103).

It is inherent in the concept of religion that it is not a mere science of God, of his attributes, of our relation and the relation of the world to him and of the enduring survival of our souls—all of this might be admitted by mere Reason, or known to us in some other way—but religion is not merely a historical or rational knowledge, it is a concern of the heart, it has an influence on our feelings and on the determination of our will. (TÜBINGEN ESSAY, 482)

XIV More on the Paradoxical and Absurd Nature of Christianity

More needs to be said about Kierkegaard's insistence that the Christian promise is somehow absurd or paradoxical. It is something which looks impossible to the reason and, just because of that, cannot be reached by reason, though in fact it is how things somehow really are. This was mentioned in my discussion of *Fragments* but it is even more central to *Postscript*.

It is worth noting, first, that Kierkegaard has quite a respect for the atheist who rejects Christianity just because of its absurdity. For the person who rejects it as 'an offence to reason' is relating more suitably to Christianity than the person who seeks to rationalize it. Thus the atheist is really nearer the truth, in rejecting Christianity as absurd, than is the Hegelian or other rationalizing philosopher of religion.[18] The one whom he despises is the person who thinks that God probably exists, or that the Incarnation probably took place.

The paradox or absurdity of Christianity has several components, but it will be enough to dwell here on the central one: namely, that the eternal launched itself into a particular moment of history in the form of a finite human being. Kierkegaard, as we saw, emphasizes that God did not merely disguise himself as a human being, but actually became one.

It may be interesting to consider this passage from Spinoza.

As to the additional teaching of certain Churches, that God took upon himself human nature, I have expressly indicated that I do not know what they say. Indeed, to tell the truth, they seem to me to speak no less absurdly than one who might tell me that a circle has taken on the nature of a square. (SPINOZA LETTER 23)

Kierkegaard is at one with Spinoza on the absurdity of the idea of the Incarnation and associated ideas, but none the less it is, he is passionately convinced, to think truly. In fact, it is just because we cannot accept it rationally, that we must accept it non-rationally through faith.

Thus it is part of the central significance of Christianity that it makes claims which look logically absurd. Rationalized versions of Christianity, which seek to make Christianity more intellectually credible, only deprive it of its most important feature.

Christianity has itself proclaimed itself to be the eternal, essential truth that has come into existence in time; it has proclaimed itself as *the paradox* and has required the inwardness of faith with regard to what is an offense to the Jews, foolishness to the Greeks—and an absurdity to the understanding. (POSTSCRIPT, 213)

But does Kierkegaard mean only that these claims *look* absurd, or that they *are* absurd? The correct interpretation on balance seems to be this.

These are our formulations of claims which God himself understands, and which are in that sense intelligible, and which perhaps we will understand in another life. However, it is beyond our powers to grasp how something which calls for a description in language which looks logically absurd can in fact be the case.

What, then, is the absurd? The absurd is that the eternal truth has come into existence in time, that God has come into existence, has been born, has grown up, etc., has come into existence exactly as an individual human being, indistinguishable from any other human being... (POSTSCRIPT, 210)

Kierkegaard suggests that Christianity is designed to be paradoxical, precisely so that its acceptance will not be a merely intellectual operation, but an act of will involving the whole of our personal energy.

Suppose that Christianity does not at all want to be understood; suppose that, in order to express this and to prevent anyone, misguided, from taking the road of objectivity, it has proclaimed itself to be the paradox. Suppose that it wants to be only for existing persons and essentially for persons existing in inwardness, in the inwardness of faith, which cannot be expressed more definitely than this: it is the absurd, adhered to firmly with the passion of the infinite. (POSTSCRIPT, 214)

The whole attempt to rationalize Christianity, whether by making it a stage in which the Absolute Idea comes to understand itself rationally, or by any other philosophical method, is an attempt to make the existence of God, and more especially his incarnation as the historical person Jesus of Nazareth, a fact among facts, even if a supreme fact. The paradoxical nature of Christianity puts a stop to the genuine Christian following any such rationalizing path, and trying to make the divine into something which he can comprehend intellectually.

The thesis that God has existed in human form, was born, grew up, etc. is certainly the paradox *sensu strictissimo*, the absolute paradox. But as the absolute paradox it cannot be related to a relative difference. A relative paradox is related to a relative difference between more or less sagacious people. But the absolute paradox, precisely because it is absolute, can be related only to the absolute difference by which a human being differs from God. (POSTSCRIPT, 217)

What we need, if our goal is access to the eternal happiness which we all (even if not fully aware of it) yearn for is an appropriate subjective response to the incomprehensible infinity of God, and his paradoxical involvement with the finite, not to grasp some 'objective' truth about the universe through our reason. Objective truth on divine matters is there for God, perhaps, but not for man.

Hegelianism is an attempt to play the role of God and see things under the aspect of eternity, as though we ourselves were eternal beings.[19] And indeed we ourselves have an eternal reality; it is eternity blended with existential contingency, however, which means that we cannot expect to understand reality *ab extra* but only as struggling beings within it.

But the absolute difference between God and a human being is simply this, that a human being is an individual existing being (and this holds for the best brain just as fully as for the most obtuse), whose essential task therefore cannot be to think *sub specie aeterni*, because as long as he exists, he himself, although eternal, is essentially an existing person and the essential for him must therefore be inwardness in existence; God, however, is the infinite one who is eternal. (POST-SCRIPT, 217)

XV Christianity is Sticking by Absolute Faith to the Paradox and the Absurdity

Thus to be a Christian demands that we make the leap of a doubly (at least apparently) irrational faith. It is irrational, first, because it is only through having faith in it that we discover it to be certainly true, and secondly, because the very content of our belief is apparently logically absurd. Passionate commitment to the absurd is of the essence of Christianity.

So faith is the one way of discovering that it is certainly true. However, the word 'certain' needs qualification, because at every moment the assurance of the Christian hope is at risk from the offence it gives to the intellect; therefore it must remain a continual struggle to believe it.

But what motivates us to engage in this struggle? For Climacus, as we have seen, it is because he has heard that Christianity holds out the promise of an eternal happiness. And Kierkegaard implies that if this is really what we want, we should not dally about looking for evidence for what of its nature cannot be proved, but launch ourselves into faith by an act of will. (See POSTSCRIPT, 385–7, 391–3, and 574.)

It would also seem to be because we are, in our fully awake moments, riddled with a sense of our own horrible sinfulness, for which Christianity holds out the only hope of being forgiven. That we should be forgiven because God, as incarnated in Jesus, has taken our due punishment upon himself is another of the absurdities to which the Christian is committed.

The Christian, then, is committed to a belief which he cannot claim to be objectively certain. Yet in a curious way, according to Kierkegaard, being aware of its objective uncertainty becomes the peculiarly Christian way of being certain of it. (This is part of what Kierkegaard calls 'the existential dialectic'.)

As soon as uncertainty is not the form of certitude, as soon as uncertainty does not continually keep the religious person hovering in order continually to grasp certitude, as soon as certainty seals with lead, as it were, the religious person—well, then he is naturally about to become part of the mass [of pre-religious people, I take it]. (POSTSCRIPT, 507)

XVI More *contra* Hegelian Christianity

Kierkegaard believed that Hegelian philosophy, with its claim to provide the philosophical and literal truth which the Christian religion presented in a pictorial form, was the greatest enemy of true Christianity in his day among the intelligentsia, while its greatest enemy for less intellectual people was the bourgeois Christianity of the Danish Protestant Church and similar churches elsewhere.

Hegel, as we saw in the last chapter, held that the universe consists in the gradual realization of the Absolute Idea, first in nature and then in human life, in which, at its climax, it comes to full consciousness of itself in the developed human mind. The Incarnation of Jesus is a symbol of the fact that humanity at its highest is that great self-actualization of the Absolute Idea which is the point of the universe.

Kierkegaard found something essentially ludicrous (not merely paradoxical, as in Christianity) in the Hegelian philosophy and in the attempt to interpret and promote Christianity in terms of it. For the Hegelian text declares itself to be, not the expression of the limited thought of a finite human being, but the registration of the process by which the universe unfolds dialectically. In fact, somehow its own unfolding is identical with that cosmic unfolding.

Likewise, Hegel's followers, especially (so I learn from Kierkegaard and commentaries on his work) various Danish theologians, thought that their own philosophical works were further unfoldings of the Absolute Idea, which had not, as it happened, completely revealed itself through Hegel. Of these the most important were Hans Lassen Martensen (1808–84), 'formerly Kierkegaard's university tutor and later Bishop Primate of the Danish State Church' and J. L. Heiberg.[20]

So it was not just Hegel, but his followers too, who regarded their philosophy not just as their own personal thoughts, but as the necessary unfolding of the basic categories and forms of reality. The project was to avoid merely subjective factors pertaining to one's own person and give oneself up to the necessary logic of the dialectical series. One pretended that one's thoughts were not those of an existing person, but the necessary unfolding of the Absolute Idea. Indeed, the Hegelians, in particular the Hegelian Christians, almost ceased to be genuinely existing persons at all, at least in their own ignored eyes.

Somewhere, indeed, one might oneself appear as an item in the series, or, more likely for most of us, some minor historical movement would appear in which one had played some little part. Knowing thus one's little part in the great world-historical process of thought and action was the most the project could do for one personally, except for the enjoyment of an abstract exercise. For it makes one's own personal decisions look meaningless, or at best necessary details in the vast march of history, as it actualizes the Absolute Idea.

Alas, while the speculating, honorable Herr Professor is explaining all existence, he has in sheer absentmindedness forgotten what he himself is called, namely, that he is a human being, a human being pure and simple, and not a fantastical three-eighths of a paragraph. (POSTSCRIPT, 145; see also pp. 120, 81, etc.)

The whole matter had become comical. Surely the philosophical writings of these Hegelian Christians somehow stemmed from the subjective character of their own little selves, selves who were not pure mind, but humble little human organisms who had to go to the lavatory from time to time. Yet they tried to identify themselves with the Absolute Idea and lose sight of their own little selves. For the pure thinking of the Hegelian system tries to have nothing to do with any existing person. (See POSTSCRIPT, 315.)

Moreover, in all honesty, what can a person care about more than his own personal destiny? Thus there was a kind of bad faith in this attempt to lose any sense of oneself as an individual whose own subjective life matters to one more than anything else. It is an attempt to avoid the one thing which truly concerns each and everyone, how to find one's way to an eternal happiness and assuage one's awareness of one's own guilt.

Thus, according to Kierkegaard, a speculative thinker must be regarded as 'absent minded' because he somehow seems to forget his own existence. (See POSTSCRIPT, 145 and *passim*.) And indeed it is intrinsic to speculative philosophy that it invites one to forget one's own existence, since it is of its essence to belittle the importance of the individual. What matters, so it tries to teach us, is the great sweep of history, the world-historical process, not any ordinary little person as opposed to world-historical figures like Napoleon or perhaps Hegel himself.

Whether our age is more immoral than other ages, I shall not decide, but just as a degenerated penance was the specific immorality in a period of the Middle Ages, so the immorality of our age could very easily become a fantastical-ethical debilitation, the disintegration of a sensual, soft despair, in which individuals grope as in a dream for a concept of God without feeling any terror in so doing but on the contrary boasting of their superiority, which in its dizziness of thought and with the vagueness of impersonality has an intimation, as it were, of God in the indefinite, and in imagination meets him whose existence remains more or less like that of the mermaids. And the same thing could easily repeat itself in the individual's relation to himself—namely, that the ethical and the responsibility and the power to act and the strong-nerved sorting out by repentance evaporate in a brilliance of disintegration, in which the individual dreams about himself metaphysically or lets all existence dream about itself and confuses himself with Greece, Rome, China, world-history, our age and the century. (POSTSCRIPT, 544–5)

But this belittling of one's own little self cannot in honesty be satisfying. And here is a great contrast with Christianity. For Hegelianism the individual person hardly matters, not at least unless he is one of the few world-historical figures. It is only in so far as one who is not a world-historical individual can identify himself with some generation of men, rather than see himself as the distinct individual he is, that he can find life worthwhile.

So the great difference between genuine Christianity and any at all Hegelian point of view, whether it professes to be Christian or not, is that the Hegelian loses all sense of his own personal significance in grasping the dialectic of world history, in which he himself is at best a footnote. For Hegelianism nothing really matters except the process of the great Whole, and 'Christianity is changed from an existence communication into an ingenious metaphysical doctrine addressed to professors'. (See POSTSCRIPT, 579, also p. 371.)

Thus, seen from the world-historical point of view espoused by the Hegelians, most human individuals seem sheer waste. What would it matter to world history whether a particular factory worker existed or not? But for Christianity that worker is all important. For God is equally concerned with every individual and the extent to which that individual relates himself to God appropriately. (See POSTSCRIPT, 135, 141, 149, 155, 159, etc.)

In short, it does not matter one iota to the genuine Christian what his place may be, or whether he has one, in world history. What matters is solely how he stands with God.

Every age has its own [special immorality]; the immorality of our age is perhaps not lust and pleasure and sensuality, but rather a pantheistic, debauched contempt for individual human beings. (POSTSCRIPT, 355)

Thus, to identify oneself with mankind or with one's generation is a radically misconceived life stance. One is oneself, and one must find one's own salvation through a proper relation to God, no matter what is going on in the world elsewhere or what others think and do. This is shown by the fact that one cannot simply take off ethically at the point humankind has reached so far. Each must take up his own ethical task, starting from scratch (see POSTSCRIPT, 345). What is more, advantages of birth or talent do not affect one's chances of eternal happiness (see POSTSCRIPT, 428).

In the animal world, the particular animal is related directly as specimen to species, participates as a matter of course in the development of the species, if one wants to talk about such a thing. When a breed of sheep, for example, is improved, improved sheep are born because the specimen merely expresses the species. But surely it is different when an individual, who is qualified as spirit, relates himself to the generation. Or is it assumed that Christian parents give birth to Christian children as a matter of course?... And yet it is of this confusion that modern speculative thought is, if not directly the cause, nevertheless often enough the occasion, so that the individual is regarded as related to the development of the human spirit as a matter of course (just as the animal specimen is related to the species), as if development of spirit were something one generation could dispose of by a will in favor of another, as if the generation and not individuals were qualified as spirit, which is both a self-contradiction and an ethical abomination. Development of spirit is self-activity; the spiritually developed individual takes his spiritual development along with him in death. If a succeeding individual is to attain it, it must occur through his self-activity; therefore he must skip nothing. Now, of course it is easier and simpler and *wohlfeilere* [cheaper] to bellow about being born in the speculative nineteenth century. (POSTSCRIPT, 345)

Two points may be worth making here. First, if Kierkegaard, not unreasonably at that time, believed in the inheritance of acquired characteristics in animals, he held a view which modern biologists reject. Secondly, in so far as he believes, as it seems from many remarks (see sections above and below), in original sin, at least if he took the orthodox view that this was inherited from some primary sinner, he did, in effect, believe in some kind of inheritance of acquired characteristics in human beings, so far, at least, as what is most important about them goes—namely, their ethical status. Indeed, he actually calls it 'hereditary' sin. (See quotation below at p. 209.)

However, this does not much affect Kierkegaard's insistence that we should not conceive ourselves morally as a particular stage in the development of the World Spirit, as Hegelianism suggests, but must take full responsibility ourselves for what we do. And it is this conception, above all, which evokes Kierkegaard's hostility to what he calls 'religious objectivism'. 'I am not just a paragraph in the great world book', as he puts it elsewhere.

Christianity, therefore, protests against all objectivity; it wants the subject to be infinitely concerned about himself. What it asks about is the subjectivity; the truth of Christianity, if it is at all, is only in this; objectively, it is not at all. And even if it is only in one single subject, then it is only in him, and there is greater Christian joy in heaven over this one than over world history and the system, which, as objective powers are incommensurate with the essentially Christian. (POSTSCRIPT, 130)

Moreover, there is a logical mistake (touched on above) at the heart of Hegelianism, according to Climacus/Kierkegaard. For Hegelian thinking, despite its claims, is essentially an abstract affair. At any rate, it claims to have the necessity commonly claimed for logic. But in so far as it professes to be logically necessary, must it necessarily fail to deal with the concrete. For abstract thinking sees things *sub specie aeternitatis*, and therefore cannot deal with the concrete, which is essentially contingent. (See POSTSCRIPT, 301, 474, 541.) Thus the Hegelian attempt to move to the level of *pure thought thinking itself* is in effect a retreat from thinking about existing reality at all. The individual becomes a monstrous hybrid between the abstract and the concrete, the eternal and the actual. (See POSTSCRIPT, 314.) Kierkegaard himself regards each of us as somehow both temporal and eternal. What is wrong, however, is to regard us as intellectual abstractions.

So the trouble with Hegelianism is that it moves purely in the realm of essences and charts the ideal relations between these. And at the level of essence, many strange things are possible and explicable. But when these things are supposed to be historically actualized, they become paradoxical. Christianity does, indeed, hold that the basic actualities passionately accepted by faith are paradoxical, but Hegelianism thinks that it can remove the paradox by treating them as though they were pure essences (in the fantasy world of the possible).

God can very well coalesce with humankind in the imagination, but to coalesce in actuality with the individual human being is precisely the paradox. (POSTSCRIPT, 581)

He [the Hegelian] will, misunderstanding, understand Christianity as a possibility and forget that what is possible in the fantasy-medium of possibility, possible in illusion, or what is possible in the fantastic medium of pure thinking (and basic to all speculative talk about an eternal becoming-of-the-deity is this shifting of the setting into the medium of possibility) must, in the medium of actuality, become the absolute paradox. He will, misunderstanding, forget that understanding holds only for something of which the possibility is higher than its actuality; whereas here, just the opposite, actuality is the higher, is the paradox, because Christianity as a proposal is not difficult to understand—the difficulty and the paradox are that it is actual. (POSTSCRIPT, 580; see also p. 581)

Another fault in Hegelianism is the principle of mediation, according to which all contradiction between different viewpoints, or different life choices, somehow vanishes via a synthesizing viewpoint or choice, which mediates between them, and endorses both, provided neither claims a position other than that particular position in the system which the mediating idea allocates to them. (See POSTSCRIPT, 474, 541, etc.) Thus Hegelianism teaches that there is, after all, no need to brace oneself to make the great choices, as, say, between a life of pleasure and a life of religious devotion. But the importance of choice between irreconcilables, of the *either/or*, as opposed to the Hegelian *both/and* is of course, centre stage for Kierkegaard. (See POSTSCRIPT, 305 and *passim*.) For the Hegelian everything has its legitimate place in our lives, when it is suitably sublated (*aufgehoben*), and thereby he tries to avoid all sense of sin. For Kierkegaard there are things on which we must turn our back.

The whole attempt to see the world *sub specie aeternitatis* is the besetting sin of Hegelianism, for it is an attempt to usurp the place of God. (Spinoza must have been similarly objectionable to Kierkegaard.) For God doubtless does see the whole of the world and of natural history in this way, but that is not for us struggling finite beings. For the true Christian, the contrast between man and God is absolute, and something which we must acknowledge in worship. (See POSTSCRIPT, 411–12.)

Hegelianism indeed strives for an identification of *man* with God, either man as a species or the individual who can spout the dialectic system. Christianity, by contrast, teaches us not to try to understand God, but rather to express the infinite distance between us and him by worship. 'And thus one also demonstrates the existence of God by worship—not by demonstrations' (POSTSCRIPT, 546).

Our existence is one of continual becoming, rather than one of completed being. But the Hegelian system attempts to transport us into a realm of pure being, where, in truth, only possibilities or essences belong. God, it is true, is eternal, but it is one of the paradoxes of Christianity that he is both eternal and historical, as an eternal Form like a number cannot be. (See POSTSCRIPT, 307.)

Moreover, Hegelianism, like, we may add, Spinozism, fails to recognize that God is a person with whom we interact by making him some kind of eternal principle operating in the world. By contrast, the medieval mind, so despised now, had a full sense of this, even if rather a childish one. People today may mock at the attempt to find some act of penance which should set them right with God, as though God was 'a pasha with three horsetails, whom such a thing could please' (POSTSCRIPT, 543).

But is it better to abolish God in such a way that he becomes a titular deity or a fussbudget who sits in heaven and cannot do anything, so no one notices him because his effect touches the single individual only through the solid bulk of intermediary causes, and the thrust therefore become an undetectable touch! Is it better to abolish God by having him decoyed into natural law and the necessary development of immanence! No, all respect for the penance of the Middle Ages and for what outside of Christianity is analogous to it, in which there is always the truth that the individual does not relate himself to the ideal through the generation or the state or the century or the market price of human beings in the city where he lives—that is, by these things he is prevented from relating himself to the ideal—but relates himself to it even though he errs in his understanding of it.... Because of the jumbling together with the idea of the state, of sociality, of community, and of society, God can no longer catch hold of the single individual. Even if God's wrath were ever so great, the punishment that is to fall upon the guilty one must make its way through all the courts of objectivity—in this way, with the most affable and most appreciative philosophical terminology, people have managed to smuggle God away. They are busy obtaining a truer and truer conception of God but seem to forget the first basic principle that one ought to fear God. An objective religious person in the objective human mass does not fear God; he does not hear him in the thunder, because that is a law of nature, and perhaps he is right. He does not see him in events, because they are the immanent necessity of cause and effect, and perhaps he is right. But what about the inwardness of being alone before God? Well, that is too little for him; he is not familiar with it, he who is on the way to accomplish the objective. (POSTSCRIPT, 543–4)

Hegelianism, moreover, attempts to identify thought and reality. Thus it claims that by pure thinking one can know how reality really is. But this identity of thought and its objects applies only to what Kierkegaard calls 'thought-objects'. (See POSTSCRIPT, 331.) Thus, as a novelist writes his novel, he creates characters who exist only as his, and eventually the reader's, thought-objects. We may say, then, that their being consists in their being thought. And so it is with abstract systems. A purely logical system may be designed, and up to a point was designed by Hegel, but its subject-matter is really just Hegel's and his followers' thought-objects. But the world does not consist of thought-objects, and if one's system is supposed to apply to the world, its evidence cannot be purely logical. Thus Euclidean three-dimensional forms have their own nature in the Euclidean system, and there are truths as to what there is (what can be constructed) on the basis of the axioms and definitions. But whether it applies to concrete reality is another question, as we have come to see in the twentieth century (the example is mine, not Kierkegaard's). That is the essential flaw in the Ontological Argument. (See POSTSCRIPT, 334.) It only shows that God necessarily exists as in an item in a metaphysical system. It does not reveal to us the reality of the living God.

In any case, the famous transitions in Hegel's system are not really always that convincing, and often stem from Hegel's own unacknowledged subjectivity. (For mockery of this, see POSTSCRIPT, 337–8.) The Hegelian will reply that all the matters of existing fact which Kierkegaard holds the system cannot deal with are there. Thinking is there, and so is acting, and so are Napoleon, probably Hegel, and perhaps Kierkegaard. Significantly, Jesus, as God incarnate, is there also. But they are there only as thought-objects, abstractions with only the properties which follow from their definition, and the system cannot tell us about them as concrete realities. Thus the system still fails to reach out to concrete existence. The good Samaritan might even occur there as a thought-object, but really good Samaritans are existing persons, not the abstractions of a metaphysical system.

However, so far as action goes, Kierkegaard wants to avoid going to the extreme (to which Sartre later went) of holding that all that matters ethically is overt action. For what matters is the intention of the action, not its results, and a genuine intention, only prevented from realization by physical infirmity, would be as ethically valuable as full action. But ethics is still concerned with concrete subjectivity, not with subjectivity as a thought-object in an intellectual system.

In the sense in which real decision can take place in subjectivity, and must always originate there, Kierkegaard insists that being a Christian is a matter of what one does, not what one believes. Christianity is not a doctrine. Thus, even if Hegelianism were true, and even if it coincided far more than it does with Christian doctrine, being a Hegelian would be a long way from being a Christian. Christianity is not a matter of what you believe, but of relating to God in fear and trembling and troubled love. (See POSTSCRIPT, 327 and 383.)

The objective interpretation of Christianity is responsible for the error and aberrance that by coming to know objectively what Christianity is (in the same way as a

research scholar, a learned person, finds it out by way of investigation, information, instruction) one becomes a Christian (who bases his happiness on the relation
to this historical knowledge). (POSTSCRIPT, 577)

The trouble with Hegelianism is that, just like the historical approach to
its claims, it does not recognize that Christianity is not a doctrine, but an
existence-communication. (See POSTSCRIPT, 379, 383, and *passim*.) Not
being a doctrine, it cannot be a stage in speculative philosophy, or a
form of it.

Objective faith—it is indeed as if Christianity had also been proclaimed as a little
system of sorts, although presumably not as good as the Hegelian system. It is as if
Christ—it is not my fault if I say it—as if Christ had been a professor and as if the
apostles had formed a little professional society of scholars. (POSTSCRIPT, 215)

It will be seen that Kierkegaard's critique of Hegelianism is appealing
here to much the same distinction as he had made in *Philosophical Fragments* between the realm of possibles, which is the only realm where there
is such a thing as necessity, and the realm of concrete reality. For Hegel's
system is supposed to be a sequence in which each item is necessarily
called for to redress the inadequacies of its predecessors. If Hegel were
merely dealing with concepts—that is, with the realm of possibles, and the
ideal relations between them—this would deserve consideration as a serious project. But Hegel thinks that he can pass from the sequence of
concepts (the so-called nature of God before the creation) to the actual
world, and lay bare the necessary sequence of concrete realities which
reflects the necessary sequence of concepts.

However, in *Postscript* there seems to be a slight shift in the view of the
realm of possibles from that in the *Fragments*. For in *Postscript* he speaks of
possibilities as abstractions from existing things (see p. 314.) This seems to
contrast with the doctrine of possibles and eternity in *Fragments*. For there,
possibles belonged to a realm with its own kind of reality, almost that of
Platonic Forms, rather than abstractions made by the human mind. Indeed, in *Fragments* there is a sense in which possibles are primary, while
existences are these possibles made actual (and thereby in a manner
changed).

However, this alteration in Kierkegaard's conception of the possible, if it
is one, does not make too much difference. It remains true, according to
Kierkegaard, that necessity only applies to possibles = essences = abstractions. Thus an exploration of possibles treated as an exploration of concrete reality is bound to miss the true character of the latter, and will see
only necessity where there is really freedom.

In this connection Kierkegaard makes the striking point that what we ordinarily call 'knowledge' of existing things, being conceptual, transforms them into possibles. So there is a sense in which one can never have conceptual knowledge of concrete realities. This applies with particular significance to our knowledge of other persons. We can only know about them by treating them as essences and thereby failing to register their inwardness and freedom.

The same is true of all historical facts. These can never be known as real living actualities. Moreover, it is only past historical events that we can know, and in knowing them, just as with other people, we cannot grasp them in their once living reality.

The only thing which we can know as a truly concrete reality is ourself as of now. For we are immediately aware of our own choosing, our own 'ethical actuality' (POSTSCRIPT, 316), which is the most basic fact about us. And it is just this to which the Hegelian seeks to close his eyes by identifying himself with some more or less tiny ingredient in the *Absolute Idea* unfolding itself in history.

It would seem to follow from this account of 'knowledge' that much of Kierkegaard's critique of Hegelianism is really a critique of any way of trying to understand concrete reality conceptually. For his point seems to be that all attempts to express the character of existing reality in conceptual thought are bound to distort it. Indeed, these remarks are not so far from a Bergsonian or Bradleyan claim about the limitations of conceptual thought in general.

Be that as it may, the *pure thought thinking itself* with which the Hegelian attempts to identify himself is a monstrous hybrid between the abstract and the concrete, the eternal and the actual. It is an attempt to get away from the fact that one is merely one particular finite thinker. (See POST-SCRIPT, 313.) The only 'I' the Hegelian acknowledges is a 'pure I', the same in all persons. But to suppose that one's thought is the activity of a pure I is an attempt to escape from the concrete world into the untroubled realm of pure essence or possibility. (See POSTSCRIPT, 317.)[21]

The speculative thinker will deny that the thinker is left out. He may even deny that he, this particular person born on a certain day and presently living in a certain town, is omitted. But this is only to say that he may make an appearance there as a pure possible, a concept. His actual concrete existence, as opposed to the idea of his existence, has no place in it and is, in bad faith, forgotten.

The fact is that speculative thinking is an attempt to have a God's-eye view of the whole world and of its development in time in one great synthetic glance. But this is the prerogative of God; to strive for such a vision oneself is an absurdity. One must deal with oneself and the world as one finds oneself in concrete experience, not attempt to be God. (See POSTSCRIPT, 301.) This self does indeed have an eternal aspect, but it is the eternal brought down to earth.

Precisely because abstract thinking is *sub specie aeterni*, it disregards the concrete, the temporal, the becoming of existence, and the difficult situation of the existing person because of his being composed of the eternal and the temporal situated in existence. (POSTSCRIPT, 301)

XVII On Becoming Subjective and Away from Objectivity

One only comes in sight, then, of religion if one eschews the so-called objective approach to it and faces up to what it is to be a finite subjective individual. The Hegelian or like-minded philosopher who seeks to understand things in a wholly objective manner can become a terrifying and insane figure.

Most people associate madness with a mind which is determined by its own subjective processes rather than by objective evidence. The person who thinks that he is Julius Caesar or imagines that he has magical powers is mad in a subjective way. It is because there can be subjective madness that people are worried about the concept of subjective truth. And certainly there *can* be subjective madness.

But one cannot escape madness by becoming purely objective. For example, someone seeking release from a lunatic asylum by repeating endlessly objective truths, such as that the world is round, only shows himself to be still a lunatic (see POSTSCRIPT, 195–6).

In any case, there is a much more terrible form of insane objectivity: that of pretending that one has no inwardness. Kierkegaard's main target is Hegelianism, but what he says is strikingly relevant to the position of those Anglo-American philosophers of today who deny the reality of their own consciousness as anything other than a computing process in the brain not essentially different from what occurs in an advanced computer.

This kind of insanity is more inhuman than the other. One shrinks from looking the first one in the eye, lest one discover the depth of his frantic state, but one does not dare to look at the other at all for fear of discovering that he does not have proper eyes but glass eyes and hair made from a floor mat, in short, that he is an artificial product. If one happens to meet a mentally deranged person of that sort, whose illness is simply that he has no mind, one listens to him in cold horror. One does not know whether one dares to believe that it is a human being with whom one is speaking, or perhaps a 'walking stick,' an artificial contrivance of Dobler that conceals in itself a barrel organ. To drink *Dus* with the executioners can indeed be unpleasant for a self-respecting man, but to get into a rational and speculative conversation with a walking stick—now that is almost enough to drive one crazy. (POSTSCRIPT, 196)

There are, in fact, certain questions which should *only* be approached subjectively. (See POSTSCRIPT, 165 ff.)

Among these questions are, says Kierkegaard,

What does it mean to die?

The objective thinker, asked what death is, will give a biological or a metaphysical answer, through which he quite fails to face up to the fact that he himself will die. Tolstoy's Ivan *Illytch* is, I suggest, an example of someone who only faced the question subjectively rather too late in the day.

What does it mean that I should thank God for the good that he gives me?

We do not do this by reciting a church formula but by intensely opening ourselves to the truth that we owe our existence and possibility of salvation to God alone, and not to ourselves.

What does it mean to marry?

An example of the objective approach to this question may be found in *Hard Times*, when Louisa Gradgrind asks her father whether she should marry Mr Bounderby (see book 1, chapter 15).

As for the big, less personal questions about which we think we would like to know the objective truth, we should bear in mind that, as existing spirits always in process of change, and whose thoughts are fleeting, we cannot grasp reality as it 'really' is by somehow reflecting it in our minds (see POSTSCRIPT, 192). That is something for God, not us. For us what is required is that we relate ourselves in an appropriate subjective manner to reality as we encounter it in our own personal experience.

To approach Christianity in an objective manner, as a doctrine whose claims are to be weighed carefully in the balance, and which is to be accepted for the nonce, until perhaps we find a way of 'going beyond it',[22] is to show oneself frightened of making a decision. This is no way to live our lives, prey to every historical or intellectual doubt.

But this is not the only thing which is wrong with the objective approach to religion and, more specifically, to Christianity. For, as we saw above, the engagement in speculative thought is a self-deceiving attempt to lose any sense of oneself as an existing person and to become pure thought thinking itself: that is, to follow the dialectical flow of concepts. (See POSTSCRIPT, 313–14.) In fact, if speculative thought were right, it would be a case more of *cogito ergo non sum* than *cogito ergo sum*. And, indeed, the speculative thinker, until some ethical decision forces itself on him, is not fully existing as a person.

[O]ne must be very cautious about becoming involved with a Hegelian and above all must ascertain who it is with whom one has the honor of speaking. Is he a human being, an existing human being? Is he himself *sub specie aeterni*, also when he sleeps, eats, blows his nose, and whatever else a human being does? Is he himself the pure I—I—something that certainly has never occurred to any philosopher, and if he is not that, then how does he, existing, relate himself to it, to the middle term, in which the ethical responsibility in and with and by existing is duly respected? Does he exist? And if he exists, is he not then in a process of becoming? And if he is in a process of becoming, is he not then related to the future? Does he never relate himself to the future in such a way that he acts? (POSTSCRIPT, 306; see also p. 404)

The modern attempt to dissolve oneself into pure thought may have appalling implications for future humanity. For one thing, it attempts to do without any confrontation with the either/or which must somehow be faced. (See POSTSCRIPT, 306–7.)

XVIII Original Sin Again and Children

In *Postscript* Kierkegaard engages further with the notion of original sin, on which we have touched in our account of *Fragments* (see section VII above). In fact, *Postscript* is soaked in this unattractive doctrine. God would love to exchange mutual love with us, but he cannot do so unless we are redeemed by the sacrifice of Christ and our faith in it. Kierkegaard constantly speaks as though our sinfulness was our own fault; but, venerable as the doctrine of original sin is, it is a weird view that we are guilty of sin without apparently any option in the matter, and that we must repent of it.[23]

It is not, indeed, to be denied that from the beginning of our life we are egotistical and insufficiently concerned with the welfare of others, or that, even if we are not villains, we all have some disreputable feelings and wishes. But surely it is inappropriate to blame us for this before we have had any chance to do anything about it. At any rate, Kierkegaard does not want Christianity to be thought of as something comfortable. On the contrary, to be Christian is really quite an ordeal, even though it is the only path to eternal happiness.

Indeed, Christianity is so disturbing that in its true form it may be best to keep a child in ignorance of it. (Is Kierkegaard perhaps criticizing the excessive piety in which he was brought up by his father?)

Christianity in its decisive form is not suitable for every age in life any more than Christianity entered into the world in the childhood of humankind but in the fullness of time. There are times in life that demand something that Christianity seemingly wants to omit altogether, something that to a person at a certain age appears to be the absolute, although in later life the same person sees its vanity. Christianity cannot be poured into a child, because it always holds true that every human being grasps only what he has use for, and the child has no decisive use for Christianity. As Christianity's entrance into the world indicates by what preceded it, the law is continually this: *No one begins with being Christian; each one becomes that in the fullness of time—if one becomes that.* A strict Christian upbringing in Christianity's decisive categories is a very venturesome undertaking, because Christianity makes men whose strength is in their weakness; but if a child is cowed into Christianity in its totally earnest form, it ordinarily makes a very unhappy youth. The rare exception is a stroke of luck.

The Christianity that is recited to a child or, rather, the Christianity the child himself puts together if no pressure is used to drive it existentially into decisive Christian categories, is actually not Christianity but idyllic mythology. It is the idea of childlikeness raised to the second power, and the relation is sometimes turned around so that it is the parents who learn from the child rather than the child who learns from the parents. It is turned around so that the child's lovable misunderstanding of the essentially Christian transfigures father love and mother love into a piety that nevertheless is not actually Christianity. There is no lack of examples of people who themselves have not previously been religiously moved but are now so moved by a child. But this piety is not the religiousness that should essentially belong to an adult, and the parents' religiousness should no more find its decisive expression in this piety than the mother herself is nourished by the milk that nature provides the child. Father love and mother love are so deeply attached to the child, surround it so tenderly, that the piety itself discovers, so to speak, what is indeed taught: that there must be a God who makes little children his own. But if this mood is the parents' entire religiousness, then they lack authentic religiousness and find their refreshment only in a sadness that indirectly sympathizes with being a child. This parental piety and the child's teachability and ease of understanding this blessedness are lovely and lovable, but it is not really Christianity. It is Christianity in the medium of fantasy-perception; it is a Christianity from which the terror has been removed: the *innocent* child is led to God or Christ. Is this

Christianity, the point of which is that it is the sinner who takes refuge in the paradox? (POSTSCRIPT, 590–1)

In speaking of the relation of children to Christianity, Kierkegaard criticizes the usual reading of 'Leave the small children alone and do not forbid them to come to me, for to such belongs the kingdom of heaven' (translation of Matt. 19: 13–15 as in Kierkegaard translation). (See POST-SCRIPT, 592 ff.). For Jesus, according to Kierkegaard, here and in the similar passage in Mark (10: 13–16) is not telling us that children are particularly ensured of entering the kingdom of heaven, but only that, to do so, adults must become like little children, something impossible for children them-selves to do, since things are not like themselves. Kierkegaard is not too clear in his own mind as to the way in which an adult must become like a little child in order to be saved. But one thing of which he is sure is that it does not mean that true Christianity is the kind of thing that children are typically taught. In fact, 'to gaze at the lovely, enchanting landscape of childhood is perdition' (POSTSCRIPT, 603). For the Christianity taught to little children is not genuine Christianity. It is suitable enough at their age, and indeed the painful rigours of true Christianity should not be inflicted on them, as it can have disastrous results (POSTSCRIPT, 589); but the cosy Christianity suitable for children is not the thoroughly painful Christianity to which we need to come as adults. Thus the idea of Christ 'as a friend of children à la Uncle Frank Goodman, or as a teacher at a charity school' (POSTSCRIPT, 588) has absolutely no place in the Christianity of an adult. Nor is the Christian able to think of children as the innocents which a mistaken reading of Jesus's saying is wrongly interpreted as depicting them.

It is beautiful and moving, and as it ought to be, that an old person feels his guilt upon seeing a child and sadly comprehends the child's innocence, but this mood is not decisively Christian. The sentimental view of the child's innocence forgets that Christianity does not acknowledge anything like that in fallen humankind, and that the qualitative dialectic defines the consciousness of sin as more explicit than all innocence. The rigorously Christian conception of the child as sinner cannot provide the period of childhood with any advantage, because the child has no consciousness of sin and therefore is a sinner without the consciousness of sin. (POSTSCRIPT, 591–2)

Kierkegaard certainly gives the impression that few of us will eventu-ally be 'saved'. We have mostly not done what we must do if we are to attain 'an eternal happiness'. But it is not too clear what the fate of the unsaved majority of us will be. Are we doomed to an 'eternal unhappiness'? (See POSTSCRIPT, 94, 369.) Kierkegaard, in this work at any rate, seems unclear about this; but I fear that he may have thought most men damned and destined for a dreadful fate after death. Yet the doctrine of original sin coheres awkwardly with Kierkegaard's insistence that the choice between good and evil is one which it is utterly up to each of us to make ourselves.

It is this gloom in which, like Pascal, he stands so opposed to Spinoza. And it is this aspect of Christianity which alienates so many people today.

The ethical immediately embraces the single individual with its requirement that he shall exist ethically; it does not bluster about millions and generations; it does not take humankind at random, any more than the police arrest humankind in general. The ethical deals with individual human beings and please note with each individual. . . . The ethical requires itself of every human being, and when it judges, it judges in turn every single individual; only a tyrant and a powerless man are satisfied with taking one out of ten. (POSTSCRIPT, 320)

We may return now to a question which arose in our discussion of *Fragments* (see section IX). Does Kierkegaard believe in the damnation of those who had no opportunity to relate to Jesus? The answer certainly seems to be 'Yes'. For he says that it is one of the grimmest paradoxes of Christianity that all will suffer perdition who have not related themselves in faith to the historical fact of the Incarnation in Palestine in 4 BC or whenever. Yet Kierkegaard either accepts this as a part of Christianity or makes his external but sympathetic observer of Christianity, Climacus, regard it as one of the paradoxes that the Christian must embrace. In this connection Climacus tells us that whereas more pantheistic types of religiousness (religiousness A) promote a feeling of sympathetic oneness with human beings at large, the Christian's sympathetic feelings must be limited to fellow Christians. Not, indeed, merely formally baptized Christians, but those who, like him, have embraced passionately the whole paradoxical contents of true Christianity, including this division of mankind into the sheep and the goats, where the goats seem even to include those whose position in time precludes their having been Christians. Kierkegaard thinks this indeed to be a horrific belief, but seems to regard its acceptance as part of the agony of being a Christian.

The happiness linked to a historical condition excludes all who are outside the condition, and among these are the countless ones who are excluded through no fault of their own but by the accidental circumstance that Christianity has not yet been proclaimed to them. (POSTSCRIPT, 582–3)

The believer expands the consciousness of sin to the whole race and at the same time does not know the whole race to be saved, inasmuch as the single individual's salvation indeed depends on his being brought into relation to that historical event, which precisely because it is historical cannot be everywhere at once but uses time in order to become known to human beings, during which time one generation after the other dies. . . . In Religiousness A, the sympathy is with all humankind, because it is related to the eternal, a relation of which every human being is assumed to be essentially capable, and because the eternal is everywhere, so that no time is spent in waiting or in sending a messenger for that which by being historical is prevented from being everywhere at once, and about whose having existence countless generations through no fault of their own could continue to be unaware.

To have one's existence qualified in this way is sharpened by pathos, both because it cannot be thought and because it is isolating. In other words, sin is no teaching or doctrine for thinkers. . . . *The pain of sympathy*, because the believer does not, as in *Religiousness* A, latently sympathize and cannot sympathize with every human being *qua* human being, but essentially only with Christians. (POSTSCRIPT, 584–5)

This recognition that it is partly luck which relates you to the saving redeeming moment gives one no right to feel superior to those born out of time.

Religiousness B is isolating, separating, is polemical. Only on this condition do I become blessed, and as I absolutely bind myself to it, I thereby exclude everyone else. This is the impetus of particularism in the ordinary pathos. Every Christian has pathos as in Religiousness A, and then this pathos of separation. This separation gives the Christian a certain likeness to a person who is happy by way of preferential treatment, and if a Christian selfishly perceives it as this, we have the desperate arrogation of predestination. (POSTSCRIPT, 582)

Climacus makes a great point that he is making it more difficult, not easier, to become a Christian. (See POSTSCRIPT, 381.) It is surely also true, as Kierkegaard perhaps admits in holding that religiousness goes beyond the ethical, that he makes it immoral to be so. Or is the idea that as God substituted a ram for Isaac at the last moment (in the key text of *Fear and Trembling*), so God does better at the last moment by those who have not related to the historical Christ (or even believed in God's incarnation at some other, or unidentified, historical moment)?

One becomes a sinner, according to Kierkegaard, in the very act of existing, and this is because until one has managed to develop a subjective *how* appropriate to the eternal, one is existing in untruth rather than truth, and the word for such living in 'untruth' is sin.

Let us now call the individual's untruth *sin*. Viewed eternally, he cannot be in sin or be presupposed to have been eternally in sin. Therefore, by coming into existence (for the beginning was that subjectivity is untruth), he becomes a sinner. He is not born as a sinner in the sense that he is presupposed to be a sinner before he is born, but he is born in sin and as a sinner. Indeed, we could call this *hereditary sin*. (POSTSCRIPT, 208)

What happens to the person who is not saved by relating properly to God, ideally by relating himself to the historical fact of the Incarnation? Kierkegaard hesitates somewhat to talk of hell, but there is a strong suggestion that eternal unhappiness is their lot. All in all, it rather looks as though Kierkegaard really did believe that all those—even those who did not have the chance—who have not related to Christ in history are cast out in darkness—or at the best annihilated. Though he cannot be said to have believed in predestination, since one can only be saved through one's own free choice, it seems that this will inevitably reflect one's state of original sin.

In order not to cause unrest by prompting any thought about an eternal unhappiness, I want to point out that I am speaking only of the positive, that the believer becomes sure of his eternal happiness in time by his relation to something historical. (POSTSCRIPT, 369)

For the believer it holds true that outside this condition [having the right subjective relation to the historical fact of the Incarnation] there is no eternal happiness, and for him it holds true, or it can come to hold true for him, that he must hate father and mother. Is it not the same as hating them if his eternal happiness is bound to a condition that he knows they do not accept? (POSTSCRIPT, 586)

XIX How Hard on the Ages before Jesus Christ: How does Kierkegaard Relate to Damnation?

Thus Kierkegaard seems to have believed that eternal happiness is open only to those who have faith in the paradox of the Incarnation (as a unique historical fact, *an eternal-becoming-of-the-deity*), and to have had some inclination to think that those who do not accept Christ as their Saviour are condemned to eternal unhappiness (whether it is Hell in a fire-and-brimstone sense or not). Certainly in *Works of Love* he says that 'Christianity discovered a danger called eternal damnation' (LOVE, 196).

Apart from objections one may feel to the idea of anyone being condemned to an eternal unhappiness, this, as has often been said, seems peculiarly unfair to those who lived before Jesus, or in places which Christianity has never reached. The best that traditional Catholic theology (as expressed superbly in all its nastiness in Dante's *Divine Comedy*) can do for the better among them is to provide them with a place somewhere between Heaven and Hell called 'Limbo', where they are bored rather than tormented. This is not very generous. In any case there is no mention of this by the Protestant Kierkegaard. Stop press: Pope Benedict XVI has just abolished Limbo.

Matters are somewhat improved by his holding that someone who really had faith that God had been incarnated in space and time somewhere and somewhen might reach eternal happiness. He would have found subjective truth even if not objective truth, much like the pagan worshipper of the idol. But the idea that, some exceptions like this apart, the fate of the non-Christian (and of many so-called Christians) is eternal unhappiness is a sad one. Kierkegaard is, indeed, particularly sad at the thought that the speculative philosopher who has never reached a genuinely inward Christian faith is likely to be damned. Does this put Hegel along with Himmler? (See POSTSCRIPT, 231–2.) Does Kierkegaard endorse the non-salvation of the sceptic which worried the old man whom Climacus met mourning at his son's grave that his son could not be with him in Heaven, in view of his scepticism when he died (see POSTSCRIPT, 236–8).

It is indeed just possible that Christianity is the truth; it is indeed just possible that someday there will be a judgment in which the separation will hinge on the relation of inwardness to Christianity. (POSTSCRIPT, 231)

While Climacus hesitated on this matter, the implication would seem to be that this is how the true Christian believes it to be, and that eternal happiness is open only to those who have related with deep inwardness to the historical Incarnation.

XX Is the Religious and Ethical Viewpoint of Kierkegaard/ Climacus Essentially Egotistical?

We have seen that Kierkegaard/Climacus often gives the impression that the proper motive for embracing Christianity is the chance it offers of an eternal happiness. To be a Christian is to take the risk of passionately holding to this faith, even though there is no adequate rational evidence for it. But is not this overriding concern for one's own eternal happiness a somewhat selfish motive, reasonable enough as one motive among others, but somewhat sickening if it is one's sole motive for living as a Christian? Does not all this emphasis on relating to an eternal happiness sound a wee bit egotistical? (See POSTSCRIPT, 392–3.)

Another disturbing feature of *Postscript* is its insistence on the impossibility of relating to the real inwardness of another human being, and that it is only in one's relation to God that one's own inwardness can come into play. For, as we saw above, the particular cannot be thought (except where it is by its own thinking of itself), therefore another person is an essence or possibility for me rather than an actuality—but faith gives me the actuality of 'the God' (see POSTSCRIPT, 326).

Does not this represent a somewhat solipsistic outlook on the world, or if not solipsistic, at least in a curious way egocentric?

For existing ethically, it is an advantageous preliminary study to learn that the individual human being stands alone. (POSTSCRIPT, 323)

The ethical grips the single individual and requires of him that he abstain from all observing, especially of the world and humankind, because the ethical as the internal cannot be observed by anyone standing outside. The ethical can be carried out only by the individual subject, who then is able to know what lives within him—the only actuality that does not become a possibility by being known and cannot be known only by being thought, since it is his own actuality, which he knew as thought-actuality, that is, as possibility, before it became actuality; whereas with regard to another's actuality he knew nothing about it before he, by coming to know it, thought it, that is, changed it into possibility. (POSTSCRIPT, 320–1)

Thus, since I cannot know another in his concrete actuality, there is no direct relation between subject and subject. When I seem to have understood another subject, his actuality is for me a 'possibility' 'thought-actuality', essence, or abstraction (see POSTSCRIPT, 321). It follows that if I do something to help him, it is not really for his sake as a concrete individual, but for the sake of the one concrete fact which takes me beyond myself, my experienced relation to God and his commands.

To me this seems the destruction of real altruism. But maybe we should not take Climacus's word, as that of a sympathetic observer of Christianity, for Kierkegaard's, as a committed Christian, on this matter. For maybe the former has not grasped the full inwardness of the latter! Besides, if this was Kierkegaard's view, he seems to have substantially qualified it not much later in *Works of Love* and elsewhere. Indeed, it looks rather like a *jeu d'esprit* rather than something to be taken quite seriously. However, there is still a trace of it in the insistence in *Works of Love* that it is always possible that what looks like bad behaviour would appear as good if only we could grasp the inwardness from which it sprang.

So let us look briefly at that work, which, exceptionally, is published under Kierkegaard's own name and which constitutes his most thorough discussion of ethics.

XXI *Works of Love*

The main thrust of *Works of Love* (1846; i.e. around two years after *Postscript*) is the necessity for the Christian to grow out of worldly self-love and embrace a life of suffering.[24] But whether the ultimate motive for doing so is the prospect of an eternal happiness beyond the grave is not too clear. Perhaps it is only for Climacus that this is the attraction of the Christianity he never quite accepts. Maybe once one has become a Christian, it is solely love of God which motivates one.

The Christian ideal of self-denial is: give up your self-loving desires and cravings, give up your self-seeking plans and purposes so that you truly work unselfishly for the good—and then, for that very reason, put up with being abominated almost as a criminal, insulted and ridiculed. (LOVE, 194)

Thus teachers of Christianity must avoid the slightest suggestion that a Christian life will make you happier in the here and now. Recommending Christianity as a cosy path to worldly happiness is the fault for which Kierkegaard increasingly chided the Danish church.

Works of Love is mainly devoted to an examination of Jesus's second great commandment, 'Love your neighbour as yourself'. Kierkegaard follows Kant in holding that the love in question cannot be a feeling, for one cannot be obliged to have a feeling, since this is not within one's control, as behaviour is.

What, then, is the love in question? Kierkegaard distinguishes three types of love: (1) erotic love; (2) love of friends; (3) Christian agapeistic love. It is only the third which is a duty, and for this reason, it alone is 'eternally secured against every change'. For both erotic love and friendship are liable to change if the loved person, as may always happen, changes and loses the features in virtue of which one loved them or if the temperament of the lover changes. One's duty to love, in contrast, cannot change, and is therefore a mode of behaviour, not of feeling.

Agapeistic love is directed equally at every human individual. It knows no preferences. But, one may wonder, if there is nothing special about the person in virtue of which one loves them, is this genuine love at all? Kierkegaard answers this by claiming that agapeistic love is a derivative of love for God, the one and only truly and eternally lovable individual. However, God has told us that the love which we owe to him as the only truly lovable being should be expressed in loving our neighbour, that is, every other human being. (See Philip L. Quinn, in COMPANION TO KIERKE-GAARD, 362.) Such love need not depend, therefore, on any special features possessed by its individual objects. What it does depend on, however, is the fact that every human being, however unprepossessing he or she may seem, bears at a deeper level the same mark of being God's special creation. So, with God's help, we should love all human beings equally as all equally bearing the divine imprint. Thus, when the differences of station in life and other features which are only the clothes in which the essential self is dressed up during this life are thought away,

then in each individual there continually glimmers that essential other, which is common to all, the eternal resemblance, the likeness. . . . If then, you should see the beggar—perhaps in your sorrow over him suffering more than he—you would still see in him the inner glory, the equality of the glory, that his wretched outer garment conceals. Yes, then you would see, wherever you turned your eye, the neighbor... In being king, beggar, rich man, poor man, male, female, etc., we are not like each other—therein we are indeed different. But in being the neighbor we are all unconditionally like each other. Dissimilarity is temporality's method of confusing that marks every human being differently, but the neighbor is eternity's mark,—on every human being. (LOVE, 88–9)

Kierkegaard, however, also emphasizes the need to see each person as an individual with his own distinctive nature, and not be concerned to require of him that he live according to precisely one's own ideas. (See LOVE, 270.)

All in all, Kierkegaard's interpretation of the commandment to love one's neighbour, as developed in *Works of Love*, does suggest a deeper way of relating to others than Climacus regards as possible. (But he often spoils things by the suggestion that in fact no human being really is very lovable.) Yet, one may well feel uneasy at some of what he says about true Christian love of one's neighbour.

For example, one may feel that in identifying love of one's neighbour with the effort to bring him to God, it reduces the requirement of self-sacrifice in a more mundane sense. (See, for example, LOVE, 136–8.) Thus it is implied that it is more important to teach the poor to show mercy than to help them by gifts of money (see pp. 321 ff.). In fact, it is a great gift to them to teach the poor to have mercy on the stingy rich.

Therefore we speak that language more correctly, we who say to the poor, the poorest of all: Oh, be merciful! Do not let the envious pettiness of this earthly existence finally corrupt you so that you could forget that you are able to be merciful, corrupt you so that a false shame would stifle the best in you! A false shame, yes, because the true shame comes first—would that it would always come—but in any case it ought to come with the money. If you acquire money and are able to give, then, only then do you have something to be ashamed about. Be merciful, be merciful toward the rich! Remember what you have in your power, while he has the money. . . . Oh be merciful! If the rich person is stingy and close-fisted, or even if he is close-fisted not only with money but just as stingy with words and repelling—then you be rich in mercifulness! (LOVE, 322–3)

Kierkegaard, in fact, saw no reason to reduce inequality, in the ordinary sense, in society. (See, for example, LOVE, 138.) What matters is to realize that we are all equal in the eyes of God, and under judgement for what we do with our own lives. Indeed, Kierkegaard seems to think that all that is sad in being poor is that one feels ashamed thereof, and argues that poor Christians have no need to feel this. The actual physical suffering involved in poverty seems hardly to have struck him.

The whole work (so it seems to me) is a strange mixture of subtly sensitive suggestions as to how we should relate to others and a somewhat morbid insistence on the thesis that in truly loving another we are very likely to make him or her hate us, because our concern will be not with their earthly fortune but with their spiritual improvement. This is how Kierkegaard interprets Jesus's strange (reported) remark that if we are to follow him we must hate our father and mother. (This remark seems rightly to have haunted him, for we have already found him referring to it in *Postscript*.)

To such a high point, to such madness, humanly speaking, Christianity can press the requirement if love is to be the fulfilling of the Law. Therefore it teaches that the Christian must, if it is required, be able to hate father and mother and sister and the beloved,—in the sense, I wonder, that he should actually hate them? Oh, far be this abomination from Christianity! But certainly it is in the sense that love, faithful and true love, divinely understood, must be regarded by the loved ones, the nearest and dearest ones, the contemporaries, as hate, because these refuse to understand what it is to love oneself, that it is to love God, and that to be loved is to be helped by another person to love God, whether or not the actual result is that the loving one submits to being hated. (LOVE, 108–9)

On the other hand, he is touching and instructive in his advice always to put the best interpretation possible on another's motives. (See LOVE, 218, 228, 234, 255.) Even if we are sometimes led astray by this, we will be the better for it ourselves than we would be as cynical 'realists' who always think the worst of people.

XXII We should Live the Religious Life without its being Clear from our Behaviour that we are Doing so

According to Climacus/Kierkegaard, religion is essentially a matter of deepening one's inward relation to God. That one is or is not doing this cannot be known from the outside. The Christian lives in the world, acting the part of a quite ordinary person, but all the time he is offering up all his activities to God. His absolute *telos* is the eternal happiness offered by God to those who relate appropriately to him, and to the fact of the Incarnation; nothing else matters to him. But he must not make others aware of his constant devotion to God; nor can he know whether others are similarly devoted. Since the religious life is lived incognito, it is difficult for one genuinely religious person to recognize another.

Related to this is the claim, which we mentioned above, that one can know only oneself as a concrete existing reality. Other people must be known only as fixed essences,—what Kierkegaard calls 'possibilities'. For when we relate to the particular by thought, we do not confront it as an actuality, and this is the only way we can relate to others, as opposed to relating to ourselves. (See POSTSCRIPT, 326 and 322.) The one exception again is God (mainly, I take it, as incarnated in Jesus), whom one can relate to in his concreteness through faith.

In so far as the religious person lives as an ordinary citizen enacting his status and its duties, he is relating himself to the ordinary values of the world. But his relation to them must be 'relative'; it is only to God that he must be related 'absolutely'. To be related relatively to the relative and absolutely to the absolute is the ideal; the former is something outward, the latter something inward. This requires that he constantly recall his total dependence on God, which Kierkegaard expresses as the fact that we 'are capable of nothing of ourselves'.

The individual does not cease to be a human being, does not take off the multitudinously compounded suit of finitude in order to put on the abstract attire of the monastery but he does not mediate between the absolute telos and the finite. In immediacy, the individual is firmly rooted in the finite; when resignation is convinced that the individual has the absolute orientation towards the absolute telos, everything is changed, the roots are cut. He lives in the finite, but he does not have his life in it. His life, like the life of another, has the diverse predicates of a human existence, but he is within them like the person who walks in a stranger's borrowed clothes. He is a stranger in the world of finitude, but he does not define his difference from *worldiness* by foreign dress (this is a contradiction, since with that he defines himself in a worldly way); he is incognito; but his incognito consists in looking just like everyone else. (POSTSCRIPT, 410)[25]

In this connection, Kierkegaard makes some comments upon monasticism. The monastics realized that what mattered was one's inner relation to God. However, they felt that this required a suitable external expression. So they wore special clothes and cut themselves off from the ordinary business of life, in order to commit themselves entirely to devotion to God. But this was to make of this devotion something external, rather than inward. In modern times the religious person must live in the world keeping his devotion to God something entirely internal.

It will be seen that Kierkegaard, or at least Climacus, was not of Wittgenstein's persuasion that an inward state must have a public expression.[26] For he seems to have thought that one's religious feeling should have no external manifestation at all. The Christian must behave in standard ways while inwardly being absolutely committed to his absolute *telos*. (See POSTSCRIPT, 408.)

Even if we reject, as I think we should, this Wittgensteinian idea, there is certainly something odd in the suggestion that being religious makes no difference to how one behaves publicly, provided one is not actually criminal (and even that is qualified, remember Kierkegaard on Abraham and Isaac). We must surely take Kierkegaard as making, in a rather exaggerated way, the point that the religious person does not give himself special airs and graces, after the fashion of the Pharisees. Nor does he make a great show of being a sinner who must repent, like some revivalists. (See POSTSCRIPT, 510–12.)

At one point Kierkegaard seems aware of the difficulty with the idea that being a Christian should make no difference to what one does outwardly. So in saying that the religious person lives outwardly just like anyone else, he explains that this does not of course include behaving criminally, but only behaving like an ordinarily respectable person. However, his form of awareness of what he is doing is quite different from that of the non-religious person. For whatever he does, he is associating it in his mind with his awareness of God. Thus, if he is performing some everyday business transaction, the others may be taking what they are doing very seriously, as really mattering. The religious person, however, is doing it because it is part of the pattern of life which he has agreed with God should be his way of being publicly in the world, and not something by which he puts any great store by for its own sake. And he will have a sense of the humour about what he is doing.[27] For others it is all important, but for him it is a kind of show life, irrelevant to what really matters, his relationship with God.[28] Or rather, it is all important for others unless they too are living the religious life similarly incognito.

Such is the view expressed under the name of Climacus, and probably Kierkegaard was then endorsing it. However, later, he very reasonably mocked the idea that one's Christian inwardness should in no way appear in one's behaviour. In fact, he was particularly scathing about the attempts of Danish pastors to remove all danger from the life of the modern Christian who might take

> seriously Christ's requirement of self-denial and the renunciation of worldly things, they have...wanted to do away with by endeavouring falsely to transform the Christian life into hidden inwardness, kept so carefully hidden that it does not become noticeable in one's life. One should be willing to deny oneself in hidden inwardness, to renounce the world, and all that is of the world but (for God's sake, shall I say?) one must not let it be observed. In this way, established Christendom becomes a collection of what one might call honorary Christians, in the same sense as one speaks of honorary doctors who get their degree without having to take an examination. (TRAINING, 246)

XXIII Bourgeois Christianity and Christian Suffering: Christianity Not Cosy

In sketching the character of what he conceives to be the true Christian life, Kierkegaard insists that it is one of great suffering. For intense suffering is the only path to eternal happiness, and is necessarily the character of the religious person's life. (This is especially emphasized in *Training*.)

Kierkegaard does not draw out the character of this suffering in detail, but presumably it consists largely in the constant self-denial for which being a Christian calls. It also includes the pain which one may feel at some of the features of Christian belief, such as the fact that it is so easy to fail to qualify for an eternal happiness, and even if one does qualify for it, pain at the thought of how many do not. There is also some pain in the 'crucifixion of the understanding' for which Christianity calls.[29] Above all, there is the sense of one's unworthiness, as a miserable sinner, of the love which God is so ready to give one, but which one continually rejects through one's failure adequately to repent and one's continued sinning (in thought, if not in deed).

Kierkegaard sums up the essence of Christian suffering as 'dying to the immediate'. However, this dying to the immediate is brought about especially by consciousness of guilt. (See POSTSCRIPT, 526.) For, as we have already seen, Kierkegaard believed that we are all guilty, and that our guilt separates us from God. However, we can only approach God and our eternal happiness by becoming intensely conscious of our guilt, and this is bound to make us suffer.

Kierkegaard distinguishes between the guilt which men may possess, or be aware of possessing, in the immediate mode—that is, in the aesthetic form of life. This is a matter of being guilty about particular things. It is the kind of guilt which is the concern of the magistrate. But the guilt which is religiously relevant is total guilt. It is guilt understood as what Kierkegaard calls a totality category. This total guilt may well become most obvious to us when we recognize ourselves as guilty of something in particular; but we are always in truth guilty, whatever we do. Indeed, according to Kierkegaard, the idea of guilt for something in particular only makes sense when it is seen as an instance of our ineradicably pervasive form of guilt. (See POST-SCRIPT, 529.) In fact, we can never be quits with guilt by any kind of punishment. (See POSTSCRIPT, 550.) On the other hand, the religious person is saved from despair by his hope for an eternal happiness, which he knows he can reach only through the suffering of constant repentance. For guilt consciousness in the full sense is bound up with the hope of eternal happiness, and the suffering which it knows is the only means to that. (See POSTSCRIPT, 540.) And here again we must distinguish the suffering characteristic of the religious life from the suffering of the ordinary man (viewing things from the so-called aesthetic standpoint), which he thinks a mere temporary disturbance in the even keel of his life. (See POSTSCRIPT, 447.)

In stressing the painful nature of the Christian life, Kierkegaard pours scorn on the cosy version of Christianity which he found typically expressed by the Lutheran pastors of the church in Denmark (and doubtless in other countries too at that time, as he would have seen it). (See POSTSCRIPT, 460 etc.)

Such worldly pastors try to present the spiritual trials of Christianity as something which belong only to the earlier stage of the Christian life, so that from now on the path of pleasure and the path of virtue gradually coincide. (See POSTSCRIPT, 403.) In contrast to the platitudes of such pastors, Climacus, as we have seen, is aiming to show how extremely difficult it is to be a Christian. (Climacus is making Christianity difficult here, as promised.) In fact, such pastors really just glorify 'bourgeois-philistinism' and do little better than mouth such saws as 'honesty is the best policy'. We are not far beyond the cosy Christmas Christianity which is appropriate enough for children.

The pastor who encourages people to think that religion will help people to be happy is badly misleading them as to the character of Christianity. 'Essentially, the religious address has [the task] of *uplifting through suffering*' (see POSTSCRIPT, 436). Thus the pastor should emphasize the fact that to be religious, one must suffer (see POSTSCRIPT, 439).

...if it is a pastor's task to comfort, then he also ought to know how, when necessary, to make the religious so difficult that it brings every insubordinate to his knees. (POSTSCRIPT, 482)

Just as for an existing person the highest principles of thinking can be demonstrated only negatively, and to want to demonstrate them positively promptly betrays that the demonstrator, insofar as he is indeed an existing person, is on the point of becoming fantastical—so also for an existing person the existence-relation to the absolute good can be defined only by the negative—the relation to an eternal happiness by suffering, just as the certitude of faith that relates itself to an eternal happiness is defined by uncertainty. If I remove the uncertainty in order to obtain an even higher certainty then I do not have a believer in humility, in fear and trembling, but an esthetic coxcomb, a devil of a fellow who, figuratively speaking, wants to fraternize with God but, strictly speaking, does not relate himself to God at all. Uncertainty is the sign, and certainty without it is the sign that one does not relate oneself to God. (POSTSCRIPT, 455)

Kierkegaard's ideal pastor is certainly gloomy, but he should also exhibit a certain sense of humour. (See POSTSCRIPT, 440.) Thus he should show his congregation how little misfortune matters by his laughter at it. (See POSTSCRIPT, 440.) For though suffering belongs essentially to the highest life, and the nobler we are, the more we will suffer, we may also enjoy laughing at the pointlessness of all ordinary forms of good and evil. (See POSTSCRIPT, 450.) However the main aim of the pastor should be to arm us for the dreadful trials which are essential features of the Christian life.

XXIV How Friendly is Kierkegaard's God?

Many react to such a highly impersonal conception of God as Spinoza's with dismay, because they want a personal God who can be their friend. And although Hegel's God may seem less distant from us than Spinoza's, inasmuch as it is through us that he is realizing himself, he is still not exactly a friend.

But if we want a friendly, loving God, it is only to a very limited extent, as I see it, that God, as Kierkegaard conceives him, would satisfy us.[30] For he is a terrible judge who will cast us out unless we grasp with a peculiarly strong passion that he has redeemed us by incarnating himself[31] and burdening himself with our sins. True, Kierkegaard praises God for his patience with our sins. (See POSTSCRIPT, 406.) But, as I see it, patience with those whose sinfulness at birth was not their own doing is no great deal.

XXV Concluding Remarks

The real challenges that we may take from Kierkegaard are the following.

First, is not all philosophical religion essentially like the religion of the man who could not find comfort in his own book—that is, to say essentially shallow, an occupation for professorial industry but not for the whole person?

Secondly, there is the point that the intellect is not an adequate tool for probing the true depths of reality and of our own self.

Thirdly, there is the more specifically Christian objection to the claim of philosophical religion that man can save himself by his own efforts.

Of these the two first are the more important from my point of view. Some of the philosophers I discuss in this book had no intention of being Christians as Kierkegaard understands this. If their philosophy is right, that sort of Christianity is wrong. But even from a non-Christian point of view, it is an arresting charge that philosophical religion is *essentially hollow*, and *demands of the intellect what it is incapable of giving.*

Notes

1. The full title-page of this reads (in translation) 'Philosophical Fragments or A Fragment of Philosophy by Johannes Climacus, Edited by S Kierkegaard', followed by the Lessing quotation.
2. At the end of *Postscript* (pp. 625–30) Kierkegaard appends 'A first and Last Explanation', in which he finally acknowledges his authorship of all the pseudonymous works and tells us that none can be identified with himself.
3. Climacus was also the imaginary author of an earlier, but only posthumously published, work of Kierkegaard called *De Omnibus Dubitandum Est.*
4. 'Commentator's Introduction' by Niels Thulstrup, in FRAGMENTS SWENSON, p. lxxxv.
5. Kierkegaard's references are simply to the following Platonic dialogues *Protagoras, Gorgias, Meno, Euthydemus*. The classic statement concerns Socrates' elicitation of the Pythagorean theorem from Meno's slave in the *Meno* and the *Phaedo*. See also *Theaetetus* §188.
6. For Kierkegaard on damnation, see at n. 11. Incidentally, Kierkegaard thought of Socrates as an existential thinker, and that it was Plato who was guilty of excessive objectivity. See POSTSCRIPT, 206.
7. On this topic, both in *Fragments* and *Postscript*, Kierkegaard is closer to doing philosophy of a standard academic type than anywhere else. Strongly influenced by Leibniz, it in fact develops a viewpoint given its finest expression by George Santayana in ESSENCE and MATTER.
8. I have changed 'follower' to 'disciple' in the translation, having taken advice from an expert.
9. Although in speaking of the need to think of Christ as though one were contemporary with his life on earth, he urges us to imagine how Jesus would have struck us then. (See esp. TRAINING, Part I.)

10. *Works of Love* (1847) is his exposition of what he thinks Jesus's instruction to love our neighbour as ourselves means. But in *Training* (p. 123) he says that 'Christ [is] infinitely more important than his teaching'.
11. Relevant passages may be found in POSTSCRIPT, 130, 231–2, 237–8.
12. Compare T. H. Green in quotation from 'Faith' in Ch. 5 below.
13. Kierkegaard is referring to one of the less attractive sayings attributed to Jesus. 'If anyone comes to me and does not hate his father and mother, wife and children, brothers and sisters, even his own life, he cannot be a disciple of mine' (Luke 14: 25–6, NEB). I am assured by a New Testament scholar that 'hate' is the right translation.
14. See LOVE, 230–1.
15. Compare the opening of Spinoza's *Emendation*, so similar and yet so different.
16. Some will think that much of what Kierkegaard says in this connection can be applied, so far as we think it well taken, to other philosophical approaches to religion: e.g. to Spinoza, on the one hand, and to some more recent defenders of Christianity, on the other, for example, Richard Swinburne. (Pascal would surely have agreed. I am not endorsing the point myself.)
17. I have adapted this to my own interpretative ends from a story told by Kierkegaard in DISCOURSES, 206–7. Indeed, I composed the story from a vague memory of Kierkegaard's story which I could not identify until Alastair Hannay found it for me.
18. 'Kierkegaard praised Feuerbach and David Friedrich Strauss for their repudiation of Christianity. He believed that "resolutely and definitely to have no religion at all is something passionate and that these two thinkers were to be praised for their forthright atheism."' I apologize to the commentator from whom this is quoted for having lost the reference.
19. For Hegel sin was an inevitable by-product of finitude; for Kierkegaard it was as much the consequence of an attempt to ape the infinitude of God. See THE CHRISTIAN RELIGION, editor's appendix, pp. 330–1.
20. HANNAY 1982, 94. See also ELROD.
21. It is perhaps worth remarking that Kierkegaard is sometimes guilty himself of talking as though 'subjectivity' were the name of a person.
22. 'Going further' or 'going beyond it' was 'an expression used by the Danish Hegelian H. L. Martensen in a review where he claimed that one should move forward from the methodological doubt of Descartes to Hegel and even beyond' (Introduction by Alastair Hannay to *Fear and Trembling*).
23. Kierkegaard's fullest account of original sin occurs in *The Concept of Anxiety*.
24. I have been guided on this paper especially by 'Kierkegaard's Christian Ethics' by Philip L. Quinn, in COMPANION TO KIERKEGAARD, 349–75.
25. Cf. *Fear and Trembling*, 67–70.
26. See ibid. 97 for some criticism of Hegel's putting the external higher than the internal.

27. This state is apparently religion A, rather than Christianity. If I follow Kierkegaard rightly, at the stage of religiousness A, humour is the form of one's relation to the formalities of the world and similar externalities; but once true Christianity is reached, with a more direct relation to the paradoxical in religion, the need for humour declines. See POSTSCRIPT, p. 531–2 footnote.

28. It is unclear how far the religious person keeps his humour at the situation to himself. At POSTSCRIPT, p. 509 Kierkegaard speaks of humour as the incognito of hidden inwardness. That implies that publicly he takes everything lightly, though actually he is deeply in earnest in so far as his real concern is his relation to God. He also emphasizes that the religious person does not let his humour at the situation be a form of pride.

29. When I was an undergraduate at Cambridge during the 1950s I went, for curiosity, to a meeting addressed by Billy Graham, and this is what in effect he asked of all of us students.

30. As an example of the unpleasantness of Kierkegaard's God, consider this. God became the historical person Jesus and paraded the world incognito. Then he blames people for not recognizing him as God, though he had done what he could to make this difficult. This is not my own comment on Christianity, for, as a Unitarian, I doubt that Jesus really did claim to be God, and even if he did, would he have blamed people so harshly for not recognizing this? See *Training*, the section called 'He will draw all', ii. 157–66. At p. 167 of the same work it is made clear that only those who have believed in him will be saved; presumably the others suffer perdition.

31. Kierkegaard does not invoke the doctrine of the Trinity in this connection.

Chapter 5

T. H. Green and the Eternal Consciousness

I Absolute Idealism

The various forms of absolute idealism which flourished in the English-speaking world at the turn of the nineteenth and twentieth century provide prime examples of metaphysicians who arrived at what can broadly be called a religious view of the world on the basis of metaphysical reasoning.

In this and the next two chapters I shall examine the thought of three of these absolute idealists with a view to the 'religious availability' of their philosophies. The first two, T. H. Green (1836–82) and Bernard Bosanquet (1848–1923), both belong to that school of British philosophy which broke away from the main empiricist tradition of their country and drew on German philosophy (as had hardly been true of any major British philosophers previously), in particular on Hegel (and to a lesser extent Kant).[1] The third, Josiah Royce (1855–1916), is the most important representative of the same philosophical movement in America. The most important British representative of this school was F. H. Bradley (1846–1924), but I am only considering his thought quite briefly in one section of the chapter on Bosanquet. A main reason for this is that Bosanquet has more to say about religion than Bradley, and is also undeservedly neglected, besides which I have already written on Bradley at length in my *James and Bradley: American Truth and British Reality*. Moreover, my own views, as expounded in Chapter 9, owe so much to his thought that Bradley may be thought of as making his entry there. I regret that lack of space and time has stopped me discussing the views of Edward Caird. Incidentally, I think that his brother John Caird's *An Introduction to the Philosophy of Religion* (1880) is one of the best books interpreting religion along idealist lines of which I know.

It has been said that the appeal of idealist philosophy at that particular juncture arose from the dismay felt by many at developments in science and biblical scholarship which were making it difficult for them to continue to believe in biblical accounts of the history of the world and the acts of Jesus. (The development of a spiritual interpretation of the world invulnerable to such threats was more an explicit goal of his philosophy on the part of T. H. Green than it was for the other two idealists whom I shall be studying.) And it is doubtless true that these philosophers helped such people by offering a religious view of the world which did not seem threatened in this way.[2] However, thinkers nowadays who suppose that this was the sole ground of their influence in their day have probably not seriously examined the purely philosophical force of their thought, perhaps because the mood of our own time makes them sure it must be all wrong.

Doubtless there are features of the idealism of that period which reflect Victorian needs and values which we may or may not have been the better for moving beyond. But there is as much reason to discount the logical positivism of 1930–50, or the philosophical materialism current from 1960 to the present (2005), as stemming from an emotional need to be rid of religion as from purely intellectual considerations. The serious thinker will attend to all arguments which have been put forward by figures of any intellectual pretensions and accept or dismiss them independently of how far their conclusions fit the mood of any particular time. That religious or philosophical opinions suited the emotional mood or needs of a particular past time is not of itself a reason for thinking them less of a serious option for all times than are ideas which suit the emotional atmosphere of our own time better.

All these absolute idealists, in their different ways, thought that ultimately Reality consists in one Eternal Mind, which Bosanquet and Royce and others called 'the Absolute' (following Hegel's use of the expression 'Absolute Idea') and which Green called the 'Eternal Consciousness'. Our minds are somehow included in this eternal being, and nature is *either* how the rest of it appears to us *or* exists only as perceived or conceived by mind at some level.

Thus these thinkers were exponents of very similar forms of absolute idealism, and there was much exchange of influence. Moreover, while they were certainly concerned to defend an essentially religious view of the world, they were quite various in their relation to Christianity. Even on the question of the existence of God, they had their differences, since some of them did, and some of them did not, identify the Absolute in which they believed with God. But this turns more on what they took to be implied by the word 'God' than what they believed about the Absolute. Of the thinkers whom I shall discuss or mention, Green, Royce, and Edward Caird found it appropriate to call the Absolute (or the Eternal Consciousness) 'God', while Bradley and Bosanquet did not.

As for their relation to Christianity, probably Green and Caird were closest to it, and Bradley and Bosanquet the furthest. But none of them provided quite what was wanted either by orthodox Christians or by anti-religious positivists. There are other Anglo-American absolute idealists also worthy of study with interestingly diverse relations to Christianity, but there is no room for an investigation of their work here.[3]

However all that may be, I myself think that they provide a by no means outmoded case for what in a very general sense may be called a religious interpretation of the world, and that, more generally, what they have to say about human beings and the world in which they find themselves has a value not merely historical. They do so more, in my opinion, than do such other major post-Kantian idealists as the Germans Fichte and Schelling. In fact, they provide the best purely philosophical case for a religious view of the world of any metaphysicians.

II T. H. Green

The initially leading figure among the absolute idealists who came to dominate British philosophy in the late nineteenth century was T. H. Green. He was a fellow of Balliol College, Oxford, and in 1878 was elected to the Whyte's Chair of Moral Philosophy.

Green's philosophy may be summed up in a much quoted passage (partially quoted already in Chapter 3 but worth quoting more fully here) from a review which he wrote of *Introduction to Philosophy of Religion* by John Caird (1880). Green is summing up what he thinks is living in the philosophy of Hegel:

That there is one spiritual self-conscious being, of which all that is real is the activity or expression; that we are related to this spiritual being, not merely as parts of the world which is its expression, but as partakers in some inchoate measure of the self-consciousness through which it at once constitutes and distinguishes itself from the world; that this participation is the source of morality and religion; this we take to be the vital truth which Hegel had to teach. (WORKS, iii. 146)

Not all would agree that that was what Hegel was teaching, but it was certainly Green's own quite stable opinion from early on in the development of his thought. In this he was much influenced by both Kant and Hegel, initially more by Hegel, later more by Kant. Thus he figures as possibly the main figure who introduced the influence of German idealist philosophy into Britain, and with it challenged the dominating empirical philosophy of our land.

In the case of Green, it is certain that his main aim was to save a religious view of the world from developments in natural science and biblical criticism which threatened traditional Christianity. The impact of Lyell's geology (with its implication that the earth was far older than the age it was thought to be on the basis of biblical analysis), of Darwinism (with its implication that there was no special creation of mankind, but that the race had developed by an evolutionary process powered mainly by natural selection), and of biblical critics like David Strauss (who had persuaded many that the miracles of Jesus and his resurrection, etc. could not be regarded as historical facts by serious students) all threatened orthodox Christian belief. What is more, these combined with the tradition of British empiricism, more especially in the person of Hume,[4] to suggest that the human race was simply one of the phenomena of nature whose existence and character arose from essentially the same sort of causal laws (even if not from precisely the same laws) as explained these. But Green thought that a demonstrable form of idealism could avoid all these pitfalls.

And it certainly was one of the appeals of Green's idealism to the considerable number of young men who fell under his influence in their Oxford days, and remained inspired by his thoughts throughout their lives, that it provided them with a form of Christianity which did not require them to ignore the development of science or challenges to the historical accuracy of the Gospels.

Nor did it only help those alienated from the Church to retain an essentially religious view of the world; it also helped some within the Church, such as Scott Holland and Charles Gore, to free their more orthodox Christianity from its fear of science and biblical scholarship. Moreover, these somewhat Greenian churchmen were also key figures in converting the Anglican Church to the kind of increased social concern which eventually led to the ideal of a welfare state and to an ethical and Christian socialism distinct from either the bureaucratic socialism of the Webbs or more Marxist types of socialism. (Key figures were Scott Holland and Charles Gore; see CARTER, chs. 4 and 5.)

Green died when he was 46, leaving his main philosophical work almost finished. It was published posthumously, edited by A. C. Bradley (1883). This was the *Prolegomena to Ethics*. But through his lecturing and published articles, his philosophical position was quite well known before then. Among those who were influenced by him was F. H. Bradley, who was an undergraduate when Green was a professor. (None the less, the whole tone of Bradley's philosophy was markedly different from that of Green, though less so in Bradley's first major work *Ethical Studies*, published 1876.) Thus Bradley's first important work preceded Green's in terms of publication, but the dissemination of Green's work was earlier.

III Green and Bosanquet

Bernard Bosanquet was also a student of Green's, and his philosophical approach is closer to his thought than is Bradley's. But there were important differences between them.

First, Bosanquet derived from Green's idea that the goal of the state should be to make its citizens *better* people rather than more *happy* people in a hedonistic sense a harshness in his attitude to the poor which was quite alien to Green. For Green always insisted that a reasonable standard of living was necessary for people to be capable of being fully moral beings.

Secondly, Bosanquet had at least a tendency to deify the state in a manner which brought him closer to Hegel than was Green. For, while rejecting the kind of social atomism for which the state was simply a policeman to control the rivalries of individuals each seeking a purely private good, and arguing that there was a common good for all, Green had no tendency to ascribe a value to the state which was not realized in the value of the lives of individual citizens.

[T[here can be nothing in a nation however exalted its mission, or in a society, however perfectly organised, which is not in the persons composing the nation or the society. Our ultimate standard of worth is an ideal of *personal* worth. All other values are relative to value for, of, or in a person. To speak of any progress or improvement or development of a nation or society or mankind, except as relative to some greater worth of persons, is to use words without meaning. (PROLEGOMENA, §184)

IV Green and the Welfare State

Green can be credited with considerable influence on political and social reform. H. H. Asquith had been a student of his, and it was under Green's influence that he approved collective action in the interests of promoting so-called positive freedom, rather than merely protecting so-called negative freedom. He can also be seen as having had some influence on the development of the welfare state in so far as that incorporated the idea that the state should act positively to promote the good of its citizens. Among those who regarded themselves as followers of Green, the social reformer and prophet of adult education, Arnold Toynbee, deserves especial mention. And although he did not come up to Balliol until two years after Green's death, it seems that R. H. Tawney was quite strongly influenced by Green's thought as mediated to him by Edward Caird (then Master of Balliol) and the continuing influence of Green's thought in the general intellectual atmosphere. (See WEMPE, 163, 265, and CARTER, ch. 6.)

V Grounds of Green's Idealism: Background

I turn now to Green's technical metaphysical position.

One might have expected philosophically idealist Christians to have looked to Bishop George Berkeley as someone who claimed to have proved the existence of God on their shared principles.[5] For Berkeley's argument is actually very powerful. However, its influence was slight. And of course Berkeley knew nothing of the threats to religion which were to come from geology, biology, and the higher criticism. (However, he was aware of the threat from Deism, of which his *Alciphron* is a critique.) At any rate, Green owed nothing to Berkeley, and almost everything to his study of Kant and Hegel. My purpose, in my discussion of each of the philosophers given centre stage in this book is not, however, to trace their place in the progression of philosophical ideas, but to attempt to understand how their philosophy purported to establish the truth of some kind of theism, or at any rate of a view of reality as somehow essentially spiritual, and then to ask whether what they offered, whether validly established or not, was religiously relevant.

Green sought to establish that the existence and nature of human beings, and more especially of the human mind, was not susceptible of a purely empirical or scientific (in the popular sense of the word) explanation. He claimed, instead, that the only possible explanation involved reference to the existence of an Eternal Consciousness which was gradually realizing itself in the temporal (as opposed to the eternal) world, more especially in the life of human beings. The chief argument for this was the impossibility of treating ordinary empirical knowledge of the natural world as itself a natural phenomenon.

The individual finite mind is, in fact, an emanation (not Green's own expression) from the Eternal Mind, or Consciousness, which is ever seeking to realize itself not just in divine isolation but by living its life in humans. And the human organism is the medium through which it seeks to realize itself, not just in eternity but in time. Thus Green's concept of a human being is dualism of a special kind. The human mind (which is somehow identical with the Eternal Consciousness or at least an emanation thereof), acts through the human body, which is part of a physical world which exists only for the Eternal Mind and us emanations of it.

[A human being], then, is a certain reproduction of itself on the part of the eternal self-conscious subject of the world—a reproduction of itself to which it makes the processes of animal life organic, and which is qualified and limited by the nature of those processes, but which is so far essentially a reproduction of the one subject, implied in the existence of the world, that the product carries with it under all its limitations and qualifications, the characteristic of being an object to itself. It is the particular human self or person, we hold, thus constituted, that in every moral action, virtuous or vicious, presents to itself some possible state or achievement of its own as for the time its greatest good, and acts for the sake of that good. (PROLEGOMENA, §99)

In reaching this conclusion, Green makes use of three claims about the nature of relations. (a) Relations between things must always be the work of a mind which is aware of them. This, he says, has been generally recognized by philosophers. While this may be an exaggeration, it is true of quite a lot of historical philosophers. (b) The character of the constituents of the physical world is wholly a matter of the relations in which they stand to each other. (c) These relations are unchanging. It will be worth clearing up just what is meant here before we enter into his argument for his idealist position in further detail.

There is something odd in the claim that the relations between the constituents of the natural world are unchanging—indeed, it seems quite obviously untrue, at least if these constituents are supposed to be continuants, that is, things in the ordinary sense. (A continuant is something which exists over time, like any ordinary physical thing, rather than stretched out in time, like an event such as the reign of Henry VIII.[6]) Once this fallen leaf was here, and now the wind has blown it there. Once I was taller than my son, now my son is taller than me—there is no question of unchanging relations here. My copy of Green's *Prolegomena to Ethics* is sometimes on the same table as my copy of Bradley's *Ethical Studies*, and sometimes it is not—thus the spatial relations between them frequently change.

On the other hand, the event of my first reading *Prolegomena* and first reading *Ethical Studies* are eternally in the same order of earlier and later, and there is no possibility of change in their relations to each other. We must conclude that when Green says that the natural world consists of things in unalterable relations to each other, he must be thinking of events rather than continuants. And there does seem some justice in saying that if we regard the natural world as made up of events, rather than continuants, then its constituents may reasonably be said to be 'unchanging'.

For what we call the real natural world is, so it is not unreasonable to claim, distinguished from illusions and fictions by the fact that the relations between the events which make up its history are unchanging. In contrast, Red Riding Hood sometimes escapes from the wolf before he devours her, sometimes she is cut out of the wolf's stomach unharmed, while sometimes his eating her is the end of her. Similarly, Dickens made various changes in his novels as planned: e.g. giving *Great Expectations* a more hopeful ending in the published version than in the story as originally intended and in the development of Walter in *Dombey and Son*. In contrast, there is only one correct account of the series of events which constituted the life of Napoleon, and only one correct account of the early years of the earth's history, whatever that may have been.[7] Human beings rightly admit to ignorance on an enormous number of things about the natural world, but they do not admit that there are alternative mutually inconsistent truths about it. And the fact that there is only one truth about the natural world can be expressed as the statement that it consists of events standing in unchanging relations to each other—for example, that of the various battles won and lost by Napoleon.

VI Green's Implicit Event Ontology

I suggest, then, that Green thinks of the world as consisting not so much of continuants—that is, of enduring but changing things, like trees or persons—as of events, a series of which constitute the 'life' and 'adventures' of such things. Whether events or continuants are the more basic constituents of the world—that is, whether the world is best described as a world of events or as a world of changing but self-identical things—has divided philosophers to quite an extent since the end of the nineteenth century. Process philosophers, such as A. N. Whitehead and Charles Hartshorne, think that events are the more basic, while the analytic philosophers P. F. Strawson and Jonathan Bennett think that continuants are.

Now this alternative was not (so far as I know) one which was much before the minds of philosophers at the time of Green or earlier. It is true that there was division over the status of minds in this respect. Hume had claimed that the self or mind was simply a series of impressions and ideas—that is to say, of events—while Joseph Butler and Thomas Reid thought that it was a thing, that is, a continuant. But, as a more general issue, the contrast between events and continuants was not much noticed, though implicitly it seems that some philosophers may have thought more in the terms of one, some more in terms of the other.

Certainly Green did not raise this issue explicitly. But I am forced to think that he was tacitly conceiving the world as a world of events. For otherwise his key principle was quite obviously false.

If this is not why Green speaks of unchanging relations, then I am baffled as to what he meant. The idea is, it seems, that there is just one (enormously complex) true story about the history of nature, and in this story every event is once and for all in a definite relation to every other event. By contrast, take any traditional oft repeated fictitious story and, as we just saw, the relations between the various events tend to vary, while the events in true factual accounts do not.

Theories about how natural phenomena operate are, indeed, different from mere narratives. The former concern laws of nature, the latter concern the history of individuals or the series of events said to constitute their lives. Now if Green had been talking about the laws of nature as unchanging relations, then he could have combined that with an ontology of continuants, rather than events, but it would not have allowed him to talk of the relations between all real things as unchanging.

He could, indeed, have spoken more circumspectly of what is unchanging about things (continuants) as being such that what they most essentially are or were at any particular time cannot change. Maybe this is what he was really thinking, but if so, he certainly did not spell it out for us. And actually I have noticed that he does more frequently talk about events than things.

So I suggest that he was making the quite reasonable claim that our way of understanding the world is to assume that there is one single (immensely complex) story about its development over time, and that this story cannot change. (A question hovers here, however, as to whether it does not change by having fresh chunks of process added to it as time moves on. On this hangs the whole question of whether the future is genuinely open or not. See below.) We may like to add to this claim about the unchanging character of the true story of the world's history: that it is governed by eternally unchanging laws.

Then his basic claim is that knowledge about anything consists in finding how it fits into this world story and with the laws that eternally govern it. Of course, we never know the whole story, but the acquisition of knowledge consists in becoming aware of more and more of it, and dismissing things once believed in which cannot be fitted into it.

VII The Human Mind is not Merely Something in the Story but is Part of the Story-Teller

According to Green, then, we are bound to take it that everything that happens (human action apart, see below) fits into this law-governed story. But what is impossible, he claims, is that our partial knowledge of it can be a part of that story. And since we do possess some such knowledge, it follows that there is something important about us which exists outside the story (and which is therefore outside space and time): namely, our knowing something of the story.

Reflecting on this, it seemed to Green that these claims can be explained only by postulating the existence of an Eternal Consciousness to which the *physical* or *natural* world and the *human mind* are quite differently related. Physical nature exists only as the object of the Eternal Consciousness, while a human mind is the Eternal Consciousness itself, obviously not in its completeness, but as bringing itself into the natural world at a certain time and place (not, indeed, as there in the sense in which natural events are there, but as viewing the world from that perspective). And in virtue of this, human actions, as determined on by the human mind, are not open to naturalistic explanation, and at least in that sense are free. (See WORKS, ii. 95.)

As such, the human mind shares in what Green calls the 'self-distinguishing' character which the Eternal Consciousness makes between itself and the world which it creates by thinking it. However, it may do this more or less explicitly, and in the latter case it is tempted to regard itself as a mere natural phenomenon whose explanation lies within the scope of natural science. But in characterizing itself to itself as much like a machine, it tries to evade moral responsibility for what it does and to indulge itself in a form of life suitable only for beasts. (The naturalistic ideas of which Green was offering this critique covered the empirical account of mind given by Hume and other similar thinkers, as well as the beginnings of an evolutionary account of how it was what it is. The former was not a physicalist view in the full modern sense, but it was in a broad sense naturalistic.) Thus Green, in effect, claimed that naturalistic treatments of the human mind are in 'bad faith' in a manner somewhat like Sartre's claim that the *For Itself* (*Pour Soi*) is continuously trying to absolve itself from the responsibility of its own freedom by pretending to itself that it belongs to the realm of the *In Itself* (*En Soi*).

This likeness to Sartre should be qualified by noting that Sartre would think that explaining one's behaviour by reference to one's character is in bad faith, just as is a more mechanistic type of explanation. For character is not a cause of action, but a description of its freely chosen nature.[8] Still, I think there is some similarity. It's hard to say whether Green was a psychological determinist or not. He was certainly not a physical determinist.

VIII The Case for Green's Idealism in More Detail

A more detailed account is perhaps necessary of Green's view (a) of the non-natural character of the human mind and (b) of the necessity of postulating an Eternal Consciousness as the ultimate basis of things.

(a) Non-natural Character of the Human Mind

To know about anything which happens over a period of time is to understand the character of certain events, and how they relate, especially how they relate temporally, to one another. The bit of history in question may be a long one such as a historian seeks to discover, or it may only be the little history of what the thinker himself (or herself—oh heavens have I got to add this every time?) has done over the last hour. In either case we know something of the filling of a certain stretch of time, within a certain space. Let us represent the little history of the thinker's life over that hour by ABCDEFGHIJKLM. Now if this knowledge becomes conscious in a thought occurring at time N, it seems that the thought somehow hovers over a time previous to, and longer than N. But if it is no more than an event occurring at N, how can it do this? Only, thinks Green, if the thought is more than a mere event in time, but is somehow one with an eternal act of knowing on the part of something out of time: namely, the Eternal Consciousness.

Really Green should have distinguished between cases where one learns only indirectly of the occurrence of a series of events and the case where one would describe oneself as having experienced the series oneself. If one listens to a symphony, then, if one has been attentive, one may be said to have experienced that symphony, as one has not experienced a great many of the historical phenomena which one has learnt of more indirectly. But one could not have personally experienced the series of sounds if one's experience had been confined to a single moment. And here another distinction should have been made between the whole symphony which one heard bit by bit, and the ultimate bits which one experienced as unified units, just as one does the spatial spread of a visual phenomenon.

The notion of the specious present, which has long been called in to help us with this kind of thing, was, I take it, unknown to Green. His concern was as to how one can experience any phenomenon spread over time, but he did not distinguish between the case where it is experienced within a single specious present from the case where it is experienced in a series of such presents. And perhaps he did not distinguish this precisely from a historical episode of some duration which one heard or read about without directly experiencing any part of it oneself. Besides which, he certainly owed us some account of the nature of memory.

We need not insist on these distinctions here, and thereby seek to improve on a certain vagueness which I think pertains to Green's own position. So let us concentrate on Green's essential message, which is that events in nature happen one after another, but there is no real unity to them across time: when one happens, its predecessors have ceased to be. We must say the same even of experiences *qua* mere temporal events. For a series of experiences, a b c d e f g is not of itself the experience, or consciousness, of the series.

By contrast, such a series of events can somehow be present to a consciousness in a unified manner such as cannot pertain to the series itself. This consciousness must then be something other than that series, something not confined to any one time, but which somehow hovers over the fleeting phenomena of the natural world and is aware of them as a unity which they cannot constitute of themselves. This consciousness cannot, then, concludes Green, be an event in time in anything like the same sense. Thus the mind itself must have something timeless about it. And as such it is not a merely natural phenomenon like those of the physical world.

Green is dealing with real issues here, but he treats them somewhat vaguely. If I tried to reformulate them in a way which I found satisfactory, I would wander too far from Green. As Green sees it, then (and here he is especially following Kant, who, it must be said, was pretty obscure on this sort of thing himself), mind can somehow be present to a series of temporally successive events in time, which (but only because it is not itself in time, at any rate in the same sense) it can synthesize into a unity. This synthesizing capacity is not an event in time, and therefore it cannot be explained empirically or scientifically, since this mode of explanation is concerned exclusively with what occurs in time (or consists in laws governing what thus occurs).

(b) The Natural World as a Story Spun by an Eternal Consciousness

So the human mind is not explicable in naturalistic terms, seeing that it brings together what is not together in nature: in particular, events distant in time from each other. But what of this vast natural world which mind finds itself in the midst of?

Green thinks it demonstrable that it can only exist as an object for a cosmic consciousness. His reasoning is somewhat as follows.

1. Relations are 'the work of mind' as almost all philosophers agree. For things can only stand in relation to each other by being synthesized into unity by a synthesizing mind. And this (we may add), if true, is as true of events as of continuants.
2. What we mean by the natural world is entirely a matter of things, or rather events, in unchanging relations to each other.
3. But the synthesizing activity in virtue of which things are mutually related cannot be that of purely human minds, since we have every reason to think that the natural world contains more than human beings are aware of.
4. It must therefore exist as cognized by a cosmic mind which knows it through and through.
5. And since the whole history of the world cannot be an event occurring at one moment in time, it can be known as a unity only by a cosmic mind which hovers over it from outside time and whose thoughts are not temporal events.
6. And since the world can exist only as cognized by that mind, that mind is its cause and creator.

235

7. But our more limited minds must also be somehow distinct from any temporal process, since we too synthesize events into unities which cannot exist at any particular moment in time. Thus our incomplete knowledge of the history of the natural world can only be such little bits of this cosmic mind's awareness of the whole story of that world as it (the cosmic mind) has decided to share with us. It cannot consist merely in thoughts which occur at particular moments of time, but must itself somehow exist outside time.

Green normally refers to this cosmic mind as 'the Eternal Consciousness', though sometimes as 'God'. For clearly he thinks this to be the concept of God to which an adequate metaphysics leads us.

I once heard a very distinguished American philosopher of our own day express an admiration for Green as having drawn a deduction from the widespread view that relations are the work of the mind. But how sensible is this view? If I look at a cup, I may notice that it is blue and that it is of a certain shape. Is its possession of these characteristics a creation of the human mind? Quite a number of thinkers would say that this was true of its colour, but not of its shape, though many would deny this. If I now notice that the cup is ON a saucer, is there any more or less reason to think that this relational fact is the work of mind than the fact about its colour and shape? It's at least not obvious why of all the things we perceive around us, relations are to be especially suspected of being mind-dependent.

It is true that whereas each of the cup and the saucer is an object which we can attend to separately, there seems a difficulty in just contemplating ON. But, however this may be, relational facts such as that the cup is on the saucer seem just as sensibly evident as the characteristics of the cup and the saucer considered separately.

Well, I do in fact think that there is a special problem, hinted at here, about relations, and I have in fact written about it quite extensively myself. But so far as Green is concerned, one can hardly say that the point is sufficiently argued. However, his argument that it can only be for mind that events belonging to different times can be brought together as part of a history is more persuasive. For it is problematic how a mind supposedly stuck in one position in time can relate what exists at that time to what existed at other times, and is therefore commonly thought to have ceased to exist.

All these problems will be considered again in connection with the philosophers discussed in later chapters.

IX Green's Psychology and Ethics

Green's ethics is based largely on his psychological theory. According to this, behaviour is caused by desire, and desire is the result of one's character as operative in present circumstances. But this is not determinism, if that implies any lack of self-determination. For my character is simply what I presently am. Moreover, it can be part of my character that I successfully change it for the better or the worse with the passage of time.

The general form of desire is parallel to that of the thought through which I cognize the world of facts. Such thought is no mere compound of sensations and images. Rather is it a creative response to my sensations, past and present, through which I constitute a world of objects for myself, a world from which I distinguish myself as its knower rather than as part of it. Such objects can only be presented to a mind which passes beyond its sensations to an object to which it attributes them. They are not parts of my thought, but they can only exist as presented to thought. (Not specifically to my thought, for, as we have seen, in fact they are objects for an Eternal Consciousness which it has decided to share with me.)

It is quite similar with the desire which is the cause of human action proper. It is no mere compound of impulses produced by my body or external things acting on it. Nor is it simply the last impulse to grab the reins, as Hobbes supposed. Rather is it a creative response to these impulses (of which an animal is incapable) which selects those which are to contribute to the formation of desire proper, such as will produce properly human action. And just as the human mind changes sensations into the presentation of an external object from which it distinguishes itself, so it changes (as an animal mind cannot) the objects of mere impulses into ideal objects[9] in which one hopes to find a personal satisfaction but from which one similarly distinguishes oneself. (But how one's desires relate to the goals of the Eternal Consciousness is quite problematic.) And as one develops one's active powers, the object in question will be envisaged as belonging to a unitary personal ideal.

Green makes two terminological proposals here. First, if the mere impulses are to be called 'desires', it can only be in a different sense from the morally imputable desire which is the cause of human action proper. Secondly, the desire which is the cause of human action proper may be called 'will', rather than desire, if we prefer. But Green thinks it better not to do so. For 'will' typically refers to something effortful, calling for resistance to the solicitations of contrary impulses, whereas the desire which causes morally imputable action may or may not be effortful in this way.

Green's psychology is usually regarded as a form of psychological egoism. For, as we have just seen, he holds that desire is always for an object in which one hopes to find personal satisfaction. Green thinks this an undeniable truth which we can learn from introspection.

[I]n all conduct to which moral predicates are applicable a man is an object to himself; that such conduct, equally whether virtuous or vicious, expresses a motive consisting in an idea of personal good, which the man seeks to realise by action; and that the presentation of such an idea is not explicable by any series of events in time, but implies the action of an eternal consciousness which makes the processes of animal life organic to a particular reproduction of itself in man. (PROLEGOMENA, §115; see also §§154, 156, 158)

But this satisfaction is not, typically, either pleasure or exemption from pain.

Thus he strongly dissociates himself from hedonistic psychology. And he uses against it an argument from Bishop Butler. (See PROLEGOMENA, §161.) The psychological hedonist, said Butler, misinterprets the fact that achievement of a goal at which I aim will always, *ceteris paribus*, give me pleasure. But this turns only on the fact that pleasure consists in obtaining what one sought; consequently, there could be no pleasure at all unless one had desires for something else. Butler is wrong, I think, in holding that all pleasure is of this sort, but some of it is, and this fits awkwardly with a purely hedonistic psychology. At any rate, Green is satisfied that it has been refuted by Butler.

But I wonder whether Green is not himself a victim of a similar fallacy to that which he and Butler attribute to psychological hedonism. Do I really only seek objects (or, better, attempt to bring about states of affairs) because I expect them to give me satisfaction, or some kind of personal good? Is it not, rather, that I find them satisfying, if I do, because that is what I wanted to bring about? (Such satisfaction does, of course, require my awareness that what I sought to bring about has occurred, but it is not the mental state of such awareness which I am aiming to bring about.)

It is true that I may often seek that in which I expect to find personal satisfaction, but it is neither obvious nor, I suggest, even true that this is always so. The most obvious exception is the arrangements people make in their wills, out of concern for the future of those they love, without necessarily expecting to witness that future personally.

Green tries to explain this by saying that either (1) we believe in an other world from which we hope to follow events in this one, or (2) that we project ourselves into the future beyond our death.

But this hardly meets the objection. For people who disbelieve in a life after death still make wills and other arrangements for the welfare of their family, etc. Nor does it seem plausible to say that this is simply because they have not adequately grasped what their total extinction would imply.

So Green's high-minded form of psychological egoism seems inadequate to the facts. There is also a doubt in my mind as to whether Green's notion of personal satisfaction does not stand for something not far from what J. S. Mill would call a 'high quality pleasure'. This doubt makes it difficult for me to come to any definite conclusion about the value of Green's ethical views. However, Green would have none of that. (See §§160 and 167.)

Even if it were the case, however, that self-satisfaction was more attainable than it is, and the pleasure of success to the man who has 'spurned delights and lived laborious days' really admitted of being set against the pleasure missed in the process, it would none the less be mere confusion to treat this pleasure of success as the desired object, in the realisation of which the man seeks to satisfy himself. A man may seek to satisfy himself with pleasure, but the pleasure of self-satisfaction can never be that with which he seeks to satisfy himself. This is equally true of the voluptuary and of the saint. (PROLEGOMENA, §160; see also §167)

Even if Green is wrong on such matters, his distinction between impulses which arise from bodily need or other natural causes and desire proper (or will) which causes properly human action deserves attention.

These [bodily] wants, with the sequent impulses, must be distinguished from the consciousness of wanted objects, and from the effort to give reality to the objects thus present in consciousness as wanted, no less than sensations of sight and hearing have to be distinguished from the consciousness of objects to which those sensations are conceived to be related.... In like manner the transition from mere want to consciousness of a wanted object, from the impulse to satisfy the want to an effort for realization of the idea of the wanted object, implies the presence of the want to a subject which distinguishes itself from it and is constant throughout successive stages of the want. (PROLEGOMENA, §85)

Even at the lowest level of human motivation, properly human desire is quite different from mere animal impulse.

Whereas in perceptive experience the sensible object carries its reality with it—in being presented at all, is presented as real, though the nature of its reality may remain to be discovered—in practice the wanted object is one to which real existence has yet to be given. This latter point, it is true, is one which language is apt to disguise. The food which I am said to want, the treasure on which I have set my heart, are already in existence. But, strictly speaking, the objects which in these cases I present to myself as wanted, are the eating of the food, the acquisition of the treasure; and as long as I want them, these exist for me only as ideas which I am striving to realise, as something I would might be but which is not. (PROLEGOMENA, §86)

This contrast with mere impulse holds even when the object of desire is merely the satisfaction of a physical appetite. For

it is contended that such appetite or want does not constitute a motive proper, does not move to any distinctively human action, except as itself determined by a principle of other than natural origin. It only becomes a motive, so far as upon the want there supervenes the presentation of the want by a self-conscious subject to himself, and with it the idea of a self-satisfaction to be attained in the filling of the want. (PROLEGOMENA, §88)

But the contrast is still clearer where something more elevated is desired than the satisfaction of a physical appetite. And the highest and most rational motivation for action is desire for one's own moral improvement as that in which, alone, one can find true satisfaction. For the goal of a person who knows wherein alone true personal satisfaction consists is his own moral perfectioning.

[R]egarding the good generically as that which satisfies desire, but considering the objects we desire to be by no means necessarily pleasures, we shall naturally distinguish the moral good as that which satisfies the desire of a moral agent, or that in which a moral agent can find the satisfaction of himself which he necessarily seeks. The true good we shall understand in the same way. It is an end in which the effort of a moral agent can really find rest. (PROLEGOMENA, §171)

But what is this end? It is the seeking of our good—so far as we really understand ourselves—as a good including the good of others. This is quite distinct from any form of mutual aid found among animals. For it is an interest in others as ends in themselves (such as I know myself to be). As such, it is not a concern for their happiness, in any hedonistic sense, such as a balance of pleasure over pain, but with their self-perfection as bound up with my own self-perfection. (See, e.g., §§236 and 315.) However, Green does sometimes speak of the satisfaction which such virtue alone provides as the only true 'happiness'. Is happiness in this sense compatible with absolute misery? If the answer is negative, there seems to be a chink left open for some form of the 'higher hedonism' here.

Personally, I see no reason why concern with others, or for social reform, has always and necessarily to be mediated by a concern with the sort of person one is becoming oneself, though doubtless it very often is. Be this as it may, Green associates it with altruism, by arguing that one cannot intelligently aim at the perfection of oneself except as something to be achieved in company with the self-perfection of other people too. And this movement towards perfection of each in unison with others can take place only in a society in which certain rules of morality or law are recognized as authoritative, that is, as the work of reason.

The idea, then, of a possible well-being of himself, that shall not pass away with this, that, or the other pleasure; and relation to some group of persons whose well-being he takes to be as his own, and in whom he is interested in being interested in himself—these two things must condition the life of anyone who is to be a creator or sustainer either of law or of that prior authoritative custom out of which law arises. Without them there might be instruments of law and custom; intelligent co-operating subjects of law and custom there could not be. They are conditions at once of might being so exercised that it can be recognised as having right, and of that recognition itself. It is in this sense that the old language is justified, which speaks of Reason as the parent of Law. Reason is the self-objectifying consciousness. It constitutes, as we have seen, the capability in man of seeking an absolute good and of conceiving this good as common to others with himself: and it is this capability which alone renders him a possible author and a self-submitting subject of law. (PROLEGOMENA, §203)

And this vision of a movement towards one's own perfection in unison with the increasing perfection of others provides us with the idea of a 'common good' in the pursuit of which all can unite: namely, the development of a society which provides the means for all persons to achieve an increasing approximation to 'perfection' (or even perhaps its achievement in some 'far off divine event') and in which each of us finds satisfaction in the satisfaction of others.

Our idea of this common good must remain imprecise for now, for to grasp it in any fullness requires an advance on human nature as it stands at present. (See §§171–9, pp. 179–88, and §§194–8, pp. 204–8.) However, we do have some sense of what changes in our life bring us nearer to it, and thus it is not a complete blank. It lies in the direction of being ever freer of merely carnal desires, and thus increasingly both altruistic and ascetic.

And limited as our own knowledge is of the ideally perfected humanity to which we are moving—moving, that is, through the efforts of moral self-denying human beings (not just asymptotically, but towards a kind of omega point in which time will be merged with eternity)—we are justified in assuming that there is such a *summum bonum* towards which the Eternal Consciousness is slowly steering humanity in the course of history. Not that each human being's perfection will be of the same kind. Probably the difference between the sexes points towards a different type of perfection, and some difference in position and power may also do so, though the perfection will not be less in one case than in another. (See §191.) Likewise, Green claims that the social reformer and the 'saintly recluse', who seeks moral purity in a life removed from involvement with the world, can be equals in moral perfection. (See §§303 and 309.)[10]

But how did a properly moral will develop in humanity? Green concurs with the view that probably the earliest approach to a genuinely moral attitude and way of life took the form of a sense of duty to one's family and of its welfare as one's own true good. (See §240.) This could never have originated in merely impulsive or instinctive life. Something new appeared on the scene when there were beings who distinguished themselves from their mere impulses and were motivated by a desire for a permanent satisfaction. And gradually this developed into a concern with a wider set of human fellows, only turning quite recently into a concern for other human beings simply as human beings. And this is not for any thinking person, whether they articulate their thought on the matter clearly or not, a concern that they should have as much pleasure as possible, but that both they themselves and other men should fulfil their full potentialities for excellence, however limited their conception of what these are. (I don't think that Green really faced the question of whether some men may be such that their fullest satisfaction must be in something which he would regard as altogether immoral.)

Did Green believe that human beings descended from animals? His attitude seems to have been that it was a plausible hypothesis not yet proved. He was quite easy in any case with the idea (just like that of the second great theorist of evolution, Alfred Wallace) that at a certain stage of animal evolution the Eternal Consciousness adopted, and therefore radically changed, certain ape-like creatures to become sharers of its thoughts and intentions (not just its objects, as in the case of other animals).

Of a moral development in this sense we have evidence in the result; and we can understand the principle of it; but the stages in the process by which the principle thus unfolds itself remain obscure. As has been already pointed out, such an end as provision for the maintenance of a family, if pursued not instinctively but with consciousness of the end pursued, implies in the person pursuing it a motive quite different from desire either for an imagined pleasure or for relief from want. It implies the thought of a possibly permanent satisfaction, and an effort to attain that satisfaction in the satisfaction of others. Here is already a moral and spiritual, as distinct from an animal or merely natural, interest—an interest in an object which only thought constitutes, an interest in bringing about something that should be, as distinct from desire to feel again a pleasure already felt. But to be actuated by such an interest does not necessarily imply any reflection on its nature; and hence in men under its influence there need not be any conception of a moral as other than a material good. Food and drink, warmth and clothing, may still seem to them to be the only good things which they desire for themselves or for others....

[But] if that interest, even in the form of interest in the mere provision for the material support of a family, were duly reflected upon, those who were influenced by it must have become aware that they had objects independent of the gratification of their animal nature; and, having become aware of this, they could not fail with more or less distinctness to conceive that permanent welfare of the family, which it was their great object to promote, as consisting, at any rate among other things, in the continuance in others of an interest like their own; in other words, as consisting in the propagation of virtue. (PROLEGOMENA, §242)

This gives a sense of the goal of human life more true to our real feelings (thinks Green) than does the psychological hedonism for which our ultimate desire is to maximize our own pleasure and minimize our own pain.

With his negative view of hedonism, I don't think Green would have thought much of the comparatively leisured life of workers today. He was even doubtful as to how far reforms which he had personally supported were not doing more harm than good, inasmuch as they promoted pleasure rather than morality. The following reported remarks of his are of interest in this connection.

Looking back upon this period from the time after 1874 ... [Green] once said to me, 'We held our heads too high during Gladstone's ministry. We thought the working-classes had made much more moral progress than they really had.' Explaining this, he dwelt with great disappointment on the use made by the workers of their half-holidays and their shorter hours. He even said that it was better they should not have a half-holiday, but should be set constantly at their work, so that they should not have time to drink. With regard to the agricultural labourers, he said that they had behaved very wrongly, doing wanton injury to the farmers by suddenly striking in the midst of harvest in hay-time, with the very object of causing the farmers loss. (Letter from C. A. Fyffe to R. L. Nettleship, Balliol College Library; quoted in RICHTER, 328–9)

As he develops his attack on hedonism, Green finds himself able to say something a little more positive about the ideal to which society should be (and under the guidance of the Eternal Consciousness eventually will be) moving as men continue the task of self-perfection.

And his message is the rather charming one that 'the only true good is to be good' (see PROLEGOMENA, §244). So the ultimate goal of human effort is a society of good persons permanently encouraging each other to live up to the standards this requires. Such is the common good which we all are, if lagardly, working towards. And the way in which we seek to be good, when we are at our best, is essentially non-competitive, since it is our aim to help others to be good as much as to be good ourselves. (Compare Spinoza, E4p37.)[11]

In book IV Green discusses at some length the contrast between moral judgement based on the intended consequences of action and that based on their motivation. The real moral quality of an act is a matter of its motivation, on whether it was done in purity of heart out of concern with the moral ideal of a holy will (to use Kant's expression) working for its own perfection and that of others. Green is confident, however, that every action done out of purity of heart will finally have better consequences than one done from a motive less lofty than that of aspiration to moral goodness in oneself and others.

Besides which, when it is the actions of others which are in question, we can only know the intention of the agent, not his true motive. It is only our own motives which are open to us. And knowing what these are requires a degree of introspective scrutiny which is not always for the best.

Thus Green shared Kant's idea that the good will was the one thing needful. But, unlike Kant, he did not think that the good will had always to be motivated by respect for the moral law as such, though he shared Kant's view of each individual as being an end in him or herself. For Green, anyone who satisfies himself in his activity as a good workman, a good father, a good citizen, with no selfish motive, is a prime example of the good will.

Somewhat in this connection Green raises the question whether there may come a time when there is no work of reform necessary, and consequently no labour for 'the holy will' to engage in. However, as long as man has an animal aspect to him, and remains liable to fall below the highest standards of feeling and behaviour, he must always abase himself before the perfection of the divine consciousness. And this time must last as long as the Eternal Consciousness chooses to realize itself temporarily in an animal form. The difference may be that while the social reformer is doing something which, as a will towards human perfection, serves partly as a means, though it is certainly also an end in itself, the value of the holy will of the ideal man of the future will be finally simply an end in itself. In short there may be more call for saints and less call for social reformers. (See PROLEGOMENA, §303, as quoted below.)

To such questions as why the Eternal Spirit does this and other things, Green's answer is that philosophy can only say how the world is, not why it is.

X A Problem about Animals

The psychology of animals, according to Green, cannot be used to explain the origins of human psychology. For it is a chief feature of our psychology that we have thoughts about, and desires for, objects which we sharply distinguish from ourselves, and it is very doubtful that this is true of any animals. (It may not even be true of the most primitive men, in which case our mental processes cannot be explained as a more developed form of theirs. See PROLEGOMENA, §204.)

It must be said that animals are problematic on Green's view of things, just as they are for the in some ways surprisingly similar viewpoint of Sartre. For Sartre the world divides into *for itself* and *in itself*. But the status of animals on this division is somewhat unclear. Surely they *are for themselves*, but equally they can hardly suffer from *bad faith*, something Sartre thinks endemic to the *for itself*.

Green quite similarly divides the world of finite things into (1) those which actually participate in the divine subjectivity and (2) those which exist only as objects for the Eternal Consciousness without participating in it. Since Green evidently thinks that animal minds cannot belong to the first class, because they lack the power to distinguish themselves from their impulses, he must think that they belong to the second class, as mere objects of, so to speak, the gaze of the Eternal Consciousness, and derivatively ourselves. But this is tantamount to saying that they have no subjective experience of their own.

He does, indeed, speak of animals as having feelings. (See book II, ch. 11, §§119–20.) But he denies (with some hesitation about some higher animals) that they can have either desires in the sense in which human activity is the result of desires or thoughts of the kind essential to being aware of the world as something distinct from oneself.

The truth seems to be that the logic of Green's position is that animals exist only in the way of non-sentient things (that is, as mere objects for a mind conscious of them), but that inconsistently, though wisely, he draws back from denying them any kind of subjective experience at all. At any rate, his clear purpose is to lump them in with the rest of the non-human natural world, as only there as a background in which the Eternal Consciousness can work out its purposes through moral agents.

XI The Eternal Consciousness and Human Responsibility

Many readers of Green, including myself, find it quite problematic how we are supposed to conceive the relation of the finite mind to the Eternal Consciousness.

It does not seem that finite minds are literally components within the Eternal Consciousness, as they are for F. H. Bradley and Josiah Royce, for example. It seems, rather, that we are something which the Eternal Consciousness has ejected from itself into time. Yet this suggests a more distant relation than that in which Green would appear to believe. For we are beings in whom 'an animal nature is the vehicle through which the divine self-realizing spirit works' (PROLEGOMENA, §302; see also §180).

There is also a problem which many people feel as to Green's views on free will. Are all my actions ultimately the actions of the Eternal Consciousness in the process of its self-actualization in time? How then can I be to blame personally for anything bad which I have done? Moreover, if it was the work of the Eternal Consciousness, presumably it is ultimately for the good (however little it may look like it). It is all very well to say that since the cause of my actions was my character operating in current circumstances, and that since I am, at any moment, my character, the action was self-caused. For my character too must have been produced by the Eternal Consciousness for its own purposes. The most obvious solution is to say that I do have a distinct reality of my own which can refuse to do what the Eternal Consciousness intends. But that seems incompatible with the idea that 'there is one spiritual self-conscious being, of which all that is real is the activity or expression'. This sort of problem bedevils Absolute Idealism, and in the chapter on Josiah Royce I shall be paying more attention to it, and on my own account in Chapter 9.

The problem here (so I believe) is associated with a profound vagueness in Green as to the nature of time and the openness or otherwise of the future. Is the Eternal Consciousness, from its own point of view, as opposed to ours, only gradually realizing itself in natural and human history, or does it realize itself in the whole of time (past, present, and future from my point of view 'now') in one eternal act?

The issue may be clarified with the aid of a distinction which J. E. M. McTaggart made between three ways in which the order of events in time may be conceived, or rather two ways and a third non-temporal way which he thinks is how they are really arranged. (See MCTAGGART, ch. 23.)

McTaggart distinguishes three different series in this connection: the A series, the B series, and the C series. Each of the three series has the same members in the same order, but ordered on a different principle.

The A series consists of moments of time (= sets of contemporary events) arranged as past or future to different degrees, or as present. The B series consists of such moments of time arranged on the basis of the relation of *earlier and later than* to each other. The crucial thing to realize is that the A series changes in a sense in which the B series does not. For if it is once true that the death of Nelson, for example, was earlier than the death of Winston Churchill, it is always true, while there has been a change in how these belong to the A series. For once Nelson's death was present, and Churchill's future, but later Churchill's death was present and Nelson's past. Thus, while the order of the events remains the same, the properties of each member which put them in that order changes.

McTaggart argued that unless the A series was real, there was no such thing as time as we ordinarily conceive it. For time requires change, and the B series does not change. But he also thought that there was something incoherent about the notion of the A series, from which he reasonably concluded that the distinction between past, present, and future is an illusion. He argued further that the B series could be defined only by reference to the A series, and that therefore, granted that the A series was an illusion, so must be the B series. However, there must be some reality which we misapprehend as a temporal series, and this he called the C series. We need not worry about precisely what he thought this last series was, and may simply understand by the C series the reality which appears to us as the arrangement of events in time, whatever that reality may be.

Our question now is whether the Eternal Consciousness (as conceived by Green) views moments of time as (1) constituting an A series (and a B series only as following from this) or (2) as a B series (but not an A series). (Leave aside for the moment the C series.) If the former, it must always be aware of one moment of time as PRESENT and all other moments as PAST or FUTURE, but which moment answers to which of these A-type temporal predicates will be in constant change. If the latter, it must view them as arranged statically in a B series, without there being any distinction between past, present, and future moments of time. Which is Green's view is quite unclear to me.

However, if McTaggart is right that the B series makes sense only if defined in terms of the A series, then the second alternative is not a real one. Drop the A series, and you must also drop the B series, according to him. The real alternative to the reality of the A series is not the B series (minus the A series) but the C series (minus both A and B series). However, this would be *much more like* viewing them as forming only a B series and not an A series, since the C series is supposed to have the same static quality as the B series. So we need not worry here too much about the distinction between the B and C series.

Now if there is a real A series for the Eternal Consciousness, it is an agent in time much as we think of ourselves as being. For it will be feeding us finite consciousnesses at every moment with fresh doses of its own reality. On the other hand, if, for the Eternal Consciousness, there is only the C series, then the idea of its gradually inserting itself into the world of space and time cannot be the real truth of the matter. If it is in some sense the creator of the world, its creation is not a temporal affair, but it must create all things in one eternal act.

Closely related to this issue is the question as to whether the future is genuinely open. Surely it can be so only if the A series is real. For if all moments of time are just eternally there, the idea of an open future is misconceived.

McTaggart, indeed, does not especially associate the idea of the A series with the idea of an *open* future, but as simply the idea that future events shift from futurity, to presentness, and then to increasing degrees of pastness. However, the view that the future is open requires that there really is no such thing as the future, but that as the present sinks into the past, a set of events which had no being at all until then come into existence as, for the moment, present.

If the reader is not familiar with McTaggart's treatment of time, and the substantial philosophical literature which has arisen around it, he may find this section rather hard to follow. So as a last attempt I shall sum up the issue like this: Does the Eternal Reality actualize itself in natural and human history in one fell swoop of creation covering all time, or does it do so gradually, bit by bit?

It is often supposed that if we humans are really morally responsible for anything, the second alternative must be true. For it is usually assumed that if the future is eternally settled, no one can be blamed for anything. However, I doubt that this is true. For Green can only allow for moral responsibility if some of the Eternal Consciousness's decisions are really our own free choices, and it seems to me that this can be true whether our choices occur in a genuinely temporal process or just stand there eternally, each in its own place in reality, but genuinely and freely causative of other bits of that reality. Still, probably most people think that without the A series and an open future, moral responsibility is an illusion.

But in the end, which view of time is taken may not much affect the issue of how we can be morally responsible if Green's Eternal Consciousness exists. For if, ultimately, it is the Eternal Consciousness's decision to act through each of us just as it does, and if this is always ultimately for the good, then it may well seem that all evil actions are always in the long run for the good. Perhaps I may still be wicked, but my wickedness will (if Green is right, or so it would seem) be something which the universe needed for its perfection. Many people find a view of this type disturbing.

XII Comparison of Virtue Ethics and Utilitarianism

In the last three chapters of Part IV of his *Prolegomena* Green compares his virtue ethics with utilitarianism both as a private ethic and as a basis for social reform.

The Positive Contribution of Utilitarianism to Reform

Utilitarianism in ethics and politics is Green's second great enemy, the first being naturalistic accounts of human nature and knowledge. However, he credits utilitarianism with some real achievements, and is much more generous to it than, for example, Bradley was in his *Ethical Studies*, partly because Bradley had much less interest in social reform than Green did, and it is in this that, for Green, its main merit has lain.

In this connection, he says that up till 'now' utilitarianism has on the whole done more good than harm. This is because it has taught men to appreciate that every human being matters as much as every other, and this has been a great gain. (See PROLEGOMENA, §332.)

Thus it has certainly contributed to the improvement of human life in Britain, especially in its remedying some of the worst features of poverty. But its task was now done, and the 'present' need is for a philosophy which has a higher notion of the goal of reform than that of maximizing human pleasure and minimizing human pain: namely, of moving towards a society in which people may become more virtuous. And despite all fallings back, what men are always seeking is to become morally better, rather than to be happier in a hedonistic sense.

Utilitarianism has no Concept of the Good or Bad Will

Moreover, utilitarianism is deeply wrong in its main ideas, and is liable to become increasingly harmful so long as it dominates social and ethical thinking. Green's hostility to the psychological hedonism on which he thinks its ethics rests, above all, stemmed from his belief that it provided no ground for distinguishing the good will from the bad will. For, in either case, so the theory claims, a man's good is always the same, the obtaining of pleasure and avoiding of pain.

Green takes little account of the work of his close friend Henry Sidgwick in divorcing utilitarian ethics from hedonistic psychology. In any case, such a divorce cannot avoid the main difficulties of a utilitarian ethic.[12]

Incidentally, as I noted above, Green seems never to realize that his own rather lofty form of psychological egoism, according to which all human action is directed at a goal in which the agent seeks his satisfaction, may be thought open to the same charge. This is doubtless because he thinks he is explaining what it is to have an end in view, not describing the ends men actually do have in view. But it cannot be said that Green is very clear on this point.

The Utilitarian Criterion of Right and Wrong is Incoherent

According to Green, the utilitarian ideal of maximizing pleasure is mean-ingless.[13] For the so-called maximum of pleasure is nothing which could ever be achieved. One reason for this is that this maximum is something spread over time rather than something ever really enjoyed. Likewise, satisfaction in pleasure is satisfaction in something inherently transitory. Virtue on the other hand, so Green thought, or at least some move towards it, can be achieved in a temporally more unified manner (see PROLEGOMENA, §§227–8).[14]

His argument here is at best obscure, as Sidgwick contended against him.[15] Surely virtue is a pattern taking place over time, and no more something to be achieved at some particular moment than is a maximum of pleasure. And in any case, since mind is supposed by Green, as one of his main arguments against a naturalistic account of it, to synthesize events spread out in time, why should it not do so with pleasure?

Green is on stronger ground when he claims that the idea of maximizing pleasure and minimizing pain runs up against the problem that no degree of success can be regarded as having produced the maximum of pleasure and minimum of pain. This is especially obvious in the case of pleasure.

For from one point of view there could always have been more pleasure produced, while from another, the maximization is always reached in any case in virtue of human psychology. Moreover, a maximization of pleasure for oneself or for people in general can never really be an aim in whose achievement people could find satisfaction.

Rather oddly, perhaps, Green thinks that hedonistic utilitarianism poses no threat to the standard morality of the day, for it is evident that, upon the whole, obedience to this standard is both in the individual's and in society's hedonistic interests. But in those tricky cases where standard morality does not tell us what, according to its principles, is right, or when we feel confident that in a certain case breaking away from it may be desirable, utilitarianism is likely to guide us into bad self-indulgent decisions. (See PROLEGOMENA, §338 also §276.)

Green, by the way, pays little or no attention to the utilitarian conception of the minimization of pain as a goal equally, or perhaps more, important than the maximization of pleasure. This is because his own ethic is entirely focused on the ideal we should set before ourselves (seeing what is bad as merely what hinders achievement of the good). This, I suggest, is a weakness in his approach to utilitarianism, though it is true that utilitarianism itself has a problem in balancing the maximization of pleasure and the prevention or reduction of pain.

XIII The Superiority of Virtue Ethics

So far as one seeks for an intellectual answer, rather than a more intuitive one (which can often be our best guide) to practical questions as to how to act, Green's view is that one must be guided by some ideal of human perfection and consider which of alternative actions will bring one nearer to it. And Green claims (as against utilitarians who think that they provide a practical test of right and wrong as no other theory does) that the ethics of virtue which he favours gives answers at least as definite as those of utilitarianism, though there are indeed difficulties in living the life of true virtue which Green explores painfully in *Prolegomena*, book IV.

Thus the individual who recognizes that all that really matters is the perfectioning of human beings can mostly judge whether he is becoming a more or less perfect person by the decisions which he makes in life. And this means that he is at least achieving something when he acts on this basis. So though the ethics of perfection cannot grind out answers to practical questions automatically, we can see the general direction in which the search for perfection must look, for it is revealed in history.

Green, like the utilitarian, thinks that much of the time the common morality of our time and place must be our guide. For it is the product so far of the ideal which has mostly actuated those who are attempting to be good. All the same, departure from it may occasionally be right, but only if it is for the sake of promoting human virtue. Special pleading in justification of such a departure must always be free of any tincture of hedonic advantage for oneself.

For most men their ideal is associated with the idea of God as setting the ideal for us and as judging how far we are living up to it. In its naïver forms the philosopher cannot support this as actual truth, though it is a helpful imaginative aid to the moral life. But the truth behind this imagination is that an Eternal Consciousness (which is related to us quite differently from that in which any human authority can be) is working through us and all things to produce a human race moving gradually nearer and nearer to perfection. Moreover, it has vouchsafed us some guidance as to what human perfection would be in the person of Jesus. Though the mature mind cannot accept the supernatural side of the Gospel stories, they give us enough sense of what he must have been like for him to play this role. (See §§317–20.)

XIV From Aristotle to Christianity

Green turns now (§§246–85)to the historical development of the idea of personal goodness or virtue. His investigation is, in effect, a comparison of the ancient Greek view of virtue, as developed most fully by Plato and Aristotle, with the more mature conception of it brought to us by Christianity.

Plato and Aristotle really said the last word about the formal character of virtue. This was that it consisted in the fullest possible realization of the individual's own potentialities in association with the similar realization of the potentialities of others. This was the 'great principle that the direction of a man's will to the highest possible realization of his faculties is the common good of every form of true virtue'. This conclusion will never need to be improved on, thinks Green. And it is in fact well summed up as what Christians, after Jesus, have called 'purity of heart', meaning that it is pursued with no mean concern for any kind of pleasurable experience for oneself or others. The earlier Greeks had conceived virtue mainly in military terms, with its chief merits being fortitude and temperance. As such, it was still the seed of all subsequent ideals of virtue, inasmuch as it put service to one's country or city above personal pleasure or any other selfish goal. But it was raised to a higher plane by Plato and Aristotle. And thereafter it came to include all sorts of concern for family and friends and a developing notion of the good which is common to them all. These developments were the work of the Eternal Reason or Consciousness as it inserts itself more fully into the temporal world.

Aristotle, as we know, with all the wisdom of Plato before him, which he was well able to appropriate, could find no better definition of the true good for man than the full realisation of the soul's faculties in accordance with its proper excellence, which is an excellence of thought, speculative and practical. The pure morality then, which we credit him with having so well conceived, must have meant morality determined by interest in such a good. (PROLEGOMENA, §254)

But the idea of virtue was still limited in two ways. First, the others in question were a narrow group of social equals. Secondly, the conception of the potentialities of man needed development.

Thus the scene was set for the Christian conception of virtue. (But did not Epicureanism and Stoicism already include an idea of the unity of mankind?) This had the same form of finding one's satisfaction in devotion to a common good for a society of persons, and performance of the duties this imposed.

The crucial difference was that the idea of who belonged to that society was vastly enlarged, so that it eventually became the society of all human persons. We hardly live up to this ideal even now, but we mostly recognize that we should.

If we are enquiring, then, for an interest adequate to account for the existence of an ever widening social union, in which the claims of all are acknowledged by the loyal citizen as the measure of what he may claim for himself, it is not in the desire for pleasure that we can find it, or in those 'particular passions,' such as ambition, which are wrongly supposed to have pleasure for their object.... It can have its origin only in an interest of which the object is a common good; a good in the effort after which there can be no competition between man and man; of which the pursuit by any individual is an equal service to others and to himself. Such a good may be pursued in many different forms by persons quite unconscious of any community in their pursuits; by the craftsman or writer, set upon making his work as good as he can without reference to his own glorification; by the father devoted to the education of his family, or the citizen devoted to the service of his state. No one probably can present to himself the manner of its pursuit, as it must have been pursued in order to the formation of the most primitive tribal or civil society. If we would find an expression applicable to it in all its forms, 'the realisation of the capacities of the human soul,' or 'the perfecting of man,' seems best suited for the purpose. To most men, indeed, engaged in the pursuit of any common good, this expression might convey no meaning. Nevertheless it is as part of, or as contributing to, such a realisation, that the object of their pursuit has its attraction for them; and it is for the same reason that it has the characteristic described, of being an object for which there can be no competition between man and man, and of which the pursuit is of general service. (PROLEGOMENA, §283)

Thus the ideals of both Christianity and the great Greek thinkers were very far from hedonism and utilitarianism. For neither was the goal pleasure, whether for the agent him or herself or for others; nor was it the actual effects of action, but its motive, which made it good. Though utterly different as their conception of the good will was, they in effect agreed with Kant and Green that what mattered ethically was the good will, and that it was this that mattered rather than results.

Yet beneath these differences lies a substantial identity. The willingness to endure even unto complete self-renunciation, even to the point of forsaking all possibility of pleasure ... the willingness to do this in the service of the highest public cause which the agent can conceive—whether the cause of the state or the cause of the kingdom of Christ—because it is part of the noble life, of the 'more excellent way,' so to do; this is common to the ideal of fortitude equally as conceived by Aristotle and as it has been pursued in the Christian Church. (PROLEGOMENA, §260)

Christianity still holds by ideas of fortitude and temperance which are continuous with those of Aristotle. But the fortitude is in the service of new goals, and the temperance has become a much fuller form of self-denial. And the realization that all human beings should be regarded as ends in themselves has considerably altered the goals of moral action. For Aristotle self-denial was for the good of the state, but for the Christian it is for a much wider range of altruistic purposes, including especially a concern for the poor and the weak. Similarly, its recognition that women are every bit as much ends in themselves (or, more simply, matter as much) as men has established a duty of control over sexual desire of a quite new and much stricter kind. (Green does not discuss Athenian homosexuality.)

Thus Aristotelian temperance became Christian self-denial. But whereas the value of the former was that it enabled one to do one's duty to the city-state, the value of the latter is that it enables one to do one's duty to all fellow humans. So while both the citizen of the city-state (as described by Aristotle) and the Christian must often resist the solicitations of pleasure, this is more demanding for the latter. For the Christian must often deny himself even the higher forms of pleasure, such as the pleasures of learning and of culture, as long as there are fellow men in conditions of degradation which crush their potentiality for any kind of excellence. This would have been hardly intelligible to the ancient Greeks (says Green), who, in a life based on slavery, could form no conception of every human being as demanding that he or she be treated as an end and never as a mere means.

On the other hand, while superficially the virtuous man of Athens might seem to have a more interesting life than a Victorian reformer, in fact a wider range of ways of fulfilling oneself through being good is open to the latter. Certainly he may have less pleasure. For, as the fiercely anti-hedonist Green sees it, it is likely that the highest type of human excellence will not just temporarily, but always, require that we have a lower self which must be crushed, and in crushing which we have less pleasure, but more goodness, than if we either succumbed to it or annihilated it.[16] (This is the only place where I find any suggestion regarding the problem of evil. See PROLEGOMENA, §276.) How very far Green was from his school friend, Henry Sidgwick, with whom he stayed on the best of terms while they ridiculed each other's philosophies in print, and doubtless in conversation!

But though the good of service to mankind rests on a recognition of human brotherhood of which the Greeks had no idea, the form to which it provides the content derives from them: that is, the form of a permanent good in which one can find one's satisfaction. And this good is essentially non-competitive, since its concern is with the well-being of each and all.

This ideal is beginning to produce a fundamental change in the relations between human beings at large. It is true that there are other forces at work, such as trade, which have enlarged the social union between men of different places and races, but only in so far as being good is the shared ideal can this remain peaceful. (Even a benevolent pleasure-maximizing utilitarianism could not do so, as Green argues at some length.[17]) Here again Green would have been saddened by the world situation as it is now in the year 2005, when there is so much hostility between different cultural groups. On the other hand, it may be true that, for example, Christians, post-Christians, and Muslims can only find peace not in separate selfish interests but by the sheer goodness of many in each group. This is not quite a tautology, for some think that enlightened self-interest will serve just as well, or better.

Unlike the quite extended comparison with Aristotle, Green says little in his *Prolegomena* as to how his ethics relates to that of Kant. (However, his views on Kant may be found in his Lectures on Kant in volume ii of his *Collected Works*.)

Like Kant, he thinks that the 'good will' is that which alone is intrinsically valuable. But, unlike Kant, this is fitted into a consequentialist ethic where actions are ideally to be chosen because they advance the cause of virtue among people generally. Thereby he gives a fuller and less abstract account of what it is that the good will is directed at than does Kant.

What, to say it again, remains odd is that Green seems never to realize that his account of action, even at its most virtuous, as always having as its goal something in which the agent can find 'personal satisfaction', is, if taken *au pied de la lettre*, egoistic in character. True, he does not conceive the satisfaction as the *goal* of the behaviour, but rather as experientially unified with it. But a psychological hedonist might similarly say that the goal of action is always something imagined as pleasurable or pain relieving rather than pleasure or pain reduction itself.

XV Negative and Positive Freedom

Green's Christianity (how far we may call it that will be considered shortly) led him to serious involvement in social reform, and to activity in local Oxford politics. His special concerns were with educational reform and the reduction of alcoholism by strict licensing laws. So before my final summing up on the relation between Green's philosophy and religion, some notice should be taken of the political position to which this led him.[18]

It was to answer a question which concerned liberal reformers that Green developed his influential and controversial distinction between positive and negative freedom. Liberal reforms up till around then had been directed primarily at removing legal restrictions on what people were allowed to do, leaving the task of the state to consist largely in the enforcement of contracts. But there was a need now, thought Green, to extend the power of the state in certain respects, such as the limitation of working hours (in particular for children) and the liability of employers for injury to their workers, even though everything contracted for had been done. The problem was to reconcile this with the traditional aim of liberals: namely, the promotion of personal freedom. So far this had been identified with the need to reduce state interference in what a man could do with his own. But this, argues Green, concerns only what he calls 'negative freedom'. Negative freedom consists merely in not being compulsorily restrained by law, or otherwise, from doing what one wishes to do subject only to the obligation to abide by a contract freely entered into.

But a more adequate notion of why freedom is desirable should attach even more importance to what Green christened 'positive freedom', which is the opportunity to develop one's own best potentialities to the full. Thus the notion of positive freedom allows the liberal to support some forms of state interference to count as extensions, rather than restrictions, on the freedom of citizens.

Green's crucial statement on this is as follows.

We shall probably all agree that freedom, rightly understood, is the greatest of all blessings; that its attainment is the true end of all our efforts as citizens. But when we thus speak of freedom, we should consider carefully what we mean by it. We do not mean merely freedom from restraint or compulsion. We do not mean merely freedom to do as we like irrespective of what it is that we like. We do not mean a freedom that can be enjoyed by one man or one set of men at the cost of a loss of freedom to others. When we speak of freedom as something to be so highly prized, we mean a positive power or capacity of doing or enjoying something worth doing or enjoying, and that too something that we enjoy in common with others. We mean by it a power which each man exercises through the help or security given to him by his fellow-men, and which he in turn helps to secure for them. (WORKS, iii. 370–1)

This comes from a 'Lecture on Liberal Legislation and Freedom of Contract' (WORKS, iii. 386) which was delivered before the Leicester Liberal Association early in 1881, and privately published later that year.

Says Ben Wempe about this speech:

Green began his lecture by pointing out the significance and timely nature of his argument. For this purpose he referred to the actual arguments levelled against two bills which had been proposed in the last parliamentary session. These two proposals by Gladstone's second cabinet were opposed on the ground that they interfered with the freedom of the individual parties to contracts. . . . [One of these was] the Employers Liability Act [which] was said to interfere with parties' freedom of contract in that it sought to reverse the burden of proof with respect to measuring out the responsibility in cases of industrial injuries. In the absence of a clause to the contrary the act held the employer to be responsible for any injuries sustained in the course of labour carried out under the terms of the labour contract.

This new kind of proposed legislation constituted a special problem for Liberals: for, while most supporters of the Liberal party were in favour of the bills proposed, it was clear that they ran counter to the classical liberal ideal of a maximum possible amount of individual freedom. . . .

In the first place Green drew attention to a qualitative change in the kind of legislation which was being sought, and, to an increasing extent, being carried into practice. While earlier reform legislation could always be classified and defended as an increase of the liberty of the individual, it would be difficult to make this claim for the protective measures that were recently proposed. (WEMPE, 151–3)

It is his conception of positive freedom, and other aspects of his political thought, which mainly evokes an interest in Green among philosophers at the present time. Indeed, I have the impression that most of those who currently interest themselves in his philosophy tend to treat his metaphysical, and even religious, views as unfortunate excrescences from which his ethical and political thought should now be detached.[19]

But for Green these views were closely tied up with his general philosophical position: in particular, that the aim of the state was to promote the virtue of its members, and that the development of human virtue represents the effort of the Eternal Consciousness to realize itself in time through human beings. It was because it promised to promote inward or positive freedom that Green approved the 1867 Reform Bill, and did not mind that it had been passed by the Tories rather than by the Liberals whom he normally supported.

Green's idea that the task of the state is to promote virtue is hardly without its problems. Certainly he recognized that it can only be the promotion of conditions favourable to virtue, rather than the direct promotion of virtue itself. (For virtue enforced by the state would not be virtue.) But what if there are some conditions favourable to virtue which a man like Green would not have wished promoted? Even resisting the temptation to drink too much when alcohol is readily available is a virtue of which strict licensing laws, such as Green actively promoted, limit the possibility. It would take us too much time to consider how far this is a serious objection, but it deserves to be considered. And, as we noted above, Green's supposed follower, Bosanquet, exhibits a wish that life should not be made too comfortable for the poor, since poverty can supply special opportunities for virtue.

Be that as it may, for Green and many other absolute idealists of the nineteenth century, the state or nation is misconceived if it is thought of as simply there to secure interests which individuals would have, but in a less protected way, in its absence. For the kind of excellence to which each of us can aspire is in large part due to the character of the society in which we were brought up and to that to which we now belong.

But Green strongly resists an inference sometimes falsely made from this fact: namely, that it is the improvement of the state or community, as some kind of supra-personal reality, that the Eternal Consciousness or Absolute is working for, rather than the improvement of individual persons. Hegel can reasonably be interpreted as holding this view, and Bosanquet was later inclined towards it, though not consistently so. And one reason, thinks Green, why it may have appealed to people who believed that the Eternal Consciousness was gradually realizing itself in humanity was that they thought, so to speak, that there was more hope for the state than there seemed to be for most individual persons.

It is a view, however, which, as we have seen, Green utterly and emphatically rejects. The only notion we can form of something of intrinsic value is a self-perfecting human person. It is only via our conception of the value of individual persons that we can think of the Eternal Consciousness as infinitely good. So when we speak of the improvement of society, that can only mean that the individual human beings who constitute it are being improved by its developing character.

XVI Green's Idealism and Religion

Green is more than ready to identify the Eternal Consciousness, the existence of which philosophy can prove, with the God of religion conceived as the enlightened modern person must conceive 'Him'. Thus conceived he can be for us all that God has traditionally been for good Christians.

God has his own eternal being, but he is also giving himself another kind of existence by inserting himself in human history. Thus the history of humanity consists in the gradual realization of the eternal divine ideal in time, though there are, for its own inscrutable reasons, many false turns along the way. But, as we have seen, while God knows what the virtue to which the human race is slowly moving will be in its higher stages, we ourselves can do little more than sense the next stages towards it to which we should be moving.

In this life of endeavour after virtue, we are aware of ourselves as at one with the Eternal Consciousness, or God.[20] Thus love of God and of one's fellow men is something which rational thought will inspire. And when we do less than well, we are going against God's will—that is, in a direction contrary to what we, as essentially at one with God, are ourselves aiming at in the deeper levels of our being. For there is a bad side to us, which it is part of the goodness of things that we should for ever struggle against.

Since it would seem that present society, and perhaps any society possible on earth, provides an inadequate context in which human beings can realize their full potentialities, we may reasonably believe that there is

259

another society, out of any ordinary line of connection with us on earth, in which we can continue our individual progress. Or perhaps somehow we do this rather as components in God or the Eternal Consciousness. These are things we cannot know. (See PROLEGOMENA, §186.)

But Green's emphasis upon the importance of the individual does seem to require that those whose lives were passed in circumstances unfavourable to much by way of personal development must somehow survive bodily death. For if it is humanity as a whole, rather than individuals, through which the Eternal Consciousness is gradually actualizing its own eternal perfection in time, that is not much comfort to those who died too early in this process.

Moreover, if the divine goal is to gradually realize itself in humanity, rather than in all human beings, then the point of early man (and doubtless of many of us now) can only have been to prepare the ground for a human perfection in which they would not share. But Green clearly rejects such an idea when he speaks of it as intolerable that some persons should only be a means to the general improvement. So it very much looks as though he thought that each of us would ultimately reach perfection even if not in the present world.

Reincarnation, I think, would have been a promising alternative. For then the divine purpose might have been to prepare the ground, through much necessary educative toil and trouble, for the sake of a morally austere utopian future in which we would all be worthy to share. But reincarnation was probably too Eastern an idea for Green. So it very much looks as though he thought that each of us would ultimately reach perfection in another heavenly world, though this does not chime too well with his general opposition to the supernatural in the popular sense of the word.

XVII Green's Philosophy and Christianity

Green's outlook might well be called an instance of the 'higher pantheism'. However, his pantheistic God is much nearer to the Christian God than is the Absolute of thinkers such as Bradley and Bosanquet. And this allows Green to regard his philosophy as saving Christianity from feeling at risk from developments in science or historiography. For it shows, so claimed Green, that the essence of Christianity can survive the abandonment of the myths with which it has till 'now' been associated. Jesus performed no miracles, and was in no literal sense resurrected or born of a virgin. These are the ways in which the Gospel writers expressed the significance of Jesus's life and message. But we no longer need them (in the nineteenth century and beyond). Nor need Christians tremble at the growth of scientific knowledge which rules out such things as the Genesis account of the origination of the natural universe and of the human species.

What Green especially insisted on was that it could be no part of what makes a man or woman a Christian 'today' that they believe in the truth of certain historical events or are resistant to developments in science.

> It is not on any estimate of evidence, correct or incorrect, that our true holiness can depend. Neither if we believe certain documents to be genuine and authentic can we be the better, nor if we believe it not, the worse. There is thus an inner contradiction in that conception of faith which makes it a state of mind involving peace with God and love towards all men, and at the same time makes its object that historical work of Christ, of which our knowledge depends on evidence of uncertain origin and value. (From 'Faith', in WORKS, iii. 260)

So, while the whole idealist movement of that time provided cheer to those who feared that their religious outlook was under threat from history and science, it was Green above all, together with Edward Caird and his brother John, who offered a form of Christianity claiming to be intellectually, morally, and emotionally sustainable. Thus there can be no doubt of the religious, and more especially Christian, relevance of Green's God.

Nowhere is this represented more vividly than in *Robert Elsmere* (published in 1888), the famous novel by Mrs Humphry Ward, in which Green figures, under the name of 'Grey', as saviour of the essence of Christian faith for a clergyman who could no longer believe in miracles, the resurrection, and the non-human aspect of the Jesus of traditional Christian faith.[21] This wonderful novel is said to have brought Green's ideas to a much wider public than would have learnt of them otherwise.[22]

XVIII The Overall Religious Significance of Green's Philosophy

It is not difficult to say what religiously inspired way of life Green's philosophy was calculated to inspire, and certainly did inspire in Green himself. It was to seek a higher level of personal excellence through one's thoughts and behaviour. And whatever else such excellence may be, it includes the effort to create the conditions for a similar excellence in others too.

If this answer is accepted to the question, what it is that we desire in desiring our own true or permanent well-being, it would seem that we have already answered the question, what it is that we desire in desiring the true well-being of others. It is the same common well-being, the same good of a society which we also desire as our own. No doubt, there are generous impulses consisting in desires to convey pleasures, simply as such, to others, or to lessen their pains. . . . But the desire for the well-being, whether as of others or as of oneself, is no more to be identified with such generous impulses, with which it may very well conflict, than those impulses that are excited by the imagination of pleasure [for oneself]. The objects of which a man anticipates the realisation in looking forward to such well-being, are objects, as we have seen, which he necessarily thinks of as realised for a society no less than for himself, for himself only as a member of a society. The opposition of self and others does not enter into the consideration of a well-being so constituted. (PROLEGOMENA, §235)

Thus, limited as is our knowledge of what the highest form of human excellence may be in the future, we have a fair idea of what it is now. It is a life of active altruism and personal purity.

This seems to limit human excellence, at least for now, to moral virtue. Artistic creativity is mentioned more as a hindrance to doing good than anything else, though a rather more positive view of it is taken in his Lectures on Kant. (See WORKS, ii. 144–5.) However, he does rather touchingly mention producing a philosophical system (provided it is edifying) as one form which it may take. (See next quotation but one.)

Such a life must, with rare exceptions, be one of willing obedience to the moral code of our day except in the rare cases when a higher moral demand beckons. But how can we know if it is a higher morality which is beckoning? Green thinks we will have a sense that it is demanding more of us, and will have more fortunate effects on the life of others. If the demand is genuine, it will be painful rather than pleasurable to fulfil it.

Religion comes into this inasmuch as we will have the sense that what we are doing is bringing the non-temporal perfection of the Eternal Consciousness into fuller realization in the temporal world. Christianity gives us our best sense of what this advance of the Eternal Consciousness into temporal life must consist in: namely, in a self-sacrificing life for others and a strong control over one's carnal impulses, and even one's chaste love of beauty, so that they are given their head only to the extent that they can serve the cause of moral development. Thus, as we saw from a passage quoted above, Green thinks it doubtful to what extent an indulgence of a taste for music is morally acceptable when there is so much work to be done in the improvement of one's own moral character and the production of circumstances in which others will be encouraged to improve themselves morally. But it is certainly not pleasure for others that the true altruist desires.

However, such a passage as the following makes the picture rather less forbidding.

When a man 'sits down in a calm hour' to consider what his permanent well-being consists in, what it is that in desiring it he really desires, it is not indeed to be supposed that he traces the desire back to its ultimate source in his self-objectifying personality, or that he thinks of its object in the abstract form of that which will satisfy the demand arising from such a personality. But if, unbiased either by particular passions or by philosophical prepossessions, he will identify his well-being with an order of life which that demand has brought into existence,[23] the thought of his well-being will be to him the thought of himself as living in the successful pursuit of various interests which the order of society—taking the term in its widest sense—has determined for him; interests ranging, perhaps, from provision for his family to the improvement of the public health or to the production of a system of philosophy. The constituents of the contemplated well-being will be the objects of those various interests, objects (e.g. the provision for a family or the sanitation of a town) in process of realisation, which, when realised, take their place as permanent contributions to an abiding social good. In them therefore the man who carries himself forward in thought along the continued life of a family or a nation, a state or a church, anticipates a lasting and accumulating possession, as he cannot do in successive enjoyments. In them he can think of himself as really coming nearer to an absolute good. Just so far as he is interested in such objects, he must indeed anticipate pleasure in their realization, but the objects, not the pleasure, form the actuating content of his idea of true well-being. A transfer of his interest from the objects to the pleasure would be its destruction. (PROLEGOMENA, §234)

The following remark by one of his students, Henry Scott Holland (who, as a canon of St Paul's, became a highly active social campaigner for the elimination of poverty by restrictions on capitalism) is significant in this respect.

He gave us back the language of self-sacrifice and taught us how we belonged to one another in the one life of organic humanity. He filled us again with the breath of high idealism. (Quoted in RICHTER, 35)

This highly serious and moral attitude is conceived by Green as that to which Christianity, in the form in which it must endure, calls us. But while simpler souls may be left with the whole narrative baggage of Christianity, it is essential that it is not made dependent upon its acceptance as anything other than an edifying 'fairy story'. All this is mythology which, as we mature, we are bound to reject as fact.

Green certainly lived out these ideals both as a teacher and by working for various social reforms and encouraging others to do so, more particularly his students, such as Arnold Toynbee and many others. Thus his philosophy functioned undoubtedly for a time as a religion, or at least as the confirmation of what was thought most significant in a religion (Christianity) for many people over the period of its main influence (which may be said to have dwindled by around 1914).

Thus, as noted above, he was active in local Oxford politics—was, in fact, the first Oxford don to be elected to the Oxford town council (not as a university representative but for the district of Oxford in which he lived). He was particularly concerned with restrictions on the liquor trade and with licensing hours (which in our own time have been abolished in the interests of what Green would regard as a merely negative freedom). For Green thought that the working man, in particular, was often ill fitted to act properly in relation to his family and other social associates if he was a prey to demon drink.

Green, as we have noted, recognized that virtue cannot be forced on people; in fact, it was a strong theme of his. But he did think that the obstructions to virtue by the existing arrangements of society could be removed, and that was what he was mainly concerned with in his own involvement in politics and social reform, and what, as a political thinker, he was concerned to promote.

Of all the philosophies studied in this book, Green's philosophy is most favourable to an essentially Christian point of view. But its helpfulness to Christianity in this regard is limited by the fact that its metaphysic is none too clear. Certainly, to me, it is much less convincing than is the thought of Bradley. It may be added that Green's strong emphasis on self-denial and negative attitude to the search for pleasure, or even happiness, is one which people of the present time (say from 1920 to 2005) tend to take a very negative view of. Nor does it show much concern for the need to protect other life forms on this planet, a need seldom recognized at that time, though J. S. Mill showed some awareness of it. However, Green did feel himself especially at one with God when out in the countryside, though the more humanized it was, the more so (thus contrasting with how people tend to feel today).

But perhaps what most stands in the way of someone today regarding him or herself as a follower of Green is his enormously over optimistic belief in progress, and his confidence that force would be playing a lesser and lesser part in relations between persons and nations from his time on. How startled he would have been by the horrors of the twentieth century and beyond! Bosanquet, as we will see, was in his own bland way an optimist, but this was because he managed to see what most people think of as evil as good. This was not true of Green. What he regarded as good was what most of us, I imagine, would agree with him as being so. (Many things which he did not care about are, surely, good too, but so are the things which he did care about.) The trouble is that things have not worked out at all as he expected. Not that a much more long-term optimism about the future of the human race has been decisively falsified and it may still be true. But humanity was certainly much less advanced than Green thought. Moreover, his view of humanity seems to have taken no account of anything beyond Europe (and presumably North America).

Be all that as it may, it is clear that Green was a noble and unselfish person anxious to save himself and others from what he saw as the demeaning characterization of human beings which is all a purely naturalistic view of things can offer. While one may not sympathize altogether with his stance on this matter, I would certainly concur that a pure materialism cannot do justice to what we are, though I would add (as Green would not) that it cannot do justice either to what animals truly are.

It is rather remarkable that at school and in early youth he was regarded as lazy, something which he must have roundly condemned in himself. Book IV, chapter 1, gives the impression of someone who may have been morbidly guilty about the very slightest backsliding or bad thought which may ever have crossed his mind.

XIX Decline of Green's Reputation

Although the character of Britain today owes a good deal to social reformers strongly under the influence of Green, attention to his political thought is now quite limited (though greater than to the metaphysics which he thought its foundation). It is true indeed that the ethical socialism which, before New Labour was elected, was touted as what it stood for, has largely been lost sight of as time has gone by. Moreover, it is often more the spirit of Bosanquet than of Green which seems to hover over our present social policies.

Among academic philosophers, Green's reputation certainly slumped badly after the First World War. This, it is said, had several causes. One reason for its fall from grace was supposed to be the 'powerful intellectual and logical criticism' (as Richter puts it) of absolute idealism by Russell and Moore. But was this really so powerful, or was it not just more suited to their time?

At a less purely logical level, it is said that

All the articles of the Idealist creed became irrelevant to the world of the twenties and thirties. The value of self-sacrifice, the importance of striving to attain the ideal, the belief in progress and in the duties owed by one class to another—all this the younger generation considered to be inflated and diffuse hypocrisy. (RICHTER, 376)

As to the first of these, it must be said that Green's argument for idealism was on the vague side, as a result of which it is difficult to say how far at times his reasoning may be fallacious. What I will say now is that the arguments *against* absolute idealism in general, particularly of what became its most celebrated exposition, in the work of Bradley, were not really all that powerful. The idealist case needed to be tightened up somewhat, but it is doubtful that its real core was vulnerable to those criticisms.

As regards the second, we have already remarked that Green's optimism about the near future turned out badly wrong in the century following his death. It may also be said that his puritanical approach took far too negative a view of any *joie de vivre* (though he is said to have had a good sense of humour in personal talk). But was the belief in self-sacrifice so misconceived? Doubtless the terrible sacrifice of many lives in the First World War made it a less attractive proposition, but it is hardly a value to be scorned when it is necessary for a good purpose.

Personally, I think that Green's philosophy is associated with what is the best of Christianity, that no one should cut themselves off from concern with the welfare of all. He has things to say about the use of money which it would be good for the plutocrats of today to reflect on. There is a certain oddity in that he bases his highly altruistic ethic on what is at base a form of psychological egoism—in this he has something in common with Spinoza. But his basic outlook is calculated to and, indeed did, promote the Christian ideal of love for one's neighbour more powerfully perhaps than did that of any other of the thinkers studied in this book. And he had a very real influence on many of the great social reformers of the next generation. (See especially on this CARTER.)

Notes

1. To consider why this happened so late in Britain as compared to Germany is not a question for a work which does not pretend to be historical. I shall only remark that the dissatisfaction of these philosophers with native British empiricism was more for intellectual reasons than because they found insufficient solace in the views of Bentham and Mill. Earlier attempts to defend Christianity on idealist grounds include J. H. Stirling in his *The Secret of Hegel* (1865).

2. As Melvin Richter points out: 'The most prominent spokesmen for British Idealism were all sons of Evangelical clergymen within the Church of England. It was an essentially religious concern which first brought Green, Bernard Bosanquet, and F. H. Bradley to the study of philosophy.' He continued: 'This is not to say that their subsequent work was dominated by the same motive. Bradley, who ended as the most antagonistic of the three to organized religion, first encountered Hegel in German theologians such as F. C. Baur. In this he repeated Green's experience. Quite literally their interest in philosophy derived from theology.... [However t]he search for an object of faith may lead men to very different positions.... Philosophical Idealism provided a broadly based set of formulae, which, when filled in with different values, could be used to support a variety of causes. In Green's hands, Idealism became a vehicle of reform, thus reflecting certain aspects of Evangelicalism and Christian Socialism. Bradley, reacting against both, created an aloof conservatism' (RICHTER, 36–7).

3. Alan P. Sell in *Philosophical Idealism and Christian Belief* examines the relationship to Christianity of T. H. Green himself, Edward Caird, J. R. Illingworth, Henry Jones, Andrew Seth (a.k.a. A. S. Pringle-Pattison), C. C. J. Webb and A. E. Taylor. This is an informative book, though it judges these philosophers negatively according as to how far they are from orthodox Christianity. A commentary on Green which I have found especially helpful is WEMPE.

4. Green's view of Hume may be found developed at length in his introduction to the edition of Hume's works edited by himself and T. H. Grose. There he argues vigorously against the atomistic nature of Hume's account of experience.

5. For Green's patronizing attitude to Berkeley, see his review of A. C. Fraser's edition of Berkeley's *Works* (1871), in unpaged appendix at the end of WORKS, iii. The general line is that Berkeley did some service for his age by his critique of the notion of matter, but that he failed (at least in his earlier works) to recognize that it was not so much *percipi* in which the existence of the natural world consisted as *intelligi*.

6. A piano concerto, or rather its performance, is an event stretched out in time, so that its beginning and its end are parts of it, but the piano on which it is played is a continuant which is, DV, wholly there at every moment at which it exists. All ordinary things—trees, ponds, mountains, planets—are continuants.

7. Obviously human accounts of these things vary, even among those which can be regarded as true, but we think that there is just one total truth about each of these. Qualify this statement as you like, but the general thrust of it is correct.

8. See THOMAS, 239–41.
9. Green uses 'ideal object' to mean one not yet actualized in the 'real' world.
10. Was Green trying not to feel puffed up above those who were less socially active? See the discussion of conscientiousness in book IV, ch. 1. It reads like a religious manual. See also the discussion of giving to a beggar at §305.
11. The idea that the only valuable feature of an individual's life is his [moral] goodness seems rather limited, even if moral goodness is given quite a wide interpretation. Sometimes Green seems to identify moral goodness with the fullest possible realization of one's potentialities. Clearly he means only potentialities to be good in some way, but should this not include potentialities for excellences not readily regarded as moral?
12. Roughly speaking, hedonistic utilitarianism holds that what one ought to do is that which will maximize the pleasure and minimize the pain of all affected by one's action, while hedonistic psychology holds that human beings necessarily always act in the way which they think will maximize their own pleasure and minimize their own pain. Classic utilitarians like Bentham and Mill held both views, and thought them somehow logically connected. Henry Sidgwick emphasized their logical independence, or even incompatibility, and held only the first view. (See his METHODS, also his LECTURES.)
13. Talk of maximizing pleasure by utilitarian thinkers should always be interpreted as including the addendum (and minimizing pain) a fact sometimes neglected.
14. In claiming permanence for it, Green again appeals to one's ability to identify oneself with it after death by projecting oneself forward in time. But we have already criticized this line of thought as somewhat specious.
15. See METHODS, 133 ff.
16. Did Jesus (whom Green thought of as presenting our best ideal) have a lower self?
17. I shall take some issue with this in the final chapter of the book.
18. Ben Wempe is especially informative on Green's notion of positive freedom. See WEMPE, 217, 151–3, and *passim.*
19. This seems to be true of Maria Dimova-Cookson, while Colin Tyler manages to be sympathetic with the metaphysics by giving it a very reductive interpretation.
20. For an interesting remark on the sense in which God has us under his eye as we behave or misbehave, see PROLEGOMENA, §§318–19.
21. He does not, however, persuade him to stay in the Church of England, and Robert Elsmere has to found his own form of Christianity without the miracles. In a much later novel (*The Case of Richard Meynell*), Mrs Humphry Ward shows how a Church of England clergyman could properly do so.

22. According to William S. Peterson, in *Victorian Heretic*, 'Green's ideas reached a larger audience through Robert Elsmere than through his own books and lectures. Generally after 1888, particularly in America, he was identified as "the Mr Grey of Robert Elsmere" whenever his name was mentioned in print.'

23. In the printed text there is a full stop here thus leaving the sentence with no main verb. I have, therefore, altered the punctuation.

Chapter 6

Bernard Bosanquet

PART ONE: EARLIER WORK

I Introducing Bernard Bosanquet

I turn now to Bernard Bosanquet (1848–1923), who once dominated the philosophical scene in Britain. He was never considered quite the equal of F. H. Bradley (1846–1924), but he wrote on a broader range of subjects, and was far busier at philosophical conferences, congresses, and so forth. He was also sometimes interestingly far-sighted as to the future, anticipating both the problem of how church buildings are to be used as Christianity declines and the development of artificial intelligences. His views on social issues were thorough and influential, but of questionable positive value.

Bernard Bosanquet was the youngest of five sons of the Revd Robert B. William Bosanquet, who had once been rector of a parish in Lincolnshire. However, by the time of Bernard's birth, he was occupied in managing an inherited estate, near Rock, a little town in Northumberland, though he still assisted from time to time with local religious services[1].

Bernard went to the public school Harrow, and then on to Balliol College, Oxford. There he was an undergraduate from 1867 to 1870, and fell under the influence of T. H. Green. After graduating, he was elected a fellow of University College, Oxford, having won the fellowship in competition with F. H. Bradley. On inheriting a private income in 1881, he resigned from the fellowship and moved to London. There he worked at his philosophical writings, and engaged in adult and in voluntary administrative work for the Charity Organisation Society (on which see below at section XXIII). In 1895 he married Helen Dendy, who worked for this organization. (She wrote a life of her husband after his death.)

He returned to formal academic life when he took up the chair of Moral Philosophy at St Andrews in 1903, where he remained only until 1908. One interesting personal note is that he was a keen amateur botanist, and his concept of science, as developed in his *Logic*, is said to have been influenced by this. (See e.g. A SHORT ACCOUNT, 35.) Later he gave the Gifford Lectures at Edinburgh in 1911 and 1912. I shall have some more to say about him as a person at the end of the chapter.

Bosanquet is sometimes thought of as simply a less interesting exponent of the same viewpoint as that of F. H. Bradley. But, though he is less brilliant as a pure philosopher, Bosanquet wrote on a wider range of issues, and is especially interesting for his views on the future of religion. I have not included a chapter on Bradley because there is scarcely room for a chapter on both, and I have thought it important to draw attention to the much more (and undeservedly) neglected work of Bosanquet. Also I have written on Bradley in some detail already. (See my JAMES AND BRADLEY.) The present book does not presuppose knowledge of Bradley's thought, and there is a short section on him in Part II of this chapter.

Bosanquet professed himself a follower of Bradley, at least after the publication of *Appearance and Reality* (in 1893), which, he said, had become his bible. Houang Kia Tcheng in his excellent 1954 book *De l'Humanisme à l'Absolutisme: L'Évolution de la Pensée Religieuse du...Bernard Bosanquet*, contends that the reading of *Appearance and Reality* changed Bosanquet from being a humanist to being an absolute idealist. The Bosanquet specialist William Sweet has told me that Tcheng exaggerates the change. Certainly Bosanquet was from early on an enthusiast for Bradley's work. *Ethical Studies* (1876) he regarded as a philosophical epoch[2] and he was a keen, sympathetic, though not uncritical student of *The Principles of Logic* (1883) from the start.[3] But it was *Appearance and Reality* (first published in 1893, second edition 1897) which, if Tcheng is right, really revolutionized his outlook.

But whether their essential doctrines were the same or not, their way of reaching them and the general tone of their expression are fairly dissimilar. Bradley's metaphysical position is based on two great principles: first, the pan-experientialist principle that there can be no such thing as unexperienced reality; second, that the truth reached for in any statement about the relations of things really concerns their belonging together in a whole more genuinely individual than themselves, ultimately in the Absolute, of which more anon.

Bosanquet would seem to have accepted these two principles, but at times he gives the impression of a viewpoint incompatible with the pan-experientialist principle and neglectful of the doctrine of the Absolute. As for relations, he offers no critique of relational thought in the manner of Bradley (which I briefly sum up later in the chapter) and never, so far as I know, discusses Bradley's argumentation on this matter. But the leading idea of his philosophy is much what Bradley reached through this critique: namely, that to understand anything is to see it as a necessary element in a systematic whole possessing a certain completeness to it, or as seeking to become or to join such a whole itself.

My watchword in philosophy is 'The reality is the whole', and in this view I, and those from whom I have learned conceive ourselves diametrically opposed to all forms of naturalism and realism, when setting themselves up for philosophies. (BOSANQUET AND FRIENDS, 296)

In logic this watchword is present as the claim that the search for truth is an attempt to fit all one's individual judgements into a more comprehensive system, one which brings one nearer to the total truth about everything; in ethics it is present as the doctrine that the individual can only find himself and act rightly when he grasps his function in a social whole, more especially the state (for it is as a citizen playing his unique role in this that a man can find his greatest satisfaction); in religion it takes the form of grasping that one belongs to a cosmic whole which is essentially good, however hard the lot it may have allocated to oneself.

Bosanquet wrote a good deal over a long period. It is difficult to be clear how far his views changed with time, apart from a few changes which he makes explicitly. For our purposes it will suffice to take his various works as developing the same point of view, except where there is clear evidence of a change of mind.

Though he professed himself an idealist, it has to be said that some of the time he writes as though nothing much separated him from a high-minded metaphysical materialism. For not only does he make it plain that this life on earth is all there is for each of us, but his treatment of mind is, as J. M. E. McTaggart complained with reference to his Gifford Lectures, indistinguishable in many of its formulations from one according to which it arises in nature without somehow being nature's foundation. We will see that this is not quite true, but Bosanquet's idealism, and commitment to the Absolute in what he thought was Bradley's sense, often seem beside the real points he is keen to make.

II Bosanquet and Christianity

On the whole, Bosanquet seems to have become increasingly unsympathetic to Christianity. In his *Essays and Addresses* (1889), however, to which we may now address ourselves first, he appears still committed to the essentials of Christianity as he interprets them, while discarding everything 'supernatural' in its teachings as antiquated or childish lumber.

There are three essays which expound a form of Christianity in which everything supernatural is dropped as so much lumber hiding what should still engage our allegiance: (1) 'On the True Conception of Another World', (2) 'The Kingdom of God on Earth', and (3) 'How to Read the New Testament'. The first was originally published as the introduction to a translation of a fragment from Hegel's 'Esthetic', while the other two were addresses given to the London Ethical Society. This, Bosanquet tells us in his Prefatory Remarks, was 'a small association in London, modelled on the more powerful Ethical Societies of the United States, which have for their object to contribute by precept and in practice to spreading moral ideas and strengthening moral influences on a non-dogmatic basis'.[4]

'How to Read the New Testament'

The aim of these essays is to interpret all important talk of another world in New Testament Christianity as referring, not to a supernatural realm to which we will go after death, and which sometimes impacts on this world, but to this world conceived in relation to the spiritual values actualized there.

This was the only other world to which Plato, at his best, ever referred, and it is this which the message of Jesus concerns. Their purpose was 'to enforce a distinction which falls within the world which we know, and not between the world we know and another which we do not know' (E&A, 94). And this is the distinction between the trifles of this world and the great spiritual values which are present in it.

Let us take a closer look first at 'How to Read the New Testament' and then at 'The Kingdom of God on Earth'. Bosanquet says that in reading the New Testament, the modern reader should put all ideas out of his head that it is an inspired work in which God has taught us a consistent body of religious truth as the basis for a church. If we want to learn from what remains valuable in it, we must first consider these writings as they were intended 'at the time of their origin, before anyone thought of them as an official revelation or as the charter of a new religion' (E&A, 133). For the idea that their authors saw them as contributions to a unified *New Testament*, to be contrasted with what we now call the *Old Testament*, is quite untrue. It was only much later that they were combined as though parts of a single work. Moreover, the attempt to find some systematic body of doctrine in the New Testament is hopeless, and not to be expected in the light of the different circumstances in which the various books were written. In particular, we should not look upon the Epistles of Paul as a kind of commentary upon the Gospels, as they were, so Bosanquet is confident, written before these. The true order of composition of the main works was, rather, (1) Paul's Epistles, (2) Revelations, (3) the Gospels.

As Bosanquet put it:

First, there came the fiery letters of the missionary to the Gentiles, with few or no facts and confused artificial reasonings, but glowing with the first flush of a great human idea; then came the prophecy of the Jewish believer, expressing his hope even in the crisis of his country's agony, which he took to be the sign of the Lord's imminent return; and, at last, after this hope had proved a delusion came the late and gradual attempts to commit to writing, and to interpret worthily, the fragmentary tradition of the life that was beginning to seem distant after the interval of more than half a century. (E&A, 140)

However, if we are concerned to understand the early development of Christianity, the vital phases are these four:

1. Jesus's teaching centring on the message, directed (primarily at any rate) at the Jews, that the kingdom of God is within you;
2. Paul's application of this teaching, in which it is extended to humanity generally;
3. the development of the divine ideal, by which Bosanquet seems to mean the doctrine of the Incarnation;
4. the development of the church as a worldly organization and power.

Bosanquet has something to say about each of these in turn, but more especially about phases (1) and (2), which are those he thinks important for us today (late nineteenth century).

FIRST PHASE IN THE DEVELOPMENT OF CHRISTIANITY: THE TEACHING OF JESUS

Bosanquet considers how far the evidence allows us to grasp what Jesus as a historical person was actually teaching. Here the main evidence must come from Matthew, especially the Sermon on the Mount.

Jesus's primary purpose was to preach the gospel of the Kingdom. And in trying to understand this,

We must clear away from our minds all such ideas as that the kingdom of Heaven means a future life in Paradise, that salvation means being saved from eternal punishment, that eternal life means living for ever in another world, or that forgiveness of sins means the doctrine of the atonement by the merits of Christ.

It is indeed possible that

Jesus may have had some such ideas, ideas which we must pronounce quite unreasonable, but tradition constantly misunderstood him, so that it is impossible to say exactly, for example, how far he believed in his own miraculous second coming. (E&A, 142)

Be this as it may, what should concern those of us who still wish to learn from Jesus are the bulk of his sayings, which are of a quite different nature. And it seems likely that most of these were actually said by someone known as 'Jesus of Nazareth', though the sayings retain their value, who-ever said them.

Now the key to the real meaning of these sayings is, according to Bosanquet, the words 'The kingdom of God is within you' or 'is already among you' (Luke 17: 21). (Bosanquet does not raise the question as to which of these significantly different translations is more correct. 'Among you' suits his philosophy better, I think.)

According to Bosanquet, this was intended as a corrective to current Jewish notions of 'the kingdom of heaven 'or 'kingdom of God'. (These are the same, for talk of Heaven is talk of God without invocation of his name, which should be largely avoided according to Jewish custom.)

This kingdom of God or Heaven was generally thought of, among the Jews, as an event due to occur on earth. It was the idea that there was a good time coming. For some of them this was to be an era of greatness and glory for the Israelites; for others it was to be a time of widespread reform and righteousness. In either case it is thought of as a future event that will occur on this earth, not in some supernatural realm. So far, so good, for Bosanquet, who detested ideas of a supernatural realm. But what Jesus did was to teach that this good time was already there for us in so far as we live according to the precepts of righteousness which he taught.

When Jesus says

'Thou art not far from the kingdom of God', it is just like saying, You have very nearly obtained salvation or eternal life, or forgiveness of sins. You have nearly brought yourself to the true will to be righteous, which *is* eternal life. And consequently the world to come does not mean a life in heaven; it means the whole good time which had begun with Christ's coming. (E&A, 143)

Bosanquet comments again that whether Jesus himself really expected a Second Coming, in which he himself would establish a righteous order, is doubtful; but what is important for us is that it consists in moral regeneration upon this earth, and that his followers were already on the way to this. (Since the publication of Schweitzer's *The Quest of the Historical Jesus* in 1906, opinion has swung against this account of Jesus's main concerns—though things may have changed more recently in Bosanquet's direction.[5])

This moral regeneration has two aspects: one of which is the theme of the Sermon on the Mount, the other of which is expressed in the parables that deal with the kingdom of Heaven, especially the parables of corn and the mustard seed (see Mark 4: 26 Matt. 13).

The first of them is that the good time coming

on the one hand, is to consist in righteousness of heart and life, in genuine human morality, in putting away the selfish will. 'He that loseth his life shall find it'. And it is to consist, for this very reason, on the other hand, in a purification of human society, and the formation of a righteous community not restricted to any nation, rank or creed.... [For if] human righteousness and love are the one thing needful, then all the barriers of class and of caste and rank and creed are condemned already, and must go. (E&A, 144)

Or at least this is the logic of what Jesus was saying, though it is unclear how far he may have continued to think exclusively of a righteous community for the Jews, or whether he realized that his ideals demanded an end to their separateness, a question which, of course, 'split the Apostolic society to its foundation, and the tradition of what Jesus did and said flatly contradicts itself' (E&A, 144). At any rate, while it is unclear how far Jesus intended his teachings for Jew and non-Jew alike, he was preaching a moral doctrine the logic of which required its universalization.

But the second aspect of the coming righteousness is a radical change in religious observance. For Jesus continually expresses his indignation at all the outward shows of religion. His message is clearly

that a spiritual religion, which demands rightness of heart and character as the only law can make no truce with idle forms and ceremonies, or with the orthodoxy of a priestly caste, or with the selfishness of classes, or the exclusiveness of nations. The kingdom of heaven, which is a kingdom of the heart and mind, must also, and for that reason, be founded on freedom and be as wide as humanity. (E&A, 145)

In this connection Bosanquet quotes such sayings as 'The Sabbath was made for man, and not man for the Sabbath' (E&A, 91).

Interestingly, Bosanquet suggests that when Jesus spoke of destroying the Temple, he meant 'that the Temple service was doomed', and that it was his disrespect for the whole ceremonial and ritual aspects of Judaism which made the rabbis wish him dead.

Incidentally, Bosanquet suggests that Jesus's indignation at priests and pedants shows that he made no claim to be God, for 'indignation is incompatible with divinity: since it would be at what one is oneself responsible for if one was God'. Bosanquet does not reflect on the fact that Christian believers in free will would claim that Jesus was indignant at behaviour which God had permitted rather than produced, while for Calvinists God produced it precisely in order to exhibit his righteousness in punishing it.

So far Bosanquet finds a message from Jesus that he thinks inspiring and civilizing. But now he turns to something with which he is dissatisfied in the teaching of Jesus and which he calls, a bit oddly, his 'sentimentalism'. This is Jesus's attack on worldliness: for example, on taking thought for the morrow. Certainly, says Bosanquet, it is importantly true that to be overcome with care and worry about the future, rather than getting on with the task at hand, is damaging, as also is concern with the trappings of 'respectability'. But Jesus is dangerously close to attacking the whole notion of good citizenship, so dear to Bosanquet.

[I]t is a perilous position to go about telling people to take no thought for the morrow, and to sell off all they have and give to the poor. The *spirit* of it is that they should give *themselves and* all that they have to the good cause; but here as elsewhere, the letter killeth. (E&A, 146)

In fact, Jesus could have learnt a thing or two from Pericles' famous oration on the virtues of the Athenians. Historically, this is a somewhat bizarre remark, but the point that Jesus's teaching must be substantially modified if the Christian is to be a good citizen is clearly important, whatever we think of it. Jesus's remark that one should render unto Caesar what is Caesar's exhibits a divorce between spiritual values and political engagement which was anathema to Bosanquet. Nor, one suspects, would he have thought much better of Jesus if he was, in fact, the social revolutionary that some think him. (How Bosanquet thought the Jews should have viewed their subjugation to Rome is unclear.)

Bosanquet ends his discussion of Jesus's teaching by saying that Jesus had no idea of founding a new religion, but was rather reforming Judaism, but in a spirit which suggests that he was moving towards the notion of 'a religion for the world'.

SECOND PHASE OF CHRISTIANITY: PAUL

Bosanquet now moves to the second phase of early Christianity (E&A, 147–53). This second phase was that of the struggle between those who wished Christianity to remain simply a sect within Judaism and those who thought that they had learnt a true universal religion from Jesus and set out to convert the world to it. The victory of the latter was above all the work of St Paul.

After deciding rather hesitantly that the struggles going on in Paul's mind must have produced a vivid hallucination on the road to Damascus, Bosanquet continues:

But however he came to his views, we have his own writings to tell us what they were and so far we are better off than trying to learn about Christ. The centre of this doctrine was what I have ventured to call the Gospel of Humanity, and was implied rather than affirmed in Christ's gospel of the kingdom. The extraordinary force of this gospel is shown by the hold which the new religion gained in Paul's lifetime in the very centre of the civilised world ... I suppose we might speak of Paul's central ideas as 'justification by faith only' [e.g. Rom. 3: 28]. To mention this doctrine fills the mind with echoes of theological dispute. I will only make two suggestions ...

First: he says in so many words [Rom. 10: 9] *what* the faith is—a belief in the risen Christ and in his Divinity—and secondly, if you ask what that belief means, for Paul, you must look for the answer in his idea of the spiritual oneness of all believers in and with Christ. There—*in* and *with* Christ—are the two aspects of Paul's doctrine. Being one *with* the risen Christ, means that the particular believer has put away his own bad will, is dead to sin, and has thoroughly submitted his heart and soul to the dominion of the good will, that is, the mind of Christ [2 Cor. 4: 10; Rom. 6: 5]. Being one *in* the risen Christ means that the society of believers form what Paul calls the 'body of Christ,' that is, a spiritual unity which is Divine and yet human, and as wide as humanity. Faith means realizing this oneness in and with Christ. This great comparison of the relation between human beings in society and that between the parts of a living body was introduced into moral thought by Plato, and has been, perhaps the most fruitful of all moral ideas. (E&A, 151)

Bosanquet quotes the most relevant passage from Plato's *Republic* at length. He then insists again that for Paul this insight is unfortunately jumbled up with all sorts of irrational things which no one should take seriously today.

Justification by faith does not mean salvation from eternal punishment, by believing historical facts. It means, as Paul says elsewhere, a new creation *of the man*, a conviction that right is the law of the world, and an entire devotion to this law which gives strength for or rather *is* a complete victory over sin. (E&A, 153)

Thus Bosanquet is able to enthuse about Paul's teaching in so far as he is claiming that salvation consists in playing our role in what Josiah Royce, who also thought this the heart of Paul's message, was to call 'the beloved community'. But in relating Paul to Plato, Bosanquet shows himself in movement to a viewpoint which was certainly not Jesus's, and not really Paul's, that the individual only matters as an organ of society conceived as an organism and that since different organs have different functions, social egalitarianism is misconceived. Thus for Bosanquet Pauline doctrine, via assimilation with Plato, is put to the service of a view of the state which is on the whole quite inimical to that privileging of the individual over earthly powers which is more reasonably taken as the message of Jesus, and somewhat differently, Paul. We will see how this led Bosanquet to a philosophy which seems extraordinarily weak on compassion, as instanced by his thorough dislike of, not merely disbelief in, the idea of any recompense after death for those who suffer in the cause of righteousness.

THIRD PHASE OF CHRISTIANITY: GOSPEL OF ST JOHN

The third phase of early Christianity is represented mainly by John's gospel. Here superstition and magic have increased painfully. The miracles become more extreme, and all the 'solemn nonsense' of the doctrine of the Trinity is coming into action. On the other hand, the universality of Christianity, as directed at all men, is now set beyond doubt. So it represents, for Bosanquet, a mixture of decline and progress. Certainly we must not lose sight of the simple sensible main message of the synoptic gospels by interpreting them in the light of Johannine mysticism.

FOURTH PHASE IN THE DEVELOPMENT OF CHRISTIANITY: THE CHURCH

The fourth phase is that of elaborate theology and church organization. Jesus and Paul would have been horrified at anything but an organizational distinction, at most, between cleric and laity. (See E&A, 156.) Some of this decline from the first fresh message is prefigured in some of the Epistles wrongly ascribed to Paul (1 and 2 Timothy, according to Bosanquet) and in the so-called second Epistle of Peter.

Bosanquet ends with some final remarks (rather patronizing of his humble audience of working men, I feel) on how to read the New Testament. (See E&A, 158–61.) Concentrate on the letters of St Paul and the

Gospels; bear in mind the order in which they were evidently written, and do not allow subsequent theory to distort grasping things straightforwardly but critically.

'The Kingdom of God on Earth'

In this companion essay or address, Bosanquet asks the question, 'What did Jesus mean by the kingdom of God (or of Heaven) on Earth?'

There are many sayings of Jesus which imply two things: (1) there is a life after death in which God will 'right the wrongs' and 'compensate the injustices of this world'; (2) in the life after death each of us will be rewarded or punished in a way appropriate to the righteousness or wickedness of the life we have lived on earth.

These were the old convictions about heaven and the kingdom of God,—that it was an invisible future world, in which wrong was to be righted, and good and bad men rewarded and punished. These fancies have not in reality a great place in the New Testament; but they were known to the Greeks and many other nations. (E&A, 112)

This whole notion of a moral government of the world is so much childish nonsense in Bosanquet's opinion, and though it may have had some good effects on human behaviour, it has also done a good deal of harm. Mature people now must utterly reject it. But though these 'fancies' are present in the sayings of Jesus, they are secondary to matters of far more importance.

To anyone with eyes to see, today, all such ideas as

compensation, rewards, and punishments, God's commands in the Bible, the authority of the clergy, ... are all fancies that men have had, just as though they were children, and being children, knew that they must be treated like children ... And so men had to learn to behave themselves, only they had to fancy that there was a parent or schoolmaster looking after them. They naturally invented the only sort of instruction they could receive. (E&A, 114)

We should set aside all such ideas as belonging to the infancy of civilization. What we should concentrate on are certain

other ideas mixed with those which we have been speaking of. The kingdom of God is within you (or perhaps 'among you'); it is like leaven; it is like a seed; it is not of this world. This might mean it is in heaven, but I do not think it does. (E&A, 114)

Bosanquet then develops the following points:

(1) Primarily the kingdom of God means a morally regenerated life on earth, a regeneration which had already started with Jesus's preaching and followers.

(2) Initially after his death it was expected that Jesus would come again, and the regeneration would occur all at once and immediately.

(3) In 'thy kingdom come, thy will be done, on earth as it is in Heaven', this expectation was mixed up with the really irrelevant superstition that there was 'another world' in which everything is just as it should be and which is the model for the regeneration of this world.

(4) In fact the kingdom of God is here on earth already in so far as God's will is done here.

Bosanquet's aim, in effect, is to rescue (1) and (4) from (2) and (3), and he presumably thinks that this is the dominant note in Jesus's own teaching. But now, asks Bosanquet, if we are to do God's will, how shall we know what his will is, and why, for that matter, should we do it?

There are two answers which belong to the childhood of the human race: (1) that we may learn it from the Scriptures; (2) that we should do it in order to be rewarded rather than punished supernaturally after death.

If argument is required, it may be pointed out, first, that the Scriptures are only as good as the morality which they preach, and we must judge how far that morality is good for ourselves; and secondly, that to do good is to do it for its own sake, and if you do it for reward or fear of punishment, you are not doing good—quite apart from the fact that it is superstition to believe in a God and supernatural realm where he metes this out.

In fact, says Bosanquet,

There is only one true way of answering these questions. We must know what is right, what we call God's will, by finding it in our own will. And we must do what is right, what we call God's will, because we find that it is our own will....

[And if] we come to think over our lives, and to ask ourselves what fills up the greater part of our thoughts and purposes, we shall find, if we are decent people, that it mostly comes back to our station in life, and the duties that are recognised by ourselves and others as belonging to it; and also in certain duties and interests usually connected with our station, which we have taken up and made our own. (E&A, 116)

Thus this address, as Bosanquet says in a note, is designed to popularize the famous chapter 5 of Bradley's *Ethical Studies* ('My Station and its Duties') and apply it to the present question.

That our station tells us what to do, and motivates us to do it, follows from the fact that it is what makes us who and what we are. And in doing it, we escape our more narrow and limited self by identifying our will 'with the good will, which is the *real* will that unites men together'. Here, then, we find Bosanquet subscribing to the doctrine of my station and its duties as basic to ethics (in fact, he does not qualify its sovereignty in ethical matters, as Bradley does) and initiating his own version of the doctrine of the general will as being the true will of each.

In expanding on these claims, Bosanquet puts rather neatly his own view on the relation between duties and rights:

I may say that I make no distinction, morally, between rights and duties. That which our station demands of us is a duty if the difficulty in doing it is in ourselves, and a right if the difficulty is in someone else. (E&A, 117)

And he illustrates this by some aspects of family life as (what we may think of as) complacent Victorians conceived it.[6]

Bosanquet explains further that the only legitimate talk of an invisible world of the spirit concerns all 'ties and relationships, these rights and duties, purposes, feelings and hopes' which are indeed not revealed to sight but to the moral intelligence. But is not all this rather tame?, he asks. Should we not have some higher ideal than that of merely performing the duties of our station. No, for the most part, such a suggestion is misconceived. Our station demands quite enough of us, as well as providing our own main proper satisfaction in life.

So one's station and its duties tells us what to do, and it also tells us why to do it. For if we do it in a committed way, not merely mechanically, we will find

the good will to be really and at bottom our own will. That is to say, it is through our station and its duties that we take hold of our humanity and bring it home to our particular selves. On the one hand, the good will is ourself; and, on the other hand, it is the common aim and spirit of our society and of mankind. (E&A, 121)

Our own personal life is good to the extent that we grasp this coming time and work out the role which our own station gives us in contributing to its fulfilment. Thus

All that we mean by the kingdom of God on earth is the society of human beings who have a common life and are working for a common social good. The kingdom of God has come on earth in every civilized society where men live and work together, doing their best for the whole society and for mankind. When two or three are gathered together, cooperating for a social good, there is the Divine Spirit in the midst of them. (E&A, 121)

Bosanquet then considers some standard objections to basing ethics in this way. Is there not a distinction between a man's being a good member of his profession, a good doctor, say, and his being a good man? Bosanquet tells us that this rests on too narrow a conception of a person's station.

Their station is a matter of the whole role they play in society. (The problems of those who hardly have such a role is not much discussed by Bosanquet. See my reference to Joe in *Bleak House*, in section XVII below.)

As for the objection that we should try to improve society, not just operate in it as it is, Bosanquet says that it is of the essence of society (he does not qualify this by saying 'of a good society') to be for ever improving itself, and one's station includes one's appropriate participation in this process. But the urge to reform, Bosanquet warns his hearers, is empty unless it pertains to the real moving processes in society. For 'a great nation, such as England, is a living real purpose, which exists, and pre-scribes our ideal to us' (E&A, 122). Whether we like to call such a nation 'a Christian community' is, once we have got beyond the whole supersti-tious side of Christianity, a matter of choice. What matters is that we should retain the abidingly important message of Christianity—(1) and (4) above, as opposed to (2) and (3)—and not whether we retain its name.

But is not a church (a denomination) better called the 'kingdom of God' rather than a secular community? Well, a church, like the Anglican or Roman Catholic denomination, is a portion of the kingdom of God just in so far as it assists in promoting the good life. 'But a family, or a nation like the English nation, is a far more sacred thing than any Church, because these are what prescribe our duty and educate our will' (E&A, 123). And a social unity like a nation is invisible, as the Kingdom of God is supposed to be, because it is 'bound together not by such symbols as buildings or creeds, or books, but by the great achievements and purposes which form the life of mankind' (E&A, 123–4).

Bosanquet now considers the challenge that what he is describing is morality, not religion, with which he may be suspected of dispensing. But that there is a distinction of a kind between morality and religion Bosanquet agrees, and he gives the following account of it.

If we are to be moral, we must believe that there is such a thing as the good. It must be a reality which exists in the world, and one with which we can engage. Morality, however, of itself gives no guarantee that it is fundamental to reality and that its cause will therefore always prosper in the end.

Religion provides this guarantee. For while morality requires the belief that the good is a reality, religion is the faith that it is the only reality, 'that *nothing but good* is a reality' (E&A, 124).

We would be paralysed morally if we did not see the good forces acting within ourselves as acting more generally in the world, through others and the community. But religion goes a stage further, and says that the good is the only reality. My bad self, for example, is not the real me, and presumably the bad society or state is not the real society or state (not e.g. the real England or Britain). And in teaching that evil is not real, we do not diminish our energy to fight it, for '[n]othing gives such confidence in a battle as thinking that your enemy is only a sham'.

Bosanquet knew no more of battle than I do, but I doubt that he is right that armies do best in war if leaders and men believe that their enemy is a sham. Surely many battles have been lost because the enemy was not taken seriously enough.

It is obviously open to question what can possibly be meant by saying that only the good is real. Was Hitler unreal, or whoever Bosanquet might have regarded as evil—with such a bland thinker, it is unclear whom he did think so, but let us say Jack the Ripper? Presumably, it means that the general drift of things is always in the end good, and that what goes wrong is a necessary element in the development of the good. We shall consider the Panglossian character of Bosanquet's thought more fully later.

Bosanquet finishes his sometimes bizarre account of what Jesus meant by the Kingdom of God on earth by quoting at length from the vow with which the 18-year-old Athenian youth was sworn in as a citizen-soldier and with a long quotation from Kant. Christianity deepened the Athenian concept of loyalty to—I almost said King and Nation—the city-state. And Kant went far to rescue the Christian message from superstition. For Kant, religion, as it becomes rational and adult, consists in the growth of morality, understood as a life based on the moral law which man dictates to himself and which is 'the will of the Ruler of the world, presented to man by his own reason'. From Bosanquet's point of view, Kant's position is largely admirable, but he is still stuck with a residual unnecessary belief in God as divine ruler of the world and in a future life. It comes close to an identification of true Christianity with true Athenian-style citizenship. (T. H. Green was an influence here. However, Green never raised the good of the state above that of the individual citizen, as Bosanquet eventually tended to.)

To conclude this summary of Bosanquet's two early papers on Christianity, I suggest, that, in his insistence on seeing the kingdom of God on earth as essentially a matter of the gradual[7] moral regeneration of humanity, he is already adumbrating some of the less appealing aspects of his later thought.

(1) A strong tendency to regard European civilization as already perfect in essentials.

(2) A corrupting tendency to interpret everything that is wrong and bad as essentially good, properly understood, this leading to a somewhat callous and insensitive attitude to human suffering. Indeed, Bosanquet's philosophy as a whole seems increasingly short on compassion, which, it may be noted, hardly figures in his account of what is of abiding value in Christianity.

(3) An idealization of the state and a morally and metaphysically dubious notion of the 'general will'.

(4) A strong element of unappealing Panglossism.[8]

It is not surprising that Bosanquet became less keen on Christianity as time went on, since his attempt to identify its ethic with that of good citizenship as the be-all and end-all of life is highly dubious.

III The Future of Religious Observance

Let us see how Bosanquet's view on religion developed in the next few years by taking a look at a talk to 'The Progressive Society' called 'The Future of Religious Observance' published in 1893 in the collection of essays called *Civilization of Christendom and Other Studies*.

He raises the question of the future of religious observance in connection with the English Sunday of the late nineteenth century. Even for those who have no religious grounds for treating Sunday as a special day, and not just like a weekly bank holiday, the dominant sabbatarianism influences our grasp of how it is appropriate to spend it. And if we go to 'ethical meetings', the Sunday ones feel different from the weekday ones. But will this continue?

Bosanquet associates this question with the further question as to what will happen to our churches (in the sense of buildings). At the moment they still provide a special social focus, where the great events of life are solemnized. But if the Church were disestablished,

The fabric would then belong, I imagine, to an exasperated sect, whose members would have to maintain it. For a long time its old prestige would continue, and wealthy persons would be found to meet the cost of maintenance. But one day the actual situation would exert its influence; many would abandon the sect in possession, which would become narrower and still more exasperated, and an apple of discord would have been planted in the centre of the village, many of whose inhabitants would feel themselves ousted from the old church at their doors. (CIVILIZATION, 5–6)

However, another possibility is that, rather than remain the home for a declining religious denomination, it will be maintained by the ratepayers as 'a valuable centre of their [the villagers'] social life and religious observance'. And by 'religious' here, Bosanquet says that he means 'something generally and obviously taken as symbolic of the best we know'. This is what has been called 'disestablishment of the clergy and not of the Church'.

This would be better than having these fine old buildings at the centre of the villages fall into neglect and disrepair. Could they not become places where youths were initiated into their role as citizens? Here again we see Bosanquet valuing what he imagines to have been the life of the Athenians above that of Christians.

And if the Athenian made his oath of service to the community on becoming of age to bear arms. I do not see why we should not have a rational confirmation ceremony, at which the individual should accept for himself the vows and intentions which, whether in church or out of church, his parents have surely conceived on his behalf. (CIVILIZATION, 10)

The problem (Bosanquet continues) is somewhat worse in towns. For here there is not the local community which could still enjoy some sort of non-doctrinal coming together in the service of universal ideals; what is more, the churches are generally hideous, at least the ones with most following, the Nonconformist ones. These bring together working men and women for focusing on their highest values. What will happen to such people when doctrinal belief commands little assent? 'Will something analogous to our own Ethical lectures serve as a meeting point for them, and as a means of guiding and concentrating their "cosmic emotion"?' (CIVILIZATION, 13).

Against this background Bosanquet puts forward some ideas of his own. He would like to see some distinctive feel about Sunday: in particular, that it should not be a day of money making. So his ideal would be that putting on shows or sports for profit on Sundays would be illegal, but that wholesome cultural events performed for the love of them should be encouraged.

Thus I should hope that before our Sabbatarianism is destroyed we may have utilised it to found a new kind of Sunday—an English Sunday, not a Puritan nor yet a Parisian Sunday. We have a great and grave responsibility in this matter. We are working to destroy superstition. Are we or are we not aiming at such a result that the Derby will be run on Sunday [and that] ... the huge machinery of Lord's and the Oval would not be set in motion. (CIVILIZATION, 15)

However, if it had to be a choice between the Puritan Sunday and the Bank Holiday Sunday, he would prefer the latter. But the best would be that it should be a time for quiet family reunion and openness to 'art, music, and literature and . . . the beauties of Nature'. We can imagine that Bosanquet would not have been too happy with our own Shopaholic Sunday, though he would have been pleased at the crowds who go to art exhibitions these days.

But how far do we want something like ceremonial religious observance to continue? Well, first, it does seem important to have some form of 'social recognition of great moments both in national and individual life'.

But, as for any weekly meeting together at all like Sunday services, we must remember that till now the minister has been more educated than most of his congregation and therefore has something to offer them in the sermon which they could not easily find for themselves. And as for ethical societies, they are an opportunity to meet a few other rational minds. But talks on life in general will become less significant as the generalists will have to talk about things on which many members of his audience know more.

It appears, therefore, very doubtful whether instruction or oratory can ever take the place of public worship. Instruction essentially deals with special matter, while public worship is supposed to meet a general need; and with the abandonment of public worship as a service of prayer and praise to a common Father, it appears to me that the only general source of cosmic emotion has ceased to exist, and that the world will have to rely on more concrete forms of sympathy depending on more definite common experience and common interest. (CIVILIZATION, 19–20)

So Bosanquet anticipates a highly educated society in the future, in which each will pursue, in groups of individuals with the same interests, his own cultural and intellectual development, but there will be no unitary celebration of the supposedly highest values. But it will be good if Sunday is kept a somewhat special day for superior occupations of the mind, by banning commercial entertainment (and presumably, though he does not say so, Sunday trading).

It may seem that these suggestions herald a splitting up of culture which will destroy unity and sympathy. I do not think so. The open secret of modern life, to my mind, is that we find the universal not in the general, but in the individual. (CIVILIZATION, 21–2)

What is to be hoped is that a tradition will form itself of Sunday being a day for social reunions and for renewing our hold 'on those works of man and nature which best typify to us the unity of the world'. If our circumstances prevent our following the suggestion of Matthew Arnold 'that it is a duty to hear or read or see something very good every day', we may at least attempt to do so 'every week'—on Sunday.

Bosanquet sums up these ideas by saying that it seems

quite possible, that in spite of a sound tradition as to the use of the weekly holiday. . . . we may in course of generations cease to possess or to recognise any general external symbol of our common human relation to the reality of what is best. (CIVILIZATION, 24–5)

If dropping the symbols meant dropping the reality, that would indeed be tragic. And there is a real risk of this, a risk which, if it materialized, would mean that the 'world would not be worth living in' and a 'baser thing than it ever has been before'. But if we abandon the symbol because we have taken hold of 'the actual spiritual world in all its various reality, then, surely, life will be nobler than it ever has been before' (CIVILIZATION, 25–6).

We have now before us a fair picture of Bosanquet's outlook on religion prior to 1893. What he really believes in is a civilization in which all, in their various stations and with their various aptitudes, participate in high culture and learning.[9] A general sense of man's unity with the cosmos will be pervasive, but there will be no communal way of expressing this sense of union. This combines a little problematically with a wish that there should be a celebration of the great events in which people commit themselves to their duties as citizens.

Many will think that religion is altogether abandoned here. Even if we take religion, in Bosanquet's sense, as a symbolization of the best that we know, it seems that he is abandoning this. Culture is the one thing needful, it seems.

In the earlier of these essays Bosanquet clings to some way in which he can still identify himself with Christianity. By the later essays it seems that he has abandoned this dubious attempt. For surely his thought is really highly un-Christian. Not only does he abandon the whole supernatural aspect of Christianity, but he dislikes what he thought psychologically motivated it, to some great extent: namely, the idea of recompense and blessings upon the good (and contrariwise for the bad).

But it is not just the supernatural side of Christianity from which he is quite distant. For surely what must be central to a de-supernaturalized Christianity must be an ethic based upon compassion and a belief in human equality as an ideal. Bosanquet has not exactly opposed these in the essays we have considered, but nor has he done anything to celebrate these beliefs and ideals. Compassion, at any rate, is notably absent, and in his later thought we will see him standing quite opposed to it, as it seems to me.

As for his idea that our commitment to the best needs little if anything by way of community expression and celebration, this is doubtful. While in many ways our society, in Britain, is much better than it was in Bosanquet's day, there is a universal tawdriness in our cultural world, which (I suggest) Bosanquet would certainly deplore, but which is partly a result, surely, precisely of the lack of communal forms of identification with the good.

But let us see how Bosanquet's thought on religion and such things developed when he constructed a more or less complete metaphysical system of his own, the main statement of which is in the two volumes of the Gifford Lectures which he gave at Edinburgh in 1911 and 1912. I shall also have a word to say about what is probably Bosanquet's most read, and maybe his best, work, *The Philosophical Theory of the State*.

PART TWO: LATER WORK

IV A Brief Sketch of the Metaphysics of F. H. Bradley

Bosanquet's metaphysical position is given its main, and lengthiest, statement in the two volumes based on the Gifford Lectures: *The Principle of Individuality and Value* (1912) and *The Value and Destiny of the Individual* (1913).

I have already indicated that Bosanquet's thought owes much to that of Bradley, though diverging from it significantly in emphasis.[10] For this reason a brief sketch of Bradley's metaphysical position may be helpful.

The central tenets of Bradley's metaphysics are:

(1) The stuff of reality is sentient experience. Every genuine reality is either an experience or a component of an experience.
(2) All the ordinary concepts with which we cope with the world are, in the last resort, incoherent, and do not apply to Reality as it really is, except in the sense that they are more or less useful tools for dealing with it for one purpose or another.
(3) Among the basic ordinary concepts which are ultimately incoherent are space, time, causation, personal identity, also goodness, wickedness, and God.
(4) The fundamental vice of our conceptual system is its relational nature. Our ordinary thinking conceives of the world as consisting of lots of

individually conceivable things, in various relations one to another, when in fact every conception of them, other than as aspects of the Absolute, must to some extent misrepresent them.

(5) It is about as close to being true as any proposition can be that the Absolute is articulated into innumerable finite centres of experience of which the Absolute is the synthesis.

(6) In fact, reality as a whole is a single timeless experience (the Absolute), of which every other reality is a component.

(7) Thus every moment of apparently transitory experience is really just eternally there in its own place within the Absolute.

(8) The Absolute is too unlike God, as the term is usually understood, to be God, but belief in God is one very appropriate way of relating to the Absolute.

(9) The natural world of every day life is, for each of us, a conceptual construction which, as finite centres of experience, we make to extend and deepen what is given in sense experience.

(10) It is just possible that the reality which appears to us as the physical world (which our construction of it somehow represents) is, in itself, a system of experiences, perhaps articulated into low-level finite centres or perhaps not (in which case proposition (9) requires some qualification).

(11) To live well is to actualize, to some significant extent, the eternal values of truth, goodness, and beauty in the apparently temporal world.

(12) Religion consists in dedication to these values, associated with the assurance that they are the ultimate determinant of how things are both eternally in the Absolute and in the world (or worlds) of space and time (which, after all, only genuinely exist as a component of the Absolute). However, it is absolutely appropriate that the religions of most men should make use of a mythology, just as science does, to promote its purposes, as just briefly specified.

(13) Whether anything ever occurs of the sort popularly known as 'supernatural' is of no religious significance. Likewise, it is religiously irrelevant whether there is a life after death for human beings (or any other finite individuals).

(14) Religion in the highest sense is devotion to a single object thought of as supremely good. But it is impossible to form any conception of this object which will be metaphysically satisfactory. The Absolute is more real than God, but not necessarily more suitable for the religious imagination.

(15) For Bradley, religion (like everything else except the Whole or Absolute) is self-contradictory. This is primarily because, on the one hand,
God has to be just one part of total reality if we are to relate to him, as
in prayer or worship, while to regard him as a part only of reality is to
debase him.

We may say that God is not God, till he has become all in all, and that a God which
is all in all is not the God of religion. God is but an aspect, and that must mean but
an appearance of the Absolute. (APPEARANCE, 396–7)

Just what role this leaves for religion for one who believes in Bradley's
Absolute is open to debate. Bradley said at one point that a new religion is
needed. I doubt that he would think that it has yet been found. However,
upon the whole, what is required is a mythology which will promote the
actualization of the values of beauty, truth, and goodness in human life,
express the sense we have in our deepest experiences that the barriers
between men, and man and nature, are all ultimately illusory, while yet
there really is a scale of values (in which there is a better and a worse)
which we should live by. And degree of value, and indeed of reality, turns
on how much supplementation phenomena require (and receive) in order
to be 'transmuted' in the Absolute as elements of its perfection.

In talking of this transmutation, Bradley often writes as though finite
things change as they enter into the Absolute. But this is not his real
message, or if it is, he is inconsistent. For there are not two of everything,
a version outside the Absolute and a version inside the Absolute. The
distinction is only in the kind of contribution they make to the Absolute,
and how much of the Whole's character is reflected in these its parts. In
truth the Whole is eternally perfect and needs everything to be just as it is
for it to be so. (It was the apparent implication that all evil is somehow
good seen in the light of the whole that fuelled the hostility of many
critics of Absolute Idealism, none more so than William James.)

Perhaps Bradley's main message as to how one should live one's life is
that it must be based upon recognition that there is no one ideal worthy of
single pursuit. For every ideal has its internal contradictions. What one
must do is judge what ideal, and for that matter belief, suits the present
circumstances, and there is no formulable rule which will tell us this.
One's life should be devoted to the good. But the good is not purely
ethical. Neither living for others nor the aim at personal perfection is
satisfactory unless each is balanced by the other. The actualizing of every
ideal is good so far as it goes, but it can be bad if it frustrates the actualizing
of other ideals whether for oneself or for others.

I end with an often quoted passage from Bradley which may be regarded as definitive of the sense in which he was an idealist, and does not serve badly as definitive of philosophical idealism in general.

Our result so far is this. Everything phenomenal is somehow real; and the Absolute must at least be as rich as the relative. And, further, the Absolute is not many; there are no independent reals. The universe is one in this sense that its differences exist harmoniously within one whole, beyond which there is nothing. Hence the Absolute is, so far, an individual and a system, but, if we stop here, it remains but formal and abstract. Can we then, the question is, say anything about the concrete nature of the system?

Certainly, I think, this is possible. When we ask as to the matter which fills up the empty outline, we can reply in one word, that this matter is experience. And experience means something much the same as given and present fact. We perceive, on reflection, that to be real, or even barely to exist, must be to fall within sentience. Sentient experience, in short, is reality, and what is not this is not real. We may say, in other words, that there is no being or fact outside of that which is commonly called psychical existence. Feeling, thought, and volition (any groups under which we class psychical phenomena) are all the material of existence, and there is no other material, actual or even possible. This result in its general form seems evident at once; and, however serious a step we now seem to have taken, there would be no advantage at this point in discussing it at length. For the test in the main lies ready to our hand, and the decision rests on the manner in which it is applied. I will state the case briefly thus. Find any piece of existence, take up anything that any one could possibly call a fact, or could in any sense assert to have being, and then judge if it does not consist in sentient experience. Try to discover any sense in which you can still continue to speak of it, when all perception and feeling have been removed; or point out any fragment of its matter, any aspect of its being, which is not derived from and is not still relative to this source. When the experiment is made strictly, I can myself conceive of nothing else than the experienced. Anything, in no sense felt or perceived, becomes to me quite unmeaning. And as I cannot try to think of it without realizing either that I am not thinking at all, or that I am thinking of it against my will as being experienced, I am driven to the conclusion that for me experience is the same as reality. The fact that falls elsewhere seems, in my mind, to be a mere word and a failure, or else an attempt at self-contradiction. (APPEARANCE, 127–8)

V Contrasts and Affinities between Bosanquet and Bradley

Bosanquet's quite frequent assertion that he entirely accepts the metaphysics of *Appearance and Reality* implies that he accepts almost all these propositions. There is no real reason to doubt that he does so, with the exception of (10), which he rejects both explicitly and vigorously, possibly influencing Bradley to look less favourably upon it. As for the rest, any divergence is probably more a matter of emphasis than anything else. To be more specific about his relation to these propositions, he says very little by way of assertion of or argument for (2), (3), and (4) (there is none of Bradley's complicated argument for the unreality of relations); he says many things which look inconsistent with (1); he certainly places less emphasis on (5) and (6); he is very clear in his acceptance of (8) and (9), but less clear in his acceptance of (7), while (11), (12), and (13) largely characterize his own position, except that he seems less favourable towards the mythology mentioned in (12).

Though the Absolute is the unique infinite individual which somehow experiences and is responsible for everything, Bosanquet agrees with Bradley that it is best not to call it 'God'. For it is, rather, the scene of the strife between good and evil, than itself good (still less, evil). However, it is perfect in a sense which means that what is good is nearer to the heart of things than what is evil. None the less, it could not be perfect unless there was a great deal of evil in the temporal world. For the temporal world is the history of the adventures of finite things, in particular souls, and souls, as finite, are bound to include contradictions which are painful and, considered in abstraction from their total context in the Absolute, bad. But there would be no goodness or perfection if it were otherwise, since these are essential to the perfection of the Absolute. Included in this perfection is a force for the good which will always have the last word in the struggles of finite things. It is this force for good which is best called 'God', if we are to retain the term at all. And evil of every sort has to be there if there is to be any nobility in human life. (See section XVI below.)

What is religion? Essentially it is noble behaviour accompanied by an elevating and calming emotion, which at times will give us a rest from the distresses involved in our necessary struggles, based on the recognition that the values for which we struggle are necessary features of an eternal Whole in which all that we could wish for, when our wishes are purged by critical reflection, is eternally realized. Religion and morality are distinguished only by the special underlying peacefulness which this knowledge, or sense, of the ultimate perfection of the universe sustains, even though most of the time we are caught up in the heat of our battles. This emotion is the distinctive experience of the religious mind, whatever the official doctrine in which it is expressed.

VI Two Tensions in Bosanquet's Thought

There are certain tensions in Bosanquet's thought which make it difficult to give a fair summary of what he stood for. Two are particularly important.

First, there is the fact, just noted, that while asserting periodically, in alliance with Bradley, that there is no reality except experience or consciousness,[11] he often describes it as a late comer upon the cosmic scene, whose role is rather to appreciate what the natural world has brought forth than to play any substantial role in creating it.

Secondly, there is the problem that (1) he describes the world as 'a vale of soul making', which seems to imply that what really matters is the excellence of individual souls, while (2) also seeming to believe that the individual hardly matters except for his role in constituting—what does really matter—great organizations such as the state. I shall explore both of these tensions in what follows.

VII Some Terminological Clarifications: 'Consciousness', 'Experience', and 'Materialism'

The first tension in his thought mentioned shows in the fact that there are long stretches of *The Principle of Individuality and Value* in which Bosanquet seems to argue for a naturalistic view of things, which looks quite inconsistent with idealism, in particular with Bradley's view that the stuff of reality is sentient experience.

Before exploring this problem further, it will be convenient to clarify my own use, henceforth, of the expressions 'consciousness', 'experience', and 'materialism'. I am among those philosophers who hold the view (contraries of which I find it hard, I admit, not to regard as insane) that consciousness cannot be identical with any purely physical thing or process if physical reality is as it is normally conceived to be. In fact, the word 'consciousness' stands for too basic a reality for its meaning to be captured in a definition. However, there are ways in which one can indicate what one is talking of to those who are not (as I must see it) simply obtuse at this point in their thinking.

There are various animals and humans around one, and one is a human oneself. Now there are two different sorts of knowledge one may have of any such individual: (1) knowing what it is like and (2) knowing what it is like to be it.

To know what a human being is like (whether human beings in general or one particular human being) is not fundamentally different from knowing what, say, an oak tree (whether a particular oak tree or oak trees in general) is like. One may be able to recognize oak trees by the distinctive shape of their leaves, or by the character of their bark, or their kind of overall shape. If one is a botanist or a biologist, one will know lots more about what oak trees are like. And the same goes for a particular oak tree. If one is observant, one may have some idea of a particular oak tree's height, of the particular form it has as a whole, and other things of that sort. But most people nowadays, rightly or wrongly, think it would be only a kind of joke to ask *what it is like to be* an oak tree or some particular oak tree. And to regard this question as a kind of a joke is to regard the oak tree as non-conscious, or as lacking consciousness. It is not that one regards oneself as ignorant as to what it is like to be it, but that one thinks the only true answer would be that there is nothing whatever which it is like to be it.

Perhaps there are people, who, stopping short of panpsychism, think of all *living* things, animals or plants, as conscious. For their benefit, one may substitute similar questions about bicycles, planets, or Swiss mountains. 'What is a bicycle like', someone who has never seen one might ask; or one might ask, 'What is the planet Mars really like?' or 'What are the mountains in Switzerland like?'. And answers are available, even if some of us would not be very good at providing them, either through ignorance or bad powers of description. But as to what it is like being them, it would seem again that the only answer is 'nothing'.

Contrast the case of a human being. One may know what a particular person is like, their sex, their height, their degree of corpulence, and so on. Knowledge of their anatomy, or of the various physiological processes going on within them, are not essentially different. They are all questions as to how space is filled up when occupied by the person.

But one may also wonder what it is like to be a particular person or a particular type of person (one should know what it is like to be simply a human being from one's own case). I often wonder what it can be like seriously to believe that materialism is true. Or I might wonder what it was like to be a eunuch in the court of a Byzantine emperor.

I often wonder what it is like to be a (mallard) duck. I hardly dare say I know, but what I do know is that there is a truth as to what it is like to be a duck, or some particular duck. This is quite different from wondering what ducks (or some particular duck) is like, something of which I have some (though quite limited) knowledge.

Before proceeding further, it will be as well to distinguish the use of 'consciousness', in the very broad sense which I have been trying to explicate, without being able to define, with some narrower uses of the expression, in which it stands only for some specific form thereof.

(1) 'Consciousness' is sometimes used as synonymous with 'self-consciousness'. Now 'self-consciousness' itself has several meanings. It can refer to a tendency to be over concerned with how one is presenting oneself to others. Or it can mean a more general tendency to reflect on one's own personality or make an object of one's own mental processes. And there are other meanings too. But in none of these meanings is self-consciousness required for consciousness as I, and I think the majority of philosophers, use the expression.

(2) A more specifically philosophical use of 'consciousness' is one in which it refers only to those experiential states which divide into a SELF confronting a NOT-SELF.[12] Thus to know what it is like to be someone looking at a particular painting, you have to know both what the painting is visibly like (not-self) and his then bodily state as he experiences it (self). (There is a problem as to whether the painting's beauty belongs to the self or not-self side. My own view is that it belongs to the not-self.) Most human experience is of this character, and so, it seems clear enough to me, is a duck's experience, but maybe there are lower organisms, or perhaps other things, in which there is no such contrast between self and not-self. So although most human *consciousness*, in my sense, includes a contrast between self and not-self, there can be forms of human consciousness in which there is no such contrast. For example, extreme pain may sometimes abolish the contrast between self and not-self, perhaps also states of extreme ecstasy, and may especially characterize some mystical and some drug-induced experiences. And who knows what the experience of some lower animals may be—apart, that is, from the animals themselves who know it immediately though, not conceptually?

Now Bradley preferred to use the expression 'consciousness' to refer only to such 'sentient experience' as includes directedness upon an object, while using 'experience' to cover also forms of experience lived through without referring to anything other than themselves. But he admitted in a letter to G. F. Stout that the broader use was becoming common among philosophers.[13]

Bosanquet is more inclined to the broader usage than is Bradley. And personally I prefer to use 'consciousness' in the broader sense. For the danger, especially in a philosophical culture more inclined to materialism than in Bradley's day, in using 'experience' as the generic expression (though

I am happy to use it as synonymous with 'consciousness' in my sense) is that it is sometimes used, apparently, to include in its extension a purely physical aspect of an organism. The distinction is important when we discuss, as we shall, the doctrine of panpsychism, because the panpsychist may think that much of nature is inwardly conscious but neither self-conscious nor with much sense of a contrast between self and not-self.

I turn now to the meaning of 'materialism'. Among philosophers today this usually refers to the opinion that nothing exists which is not physical. And to be physical, in this connection, I suggest, is to fill out a part of public space or be a part of what does so. Sometimes the expression 'physicalism' is preferred, perhaps because 'matter' has a rather old-fashioned sound.

The materialist, in this sense, must either deny the existence of consciousness or interpret it in a strictly materialist way. There are a number of alternative ways of doing this. It may be said that consciousness is what produces the kind of behaviour which we ordinarily take as a sign of its presence, and that since what does so are certain processes in the brain, these are what consciousness is. Then again consciousness may be identified with a computer-type program on which the brain operates.[14] There are other alternatives too, but all boil down to the claim that the existence of consciousness consists in the fact that a physical part (the brain) of a physical organism has certain causes and effects or performs certain functions. The modern materialist does not claim that this is something which can be known by purely a priori philosophizing, but holds that it turns out empirically that there is nothing non-physical to which the term 'consciousness' applies. The same goes for all types or instances of consciousness, such as conscious desires or thoughts.

This is the kind of materialism which I think insane when the issue is fully understood. For whatever physical facts are known about an organism, inferring that it is conscious is to move to a different kind of reality. A simple way of contrasting 'consciousness' with the physical is that there is nothing physical to which only one person has special cognitive access, whereas I do have a special 'privileged access' to my own consciousness. This does not mean that I may not misdescribe it (as indeed do all materialist philosophers), but that I know what I do know about it in a more direct way than do other people.

The expression 'privileged access' comes from Gilbert Ryle's *The Concept of Mind*. He used it to refer to what he thought a mistake, and deployed it negatively to attack any kind of mind–body dualism. But though one can argue as to how the matter should be expressed in detail, it remains obvious that we do have a kind of privileged access to our conscious states.

Materialism in the strong sense which I have been describing was hardly dreamt of till around 1920. So when philosophers prior to that talked of *materialism*, they usually meant either (1) epiphenomenalism, the view that consciousness is a product of brain processes, which do not act back on the brain, or (2) the less extreme view that, even if consciousness has some limited causal efficacy of its own, it is entirely dependent for its existence upon the brain, and has no possible home except in brain-possessing physical organisms.

And since I am talking about a philosopher writing before 1920, and there is no other convenient expression for this purpose, I shall use 'materialism' to refer to the disjunction of (1) and (2), distinguishing the first as strong materialism and the latter as weak materialism. In contrast to these stands the more extreme modern view which seems to me 'insane' and which is best called 'physicalism'. With these terminological clarifications, I shall now consider certain stretches of *The Principle of Individuality and Value* which have a curiously materialist (in our now settled sense) air to them.

VIII Materialist Tendencies in Bosanquet's *Principle of Individuality and Value*

In Lecture V of *The Principle of Individuality and Value* Bosanquet examines the origin of mind in the universe. He holds that it comes on the scene when cosmic evolutionary processes produce organisms with a suitable kind of internal physical complexity, in particular in their brains. The great question has always been how something so different as conscious mind can arise from a purely physical world.

Bosanquet is especially anxious to challenge one viewpoint on this matter which he finds too widely current among his contemporaries. This is the panpsychist view that physical nature, as a whole, is composed of sentient individuals, and that our kind of consciousness is produced by some special type of complexity or aggregation in the pervasive flows of sentience always present in the universe. For more discussion of this, see section XI below.

Bosanquet thinks the more satisfactory view is that significant wholes so act upon their parts as, other things being equal, to maintain themselves in existence with the same essential character. Such a significant whole for

Bosanquet is a concrete universal inasmuch as it holds sway over its instances so that they continue to exemplify it until external circumstances crush it.

The totality of physical nature is itself such a whole. But it gradually produces lesser such physical wholes with a special kind of internal complexity and sensitivity to the world outside them and with an overall character which acts as a main determinant of the behaviour of their parts. One may speak of the parts as acting according to the spirit of the whole, but 'spirit' here simply means this controlling nature, not anything mental. Wholes may have a spirit, in this sense, without having any kind of consciousness at all.

All laws of nature are really instances of this, a matter of the parts of a whole doing whatever is required in particular circumstances, so that the whole remains the same in its most essential properties. In the case of the laws of physics, the whole in question is simply *physical nature as a whole*. However, as a result of these basic physical laws, individuals are generated whose parts act so as to sustain *them*, rather than *merely nature as a whole*, in their overall character. That they do so may or may not be simply a special case of the operation of the basic physical laws, but it may be that fresh laws, modifying the operation of the basic laws, thereby apply to the parts of such wholes. Bosanquet is open-minded as to which is the case; it makes no essential difference to the fact that nature as a whole produces these smaller self-sustaining wholes.

Be that as it may, Bosanquet certainly looks at nature as being such a self-sustaining whole itself and as containing these lesser such self-sustaining wholes. And he thinks it quite appropriate in such cases to speak of the guiding spirit of the whole as governing or influencing the behaviour of its parts. This may be true, from Bosanquet's point of view, both of plants and of certain human societies. The character of many wholes, such as plants and animals, includes, of course the potentiality, under favourable conditions, to move through a characteristic life cycle, and even jointly or singly to generate heirs.

But we must be careful not to identify spirit with mind. Trees have a guiding spirit in this sense, in virtue of which they grow and keep themselves alive under the right conditions, but Bosanquet is determined not to ascribe mind to them. They are not conscious.

Moreover, even if some of these wholes are conscious, it does not follow that their consciousness is what controls their behaviour. If one supposed, for example, that trees and plants possess an individual consciousness (which Bosanquet thinks altogether implausible), it would be folly to conclude that what they do is controlled by it. For that would suggest the absurd idea that a plant could have thoughts about just what needed to be done at every moment. After all, even in our own case, that of conscious human beings, our bodies maintain themselves to a very great extent independently of our thoughts about them.

So it is characteristic of the natural world, first, that it is a whole which maintains its character through the behaviour of its parts, and, secondly, that it tends to produce subsidiary wholes which also maintain their character (and even spread it) by the behaviour of their parts. And up to a certain level this goes on without any consciousness being involved.

Is nature teleological, as thus described? Not so, humans and animals perhaps apart, if teleology implies guidance by conscious aims. But should it be considered as unconsciously teleological? Only if this refers to the guidance of parts by wholes in the sense explained. And if we do speak of it or its non-human parts as teleological, we must be constantly on guard that we do not think of this as implying consciousness.

But, though consciousness is not required for teleology, maybe when it does arise, a new type of teleology is born in which individuals are guided by 'the pursuit of conceived goals'. This might be called conscious teleology. But, warns Bosanquet, we must not be over ready to suppose it present, wherever the teleology of something non-human reminds us of guidance by human purposing, since there is no clear limit to what unconscious teleology can achieve.

I am not concerned to maintain that purposes do or do not operate in nature; it seems doubtful what the question can mean. What I am interested in pointing out may be taken to mean almost the reverse, viz. that Nature below conscious intelligence, and Providence, if we like to call it so, can achieve, without the help of a relevant explicit consciousness, results of the same general type as those which are ascribed to the guidance of finite minds. (PIV, 145)

But where, then, exactly does consciousness come in? Bosanquet's surprisingly modern answer is that, at a certain stage in the development of nature, physical representations of the environment, and mechanisms for reacting to it, at a certain 'centre' within an organism, give it such an intense inward unity, that the universe, so to speak, requires that it leads on to an even intenser kind of inwardness which only consciousness can supply. (See PIV, 291.)

Bosanquet is far from denying that consciousness is a quite fresh kind of reality, whose occurrence could not have been predicted before the event (and not merely because there would have been no one to make the prediction). There is no question of his reducing consciousness to something physical. None the less, its occurrence is not altogether a mere brute fact without explanation. For consciousness is, in a sense, the next stage in a development intrinsic to the physical character of high-level organisms, the development towards an ever greater intensity of being and of ever subtler life-conserving responses to the environment.

But is consciousness, according to Bosanquet, a genuinely causal agent, so that what a conscious organism does is to a considerable extent inexplicable in purely physical terms—that is, in terms of unconscious teleology? Upon the whole, Bosanquet's answer is positive, but he is remarkably tolerant of a negative answer as an option which he does not altogether reject. Thus he often seems to be advocating strong materialism as defined above (if not quite physicalism).

There is nothing in the contact of men with their machines to show... that the human consciousness is not mechanically constituted; there is certainly no observable point in the construction or control of a machine at which anything but mechanical interconnection takes place between the producer and his product. (PIV, 143)

He means (I think) that it is (epistemically) possible that our consciousness may not, in fact, play any part at all in causing our behaviour, and that the latter may always be mechanistically determined by purely physical processes, just as is the behaviour of 'intelligent' machines. Bosanquet here brilliantly extrapolates from the technology of his day to the concept of the brain as a kind of natural computer.

If this were indeed so, holds Bosanquet, it would not show that consciousness is a pointless excrescence in nature, such as epiphenomenalists tend to view it. Its point would be, rather (and indeed, this is a large part of its point in any case), not to produce results in the physical world but to be a centre of appreciation of what has been achieved by the *nisus* of the physical to form more and more intensive wholes. It would be a 'supervenient perfection' (PIV, 202) rather than a causal agency. Of course, to talk of 'its point' suggests something beneficent which is responsible for the world, but this is only hinted at here as an almost hidden reference to the Absolute.

And even if it is a causal agent in its own right, it should not be thought of as a sharply distinct factor interfering with brain process, as it is according to standard dualism. Rather is there a single psycho-physical individual whose character determines both that its parts and itself as a whole behave so as to maintain it (including a tendency for a characteristic development over time as part of its character).

Altogether Bosanquet seems somewhat ambivalent as to whether he is more drawn to the view that consciousness does, or that it does not, play the part which it seems to play in the causation of our behaviour: remarks such as the following certainly seem to suggest the latter alternative, though it is a bit hard to believe that he really wished to commit himself to it. 'Consciousness, we repeat, neither creates a higher organism nor works it. It is rather the indispensable means of reaping the final and supreme result of the organism's complex adaptation' (PIV, 197).

What is, at any rate, surprising in the work of a famous idealist philosopher is just how easy it would be to cull from the pages of *The Principle of Individuality and Value* a fine exposition of a totally materialist philosophy. But we can no longer keep at bay features of Bosanquet's thought which sound a different note. However, these are of two types. First, there are features of it which supplement rather than contradict this purely materialistic account. Secondly, there are features which prima facie actually contradict it. Let us confine ourselves to the first for now.

IX Laws of Nature

In so far as Bosanquet's text strikes a surprisingly materialist note much of the time, it should be stressed that it would be a materialism significantly different from that of a Hobbes or a physicalist of our own time. First, there is no suggestion that he wishes to reduce so-called secondary qualities to primary qualities. He has no inclination to suppose that nature could be adequately described in a language of pure physics.

And, perhaps more importantly, he had, as we have been seeing, a very special view of laws of nature according to which they are really what the spirit of some whole imposes upon its parts. As we might put it, all causation is holistic, that is, the control of its parts by some whole.

In this connection he criticizes those empiricist philosophers who think that to learn about a law of nature is to know how reality repeats itself. Their scientific ideal is to explain the whole of nature as a system in which events of type A are always followed by events of type B. Bosanquet insists that this is wrong. Essentially he is making the correct point that laws of nature are normally formulas which explain what happens at any particular moment as logically following from the formula in conjunction with antecedent circumstances. The law of gravity is not primarily telling you that your dropping a glass is just like all sorts of other cases where people have dropped glasses. (The motion of the planets round the sun seems something quite different.) It is, rather, telling you that there is an identical principle which gives quite different results in different circumstances. That the laws of nature remain the same over time does not imply that the world is a highly repetitive one; rather, the opposite is true. In this connection Bosanquet utilizes the concept due especially to Hegel, that genuine identity is always an identity-in-difference. Bosanquet claims on this basis that to understand an identity-in-difference is to grasp how an identical principle produces different results in different circumstances.

This criticism of the idea that the archetypal form of a law of nature is to the effect that A is always followed by B, without any difference between A and B on each occasion, seems right. But Bosanquet is even more contemptuous of the idea that a law of nature is to the effect that something *merely resembling* an initial A will always be followed by *something merely resembling* an initial B. No, what is required is a genuine identity, but one which is also a difference. For a genuine identity is not merely a matter of different symbols or representations of one thing. Rather, it is a matter of precisely the same thing being present in different locations in the universe, and in virtue of this difference of location being different in itself.

The insistence that precise causality does not imply exact repetition allows Bosanquet another swipe at panpsychism. For the wretched panpsychists, he says, who are anxious to conceive the fundamental units of nature as mental, usually believe themselves obliged to deny that their behaviour is altogether governed by natural law. This is because they suppose that an individual's consciousness is displayed above all in the unpredictable freedom of his acts. They therefore suggest that nature is not really as precisely determined by inflexible laws of nature as it seems, and that the regularity is statistical rather than precise.[15]

Such thinkers are barking up the wrong tree, according to Bosanquet. The laws of physics may not suffice to explain human behaviour, but this does not mean that the latter is not governed by another type of law, in which a fresh kind of whole determines the behaviour of its parts. For the very same laws of human nature, just like the laws of nature at large, can and do continually produce quite fresh results as circumstances change and individuals develop. The panpsychist, therefore, objectionable as is his viewpoint, has no need to argue that nature may be less deterministic than it seems.

But if human behaviour, as Bosanquet supposes, is governed by its own special laws which go beyond physics, why is it often so difficult to predict? Here Bosanquet makes a point akin to one which Karl Popper made against 'historicism'. Certainly one cannot predict what (say) a great writer will produce next. One could only do so by creating his novel in advance of him. Nor can one predict what scientists will discover without discovering it oneself. (See VDI, 8.) Even if all this is covered by law, one cannot arrive at such predictions without a knowledge of what there is to be discovered, something *ex hypothesi* not yet known. Nor can one predict the scientist's mental processes as they develop internally without being of similar intellectual power and imagination oneself.

For although a person's character together with his current circumstances necessarily determines what he will do, this is not something which could be charted in advance in a manner lending itself to standard deductive techniques. Of course, we often can know a person's character (or human nature in general) well enough to make quite a lot of predictions about him, but we cannot know it well enough to predict his behaviour in all cases. For at his birth a new kind of whole appeared with laws of behaviour with features of which no one could have known in advance.

Bosanquet's views on this may become clearer if we relate them to his views on artistic creation. According to him, the finest artistic work is the result of the artist having been captured, so to speak, by a sense of some aesthetic whole which requires just such details as his work has in order to be actualized. Only an artist captured by that same whole could predict the final product. Thus, to whatever extent *The Brothers Karamazov* is a successful work, everything in it is necessary to produce a whole which Dostoevsky intuitively sensed from the start. In so far as that is not so, it is less than a perfect work. In either case the work will be the product of two wholes: Dostoevsky's mind and its having been captured more or less successfully by some aesthetic whole. Thus Dostoevsky's creativity is as truly the logic of an idea working itself out as is a discovery in mathematics.[16] 'The essential for philosophy is to dismiss as self-contradictory all attempts to set the creativeness of mind in opposition to its systematic lawfulness' (VDI, 4).[17]

X Contradiction and Wholeness

So far, so good. However, we will not have fully grasped Bosanquet's conception of the relations between wholes, parts, and the laws of nature until we have explored a somewhat Hegelian theme in his metaphysic: the thesis that somehow the motivating force of all that goes on in the world is the struggle of finite things to free themselves from contradiction. So let us explore this theme a little.

Bosanquet shares the belief of Hegel and Marx that there are real contradictions in nature. This is a view of which philosophers of the analytic
tradition have been highly critical, arguing that it is only propositions
which can contradict each other or be self-contradictory, and that propositions do not belong to nature in any relevant sense.

But things are not as simple as that. For surely people who affirm
contradictory propositions are properly described as contradicting each
other. And if people can contradict each other, surely they can contradict
themselves. In which case, nature, presuming that it includes human
beings, can contain contradictory elements. To this it will be replied by
the enemies of contradiction in nature that the contradiction is between
the propositions which each affirms. Or if there is a sense in which there
can be self-contradictory things, it is really the concept of such a thing
which is self-contradictory (like a round square), for which reason there
can be no real thing in nature answering to it.

However, let us make a more positive attempt to understand the claim
that there are real contradictions in nature. Bradley thought that most of
the things postulated in ordinary thought are self-contradictory. They are,
therefore, mere appearances of Reality, not themselves real. What he
means by this (at least, this is how I find it best to understand him) is
that, although the postulation of such things is an essential feature of the
thinking through which we (whatever we really are) cope with reality
(whatever it really is), when we think matters through, we discover that
there cannot *really* be such things, since in the last resort, they are self-
contradictory just as round squares are. However, it is so essential for
ordinary purposes to think in terms of there being such things that it is
appropriate to say that they *do exist but only as appearances.*

Physical objects, for example, could not exist as we conceive them. For
our idea of them contradicts itself as to which of their properties belong to
them independently of our perceptual consciousness of them. However,
we are adept at using whichever side of the contradiction is most useful for
the particular purposes we have in hand at any moment.

Thus, if we found it for some reason convenient to speak of round
squares, we could say that round squares do exist, as appearances, but
are self-contradictory. It is after this fashion that some scientists have
spoken of 'wavicles' which are both waves and particles, though being a
wave and being a particle are admitted to be contraries.

But matters are worse than this. For we who think these self-contradictory thoughts are mere appearances ourselves. One reason for this is that
there is no coherent answer to the question of what is required for my very

own self to exist in the future, after dramatic brain surgery or after death. (I am, it will be seen, using post-Bradley illustrations.)

Such an account of the sense in which contradictions may exist suits much of what Bradley says, and some of what Bosanquet says. However, it hardly serves to explain the sense in which Bosanquet thought that contradiction and its resolution was the key to all process in the world. For that we need a more 'realist' account of how there can be contradictions in things. So let us see how Bosanquet may have conceived this.

An initial suggestion for such a more 'realist' interpretation of the claim is this. May there not be two forces at work in some part of the world, each of which, left to itself, would produce a result incompatible with the result which the other would produce? These may be described as contradictory of each other and the whole, which includes them both, as itself self-contradictory.

This sounds fairly straightforward, but thought through it has some difficulties. Does it make sense to ask what result something would have if left to itself? Do not the effects of a thing always depend upon the context in which it exists? So what does 'left to itself' mean?

Still, something like this is evidently part of what Bosanquet means, since he was a convinced Darwinian, and regarded evolution by natural selection as the most fundamental explanation of the way in which the living world changes. And this can be interpreted as the gradual resolution of conflict between species by the formation of larger systems (eco-systems as we would say now), in which various species live if not exactly in harmony with each other, at any rate in a fairly stable fashion. Similar remarks apply perhaps to the state.

Bosanquet, then, unlike T. H. Green, was able to bring a spot of Darwinism into his system. But I doubt that this quite does full justice to what Bosanquet means by saying that finite things are all internally contradictory. Perhaps we should seek a clue in the title of PIV, Part One, lecture 5, 'Self-consciousness as the Clue to the Structure of Reality'.

In the light of this I suggest that what Bosanquet means is that every self-conscious being has two concepts of itself, one as something complete in its own right, the other of itself as essentially incomplete. These conceptions contradict each other. The contradiction is resolved, however, once the individual realizes just how he can belong to a certain larger social whole in which he has his own limited individuality precisely by playing his own distinctive part in it.

Bosanquet can then say that the way in which a self-conscious being conceives himself is so much part of his nature that the contradiction in

his conception of himself amounts to his being a self-contradictory existent. We can say further that in individuals who thus conceive of themselves in a self-contradictory manner, actual tendencies of behaviour arise
which are in conflict with each other in the sense that they are struggling
for something essentially self-contradictory, struggling, as it were, to be
round squares.

But if this is the sense in which conscious individuals are self-contradictory, how can it be used to give sense to the idea that nature as a whole
is powered by the self-contradictory character of its components, even
when they are completely without consciousness? Bosanquet must hold
that there is some physical analogue (not implying consciousness) to the
contrast between rival self-images found in conscious beings. He must
hold that somehow every individual thing in the universe has some kind
of internal drive to be something of a certain sort, where the sort is in some
manner incoherent. Their *conatus*, to use Spinoza's term, is one which
cannot be successful, since the essence they are trying to preserve is one
they do not really have, since it is an impossible one. Their only solution is
to either make themselves, or find that they really are, components in a
larger whole which would, or perhaps even eternally does, provide them
with an essence which is a modified and self-consistent version of that
false essence at which their *conatus* is directed.

So we may sum up Bosanquet's view as being that every part of the
universe has a striving within it to shake off its internal contradictions,
and to be a complete individual whole, or, if this is impossible, to be
completed in a more comprehensive and less self-contradictory whole.
Since in the end nothing is a complete individual whole except the total
universe, it follows that everything in it is striving for completion. Moreover, the incompleteness of every finite thing takes the form of internal
contradiction. There are antagonistic elements within it the effort to
resolve which forces it to struggle to be a part of a larger whole in which
these elements will be reconciled. And though in the end there is one great
whole, the Absolute, within which all antagonistic elements are reconciled, some lesser wholes are more individual, and more reconciling of the
struggles within them, than are others.

XI The Emergence of Mind from Nature

A suitably abbreviated version of *The Principle of Individuality and Value*
could yield an impressive short book expounding a form of philosophical

materialism of one sort or another. Abbreviating a little less, one could produce a book in which matter (purely physical reality) is supplemented by the Absolute without disappearing as a reality in its own right.

A paragraph which would figure significantly in such a work would be the following.

> We shall find, then, that the absolute must under certain conditions appear as a soul with a capacity for forming a self, because the stuff, and pressure for utterance, are there to which nothing less than a soul can do justice. There will be...no motive whatever to level down the nature of consciousness to that of the psychical or physical foundation; on the other hand there will not be the smallest presumption that the psychical or physical stuff in which the Absolute has deigned to become self-conscious is unfit, because itself an externality, to be the instrument of the manifestation of which it has become the occasion, and no motive, therefore, to level up as is attempted by Panpsychism. What could be higher, short of the Absolute itself, than a being which is directly its organ for appropriation and appreciation of some context and province of experience? (PIV, 191)

We must pause for a moment over the expression 'psychical or physical stuff'. This must be understood, presumably, in a manner in which the psychical is not necessarily conscious, and consists simply in matter organized in a particular way, characteristic of organisms. For the whole point of this passage is that animal and human consciousness arises from what is non-conscious. It is only when organisms arrive with brains which improve their survival chances by relating them more flexibly to the environment that the Absolute 'thinks', so to speak, that it would be a pity if they were not allowed consciously to appreciate the world around them and what they were doing in it. (See PIV, 198–9, 220, and *passim*.)[18]

> The approach to the nature of mind has been for us, always on the basal conception of a centre of a world, an approach to a wider apprehensiveness and responsiveness.... We argued that the growth towards teleology was simply the growth towards individuality of the whole recognised by the centre. Of course there is a gap between external relation and conscious apprehension and response; but, especially considering the intermediate realm of mere life, it involves, for our point of view, no change of principle. On the hypothesis of [mind/body] interaction [in contrast] you destroy continuity by extracting the principle of unity, and then setting it, empty, to act *ab extra*; it is a different thing when you keep it within the concrete to which it belongs. All that happens, on our view, is that when you come to matter which has been granted life and consciousness, its capacities of apprehension and response open up in a new significance and become the focus of a new kind of whole. (PIV, 198–9)

The general picture which arises from such passages is this. Something called the Absolute is somehow the source of a physical world, in which it expresses itself, but this world is in large tracts quite without any consciousness of its own. Consciousness arises only when, as a result of evolution governed by natural selection, organisms arise with brains. Such organisms are enabled, as a result of purely physical processes, to 'look after' their own welfare by behaviour caused by purely physical signals and representations occurring in their brains. However, when this purely physical development of organisms reaches a certain level of complexity, the Absolute provides them with their own finite consciousness in which actual conscious awareness and appreciation of its surroundings and circumstances occurs.

This conception of the world to which much of what Bosanquet points is not at all idealist if that means reducing everything to mind, either as a mode thereof or as its object. Nor is there much to suggest that Bosanquet wants us to think of the unconscious physical world as there only as an object of the Absolute's consciousness, in Berkeleyan fashion.

We should also note how Hegelian Bosanquet's conception of cosmic and human history often seems: namely, as powered by a dialectical process which continually creates and resolves contradictions, a process which, for Bosanquet, takes the form of a striving, not necessarily conscious, to create wholes with increasing degrees of 'individuality', however precisely that is to be understood.

XII Hegelian versus Bradleyan Loyalties

But this cannot be Bosanquet's final view, even if he sometimes seems to forget what that final view is. For his more considered view of the Absolute (not far from Bradley's) is that it is the ultimate container of everything which exists, and that both it and all its contents are somehow experiential. But not only is it the ultimate container, it is also the ultimate goal of conscious or unconscious striving on the part of all the partial realities within it. Every finite thing is seeking its quietus within it, notwithstanding the fact that it is really in it already!

I remarked above that Bradley often speaks as though things changed when they entered the Absolute, and that this is inconsistent with the true logic of his metaphysics. Bosanquet does the same, in that he often speaks as though there were two phases in the existence of each finite thing. In the 'first' phase (even if not *first* in a temporal sense) it is full of contradictions, that is, possesses predicates which it cannot satisfactorily combine. This causes it dissatisfaction so that it struggles to free itself from the contradictions by looking for consummation in the Absolute. When this 'second' consummatory phase is reached, the contradictions disappear, because the Absolute finds a way of uniting them.

But in expressing themselves like this both philosophers are misleading their reader and, it would seem, sometimes themselves as to their main message. For this is that every finite thing is eternally part of the Absolute, not merely striving to become part thereof. (See VDI, 257–8.) Nor are things eternally in the Absolute in the sense that there is a phase of them eternally there and another phase of them in which they are self-contradictorily isolated.

The fundamental position of our thinkers is, surely, that the conception of finite things as separate individuals existing in their own right, is a conception which never truly applies to anything. However, it is a conception which finite self-conscious beings apply to themselves.

As a result, they see themselves as in possession of properties which they cannot satisfactorily unite, and this causes them frustration. What they do not realize is that though *they* cannot unite them satisfactorily, *the Absolute* eternally does so. And there are steps available to them which to some extent free them from this false self-image and bring relief—this being a process in the reality which appears to us as Time.

But what of non-conscious things? Here Bosanquet should hold that, as we conceive them, they are indeed self-contradictory. So the struggle as it relates to them is really the struggle of finite conscious beings to conceive them more adequately in their true character as components within a larger whole of things (ultimately the Absolute) more adequately understood.

This struggle on the part of finite conscious individuals to grasp their true place, and that of their objects, in the Absolute sounds like a process in time. But if time is in part an illusion, as we shall be seeing it presumably is for Bosanquet, as it was for Bradley, the struggle is really a non-temporal series of what seem to themselves (unless the series culminates in states of mind of high enlightenment) to be the temporally successive conscious states of a single conscious individual (but which are all in truth components in the eternal fullness of the Absolute).

Thus, what powers the world, at any rate looked at as a process in time, is the effort of beings who conceive themselves as cut off from the total reality to conceive themselves and the things around them in their true eternal being.

Thus we approach the study of finite self-conscious creatures, prepared to find in them the fragments of a vast continuum, fragments in a great measure unaware of their inherent character [just as citizens may be to the state] ... It is able, as we have seen, to concentrate in itself and to represent only a limited range of externality, and in this limited range it is always inclined, just because of the limitation, to suppose its being self-complete. But yet, belonging as it does to the continuum of the whole, and unconsciously inspired by its unity, it is always passing beyond its given self in the attempt to resolve the contradictions which infect its being and obstruct its self-satisfaction. This double being *is* the nature of the finite. It is the spirit of the whole or of ultimate reality, working in and through a limited external sphere. Its law is that of the real; its existence is the existence of an appearance. (VDI, 11–12)

If this is right, Bosanquet is, finally, less close to Hegel than he has seemed to us so far. For Hegel there are real contradictions in the things which come into existence in time. For Bosanquet, the contradictions pertain to the conception that ordinary finite beings have of themselves and of the world which they inhabit rather than to them as they truly are.

XIII Does Nature Only Exist as the Posit of Finite Mind?

In section VIII above ('Materialist Tendencies') we found Bosanquet arguing that finite consciousness comes on the scene only when physical processes acquire a degree of richness which calls for conscious appreciation.

But what exactly are these physical processes in their real nature? For Bosanquet explicitly commits himself elsewhere to the idealist view that nothing but experience or its contents exists. (See PIV, 135.) So, presuming that he is a consistent thinker, the physical world must either be itself somehow experiential or be a content of experience. But whose or what's experience?[19]

There are basically four options for a philosopher who holds to the 'all is experience' principle and to the existence of an Absolute.

1. The panpsychist view that the physical world consists, in its inner nature, of innumerable streams of mostly low-level experience and that each such stream appears to us as the history of a physical object, the totality of these physical objects constituting the physical world. And a panpsychist who is an absolute idealist must hold that all these streams are processes going on within the Absolute together with, or as including, the streams of human and animal consciousness. But Bosanquet is absolutely dismissive of any form of panpsychism.

2. A somewhat Berkeleyan view that the whole physical world exists as an object of perceptual, or quasi-perceptual, experience within the Absolute, and that parts of this are reproduced again in finite minds. Is this perhaps Bosanquet's view?

3. The view that the physical world (as opposed to the Absolute) is a construction which each of us makes on the basis of our perceptual experience, a construction which treats every given perceptual field as part of a much larger whole of the same sort, and that our constructions converge in such a way that we can talk of one total physical world common to us all. There are passages in Bosanquet's *The Essentials of Logic* (1895) which suggest this view.[20] But, if (most of) the physical world exists only as an explanatory construction on the part of finite centres of experience, it is a trifle misleading to speak of finite consciousness as a late comer on the scene, as we have seen Bosanquet asserting.

4. According to the fourth view, the Absolute experiences the whole physical world from within (rather than perceiving it from without, as supposed by (2)), somewhat as we do our own bodies, though more completely. The existence of the physical world consists in its being thus experienced as the body of the Absolute. But although the Absolute Experience is unitary, its experience of some bodies (high-level organisms) has a certain sense of separateness from the rest which constitutes them finite centres of experience. Other bodies are not individually conscious.

This fourth view could be either pantheistic or panentheistic. That is, we could either think that the Absolute Experience consists in its feeling of the physical world from within, or that it consists rather in a larger experience of which this is just one part or aspect.

It is this fourth view which seems to me best to bring what seems materialistic in Bosanquet's thought into harmony with his absolutism and pan-experientialism. And such a view is strongly suggested by such passages as this:

The suggestion would be that the universe is, as a whole, self-directing and self-experiencing; that minds (such as ours) are members of it, which play their part, taught and moulded through Nature, in the work of direction, and a very essential part in the work of appreciation. But the supreme principle of value and reality would be wholeness, completeness, individuality, and not teleology. (PIV, p. xxv)

On the other hand, there is also much in the two series of Gifford Lectures which suggests, rather, that his position is (3). In fact, this does seem to be his position when he was at his most careful.

But though the materialist-sounding account of the origin of finite consciousness is not actually inconsistent with (3), there is something a little strange about their conjunction. For it implies that the physical world is a compulsory fiction created in finite minds, and that it is part of this fiction that these minds are not only the product of this fictitious world but that most of what they achieve is achieved by it rather than them.

At any rate, if (3) is Bosanquet's most considered position, there are two different ways in which one may think of the relationship between finite mind and the physical world, the first the more useful for science, the second more metaphysically true. (a) For the purposes of natural science we should think of finite mind as nothing more than an emergent feature of animal life, arising in a universe which is mostly non-conscious, thereby treating the physical as more basic than the (at least finite) mental. (b) But for metaphysical insight one should recognize that the physical world is a construction on the part of finite minds, thereby thinking of finite minds as the more fundamental. One may explicate each view further by an appeal to the Absolute, in the first case, as related to the physical world as a whole rather as the minds of conscious organisms are to their bodies, in the second case, as a guiding totality to which all such finite minds belong. Of these, (b) is the more fundamental and metaphysically true of the world as the scientists best 'construct' it.

Something like this is supported by such a passage as this.

> It is plain that when engaged in one thing we cannot be engaged in another...In moments of detached analytic labour—say, when occupied in experimental research—we necessarily set aside the 'relativity' of the 'external' world to some kind of knowledge or apprehension, and treat it *ad hoc* as a self-existent reality which we have to take as given. (PIV, 279)

If this is his position, then presumably it is the metaphysical view that the physical is a construction by finite minds which is the more ultimate truth (though how well this fits with his view that truth itself is a maximally coherent and comprehensive construction on the part of finite minds is open to question).

Some further light on all this is thrown when Bosanquet starts, in his second series of Gifford Lectures, making use (without much initial explanation) of the conception of 'a world', and of the individual finite self as 'a partial world' struggling to be more than partial.

> What is certain, and what matters to us, is that the finite self is plainly a partial world, yet possesses within it the principle of infinity, taken in the sense of the nisus

towards absolute unity and self-completion. It is both a concentration of externality and a fragment of the Absolute. (VDI, 4; see also what precedes this passage)

This seems to mean that each of us constructs our world, as an imaginative extension of our varying perceptual fields, powered by the urge to integrate the perceptually given into a maximally comprehensive and self-explanatory whole. For more ordinary purposes, at the level both of common sense and of science, the whole aimed at is spatio-temporal. For the enlightened philosopher, however, and perhaps even for the merely religious, the whole throws off its spatio-temporal character and becomes that of an absolute Eternal Consciousness embracing all finite centres of experience. (I am not here distinguishing between 'experience' and 'consciousness'.)

I have used the expression 'each of us' just now for the sake of simplicity. We should bear in mind, however, that the self is actually part of the constructed world, and that the construction is something occurring within the finite centre rather than performed by it. Bradley, at any rate, would add that a person is not a construction made solely within his own centre of experience but in co-operation with other centres too, and probably Bosanquet would agree.

This implies that when Bosanquet speaks of consciousness as a late arrival on the natural scene, he means that it is so from a pre-metaphysical point view; that is, it is thus that it figures in the world of pre-metaphysical construction. Thus the self figures twice, once as the author of the world and again as a character in the world.

It [the finite self or partial world] is both a concentration of externality [= merely physical system] and a fragment of the Absolute. It has the lawfulness of the logical spirit working towards totality within a fragmentary context. (VDI, 4)

Irwin Schrödinger put a similar point extremely well as follows.

Sometimes a painter introduces into his large picture, or a poem into his long poem, an unpretending subordinate character who is himself. Thus the poet of the *Odyssey* has, I suppose, meant himself by the blind bard who in the hall of the Phaecians sings about the battles of Troy and moves the battered hero to tears. In the same way we meet in the song of the Nibelungs, when they traverse the Austrian lands, with a poet who is suspected to be the author of the whole epic. In Dürer's *All-Saints* picture two circles of believers are gathered in prayer around the Trinity high up in the skies, a circle of the blessed above, and a circle of humans on the earth. Among the latter are kings and emperors and popes, but also, if I am not mistaken, the portrait of the artist himself, as a humble side-figure that might as well be missing.

To me this seems to be the best simile of the bewildering double role of mind. On the one hand mind is the artist who has produced the whole accomplished work, however, it is but an insignificant accessory that might be absent without detracting from the total effect. (SCHRÖDINGER, 147–8)

Bosanquet's notion of *a world*, however, is somewhat elastic, and its extension includes all sorts of wholes which figure prominently in his philosophy, such as cultural groups, forms of art, individual works of art, and so on. These are perhaps real sub-unities within the Absolute, our awareness of which is mediated through our awareness of the constructed world of space and time. And all these sub-unities are somehow striving to be ever more unitary, ultimately through discovering their locus within the Absolute.

XIV Bosanquet on Panpsychism

In the light of the last section it will be necessary sometimes to distinguish two levels of discourse in Bosanquet. At one level, which we may call the *realist level* (that of daily life and at a more sophisticated level of natural science) statements are made about the constructed universe without reference to the fact that it is a construction. Speaking at this realist level, we may say that mere physical processes are probably prior to any finite mental processes. We will need, however, even when still speaking at the realist level, to include the existence of the Absolute as somehow expressing itself in the operations of nature. Thus, though discourse at this realist level will not be idealist in the sense of holding that to exist is to be experienced, it will be idealist in a larger teleological sense.

At the other level, which we will call the *idealist level*, reality is conceived as a system of finite centres (falling within and inspired by the Absolute) which construct a largely shared natural world between them, in the temporal development of which they are late comers.

The realist view might be called practically useful or necessary mythology, the idealist view an approximation to literal truth. (This contrast is in terms of something like a correspondence theory of truth, which Bosanquet would have rejected. However, I think it necessary for understanding his position better than he may have done himself.)

It must be admitted that Bosanquet does not seem adequately aware that he should distinguish between these two levels of discourse. In fact, I have an uneasy suspicion that he was in some confusion as to which position he really stood by. However, it will be convenient for us to make the distinction on occasion.

With this distinction clear, let us consider why Bosanquet was so opposed to the doctrine of panpsychism which has appealed to a number of philosophers in the idealist tradition as allowing them to take the natural world more realistically than their idealism might otherwise force them to. For such philosophers there is a problem because, on the one hand, they hold what may be regarded for our purposes as almost the defining feature of idealism, that nothing exists except experience and its contents, while wishing to avoid the 'cosmic impiety' (Santayana's expression) of reducing the vast physical cosmos to something little better than a fiction. Among such philosophers are Josiah Royce (as we shall see in the next chapter) and, at least at one stage in his intellectual development, A. E. Taylor. (See his *Elements of Metaphysics*, book III, ch. 2.) Moreover, Bradley seems to have thought that it might be true, and may well have been held off from actually embracing it by Bosanquet's strong objections to it. (See APPEARANCE 238–41.)

Bosanquet's opposition to panpsychism is most easily understood when he is operating in the realist mode. Consciousness, as it seems to Bosanquet when operating in this mode, is not so much there to *do* something in the natural world, as to appreciate what purely physical processes have done. And even if it does *do* something on its own account, its appreciation of the world is just as, if not more, important.

But if we once recognize that the main (or even a main point) of consciousness is that the world be appropriately appreciated, we should also recognize that this is a value to which consciousness, on the part of inanimate things, or even plant life, could contribute little or nothing. For if such things need to be appreciated, the appreciation is much more effectively done by us than it could possibly be by them.

Why should not a plant enjoy its own being, or a mountain or the sea feel its own power and persistence? Of course we are here in a region with but little to sustain conjecture, but it seems worth observing that appreciation is of less interest as its object loses distinctness, and that, according to all presumptions of analogy as well as definite evidence, the capacity of consciousness for distinctive apprehension must diminish as we go down the organic scale. We involuntarily ascribe to the higher animals some appreciation, analogous to ours, of their own grace and splendour. But even here we probably overstate. . . .

Suppose a mountain or a lake to have a dim subjectivity of its own, this consciousness can neither guide itself, nor again appreciate itself as the poet and artist can appreciate it. Whether or no it possesses a subjectivity, its subjectivity does nothing in the finite world. Its function is that of an object to the subjectivity of another, an externality correlative to finite mind, not that of a being which is itself a subject of finite mind.

316

Thus Pan-psychism seems to me a gratuitous hypothesis, depending on a hasty resolution of the responsiveness of Nature to mind by help of the idea of resemblance, and wholly failing to recognise the complementary functions of subjective mind on the one hand and externality on the other as together essential to any complete form of conscious experience. (PIV, 364–6)

Moreover, to attempt to reduce external nature to something internally mental, so thinks Bosanquet, is not to realize that it is precisely as the other of mind that it matters, an otherness of which panpsychism seeks to rob it. 'External nature, then, on the view here suggested, is not a masked and enfeebled section of the subject-world, but is that from which all finite subjects draw their determinate being and content' (PIV, 369).

In so far as he is thinking in the realist mode, Bosanquet seems to be making two points. First, the origin of mind in the universe must be explained as arising from unconscious processes which the Absolute sustains largely in order that they shall one day give birth to finite consciousness. Secondly, once mind is there, it needs a real external nature as the field of its mental and physical operations, a nature which provides raw material for its own development. Mind which thus emerges from nature is capable of having a much richer form of life than it could have had if it had only other minds to deal with.

If we try to understand the value of externality at the deeper idealist level, we must presumably hold that every finite consciousness, of a type like ours, divides, under the guidance of the Absolute (that is, as moulded by its holistic character) into self and not-self, and that the not-selves are sufficiently congruent with one another and interactive for the selves to think of themselves as living in a common world. And this constructed common world is necessary in order that they shall live lives of any worth, lives that is which require honest work and toil, communal living in societies, and shared appreciation of the beautiful.

Bosanquet sums the matter up in the rather ambiguous statement: 'The external must be frankly accepted, as a factor, actual but not ultimate, in the universe' (PIV, 146).

XV The World should be Interpreted Teleologically in a Deep Sense of 'Teleological'

So there are two ways of thinking of the world: we may think of it in the realist mode, or we may think of it in the idealist mode. However, thought in each mode converges on one common idea: namely, that the universe as a whole ultimately consists of one great cosmic experience, to the perfection of which each finite thing makes its own special contribution. In that sense everything has a purpose, or at least a point, whether we can grasp what it is or not.

However, Bosanquet is anxious to repudiate any crude teleological interpretation of the universe. It was not designed to produce certain results, for there is no designer (only the all-containing Absolute), and nothing is there merely as a means to something else.

The question for this lecture is what help we get from the notion of a mind which purposes or desires things, in appreciating the worth of factors in the universe. The idea called 'Teleology' is that you find something valuable when you find what has been the purpose or invention of some mind, human or divine...

But to be desired by a human mind is almost no proof of value for their desires are constantly wrong; while it is impossible seriously to treat a mind which is the universe as a workman of limited resources, aiming at some things and obliged to accept others as means to these....

[All the same] there is a teleology (if the word is to be retained) deeply rooted in the universe, wholly above and beyond any plan or contrivance of a consciousness guiding or directing the universe, but expressing itself, for example, in conjunctions and results of the co-operation of human minds quite beyond the knowledge and intentions of any of them; and, again in the character and formations of inorganic nature altogether below the region of intelligent action... The conclusion would be that the value of the universe, or its capacity to constitute an experience without defect, lies much deeper than in what is commonly called teleology; which is understood to imply direction by a supreme mind outside or above the universe, and by finite minds within it. (PIV, pp. xxiii–xxv)

Two questions especially confront us now. Is there anything general, but not altogether vague, which we can say about the point of things in general? Secondly, if the universe is perfect, why does so much of it seem to be so nasty?

In this section I shall be concerned only with the first question, and I note first that Bosanquet seems to have two answers to it.

Bosanquet's first answer to the first question is that the universe is above all a vale of soul building; that is, it exists for the production of souls in possession of excellences of various sorts.

His second answer is that the individual hardly matters except for his role in constituting what does really matter: namely, certain great social wholes and supra-individual achievements, such as nations and cultural traditions.

But these answers seem inconsistent. If the one great point of things lies in the production of great individual souls, then it does not lie in the production of supra-personal wholes. If it lies in the production of great supra-personal wholes, then it does not lie in the production of great individual souls. Of course, one might regard both as possessing value, but Bosanquet is anxious, it would seem, to find some master principle, and, if so, he must choose between these too.

However, Bosanquet attempts to reconcile the two answers in passages like the following.

The universe is not a place of pleasure, nor even a place compounded of probation and justice; it is, from the highest point of view, concerned with finite beings, a place of soul-making. ... It is for the moulding and greatness of souls that we really care.

This observation has to be reconciled with what we said above as to the relative values of the particularity of the particular centres of mind compared with the value of mind as such. But this reconciliation ... is not in principle difficult. The destiny or conservation of particular centres is not what primarily has value ... What has value is the contribution which the particular centre—a representative of certain elements in the whole—brings to the whole of which it is a member. (PIV, 26–7)

This does to some extent provide a synthesis of more individualist and more supra-individualist elements in his thought. However, it gives the second answer priority, and sees the first to be an inference from it. What really matters is the creation of such things as great cultural traditions, fine cities, stupendous technological advances, and above all great nations of which the glory is no mere sum of the values realized in the lives of individuals. But none of these things can be realized except in individual centres of consciousness (leaving the Absolute aside, which anyway achieves its good through the individual centres into which it pluralizes itself). So the individual centres are necessary conditions of these great values, but it is the supra-personal values, as realized in individual centres, which really matter.

It is, indeed, his association with the second answer which has disturbed many of his readers. For it is a famous, perhaps infamous, part of Bosanquet's philosophy that what really matters is neither the fate nor the moral character of individual human beings, but the character of the communities they form (especially states and nations) and the historical development of certain great transpersonal processes like art and science. And in neither of these cases, so Bosanquet often insists, can the value of

319

the whole be a mere sum of values realized in the lives of individual persons. The value of Britain is not the sum of values realized in the lives of Britons; nor is the historical development of art the value of individual acts of creation or appreciation. (Contrast this with T. H. Green, as quoted on p. 227 above.)

Thus, although Bosanquet's idea of the world as a 'vale of soul making' comes from Keats, his conception of the vale is very different. Keats's idea was that this life is designed to prepare souls for a glorious life together in a realm beyond death (perhaps after a purgatorial process of improvement).[21] Yet Bosanquet was anxious to dissociate it from any hopes for a future life. (See VDI, 66–7.) Such hopes had little appeal to him. This fits in well with the insistence that it is not so much individual persons who matter as the great wholes to which they belong, but hardly with the idea of human life as a vale of soul making. Keats was expressing an individualistic view of reality, while for Bosanquet it was an inference from a decidedly non-individualistic view.

Perhaps Bosanquet could argue that a main thing which makes a civilization great is its having given birth to certain great heroic individuals. Perhaps so, but one should bear in mind that he, like Bradley, was, on the whole, against the excessive celebration, whether by J. S. Mill or by Nietzsche, of great individuals at the cost of the decent ordinary man. Mill's tendency to identify individuality with eccentricity (in his *Essay On Liberty*) particularly annoyed Bosanquet.[22]

Thus, great values such as goodness (which I am glad to say that the often harsh Bosanquet replaced by kindness in later works), truth, and beauty are realized through processes which no single person can create or enjoy. So, for example, the great sweep of (European) art history is of more value than the sum of the value of the individual pictures considered one by one (still less the pleasure taken in their creation or enjoyment by individual persons). Nor is it the achievement of great single individuals. The work of a Michelangelo, a Beethoven, and a Shakespeare arose in cultures which were ready for them, and in which there were people who could appreciate them.

As compared with these great transpersonal processes, it matters little that some individuals have a hard time of it. Besides, most lives are made better by suffering. A man who has not suffered is no better than a country which has never gone to war! However, the quality of their souls does matter, understood as the making of souls for the wholes to which they belong, for it plays a large part in his discussion of the problem of evil, as we shall see in the next section. And some tension, remains, I believe between the ideal of soul making and the ideal of great collectivities.

Bosanquet often gives the impression that the real justification of human life is the development of specifically Western civilization. I would guess that he would have thought that non-Western civilization is mainly of value as some kind of necessary associate of this. (For Bosanquet, the value of African art would have been at most its influence on Picasso *et al.*)[23]

If somehow it is civilization which is the object of the teleology present in human life, how does it operate? Bosanquet's rather surprising answer is that it does so by natural selection and, at a later stage, social selection.

As a partial expression of the world, formed by its surroundings, soul may be said to be moulded by natural selection, although more especially in the shape of social selection; for mind has its main environment in mind, and there is far more room for contrivance and initiative than in mere natural selection. (vdi, p. xxiii)

But is there no value in any aspect of nature other than the human? Bosanquet would perhaps grudgingly ascribe a certain value to the lives of animals. But, as for anything else in nature except as an object for human appreciation, perhaps not. But here the question of how realist is Bosanquet's view of the physical world haunts us once again. If it is experienced throughout as the body of God, that doubtless fills the world with a great deal of value other than the human. But if it exists only as a presentation which the Absolute gives itself via human minds, its possible value seems substantially reduced.

In any case, the universe as a whole ultimately consists of one great cosmic experience, to the perfection of which each finite thing makes its own special contribution. In that sense everything has a purpose, or at least a point, and it is a task for an idealist philosophy to suggest how this may be so in representative cases.

XVI The Problem of Evil

This leads us on to the problem of evil (our second question above). However, no such problem, in its usual form, arises for absolute idealism. For this contains no doctrine of a creator God with beneficent designs. Moreover, it conceives all things as somehow necessary, not chosen as the best of possible alternatives.

Disclaiming, as throughout, all attempts at a *théodicée*, because we do not regard the universe as ruled by an omnipotent moral person, we must attempt to consider the connection and real facts of things with an open mind. (VDI, 218)

However, the absolute idealist (Bosanquet, as we have seen, very much among them) does believe that the universe is somehow perfect and that everything in it plays its part in making it so. For otherwise the Absolute, which is the consciousness of the Whole, would be discontented, and discontent implies an itch to be on to something else, which is impossible in a timeless being. (See section XIX below.) Therefore the absolute idealist is faced with the problem of how such perfection of the whole is compatible with the apparent badness of so many of the parts. Thus he has his own problem of evil, even if it is not quite the same as the conventional theist's.[24]

Bradley was prepared to joke that this is the best of all possible worlds, and that everything in it is a necessary evil. (See APPEARANCE, p. x.) But, joking apart, he was content to remain largely agnostic. Bosanquet is more determined to find a serious answer.

His answer, in essence, is that 'the troubles and adventures of the finite arise from one and the same source as its value; that is, from the impossibility of its finding peace otherwise than as offering itself to the whole' (VDI, 18). Thus, every finite being is in some manner seeking completion in the Absolute.[25] Actually, it always is thus completed. But it is of the nature of the finite not to grasp this, apart from exceptional moments of enlightenment. Thus a finite mind (at any one stage of its apparent temporal existence) suffers from internal contradictions which are, indeed, resolved in the absolute experience, but not within its own limited experience. And it yearns to be one with the Absolute Experience from which it is, from its own point of view, cut off.

For many the problem of evil revolves around the question of why there is so much suffering in human life. This is sometimes answered by arguing that great human suffering is a *necessary means* to some greater good. But, says Bosanquet, this could only be so if God or the Absolute is like a human artificer who has to do the best he can with limited materials. No, somehow the suffering itself must be a good—good, that is, as what it really is, an element in the perfect whole of the Absolute, conceived outside of which it is always to some extent misconceived. (There is an echo here of his early essay 'The Kingdom of God' discussed above.) And Bosanquet is uncomfortably ingenious in giving examples suggesting that this is so.

I turn now to two mistakes with which Bosanquet charges those who think the empirical facts are incompatible with the cosmic optimism of absolute idealism. The first is a hedonic theory of value. This once accepted, it is supposed that the universe can be perfect only if it contains more pleasure than pain, and if what pain there is can be interpreted as a necessary means to a general maximum of pleasure and minimum of pain. Bosanquet meets this with an absolute denial of this hedonic theory. And it is not for finite minds to settle the degree of suffering required in human life in order that it contribute the best that is in it to the filling of the universe. (See VDI, 158.)

The second reason is that we think about the universe, or Absolute, as though we had rights as against it, and judge it ill because these are not satisfied. But the ethics of rights belongs to 'a world of claims and counter-claims', important for the organization of human society, but not as a basis for a judgement about the universe.

The chief trouble with appeal to the notion of duties and rights in this connection is that it rests on a misconceived belief in the ultimate reality of the finite individual. No, it is larger wholes than this, and ultimately the largest whole of all, which are what truly matter. (Here again the notion of soul making seems to be pushed to second place.) There is no reason at all why the universe should arrange things so that each has equal shares of happiness or, alternatively, that happiness is proportionate to merit. That it postulates a God who will do so is, for Bosanquet, one of the worst features of orthodox theism. For religion should teach us not to care too much about our own fate. 'Ask not', Bosanquet might have said, 'what the universe can do for you but what you can do for the universe.'

For this world of 'relational morality with its machinery of duties and rights, for the finite being who takes himself seriously as finite' is an illusion. 'There *is* no such world of isolated terms in relations' (VDI, 133).

Comparing different persons as separate units, and their fortunes in the same way, we are struck by inequalities. And in the face of these inequalities, standing on the ground of separable and comparable terms, characteristic of this whole world of claims and relations, we are led to frame some sort of *prima facie* scheme of claims or pretensions, dealing with some kind of apportionment of external advantages to individual units—apparent finite individuals—each to each. (PIV, 144)

But, contends Bosanquet, the whole notion of fairness and justice which characterizes the world of claims and counter-claims contains contradictions. Should it be the weak who have compensatory advantages or the strong who have the reward of merit? But in spite of these difficulties, when we regard each other as finite units in a world of externality we tend to frame schemes of apportionment according to which, by some rule or other, each separate unitary being has some claim to a separate unitary allotment of happiness or opportunity or reward—of something which should be added to him, it seems to us, by God or man or nature or fortune. And when our scheme proves wholly and absolutely alien to facts, we foster a pessimistic sense of injustice. We ask, 'Why is it not as we so reasonably expected?' (PIV, 145)

So for Bosanquet, all ideals, both of equality and fairness, are immoral and incoherent.[26] What each should have, and necessarily does have, is just what he needs to play his own special part in constituting the ultimate and perfect whole.

> The Hegelian inclined Bosanquet
> Said 'its really, you know, rather wet
> To expect each finite chappie
> To be well fed and happy
> For the Absolute ain't in our debt.'

Bosanquet, it seems, rather glories in the fact, as he thinks it, that there is no compensation hereafter for good people who have suffered greatly in this life.[27] For one of the few things he still likes in his old age (so he tells us) about Christianity is its notion of vicarious atonement, or, more generally, of one person suffering for the good of others.

I may venture perhaps to explain the light in which this contrast of worlds appears to me by referring once more to a phase in my own experience. When critical ideas directed against current orthodox Christianity first made an impression on my mind, it was more than anything else the doctrine of vicarious atonement, literally construed, that seemed shocking and unjust. And it was with some interest, and not without surprise, that, taking stock of one's convictions after a long development, one found that what was obviously the intention of the doctrine in question, so far from remaining the great stumbling-block in Christianity, had become pretty nearly its sole attractive feature. One had passed, I suppose, from an individualistic rationalism to an appreciation of the world of spiritual membership. (VDI, 147)

Thus the doctrine of atonement may be seen as symbolizing the fact that in virtue of our unity one with another we must all suffer for each other without asking for fair shares in life. (See VDI, 148.) It is, indeed, to be expected that the best will suffer most, and this is what they should welcome.

We feel that to make a great poet, say, the richest man in his community, would be irrelevant and self-contradictory. It is not what he wants, and would probably choke his work and do enormous social mischief. (VDI, 155)

In a world of soul making there must be a good deal of suffering, and it will be where great souls are made, rather than where it is 'deserved', that it will occur. In this connection Bosanquet tells us that he has been reading

the terrible story of certain campaigns in the American Civil War... [And] I might be challenged, 'Would I maintain that such things could exist in a just universe?' I am not going to answer the challenge, but to point out what I hold to be an absurd implication in it. Am I, an elderly gentleman almost tied to his arm-chair, to be asked to dictate the limits of heroism and suffering necessary to develop and elicit the true reality of finite spirits? (VDI, 157)

It is not for finite minds to settle the degree of suffering required in human life in order that it contribute the best that is in it to the filling of the universe.

I venture these remarks because I seem to observe an extraordinary eclecticism in the toleration of pain and trouble, as if Marathon and Salamis were somehow obviously fine and desirable events, while modern battles of a less picturesque type, and attended no doubt by miseries on a more enormous scale in the way of neglected wounded and the like—not to speak of the thousand-fold horrors of our civilisation in its grimmer and dirtier parts—were obviously and self-evidently to be ruled out as intolerable. (VDI, 158)

This was written in 1913. Did Bosanquet look on trench warfare in this light? Like most civilians then, he probably had no idea of its horrors, but perhaps, if he had, he would have stomached them with the same aplomb.[28] And how much by way of great souls did it create? But suffering, injustice, and accident are essential features of a world in which there is going to be great value, and Bosanquet is full of examples which he thinks point up this fact.

For us, however, the conviction that reality implies perfection does not carry the consequence of excluding or minimising imperfection and consequently it supplies no driving force in favour of the postulate before us [that pain is not a deeply inherent feature of reality and may disappear in time]. Our theoretical prepossession in some degree even leans the other way. It is part of the paradox of our finite-infinite being that we are bound to maintain the combat against evil and no doubt in a great degree against pain, not merely without anticipating, but even without whole-heartedly desiring, their entire abolition in every possible shape with all their occasions and accessories. For we can hardly understand what of life would survive such an abolition. And perfection itself, so far as we see, would lose some essentials of its being. The Utopian temper as a rule seems dull and inhuman; and, as I remarked above, there is something mediaeval in the worst sense about the idea of a future in which—to take a typical instance—tragedy is to be enjoyed without any tragic experience. (PIV, 179)

I hope that the reasoning of this lecture has reinforced a conclusion in the former volume, to the effect that the issue of optimism and pessimism must not, and indeed cannot, be treated as a question of the quantitative balance between pain and pleasure, but rather from an organic standpoint as a problem of the function of pain in soul-making, and its transformation in the higher experiences, not its neutralisation or submergence by an overbalance of an opposite. In general we may say that this problem should be argued on the basis of value and not of pain and pleasure. (VDI, 182)

So optimism or pessimism about the ultimate nature of things should be judged neither by hedonistic criteria nor by the extent to which it gives individuals that to which they have a right.

And, as for the hedonist's judgement of the world, even if we thought his sense of values appropriate, it is doubtful that it should lead to a pessimistic conclusion. For there is much pleasure, surely, in lives with which we find it hard to empathize, such as the barbarian chief just mentioned as also in the poor of our own society.

If he [the critic] means to found his complaint on suffering as such, then he must go to the facts of suffering as such, as actually felt by the sufferers, and must not bring in our moral ideals to eke out the sense of failure. He must analyse the actual life of heathendom or of Europe in the dark ages or of the poor in our great cities, or any other type of life he chooses on which to rest his case...

And if anyone speaks of 'slum-life' as a whole and treats it as not worth living, he writes himself down as a victim of class prejudice and conventional superstition. (VDI, 218–21)

But perhaps people will object that it does not meet the higher criterion of adequately promoting 'moral or cultural development' on the part of humanity. But in this connection we should have learnt from Rousseau that what matters most are the values of 'love, and courage, and self-sacrifice' and that these do not require high intellectual achievement. (See VDI, 220.) This seems rather different from what he often says about civilization.

Is there, then, any appropriate criterion for judging the universe as a whole? Yes, 'the test is the satisfaction of our criticised desires' (VDI, 221). And Bosanquet thinks it stands up well thus judged. (Bosanquet adds that in judging it we must avoid the idea that its value lies only in a future for which the rest is merely preparation, for the Absolute is as truly present in every here and now.)

As for myself, it seems to me that Bosanquet shows some lack of imagination in treating human suffering so lightly. It is difficult at any rate to avoid the thought of Dr Pangloss when reading such a passage as the following.

There is evil, then, with the Absolute, but the Absolute is not characterised by evil. That is to say, there is nothing in evil which cannot be absorbed in good and contributory to it; and it springs from the same source as good and value.... It is true, good as good involves evil, but good as absorbed in perfection only involves evil as absorbed within good. And so, if we think of judging the universe, we should remember that our highest form of judgement is not the judgement of good and evil; not even if we take good to imply an attitude to all that has value, the widest meaning of morality. Our highest judgement is the judgement of perfection, and raises a different problem from the judgement of moral good and evil in their widest sense. The universe may be perfect owing to the very fact among others, that it includes, as conditions of finite life, both moral good and evil. (VDI, 217–18)

But since the value of the universe is not to be evaluated hedonistically, let us consider further what does constitute its value, and indeed value in general, for Bosanquet.[29]

XVII Bosanquet's Conception of Value

Referring obviously to G. E. Moore's *Principia Ethica* (1903), Bosanquet remarks:

It has been maintained that good is undefinable.... Definable, I should urge, is just what it is; describable, perhaps, is what it is not. We cannot describe perfection; that is, we cannot enumerate its components and state their form and connection in detail. But we can define its character as the harmony of all being. And good is perfection in its character of satisfactoriness; that which is considered as the end of conations and the fruition of desires. (VDI, 194)[30]

More fully, Bosanquet's not altogether clear account of values may perhaps be summed up in the following nine points.

Definition of Value

(1) Value can only exist as experienced. In short, existing values must either be experiences or contents of experience.
(2) To be valuable is to satisfy (or be capable of satisfying?) in a complete and enduring way. (Satisfy whom? Perhaps in the end the Absolute, but *en route* to this, appropriate human beings, open to the experiences in question.)

(3) The satisfaction which constitutes value must be able to stand up to criticism (as great works of literature can stand up to literary criticism). Human beings capable of experiencing some particular value will converge, after criticism, in the degree of satisfaction they find in it.

(4) Bosanquet does not hold that the real value of a state of consciousness is independent of its 'objective relations': e.g. that a belief's truth or falsehood is irrelevant to its value. This is not, however, to say that it is not determined by its own character, but that its own character includes its 'objective' relations, not just by an optional enlargement of what counts as its own character, but because its relations to what is outside it are inside it. This is not Bosanquet's own language, but it is what he is evidently getting at.

(5) Thus judgements of value can be more or less correct, since discussion and argument can alter what we find satisfying and how far.

(6) There is, in fact, no more important aspect of education than that of being trained as to what one likes and dislikes: that is, to what one finds or does not find satisfaction in.

(7) Values cannot be summed in any simple arithmetical way. The value of a life is not the sum of the values of its temporal phases (still less of individual sensations) as these might be reckoned independently. The value of a society is not the sum of the values of the lives of the individuals within it each considered on its own. This turns partly on a point not specifically concerned with value: namely, that considered on their own, individuals and their experiences are misconceived.

(8) In fact, things (whether they are thoughts, acts, feelings, works of art, or whatever) possess value to the extent that they are organized wholes with parts in constructive rather than destructive relations one to another, each contributing its distinctive bit to the overall character of the whole.

(9) It appears then that the perfection of the Absolute consists in its being an infinitely satisfying experience. One may speak of this as the experience which the Absolute has, but in fact the Absolute simply is the total experience of which all finite experiences are components. However, these latter are more or less satisfying, within their own bounds, and this, together with the contribution they make to the various totalities to which they belong, determines their relative value. It should be remembered, however, that even within their own bounds they possess a character which is, more or less evidently, intrinsically bound up with that of the various wholes which they help constitute as parts thereof.[31]

Value of Individual versus Value of State

This account of value is closely related to Bosanquet's somewhat ambivalent attitude to the value of persons. As opposed to the kind of utilitarianism for which value pertains to individual sensations, or moments of consciousness, Bosanquet stresses that what matters is the quality of a whole life. But he also wishes to stress the relative unimportance of the fate of the individual as compared with the values realized in the nation-state.[32]

This is, however, because what an individual truly is, is a mode in the life of something larger than himself, in particular the state. To this I am inclined to object that while this seems a reasonable account of someone well educated in the history and culture of his nation, it is more doubtful with regard to those who are not. The ignorant person does not grasp the role he is playing in his society, and in many cases, his personal consciousness would seem to be uncoloured by what is best in it.

Value of Experiences as Actually Felt

It is instructive in this respect to think of Joe in *Bleak House*, who 'knew nothink'. Dickens depicts him as having no part in his country's civilization, being quite ignorant, for example, of what churches were. (Faced with examples like these, Bosanquet's tendency to see a silver lining in even the worst human fates, as essential to soul making, seems harsh indeed.)

Moreover, Bosanquet's view, tabulated above as (7), that, considered on its own, someone's state of mind is misconceived is problematic. For it seems to contrast the felt quality of someone's life with its real character. Yet, surely its felt quality is just what it essentially is. To this Bosanquet should, in my opinion, respond that, though its larger context may not be part of what the individual feels, it is still true that just such an experience could occur only precisely in that bit of reality. Joe knew virtually nothing of Christianity, but his experience had a quality which could be actualized only in a formally Christian country. If everything is a necessary feature in the perfect whole, what is evil?

Evil arises especially when a man cannot bring all that is in him into harmony with the more immediate whole harmonious membership of which constitutes his good. (VDI, 210)

The stuff of which evil is made is one with the stuff of which good is made. No tendency or desire could be pointed out in the worst of lives or of actions which is incapable of being, with addition and readjustment, incorporated in a good self. There would not be the contradiction of good and evil if there were not this community of nature as in pain and pleasure, or in error and truth. The essence of the evil attitude is the self-maintenance of some factor in a self both as good and also as against the good system. It is, as we saw above, good in the wrong place, and therefore wrenches the whole nature of the soul out of gear. (VDI, 215)

The trouble is that if the Absolute is perfect, then every lesser system is ultimately congruent with the greatest whole to which it belongs: namely, the Absolute. So it seems that things only seem evil when you focus attention on some insufficiently large totality of which they are a part.

Bosanquet's reply is, I think, that although everything is necessary for the ultimate good, some of it is none the less rebellious against the ultimate perfection which it helps to constitute (see VDI, 219). And that is essentially what moral evil is.

Wickedness

Wickedness is not a subject on which Bosanquet has much to say. What he does say is very close to Bradley.

Even the best of us have impulses which do not cohere harmoniously either with each other or with the main block of our personality, but which occasionally take the controls in our worst moments. When they do, we are behaving badly. But when such impulses organize themselves into an often successful rival to the dominant personality, we have a really wicked person. So in the wicked person

his ineradicable passion for the whole [i.e. for a whole as such] makes it inevitable that out of the superfluity which he cannot systematise under the good, he will form a secondary and negative self, a disinherited self, hostile to the imperative domination of the good which is, *ex hypothesi*, only partial. (VDI, 210)

Bosanquet's treatment of the problem of evil, and in particular of the place of wickedness in the world, seems somewhat inadequate. For a more adequate approach to evil from the point of view of absolute idealism, one must turn to Josiah Royce. As for my own view, as an absolute idealist, the best solution I can find is that everything is so necessarily linked up with everything else that if the universe were to have any of it, it had to have all of it. Thus the evils are necessarily bound up with the good in the universe, which finally tips the balance in its favour; but they are not contributory (for the most part) to that good.

XVIII Proof of the Existence of the Absolute

I am working with the idea which I have maintained throughout, that the universe is one, and each finite mind is a factor in the effort which sustains its unity. (VDI, 103–4)

By the Absolute, as we have largely seen, Bosanquet means, as did Bradley, one unitary cosmic experience which includes everything which in any sense is. The relation of its components to the total absolute experience is of the same generic sort as is that of our various sensations, feelings, and thoughts to the state of consciousness to which they belong. The richness of its contents is altogether beyond our direct imagining; but it is not a mere all-containing dump, but an organized and harmonious experience in which every finite experience has its own unique locus.

Bradley has a fairly clear-cut proof of the existence of the Absolute, turning on the fact that the reality behind the relatedness of things in the world is their union within an absolute experience.[33] Bosanquet gives the impression that he went along with everything in *Appearance and Reality*, but he never actually discusses Bradley's proof. And in his main metaphysical opus, the Absolute enters the scene without any opening proof of its existence. There is, however, an attempted proof later in the work, which Bosanquet calls the argument from *contingentia mundi* (*the contingency of the world*) (see PIV, 262).

The argument is this. Everything contingent exhibits contradictions when considered in isolation. But the ultimate truth about reality cannot contain unresolved contradictions. Now the contradictions of finite things can often be resolved to some extent by considering them as components in more comprehensive but still finite wholes which themselves are parts of something larger. However, they can never be completely resolved thereby; even if the original contradictions are overcome, other, fresh ones arise at the new level. Thus, since everything finite contains contradictions, which must be resolved in ultimate truth, there must be an infinite reality, to which everything finite belongs as a component, and in which the contradictions of finitude are resolved. This is the Absolute.

Now everything which exists is either an experience or a component in an experience or only something usefully posited within an experience. And since the Absolute obviously cannot be either the second or third it follows that it must be the first. So it must exist as one 'vast' all-including experience.[34] (See PIV, 268.)

So the Absolute exists. But do we have any reason to believe that the Absolute is supremely good? May not a pessimistic conception of its character be as satisfactory logically—and empirically perhaps more so?

We have seen the a priori grounds for regarding the Absolute as *perfect* in some valuational sense already. The one great Whole must be not only logically consistent, but somehow satisfactory in some richer way which deserves to be called perfection. For the unsatisfactory and often decidedly bad character of individual things is a matter of the struggle within them of predicates (what verbal predicates stand for) to affirm their existence as against other elements within these things which are incompatible with them. Thus the Absolute brings not only logical peace, but valuational peace, since as aspects of the Absolute there is no quarrel between them. Hence for Bosanquet the resolution of all logical contradictions must involve some kind of valuational perfection.

The Absolute, then, is perfect in the sense that it contains no (unresolved) contradictions, logical or moral. Bosanquet, however, holds back from calling it good. Certainly it cannot be good in the sense in which a person is, for the Absolute is not a person at all.[35]

Secondly, its perfection is not of a hedonistic kind, since a hedonistic conception of value is radically wrong. Moreover, tension does not entirely disappear in the Absolute. The finite mind progresses through the resolution of contradictions. When these contradictions are resolved, a sense of tension remains, or the solution would not be experienced as a resolution. In the Absolute, contradiction will not be there in the same way (e.g. as a stimulus to development), but some sense of itself (or of its included components) as continually but timelessly passing out of and then regaining itself will be there. It follows that pain and evil are essential aspects of the Absolute's self-possession and perfection.

Thirdly, it is rather the scene in which good is eternally triumphant over evil than itself the triumphant good.

Fourthly, it guarantees that there is no ultimate waste of anything. All the apparently unfulfilled great human aspirations, for example, are either in some way satisfied or add to the value of the world precisely by their frustration.

So, though the Absolute is not exactly good, its perfection is maximally valuable in a sense which goes beyond logical coherence and comprehensiveness, as usually understood, although entailed by these. And its overarching value entails that everything finite possesses positive value, considered as filling just the slot in reality which it does fill—that is, considered in its true nature. And the somewhat bland Bosanquet has no difficulty in finding a positive value in many of the things which tenderer souls see as blots on the face of the universe.

XIX Time and the Absolute

Of all the absolute idealists, it was Royce who put forward the clearest views about the relation of the Absolute to time. Bosanquet is often confusing on the matter. But in order to make sense of his position, I believe that we must ascribe the following view to him.

All the experiences which, as we would put it at any moment of our lives, have ever occurred, are occurring, or ever will occur are eternally just components of the eternal Absolute. The ultimate truth of the matter is that there is no coming into existence and going out of existence. We have the contrary impression, because it is a character of every finite experience belonging to an apparently temporal series to feel to itself as a transitional point between experiences which are in the process of ceasing and experiences about to be. Thus my experience at any moment is an eternal reality which is eternally under the false impression that it is in the process of giving way to a different experience, as another experience gave way to it.

This is, in my opinion, the truth of the matter. And my own way of arguing for it is somewhat as follows. If we think that once something has happened, it remains true that it did so even if the matter is quite forgotten, we must suppose that the past has some kind of reality. But what kind of reality could it have other than as something which is present from its own point of view? If we give it some more shadowy existence, that is relevant only if the shadow is of something real, the real past event. So the past must just be *there* as the present is. But if the past in its own essence is as much present as what I, at any particular moment, call 'the present', it follows that the future is so too. For my own present experience is a sample of the future: the future, that is, from the point of view of something which is intrinsically as present as it is. But the future of one event present in itself can hardly be of a quite different ontological status and character from the future of another event equally present in itself. Thus all moments of time are just eternally there. (I present this argument more fully in Chapters 8 and 9.)

From this it follows that total reality is a changeless or eternal whole containing innumerable events which are past, present, and future from the point of view of any one of them, but are not so in any absolute way. Thus, time as we ordinarily conceive it, is an illusion, for as we ordinarily conceive it, the past is somehow different in its nature from the present, and the future different again from both.[36]

The essentials of this conclusion about time find additional support, I believe, in relativity physics (though some deny this), but may be argued for, as here, on purely metaphysical grounds. What absolute idealism adds is that this total reality is one great Cosmic Experience.

This is surely the view to which Bosanquet's basic principles commit him. But he neither states it clearly, nor always speaks consistently with it; indeed, he seems to have had only a limited appreciation of its significance.[37]

Bosanquet sometimes explicates the relation between finite and absolute experience by comparing it to the relation between immature and more mature thinking when the latter places the former in a better understood larger conception of things.

Thus the Absolute is said to stand to us as 'the high water-mark' of that effort to understand things as deeply as possible which powers each individual's own thinking. The idea is that each of us strives constantly for as full a grasp of reality as possible, and that this striving usually meets with some success as we age, but that the Absolute contains the final consummation of that urge. Or again, we may feel that our own thoughts are included in a larger context in the thought of some greater human mind (Bosanquet refers to Dante in this connection).

But though this may do as a way of giving more content to our conception of the relation between the Absolute and ourselves, Bosanquet ought to have been more careful to stress the great contrast. For certainly our earlier thoughts cannot be literally parts of our later thoughts;[38] nor can my thoughts be literally contained in Dante's or Einstein's. Yet my thoughts and feelings, as opposed to thoughts with the same but enriched content, are literally contained in the Absolute, if absolute idealism is right.

Bosanquet may have slid into this view because, like Bradley, he thought that the idea of purely numerical difference between two experiences wrong-headed. Two experiences A and B cannot be merely numerically different; to be two, they must have different contents. From which it may seem to follow that if the content of an experience A is included as a 'sublated' element in the content of an experience B, then the particular experience A is similarly included in the experience B. But whatever particularity is, exactly, it cannot be shed so lightly. My neighbour at a concert may be better educated musically than I am A, and thereby his experience of the music may be, as it were, an enriched version of my own experience. But his experience does not literally contain mine as mine does both the sounds as heard by me and my backache. And however similarly two people at a concert may experience the music, there are still numerically two experiences.

Bosanquet could say quite rightly that the music as heard by one person and by another is an identical content within both their distinct experiences. From which it would seem to follow that if, somewhat *à la* Proust, I could completely recapture in my imagination an experience in my past, then my later experience would include the earlier one. However, for Bosanquet and like-minded thinkers, the identity would be an identity-in-difference, and the element of difference would keep them up apart to a point. But I take it that this would not be the manner in which each experience of mine is supposed to be contained within the Absolute, for the element of difference is an illusion.

Thus the absolute experience (*contra* what Bosanquet sometimes implies) includes all other experiences in a way in which my later experiences never similarly include my earlier experiences. For my later experiences will always lack the distinctive timbre of those which I lived through at an earlier time. These contrasting timbres may come together in the Absolute, but only a moderate attempt at introspection will show that the earlier timbre, in its fullness, is not included in the later experience. If I listen to the same performance of the same music (as electrical recording now makes quite usual), my later, perhaps richer comprehension of its structure may make the content of the one experience include that of the other, but there will still be an apartness which makes this inclusion a different kind of thing from the inclusion of both within the Absolute.

Another way in which Bosanquet tries to clarify our relation to the Absolute is by comparing it to that of how his characters relate to the mind of a great writer. Thus, so the suggestion runs, I am related to the Absolute somewhat as Mr Jingles (in *Pickwick Papers*) was related to the mind of Dickens as he composed the novel.

How good is this as an analogy for our relation to the Absolute? The answer depends on how we understand the novelist and his characters. If Mr Jingles is an intentional object of certain mental acts of Dickens, and thereafter his readers, then, as intentional objects are usually understood nowadays by philosophers, he is not part of Dickens's mind, any more than you are when I think of you. On the other hand, it is a differently illuminating way of conceiving how the characters in a great novel relate to the mind of the novelist to say that they are produced by distinct thought tendencies within him, each of which has a certain *conatus* in a

Spinozistic sense of its own. Taken thus, I believe the comparison a rather good one. (See the last paragraph on PIV, p. xxxvii, and pp. 370–86.)

As regards the Absolute and time, Bosanquet is confident 'that the Absolute is non-temporal', something which follows inevitably 'from the idea of completeness or perfection' (VDI, 257). In this connection Bosanquet warns us not to suppose that the real value of the universe must lie in the future. 'Values are distributed all over the temporal revelation of the Absolute, not reserved for a climax' (VDI, 220). '[T]he finite self like everything in the universe is now and here beyond escape an element in the Absolute.' So although Bosanquet, as we have seen, by talking of how things are 'transformed' in the Absolute, occasionally writes as though things passed into the Absolute, after first existing separately, he is also anxious now and then to alert us to the mistake that this would be.

We must surely distinguish the conception of changing or progressing as a whole from the conception of uniting in a self-complete being characteristics which for us demand succession. (PIV, 244)

XX Bosanquet and the State

The Philosophical Theory of the State is probably Bosanquet's most widely read work today and, since it has been harshly criticized for promoting a kind of worship of the state, it must receive some attention here.

In this work Bosanquet criticizes views of the state and its laws and institutions which present it as a necessary evil whereby we give up some of our natural liberty for the sake of preventing various mischiefs which would otherwise threaten us. For this suggests that an individual is most truly himself when left free of social bonds. But the truth is that, rather than a limitation upon his freedom, it is only as a citizen of a state that any human being can adequately fulfil himself. Moreover, the state is not some alien force; rather are its laws and institutions the expression of my own true self. Indeed, I am only myself as a component of a greater self, the state or nation, in which I live in accordance with my true identity-in-difference with all other persons.

Bosanquet defines the state as follows: 'By the State, then, we mean Society as a unit, recognised as rightly exercising control over its members through absolute physical power' (THE STATE, 172).

There is an ambiguity here as to whether we can ascribe to the state only what it supports with force, or whether, granted it has such force, it still possesses other features. Upon the whole, it seems best to understand him as holding that a state must possess such powers, but that its life and action are not restricted to their exercise. It is to be noted that, for Bosanquet, what purports to be a state is only genuinely so if it exercises its power rightly (which means, for Bosanquet, as promoting an excellent form of life).

The first historical examples of what a state should be were the Greek city-states. However, the modern nation-state is a more advanced type of Social Whole which is equally, though differently, excellent.

Bosanquet is sometimes supposed to have seen conscious participation in the workings of a great nation as the highest form of religion. He has invited a good deal of hostile attention for this position, most notably from L. T. Hobhouse in his *The Metaphysical Theory of the State* (1918), which saw him as an exponent of that same state worship which, from Hegel to the Kaiser, was at work in producing the First World War.

There is some excuse for this reading of him. However, for the most part, Bosanquet is simply insisting, as against more social atomist political theories, that human beings can only realize themselves in a fully satisfactory way as members of a society with some shared values, and this (if it is to be adequate) must include citizenship of a spiritually united nation wielding state power.

Liberals (from J. S. Mill to Isaiah Berlin) will object that any such view justifies imposing one particular form of life upon everyone whether it suits them or not. The job of the institutions of the state, for such liberals, is simply to preserve that minimum of social harmony within which each can pursue his own vision of the good in his own way and presents no further ideals of its own.

To this Bosanquet might object that the idea that each individual, or group, should be left to pursue their own good in their own way tends to trivialize these more private ideals on the grounds that they are simply a matter of personal preference. But if there is some real best form of life (within which, of course, different individuals play different roles), then the state should surely promote it, even if not enforce it. Moreover, social harmony does require some common sense of values which have more content than merely that of unsympathetic coexistence. (How far this is true is quite a hot issue in current debates (2005), about immigration. See below.)

Thus the purpose of the nation-state is to promote the best possible form of human life, and any particular nation wielding state power must rest on a shared conception of this. However, this is importantly qualified by the insistence that the activity which constitutes this must be voluntary, not enforced. The proper use of state power is limited to removing hindrances to the good life. (This is an idea deriving from T. H. Green.) So, although its *goal* is positive, its *means* are negative. The sole thing it should do by force is remove hindrances to the fulfilment of impulses towards the good which, with these removed, will issue in fully voluntary actions.[39]

Thus, while Bosanquet rejects the liberal view that the state is only there to keep the peace between individuals and groups with essentially incommensurable visions of the good life, and has no values of its own to promote, he objects strongly to the state taking on what can only have value if done freely by individuals.

However, though it must not enforce them, the nation must know what the ideals are to which it is removing hindrances. It knows and acts on these ideals in virtue of the General Will (a concept which Bosanquet takes over from Rousseau, but substantially develops), which is the deeper self of all the citizens.[40] For what an individual person *really* wills and *apparently* wills *in his moment by moment volitional consciousness* are distinct; his *real will* is directed at what would truly satisfy him, rather than at what he thinks from time to time will do so. And what would really satisfy him is a social life lived according to a certain set of values shared by all those with whom he has to deal. And it is this set of values which, as a result of the pervasive psychological relations between all citizens, constitutes a nation proper with a General Will.

Bosanquet even talks of nations (and other genuine social wholes) as *minds*.[41] He is not claiming, indeed, like Josiah Royce (as we shall see in Chapter 7) that there are states of consciousness which pertain to the nation other than as mediated by individual persons. His idea is rather this: just as my consciousness at any time is imbued with my own particular ways of thinking and feeling which will outlast and precede these its momentary instances; so are these imbued with the ways of thinking and feeling which constitute the culture of my country and which derive in large part from a history which preceded my existence. Therefore just as an individual's mind is an identical universal present in his particular thoughts, feelings, and deeds (as his own particular outlook on things), so is the national culture (derived from the nation's history) a universal present in varied forms in each citizen's style of living and thinking. Even when we disagree with one another sharply, we do so in terms set by the national culture and impossible without it.

Bosanquet's celebration of the national mind would certainly require rethinking if he had foreseen the multicultural character of the Britain of today. Those who are not rebelling against this will claim that it is good that there is a plurality of cultures from which each individual should draw what suits him best. Still, it does seem that there is a gradual process whereby some largely accepted identity of viewpoint cohabits with what distinguishes each from each other.

The more usual view today is that it is desirable for each of us to get beyond their own culture, and learn how to live as an individual enriched by the best in every culture on which they can draw. Thus, it may be argued, these cultures are there to be drawn on by individuals, rather than the individuals being there to enrich the culture. And this does seem to go against the main tenor of Bosanquet's thought. So its relation to the modern ideal of pluralistic societies is problematic.

Be that as it may, Bosanquet thought of the nation as a greater Self of which each of its citizens is a component, reflecting individually its wholeness from the perspective of their particular role in it. This is especially evident in his theory of rights. For this is based on the claim that one's true identity is determined by the particular role which one plays in the nation both *qua* state proper and as cultural and historical unity. (See THE STATE, 191.) This role or position is what gives one rights, for a person's rights are a matter of what others may be forced to do to allow him to fulfil that position properly, this constituting their obligations or duties. One should not speak, however, of a duty to fulfil one's own position properly, for this requires voluntary moral action which would cease to be such if enforced.

Does then the Nation-State (in Bosanquet's opinion) exist for the sake of the individual, or vice versa? Bosanquet, as we have in effect seen, is misunderstood if we give either answer. For the state is only actualized as something having value through the activities of its citizens, while these activities are only valuable as elements in the total life which the state lives through them.

So important is the nation for Bosanquet that he shows a distinct tendency to favour a turning of religious feeling from direction towards God to direction towards one's nation. (We saw this idea already in his early papers on Christianity.) However, *The Philosophical Theory of the State* is not concerned mainly with religion and it is fairer to look elsewhere for Bosanquet's precise religious position.

XXI What was Bosanquet's Religion?

Bosanquet said once that his creed was really civilization (see n. 9). But that hardly does full justice to his religious outlook. If we look at his work as a whole, I suggest that it always remained close to what he expounded in his early talks on Christianity (discussed in Part One of this chapter) except for the important point that now the attempt to associate it with the essential message of Jesus is abandoned. But religion remains, for Bosanquet, a frame of mind and style of living which does not turn on membership of any specifically religious organization. In his later years he started going to a Friends Meeting House, though his marriage to Helen Dendy and his own funeral were at a Unitarian church. But he persistently avoided taking part in the formal worship of the two universities at which he worked: namely, Oxford and, much later, St Andrews.

Ethics and religion were always very close for Bosanquet. The essential difference is that for ethics the good is something to be sought, whereas religion adds that the world has somehow already eternally found it. Ethics, he still holds, is mainly a matter of 'my station and its duties'. Each of us has such a station and tasks to perform deriving from it. These tasks, you will recall, are our duties, while our rights are what others must do or refrain from doing to allow us to fulfil them.

So what does the personal religion of Bosanquet amount to?[42] I find the following four central features in it: (1) good citizenship; (2) high culture; (3) personal courage, each of which, for the religious man, are bathed in the fourth component: (4) cosmic contentment.

Cosmic contentment is the faith (which is a matter of both belief and emotion) that the world is perfect, and good always dominant over evil, while everything nasty in it is a necessary factor in the universe's perfection.

I turn now the first three heads.

(1) Good Citizenship

The good citizen loves his state or country more than he loves himself, perhaps more than he loves anything. Fate, or his own fate-determined efforts, have made him a soldier, a statesman, a professor, a stonemason, a rich man, a poor man. Each of these positions in society imposes its own special duties and determines the associated rights (what will allow the citizen to perform his duties properly). The duty-determining roles also include such things as being a spouse, or a parent, and, presumably, also being a child (though perhaps they should not be called duties of citizenship).

The duties of a citizen also include the duty, according to one's own circumstances, of assisting others to perform their duties and also to develop the other features of religion to which we now turn.

(2) High Culture

The religious man, or at least the modern religious man, will either be a highly cultured man or will be doing his best to make himself one. He will enjoy the great classics of literature, of painting, of music. Here again, as in his early discussion of the future of religious observance, there is an echo of Matthew Arnold's advice to read something excellent each day or at least once a week for ordinary toilers.

These classic works of art will (one may be sure) be primarily celebrations of human life and of nature, rather than denigrations of it (Margaret Gillies rather than Francis Bacon). And in the background of the person's enjoyment will be a general sense of the greatness of the universe which has brought them forth. Upon the whole, it does seem that 'civilization' was his highest value and, so far as he could see, that of the universe too. For mere luxury he always felt contempt.[43]

High culture may be taken as including all attempts to understand the universe, whether human or natural.

Bosanquet does, however, in his later work lay some stress on the love of nature (that is, of the less humanized features of the globe). In particular, enjoyment of the beauties of nature will both cause and be caused by one's cosmic contentment.

(3) Personal Courage

One will not be a pleasure seeker, and will wish no more for one's own happiness than the sense that one is playing one's own proper role in a greater whole—more immediately, some human organization, and ultimately the great spiritual cosmos of which we are each a fragmentary manifestation or component. Rather will one put up with whatever sorrow comes one's way as providing a chance for the ennoblement of one's character.

(4) Cosmic Contentment

Finally, we have a certain sort of cosmic contentment. This is the faith that the whole great thing is perfect, that it includes both good and evil, but that the good is eternally victorious over the evil. There will also be some more or less distinct realization that time is unreal, and that all is eternally there in the eternal Absolute. And there will be acceptance that it is the role of the finite to contain imperfections and often painful struggles as essential elements in the Absolute's eternal perfection.

Under this heading comes what Bosanquet on occasion calls 'cosmic emotion'. This may have some resemblance to what has sometimes been called 'the oceanic feeling'. However, it will not function for him as an escape from human affairs, as it often does. It is simply the grasp that all our struggles and tribulations are part of a system which is ultimately perfect.

The citizen knows that the state to which he is loyal has something unique to contribute to the Whole, and he loves it as such. The man of high culture sees great art as a special revelation of the Absolute's perfection, and the courageous man is sustained by his confidence that what he values most will be preserved eternally by the Whole.

Perhaps Bosanquet's best brief statement of his religious outlook is this:

If you claim nothing for your finiteness but to repose on the perfection of the whole through your recognition of your spiritual membership, you have a position which is secure with the security of the whole itself. (VDI, 229)

What should we think about Bosanquet's philosophy as an illuminator of religious issues? Consider first some things usually associated with religion which are lacking or have only a very secondary place in Bosanquet's outlook.

(1) God

What about God? If by 'God' we mean a personal creator of the universe, Bosanquet does not believe in him. However, he recognizes that belief in God, and devotion to him, has been a key element in humanity's religious sense. And surely, despite his disclaimers, Bosanquet's Absolute is at least a pantheistic God.

(2) Institutional Religion

What about organized religious faiths and associated ceremonies, rituals, prayers, and so forth? For Bosanquet these are to be valued to whatever extent they are (for human beings at a certain level of development) supports of true religion, as Bosanquet understands it. But Bosanquet thinks that humanity is likely to outgrow the need for such organizations.

(3) Love and Compassion

What about love, for example: love as the principal value from the point of view of Christian teaching? Well, Bosanquet does, as noted above, at one point substitute for 'Goodness, Truth and Beauty', 'Love, Truth and Beauty'. However, love in the two central senses of 'personal love between human beings' and 'compassion' does not figure very largely in his work.

Particularly absent, as it seems to me, is compassion. His comments on those who seem to have had a raw deal out of life are usually to the effect that they were the better for it, enabling them, for example, to reach peculiar moral heights. Thus, anything like a welfare state was anathema to him. These tough attitudes towards suffering are reflected in his involvement in social work (see section XXIII below).

(4) Life after death

Bosanquet insisted in his early work that the deeper and only acceptable sense of 'eternal life' was that in which it stood for this present life when transformed by devotion to eternal values. He had nothing but contempt for any religion for which individual survival of death was important. In his later metaphysics he did not discount the possibility, but what is important is the confidence, provided by a legitimate religious faith, that what we most rightly value is eternally preserved and even victorious within the Absolute.

The question of personal survival of death is discussed in chapter 9 of *The Value and Destiny of the Individual*. Here he stresses that the answer may well not be a straight yes or no, since it depends to a great extent on what one chooses to regard as oneself. Our life on this earth is an experience which is eternally there in the Absolute; its sense of its own passing away is an illusion. And, as experienced in the Absolute, it is certainly experienced as pertaining to larger wholes than we are clearly aware of in our terrestrial life. Perhaps some of the most significant such larger wholes do include stretches of apparent time in which something describable as myself continues after death, but equally perhaps not. Or rather, it is bound to be a matter of degree, for certainly if I identify myself with what I most intelligently value, this will be present in the future as much as it is now, for such values are actualized everywhere and everywhen.

The truth is that it is quite problematic what it makes sense to wish with regard to one's own existence after death. The personal relations (that of parent to child, for example) can hardly continue, not at any rate if we look for maturation rather than a pointless preservation of what belongs to another time. Moreover, the higher self which we may long for would be one in which our separateness from others is less sharp than it seems in this life, even reduced as it is at the higher levels of morality and culture.

It is thus no juggle, no 'faith as vague as all unsweet,' to offer the eternal reality of the Absolute as that realisation of our self which we instinctively demand and desire ... [I]t is not in principle the bare continuance of what we now seem to ourselves to be, which our heart is set upon. It is not the unbrokenness of the link of personal recollection. It is the security, the certainty, of the realisation of what we care for most, in the Absolute; and this does not mean in a remote and supernatural world, but in the fullest experience and throughout the universe of its appearances. (VDI, 288–9)

And it does not matter if 'we' are to be aware of it or not—since it is a matter of degree whether 'we' as such will be there.

We know that what we care for, in so far as it really is what we care for, is safe through its continuity with the Eternal. It is in this assurance that there is comprised, in principle all that we long for in the desire of our own survival. (VDI, 261)

Bosanquet reflects at the end of Chapter 10 of this book on how humanity may develop in the future. Constant improvements in technology may teach us that what they provide are not what really matters. It may be that there will be a deeper sense of our spiritual unity with one another in the Absolute, but we must not think that the point of the universe is to lead up to some great consummation. Its point lies equally in its appearances at all times and places.

Since Bosanquet set such value upon high culture and a spiritual sense of the oneness of humanity with itself and with nature, one wonders what he would have made of European civilization a century or so later. Surely he would have been shocked at the taking over of high culture by pop culture, and by the trashiness of much of the modern media. He might have wondered whether, after all, he was wrong to think that spiritual values did not need to be communally expressed in some form of religious observance of a liberal, non-fundamentalist kind. For now what people are mainly offered is a choice between religion of the crudest kind, often fundamentalist in character, or complete detachment from any kind of religious symbols or institutions.

(5) Jesus Christ and the New Testament

We have surveyed his earlier views on Jesus, Paul, and the New Testament. He offered an interpretation of their teaching as a this-worldly call to a life in the light of higher values. Later his interest in the New Testament seems to have waned, and there is nothing about Jesus in his metaphysics. And with this went that increasingly uncompassionate outlook of which I have just spoken. So in the end, Christianity would seem to have been for him at best just one strand in what he really rejoiced in: namely, European civilization as the presently (that is, in his time) high-water mark (PIV, ch. 10) of the Absolute's achievement. Nor is there any sign of any shaking of his confidence in this at the time of the First World War, when, of course, he was rather too old a dog to learn new tricks.

XXII *What Religion Is*

Bosanquet presents what we may take to be his final thoughts on religion in the meditative little book of his old age, *What Religion Is*, published in 1920 a year before his death). Its essential message is:

To be one with the supreme good in the faith which is also will—that is Religion (RELIGION, 79)

Concerning this book his wife says:

He had felt deeply the need of many who could not accept the ordinary forms of religion,—'persons who, while feeling the necessity of religion, are perplexed by the shape in which it comes before them.' He was also painfully impressed by certain developments which arose out of the sorrows of the war, feeling that many were being led to seek consolation where they could find no lasting satisfaction, and longing to help them on to firmer ground. The little book is the culminating expression of his lifelong passion for helping others to find happiness where he had found it himself—in the life of the spirit. (A SHORT ACCOUNT, 141)

The essential themes are as follows.

1. The duties of religion are the same as those of morality. There is one important difference, however. At the purely moral level there is a sharp distinction between what I should be and what I am, and between how the world should be and how it is, and if I do not manage to do what is right, I am a moral failure. At the religious level, however, I act in the assurance that the good is the only reality and that evil, including my evil self, is unreal, and this empowers me to do right, as it is hard to do without religion's aid.

2. Religion is not a matter of philosophical proof or argument, but consists in the experience of 'oneness with the supreme good in every facet and issue of heart and will' (RELIGION, 32).[44] It is the felt reality of our 'unity of will and belief with the supreme good' (ibid. 30) and the consequent commitment of the will to play our part in constituting the perfection of

the Whole willingly, rather than perforce. (I am elaborating a little on his actual statement of this theme here.)

3. There may or may not be something after my death which should count as my continuing self, but this is quite inessential to religion. Indeed, religion has nothing to do with any special expectations about the future, whether for myself, mankind, or the natural cosmos. What matters is that I can live in the eternal in my day-to-day life, by identification of myself with the great values of love, truth, and beauty. We must avoid interpreting our unity with the eternal perfect whole as having anything to do with remote events.

4. More generally, religion is not concerned with the order of events in time. Each period of history realizes the eternal perfection of the Whole in its own particular way.

5. Evil is an essential ingredient of this perfection. The eternal must actualize itself in the finite and temporal, and the finite is necessarily full of struggle and frustration. Serious attempts to imagine a better world than this are vacuous. We cannot know that some life which seems full of deprivation might not have been better if it had been less troubled.

You may rightly try to hinder what you think hardship or defect. But it is far beyond the facts to say: This or that privation or deprivation is abnormal, an injustice, a necessary spiritual loss. The man, say, is blind. Is he so far less than a man should be? Would Mr. Fawcett have been less or more if he had had his sight? Who can tell? And Mr Kavanagh, if he had had his limbs? One has a bad wife, another a bad son. How can we say what he makes of his burden? We are not entitled to judge that the unique being and equipment which the universe lays upon each individual is such as to impart and defeat the possibilities of good. We must not assume that things would be better if we could make him and his conditions over to suit our smoothed conception of what a man and his life should be. (RELIGION, 56)

It may be remarked that Bosanquet's discussion of evil in this work is entirely of the deprivations and suffering which ennobles those who rise above them. There is not a word in this book about evil men. Rather is it implied that everyone is both good from one point of view (that of the ultimately real) and bad from another (that of the merely existing).

Thus, through Bosanquet's Panglossian spectacles, everyone is really doing their best in circumstances 'designed' to call it out from them. Suffering is inevitable and not really bad, and moral evil has its proper place in the universe.

6. Prayer and worship and all sorts of religious institution matter only as techniques for sustaining religious faith. Any attempt to give a coherent theoretical basis to them is beside the point, because they are of no ultimate religious significance.

7. Although he does not discuss religious organizations in this work, Bosanquet clearly stands by his view that the religious consciousness of modern man probably no longer needs any sort of institutional expression.

But what, we may ask, once more, of God? I can only repeat that, although Bosanquet occasionally uses the word 'God' to stand for the eternal perfect whole of which we are all constituents, his more considered position is that if we continue to use the word at all, it should be as denoting the forces for good which eternally triumph over evil in the Absolute.

What Religion Is is certainly gentler than much of his earlier writing, and the association of religion with love of country is scarcely mentioned, only the value of loyalty to some whole greater than oneself. In some ways it may therefore make a better impression on the modern reader.

XXIII Mr and Mrs Bosanquet and the Charity Organisation Society

It seems to me that Bosanquet's philosophy, whether one likes it or not, does support a philosophy of life which amounts to a religion. And from what I have read about him, he seems to have lived just such a life himself. There is a certain complacency about the philosophy and, such is my impression, about the man. But his attitudes have a strong side too.

We saw at the beginning of this chapter that Bosanquet gave up his Oxford position in 1881, having inherited enough to live as a man of private means. Thereafter (except for his short spell from 1903 to 1908 as a professor at the University of St Andrews) he devoted himself to his own writings, gave lectures to the London Ethical Society, and did voluntary work for the Charity Organisation Society (COS). There is a very good account of this society in Alan McBriar's *An Edwardian Mixed Doubles: The Bosanquets versus the Webbs*.

The COS was founded in 1869 to bring various charities for work among the poor under a common umbrella through which they could work more effectively. It was, however, driven by a quite harsh ideology. And this owed a good deal to T. H. Green's philosophy as interpreted by C. S. Loch, who was for a long time secretary of the society. He had been a friend of Bosanquet's at Balliol, and the two of them were much under the spell of Green.

In 1895 Bosanquet married Helen Dendy, whom he had met through the Ethical Society and the COS. She was working for this organization as a salaried social worker, and subsequently continued as a dominating figure in it as a volunteer and writer of several books on social problems. She fully shared the society's tough attitudes, and regarded most poverty as the result of curable character defect. For example, she said that *'there is always some reason* why the man who knows his trade cannot get employment', meaning that it was in some way the result of moral failing (THE STANDARD, 275). Likewise, in her *The Strength of the People*, making somewhat light of poverty as such, she said: 'The undernourishment of school children might be the result of the ignorance of parents rather than of their poverty' (quoted in MIXED DOUBLES, 150). What was required to reduce poverty, so McBriar expounds her saying, was the dissemination of 'the *will* of the individual to preserve his independence. Anything that undermined that will to independence, even if it were the provision of old-age pensions[45] that relieved workmen from having to think of providing for their future or the provision of school meals, which removed from parents, more especially fathers, the responsibility of providing for their offspring, would have fatal social consequences'[46] (ibid. 151). 'The strong can help the weak, there is doubt about that; they may even help the poor to be less poor; but money will play a very subordinate part in their work' (ibid. 152, quoting from STRENGTH).

This was the view of both Bosanquets, who seem to have been entirely at one on all social issues.[47] For Bosanquet, at any rate, this was an application of Green's principle that the aim of social reform was to make people morally better, rather than more comfortable. But in the case of Bosanquet, this principle led to conclusions much less attractive than those of Green himself.

For while Green and Bosanquet both accepted that our goal should be a society of morally good people, there was a significant difference in their deduction from this belief.

As Bosanquet and his wife understood this principle, charitable help to the poor was usually more apt to make them morally second-rate welfare-dependent wastrels rather than better people. Thus they should be helped only to the extent of putting them on the path of dealing with their problems themselves. (It was helpful if they went hungry from time to time.) Even if there is an element of truth in this idea, it was adopted in a very harsh form by the COS, and Bosanquet was at one with its other organizers. For its ideal was to such an extent that its clients must be taught to take their own responsibilities that it was careful not to do too much for them.[48] Green, in contrast, had thought that a decent standard of living for all should be pursued by the state, because it was the necessary background of moral goodness, whereas Bosanquet thought that the state should do little or nothing to promote the material welfare of the poor, since it was the task allotted to them by the Absolute that they, and more especially the father of a family, should have the chance to become morally good by taking responsibility for saving for old age (thus state pensions would be an evil), and feeding his children (thus free school dinners would be an evil). Similarly, he opposed free medical care for the poor (which would discourage the virtue of thrift) and outdoor relief (as opposed to the workhouse) because it would encourage laziness—while the disabled should give their relatives the chance of moral excellence by looking after them. And he disapproved of any kind of dole for the unemployed for similar reasons (while gifts for the well-off did not change them morally (see CIVILIZATION 344). All this from a couple living on inherited money!

Helen Bosanquet and other representatives of the COS served on the Royal Commission on the Poor Law of 1905–9. Also on it was Beatrice Webb. Each of these women represented both their own views and their husband's (Bosanquet and Sidney Webb, respectively). Mrs Webb was a somewhat lone opponent of the general tone of most of the commissioners, whose ideology was primarily that of the COS. This led to her finally dissociating herself from the Majority Report, a large part of which was written by Helen Bosanquet. (It is controversial how much Bernard assisted her in writing it, though it certainly expressed their shared views.) Instead, she engaged in private research on the whole issue, and eventually produced a Minority Report in opposition to the Majority Report). Thus the Majority Report reflected the dominant view of the COS that it was primarily moral failure which led to destitution, while the Minority Report expressed Mrs Webb's view that it was primarily social factors (and not these mainly as affecting the character). The long dispute between the Bosanquets and the Webbs cannot be charted here. (See MIXED DOUBLES for a fascinating account of this.) Neither side can be said to have triumphed totally, and serious reform did not take place until after the 1914 war.

Personally, I find it difficult not to sympathize with J. A. Hobson in his remark *re* the views of the Bosanquets and the COS generally that 'There is ... an insidious attraction for the well-to-do in this notion that destitution is but the natural working out of human character' (MIXED DOUBLES, 342). On the other hand, the limitations of the Webbs's perspective are shown by the fact that much later they fell hook, line, and sinker for the supposed enchantments of the Soviet Union.

It might be thought odd that Bosanquet believed that the state or nation was a moral organism, while being so resistant to anything approaching what today is called 'the welfare state'. The answer is given by a distinction which he made between moral socialism and economic socialism. Moral socialism regards us all as members of the state conceived as an organism, who should live their lives as their personal dedication to the goodness of the whole, while economic socialism conceives individuals as mere atoms who must be forced to do what the greatest benefit of the greatest number requires, while easy welfare provisions turn their recipients into parasites upon, rather than living member of, the whole. (See CIVILIZATION, ch. 10.)

Thus, for Bosanquet, what made the state an individual, even a *mind*, was the fact that there was a culture, a general sense of how to behave, which was a common essence present in all except the worst of its citizens, not something dependent upon the control of citizens by government. However, the fact that it was an individual at its best, more worthy of love than most people belonging to it, did mean that it had the right, in its own interest, to control individual citizens by force when this was necessary for the good of the whole. So Bosanquet was not against a good deal of state control where necessary, provided it served to improve people rather than spoonfeed them with the comforts of life. Another contrast between Green and Bosanquet was that, while Green worried that cultural activities on the part of the well-off might encourage escapism from the duty to improve society, Bosanquet thought that the excellence which should be encouraged by the state included, as a large part of it, engagement in high culture, at least for the nobs, with the possibility of some trickle down to the poor. Here we intellectuals may feel more at ease with Bosanquet, though whether we should or should not do so is another matter.

Whether Bosanquet's deduction from the primacy of the production of virtue (rather than happiness) was more or less logical than Green's deduction, Green's certainly led to a more humane practical ethic. As for Bosanquet's role in the COS, he only worked on the administrative and organizational side. He did not meet actual clients, as he would not have known what to say to poor people (so his wife reports). But he certainly was one of its main ideologists. And I must say that to me this ideology is pretty repellent, and made Bosanquet and his wife into a powerful opposition to any developments at that time which heralded the welfare state as it came into being in Britain in 1945 and still continues a troubled existence.

I end by repeating that Bosanquet's real religion was that of *civilization*. And he was certainly a rather earnestly cultured man, and clearly a good friend of his intellectual peers, ever anxious to learn something from those of opinions adverse to his own.

Notes

1. On biographical matters I am grateful for some help from William Sweet. I have also used the life of Bosanquet by his wife (A SHORT ACCOUNT) and the very informative *An Edwardian Mixed Doubles* by A. M. McBriar.
2. 'Life and Philosophy'. See also TCHENG, 38.
3. Witness *Knowledge and Reality* (1885).
4. For more on the Ethical Society see A SHORT ACCOUNT, 44–5. The lecture on reading the New Testament 'led to the formation of a class of working men to study the subject under Bernard's guidance, an episode to which he always looked back with pleasure'. See also RICHTER, 118–20. See also MIXED DOUBLES, 5 and 12.
5. See e.g. MACKEY and TEMPLETON, and the writings of D. Z. Phillips.
6. For a careful study of Bosanquet on rights, see SWEET.
7. I feel bound to say 'gradual', though actually Bosanquet has a pretty rosy view of human nature throughout the ages, at least in Europe.
8. It may be thought that what particularly alienates us now from Panglossism are such things as the Holocaust and other twentieth-century horrors. But Bosanquet remained in Panglossian mood during the First World War, and after all there had been horrors enough in history before his time. For a later example of his Panglossian see THE STATE, 272.
9. 'My faith is in civilisation and I have no need of any other creed' (*Aspects of the Social Problem* (1895) quoted by Tcheng in French (TCHENG, 49)).
10. An interesting comparison between the two thinkers was made by J. N. Muirhead: '[I]t is certainly true that with all their deep-seated theoretic agreement there were perhaps no two philosophical writers of the time who contrasted with each other so completely in temperament. However we describe the difference, as that between rationalist [Bosanquet] and mystic [Bradley], radical and conservative, simple and complex, classic and romantic, it was a sufficiently striking one' (BOSANQUET AND FRIENDS, 246).
11. I note, without comment, a tantalizing remark which Bosanquet made in a letter to C. J. Webb in 1923: 'I didn't say anything about Naturalism [in a previous letter]. I don't think it important; the universe is so obviously experience, and it must all be of one tissue' (BOSANQUET AND FRIENDS, 243).
12. One usage would be that the self side is conscious of the not-self side, and less immediately of what the latter may be said to represent.

13. Bradley and Stout corresponded on Bradley's restricted use of the word 'consciousness'. In a letter to Bradley dated 31 Jan. 1893, Stout says that it is now established philosophical English usage to use 'consciousness' as 'the most general & indeterminate word in the vocabulary of Philosophy & Psychology' [for experienced mental states] and that Bradley's attempt to restrict 'consciousness' so that it applies only to states of sentience in which there is direction of something mental upon an object is unlikely to win general acceptance. Bradley replies in a letter of 3 Feb. the same year: 'I suppose "consciousness" is now fastened on us but it seems to me an awkward term, & "unconscious" is worse' (*Collected Works of F. H. Bradley*, iv. 63–6).

14. There is an effective critique of some of these positions by Ted Honderich in his book *Consciousness*, though I cannot quite go along with his own position for which, none the less, consciousness is somehow something physical which exists only in brains.

15. Since Bosanquet, quantum physics seems to confirm the view that the laws of physics are statistical rather than fully deterministic. But Bosanquet could still maintain that it is foolish to associate the presence of mind with indeterminism.

16. It is worth noting that Whitehead quite similarly relates logical and aesthetic relations. See ADVENTURES, 373, also J. S. Bixler's 'Whitehead's Philosophy of Religion', in SCHILPP, 503.

17. Bosanquet's view of the spirit of the whole extends to Logic. 'By Logic we understand, with Plato and Hegel, the supreme law or nature of experience, the impulse towards unity and coherence (the positive spirit of non-contradiction) by which every fragment yearns towards the whole to which it belongs, and every self to its completion in the Absolute, and of which the Absolute itself is at once an incarnation and a satisfaction. . . . It is the strict and fundamental truth that love is the mainspring of logic' (PIV, 340, quoted in A SHORT ACCOUNT, 58).

18. 'Mind is the meaning of externality, which under certain conditions concentrates in a new focus of meaning, which is a new finite mind. When we speak of the making of souls, we mean nothing more than the moulding and relative perfecting of minds' (PIV, 220).

19. It is interesting that Bradley very much objected to the chapter on Nature in this book. See BRADLEY LETTERS, 172.

20. Take the following passage as an example:

Thus, for the purposes of Logic, we must turn our usual ideas upside down. We must try to imagine something of this kind. We have all seen a circular panorama. Each one of us, we must think, is shut up alone inside such a panorama, which is movable and flexible, and follows him wherever he goes. The things and persons depicted in it, move and act upon one another; but all this is in the panorama, and not beyond it. The individual cannot get outside this encircling scenery, and no one else can get inside it. Apart from it, prior to it, we have no self; it is indeed the stuff of which oneself is made. Is everyone's panorama exactly the same? No, they're not exactly the same. They are formed round different centres, each person differing from all the others by individual qualities, and by his position towards the points and processes which determine his picture. For—and here is the remarkable point—every one of us has painted for himself the picture within which he is shut up, and he is perpetually painting and re-painting it, not by copying from some original, but by arranging and completing confused images and tints that are always appearing magically on his canvas. Now this magical panorama, from which the individual cannot escape, and the laws of which are the laws of his experience, is simply his own mind regarded as a content or a world. His own body and mind, regarded as things, are within the panorama just as other people's bodies and minds are. The whole world, for each of us, *is* our course of consciousness in so far as this is regarded as a system of objects which we are obliged to think. (THE ESSENTIALS, 14–15)

21. See KEATS, 26–268 (long letter to his brother and sister, 14 Feb.–3 May 1819).

22. 'In the same way, the connection of originality and eccentricity, on which Mill insists, appears to us today to be a fallacious train of thought; and, in general, in all these matters, we tend to accept the principle that, in order to go beyond a point of progress, it is necessary to have reached it; and in order to destroy a law, it is necessary to have fulfilled it' (THE STATE, 57).

23. But although Bosanquet often gives the impression that all that really counts in human life is the development of Western civilization, he defends his optimistic view of things at one point by exhibiting a (perhaps alarming) sympathy with what he supposes to be the life of a primitive chief (his slaves are not mentioned!): 'I should have said that prima facie the poor and the benighted heathen were more light-hearted—we are now speaking of facts and not of "oughts"—than the well-to-do, cultivated, and respectable Christian. ...If...you go, without moral prejudices, to pleasure merely, you must remember that, say, a savage or barbarian chief, whose life, if I had to live it, would be to me prolonged hardship, terror, and remorse, probably enjoys his existence as much as I do mine, or more. And he would certainly prefer to be shot a dozen times rather than, well warmed and well fed, to sit in my armchair and try to read Hegel.'

24. For some early thoughts of Bosanquet on the problem of evil and the claim that pain is not an evil, see his article 'On our Right to Regard Evil as a Mystery'.

25. '[E]very fragment yearns towards the whole to which it belongs' (PIV, 340). In support he appeals to Plato, *Phaedo* 75B.

26. He gave a talk at King's College for Women, around the period of the First World War, called 'Is Compensation Necessary to Optimism?' which I have not managed to get hold of, but which is presumably on this subject. See A SHORT ACCOUNT, 131.

27. Bosanquet's hostility to those who think that pessimism can be avoided only by believing that we will eventually be compensated for our sufferings is already expressed in a letter to Bradley of around 1883. See BRADLEY LETTERS, iv. 6.

28. However, his wife says, *re* the 1914 war, 'How deeply also he felt the pain and suffering of the soldiers even I hardly realised at the time, though it was brought home to me keenly in the future' (A SHORT ACCOUNT, 137).

29. It is worth noting that Bradley, though he would certainly not have called himself a hedonist, was much more concerned to claim that there was more happiness than unhappiness in reality.

30. For more implied discussion of G. E. Moore's position, see *Some Suggestions in Ethics*, ch. 3. Moore could have had a heyday attacking this.

31. Another way of putting it is that the value of anything short of the great Whole is the degree to which that Whole is 'present' in it; for, while 'present' in every one of its parts, it is not so equally. That is to say, some contain more guidance to the character of the whole than do others.

32. The relation of value to consciousness, and 'part-values' to 'whole-values', is discussed importantly in relation to Green, Kant, hedonism, G. E. Moore, and Sidgwick at PIV, 302 ff.

33. I have discussed this proof particularly in 'Bradley's Doctrine of the Absolute' in STOCK, also in JAMES AND BRADLEY.

34. It will be seen that this argument is a posteriori inasmuch as it depends upon the existence of something. Bosanquet does not argue as neatly as above, but I think that it is what he is trying to say.

35. The occasional reference to the Absolute as a supreme self is, I think, somewhat misleading as to Bosanquet's real view.

36. I develop this line of thought more fully in Ch. 9, sect. X. For a more adequate statement, see *The Vindication of Absolute Idealism*, 30–3, 238–9, and *passim*; JAMES AND BRADLEY; Part 2, ch. 4, sect. 3; 'Hartshorne on the Past'; 'The Unreality of Time'. There is more on this in Chs. 8 and 9 below.

37. Consider in this connection such passages as the following (see, indeed, the whole discussion on PIV, 372–9).

> So far from it being a strange or unwarranted assumption that the experiences of conscious units are transmuted, reinforced, and rearranged, by entrance in to a fuller and more extended experience, the thing is plain fact, which if we were not blinded by traditional superstition, we should recognise in our daily selves as a matter of course. We, our subjective selves, are in truth much more to be compared to a rising and falling tide, which is continually covering wider areas as it deepens, and dropping back to narrower and shallower ones as it ebbs, than to the isolated pillars with fixed circumferences, as which we have been taught to think of ourselves. (PIV, 372–3)

38. However, that they are so is a main doctrine of McTaggart's.

39. We might note in this connection that Bosanquet thinks that 'civilised life' requires that no individual belongs to more than one state, since the state must be the arbiter in any conflict an individual may find between the demands on him of different social groupings (THE STATE, 173).

40. 'This indestructible impulse towards the Good, which is necessarily a common good, the substantial unity and filling of life by the interests through which man is human, is what Rousseau plainly has before him in his account of the General Will' (THE STATE, 103). And in being forced to meet the demands of the state, I am being determined only by my own larger self as against my passing moods, for the state embodies each individual's own real will.

41. As indeed he must do, on his own principles, if they are to be wholes more valuable than any individual person, as he thinks they are. 'Explanation aims at referring things to a whole; and there is no true whole but mind' (THE STATE, 40).

42. For a treatment from a slightly different point of view, see William Sweet, 'Bernard Bosanquet and the Nature of Religious Belief'.

43. The desires of the civilized man would 'not be artificial desires stimulated and elaborated into a tyranny of the machinery of life by the self which gropes for more and cannot find the "more" which it needs' (THE STATE, 136).

44. This shows a limited sympathy with those to whom we are replying in this book: Pascal, Kierkegaard, and indeed William James. But he is not really at one with them, for clearly he thought a proper philosophical understanding of such things helpful in promoting them. After all, that is why his wife said that he wrote *What Religion Is*.

45. See also THE STANDARD, 104–5.

46. On the possibility of free medical treatment for the poor, Helen Bosanquet commented: '[We certainly do not favour] the ideals of those enthusiasts who contemplate unfettered and unintermittent medical control, supervision, and treatment of every human being from the cradle to the grave...A race of hypochondriacs might be as useless to the State as a race of any other degenerates...We are not inclined, therefore, to make medical assistance so attractive that it may become a species of honourable and gratuitous self-indulgence' (quoted in MIXED DOUBLES, 298–9, from the Majority Report of the Royal Commission on the Poor Law, for which see below).

47. For Helen Bosanquet's views of such things, see THE STANDARD, esp. chs. 6 and 9. Both Bosanquets thought it a good thing that potentially feckless workers should go hungry. 'A little wholesome starvation' might do a feckless worker no end of good (THE STANDARD, 271). And Bernard Bosanquet says somewhere that it is good for a man sometimes not to know where his next dinner is coming from.

48. The view that Bosanquet was much more conservative, and unsympathetic to the poor, than others inspired by Green's teaching is criticized by Matt Carter in his *T. H. Green and the Development of Ethical Socialism* (especially in ch. 3).

Carter says that Bosanquet was all in favour of state interference where it would be helpful; where he differed was in what he thought, as a matter of empirical fact, the poor needed. But the view that the destitute are usually more in need of a stiffening of their moral fibre than a handout is a harsh one. One has the impression that both Bosanquets felt that happiness which did not arise from hard work was rather contemptible.

Chapter 7

Josiah Royce

I Introductory

Josiah Royce (1855–1916) was born in 1855, the son of so-called Forty-Niners, at a gold mining camp at Grass Valley, California. His father, having little success as a miner, was, first, a commercial traveller and then a fruit vendor. As a boy, Josiah often heard his elders say that 'this was a new country'. Looking at the 'vestiges left by the former diggings of miners', he wondered what this could mean, and decided to devote his life to finding out. Later he actually wrote a history of California, and his philosophy owes much to his childhood pondering of this question.

Royce studied science and literature at the new University of California in San Francisco, and on receiving his Ph.D. (after studying in Germany) he became a lecturer in the English department there. But though there are many literary references in his philosophy, it was to philosophy that he wished to devote himself. Thus he wrote to William James at Harvard that there was no fellow philosopher within some thousand miles or so (how many are there in California now?), as a result of which James found Royce first a temporary, and then a permanent, job at Harvard. Much in the philosophies of both James and Royce results from their friendly intellectual sparring.

Royce came from a much humbler background than most (or all?) of the Faculty at Harvard, and this increased a certain innate awkwardness in his social relations. His loud voice and strikingly red hair made a strong, but sadly, not always a pleasant impression on others. He is also said to have stopped people on passing them and insisted, like Socrates, on challenging them as to their opinions. And probably he was not always too polite in the objections he raised to them. Certainly he tended to write pretty harshly of philosophical work of which he thought poorly.

He had periods of great depression (coupled with serious insomnia), from which he sought release, not without success, by going on long sea voyages. Indeed, in 1888, after something of a nervous breakdown, he went off to Australia for six months. On his voyage there he had some interesting discussions with the rather contemplative captain of the ship, who once asked him what he taught his students. Royce replied by telling him about a man who had gone to the wrong place for a lecture by Mark Twain and heard someone else, whom he thought was Twain, giving a quite different lecture. Asked whether Mark Twain was funny, he answered that the talk was indeed funny, 'but then, you see, it was not so damned funny'. Adapting this, Royce said that he taught his students 'that the world and the heavens, and the stars are all real, but not so damned real, you see' (see CLENDENNING, 155). Royce periodically thereafter went on sea voyages to deal with periods of mental fatigue, and managed to do much of his writing on board ship.

Perhaps the worst period in his life was when the beloved eldest of his three sons, Christopher (1882–1910), a man of great promise, became pretty well insane, at about the age of 28, and had to be committed to a mental hospital for the rest of his short life.

Later in Royce's career, the increasing scepticism of younger philosophers regarding the claims of absolute idealism was another cause of depression, although he continued to be respected as a major philosophical figure. These sorrows, together with a certain innate tendency to pessimism, should be borne in mind when we examine his grapplings with the problem of evil.

Though it will not be considered here, he took a skilled interest in (and even contributed to) the development of symbolic logic, concerning which his colleagues knew little, and he was the first to initiate the teaching of it at Harvard and perhaps in the USA. In fact, the important logician (and philosopher) C. I. Lewis (who, as perhaps few have noticed, said later in life that he thought perhaps absolute idealism was right[1]) first learnt his logic from him.

He seems to have been happily married to a somewhat eccentric lady, Katharine née Head, who sometimes told visitors that all philosophy was 'just drivel'. There was a fanciful tale that Royce (who was a brilliant linguist, able, among other things, to read Sanskrit) wrote his books in German, and that Katharine translated them into English (CLENDENNING, 331).

I shall discuss the following themes from Royce:

1. Royce's proof of the existence of God in *The Religious Aspect of Philosophy*
2. Ethical theory in *The Religious Aspect of Philosophy*
3. The problem of evil in *The Religious Aspect of Philosophy*
4. The panpsychism of *The Spirit of Modern Philosophy*
5. The Four Conceptions of Being in *The World and the Individual*
6. Time and eternity and the worlds of description and of acquaintance (mainly in *The Spirit of Modern Philosophy*)
7. The notion of the beloved community in *The Philosophy of Loyalty* and *The Problem of Christianity*

I will conclude with a comment on Royce as religious thinker and man.

Royce's thought underwent some development over his life. Since for the most part I prefer the earlier thought, I shall deal both with his earlier and later works, the former to do justice to myself, the latter to do justice to Royce.

II Royce's *The Religious Aspect of Philosophy*

(a) Proof of the Existence of God

Anglo-American absolute idealists were united by their belief in the existence of an infinite consciousness (or something close to this) which somehow includes everything else which there is. This is usually referred to as the Absolute (though T. H. Green called it an 'Eternal Consciousness'). They disagree, however, as we have seen, as to whether this Absolute or Eternal Consciousness is sufficiently like God as he is traditionally conceived to be called 'God'. Bradley and Bosanquet, for example, thought that it was not, while Royce and Green believed that it was.

I shall now consider Royce's attempt to prove the existence of God or the Absolute in the first, and perhaps most attractive, of his philosophical works: namely, *The Religious Aspect of Philosophy* (1885). He does so on the surprising basis that there could not be such a thing as error if God did not exist, and yet clearly there is such a thing.

Royce regards the idea that there is such a thing as error as beyond doubt. For if the belief that there is error is true, then there is such a thing, while if there is not such a thing as error, then the belief that there is, is itself an error, and so, once again, there is such a thing.

There are some problems about arguing for the existence of error in this a priori way, into which I shall not enter. But surely no one is going to deny that there is such a thing as error, and if he can be shown that from this it follows that God exists, surely he has proof enough of God's existence to satisfy anyone. So let us grant that there is such a thing as error without any quibbling.[2]

The argument runs like this. In order for error to exist, two conditions must be satisfied. First, a mind must identify an object as that of which it is thinking, and secondly, it must ascribe some character to it which it does not, in fact, possess. And there is a problem as to how these two conditions can be satisfied.

For consider, first, that the object that the mind identifies must, so it might seem, either be a content of its own consciousness, such as one of its own ideas, or something outside it. In the former case, it can hardly be mistaken about it; so it seems that when thought is erroneous, it must be concerned with something other than and lying beyond its own contents.

If a mind identifies some object beyond itself, it must presumably do so as that which answers to some idea it possesses: that is, as answering to some description which the mind gives to itself. But if there is an object which answers to that idea or description, then that mind is in possession of the truth about it. To suppose that it does not answer to that idea is to suppose that the mind is not thinking about that object. Rather, is it thinking about whatever object it is which answers to its idea, and about that object it must be right (even if it exists only as an object of its own thought). Hence there is no possibility of error.

Since, however, there is such a thing as error, there must be some deficiency in this account of how the mind can home in on something lying beyond its own bounds. This deficiency can only be remedied, according to Royce, by recognizing that both the individual mind and its object are contents of one overarching absolute mind (= God, or the Absolute).

To see how this would remedy the deficiency, consider that, although one cannot be in error about a content of one's own consciousness,[3] one can entertain a false thought about it. Thus I can direct my attention upon a blue shape in my visual field, and think the thought that it is red, though realizing, of course, its falsehood. Similarly, an infinite mind which includes absolutely everything as a content of its consciousness could contain all sorts of false thoughts about such contents. To it the falsehood of these thoughts would be evident. However, a finite mind which was only part of the Absolute Mind might contain one of these false thoughts without containing that direct confrontation with its object which would show that it was false, and thereby take it as true. (We saw that Spinoza had a slightly similar idea.)

Suppose the Absolute has the thought that a predicate F applies to a certain individual X of which it is immediately aware as one of its own contents and at the same time recognizes that X does not really possess the property F. Then, if there is a finite mind which is only a part of the Absolute Mind, it may have the false thought that X has the property F, because, while it has a clear enough idea of F, its idea of X is too feeble to manifest its falseness. And this, claims Royce, is the only possible explanation of our capacity to have false thoughts.

Thus, when I think falsely, the Absolute Mind contains the thought that a certain object has a certain property while knowing, from its direct awareness of the object that the thought is false. However, my consciousness is only a fragment of that totality and contains only the false thought, though it is continuous in the Absolute with a direct confrontation with its object which reveals its falsehood. This is what error, granted it exists, must really be. As to why there is such a thing, Royce holds that the Absolute's grasp of the character of its own contents is enriched by the correction it contains of what is thought about them in these fragments of itself. And that correction of our false thoughts in the Absolute, in which their true object and its character are fully displayed, is a deeper version of ourselves, whose gradually fuller realization in our lives, here and in the hereafter, is what gives them significance.

Royce's argument is a good deal better than it may strike many readers as being at first. For although not satisfactory, just as it stands, there is more to it than impatience with its conclusion may allow some contemporary philosophers to recognize.

Its defects as it stands are indeed several. First, it rests on the supposition that falsehood always consists of wrongly ascribing a predicate to a subject. But this is not evidently so of false existential beliefs, positive or negative. To believe that there are such things as unicorns, or that there are no such things as horses, is not to believe of certain things that they do or do not answer to a certain predicate (or at least so it is usual to believe nowadays, though Royce himself, as we will see, talks of the 'ontological predicate'). And there are other types of belief which also seem not to be of this simple subject/predicate type.

But even if recognition of this point would reduce the snappiness of Royce's proof, its main thrust could be preserved provided he could win our agreement to the fact that there are false beliefs of the subject/predicate type he requires, whatever other kinds of falsehood there may be as well. And surely he is right that we are sometimes in error about the character of particular things.

Consider any erroneous belief of the required kind—say, the belief, on my part, that my friend Jack Robinson is honest (although in fact he is not). Royce will say that there is a problem as to how it is *that* Jack Robinson, rather than someone else with the same name, of whom I am thinking. For the idea I have in my mind is of a man, who, along with other things, is honest, and this is an idea to which Jack Robinson does not answer. How then can it be of him that I am thinking? But if I am not thinking of him, I cannot be wrong about him. (Royce, indeed, says that I am simply right about my own Jack Robinson—neglecting the point that I am also wrong in thinking that such a person exists. However, this is not essential to his contention that I cannot be wrong about Jack Robinson himself.)

There is, however, a rather obvious reply to Royce's argument even thus reconstructed. For surely I can identify Jack Robinson by a description which does uniquely identify him, and which does not include the erroneous predicate. Thus I may identify him as the man who looks a certain way, lives in a certain place, whom I have met on certain occasions, etc., all of which do truly identify him, and then go on to think falsely that the man thus identified is honest. This is roughly the analysis of it given by Bertrand Russell's theory of descriptions. It, or something close to it, was once almost universally accepted by analytic philosophers in the mid-twentieth century.

However, recent discussions of *de re* thoughts and beliefs may encourage us to regard Royce's argument with more respect. (A *de re* thought of the kind relevant here applies a description to a thing identified otherwise than by, and more directly than by, any description.) For many philosophers have come to think Bertrand Russell's account, of how our thoughts may refer to things other than immediate contents of consciousness, inadequate, as putting us at too great a distance from the world. Surely, they argue, when I have a thought about some particular person or thing in my environment, I am not just thinking that there is just some one otherwise unidentified something which answers to a certain description, and that whatever does so also answers to another. Rather, am I thinking about precisely that thing, and could not have had that thought without being appropriately related to just that thing. Something else which might have answered instead to the same available identifying description would not have yielded the same thought. Thus suppose that, while driving somewhere, I think that a certain rock which is blocking the road is too hard for me to lift. Surely (so it is argued) I could not have had just that very thought if instead of that rock there had been another one there, visually just like it, even if my purely subjective state would have been the same in either case.

Elaborate arguments have been given for this claim. And more generally, there is a widespread feeling that only genuinely *de re* beliefs can put us into the kind of direct contact with the environment which it seems reasonable to suppose that we have. It is also sometimes said that only beliefs with a *de re* character can influence our behaviour.[4] However, it seems to me that if there must be an element of '*de re*-ness' in all practice influencing beliefs, this may pertain only to such indexicals as 'here', 'there', and 'now' (with the rest done by description). Thus it is far from showing that my belief about the rock, in my example, would be a different belief if it had been a different rock.

I cannot enter into this matter further, beyond allowing that there is much to be said for the claim that an adequate account of belief will show that the mind is often put thereby in a more direct relation to particular things beyond its own contents than that of simply containing a description which they match. Yet, on most contemporary accounts of *de re* belief, one's relation to what one is thinking about remains strangely external. The picture is of some kind of inchoate mental activity, which is only the belief or thought it is, or even belief or thought at all, because it occurs in the right spatial or causal relation to it to be described as about it.[5] It could have been just the same subjectively, that is, so far as what it was like to live through it went, without having been the same thought or even a proper thought at all.

In contrast, Royce can be taken as giving an account of genuinely *de re* thought which does not make its being about what it is about so extrinsic to what it feels like to have it. For if I am a component in an Absolute Mind in which my thought directly confronts that which it is about, then perhaps something of the nature of that direct confrontation permeates my thought even within its own bounds. In short, on Royce's view, there is no hard and fast divide between what is in my mind and what lies beyond it. Doubtless there is much that is mysterious in this, but perhaps there is something essentially mysterious about the directedness of thoughts on things beyond which cannot be captured in more common-sense accounts. Even if we are determined to fight our way out of such mysteries, we should recognize the force of Royce's case.

The two other main themes in *The Religious Aspect* are the foundations of ethics and the problem of evil.

(b) The View of Ethics taken in The Religious Aspect

For the Royce of *The Religious Aspect* the basic problem of ethics is whether (a) a moral judgement expresses an act of will or of preference, or whether (b) it expresses a cognition of some special kind of fact. If the former, it seems a personal preference with no logical obligation to conform to anything beyond itself; if the latter, it is unclear how it motivates. This is a fine statement of one of the main problems about ethics in subsequent moral philosophy: namely, whether moral judgements primarily express conations and emotions or thoughts proper.

Emotivism holds that moral judgements express an attitude of being in favour of or against something and cannot be true or false in any factual sense, any more than 'Please don't say things like that' can be true or false. Ethical realists hold that moral judgements are factually true or false, but have difficulty in explaining why it is odd to say something like 'I know that it is wrong', yet not be in the least worried about doing it. No one seems to credit Royce with having put the problem so well and having provided such a valuable answer.

Royce's answer is that one cannot have the idea of a desire (unless in a purely verbal way) without some participation in it, at least to the extent of looking with some favour at situations which would satisfy it. For the most adequate representation of a desire in thought is itself a kind of mini-desire. It follows that the more one grasps about what other people, and animals, are like, including in particular what they are striving for, the more one sees some value in their attaining their ends. One will, of course, have one's own aspirations, but the more steady one's grasp of reality, the more one will see these as just some among the numerous aspirations which fill the conscious world. But the aspirations of different individuals are to a very great extent contrary to one another. How can one deal with this, once one accepts the prima facie desirability of satisfying each? The only way is to form an overall aspiration that the behaviour of oneself, as of all others, should be such that the aspirations of all conscious beings are harmonized, through such modification of them as this requires. Thus the key principle of ethics is so to act that one contributes to a universal harmony of effective aspiration.[6]

Indeed, according to Royce, who, in this connection, had a good deal in common with Schopenhauer, egoism and malice rest on an illusion, the illusion that our own feelings, and in particular our own sufferings, have a kind of privileged reality in comparison with which the feelings of others have only a shadowy kind of existence.

What, then, is our neighbor?...He is not that face that frowns or smiles at thee, although often thou thinkest of him as only that.

...Thou hast regarded his thought, his feeling, as somehow different in sort from thine. Thou hast said, 'A pain in him is not like a pain in me, but something far easier to bear.' Thou hast made of him a ghost, as the imprudent man makes of his future self a ghost. Even when thou hast feared his scorn, his hate, his contempt, thou hast not fully made him for thee as real as thyself. His laughter at thee hast made thy face feel hot, his frowns and clenched fists have cowed thee, his sneers have made thy throat feel choked. But that was only the social instinct in thee. It was not a full sense of his reality.... Of thy neighbor thou hast made a thing, no Self at all....

Have done with this illusion, and simply try to learn the truth. Pain is pain, joy is joy, everywhere, even as in thee.... The result of thy insight will be inevitable. Seeing the oneness of this life everywhere, the equal reality of all its moments, thou wilt be ready to treat it all with the reverence that prudence would have thee show to thy own little bit of future life. Lift up thy eyes, behold that life, and then turn away, and forget as thou canst; but, if thou hast known that, thou hast begun to know thy duty. (RELIGIOUS ASPECT, 156–62)

This seems to me a true account of how we ordinarily feel about each other, and also to justify the claim that egoism rests on an illusion of which compassion is the correction. And although for Royce it is associated with the belief that we are all components in a single divine mind, this is a claim about ethics which may commend itself to people who altogether reject the metaphysical claims with which Royce associates it.[7]

Royce's idea is that imagined pain (or pleasure) affects one like experienced pain, but not so strongly. It would be impossible for this reason to care no more about one's present pain, than about someone else's. For in the first case one's response is to an actual pain, while in the second it is to an imagined or conceived pain. Thus, although imagined pain affects one like experienced pain, it does not do so as strongly. But this does not apply when it is anticipated pain that is in question.

(c) The Problem of Evil in The Religious Aspect

Among the most impressive lines of thought in this his first philosophical book is his treatment of the problem of evil. Though this arises in a somewhat different form for an absolute idealist like Royce than for a

Christian theist of a more traditional type, it certainly does arise. This is because Royce is sure that God, or the Absolute, is good, nay perfect. So the problem for Royce is how he can reconcile the claim that everything which happens is ultimately a contribution to the perfection of the Absolute with the existence of evil.

But, one might ask, why not simply accept that God, who is identical with the world, is not altogether perfect, and that he is at best like the curate's egg, good in parts?

Royce's main reason for regarding God, or the Absolute, as perfect turns on his conception of what it is for a finite person to act wrongly—namely, as we saw just now, to act with a mind closed to the equal plangency of consciousness everywhere.

For Royce, then, wickedness consists in a limitation of one's attention to just one aspect of one's situation and possible courses of action. As he says in a later work:

To sin is *consciously to choose to forget*, through a narrowing of the field of attention, an Ought that one already recognizes. . . . All sin, then, is sin against the light by a free choice to be inattentive to the light already seen. (W&I 2, 359)

Thus the wicked man simply closes his eyes to the real nature of all the suffering which he is causing others. But the Absolute cannot close its eyes to anything, therefore it must be completely good morally.

Royce's solution to the problem of evil is that the highest good is the overcoming of evil, especially moral evil. We experience this directly in ourselves, for the best feelings we ever have are those we enjoy when we rise above our worse nature, with its selfish, cowardly, or cruel impulses (impulses so hostile to the aspirations of others that they cannot be harmonized in any unified ideal for humanity, unless in some altogether transformed shape), and move in the free air of self-control. This is far superior to the experience of those who have no bad aspect to them. The same must be true of the universe. It nurtures bad men, but they are there to be conquered in the good fight in the absence of which life would be simply anodyne. 'Only through the conquest of this evil-doer and his deed, is the final perfection to be won' (W&I 2, 366). This remained the essence of Royce's view of the place of evil throughout his philosophical career. (See, for example, W&I 2, 365 ff., 398, 409–11 ff.) However, he had not at this stage arrived at his later view of what is usually called natural evil, e.g. pain. This turns on a form of panpsychism which he advances in his later works. Pain, and indeed all our especially physical feelings, according to this later doctrine, result from our relations with the obscure life of (what appears to us) as unconscious nature, with whose mysterious sentience and strivings we are, without knowing how, sympathetically involved, in a manner which in some frightfully last resort is a necessary feature of the perfection of the eternal whole (w&i 2, 384).[8]

III The World of Description and of Acquaintance in *The Spirit of Modern Philosophy*

Royce's next philosophical book, *The Spirit of Modern Philosophy* (1892), was based on public lectures delivered to the intelligentsia of Cambridge, Mass. In Part One he examines the philosophies of Spinoza, Kant, Fichte, Hegel, and Schopenhauer, while Part Two presents Royce's own metaphysical views as they had developed since (but in harmony with) *The Religious Aspect*. Most important is Royce's distinction between the world of description and the world of acquaintance. The first is the world as described by science, and prosaic common sense, while the second is the world of the immediate experience which constitutes our inner emotional and sensory life. The first concerns the abstract structure of things, the second their inner conscious life, if they have one. Ordinary human communication utilizes the concepts of the world of description, while the concepts of the world of acquaintance are of a more private nature.

Royce's next step is to show that the world really consists throughout of things which do have an inner life, and thus inhabit worlds of acquaintance. (It must do so, since the only thing we can conceive of in a fully concrete way is something subjectively felt, like thought or desire.) However, these worlds are not altogether private, since all finite minds are united in the Absolute through which they, to some extent, permeate each other in social relationships. (Unlike W. K. Clifford's 'mind dust' theory, Royce's panpsychism did not regard mind proper as a late comer in the cosmos evolved through the aggregation of primitive mental particles.)

IV *The World and the Individual*

(a) The Four Conceptions of Being in the World and the Individual

I shall now say something about the way in which these themes were developed in some of Royce's later work. First I shall consider the metaphysics of *The World and the Individual*, the two volumes of which constituted the first and second series of the Gifford Lectures which he gave at Aberdeen in 1899 and 1900.

Royce opens by explaining that he will, in accordance with the Gifford Bequest, examine the possibilities of natural religion: that is, consider how far reason, rather than revelation, can conclude to the existence of God and of human immortality. But before considering the question of the being of God, and of our soul, conceived as something immortal, the metaphysician will first want to know what it is for anything at all *to be*. For the deepest problem of metaphysics is not what there is but what it is for anything to be. I remark in passing that this is one of numerous places where previous philosophers have done what Heidegger says they do not do: namely, reflect on Being rather than beings (see w&ı 1, 10–15).

So Royce sets out, before advancing to any more specific existential question, to consider the ontological predicate, *being* or *existence* or *reality* (all of which he pretty well equates). And he identifies this with the question of what is meant when we consider whether the object of some idea is real or existent, thus of what the difference is between ideas of things which do exist and ideas of things which do not. (See w&ı 1, 19 ff.)

This approach, it must be said, begs some questions, for it implies from the start that there could not be a world of which no mind had an idea. Thus, in the process of summarizing his results on Being, he says that we must continue to bear in mind that 'the world is real only as the object of true ideas, and then your fundamental problem at once becomes that of the essential relation of idea and object' (w&ı 1, 431).

Before embarking on our account of Royce's position, a word must be said about his use of 'idea'. As is true of many philosophers until quite recent times, there is a tendency to use this word in a rather slippery manner. Among other ambiguities is one as to whether an idea is something properly expressed by a 'noun phrase' or by a 'that clause'. In short, is the object of an idea a thing, or is it rather something's being the case? Modern readers are inclined to think that such varied thinkers as Descartes, Spinoza, and Hume are less clear than they should be on this point.

I believe that part of the explanation of an apparent wavering on this is that actually these thinkers tended to a reism of a type which, so far as I know, was first properly formulated by Franz Brentano. According to reism, the object of a mental act is always a thing, a something of such-and-such a character. This thing is the object of a presentation, and along with the presentation there is typically an act of affirmation or denial. Or, on an alternative view, that of Spinoza, and rejected by Brentano, the presentation is essentially affirmative of its own nature, unless cancelled by other presentations.

What this comes down to is that, in a sense, all judgements are existential (though existential propositions as such slip away like all other propositions). We have the presentation of some possible (or perhaps impossible) object, and we affirm or deny it, which is to say that we either affirm it as a reality which exists, or deny it as a non-reality which does not exist. The thing may be a state of affairs, rather than a concrete object; even so, it is most properly formulated in a noun expression, such as 'the killing of Julius Caesar by a group of conspirators including Brutus'.

Allowing states of affairs in may seem to deprive reism of point: however, the denial of a real logical difference between an expression like 'Julius Caesar' and 'Julius Caesar crossed the Rubicon' is far from vacuous. According to the reist, each refers to something which can be affirmed as an existent or denied as a non-existent. If this is once realized, the question as to whether a 'that clause' or a 'noun phrase' is the proper expression of an idea is no longer a troubling one. An affirmative sentence is simply the vehicle for affirmation of an object, while a negative sentence is simply the vehicle for the denial of an object.

Without necessarily ascribing precisely Brentano's reist theory to Royce, I suggest that he implicitly assumes something much of this sort. If so, it explains why Royce treats the problem of what it is for an idea to have an existent object as essentially the same as what it is for a judgement to correspond to a fact. So for him the question as to what *being* is becomes the question of what it is for an idea to have a real object.

Royce claims that there are four main conceptions of what it is for the object of an idea to be real. There is the realist view, the mystical view, the critical rationalist view, and 'the fourth conception of being' which Royce himself advocates after claiming that each of the others leads to contradictions.

So let us see briefly how he expounds each of the first three views, and argues that each of them is incoherent or internally self-contradictory. I must say that some of his efforts in the latter direction seem to turn on rather simple fallacies or question beggings. There is some truth in William James's comment to Dickinson Miller in 1889.

After teaching *The Conception of God* I have come to perceive what I didn't trust myself to believe before, that looseness of thought is R's *essential element*.... And yet I thought that a mind that could talk me blind and black and numb on mathematics and logic, and whose favorite recreation is work on those subjects, must necessarily conceal closeness and exactitudes of ratiocination that I hadn't the wit to find out. But no! he is the Rubens of philosophy. Richness, abundance, boldness, colour, but a sharp contour never. (PERRY, i. 810, quoted CLENDENNING, 209)

Even so, there is a good deal of interest in what he has to say about these different conceptions of *being*.

(b) Critique of the Realist Conception of Being

The realist view of what it is for the object of an idea to be real is for it to have an existence quite other than as a mere object of thought. And this is taken as implying that the idea could have been just what it is even if its object had not existed, and the object could have been just what it is even if no idea of it had ever existed.

Royce's summary of what realism is (w&1 1, 62–7) seems well taken. I doubt if the same can be said of his criticism of it (w&1 1, 91–138).

He says that he will first consider realism taken in its most extreme form and show that such independence of object and idea is incoherent. Having disposed of that, he will consider whether some qualification of the extreme version can be made which will save it (w&1 1, 115).

Basically, his argument consists in an objection to the very idea of a world consisting of independent beings, each of which could cease to exist, or never have existed, without this making any difference to the others. His argument is in part (as he himself says in an appendix) derived from Bradley.

Since I myself accept something like Bradley's arguments against a world consisting of genuinely independent objects, I go along with the general spirit of Royce's point here. However, I don't think that he makes it at all well. Bradley's account requires some regimentation to be convincing, and Royce's requires even more.[9]

The more specific Roycean claim is that independent beings could have no quality in common. For if they did, the total destruction of either one of them would include the destruction of that shared quality, in which case it would no longer be there to qualify the other.

But an idea and its object must always have a quality in common with each other, says Royce. For the idea must somehow itself possess the quality in order to attribute it to its object. (Without worrying about details, presumably it is true that the idea must possess the quality in some sense, even if not in the same way as its object does.) But if they do have a quality in common, then they cannot be independent. For they are only independent if the total destruction of the one would in principle leave the other unaffected. But Royce thinks that he has shown that this is impossible.

This, it must be said, turns on a quite unnatural way of understanding the notion of a world of independent beings. For clearly a distinction between universals (= qualities here) and particulars is essential to any serious realism of this sort. The sane realist view is that there is no necessary connection between the existence of one particular in possession of whatever qualities it has and the existence of any other particular in possession of whatever qualities it has, however much of an overlap there may be in the qualities which they separately possess. There need be no suggestion that if one independent being is destroyed, then everything else which shared a quality with it will lose that quality.

Royce then argues more broadly that things which are independent of each other in the realist's sense can never have anything whatever to do with each other. But if that is so, they cannot have to do with each other even in the sense in which an idea and its object do. In short, there is no possibility in the realist's world of an idea having an object, hence no distinction can be made between ideas which do have real objects and those which do not. (See w&ı 1, 19 ff.)

Having refuted (to his own satisfaction) this strong form of realism, Royce turns to a qualified form of it, for which things are only partially or relatively independent of each other. However, if this is to remain a genuine form of realism, and not some other conception of being, then things must consist of two parts, one the existence of which is, and the other the existence of which is not, independent of the existence of anything else, and in particular of any idea of them. But if so, contends Royce, since the independent part is vulnerable to just the same objections as is the whole object on the unqualified form of realism, there is no escape for the realist here. (See w&ı 1, 196–201.)

So far as there is much real force in Royce's argument, I suggest that it comes to this: that purely external relations between an idea and its object do not explain how the idea targets the object, and that external relations are the only possibly relevant ones available to the realist. With this I essentially agree, but I wish that Royce had argued his case better.

(c) Critique of the Mystical Conception of Being

Royce now turns to his second conception of being or reality. (See w&ı 1, 77–87, 185–222.) This is the mystical conception which Royce, quite rightly, associated with the outlook of Advaita Vedanta.

On the mystical conception, '*To be* means to quench thought in the presence of a final immediacy which completely satisfies all ideas' (w&ɪ 1, 186). The mystic thinks that reality is encountered only when we cease to have mere ideas about it and come right up against it, or, rather, are wholly immersed in it. So long as we are in any way separated from the object of our thought, we do not know its true nature or even in what sense it is at all. It follows that reality only shows itself in its true colours when all ideation ceases. So genuine reality, or being, for mysticism, 'is the ineffable immediate fact that quenches ideas, and that makes them all alike illusory' (w&ɪ 1, 266).

Superficially this conception of being may look like that associated with absolute idealism, for certainly it implies that reality is some kind of spiritual unity. But if it is a form of absolute idealism, it is, from Royce's point of view, a bad form of it. For the Absolute, as Royce conceives it, is not something to which we can fly, in this our ordinary life, for comfort and escape. Rather is it an Absolute which can realize itself only through our suffering and effort. Thus his objection to mysticism includes a strong ethical element. For the mystic tries to escape from the truth that life is real and life is earnest. (See w&ɪ 2, 394–9.)[10]

Royce's technical objection to mysticism is fairly straightforward. If the ideas are completely extinguished, so he argues, then there is no idea whose object can be characterized as real or fictitious; yet, as Royce sees it, the problem of *being* is precisely as to how this characterization is to be understood. This, as I have remarked already, is a highly question-begging way of raising the question of what being is. For it is far from clear that the one proper way to deal with this question is to ask what it is for an idea to have an object. It should, at any rate, be a conclusion of an argument for idealism, not a premiss used in support of it. Moreover, it is not even clear that every idealist need accept it at all. For if idealism is the view that everything which exists is experienced, it does not follow that everything which exists is the object of an idea. (What about ideas themselves?)

A rather better argument is that, after all, the ideas which are quenched in the mystic's ideal immediacy were there initially, and must have had their own being. But they could not have had their own being if all being were of the mystical kind. In short, the mystic tries to deny his starting-point. There can be no ideas with a real object if there are no ideas. Thus the mystic's false Absolute is nothing apart from its contrast to our ordinary state of restless finitude. So he must grant the latter's reality, to get the contrast, and deny it, because it is only the mystical state in which it finds its quietus which is real (see w&ɪ 1, 394–9).

(d) Critique of the Critical Rationalist Conception of Being

Royce moves next to a consideration of what he calls critical rationalism (w&i 1, lectures 6 and 7), a conception whose partisans tend to be politically to the left of centre (see w&i 1, 240). According to this, *to be is to be a compulsory object of thought under certain conditions*—otherwise put, *to be is to be posited by a valid or verifiable idea.*

As Royce first formulates it, critical rationalism says that '[t]o be real now means, primarily, to be valid, to be true, to be in essence the standard for ideas' (w&i 1, 202). This becomes the view that the truth of an idea is primary, and the being of its object is a matter of its being posited in a true idea (= thought or belief). It is not so much the being of its object which makes a thought true as the thought's truth which constitutes the being of its object, while truth consists in the compulsion we are under to affirm the true idea, if we once put it to the test, by way of calculation or observation.

This does, in a fashion, make the reality of things the creation of thought or language, but Royce does not hold this against the theory.[11] There are, after all, many things which, on the one hand, are rather obviously our own human constructions and which yet, on the other hand, when once constructed, are by no means the mere playthings of our wishes. Mathematical objects, after all, so thinks Royce, are, on the one hand, free creations of the mathematical mind and, on the other, resistant things with characteristics which no finite thinker deliberately gave them. The same is true, in a somewhat different way, of such readily spoken of things as the British constitution or the current market prices of stocks and shares. In all such cases it seems that the reality of the object stems from the validity or verifiability of the idea, rather than conversely.

If this conception of *being*, of which he sees Kant as the main begetter, is developed further in an attempt to cover all cases, it becomes the claim that a true idea is one which informs you that under such-and-such circumstances of experience, you can expect to get such-and-such further experiences, while *to be* is simply to be referred to by a truth of this type.

The physical world, for such a theory, is a system of possible experiences which will be actualized under certain definite experiential conditions. He refers to both Kant and J. S. Mill in this connection, and says some interesting things applicable to much of the verificationist doctrines which were to typify the philosophy of the twentieth century. (See w&i 1, 233–9.)

Royce has much respect for this view which he sees as the dominating modern view for empirically minded men of science. But though representing a useful approach for our less than final purposes, it cannot supply a fully satisfactory answer to the question of *being*.

For one thing, there is a problem as to what 'possibility' means when reality is equated with a system of possible experiences. Certainly it does not mean mere abstract conceivability (see w&i 1, 229, 243). Related to this is the philosophical problem of counterfactual conditionals, which Royce touches on (ibid. 260–1). Must there not be something more ultimate which determines which such possibilities are real, or which conditional statements are true, even when we do not put them individually to the test?

However, Royce's main objection is rather different. Our thought, he says, is always trying to be about the truly individual, and yet the truth which can be cashed in ideas conceived as only having this if–then type of meaning is always general. Thus my life rests upon the sense of those I love or hate as absolutely unique individuals, not merely as types. But the verifiable ideas I have about them are always general in character. (See w&i 1, 241; w&i 2, 431–3.) They tell me that under such-and-such general types of empirical circumstance, I shall have a certain type of experience, and this does not of itself target my thought on to anything unique.[12]

Royce's treatment of this theme, as indeed of all that I have reported so far, is pretty hazy in its details. For example, he seems to say that every thought is really an attempt to target and characterize a unique individual, but that every thought, so far as our finite experience goes, fails to do this. But does every thought try to do this? Surely thoughts of an *All A's are B's* or *Some (or Most) A's are B's* type are not trying to do this. Royce does consider this point, but in what seems to me a highly confused manner (see, for example, w&i 1, 270–90), but perhaps what he is getting at is something like this. In judging that *All A's are B's*, I am always seeking deep down some more specific encounter with each of the A's and finding it to be B in its own individual way. But be that as it may, it is simpler to take Royce's point not so much as concerning all thought (though he says that it does) as concerning just such thought as aims to characterize a single individual or situation. (I made a similar suggestion when discussing the account of thought given in *The Religious Aspect*.)

Royce, in effect, dismisses ostension (pointing or some mental equivalent thereof) as a way of targeting some particular individual as the object of one's thought. For what one gets in supposed contact with an individual (such as when one believes oneself to be pointing at it and thereby distinguishing it from every other individual) always consists in having experiences of a certain general type which one could get from another individual too. (See w&ı 1, 290–300, and w&ı 2, 159.) And Royce assumes (without stating) the principle of the identity of indiscernibles and, more specifically, that an individual can only be fully targeted by a unique description, which he associates with its unique filling of some particular role in the universe as a whole. Here again there is quite a similarity to themes in Bradley (and some, at least apparent, divergence from *The Religious Aspect*).

A positive feature of the third conception of being, as opposed to the first two, is its recognition of the propulsive force or conative thrust towards some kind of fulfilling experience which Royce thinks is a feature of all ideas, considered as psychological phenomena. What is lacking, however, is the recognition that an idea's goal is a genuine encounter with the object which it is reaching out to as a unique individual. Here the mystical conception (though certainly not the first conception, which saw the cognitive relation as an entirely passive one) may seem to have been more satisfactory, but it destroys itself by denying the reality of our ideation as the necessary complement of the object which it seeks.

To show how fundamental his four conceptions of being are Royce says a little about the way different social attitudes tend to be associated with each of them. For example, realism is, he claims, the philosophy of conservatism and good social order because it encourages the view that things are what they are, and not malleable to our choices, so that the *status quo* is not to be challenged.[13]

In contrast, the partisans of critical rationalism tend to be politically to the left of centre. As for the influence of the mystical conception of being, Royce is interested in it especially as a liberator from any sort of dessicated dogma. (This contrasts somewhat with his criticism of it elsewhere as tending towards social escapism.) It is unclear what the political associations are of the fourth conception of being, to which I now turn. Perhaps some form of ethical or idealist socialism (to which Royce seems to have inclined).

(e) The Fourth Conception of Being

This fourth conception is Royce's own, and it is presented in lectures 7 and 8 of w&ı 1.

First, however, I must say something about a distinction in terms of which Royce discusses the whole issue of how an idea stands to its object, but which it has been convenient to leave in the background till now. Royce regards every idea as purposive, as belonging to our willing nature as much as to our cognitive nature, which (he says) can only be distinguished through an abstraction for certain limited purposes. And on the basis of its purposiveness Royce says that every idea has both an internal and an external meaning. (See w&ı 1, 24–6.) The internal meaning is the idea's purpose in so far as that is presently realized in consciousness; the external meaning is the total, not presently actual, experience which would fulfil that purpose completely. In a manner which I find quite confusing, he regards virtually every component of consciousness as an idea in this sense, with these two types of meaning. Thus if someone is singing a song, then the part of the song which is more or less successfully sung at any one moment (one specious present) is the internal meaning of that moment of singing, but it is the song which you are trying to sing as a whole which is its external meaning. Even if it is only sung 'in your head', you may feel that you have or have not got it right. (This example is not without its problems.)

How are we to understand this in the case of more obviously cognitive ideas, say the idea of Abraham Lincoln having been shot at the theatre? In effect, Royce seems often to conceive the internal meaning as roughly equivalent to what, after Frege, we may call the idea's 'sense', and the external meaning as the idea's 'reference'. Or again, we might say that the external meaning of an idea is the object as it really is, while the internal meaning is as much of its character, real or supposed, as our thought presently specifies.

Royce now interprets the search for the relation between an idea and its object as the question of how internal meaning relates to external meaning. And this leads him to his fourth and final conception of being, the conception which he himself endorses, claiming that it includes everything that was on the right lines in the other three conceptions. (See w&ı 1, 386–7.) According to this, the contrast between internal and external meaning is not as absolute as it at first appears. Rather is the latter a fulfilment which is secretly implied in the former. What this comes to is that *reference* is completed *sense*.

I turn now to Royce's advocacy of his fourth conception of being. Says Royce, it is common to regard an idea as true if and only if it corresponds to its object. Royce does not reject this on an appropriate interpretation. But what, he asks, does 'correspondence' mean here? And what settles which object a true idea must correspond to?

As to the correspondence, it does not have to be that of a pictorial likeness, though it may be. What is required is that it correspond to its object in precisely the way which the idea itself requires of itself. That is, it is somehow (Royce hardly tells us how) implicit in the idea that it corresponds to an object in a particular kind of way. This is analogous to the fact that a map corresponds to what it maps not simply in some way or other, but according to the mode of projection specified by the atlas.

But the atlas must also indicate which part of the earth it is supposed to be a map of, and an idea must similarly somehow indicate what it is that it is trying to correspond to in the specified way.

So a true idea must *both* pick out its object *and* lay down the kind of correspondence which it professes to have to it. (See w&ı 1, 300–11.) A false idea will be one which successfully picks out its object, but does not have the intended correspondence to it.

Now I must say that Royce's discussion becomes very murky around here, but his solution to the problem seems to be this. We have this problem because we set up in our minds a complete barrier between the internal meaning of the idea and its external meaning: that is, roughly between its sense and its reference. But if we reflect on the case of someone singing a song, we will see that each stretch of the song owes its experienced character to its being just that bit of just that whole. This is our clue. The external meaning is precisely that which fills out the particular feeling of striving which is present in the idea as a passing psychological event, and which constitutes its internal meaning. Thus the external meaning is the one thing which satisfies the purpose felt as present in the idea. It is the object to which the idea is in process of corresponding (in its own more or less implicitly chosen way), a process, however, which need not be an event in this our everyday world. And a real object is one to which such an idea is reaching out to and which fulfils the purpose implicit in it.

But surely if an idea is false, its object defeats rather than fulfils our purpose? No, says Royce, for our purpose was to have the adequacy of our idea settled in a particular manner, and this the misconceived object does as much as does the correctly conceived one. Moreover, we wanted this adequacy of our idea to be settled by something completely individual, not specifiable in the generalities which exhaust what things can be according to the third conception of being.

So in the end, Royce seems to think that every idea is somehow at the deepest level true, though that fragment of it which is the present thought of a mind like ours may mistake the nature of the reality which it targets.

In reaching this conclusion, Royce, it seems to me, prevaricates between two positions. According to the first, the idea implicitly or mystically so adumbrates the actual character of its object that at some deep level it knows its own truth or falsehood. On the second, it merely points us towards a bit of reality whose being this or that is what settles whether it is a true or a false idea while containing no inherent pointer as to which it is. Royce's account tends to take the second form when he is trying to persuade us to accept his fourth conception, but it is the first from which he deduces his important metaphysical results. (See w&ɪ 1, lecture 7 from p. 300 onwards, also w&ɪ 2, 270–1.)

In endeavouring to persuade us that our thought does somehow adumbrate the full character of its object, without our having any clear consciousness of this, Royce elsewhere makes a comparison with the phenomenology of trying to remember a forgotten name. You don't presently know what the name is, but when you finally remember it, you realize that it is precisely what you were grasping for. It is the same phenomenon as William James (though not in connection with the Absolute) described as there being, so to speak, a hole in your consciousness which only just that name will fill, though you cannot presently fill it.[14] Thus all our thoughts refer to things whose full character is known to us at that deep level of our being which is not cut off (however much it seems to itself to be so) from the total awareness of all things by the Absolute. (There is something rather like Plato's view of knowledge as reminiscence here.)

So the object of an idea must somehow fulfil in a more complete way the purpose which is adumbrated in the idea of it. And it is the relation of the part to its proper whole, as a fragment of song is to the song as a whole, that constitutes both the reference and the truth of the idea. (Presumably Royce must think that each fragment of a song is a true idea of the song as a whole.)

Thus, says Royce,

what the idea always aims to find in its object is nothing whatever but the idea's own conscious purpose or will, embodied in some more determinate form than the idea by itself alone at this instant consciously possesses. (w&ɪ 1, 327)

This leads, according to Royce, to the fourth conception of being for which:

What is, or what is real, is as such the complete embodiment, in individual form and in final fulfillment, of the internal meaning of finite ideas. (w&ɪ 1, 339)

In short, *to be* is *to be the fulfilment of a particular kind of purpose*: namely, that which characterizes ideas.

Or rather, this is what he should say, for surely all he should have claimed is that it is the fulfilment of the *cognitive* purpose of an idea: namely, the purpose of identifying and corresponding to something. But on the rather flimsy ground that there is no sharp distinction between willing and thinking, he virtually identifies them, so that what satisfies thought must in the end satisfy will, and vice versa.

Royce is less wise than Bradley here, who, in identifying truth with satisfaction, makes it clear that he has in mind intellectual satisfaction. (True, at a later stage he says that intellectual satisfaction cannot be sundered from other types of satisfaction, but at least he takes this as something to be argued for.)

It seems to me, in any case, that Royce is open to two charges: (1) He fails to distinguish intellectual from 'passional' satisfaction. (2) He fails to distinguish the satisfaction of finding out the truth about something from being pleased at what that truth is.

Moreover, he is open to a third charge, which is that, having decided that to be real is to be the fulfilment of the purpose (the external meaning) of an idea, he seems to make the unjustifiably optimistic inference that all purposes are satisfied, if not here and now and obviously, then at some more fundamental level of being where the idea becomes conscious of its deeper, rather than its empirically apparent, goal. But even if to be real is to fulfil a purpose, it surely does not follow that all purposes are fulfilled.

Still, while it may not follow from the fourth conception of being that all purposes are satisfied, it does follow, if intellectual and passional satisfaction necessarily go together, that in the end everything, seen in the light of the whole, is satisfying, and thus good, since each fulfils the purpose its fulfilling of which is its existence. And Royce seems to think that ultimately every idea initiates a process which will ultimately (in time or out of time, see below) terminate in the satisfaction of finding its object, since it itself adumbrates the process through which it will do so. We must take it that all the horrors of life are necessary as phases in a process of ideation which can reach its true object only through them. I don't myself find any advance here on the impressive treatment of evil in his earlier work.

The following quotation from a private note to a friend written in 1905 casts interesting light on his interpretation of the human lot.

God is good, but unless you take the trouble to find out that fact for yourself, and in your own way, you will not find it out at all. And owing to the magnitude of the goodness, the trouble of finding it out is considerable. The task lasts a long time, in fact, forever. It is my task. I 'drop stitches,' throw away work half-done, forget, ignore, repent, learn, rise, grow, &c. because I am to become infinite in my own way and because I am to come to view that as God's way only through first learning it to be mine. Hence my trust in God involves an endless discontent with all my own fragmentary views of myself and of him. Why am I a fragment?—Answer: because it is well that God should learn (as he eternally does learn), just *my* way of becoming infinite through overcoming imperfection. Have I prophetic insight into God's will? No; I have only whatever good sense to guide me upwards I can get in the school of life as I go along. Shall I disagree, fight, struggle? Yes.—Why if all is good?—Answer: because I thus win my right to see the good in my own way. Shall I help, harmonize, agree, resign myself, submit, trust, and so on?—Yes, whenever that helps my brothers and myself to see better our relation to God.— In a word, the being of God is one,—the seeing of God is manifold. Therein lies the pluralism and the conflict. (communication to R. G. Cabot, May 1905 quoted by CLENDENNING, 289–90)

Be that as it may, Royce reaches his familiar conclusion, in chapter 8 of w&I, 1, though by weaker, or at least obscurer, reasoning than he did in, for example, *The Religious Aspect*, that our ideas and their objects must belong to a larger experience which includes them both as its components. For just as the full meaning of a short snatch of a familiar song lies in the whole song which includes it, so must the meaning of any idea of ours consist in a larger whole to which it belongs, and the only possible whole in which all ideas can be united with their objects is the spiritual unity known to philosophers as 'the Absolute'.

So Royce makes a common absolutist claim that all our ideas are really ideas of the universe as a whole, since it is only via its unique role in the total world system that any individual can be properly individuated. In my contact with another person, I regard myself as dealing with an individual, not a type. Proper confrontation with him or her as an individual would be confrontation with the whole world regarded from the perspective of one particular position within it.

Royce thinks that this fourth conception of being has all the virtues and none of the defects of the other conceptions. The object is other than the idea, as on the first conception, but its relation to it is internal rather than external. And the object is something directly experienced, not indeed by us *as finite beings*, but within the Absolute, where it does not extinguish the idea as it does for mysticism, since at that level idea and object confront each other with equal immediacy. On this fourth conception the object is empirical (in a rather stretched sense), as it is for critical rationalism, but it is individual as an object cannot be for that theory. For, while the third conception implies that our ideas can refer only to types of thing, the fourth conception explains how they can refer to true individuals.

So much for Royce's perplexing fourth conception of being and its grounding of the Absolute. The argument of *The Religious Aspect* was, to my mind, more convincing. However, shaky though his discussion is, there is some truth in his classification of types of philosophy according to which of these four conceptions of being they turn on, though Bertrand Russell hardly fits his characterization of realists as conservatives.

(f) The Absolute and Time

According to Royce, the Absolute must hold all experiences—that is, everything—together in its eternal grasp. From its point of view, there is no shifting of events from future to present, then past. On the other hand, the Absolute does enjoy all those experiences which constitute the historical world as in temporal relations with one another.[15]

To suggest how the Absolute does this, Royce appeals to the notion of the specious present, something which loomed large among the philosophers of the Golden Age of American philosophy, playing a significant role in the thought of each of James, Royce, and Santayana. When you experience a change which falls within one specious present, events experienced as belonging to different moments within a very short stretch of time are experienced together as an immediately given unity. That unity, however, has its own temporal character, so that its elements stand to each other in the relations of earlier, later, or simultaneous.

However, it is a fact quite distinct from this that one such unitary experience follows on another in time. Certainly, we have a sense that the present unitary experience is passing away even as it comes into existence, redolent of what occurred previously and anticipative of what is to come. However, we do not actually experience that passing away, we experience only that false sense of passing away suggested by the temporality holding within each finite specious present.

From the point of view of the Absolute, by contrast, all those experiences which form the life of historical beings are, indeed, given in their proper temporal relations to one another within one great specious present, but there is no question of their replacing one another and falling into and out of being. For although the feeling of doing so is essential to the individual character of each, for the Absolute they are simply components positioned temporally within its own eternal or, as I like to put it, frozen specious present. (Though I think that my account of Royce's intentions here is correct, I have somewhat amplified on some points in the light of views of my own reached partly under Royce's influence.[16])

I should remark that Royce evidently holds that our time series is the only time series which the Absolute experiences within its own eternal specious present. Bradley, by contrast, held that there are in all probability centres of finite experience which belong together in quite different time series from ours, united, indeed, with us within the Absolute, but such that events in their lives have no temporal relation at all to those in ours. Somewhat in this connection it should be mentioned that, according to Royce, the Absolute has in some eternal act freely chosen the possible world which is actualized. (See, for example, w&i 1, 433, 449–50, 460.)

However, what is highly important for Royce's metaphysics is his suggestion that different conscious creatures have specious presents of very different durations from ours. For example, there may be beings for whom a century is a moment. Such a being may enjoy an experience lasting the whole of what we call the nineteenth century, which for it is as momentary and unitary as an experience of a couple of seconds is for us.

(g) Panpsychism in The World and the Individual

This conception plays an important role in Royce's panpsychism (see esp. w&i 2, lecture 5). Royce is dissatisfied, as I believe every idealist should be, with regarding nature at large as existing in a full sense only as an object of the perceptions of human beings and animals, and only in the Absolute as containing these. (Nor does it do justice to the reality of nature to add thoughts to perceptions, whether ours or only the Absolute's.)

We must unlearn 'the atrocious Philistinism of our whole race which supposes that Nature has no worthier goal than producing a man' (w&i 2, 231). 'Where we see inorganic Nature seemingly dead, there is in fact, conscious life just as surely as there is any Being present in Nature at all' (ibid. 240).

So Royce holds that natural objects at large are in fact the appearance to us of centres of experience with which we are unable to get in personal contact, largely because our specious presents are of such a different span. The slow changes of the mountains may be, for them, the speediest of adjustments to the environment, while the things of the sub-microscopic world may run through what, for them, is a long lifetime of distinct experiences in what for us is a fleeting second. (See w&ı 2, 224–33, 240.)

Basic to Royce's panpsychism is the distinction, which I discussed briefly in section III above, between the world of description and the world of acquaintance. Each of these is the posited source of our perceptual experience, but conceived in different ways. The world of description is conceived as operating according to discoverable and unchanging laws of a type which make it available as raw material for the industrial arts and for increasingly successful technological manipulation. The world of acquaintance, by contrast, is conceived as a system of interacting conscious and purposive individuals whose reality is of the same generic type as that with which we are acquainted in ourselves and in those with whom our relations are personal. Modern man thinks that only a part of the real world is a world of acquaintance, while the whole of it is a world of description; but in fact reality is a world of description to a much more limited extent than he supposes, while it is a (largely hidden) world of acquaintance through and through. Even science, thinks Royce, (writing at the end of the nineteenth century) is beginning to reveal this, inasmuch as those laws which are supposed to apply identically at different times are coming to look more and more like useful ideal constructions, while evolutionary theory, which is concerned with essentially unrepeatable phenomena, is suggestive of something more like mind than mechanism.[17]

My hypothesis is that, in case of Nature in general, as in case of the particular portions of Nature known as our fellow-men, we are dealing with phenomenal signs of a vast conscious process, whose relation to Time varies vastly but whose general characters are throughout the same. From this point of view, evolution would be a series of processes suggesting to us various degrees and types of conscious processes. These processes, in case of so-called inorganic matter, are very remote from us; while, in case of the processes which appear to us as the expressive movements of the bodies of our human fellows, they are so near to our own inner processes that we understand what they mean. (w&ı 2, 226)

Royce develops this further by the elaborately argued claim that the events during any stretch of time as conceived by natural science form a 'compact' series, while a series of events in the world of acquaintance are 'well ordered' (i.e. are like the series of natural numbers). That is, for science, there are always events which occur between an earlier event and a later event (and every predicate has degrees such that between any two precise degrees there are others); in short, there are no neighbours in the world of description, while the personal world of acquaintance is entirely composed of neighbours.

Although I am a panpsychist myself, for reasons not so dissimilar to Royce's, I cannot regard all consciousness as associated with the service of lofty ideals to the extent that Royce does.[18] The world is not less magnificent than Royce depicts it, but I believe it is less ethical.

(h) Our Eternal Selves and Collectivities

Our temporal experiences, transitory as they seem to themselves, are, then, included at their proper temporal positions within the eternal Absolute's unchanging specious present. But some other constituents of the Absolute experience themselves as eternal just as the Absolute does itself; indeed, the containment of our temporal experiences within the Absolute is via their inclusion in certain such intermediate self-consciously eternal unities.

Two of these are particularly important. First, corresponding to each of us there is an eternal being, our true or total self, which experiences our life as a whole, and its relations to the rest of reality, in the eternal specious present of the Absolute. (See w&i 2, 149–51, 425, 433–6.) Each momentary phase of our consciousness is a dissatisfied fragment of this total self, and all its strivings are for a fulfilment which is only satisfied at that eternal level. 'For the goal of every finite life is simply the totality whereof this life, in its finitude, is a fragment. When I seek my own goal I am looking for the whole of myself' (w&i 2, 135).

For what makes each of us an individual self is the particular life project on which, more or less unwittingly, we are engaged, and life must be unsatisfactory until we get some grasp of what this is and act accordingly. However, the true nature of our project, and its particular place in the total divine project in which reality as a whole is engaged, is only known to our eternal selves. Thus it is only they, consciously living in eternity, which know true peace; our temporal task is to strive to realize that role as far as we can in time, a striving which must always be full, to coin a phrase, 'of blood, sweat and tears'. (See w&i 2, 272–90.) Royce's objection to mystical religion is that it looks in the temporal realm for that peace which can only be found in eternity, where our eternal selves summate all our fleeting experiences into a uniquely valuable whole.

Secondly, there are eternal beings which are similarly the eternal selves of certain social or biological collectivities, unifying the experiences in time of all their members in one summatory experience where their particular contribution to the universe is grasped (see w&ɪ 2, 231). There will be more to say about this when we move on to Royce's later ethical philosophy of *loyalty to loyalty*.

If we complain that it is small comfort for us, in that state of dissatisfaction which Royce thinks a necessary feature of temporality, that our apparently momentary experiences are combined to produce joy and peace for these eternal totalities, Royce answers that we should not think of them as remote, for it is only through such totalities that our present experience is genuinely related to anything beyond itself, as it is of its nature to wish to be. Moreover, for reasons I shall not go into, Royce thinks that our lives have no ending *sub specie temporis*, but that something nearer the peace of eternity is their ideal limit.[19]

The World and the Individual finally emerges from these somewhat remote speculations to the treatment of more down-to-earth problems of morality and religion which he thinks that they imply. But for my treatment of Royce's ethical position subsequent to that of *The Religious Aspect* I shall move on some seven years to his *The Philosophy of Loyalty* (1908).

V *The Philosophy of Loyalty*

The Philosophy of Loyalty (first given as public lectures in Boston) initiates a somewhat new phase in Royce's thought.[20] In this book he puts forward an ethical doctrine according to which ethics should be based on a foundational principle which he calls 'loyalty to loyalty'. This is presented both as a solution to the philosophical question of the basis of ethics and as a guide to living for the morally perplexed.

Royce's argument for this theme starts with a psychological claim: namely, that the isolated individual, who does not experience himself as belonging to a Whole greater and more important than himself, is wretched. This wretchedness can be alleviated only if he finds some great cause to which he pledges total loyalty. By a *cause*, Royce means primarily some concrete, but supra-personal object, like a nation, rather than some social reform, such as the abolition of slavery, though he is not altogether clear on this.

Instances of such loyalty are the devotion of a patriot to his country when this devotion leads him to live, and perhaps die, for it; the devotion of a martyr to his religion; the devotion of a ship's captain to his ship, even to the point of going down with it when others have been saved. Later examples of loyalty include 'a family, a church, or such a rational union of many human minds and wills as we have in mind when we speak of a science or an art' (LOYALTY, 308).

Royce explains more fully why a life not thus dedicated to a cause is so unsatisfactory by reference to the way in which people are normally educated morally. This consists in being subjected to family and social pressures which teach the individual as he grows up that he must conform to certain *mores* if he is not to get into trouble with his elders and associates. Moreover, he internalizes these *mores* by that innate tendency to imitate others which is a universal characteristic of human beings. (Royce published some psychological articles on imitation. Here it plays a slightly different role from in *The Religious Aspect*.) But while these pressures influence him to a degree of social conformity, they also intensify his own self-will, which encourages him to rebel against these constraints. The result is a constant tension between what he personally wants to do and what he has been taught he ought to do.

He can only escape this miserable condition if his moral sense and his own personal self-centred emotions can somehow be brought together. And this can happen only if he develops a passionate love for something greater than himself, which becomes the chief motivator of his behaviour and determines what he thinks he ought to do. And this is what Royce means by a life lived in loyalty to a cause.

But, Royce realizes, there is much loyalty in the world to evil causes. The members of a crime syndicate may be passionately loyal to their essentially evil organization. What, then, makes some causes good, and some causes evil?

Royce answers that, in so far as a person loyal to his own cause recognizes the supreme value of loyalty in general, he will wish all men to have a cause to which they are similarly loyal as he is to his. This will relieve them from the tension between their social duties and their personal inclinations. It is not desirable, however, that all men should be loyal to the same 'cause'. The ship's captain wishes other captains to be loyal to their ships as he is to his—he does not wish them all to be loyal captains of the same ship. This realization should inspire in us an overriding loyalty to loyalty, a commitment to live so that loyalty spreads among humankind, so that each person, or group, is loyal to their own cause.

Thus, says Royce, each person should resolve his own problems by choosing an object of his own loyalty. This must be something which stirs him with active emotion, but it must also be something which encourages others to be loyal to their own cause. What is bad in human life is that people are loyal to causes which can only prosper if the objects of the loyalty of others are imperilled or destroyed. Choose your own personal cause, Royce advises us, 'for the sake of the spread of universal loyalty'.

Royce notes that the desirability of periodic war has been argued for by some thinkers on the ground that it provides the occasion for the supreme loyalty of those who are prepared to give their life for their country. (See LOYALTY, 13.) But he will not agree to this. For, claims Royce, in war, one wishes the object of the other side's loyalty to come to grief. And since loyalty is the supreme good, whatever hinders others from the chance to have their own object of loyalty is a supreme evil. (See ibid. 116.)

This seems a rather inadequate ground, on Royce's part, for deploring war. It is doubtful that a war normally destroys the loyalty of the losing side. Indeed, Royce himself contends that loyalty to a lost cause can be of a particularly potent type (see LOYALTY, 284, 276–91, 319). For the defeat of the cause can especially intensify loyalty to it and give a fuller view of what that cause was. Indeed (as Royce says elsewhere), the death of Jesus, apparently a defeat, vitally promoted the development of a religion of which his death was the central symbol (ibid. 292–3).

Be that as it may, Royce's ideal for the human future is one in which the world consists of groups of individuals, each group having its own shared object of loyalty, and such that the special loyalty of each group promotes the loyalty of other groups to their particular cause, *and is ultimately the object of their adoration, just because of this*. As, perhaps, a fan's loyalty to his own football team may be based on a more fundamental loyalty to the game itself.

Royce goes so far, in his claim that loyalty is the supreme human good (provided special loyalties are associated with an overriding loyalty to loyalty), as to say that all the commonly recognized virtues, in so far as they really are virtues, are 'special forms of loyalty to loyalty'. And he goes on to explain the nature of conscience by reference to it (see LOYALTY, 172–95). Your conscience is in the first place the demand laid upon you by the object of your loyalty, and then by a more fundamental loyalty to loyalty itself.

In this connection Royce introduces a voluntarist reflection as to how one's life should be guided by loyalty. Any individual's loyalty will be complex, a unity of a variety of more specific loyalties. But what if your loyalties come into conflict? Then you must choose that loyalty which best serves the purpose of making you a loyal person, in a manner not threatening to the loyalty of others. And if you cannot work out which loyalty this is, then you must *decide*. Loyalty to loyalty requires thereafter that, unless some quite new light is thrown upon the matter by increasing knowledge, you stick loyally to your decision, even if you cannot be sure that it is the right one. Thus loyalty to loyalty requires decisiveness.

Royce adumbrates some metaphysical implications of this uniquely redeeming nature of loyalty. Loyalty 'links various human lives in to the unity of one life' (see LOYALTY, chs. 7 and 8 *passim*). Thus in being loyal to something supra-personal such as a nation or, indeed, humanity as a whole, I must implicitly believe that it is as much, or even more of, a real unit than I am. This requires that it has its own supra-personal self-consciousness, and this will be a distinct component within the Absolute Experience just as is each individual human consciousness.

The supreme value of loyalty is peculiarly fitted too to show the necessary role of evil in the world. For

what would be the universe without loyalty and what would loyalty be without trial? And when we remember that, from this point of view, our own griefs are the griefs of the very world consciousness itself, in so far as this world-life is expressed in our lives, it may well occur to us that the life of loyalty with all its griefs and burdens and cares may be the very foundation of the attainment of that spiritual triumph which we must conceive as realized by the world spirit. (LOYALTY, 393)

Many objections to this moral outlook will spring to the mind of almost everyone, especially since the years subsequent to Royce's day have faced us with a plethora of loyalties which have been and are extremely harmful, and in many cases downright evil. It has been well said that:

Very few of the individual members of a lynch mob would by themselves hang a man; joined together in community they do so with exhilaration. Few people have had a stronger sense of community than the SS. Theirs was so strong that they were able to deny individuality, and therefore humanity, to those outside the group.[21]

In fairness to Royce, it should be emphasized that he discusses such objections (though he doubtless never conceived of such extremities of horrific loyalty as were still to come and to be widely known about) and refines his concept of loyalty in ways which he (at least) thinks meet them. Thus he considers at length the objections of an individualist who thinks it deeply damaging to submerge oneself in some movement on to which one puts the responsibility for all one's decisions. His reply, chiefly, is that the loyalties compatible with loyalty to loyalty are those which one has clear-sightedly chosen and brought to the bar of the higher loyalty of loyalty to loyalty. Even so, one may be inclined to object that loyalty is a dangerous escape from taking on the burden of moral decision for oneself and casting it on an authority which is often less moral than most people would be as so-called isolated individuals.

VI *The Problem of Christianity*

I turn now to Royce's book *The Problem of Christianity* (1913). This work was given first (in part) as a series of lectures at the Lowell Institute in Boston and then, in a complete form, as a Hibbert Foundation lecture series at Manchester College, Oxford. To a considerable extent this book sets out to father the principle of loyalty to loyalty on St Paul.

As a prelude to our examination of this, I shall broach the question as to whether, as some have thought, the notion of a community, and more especially that of a community of interpretation (on which see below), is now meant to do the work which the doctrine of the Absolute did in his philosophy up till then, and in fact marks his abandonment of it.

For while there is no difficulty in associating *The Philosophy of Loyalty* with Royce's earlier doctrine of the Absolute, this is more problematic with *The Problem of Christianity*. At least, Royce certainly says things which can give the impression that the doctrine of community developed in this work replaces the old doctrine of the Absolute. He claims, for example, that it provides the key to one of the thorniest issues in metaphysics: that of the relation of the One to the Many. (See POC, 235.) And what is more, it is said to explain how the individual has access to a world beyond himself and shares a common world with others with whom he can communicate.

These are pretty well the same problems as those which he had claimed in his earlier work could only be solved by the doctrine of the Absolute. (Personally, I think that he was right about this.) It is difficult to avoid concluding that, at the very least, the doctrine of the Absolute now had much less hold on him than previously.

Despite all this, Royce assures us explicitly that the metaphysical views advocated in *The Problem of Christianity* are compatible with, and by no means a recantation of, his earlier metaphysical views. It is simply that here he is concentrating on that feature of the world which makes it a world of interpretation. He still holds that the world as a whole is one all inclusive Divine Thought. And when he says, in a manner we shall be exploring shortly, that the world is a community of interpretation, he says also that the all inclusive Absolute Mind is itself the ultimate interpreter of everything (including itself).

The truth would seem to be that he was unwilling to abandon the old doctrine, but no longer wished to give it centre stage. But whether this suggests some doubt about the old doctrine is unclear. It may be simply that he felt that he had said enough about the Absolute in his earlier writings and wished to make new explorations not dependent upon its postulation. But it is also relevant that in his later years Royce suffered periods of depression, because the younger generation of philosophers were turning against his style of philosophy. In which case, keeping rather quiet about the Absolute may well have been part of a strategy to answer the challenge of pragmatists, such as Dewey, and a little later of such 'new realists' as E. B. Holt and R. B. Perry, who saw his absolute idealism as too remote from everyday reality and without bearing on the real problems of modern life.

In this connection Royce dismisses indignantly any idea that his philosophy was an abstract system unrelated to practical questions as to how we should live (see POC, 39). The result was a determination to emphasize its relevance to practice, and play down whatever could be seen as remote from empirical fact and real social issues.

Thus he insists that his view of religion, and in particular Christianity, is based on empirical data as much as on mere abstract reasoning. (See POC, 39–41.) He also stresses, in a manner which has led some commentators to see an existentialist character to his later thought, that commitment to a religion is never purely the result of logical ratiocination or inference from experience, but as much or more an act of will. (See LOYALTY, 229–30.)

Since James had similarly claimed that his account of religion in *The Varieties of Religious Experience* was empirically based, Royce explains that, great as that work was, it suffered from its insistence that true religious experience was what occurred in its fullest form to individuals only in their own (humanly speaking) solitude and independently of religious institutions. Such institutions provided, according to James, only a second-rate form of religion, a shadow of that which had inspired their original founders. But this is far from the truth, according to Royce, for the true religious experience is social, and occurs when an individual lives as a member of a beloved community. (See POC, 40; see also SOURCES, 34, 43–4, 61–5, 73–5.)

Royce initially presents Christianity as developing a way of life based primarily on certain empirical truths about human nature and society. Only after discussing them as such, does he consider whether they point to anything about the cosmos in general; in short, do they have a metaphysical implication which can be accepted as true?

Paul had a More Important Message than Jesus

Royce begins his examination of Christianity by disclaiming any concern with the life and personality of Jesus as quite outwith his competence and, in fact, as he sees it, of little religious significance. What he is concerned to discover is whether Christianity still has an essential message for humanity which is valid today, and will be in the future, and which is quite independent of any historical facts or myths about Jesus.

His answer is that it does indeed have such a message. But it is to be found, not primarily either in the teachings or the reported life of Jesus, but rather in the life and work of St Paul. In fact, Jesus left us with teachings which, without their development by Paul, lacked any adequate content. So it is not Jesus or, indeed, even Paul as an individual who is the true founder of Christianity, but the early Christian community, under the leadership of Paul that was so. (See POC, 222–3, also 367.) But the enduring message is independent of Paul's Christology.

Original Sin and Salvation

For Royce the fact (1) that, as a single individual, man is lost, and (2) that he can be saved only as a member of a beloved community constitute what he regards as the first two great ideas stemming from Christianity: original sin and redemption. The third great Christian idea is (3) the doctrine of the atonement, to which Royce similarly gives a novel twist.

For Jesus the two great commandments were love of God and love of one's neighbour, and both of these are individual persons. For Paul there was, however, a third supra-personal individual, the Christian community, conceived by Paul as somehow the Body of Christ, whom it was salvation to love. (See POC, 92–3.) And the lasting legacy of Christianity (as Royce sees it) is not what, without Paul, one might take to be Jesus's simple message of loving one's neighbour as a mere individual. Rather, it is Paul's conception of how individual Christians are related to the Christian community, and only via that to each other. Jesus, for Paul, was essentially the personalized symbol of the unity of the Christian community, or, more dramatically, as the Christ of whose body all Christians were members. But his importance is strangely played down by Royce.

Royce then suggests that Christianity has never made as much as it should do of the idea of the Holy Spirit. (See POC, 233 ff.) Or at least, this is true so far as theoretical treatment of the grounds and nature of faith go. But the doctrine of the Holy Spirit, as realized in an ideal community, is really the most important feature of Christian doctrine. (He suggests that it was originally a replacement of Paul's conception of Christ himself as the spirit of the community.)

Thus the great message which Christianity still holds for us today is that the salvation of individuals lies in their membership of a beloved community, loyalty to which is the basic motivation of all they do.

The Atonement

The idea that Christ died on the cross so that he, rather than we, should suffer the punishment which our sins deserve has made many Christian thinkers uneasy. Among other reasons for this is that the notion of vicarious punishment seems to many people a moral absurdity. (Compare Royce on this with Bosanquet.) However, Royce offers his own interpretation of the doctrine of atonement by considering the case of a 'traitor' to the ideals which he had committed himself to live by. Such a sin can never be annulled as a blemish in the universe.

But there is one way in which the sin can be atoned for vicariously by a nobler spirit than the sinner. This will happen if its occurrence is made the basis for the development of a greater good, which could not have been reached without that sin. This does not annul the sin, which remains a permanent blemish in the world; but it does enable the sinner to be reconciled with the community which he has betrayed by his sinning. A sin is atoned for, then, when some nobler spirit brings about a good, which could never have come about without the sin. This is what Christ is deemed to have done by leading men to a higher form of life than they could ever have reached except as repentant sinners. And this is how humanity as a whole should seek to redeem much of its dreadful history. With this, Royce further enriches his concept of the way in which evil is a necessary feature of a supremely good world.

One might expect Royce to have used Judas as an example of such a traitor. For his betrayal of Christ was the occasion, if not the main cause, of the crucifixion, and this in the end led to his followers developing a higher notion of what they were about as a struggling community than they might otherwise have attained to. However, Judas is never mentioned.

What is a Community?

Salvation for the individual by devotion to a beloved community is clearly (for Royce) the most important of St Paul's teachings and the practice of the early church initially under his guidance. And this leads Royce to discuss various different ways in which human beings are more or less significantly united, even if, in the first two cases only briefly.

One thing which differentiates us from earlier generations of Christians is that we have learnt that the earth, and we humans who live upon it, are part of a vast cosmos in which we seem to be insignificant little bits. (See POC, 232.) So it is hard for us now to see the development of human life as the central fact about the universe. But, suggests Royce, there may be reason to think that the rest of the physical universe is not quite so alien from us as a mere scientific account of it might suggest (this fits in well with his earlier thought).

Royce distinguishes three types of unit to which individuals belong. (See LOYALTY, 242–3.) First, there are mere crowds; secondly, there are mere aggregates; and thirdly, there are communities proper.

A crowd is a group of people engaged in some shared activity in which each person is aware of the part he is playing in it. But its existence is very short term, and there is no shared memory, expectation, or long-term purpose uniting it.

Still less unitary is a group which we might call a mere aggregate (not a term actually used by Royce). An example might be a group of people who just happen to be all shopping at the same place at the same time.

Thirdly, we come to the idea of a true community:

But a true community...has a past and will have a future. Its more or less conscious history, real or ideal, is a part of its very essence. A community requires for its existence a history and is greatly aided in its consciousness by a memory. (POC, 243)

Royce's notion of a community is best explained by relating it to his account of an individual self (at least as it exists in time). All finite human thought, according to Royce, occurs in a momentary NOW. Such thought is aware, at least implicitly, that it is carrying on a purpose originated in earlier momentary states of consciousness, and it contains the willing of some future state of consciousness. This awareness of a past which it regards as its own, and a future which it wills or anticipates as likewise its own, is what constitutes it a phase in the life of a self.

This account is close to William James's view that my past, the past of the person thinking these current thoughts, is mine in virtue of my adoption of it as my own, and that something similar applies to my future.[22] Similarly, for Royce, a community exists when there are a number of human selves who share much of the same past and much of the same future (see POC, 246 ff.). This past and this future consist primarily in events before or after the death of these human selves. For in the case of a community there are events in the past, most typically of the ancestors of these selves, which each member of the community adopts as belonging to his own past, and hoped-for events in the future which each member of the community adopts as belonging to his own future. This adoption of a common past and common future by finite selves, which grounds the existence of a community, is closely akin to the adoption of its past which gives each individual self its own personal identity.

The key to understanding this is to recognize that the self at any one moment, what we may call 'the momentary self', ideally extends itself into both past and future. But similarly, it can and does ideally extend itself into the past of its community and also into its hoped-for future.

May not the members of a community thereby share the same present as well as partly the same past and future? Royce does think that this is possible up to a point, but says that it is derivative from the sense of unity with others which turns on a common past and hoped-for future. Royce, it is interesting to note, thinks that the past shared by members of a community may, to a greater or lesser extent, be mythical. (He is certainly right that myths may be a large part of what unites human beings in a community.) Likewise, the expected future, such as the new Jerusalem, may never come. But there must be *some* real past in common for the existence of a community.

One might ask what makes you and I distinct conscious individuals if we belong genuinely to a common community. The answer is that Royce recognizes that at any one moment my consciousness and yours are, so far as we are concerned, quite distinct. But one's consciousness as it is just at one moment is not you or I. It is only the consciousness of a self in so far as it interprets itself as a phase in the life of a continuing individual. But equally, it interprets itself as belonging to a community with a conceived past (and likely future). Moreover, each of us embodies a distinctive purpose, and this purpose (whether conscious or not) is one specific component in the more complex purpose of the community, and therefore is as truly a phase of the mind of the community as of the individual. And it is the demand of the universe that these purposes will move asymptotically to fulfilment that provides Royce with a ground for believing in personal immortality in a divinized community. (Compare at section (h) above.)

This is important for the understanding of Christianity. For the early Christians saw their community as a continuation of a process described in the narratives of the Hebrew Bible.

It is curious that Royce seems to regard this sense of sharing a common past as a distinctively Christian development. The case is, surely (to take one significantly related case), that it has always been as much, or more, of a feature of the community of Jews. It would have been better, I suggest, if he had thought of Judaism and Christianity as sharing a past as a single community, which, at a certain point in history, had bifurcated into two separate continuations of itself. Royce, however, evidently thought that Paul and the early Christians had a better idea of how they were all members one of another than had the un-christianized Jews. One important feature of this was that Christians regarded the crucifixion and resurrection of Jesus as belonging to their own past, because in some sense they all lived within Christ. As communities of memory and hope develop, the members become ever more closely linked by a shared love of the community's present activities. (See POC, 266–8.)

The modern America, remarks Royce, risks being less of a beloved community than less advanced nations, such as Japan can still be (while federal power reduces the possibility of individual states being so). For a very complex co-operating society may be so little grasped as a whole by its members that it fails to be a community in the proper sense. This is a danger of modern society. (See POC, 262–5. And on the contrast between Japan and the USA, see LOYALTY, 71–7 and 232–44.)

This can be remedied only if there are occasions of common celebration of the community's shared past (and expected future) such as can unite all its members in the love of it. Then, indeed, each can feel devotion to the community as it exists now, ignorant as he must remain of much of its detailed activities. (See POC, 266.)

A community must have a history, for it is in virtue of the 'memories' held by all its members in common that it is a community (POC, 244 ff.). But this is just another example of what is true of the self of an individual person.

The rule that time is needed for the formation of a conscious community is a rule which finds its extremely familiar analogy within the life of every individual human self. Each one of us knows that he just now, at this instant, cannot find more than a mere fragment of himself present. The self comes down to us from its own past. It needs and is a history (POC, 244)

And it is much the same with a community.

True, we cannot share personal memories, but we can share ancestral members, so that memories of a community may genuinely have a past in common. (Royce illustrates this by the way in which a Maori speaks of himself as having come over in the canoe in which his ancestors are believed to have arrived in New Zealand; see POC, 246.) In order that this may be so, however, individual selves must be able to communicate with each other. And this ability to communicate is the equivalent at the community level of what is known as the unity of consciousness at the individual level.

Royce makes a distinction between communities of memory and communities of hope. The former are composed of human beings who share a common past, the latter of ones who share a common expected future. In fact, of course, communities are normally communities of both kinds.

The Christian community shares, as its most significant communal 'memory', the crucifixion and resurrection of Christ, in virtue of which all its members feel themselves saved. (See POC, 257.) It is also a community of hope, of the general resurrection and the eventual kingdom of God to which all Christians belong. (See POC, 258–9.)

All this shows that human life exists at two levels: at the level of the community and at the level of individual persons. (See POC, 251.) Each of these is as genuinely real as the other.

Royce, we may note, insists that a community is normally an agent in its own right (its agency is not just the logical resultant of that of the individuals who belong to it).

For our purposes, the community is a being that attempts to accomplish something in time and through the deeds of its members. These deeds belong to the life which each member regards as, in ideal, his own. It is in this way that both the real and the ideal Church are intended by the members to be communities in our sense. An analogous truth holds for such other communities as we shall need to consider. The concept of the community is thus, for our purposes, a practical conception. It involves the idea of deeds done, and ends sought or attained. Hence I shall define it in terms of members who themselves not only live in time, but conceive their own ideally extended personalities in terms of a time-process. In so far as these personalities possess a life that is for each of them his own, while it is, in some of its events, common to them all, they form a community.

Nothing important is lost, for our conception of the community, by this formal restriction, whereby common objects belong to a community only when these objects are bound up with the deeds of the community. (POC, 254–5)

As communities of memory and hope develop, the members become further linked by the shared love of the community's present activities. (See POC, 266–8.)

Royce thinks that a completely naturalistic account of communities is impossible. (See POC, 270.) For the love of each individual for his community as a whole cannot be explained by a purely naturalistic psychology. Thus in some sense such love 'comes from above'. And this can only be explained if the universe itself is a genuine community. (Love of the human race is a step to grasping this.)

Royce insists, however, that the existence of a beloved community does not depend upon any mystical blending of its members in a unindividualized mush. (See POC, 256.) Nothing mystical of this sort is required in order that there be a community. The selves in a community continue to exist as separate beings each with his own distinct consciousness.

Still the community's members may well harbour the *wish* for some complete grasp of the community's life, a grasp which would involve some kind of blending. And Royce is more than ready to hold that this may actually occur. But this is not so much what makes a community a community, as an occasional result of its existence.

The distinctiveness of the selves we have illustrated at length in our previous discussion. We need not here dwell upon the matter further, except to say expressly, that a community does *not* become one, in the sense of my definition, by virtue of any reduction or melting of the selves into a single merely present self, or into a mass of passive experience. That mystical phenomena may indeed form part of the life of a community, just as they may also form part of the life of an individual human being, I fully recognize.

About such mystical or quasi-mystical phenomena, occurring in their own community, the Corinthians consulted Paul. (POC, 255–6)

And Paul insisted that this did not need to happen, and on the whole it was better that it did not happen.

Royce, it seems, was anxious that his account of communities should not depend on his old notion of supra-personal forms of consciousness, so that his account might be more acceptable to naturalistic thinkers who would be sceptical of any such idea. But, as for himself, he did, I think, still believe in them, though not as a mush.

The Community and Peirce's Theory Of Signs

In the later part of the book Royce relates what he has said of Christianity to a 'doctrine of signs' which he has reached largely under the influence of C. S. Peirce.

The Christian view of life is dominated by the ideal of the Universal Community. Such is the thesis defended in the first part of this series of lectures. The real world itself is, in its wholeness, a Community. This was the metaphysical result in which our study of the world of Interpretation culminated. (POC, 343)

So for Royce the account of the nature of the universe which best suits the essential message of Christianity, as delivered primarily by Paul, rather than by Jesus, is one which regards it as essentially a social universe.

To give more precision to this view of the universe, Royce presents a brief account of C. S. Peirce's theory of signs, by which he has been much influenced in developing it. It will be easiest to explain this theory here by an example of Royce's. Suppose that an Egyptologist manages to translate an ancient Egyptian inscription into English. Then there is a three-term relation which, Royce and Peirce claim, cannot be reduced to two-term relations. The terms are (1) the Egyptian text, referred to as the sign; (2) the translation, that is, the English text; and (3) the English reader to whom the text is interpreted, let us call him (Royce has no definite term) the interpretee. The theory of signs asserts that all communication has this triadic structure. It also claims that the process of interpretation is in principle endless, since the sign, the English text, which is the interpretation in this case, itself will need to be interpreted if it is to be understood in future, as again will that interpretation, and so on indefinitely.

Royce now claims that the universe is entirely composed of such triads of interpretation. Thus every event in the universe is a sign which a second event interprets to a third event. The most obvious illustration for this is the stream of ideas which follow one upon another in our own minds. Whenever such an idea occurs in anyone's mind, it has to be interpreted by a second idea which explicates it so that it will be understood by a third idea.

It is only because our ideas are a series of interpretations that we can have any knowledge of the past or future. A being whose mind did not consist in a series of signs would have no sense of anything other than the present moment; for a mere percept or concept does not wear its meaning on its sleeve. It is only because we interpret a present idea in our minds as an idea of something past or future, that we can have any sense of anything beyond the present. The same applies to communication between individuals. The words I utter can only be understood by a hearer in whom a mental event occurs (that of hearing the sounds) which provides a sense of what the words mean to an act of understanding.

This thesis is hard to follow in detail. Its hard to see, for example, how both the second and the third idea are to be interpreted subsequently unless the series of ideas branches out in some strange manner. But

Royce is satisfied that it makes sense to suppose that every event which occurs is a sign which an act of interpretation passes on to an act of understanding.

> Our memories are signs of the past; our expectations are signs of the future. Past and future are real in so far as these signs have their real interpretation. Our metaphysical thesis generalizes the rules which constantly guide our daily interpretations of life. All contrasts of ideas, all varieties of experience, all the problems which finite experience possesses, are signs. The real world contains (so our thesis asserts) the interpreter of these signs, and the very being of the world consists in the truth of the interpretation which, in the whole realm of experience, these signs obtain. (POC, 348)

This grounds what Royce thinks is an all important supplement to his account of a community, by showing that all proper communities are communities of interpretation. Suppose that I am able to interpret you to some third person so that they grasp something of what you really think and feel. Then I, my account of you, and the third person form a minimal community of interpretation linked by the triadic relation just explained.

But the communities which really matter are those of some large number of members bound together by a complex system of such triadic relations. And in fact all the various types of community which Royce has been explicating are rich and complex species of communities of interpretation. In such communities each member has a will to interpret other members to each other. But, of course, no such interpretation in our present form of life is perfect. I cannot explain completely what you are to another in any fully adequate way. But in all such communities there is a more or less explicit aspiration to some complete understanding of all by all. And this is that far-off divine event towards which we all struggle.

What, then, is the appropriate attitude of the will to the world on the part of one who interprets it as a system of interpretations such as Royce has described? Royce identifies three basic attitudes of Will with which men may face the universe, and considers which is the most appropriate if the doctrine of signs is recognized as true. (See POC, 351–6.) The three attitudes of the Will are these.

(1) A will to live—that is, to assert oneself as an individual. This may take all sorts of forms. A person whose attitude of will is of this kind will recognize that other persons are self affirming in just the same ways as he is. In so far as it helps his own self-affirmation to co-operate with them, he will do so. But should there be a conflict of will between them, he will

take the most selfish option and look out only for his own personal advantage.

(2) He may look askance upon this world of willing beings, and adopt an attitude of passive resignation. He may deny the will to live in the way that Schopenhauer understood the saintly to do. This is a Buddhist attitude, but Schopenhauer is quite wrong in associating it with Christianity.

(3) The third kind of will is that of the loyal individual. In being loyal, he is neither self-assertive nor life-denying. His life is dictated, rather by his loyalty to his cause. Thereby he escapes the misery pertaining to each of the first two attitudes. (See POC, 355 ff.)

And it is just this attitude of the will which is the one which the doctrine of the world as world of interpretation of signs must promote.

According to the theory of signs, I know my fellow man, not by an argument from analogy, but by signs reaching me from him which I know must have a more complete interpretation than I can give them. And this interpretation is one he must be giving them just as I constantly interpret my own ideas to myself. But the theory of signs advises us that every existent or occurrent thing is, in truth, a sign which receives an interpretation (if not by us, then by some other mind). So everything in the whole world must be interpreted, and thus have its place in someone's mental life. The universe itself must finally be its own interpreter, and this, so Royce seems to hold, implies that it is a unity held together by acts of interpretation. Thereby Royce aims to give individual persons more by way of a separate life of their own than they were allocated by his earlier monism. Yet it also seems that he would not wish to discard his old position.

At any rate, the loyal person's attitude to the world is neither selfish nor resignatory, but a life of active devotion to a cause. And this is ultimately the attitude of Christianity, of which, as we have seen, Paul, rather than Jesus, is the great exponent. On his own, the individual is lost, and he can be 'saved' only by being a devotedly loyal member of a community.

Practically I cannot be saved alone: theoretically speaking, I cannot find or even define the truth in terms of my individual experience, without taking account of my relation to the community of those who know. This community, then, is real whatever is real. And in that community my life is interpreted. When viewed as if I were alone, I, the individual, am not only doomed to failure, but I am lost in folly. The 'workings' of my ideas are events whose significance I cannot even remotely estimate in terms of their momentary existence, or in terms of my individual successes. My life means nothing, either theoretically or practically, unless I am a member of a community. I win no success worth having, unless it is also the success of the community to which I essentially and by virtue of my relations to the whole universe, belong. My deeds are not done at all, unless they are indeed done for all time, and are irrevocable. (POC, 357)

This ethical outlook points to the metaphysical truth that the whole world is one great community of interpretation.

As already noted, Royce does rather give the impression that this is a new account of the world replacing his old idea of it as a single divine thought. But since he assures us otherwise, I suggest that he is now formulating new ideas without, perhaps, having adequately thought out how they relate to his earlier positions, positions which he has no thought of abandoning.[23] None the less, he assures us that all communities of interpretation are included in the one Divine Thought, itself a community of interpretation, which, indeed, is itself the ultimate interpreter of everything (including itself).

We may sum up Royce's views on Christianity thus: The purpose of religion is to bind men together in a loving community, and the early Christian church, under the guidance of St Paul, is the best instance yet of such a community. But we must now pursue whatever means we find most helpful for binding humanity in general into a loving community, taking inspiration from that early community, while abandoning most of its credal basis. (See POC, 404.)

VII Concluding Comment on Royce as Religious Thinker and Man

That Royce's doctrine of the Absolute, and the associated claims about loyalty and community, do provide a definite answer to religious questions is clear. Though it would not support Pascal or Kierkegaard in their commitment to the full Christian message as they understood it, they could not reasonably charge Royce's God with being religiously irrelevant. Belief in such a God could undergird and even promote a genuinely religious attitude to life.

But quite apart from any criticism one might make of Royce's actual arguments, it is doubtful that many people would be altogether happy with Royce's view of what religion is, or should be, about. And there is something questionable in seeking to make loyalty to loyalty the one end to which all that we do should be subservient. Is a committed musician to be 'loyal' to music as a way of encouraging others to be loyal to some other worthwhile 'cause'? The musician might justify himself to others (such as T. H. Green or Leo Tolstoy) who complain that he should be engaging in something more socially beneficial by speaking of the way in which music can unify people and perhaps even inspire them to high ideals, but this can hardly be the main driving force of his life. My ultimate commitment, the Roycean will say, is to encourage commitment in the world. But surely to do this requires that people have commitments not derived from a commitment to commitment. Besides which, there is something logically odd in making loyalty itself the proper ultimate object of our loyalty, even if it is not quite a definitional circle.

Worried about William James's assertion that the only good of absolute idealism is that it allows us 'moral holidays' in which, at peace with the world, we do not think it our job to go about improving it,[24] Royce is ever anxious to insist that his absolute idealism gives no excuse for taking any such holidays from ethical effort. So much so that none of the peace which some religions offer their devotees is catered for by Royce.

Associated with this is Royce's peculiarly negative view of mystical experience. This may reduce the appeal of Royce's conception of religion for many of us and, at a less lofty level one may doubt that it is really so awful to do some things because you personally enjoy them.

Compare this with what G. E. Moore thought were the chief values: namely, personal affection and the enjoyment of beautiful objects. Moore was doubtless wrong to treat these as far and away more valuable than anything else, but they certainly are valuable. Yet they can only be recognized as such by the philosophy of loyalty through a highly strained use of terms. Should not most of the highest loyalties, in Royce's extended sense of the term, be to values not well described as themselves forms of loyalty?

In so far as Royce is saying that we are 'lost' so long as we think only of ourselves, he is right, but it seems a stretching of the word to call all love for others, whether for individuals, human or otherwise, or for mankind or the animal kingdom at large, a form of loyalty, let alone loyalty to loyalty. And although Royce was a devoted reader of poetry, beauty does not play much part in his religious message. Still, I would not deny that human brotherhood (= personhood), is both as an end and as a means at the very highest level of values, and this is perhaps what Royce is really thinking of.

VIII Conclusion

What bearing does Royce's view, for anyone who accepts it, have on religion? Well, the upshot of Royce's metaphysics so far as religion goes would seem to be this:

(1) We must accept a lot of suffering in our lives, recognizing that this is necessary both for the good of the universe and ourselves.

(2) We know that we will have a life after death in which we will be able to move further in the path of virtue.

(3) We must live in full recognition that the welfare of other conscious persons matters *as much as* our own, that of animals matters *as truly as* our own, and that the whole of nature is worthy of our devotion.

(4) The only way in which we can find salvation from what is otherwise bound to be a miserable existence is to devote ourselves to some cause. (This belongs more to his later philosophy.)

(5) Adhering to this cause will either go along with, or be identical with, belonging to some group of persons to which we will be loyal.

(6) We can choose our cause for ourselves, but it must be one which will help other persons in their loyalty to whatever causes or groups they devote themselves. Ultimately, we should be loving and loyal towards the Universe, realizing that this is a divine being.

It seems to me that this is relevant to religion, however far we may or may not accept it. The effect of accepting this doctrine should be that one will have the encouragement, when all one's efforts to do the right thing seem to lead to nothing or to worse, that unselfish and loyal action will never be wasted; that one's life should be altruistic and loyal; and that the universe will exhibit itself as something worthy of worship or devotion.

I have found it hard to say to what extent Royce can be said to have lived by this creed. One has the impression that he must have been a really loyal member of his university and department, and that he was conscientious as a teacher. But he was involved in two great quarrels, at least one of which seems to stem from a certain lack of sympathy with others. There were also some great tragedies in his life, in particular the insanity of his son. It seems that Royce did find some comfort in his metaphysical religious faith (see CLENDENNING, 312). Another great grief for him was the conduct of his beloved Germany in the First World War, in particular the sinking of the *Lusitania* in 1915. This grief does seem to have hastened his death.

To what great cause did Royce most fully commit himself personally? The answer is perhaps that it was to his own most deep relations to others, which one should never betray. Perhaps also to his family, and to his somewhat strange relation to his wife.[25] But perhaps the larger cause and group to which he felt he primarily belonged and sought to be loyal was the philosophical fraternity. In any case, whatever may be true of him as a person, his philosophy provides a definite view of the good life.

I suggest further that Royce had to fight against depression stemming from his sometimes quite difficult life, and that his metaphysics served to alleviate this. And this seems to me a perfectly reasonable service which a religion can provide.

Royce's stress on the importance of community makes one wonder how it could be the basis for a purely personal religion, but it could certainly serve to support someone in their membership of a church—though this does not seem to have been something which it did for Royce himself. Indeed, Professor John Clendenning (his biographer) has told me that, so far as he knows, Royce was, after 1875, a member of no church or organized religious group. This is odd, considering his profoundly religious orientation to philosophic issues. On Sundays he habitually took solitary walks and other excursions as ways to relieve the tedium of weekly obligations. Unlike other religious persons, he did not seek spiritual refreshment in Sunday services.[26]

The kind of person who most commanded his admiration is well illustrated by his account of a historical event. In 1642, shortly before the English Civil War, Charles I illegally entered the House of Commons, accompanied by soldiers, and asked the Speaker to identify certain men who had offended him.

[T]he speaker at once fell on his knee before the King and said: 'Your Majesty, I am the Speaker of this House, and, being such, I have neither eyes to see nor tongue to speak save as this House shall command; and I humbly beg your Majesty's pardon if this is the only answer that I can give to your Majesty.'

Now, I ask you to view the act [not for its historical importance but] merely as an instance of a supremely worthy personal attitude. The beautiful union of formal humility... with unconquerable self-assertion . . . the willing and complete identification of his whole self with his cause . . . these are characteristics typical of a loyal attitude. . . .

Well—here is an image of loyalty. Thus, I say, whatever their cause, the loyal express themselves. When any one asks me what the worthiest personal bearing, the most dignified and internally complete expression of an individual is, I can therefore only reply: Such a bearing, such an expression of yourself as the Speaker adopted. Have, then, your cause, chosen by you just as the Speaker had chosen to accept his office from the House. Let this cause so possess you that, even in the most thrilling crisis of your practical service of that cause, you can say with the

Speaker: 'I am the servant of this cause, its reasonable, its willing, its devoted instrument, and, being such, I have neither eyes to see nor tongue to speak save as this cause shall command.' Let this be your bearing, and this your deed. Then, indeed, you know what you live for. And you have won the attitude which constitutes genuine personal dignity. What an individual in his practical bearing can be, you now are. And herein, as I have said, lies for you the supreme personal good. (LOYALTY, 102–7)

To conclude, let us reflect briefly on his doctrine of the inclusion of all things in God, or the Absolute. For this, even if it fell somewhat into the background in his last work, is central to most of his thought. And we might ask, granted that the Absolute, as Royce conceives it, does really exist, what does this matter to us? Taken together with his doctrine of loyalty to loyalty, the answer is, I suppose, that it gives us the assurance that the universe is on our side if we devote ourselves to promoting human and even extra-human brotherhood.

However, Royce's Absolute is a rather forbidding individual. It is basically pleased with the world as it is, and pleased that this contentment depends upon the restless struggling and enormous suffering of the finite individuals which belong to it as we do, without seeming to have much enthusiasm for our more joyous moments. Positive reward for any achievement of ours comes at a level that we, as personal centres of consciousness of the human type, cannot reach, for it belongs only to those living at a more eternal level, even if they are eternal versions of ourselves. Royce's Absolute hardly seems something which we might contemplate with joy, let alone worship.

None the less, if Royce's metaphysics were right, it would definitely have religious implications. It is not mere idle word-play. It is calculated both to prompt us to moral effort and to cope with our sorrows as all for the good in the end. But though I myself believe in the Absolute, conceived as an Eternal Consciousness within which all things live and have their being, without exactly moving, Royce's account of it, and of its demands upon us, seems to lose something of 'that peace of God which passes all understanding' which one would hope that it might occasionally offer.

Notes

1. See his autobiographical essay in *The Philosophy of C. I. Lewis*.
2. The presentation of Royce's argument in this section is borrowed from my *James and Bradley*.

3. This would not be admitted by all philosophers today. One reply, sometimes favoured by A. J. Ayer, is that error about one's present state of consciousness is not factual error, but verbal error—the wrong words have been used to pick out what is none the less recognized for what it is.

4. See Gareth Evans, *The Varieties of Reference*; Saul Kripke, *Naming and Necessity*; Colin McGinn, *Mental Content*; and various authors such as Tyler Burge in Andrew Woodfield, *Thought and Object: Essays in Intentionality*, and P. Pettitt and J. McDowell, in *Thought and Context*.

5. William James sometimes proposed a view much like this. What for him determined its object and its truth was that it promoted useful behaviour in relation to it. This was developed, indeed, as a reply to Royce. The modern externalist rather less plausibly sees its object as determined by a causal chain from the object to the current mental activity.

6. It has been objected to this kind of theory that it leaves the really moral person with no specific aspirations of his own, only the aspiration to see the aspirations of others realized. The answer must, surely, be that he is allowed his own more personal aspirations, but that these must go in to the boiling pot along with those of others, so far as known, with the additional point that there are things he must do for his own good which others could not or would not do. (Cleanliness requires that, for the most part, each adult person does his best to keep himself, rather than others, clean.) Royce in effect deals with this in his 'philosophy of loyalty' by stressing that each of us should have his personal cause, but that he should eschew any cause which works against other people having theirs. See below at p. 387.

7. Charles Hartshorne, as we shall see, takes a not altogether dissimilar view, but treats our usual egotism as too easily dealt with by reasoning. Moreover, the fact that past pleasure and pain positively or negatively condition our later behavioural inclinations is not mere contingent fact, but part of the essence of personal identity.

8. This idea of our sharing dimly in the feelings of the inanimate things in our environment is rather like an aspect of Whitehead's thought.

9. I discuss Bradley's argument for this in *James and Bradley*, 393–405.

10. See also the essay on Meister Eckhart in *Studies of Good and Evil* (1898). Was Bradley's conception of *being* mystical? Royce was probably right: 'Mr Bradley's account of the Absolute often comes near to the use of mystical formulations, but Mr Bradley is of course no mystic; and nobody knows better than he the self-contradiction inherent in the effort to view the real as a simple unity, without real internal multiplicity' (W&I 1, 549).

11. Otherwise put, according to Royce, it is the philosophy of *as if*, in contrast to the realist philosophy of *how things really are* (W&I 1, 243).

12. '[W]e men have never experienced the direct presence of any individual whole whatever. For us, individuals are primarily the objects presupposed, but never directly observed, by love and by its related passions' (W&I 1, 585).

13. However, extremes meet, and realism can also become anarchistic through conceiving the self as an independent being with no genuine ties to anything or anyone else, as in Max Stirner's *Der Einzige and Sein Eigenthum* (w&ɪ 2, 283 and n.).

14. See *Spirit*, 373–4. Compare James, *Principles*, 251.

15. From the Absolute's point of view, then, to use McTaggart's language, as explained in Chapter 4, the A series is unreal, but the B series is real, or more real. If we are to speak of a C series, it must, I think, for Royce, be the position in a quasi-temporal series belonging to the 'frozen specious present' of the Absolute.

16. See next section. See *James and Bradley*, Part 2, ch. 4, §3; T. L. S. Sprigge, 'Hartshorne on the Past', and 'The Unreality of Time'.

17. See w&ɪ 2, 214, 225, etc. 'We know that Nature, as it were, tolerates our mathematical formulas. We do not know that she would not equally well tolerate many other such formulas instead of these' (w&ɪ 2, 225).

18. 'It would not be true that Nature sometimes, in an exceptional way, pursues ideal goals. On the contrary, every natural process, if rightly viewed from within, would be the pursuit of an ideal' (w&ɪ 2, 231).

19. Briefly, this is because death must have a purpose (since to be is to have a purpose). This it can have only if the projects it seems to cut short are *aufgehoben* in a higher personal project, the grasp of which must pertain to the Absolute via my eternal self. Moreover, since every fulfilment of a purpose produces a situation which makes fresh demands, there can never be a complete fulfilment of one's purposes in time, but there must be an infinite series of purposes successively fulfilled in ways creating further purposes. (See w&ɪ 2, 436–43.) Some similarity to both Kant and McTaggart here may be noticed.

20. Around the same time he published *Race Questions, Provincialism, and Other American Problems* (1908). He shows himself extremely sceptical of any idea that some human races are superior to others in innate mental endowment, and argues that the solution to the racial problem in the American South is to escape from irrational prejudices and bring black people into the administration of law, etc.

    In 1911 Royce gave a series of lectures at Lake Forest College, 'a small coeducational Christian college' near Chicago. This became a book, published shortly after, called *The Sources of Religious Insight* (1912). Among other themes, it stresses the social nature of religious experience, as against William James's tendency to think of it as something essentially solitary.

21. Alan Massie, in the *Scotsman*, 23 Oct. 1996.

22. PRINCIPLES, ch. 10.

23. Besides which the view of the Absolute taken in w&ɪ is already more pluralistic than that of RELIGIOUS ASPECT.

24. PRAGMATISM, 75–6.

25. This remark is based on something which Professor Clendenning, the author of an outstanding biography of Royce, told me in an exchange of email letters.

26. Again I am most grateful for this information provided me by Professor Clendenning.

Chapter 8

Process Philosophy and Theology: Whitehead and Hartshorne

'Process philosophy' is an expression used primarily for the philosophy of A. N. Whitehead (1861–1947) and Charles Hartshorne (1897–2000) and for the work of their followers. Other philosophers are sometimes called process philosophers because their basic outlook is similar. Among such philosophers are William James and Henri Bergson. What unites them is their emphasis on change in their characterization of reality. Before moving to the main topic of this chapter, I shall say something about William James as a process philosopher. (Bergson's philosophy would have to be treated at greater length, if at all.)

PART ONE: THE PROCESS PHILOSOPHY OF WILLIAM JAMES

His Conception of Truth and Reality

James, as everyone knows, promoted a pragmatic conception of truth, according to which a belief is true if and only if it works. And the main types of working which he stressed were (1) providing guidance as to how one must act to obtain desired results and (2) producing satisfying and useful emotions.

What not everyone knows is that he combined this with an effort to grasp the nature of reality in a more intimate way than mere conceptual thought could provide. This was to sink oneself in the flux of experience without attempting to conceptualize it.

However, after doing so, one might be able to return to the world of thought and enrich one's view of reality on the basis of what one had learnt by this non-conceptual adventure. On this basis (and others) James came to hold to the view of panpsychism according to which reality consists in innumerable flows of feeling interacting with each other. The consciousness of a human being is one special kind of such flow of feeling, typified, among other things, by the high level of conceptual thinking which it contains.

This is enough to make him a process philosopher. But what are of more interest for present purposes are (1) his belief in contra-causal free will and (2) his view of God.

James on Free Will

For James, each of us has free will. That is to say, when various ideas of what I might do, at any important juncture in my life, suggest themselves as possibilities in the light of my factual knowledge, it is not always the ideas that determine, as opposed to influence, which of these things I do. No, it is sometimes an uncaused act of free will on my own part.

James on God

First, he thought that the attempt to prove the existence of God by philosophical arguments was always hopeless, and even if it was not, it would lead to an unsatisfactory conception of God. Thus James is to be counted among the enemies of 'the God of the philosophers', along with Pascal and Kierkegaard.

Secondly, he thought that the traditional Christian view of God, according to which he was omnipotent, omniscient, and absolutely good, was fatally flawed by the fact of evil. To resolve this, James advocated the conception of a finite God, an individual much more powerful than ourselves, but still not all-powerful (and perhaps not all-knowing). (The existence of God over time would be, just like our existence over time, a matter of a stream of experience occurring, in this case of experience suitably called 'divine'.) This God is attempting to make the world better and better, for the world (consisting of streams of experience other than his own) is an external fact with which he has to cope just as you and I do. Now if I wish to commit myself to the same task, I can do it better if I relate to God in such a way that we work together for the amelioration of things. I may do so simply by believing in his existence as a being who will steer what I do to the best results possible. But I can also receive a special kind of help from him if I have 'religious experiences' of association and unity with him.

God, as James conceived him, is like the God of Whitehead and Hartshorne (which we are to discuss shortly), a God who does not remain statically the same over time. Not that James stresses this as much as they do, but it is an obvious application of his viewpoint. For how can God address himself to the new challenges presented to him at each moment by acts of free will on the part of human agents, and maybe other agents too, without his state of mind changing? And since the future is open, God cannot be sure of what is coming, and must often develop a fresh strategy to make the best of what does come. Thus James joins process theology in rejecting the traditional idea that God never changes.

On what grounds did James adopt this view? Partly he held it for true because it was useful pragmatically for encouraging us in the work of ameliorating the world. But, partly in a more realistic vein than that suggested by his pragmatic view of truth, he thought that the existence of God provided the best explanation of the religious experiences of mankind. For in religious experience we seem to be in contact with something divine in the depths of our being, where our subliminal or semi-unconscious self appears to be in touch with something else which can enrich our life. And although these experiences are often interpreted as pointing to the existence of an infinite rather than a finite God, it is a more credible and more satisfying view that he is not all-powerful and all-containing, but simply the major and most benevolent single power in the world who has to do the best he can with often refractory material. But both he and each of us will do so much better with the aid of the other.

James's views were advanced as an alternative to the monistic metaphysics of Josiah Royce (his close friend) and F. H. Bradley and other absolute idealists. Though he had once found their arguments uncomfortably strong, he thought that their outlook promoted the immoral idea that all apparent evil is really good, when understood as a phase in the life of the Absolute.

This is of course an extremely summary view of James's position, leaving aside all manner of subtleties and qualifications and the fact that even in proposing these ideas he accompanied them with suggestions as to alternative possibilities which should not be dismissed. None the less, I think it is essentially a correct summary of the viewpoint to which he most inclined.[1]

PART TWO: WHITEHEAD AND HARTSHORNE

I Biographical

Whitehead and Hartshorne are recognized as the founding fathers of *process philosophy* as a fully worked out metaphysic, and it is to their philosophies that the term will refer for the remainder of this chapter.

God figures largely in the philosophies of both, as do religious issues in general, and their works have inspired a quite flourishing school of *process theology.*[2] But before examining their philosophy, a word about the sort of men that they were.

A. N. Whitehead had a highly distinguished academic career and received many academic honours. From 1884 to 1910 he was a lecturer at Cambridge, and worked mainly on mathematics and logic, collaborating with Bertrand Russell in the writing of *Principia Mathematica.* In 1910 he moved to London, and in 1914 became Professor of Applied Mathematics at the Imperial College of Science and Technology. There he worked mainly on the philosophy of science. In 1924 he moved to Harvard. It was while at Harvard that he developed the metaphysical system to be discussed in this chapter, though *Process and Reality* came into existence as Gifford Lectures delivered in Edinburgh in 1927 and 1928.[3] He found American academia more open to his type of philosophizing, and his largest, but by no means his only, influence has been on American philosophers and theologians.

As an indication of how his religious outlook developed I shall do best by quoting from Victor Lowe's biography of him.

Whitehead was raised an Anglican. A flirtation with Rome was followed, in the mid-1890's, by his becoming an agnostic; he remained one for a quarter of a century. After World War I, in which many of his pupils and one of his two sons were killed, he gradually developed his own philosophical theism. He conceived of God, the supreme monad, not as omnipotent Creator but as eternally with the temporal world, systematically interacting with it in two ways. God's 'primordial nature' is the source of all possible values; it is, he wrote, 'the acquirement by creativity of a primordial character.' God's 'consequent nature' receives, transforms, and keeps forever the monads that have perished in the temporal world; thus God grows with the world, and is always in process. Whitehead did not include his highly original concept of God in the categoreal scheme of *Process and Reality,* but fitted the concept nicely onto the scheme. I think the scheme logically required this addition. (LOWE, i. 5)

It seems that his return to a personal religious faith was strongly influenced by his need for something to help him cope with the slaughter in the First World War, in which his son Eric was killed.

When I [Victor Lowe] asked Bertrand Russell about his view of Whitehead's turn to religion, he gave it flatly and crudely: 'Eric's death made him want to believe in immortality.' It would perhaps be more accurate, because less explicit, to say what Jessie [Whitehead's daughter] immediately said when I brought up this subject: 'Eric's death is behind it.' (LOWE, ii. 188)

For without some belief for which human life is not more than 'a flash of occasional enjoyments lighting up a mass of pain and misery, a bagatelle of transient experience' (LOWE, ii. 188), he would have found things intolerable. The fact that his theism provided him with comfort in his grief does not of course show that the comforting beliefs were not true. Perhaps, so a theist might argue, God here provided him with what he needed. At any rate, it would seem that so far as religion did something for him other than provide a coping stone for his metaphysic, it was as a source of comfort and encouragement.

He certainly never accepted orthodox Christianity. (Nevertheless, his thought in association with that of Hartshorne has had considerable influence on Christian theology since his day.) Jesus did not figure especially prominently in his thought, it would seem. Although Unitarianism held out a certain attraction for him, he never joined the denomination (see LOWE, ii. 197). And he had especially the Anglican Church in mind when he made the following remark:

A system of dogmas may be the ark within which the Church floats safely down the floodtide of history. But the Church will perish unless it open its window and lets out the dove to search for an olive branch. (LOWE, ii. 194)

Charles Hartshorne was born in Pennsylvania, where his father was an Anglican clergyman. He served in the First World War as a medical orderly. He took his Ph.D. at Harvard, where he met Whitehead. He had already arrived at a philosophical position not unlike Whitehead's, and continued to develop it in relation to, but not entirely in agreement with, Whitehead's. A postdoctoral fellowship took him to Germany, where he had classes with both Husserl and Heidegger. But neither of these thinkers influenced his philosophy as much as C. S. Peirce, whose collected papers he edited with Paul Weiss. Hartshorne spent his teaching career at three institutions: Emory University, the University of Texas, and in the last phase of his career, the University of Chicago, where he was a dominant intellectual force in the School of Divinity, despite the fact that he was housed in the Philosophy Department. Hartshorne never owned an automobile; nor did he smoke or drink alcohol or caffeine; he had a passion for bird song, and became an internationally known expert in the field. Although Hartshorne, so I have been told, liked to associate himself vaguely with the Anglican tradition, in effect, he and his wife became Unitarians, though definitely Christian Unitarians ('Christian' being an epithet which some Unitarians of the present time find too restricting). And it seems to me that, though I cannot fully accept process metaphysics, since I have a different view of time and of human freedom, it is one very suitable background for a Unitarian commitment.[4]

II Views Shared by Whitehead and Hartshorne and now Definitive of Process Philosophy, or at least Theology

What unites the philosophers includes the following:

1. Both believe that the basic stuff of the world is experience, which (with the exception of God for Whitehead) comes into being in what William James called 'drops of experience' or, less metaphorically, 'momentary experiential wholes'.

2. Each believes that each such momentary whole prehends (that is, is aware of, and even in some sense absorbs) earlier such wholes and makes itself into a unitary reality with these prehended past wholes as its raw material.

3. Each believes that, as it ceases, each of these wholes enters into God, where they remain for ever thereafter; it is only in virtue of this that there is a definite and complete truth about the past.

4. They share a belief that somehow creativity is a basic feature of reality.

In many respects process philosophy is the antithesis of absolute idealism of the type promoted by Bradley and Bosanquet (and for which my own support will be given in the next chapter).[5] Yet there are respects in which Whitehead quite consciously favours absolute idealism over other metaphysical systems. (*Process and Reality*, the definitive statement of his process metaphysics, is so called to relate it to, and contrast it with, Bradley's *Appearance and Reality*.) What he shares with it in particular is the belief that in the account of nature given by natural science, or in a metaphysic deriving from science, the fact of the modification of things and their behaviour by their environment at any particular time fails to be realized. Both types of philosophy, absolute idealism and process philosophy, hold that many of the concepts of both ordinary common sense and the sciences are pragmatically useful abstractions, almost essential for practical purposes, but liable to distort our conception of reality if not qualified or enriched by insights of another kind. It is in this spirit that Whitehead agrees with Bradley that reality cannot be reduced to 'a bloodless dance of categories'. This is quite important from the point of view of religion, since both the process philosopher and the absolute idealist hold that the concepts of science can never do full justice to reality as it is actually experienced and that there is some fuller glory in the world than science can ever report.

In the following account of their thought, I shall spend rather more time on Whitehead, partly because his work is so difficult to grasp that it needs a fuller exposition. In any case I shall note the chief points on which they diverge.

Heraclitus v. Parmenides

III God Changes

Both philosophers reject the traditional idea that God does not change.[6] There is indeed something which remains the same throughout his everlasting existence, but there is also much that changes. This comes about mainly or entirely from the fact that he is in continual interaction with the world of finite things and creatures.

Change or process is, rather less strangely, the most basic feature of nature or the totality of finite existence. It has been the great mistake of traditional philosophy to identify genuine reality with the permanent. *Being* is at best a mere abstract aspect of the full concrete reality of *becoming*. Or such is Hartshorne's view, somewhat qualified by Whitehead's doctrine of eternal objects (on which see below).

Thus for process philosophy nature is composed not so much of continuants (that is, the supposed things of daily life which retain their identity over time as they change in their less fundamental characteristics) as of events. These take over from previous events as those sink into the past, enjoy their own brief moment of (present) existence, and are then superseded by further events. Strikingly, each to some extent chooses its own character: that is, what it makes of the data provided it by its predecessors.

IV Event Ontology versus Continuant Ontology

Personally, I think that the opposition between those who hold a continuant (or enduring individual substance) and an event ontology is rather exaggerated on both sides. Is there any real difference of view between saying that a certain series of events, each exemplifying the same 'personal' essence and with a certain kind of continuity, has taken place, and saying that a certain individual has lived through a series of mental states and activities? At best, they are ways of saying the same thing in a way suggestive of one moral perspective rather than another.

It is interesting that, as Hartshorne notes, India gave birth both to the extremest monistic position (Advaita Vedanta) and the extremest pluralistic position (Buddhism). (See SYNTHESIS, 177.)

It will be seen in the next chapter that I support metaphysical monism: that is, the belief that there is one Eternal Consciousness, or Absolute, in which all finite things are contained. This, however, allows for either an event or a continuant ontology so far as ordinary finite things go, while the Eternal Consciousness belongs to neither category. (The reader should note that by 'finite thing' I refer to things belonging to the ordinary world of space and time, as opposed to what is *infinite* in the sense of being timeless and complete (fully describable without reference to anything outside it) as perhaps only the Eternal Consciousness is. This is not the mathematical sense of 'infinite'.)

It may be said that an event ontology allows for a bifurcation of selves as a continuant ontology does not. (The possibilities of bifurcation are explored at length by Derek Parfit in his *Reasons and Persons*.) But I doubt this. For essentially the same debate is possible in either a continuant or an event language. Believers in persons as continuants can disagree as to whether one person could possibly divide into two. Equally, believers in streams of personal consciousness can disagree as to whether these streams can divide into two distinct streams at a certain time (and perhaps join up again).

Hartshorne, again like Parfit, and likewise stressing its affinity to Buddhism here, claims it as a great recommendation of an event ontology that it shows that egoism is illogical. For concern with one's future self is as much concern with something other than oneself now as is altruism. But even if this is a correct inference from such an ontology, which is open to doubt, it hardly addresses the important fact that egoism is more psychologically dominating. Moreover, since Hartshorne thinks that each momentary subject probably exists (except as something past whose choices are at an end) for just about one-tenth of a second, it is difficult to see it as a real decision maker. The decision must be extraordinarily quick. (See SYN-THESIS, 175.) I discuss this further below at section XIV(c).

It also suggests that if concern for one's own future is a form of altruism, then one need never be ashamed that one has behaved selfishly, since the difference will be only that one has decided to help one future individual rather than another.

One argument for an event ontology given by Hartshorne is that at the level of micro-physics it is compulsory, since many sub-atomic occurrences cannot be expressed as the momentary states of a continuing entity. But cannot the continuant ontologist regard these as individuals of the same ontological type as continuants which just happen to last only a moment? Perhaps it would be a bit strained to do so. Still, I remain doubtful that anything genuinely different is being said by the continuant ontologist and the event ontologist as regards ordinary enduring objects.

I do up to a point agree with event ontologists that their language is the more basic. There are philosophically important things that it is awkward to say in the language of continuants which are more readily said in the language of events (though the converse is also true). I even agree that an event language may get more to the root of things than a continuant ontology. All that I am denying is that the difference is as great as process philosophers (and perhaps Buddhist) thinkers suppose. For I doubt that the event ontologist is doing more than clarifying what is in effect meant in the language of continuants, when this is used in an ordinary manner, rather than as the exposition of a philosophical theory. Still, such clarification can be helpful. (Hartshorne's most elaborate statement known to me of the importance of an event ontology is in chapter 9 of SYNTHESIS.)

Whitehead's Actual Occasions and Eternal Objects

Be all that as it may, Whitehead, in particular, associates his commitment to an event ontology with a critique of one aspect of the Platonic inheritance of Western philosophy according to which ultimate reality is eternal and unchanging. This derives, he suggests, from the fact that Greek mathematics could not deal adequately with the form of temporal facts, but only with truths about eternal geometrical and numerical entities. From this it was inferred that precise knowledge could only be of a realm in which there is no change, and that therefore this alone is real. Thus 'the final outcome has been that philosophy and theology have been saddled with the problem of deriving the historical world of change from a changeless world of ultimate reality' (MODES, 81–2; see also p. 93).

417

Aristotle, it must be said, took time much more seriously. However, he is responsible, as Whitehead sees it, for another main error which has plagued philosophy: the notion of substance. The sense of 'substance' here in question is that in which Aristotle talked (in Greek) of 'primary substances' which are more or less what I have been calling (following a modern usage) 'continuants'. However, in calling them substances, it is being claimed further that they have a certain sort of completeness such that it even makes sense to imagine one of them existing quite alone independently of anything else. Moreover (on the Aristotelian and traditional view), a full description of what a substance is can be given by predicating universals of it, while in no wise can one substance be predicated of another. How it is related to other things is no part of its inherent being. It exemplifies universals, but never another substance.

Whitehead rejects this on two grounds. First, the nearest thing to primary substances which really exist (in a manner more often called *occurring* rather than *existing*) are momentary events (which Whitehead calls 'actual occasions'), which do, indeed, have a certain sort of completeness and even isolation in their moment of occurrence from what is going on at the same time. But as they only last a moment, they are certainly not continuants. Secondly, one actual occasion can be predicated of another, from which it follows that no actual occasion can be described completely in terms of universals. An adequate description of any one of them requires reference to other actual occasions which have entered into them (have been objectified in them in Whitehead's terminology). However, the actual occasions which have entered into a present one all belong to the past. Simultaneous actual occasions are cut off from each other. That is, within each event as it is present are many past events which have entered into its being, so that its past (or on a more extreme view, all past events) could be read off from what it now intrinsically is. Thus the Aristotelian view that one substance (or the nearest thing to a substance in Whitehead's system) cannot be predicated of another is abandoned.

Here an important theological difference between Whitehead and Hartshorne must be noted. According to the latter, God himself consists in a sequence of events united by the fact that each exemplified the unique divine essence. But Whitehead takes a different view. For him, actual occasions are indeed momentary events, but they belong to a broader class of realities called 'actual entities'. The one member of this class which is not an actual occasion is God. For God is not a momentary event, but an everlasting reality. So, while actual occasions come to a conclusion and exist only as the past of fresh actual occasions, God never ceases to be present. None the less, despite his everlastingness, to a large extent he exemplifies the same basic structure as does every momentary actual occasion. What this implies about God is quite difficult to understand, as we shall see.

For Whitehead, there are two main types of reality, the timeless and the temporal: that is, eternal objects, which are the forms and characters of all possible things, whether those things exist or not, and momentary events, known as 'actual occasions', together with the very special 'actual entity' God. And God has two aspects to his being: first, his primordial character, which consists in his never changing survey of the whole realm of eternal objects, and, secondly, his transactions with actual occasions as they go into and out of existence as subjectively aware beings.

Thus

there are two ultimate types of existence implicated in the creative process, the eternal forms with their dual existence in potential appetition and in realized fact, and realized fact with its dual way of existence as the past in the present and as the immediacy of the present. Also the immediacy of the present harbours an appetition toward the unrealized future. (MODES, 84–5)

For Hartshorne, in contrast, even the forms and characters of things are temporal in the sense that they only acquire being as created at some time within an event.

My view here is the Peircean one ... that all specific qualities, i.e. those of which there can be negative instances in experience, are emergent, and that only the metaphysical universals are eternal, something like Peirce's Firstness, Secondness and Thirdness [a division which Peirce made between three basic types of existence]. I do not believe that a determinate colour is something haunting reality from all eternity, as it were, begging for instantiation, nor that God primordially envisages a complete set of such qualities. (SYNTHESIS, 59)

Thus he thinks that every painting (as seen) includes a specific version of each of the colours on it, with no hold in reality at all before this.

Part of his reason for this is that he thinks you cannot separate off the specific character of a quality from the context in which it occurs. Personally, I think that the idealist notion of identity-in-difference copes best with this matter. According to this, any two occurrences of one and the same universal are indeed bitten into by their context, so to speak. So there is an element of difference, but there is also an identity which is as genuine an identity as can be. But this is a matter on which I cannot enter further here. (A simple example to make the point is that a stretch of sound from two different symphonies could contain precisely the same few bars, but their character as heard in the context of one symphony and in the other would in a sense sound differently. Something approximating to this is true of the use that Bruckner made of Wagner's music.)

However, Whitehead does not set his eternal objects in a realm to which time has no relevance. For it is of their essence to be necessarily related to the possibility of being actualized in process. Indeed, nothing at all can be conceived properly except in some relation to temporal process.

The nature of any type of existence can only be explained by reference to its implication in creative activity, essentially involving three factors; namely the data, process with its form relevant to these data, and issue into datum for further process—data, process, issue. (MODES, 93)

None the less, Hartshorne's universe is more purely temporal than is Whitehead's. (In the next chapter I shall argue that the truth is with neither of them, and that Reality as it really is, is eternal through and through.)

V Simplified Account of the Structure of an Actual Occasion for Whitehead

Whitehead lists eight types of entity to which he ascribes existence, or being: (1) actual entities, all of which except God are actual occasions; (2) prehensions; (3) nexus; (4) subjective forms; (5) eternal objects; (6) propositions; (7) multiplicities; (8) contrasts. Of these the ones on which it is best to concentrate in a short account are (1)–(5). (7) and (8) exist only in a somewhat secondary sense. (6) stands for what is more naturally called a fact, e.g. the fact that a certain particular has a certain character.

I now turn to the nature of actual occasions (for which see esp. PR, Part II, ch. X). These are the pulses of experience which are the fundamental constituents of the universe as a concrete reality. (Eternal objects are, by contrast, abstract.)

The first thing to be emphasized is that although each actual occasion is but momentary, it includes a process within it. That is, it goes through a series of internal changes during its brief span of existence as something with 'subjective immediacy'. In its phase of subjective immediacy, it is actually experienced or felt. 'Experienced or felt by whom or what?', you may ask. The only possible answer is experienced or felt by itself. However, after its phase of subjective immediacy, it takes on an 'objective' character in which it is experienced by other actual occasions, but no longer by itself. Simplifying enormously, we may say that each momentary experience or actual occasion 'starts' with a 'prehension' (in Whitehead's terminology) of innumerable past experiences which have just ceased to exist as subjectively immediate.[7] But although they have lost their subjective immediacy, they still exist though in a very different manner. This they do precisely by being objectified into the subsequent actual occasions which, prehend them.

A *prehension* is an act of awareness which a present actual occasion directs upon a previous actual occasion or rather at some feeling (prehension) which existed within it.[8] But it has its own particular way of prehending it, called its 'subjective form', which will not be the same as the way in which other occasions prehend that same earlier occasion.[9] The subjective form seems to be determined by the subjective aim. This is the kind of wholeness at which the occasion is aiming at throughout the concrescing process.

> The process of concrescence is divisible into an initial stage of many feelings, and a succession of subsequent phases of more complex feelings integrating the earlier simple feelings, up to the satisfaction which is one complex unity of feeling. (PR, 220/337)

The most surprising feature of this view is that when one actual occasion B prehends another earlier one A, then A actually itself enters into B, becoming really a part of it. Or, to be more precise, some part of A (just some of its 'feelings') becomes part of it. True, this has lost something in becoming part of B—it has lost its subjective immediacy. But it is still that part of A, become object rather than subject, that enters into B, not a mere representation of it. Thus Whitehead is able to say that there can never be an adequate description of what B inherently is which does not refer to A, or a feeling of A, as having entered into it. (See, for example, PR, 229/350.) That at least seems to be the implication of such passages as the following.

> The antithetical terms 'universals' and 'particulars' are the usual words employed to denote respectively entities which nearly, though not quite, correspond to the entities here termed 'eternal objects,' and 'actual entities.' These terms, 'universals' and 'particulars,' both in the suggestiveness of the two words and in their current philosophical use, are somewhat misleading. The ontological principle, and the wider doctrine of universal relativity, on which the present metaphysical discussion is founded, blur the sharp distinction between what is universal and what is particular. The notion of a universal is of that which can enter into the description of many particulars; whereas the notion of a particular is that it is described by universals, and does not itself enter into the description of any other particular.

According to the doctrine of relativity which is the basis of the metaphysical system of the present lectures, both these notions involve a misconception. An actual entity cannot be described, even inadequately, by universals because other actual entities do enter into the description of any one actual entity. Thus every so-called 'universal' is particular in the sense of being just what it is, diverse from everything else; and every so called 'particular' is universal in the sense of entering into the constitutions of other actual entities. The contrary opinion led to the collapse of Descartes' many substances into Spinoza's one substance; to Leibniz's windowless monads with their pre-established harmony; to the sceptical reduction of Hume's philosophy—a reduction first effected by Hume himself, and reissued with the most beautiful exposition by Santayana in his *Scepticism and Animal Faith*. (PR, 48/76)

It is true that at times Whitehead does speak of the earlier phase as being represented in the later, but on the whole he seems to think that it is there itself. This idea of A actually entering into B has seemed sufficiently peculiar for one distinguished commentator to deny that this is intended. For, according to William Christian, what becomes part of B is an eternal object which has ingressed (entered) A and now ingresses into B. (See CHRISTIAN, *passim*.) But if this were all there were to it, it would seem that the actual presence of one particular in another, which Whitehead mostly so stresses, would be lost.

In the case of Hartshorne, it will be seen, there is no doubt that the past object is meant to have actually itself become part of a later object. But whatever the niceties of interpretation, Whitehead certainly held that there was a connection between B and A, such that the existence of B is inseparable from the fact that A did exist and was in close proximity in space and time to B. It is thus that Whitehead thinks that his account of actual occasions explains why generalized scepticism about the past (and, in general, solipsism) can be dismissed.

I must say for myself that there is something very strange about this view. It is straightforward enough to talk about one thing being put inside another thing. It happens whenever I put a coin in my wallet, or, more dramatically in organ transplants. But in these cases it is an enduring thing, a continuant, which is shifted in its location. But since actual occasions are events, and events, what is more, which, according to Whitehead, cannot overlap in the region of space and time which they occupy, it is doubtful whether the idea is intelligible.

At any rate, Whitehead's view is that each actual occasion has as its first phase an awareness of all the past occasions which have thus entered into it. These are the raw material out of which it will give itself a definite character to pass onto subsequent occasions. So it goes through a process of self-creation: that is, of making out of the data supplied it by past occasions a new whole. This process of self-creation is its phase of 'concrescence'. When this is finished, it has given itself a definite character, and is ready to be 'objectified' into subsequent occasions.

The above should be qualified by a reference to so-called negative prehensions. Absolutely all past actual occasions are prehended. However, these prehensions are of two sorts: positive and negative. The former, so to speak, digest their objects, the second, so to speak, excrete them (or parts of them) (my terminology). What decides which will be which? Answer: even at the very beginning of the process, the actual occasion has a certain, perhaps as yet vague, subjective or ideal aim, of making of itself something with a satisfyingly complete final character. And what cannot contribute to this aim is, as I have put it, excreted.

So there are three main phases in the concrescence of an actual occasion:

1. All past occasions are 'objectified into it'.
2. Some are retained, some expelled, by positive and negative prehension.
3. It creates a new unity out of them, guided by its subjective aim. (This final definite character is called the actual occasion's 'satisfaction', and Whitehead says that in a certain manner this is a brief resting-place before the actual occasion loses 'subjective immediacy'.)

Concrescence finished, the world is left with a new object with a character never found in reality at all till now. This new object is available for entry into all subsequent occasions for positive or negative prehension, if not immediately, then by a chain of intermediary occasions which objectify themselves into one another. In this way it becomes one of the causes of what happens in the future, though causation is never deterministic, since every occasion has a minimum of freedom. (See especially PR, 212–15/322–8.)

However, it is by no means only parts of earlier actual occasions which enter into a new actual occasion; many eternal objects do so too. These include the eternal objects which characterized the earlier occasions. But it also becomes aware of other eternal objects which God prompts it to prehend as interestingly related to these. (This is called their conceptual prehension.[10]) And after comparing the character of these 'new' eternal objects with the 'old' ones, it selects from among the former those which it will be best to use in combining the positively prehended past occasions. (Of course, the eternal objects are *new* or *old* only in so far as their entry into concrete reality goes—they are eternally just there in the realm of eternal objects, prehension of which constitutes God's 'primordial' nature.)

So each actual occasion gives itself a new overall character which is a fresh synthesis of all the data it has received from earlier occasions. This is ideally a never before actualized eternal object which God has suggested for this purpose. But God does not force his suggestion upon the occasion, and it can be rejected. (This seems to imply some flexibility in the 'subjective aim' which is said to guide the whole process of concrescence.)

Whitehead emphasizes that such freedom as the lower sorts of actual occasions have is minimal. Their synthesis is almost mechanically created in a habitual manner. They are, it might be said, rather lazy. There may, however, be a moment of wavering between this and an alternative eternal object, an alternation which presents itself to physics as 'wave-lengths and vibrations'. But higher actual occasions, such as those whose succession constitutes our subjective biographies, do have a more substantial freedom, as just indicated. It is only higher actual occasions such as those which constitute our biography which can do much by way of accepting or rejecting what God suggests.

But it is rather unclear to me how much choice even such a higher occasion is meant to have. Sometimes it seems that it has to either take or leave what God suggests, since there is only one eternal object on offer. Yet how can it do the latter except by choosing some other eternal object similarly offered? So I take it that God offers it alternatives, some of which he regards less favourably than others.[11] And it is the adoption of one of these alternatives which brings real novelty into the world.

Apart from the intervention of God, there could be nothing new in the world, and no order in the world. The course of creation would be a dead level of ineffectiveness, with all balance and intensity progressively excluded by the cross currents of incompatibility. The novel hybrid feelings derived from God, with the derivative sympathetic conceptual valuations, are the foundations of progress. (PR, 247/378)

Thus each actual occasion may be said to have both its efficient cause in what it inherits from the past and its final cause in the eternal object, which, with God's assistance, it selects as the best way of making a satisfying unity of this inheritance. (See especially PR, 219/334 on all this.) But the efficient cause does not determine its precise character, only the parameters within which it chooses its final 'objective' character.

All this seems a bit remote from what it actually is to do something rather than just have experiences. The retort must be that our actions consist in interaction between various societies of actual occasions which are perceived in the gross (by the category of transmutation) as organisms moving about and acting on each other in space and time.

VI Actual Occasions and Time

The various phases of concrescence of an actual occasion follow on each other, but this is not a temporal succession. Or, if it is a temporal succession, it is to be distinguished from the more standard temporal process, which consists in one set of actual occasions receding into the past and giving way to the next set. There are thus two types of succession. On the one hand, there is the succession which consists in the set of actual occasions at one moment giving way to another set of contemporary actual occasions. On the other hand, there is the succession which goes on within an actual occasion. We might call the first external time, and the second internal time.[12]

It must be noted that, considered in clock time, an actual occasion lasts not a mere instant but a brief period of time. Thus the time process is atomic. That is, it consists in a succession of events which come into existence, so to speak, all at once. That they are not momentary means simply that there could have been more actual occasions occurring at that moment of clock time than there actually were. Indeed, during the moment at which some one actual occasion came into existence all at once, there may have been a succession in external time of a series of actual occasions coming into existence in turn. Thus time is infinitely divisible (because there always could have been more concrescing actual occasions within any stretch of clock time), but is not infinitely divided because the actual number will be finite.

Whitehead claims that this view of time (called 'the epochal theory of time') as coming in complete wholes (actual occasions) alone meets what is valid in the problems posed by Zeno (when features of it which depend on the limited mathematics of his time are removed, as they can be). This is one of the few cases where he actually gives an argument in favour of one of his claims. For Whitehead does not think that a metaphysical system like his should be established on the basis of argument in the usual sense. The method of speculative metaphysics is to use experience as the basis for elaborating a system of ideas which is to be tested by its ability to provide a place for everything which it is generally admitted that there is.

Speculative Philosophy is the endeavour to frame a coherent, logical, necessary system of general ideas in terms of which every element of our experience can be interpreted. By this notion of 'interpretation' I mean that everything of which we are conscious, as enjoyed, perceived, willed, or thought, shall have the character of a particular instance of the general scheme. Thus the philosophical scheme should be coherent, logical, and, in respect to its interpretation, applicable and adequate. Here 'applicable' means that some items of experience are thus interpretable, and 'adequate' means that there are no items incapable of such interpretation. 'Coherence', as here employed, means that the fundamental ideas, in terms of which the scheme is developed, presuppose each other so that in isolation they are meaningless. (PR, 3/5)

VII Whitehead on Ordinary Macroscopic Objects

Something must now be said as to how it is that we do not consciously prehend individual actual occasions, but only those groups or 'societies' of them which constitute the ordinary macroscopic objects of daily life. This occurs through a phase in the concrescence of an actual occasion (which I have so far ignored) called 'transmutation', in which the prehensions of many individual actual occasions are fused so as to make them seem like a single genuine individual, which, in fact, only single actual occasions are. These things which seem like genuine individuals to us (that is, to the series of actual occasions which constitute our mental life) are nexuses.[13]

Thus the ordinary things of daily life, such as trees, tables, animals, or human bodies are each, in reality, an enormous number of actual occasions connected to each other in an especially intimate way (that is, their objectification into each other is peculiarly strong). But by the process of transmutation they become, for the concrescing actual occasion into which they have been objectified, as though they were just one entity. (I must say that 'transmutation' does not seem to explain this process, but merely gives it a name.)

Nexuses of course are of different types. Animals, taken *in toto* (mind and body) are nexuses subject to the guidance of one top actual occasion (or series of such). They are monarchies. On the other hand, plants probably, and stones almost certainly, are democracies, for no one of the actual occasions constituting them has pretensions to be in charge.

Nexuses are sometimes called societies of actual occasions. And these societies divide into several types.

(1) There are societies which constitute ordinary physical objects. At any one moment there is a set of contemporary actual occasions which are what the physical object really is then. At the next moment it consists in another group of such occasions, which follow on from the previous ways in an especially intimate way. Or to be more accurate, as White-

head sees it, at any one moment only a part of such things exists, for the real things are stretched out in time as well as space.

(2) Some societies do not contain contemporaries, but only one actual occasion at a time, which carry on from each other in a distinctively personal way. An individual human consciousness is a society of this kind, and in virtue of this they are called societies possessing personal order. (See PR, 90/138. I must say that I think it a very odd use of the word 'society' to apply it to something of which only one member exists at any one time.)

(3) Some societies have a dominant actual occasion, or series of actual occasions, which occupies a special role in deciding what the rest of the society will do. As conscious human organisms, this is what we are.

These nexuses which constitute ordinary macroscopic objects may seem far from those objects as they appear to us. They are rather less remote from the character which they wear for science, as made up of groups of atoms, etc. However, Whitehead up to a point interprets them (at least in *Science and the Modern World*) as rather nearer to their visible or audible character than science seems to. For he holds that so-called secondary qualities are out there in the world. Thus the colour of an object actually travels from its surface along the light waves to that event within the brain which is our seeing of it and to which the song of a bird is similarly transmitted through space and relevant brain events. That is, it is some-how being experienced by the whole series of actual occasions which constitute (or are the inner being) of all these physical processes.

Locke ... places mass among the primary qualities of bodies. In short, he elaborates a theory of primary and secondary qualities in accordance with the state of physical science at the close of the seventeenth century. The primary qualities are the essential qualities of substances whose spatio-temporal relationships constitute nature. The orderliness of these relationships constitutes the order of nature. The occurrences of nature are in some way apprehended by minds, which are associated with living bodies. Primarily, the mental apprehension is aroused by the occur-rences in certain parts of the correlated body, the occurrences in the brain, for instance. But the mind in apprehending also experiences sensations which, prop-erly speaking, are qualities of the mind alone. These sensations are projected by the mind so as to clothe appropriate bodies in external nature. Thus the bodies are perceived as with qualities which in reality do not belong to them, qualities which in fact are purely the offspring of the mind. Thus nature gets credit which should in truth be reserved for ourselves: the rose for its scent: the nightingale for his song: and the sun for his radiance. The poets are entirely mistaken. They should address their lyrics to themselves, and should turn them into odes of self-congratulation on the excellency of the human mind. Nature is a dull affair, soundless, scentless, colourless; merely the hurrying of material, endlessly, meaninglessly.

However you disguise it, this is the practical outcome of the characteristic scientific philosophy which closed the seventeenth century.

In the first place, we must note its astounding efficiency as a system of concepts for the organization of scientific research. In this respect, it is fully worthy of the genius of the century which produced it. It has held its own as the guiding principle of scientific studies ever since. It is still reigning. Every university in the world organizes itself in accordance with it. No alternative system of organizing the pursuit of scientific truth has been suggested. It is not only reigning, but it is without a rival.

And yet—it is quite unbelievable. (smw, 71–2)

As against this view Whitehead sought to make nature something more concrete and appealing, and his rather strange view of secondary qualities as felt by the external stimuli to our perception of them is the only one which allows them some kind of objective reality which his main principles allow.

Hartshorne rejected this surprising realist view of secondary qualities, holding, for example, that colours come into existence only with eyes. However, he was prepared, if I follow him rightly, to allow that secondary qualities may pertain to the neurons in our brain, and even to some of our other bodily cells, but are unlikely to be similar to anything outside human or animal bodies. (See Griffin, 'Hartshorne's Differences'.)

VIII Whitehead on Causation

Whitehead claims that his account of the relation between successive actual occasions dispels the mystery of what causation is which has haunted philosophy, especially since Hume. Not, of course, that he believed in deterministic causation; but he did believe that the character of the world at one moment put definite limitations upon what could happen next and in the lower orders of reality effectively settled it.

Traditional notions according to which substances carry no essential message, says Whitehead, about their past are bound to have problems with causation. The problem is even worse for empiricists like Hume, for whom each event has a complete character in its own right, with no necessary connection with anything past or to come. (Indeed, the logical consequence of this is that no one can rationally avoid solipsism.)

Whitehead thought that his notion of the real entry of the past into the present (and thence future) somehow explained causation. Hume found nothing in causation but one damn thing following on another according to a rule for which there was no ultimate rationale. But, according to Whitehead, somehow we do experience one thing making another thing happen or, rather, strongly influencing it to happen, when we search for it in our more basic somatic and emotional feelings.

This can be understood more fully (according to Whitehead) once we distinguish two types of perception, perception in the mode of presentational immediacy and perception in the mode of causal efficacy. The former gives us (under ideal conditions) the bright sunlit world of sight and the sonorous world of sound, while the latter consists in one's sense of one's own body and a dim sense of the surrounding world and what it is doing in it. Thus, in visual perception everything is clearly presented, but there is no real efficacy, no sign of anything making anything else happen. Through bodily experience, in contrast, we experience real causation. We do so for example when a flash of light *makes* our eyes blink. This is an experience of something which the body is forced to do, not a succession presented to sight. And more generally (though Whitehead is short on examples) we feel other bodies acting on us and one part of our body on another, something which no merely visually presented succession can display. What vision does, however, is steer us more efficiently around the world of whose existence bodily sense makes us undeniably aware.[14] (See PR, 173–5/263–9.)

For what gives us our sense, and not mere sense but knowledge, of causation comes from the other type of perception (perception in the mode of causal efficacy), through which we experience our own bodies. This is less precise in its message but exhibits real causal processes going on.

The former mode [perception in the mode of causal efficacy] produces percepta which are vague, not to be controlled, heavy with emotion: it produces the sense of derivation from an immediate past, and of passage to an immediate future; a sense of emotional feeling, belonging to oneself in the past, passing into oneself in the present, and passing from oneself in the present towards oneself in the future; a sense of influx of influence from other vaguer presences in the past, localized and yet evading local definition, such influence modifying, enhancing, inhibiting, diverting, the stream of feeling which we are receiving, unifying, enjoying, and transmitting. This is our general sense of existence, as one item among others, in an efficacious actual world. . . .

[In contrast, the] percepta in the mode of presentational immediacy have the converse characteristics. In comparison, they are distinct, definite, controllable, apt for immediate enjoyment, and with the minimum of reference to past, or to future. We are subject to our percepta in the mode of efficacy, we adjust our percepta in the mode of immediacy. (PR, 178–9/271)

Since real causation cannot be cognized by the distance senses of vision and hearing (perception in the mode of sensible immediacy), while these provide the sole data on which empiricists like Hume base their theories, such theorists have found causality a problem, and have only been able to explain it inadequately in terms of constant conjunction.

It seems to me that the example of blinking is not a helpful example for Whitehead's view on causation. For, according to his metaphysic, the cause only influences the effect to contain something of its own character, but still leaves it an element of freedom as to how it combines its data into what sort of whole (at the level of satisfaction). Yet it seems that the blinking of an eye is a clear case of causation where the effect is completely involuntary. How far has Whitehead really helped us to understand causation, and along with this, exhibit why we need not be troubled by those sceptical worries about induction which have haunted philosophy since Hume's insistence that there was no necessary connection between cause and effect? I am inclined to think that Whitehead was on to something here, though I would not endorse the details of his account. For one thing, 'objectification' and 'prehension' seem to me notions riddled with problems. On the other hand, I do think it true that our present experience carries with it a valid sense that it could only have occurred in a social and physical situation, stretching quite far into the past, of which we have quite a good and undeniably true more or less specific idea. As for induction, we can be sure that the future is one which is fit to be a continuation of this present time, along with its history.

A word should be said here about the laws of nature on Whitehead's view. According to Whitehead, the world process moves through changing cosmic epochs, and each epoch has its own laws of nature (and even its own spatial geometry). 'Thus the laws of nature are merely all-pervading patterns of behaviour of which the shift and discontinuance lie beyond our ken' (MODES, 143). That these patterns of change remain largely constant for so long is due only to what we called the laziness of the actual occasions which constitute the inanimate world, which in most respects are content to carry on in the old way as the past from which they issue is objectified within them. Though in principle they may do what they like in making something new out of what they receive from the past, the normal thing (at least in what passes for the merely physical world) is for them to repeat the dominant way in which the past actual occasions have interacted and followed one upon another. And this means that the world carries on as usual, with real originality occurring only in human minds and only there to a limited extent for most of us. Only if actual occasions of a highly creative character occur, do the normal forms of transition get changed. (See MODES, 100.) And when this happens on a large scale, we move to another cosmic epoch, in which the originality of the finest human minds may extend to the world at large.

Hartshorne, I believe, largely agrees with this treatment of causation, induction, etc.

IX Whitehead on Science and What It Leaves Out

For Whitehead, science is the one and only path to one sort of truth: namely, the truth about the logico-mathematical structure of things. But it leaves out the full concreteness of whatever it describes.

One of the most striking ways in which Whitehead thinks this so comes from his belief that there are no repetitions in reality. That is, no ultimate individual is exactly the same in character as any other. For each has a unique position in reality, and is uniquely related to other unique things. And this enters into its very own character within its own bounds. In contrast, it seems to be the standard scientific view (both in Whitehead's time and now) that two atoms, or two temporal stages of two different atoms, in different spatio-temporal positions may be absolutely identical in character.

This goes with Whitehead's view that the world is quite novel at each moment. That is a large part of what he means by speaking of the constant creativity of reality. (This constancy, and some basic structural features—as, for example, the abstract structure of every actual occasion—being its only constant character.)

It seems to me that there is a certain problem in Whitehead's thought here. For the novel character of each actual occasion (in its stages of satisfaction, for which see below) was, so to speak, waiting for it in the realm of eternal objects and 'ingresses' into it from there. But are not eternal objects precisely what one would expect to allow for sameness across space and time? Hartshorne avoids this problem, but only by what seems to me an ill-advised rejection of the realm of eternal objects. But I shall not enter into the matter further here and shall ignore it in what follows.

X Panpsychism

1. For Whitehead, each actual occasion is, as it has been put, a drop of experience or feeling. So reality consists simply in innumerable such drops which affect each other in a variety of ways. But there is some difficulty in knowing quite how to take the words 'experience' and 'feeling'. The most obvious interpretation is that these drops are brief moments of consciousness. And this suggests that Whitehead is a panpsychist, for whom the world is composed entirely of sentient individuals (individuals such that there is something which it is like to be them). However, we are warned against this by various commentators.

2. This is usually because they think panpsychism too absurd a view for Whitehead to have held it. But it is mere prejudice to reject panpsychism as absurd until you have investigated its claims. Moreover, we should try to understand Whitehead without presupposing that they will not seem strange to the conventional mind.

Still, it is true that Whitehead himself certainly denies that all actual occasions, or all aspects of them, are 'conscious' as he understands the term. And from one point of view this makes his philosophy more plausible. For if actual occasions need not be conscious, or not wholly so, that explains why one's mental state as one introspects it (or retrospects one just past) does not seem to have the elaborate structure ascribed to it by Whitehead.

And certainly I, and presumably others, cannot find in my conscious experience anything corresponding to the whole elaborate process of concrescence, ideal aim, and final 'satisfaction' of which he talks. If much of this is unconscious, then matters are a little improved. Yet in other ways his doctrine becomes more obscure.

3. As Whitehead uses the expression, consciousness is predicable of actual occasions containing an act of judgement of a certain sort. In such judgements the character of some particular thing (normally a nexus of actual occasions rather than just one) prehended physically is compared with some eternal object prehended conceptually (that is, not through the medium of some past actual occasion into which it has 'ingressed') and noted as similar or dissimilar to it to some degree. The idea of such a relation between the character of some particular thing and an eternal object is (in Whitehead's terminology) 'a proposition'. As such it may enter our mind without being judged as true or false. But if it is so judged, correctly or incorrectly, to be true or false, then we

have consciousness. In this case we feel 'the contrast of theory, as mere theory, with fact, as mere fact'. We have consciousness also, I think, if a proposition is recognized as a way things might have been (PR, 188/286; see further at PR, 267 ff./407 ff.).

Personally, I prefer to use 'consciousness' to refer to any genuinely lived experience, whether it contains any sort of judgement or not. This could be a merely verbal divergence from Whitehead. (Compare Ch. 6, section VII.)

However, the thought lingers that for Whitehead 'feeling' includes much that is unconscious, even in my sense—things which are not part of what makes it like the feeling subject as it then is. But if this is so, then he seems to have abandoned what he calls the reformed subjectivist principle.

4. This is the claim that there is no unexperienced reality.

The difficulties of all schools of modern philosophy lie in the fact that, having accepted the subjectivist principle, they continue to use philosophical categories derived from another point of view. These categories are not wrong, but they deal with abstractions unsuitable for metaphysical use.... They have generated two misconceptions: one is the concept of vacuous actuality, void of subjective experience; and the other is the concept of quality inherent in substance. In their proper character, as high abstractions, both of these notions are of the utmost pragmatic use. In fact, language has been formed chiefly to express such concepts. It is for this reason that language, in its ordinary usages, penetrates but a short distance into the principles of metaphysics. *Finally, the reformed subjectivist principle must be repeated: that apart from the experiences of subjects there is nothing, nothing nothing, bare nothingness.* (PR, 167/253–4, my italics)

Such fulminations against the vacuous actuality ascribed to matter on standard philosophical (and common-sense) views are hard to understand if he is not rejecting the idea of things which are actual, without in any way being experienced, in a pregnant sense of 'experienced'. It also goes with his commendation of F. H. Bradley for his insistence on the basic nature of feeling. For Bradley certainly used 'experience' and 'feeling' to refer to genuinely subjective states.[15]

5. Besides which, in describing actual occasions, even those which are unconscious in his sense, he uses such psychological expressions as their 'emotional intensity', 'decisions' which they take, and so on, and this seems to confirm that they are, in a broad sense, conscious even if they are not so in Whitehead's restricted sense. For I don't see how something which doesn't really feel itself can be emotionally intense to any degree.

Among many passages which might be quoted in this connection I give just one:

The primitive form of physical experience is emotional—blind emotion—received as felt elsewhere in another occasion and formally appropriated as a subjective passion. In the language appropriate to the higher stages of experience, the primitive element is *sympathy*, that is, feeling the feeling *in* another and feeling conformally *with* another. (PR, 162/246)

This certainly seems to say that physical experience is emotional, even if it is only in the higher forms of experience that it can properly be called 'sympathy'.

It may be said that this is a remark about physical experience, rather than physical existence, and does not concern what is merely physical. But this is to forget that for Whitehead 'experience' is an expression applicable properly to every physical process. So what is being said is that all physical process is emotional, whether 'blindly' or otherwise. This, and many other passages which could be quoted, seems to make clear that physical processes are all felt in the same basic sense in which I can feel a headache. (See, for example, PR, 267/408, where he speaks of physical energy as consisting of 'throbs of emotional energy'. See also PR, 116/178.)

6. Another thing which Whitehead says on this topic is that some of the content of high-level actual occasions is conscious, some of it unconscious.

This account agrees with the plain facts of our conscious experience. Consciousness flickers; and even at its brightest, there is a small focal region of clear illumination, and a large penumbral region of experience which tells of intense experience in dim apprehension. The simplicity of clear consciousness is no measure of the complexity of complete experience. Also this character of our experience suggests that consciousness is the crown of experience, only occasionally attained, not its necessary base. (See also PR, 267/408; 85/130–1; 266/406)

This may be true enough if we take 'conscious' in Whitehead's sense. But in the broader sense in which everything genuinely felt is conscious, it surely cannot be. Yet it seems to me impossible that something which has the unitary quality attributed by Whitehead to actual occasions can be part unconscious (in the sense of not really felt) and part conscious (really felt). For that divides the actual occasion into two different sorts of parts (the conscious and the unconscious), from which I think it would follow that it cannot be a real unit such as Whitehead's actual occasions are supposed to be. Certainly some features of our experiences are dim and, as it were, in the background. But this is a feature of them as they belong in our consciousness, not the fact that they are, so to speak, half in and half out of it.

7. I conclude that Whitehead was a panpsychist who identified reality with felt experience, and that all such expertise comes in momentary wholes which he calls actual occasions, but that his position is problematic, because our actual experience quite lacks the complexity which he describes these wholes as having.

I admit that there is a case against using 'conscious' in such a broad sense as I do. However, it seems to me that without doing so, one runs the risk of making the doctrine of panpsychism less challenging than it really is.

8. Perhaps I should make it clear that I am far from denying that we have unconscious experiences. But these experiences really do not pertain to the whole which is our genuinely lived-through conscious life. They must consist, I suggest, in streams of experiences distinct from the 'dominant' experience which expresses itself in speech and deliberate action and which refers to itself by the first-person pronoun or the similarly dominant stream of experience of animals, and probably other things too. Of course this 'unconscious' experience influences our conscious or personally lived through experience, especially by producing thoughts and feelings which, while certainly conscious in our broad sense, are so only as lurking in the background. And in cases of multiple personality, doubtless it is one of these other streams which takes command of all deliberate speech and action, pushing the previously dominant stream of experience on one side. Moreover, like our conscious experience, they are part of what constitutes the inner nature of brain process, and like this, they are conscious in themselves, merely cut off from the dominant consciousness though intimately influencing it.

9. Hartshorne, at any rate, was openly a panpsychist, though he preferred the term 'psychicalism' to 'panpsychism'. He is confident that the world consists entirely of experiences: more specifically, of streams of experience. He accepts something like Whitehead's notion of prehension. Likewise, he thinks that past experiences literally become parts of later experiences (indeed, all of them do so enter into God). I cannot

personally accept this, but at least Hartshorne is not lumbered with the whole apparatus of Whitehead's account of concrescence, etc. For by an experience he simply means something genuinely lived through, as what it is like to be a certain individual at a certain moment. I don't think that such experiences are divided into a conscious and an unconscious part. A summarizing statement is this: 'Apart from experience, the idea of reality is empty, as some though not all philosophers admit' (SYNTHESIS, 6).

Thus it is much easier to get a handle on what Hartshorne means by the claim that the world is composed of experiences than what Whitehead means. It means simply that the world consists of innumerable streams of experience which are generically like our own stream of consciousness, though of course mostly being somewhat 'dim' in various meanings of the word.

10. And from this account of the fundamental constituents of reality, Hartshorne draws the interesting conclusion that it cannot be wholly determined by anything in the past. For one's total state of consciousness at any moment is a unitary whole in which all sorts of perceptions, thoughts, memories, and so forth are synthesized. And each state of consciousness has its own unique character, which cannot have been put together mechanically by any psychological or physical law governing how its parts came together. For it simply does not have parts in the sense of components which could have occurred without any difference at all in other wholes. So each whole of experience is a fresh creation, which Hartshorne interprets as the product of its own free will. (See SYNTHESIS, 5–8.)

Thus it is not the precise character of a momentary experience which is determined by its past but only the options which are open to it. The fact that *most* moments of experience give themselves a character which is only very slightly novel, in its context, is not known about individually. For, human experience apart, we know little of individual moments of experience, only their gross effects upon us (or the place they hold in an abstract structure). So it may easily look as though nature is deterministic, and that no free choices (within narrow limits) are going on in most of it.

This is rather persuasive, and does, I think, show that total experiences have a character which is not altogether settled by general laws. I do not see, however, that it shows that there may not be a certain necessity with which they follow on one another. So though, for this and other reasons,

I agree that physical determinism is a dubious claim, it does not follow that determinism is false; that is, it does not follow that there is any real openness as to what will follow on from one moment to another, either in an individual consciousness or in some more comprehensive reality. But I fully concur with Hartshorne's panpsychism, which does not suffer from the artificial structure to which Whitehead thinks every experience must conform.

11. Before we leave the panpsychism of our process philosophers, it should be pointed out, as Hartshorne frequently does, that it does not imply that every identifiable physical thing experiences its own existence. A house, for instance, and according to Hartshorne, even a tree, is composed of self-experiencing units but is not itself self-experiencing, any more than a cricket team is, each member of which is certainly conscious. Royce's panpsychism is somewhat different, inasmuch as he says that there can be things which are unconscious in virtue rather of the fact that they exist as part of things or processes which are conscious. (See W&I 2, 233.)

XI Space and Time in Process Philosophy

(A) Whitehead's Internal Time is not the Specious Present

It is very natural to suppose that the process of concrescence within an actual occasion is the same as what others describe as the experience of a specious present. And Whitehead gives some excuse for this interpretation. Indeed, it seems to have been his actual view when he wrote *Science and the Modern World*. (See SMW, 130.) Moreover, that seems to be how other process philosophers have understood, or developed, the notion of this process. But it is doubtful whether it is correct.

To decide this, let us see what the doctrine of the specious present has meant as advocated by other philosophers, and which I would myself endorse.

The doctrine can take several forms, but what seems to me the most satisfactory version is one which is advocated by William James in chapters 9 and 10 of his last work, *Some Problems of Philosophy* (also Royce and Santayana).

Without entering into too much detail, this doctrine may be summed up thus. A stretch of experienced time has two aspects: (1) it is a series of total momentary (but not instantaneous) experiences, and (2) within each total momentary experience there is a short temporal process which is experienced as a unity. There is a distinction within the total experience between its earlier and later phases, but these come together as the content of a single experience just as left and right do, above and below, near and far, in the experience of a volume of space. Thus, in hearing a piece of music, there is a series of total experiences, each of which is the experience of a short stretch of the music experienced as a unity.

Think of it like this. There is nothing which can be called a single experience which you have enjoyed during any single day, or even during any single half-hour. On the other hand, if you see a flag flapping, a short stretch of such flapping is experienced as a unity. Or contrast actually seeing the hand moving on a clock and having distinct experiences each of it in a fresh single position. (It makes a difference whether the clock is digital or analogue, but the same contrast exists in each case.)

For James, as for me, this is not just an account of time as experienced. It is also true of time in general, granted the truth of panpsychism, which I join with the James of that period in endorsing. However, since there are many streams of experience, time must be conceived as composed of many such stretches of experienced time. There are various alternative ways of conceiving how these many distinct stretches of change combine to form a single world time (or something close to it), but I shall have to leave that unexplored here.

Let us now consider just one single stretch of experienced time and represent it as consisting of

/fghij/klmno/pqrst/uvwxy/

where each group of five letters, enclosed within a forward slash, represents a specious present.

It is to be emphasized that f does genuinely come before g, g genuinely does come before h, h genuinely does come before i, i genuinely does come before j. But it is also true that j genuinely comes before k, o genuinely comes before p, and so on. So what is the difference between (say) /fghij/ and j/klmn? The answer is that the former is a single unitary experience as the latter is not. (Doubtless k is, so to speak, redolent of j, but it is a kind of echo of it, not j itself, so that whereas i and j are elements of a unitary experience, it is only an echo of j which is part of the same experience as k.)

Now this seems very like Whitehead's view of a series of actual occasions such as constitutes the 'life' of a single experiencing individual. (Even if not all experiences belong in what can be regarded as the life of such a single continuant, some do: namely, those which form what he calls a personal society.) For does not an actual occasion similarly have a series of phases which may be represented as fghij? Moreover, both James and Whitehead count it in favour of this view that it solves Zeno's most famous paradoxes. (See PR, 35/55, 68–9/106–7, and 307/468.)

All the same, there is this big difference. For on Whitehead's view (at least in PR) f does not really come temporally before g, or g before h, or h before i. In short, the process fghij is not a temporal process, whereas on James's account it is. Certainly Whitehead is clear that the duration of an actual occasion is by no means instantaneous in clock time. But the duration in clock time is more a matter of how it stands to a larger system of reality than itself alone.

It took me some time to realize just how different Whitehead's view is from the one which I have learnt from James and others. Yet it does have quite a lot in common with it. For both theories make any stretch of time not a continuum, but a 'well-ordered' series of experiential units including a process within them, and which each take a certain length of clock time. Within that period of clock time there could have been more such experiential units, and there is in principle no limit to how many more. In that sense, time is infinitely divisible in principle, but in fact is divided into ultimate units of duration.

Now I find James's view much more persuasive, if only because the process of concrescence as Whitehead characterizes it seems quite unlike anything which I believe myself ever to have experienced, whereas my experience does seem to me promisingly described by James. It is indeed extraordinarily difficult to know how one should describe the temporality of one's own experience, but James seems at least to be firing in the right direction, as Whitehead does not. Of course, a supporter of Whitehead will say that the process is not meant to be fully conscious—but I have already expressed some doubt about this claim.

Related to these matters is the question of how long in clock time an actual occasion lasts. And how long does a specious present last on James's account?

Hartshorne, whose epochal theory of time is, I believe, nearer to that of James than that of Whitehead, suggests that a human specious present lasts about one-tenth of a second. (See SYNTHESIS, 175.) I should have thought it rather longer, but that is not my present concern. Should we then take it that this is about the duration in clock time of an actual occasion for Whitehead, or at least of an actual occasion such as a human mind lives through? I do not know the answer, since I find the notion of an actual occasion conceived as having no temporal process within it so obscure.

However, Hartshorne in the same chapter rather interestingly discusses why our experience as it unrolls does not seem to come in distinct moments (SYNTHESIS, 194). The answer is that we only perceive it vaguely, and therefore are not aware of the joints. But if these moments of experience are something which we really live through, this is hardly satisfactory. For even if we are not (and indeed, cannot be) casting a mental eye over our momentary experiences at the time at which we have them, and so cannot characterize them on the basis of introspection, we should be able to learn something about them through retrospection. (Compare Bradley in 'Our Knowledge of Immediate Experience', ETR, ch. 6.) My own suggestion of a better answer is that we do not experience the transitions between experiences but only the experiences themselves, and these are not composed of distinct constituents. (I have discussed all this at some length in JAMES AND BRADLEY.)

But the whole matter will remain problematic so long as it remains obscure whether actual occasions are supposed to be real, subjectively felt experiences, which we can recognize in our own experience, or merely posits in a theory.

10. I should remark, to avoid misunderstanding, that James was earlier committed to a quite different notion of the specious present. This is presented in his *The Principles of Psychology*, chapter 9, before he moved to the conception of it which I have just sketched.

That other conception of the specious present does not take it as consisting in an ultimate unit of time which is experienced as a whole, and is not an 'instant' as that has usually been conceived. Rather, on this view there are instants, but at each instant something of the past is also included as experienced, though not as genuinely stretched out in time. But in the later position there are no instants of time, only drops of experience which include a temporal process within them.

I explore James's different conceptions quite elaborately in my JAMES AND BRADLEY, 198–214, to which the reader is invited to refer if he or she wishes a more thorough treatment of this whole issue.

(B) The Nature of Space is Problematic for any Form of Panpsychism

There are some difficulties in grasping how a world which really consists in streams of actual occasions can answer to the descriptions which we give of it at a common-sense level. Moreover, we largely identify individual things by their present position in space, and events by their position in time. The position of events in time, according to process philosophy, is not without its difficulties, but their position in space is still more problematic.

Space, as it seems to me, poses something of a problem for any form of panpsychism, whether it be associated with process philosophy or not. For space is that which allows many actual occasions or distinct total experiences to exist together at one moment, and it is quite difficult to see what this togetherness is. Certainly it seems impossible that your stream of experience, mine, and those which constitute the inner being of all the basic components of the universe could be in space as we are accustomed to imagine it. As I shall shortly be advocating panpsychism myself, this is an issue which concerns me as much as it should any process philosopher. Whitehead, indeed, discusses the nature of space at length, but little attention is paid to it (so I have found) in most commentaries.

Time, then, for Whitehead, consists in the continual 'perishing' of actual occasions as subjectively immediate, and their 'objectification' in other occasions, and more eminently in the never completed actual entity, God. However, within each actual occasion there is a process of another kind: the internal process through which it combines the occasions belonging to its past into a freshly synthesized whole. Matters are complicated, however, by Whitehead's version of relativity theory.

Hartshorne's conception of both experience and time is more straightforward. God is a series of momentary, but infinitely comprehensive, experiences, each exemplifying the same divine essence, but enriched by a fresh synthesis of this with all the experiences which have ever occurred (these being now all parts of its own being), and each in the process of preparing these as the data out of which the next generation of experiential units will weave their own character. For Hartshorne there is an absolute NOW, and metaphysics will eventually show how this is compatible with relativity theory. But he and Whitehead agree that time consists in a process in which experiences lose their presentness, but become parts of the experiences which follow them. Not that this account is without its problems, but it provides a reasonably clear idea of the nature of time.

As for space, Hartshorne, in what I know of his work, scarcely says much about it, but simply takes it for granted. Whitehead, in contrast, has said a lot about space in a highly technical way. I must limit my discussion to my faltering understanding of the relevant parts of *Process and Reality* and other closely related works.

A point which I should mention but shall not much examine is that Whitehead regards space and time as jointly constituting what he calls the 'extensive continuum'. Since he clearly distinguishes the spatial dimensions of this continuum from its temporal dimension, we can reasonably discuss the nature of space and the nature of time as distinct issues. Another important point is that, so far as space goes, our space is just one form which it can take and in which it answers to Euclidean geometry or at least to a geometry which we can treat as Euclidean for most ordinary purposes. But fortunately there is no need for any detailed geometrical examination here (for which I am ill fitted).

As a first shot at what space is for Whitehead, consider this:

The title of one outstanding philosophical treatise, belonging to the generation now passing, is 'Space, Time and Deity.' By this phrase, Samuel Alexander places before us the problem which haunts the serious thought of mankind. 'Time' refers to the transitions of process, 'space' refers to the static necessity of each form of interwoven existence, and 'deity' expresses the lure of the ideal which is the potentiality beyond immediate fact. (MODES, 101)

We normally think of space as that whole in which things can exist together at any particular moment of time. However, we confront straightaway the claim of Whitehead that contemporary actual occasions are, while they are 'subjectively immediate', out of all real connection with each other. In particular, they cannot prehend each other.

For the only other occasions which an occasion prehends are those in its past. The reason for this is fairly simple. The contemporary actual occasions, while they possess subjective immediacy, and have not yet become objectively immortal in later occasions (and in God), are each producing their own new objective character by working on the data supplied by previous occasions (and the eternal objects which they prehend). And, because each is busy with its own self-creation, it cannot interrupt this by obtaining fresh data from the others.

So at a particular moment of time, the actual occasions occurring then are cut off from each other. They will, however, be in contact again when they exist as prehended objects within the actual occasions which replace them. So if space is the basic way in which contemporary occasions are able to be together and act on each other, it seems to follow that their spatial relations are really a matter of their future connections (as determined by their past and their self-creation when subjectively immediate).

All right, perhaps; but what is the space in which they are together afterwards? This seems problematic to me even if we ignore the problem posed by relativity, that there is no absolute simultaneity. It is with some trepidation that I discuss the matter at all, since Whitehead has written many highly technical treatments of time and space, much of which I have not studied and much of which is well beyond my intellectual resources. But I am troubled by something which I believe is not a technical problem about space, such as requires a complicated mathematical treatment, but something much more general about it. I am concerned, I should add, solely with space as he conceived it at the time of *Process and Reality*. For his discussions of time and space in earlier works such as *The Concept of Nature* are prior to the development of the metaphysics of process which is my concern.

My problem is that I seem to find three different accounts of space in Whitehead's process system.

(C) First Interpretation: The Perspectives on Nothing Conception of Space

If one takes one's clue from *Science and the Modern World*, in the chapter on 'Relativity', one might suppose his view to be the following.

Every actual occasion is presented to every other one in a spatial arrangement perceived or prehended from a certain perspective. The position in space of any one of them is then determined by two facts: (1) the perspective from which it prehends other actual occasions and (2) its position in the perspectival field of all the others.

Perhaps this somewhat reductive and rather Leibnizian view of space is the position of *Process and Reality*.[16] If so, I find it troubling just as it stands, without some account of a reality on which these various perspectives are perspectives. For surely these perspectival facts must have a more realist foundation in a non-perspectival but somehow spatial arrangement in which the actual occasions stand to each other. Because it seems to deny this, I shall call it *the perspectives on nothing view*.

If this view is metaphysically correct, real space is quite unlike space as we ordinarily conceive it, much more so than a process view of time is, at any rate in the hands of Hartshorne, and would be in Whitehead's too if we took the process of concrescence as a temporal process, occurring within a specious present, as Whitehead does in *Science and the Modern World*. (However, we have seen that this seems not to be his position in *Process and Reality*.) For the temporality of the world can reasonably be conceived as at least analogous to the temporality which holds within a specious present, but the view that space exists only as a construct out of innumerable distinct perspectives on it makes it altogether remote from what we normally think of space as being. The space of the life world may be a human or animal construction rather than an objective fact, but as we live our construction, it is the latter.

(D) Second Interpretation: The Real Voluminous Conception of Space

Once I thought that his view in *Process and Reality* was not this, but rather the view that each actual occasion has a real inherent and experienced voluminousness of its own, and that it is thus that it fills out a spatial region. In which case, presumably this voluminousness is part of the voluminousness which constitutes the total space in which all things exist at any one moment, even if they are not then in causal interaction. But I remain unsure as to whether this is really his view. This may be Hartshorne's view, and whether or not it is quite Whitehead's position, it deserves exploration. I shall call it the *real voluminousness* view.

On this interpretation, an actual occasion is spread out in public space and time, just as it is spread out in the space and time of its own immediate experience—in fact, the latter is just a fragment of the former.[17] This seems to me much more persuasive in the case of time. But that it can be spread out in public space in any genuine way, I find it hard to believe. Moreover, even as an account of time, while it would be quite persuasive on the *Science and the Modern World* view, it is much less so on his later view that concrescence is not really a temporal process at all.

Certainly a total moment of experience is spatial in the sense that it feels like a stretched-out whole in which my body is somehow at the centre with other things stretching out from it. But this cannot be how it really is, for the world as a whole cannot have me in this central position; nor can it have that absolute sort of nearness and distance which things have within one's somatico-perceptual field. So real space must be something quite other than space as we experience it. And I can only conclude that it is something like the abstract structure of the possibilities of communication and influence between different centres of experience (this being determined for an absolute idealist by some arrangement within the Absolute). This theme is developed in the next chapter.

This real voluminousness view, then, that space and time characterize the whole world in just the same way as they characterize each actual occasion, or momentary experience, but on a larger scale, is quite persuasive, whether finally acceptable or not, in the case of time. But it is much less so in the case of space. For the spatial voluminousness which does indeed belong phenomenologically, and therefore truly, to our moments of experience, cannot be a part of a larger voluminousness to which my experience at a moment and yours both belong.

But nor can I be satisfied with the perspectives on nothing view that what unites us is that we each have a perspectival presentation of each other. For this leaves us with a world without any real wholeness to it.[18] I, at least, find this incredible. (But what of God? Is he not the ultimate unifier of the world?)

(E) Third Interpretation: Space as a System of Vectors Passing through Distinct Actual Occasions

So, as my third attempt to understand Whitehead's view of space, I turn now to what he says about 'Strains' in Part IV, chapter 4, of *Process and Reality*. And if I come anywhere near understanding this, he says there that there are straight lines, or vectors, passing from the centre of consciousness *in* my body *into* regions outside it. And ordinary perception by way of the distance senses consists in the fact that sensa derived from the past are projected on to regions which I identify by the direction and distance of straight lines which pass through me to them.

But this seems to be a version of the view that the voluminousness of public space is basically of the same kind as the voluminousness of my body and my environment as I experience them. And the same difficulty holds. Can there really be straight lines from the space which has me at the centre to a space which has you at the centre? Obviously we commonly believe in such a space, but I can't conceive how it could be a reality. But if what is in question is a space without a centre, then it is no part of our experience and cannot figure in a world in which experience is all.

(F) A Question about Shape

Another question I would put to process philosophers is: Do actual occasions have a shape, and if so in what sense? For surely, if they are in space, they must have a shape, granted that mere points are explicitly excluded as real existents by Whitehead? In fact, I could also do with some help on the shape of nexuses.

As a final comment, I remark that Whitehead and Hartshorne speak of the universe as an 'ocean of feeling'. But it is hard to accept this as a metaphor for describing their position, granted (1) that contemporary actual occasions are quite cut off from one another and (2) that actual occasions are connected only after their existence as actually felt individual feelings (i.e. when objectified in something later than their own moment of subjective immediacy).

(G) God and Creation

The traditional Judaeo-Christian and, I believe, Islamic view is that God created the world *ex nihilo* at the beginning (whether of time or of the universe). Before that (if there was a 'before that') there was nothing but God.

But so far as I can see, neither of our process philosophers went along with this. Rather, God and actual occasions have always been there, way back through an infinite past. Personally, I find the conception of an infinitely extended past (and for that matter, future) quite problematic, but many wise minds think it coherent and probably true.

God is, of course, intensely creative according to both philosophers. For at every moment he is doing his best (which must be *the* best, or *equal* best) to bring all the plurality of what is going on—that is, all that is going on in and between actual occasions, and all that has gone on—into the most harmonious whole he can manage. And this is not settled deterministically, but is an exercise more like that of artistic creation. Also, as a means to this, he is feeding each actual occasion as it first comes into existence (or becomes, as process philosophers say) with a subjective aim by which it can create something good out of itself.

Thus God is not exactly the first cause. Rather is he an essential condition of the existence of anything at any time.

(H) Time and Relativity Theory

I shall start in this section with the view of Hartshorne. According to him, the present exists, and so does the past (as objectified in God), but the future does not exist. The universe is always being added to by what was simply not part of reality at all previously. And simultaneity is an absolute, not something relative to a particular perspective on the world. For events are simultaneous which are *now* together, and continue to be so (derivatively from this) when they are not *now* at all.

Whitehead, in contrast, thought that no two actual occasions share precisely the same past, present, or future. Consider an actual occasion X. Its contemporaries are those with which it can have no causal relations. Suppose now that Y and Z are two of its contemporaries. One would expect that everything which was past for one of these three would be so for the other two. Similarly with present and future. However, according to White-head's own theory of relativity, just as for Einstein's (from which Whitehead's differs significantly), there may be—nay, are bound to be—events which belong to X's future but to Y's present and to Z's past. Thus there is no COSMIC NOW. (See PR, 65–6/101–3.)[19]

This surely is problematic for a process philosophy which wants to regard the future as absolutely open. For it implies that the future is absolutely open, but only so from the point of view of certain specific actual occasions. This even carries a hint of the eternalistic view of time, to which I shall lend my support in the next chapter. For eternalism, all times are eternally just there in the Divine Mind, or Absolute. Futurity, present-ness, and pastness are relative, not absolute, matters.

A simple way of directing oneself to the issue is to consider how it stands with God, for process philosophy. Surely God has no call to identify himself with one actual occasion rather than another for regarding things as past, present, or future. So if the future is open for him, as process philosophy insists, it seems that from his point of view, which must be the absolute truth, past, present, and future are absolute matters. What lies in his future cannot somehow be present from another perspective.

It is, indeed, difficult to think the matter out. But Hartshorne, at any rate, thought that process philosophy required that there be an absolute NOW.[20] For if no two actual occasions ever have the same past, then there is no such thing as THE PAST and no such thing as THE NOW. But that threatens the notion of a completely open future. For if what is future for one actual occasion may be past for another, while each of these occasions falls within the other's present, then the notion of what is future, and thus open, seems to be relative to a particular occasion. It follows that there is no such thing as that which is quite absolutely unsettled so far as its determinate character goes. Yet that there is such a thing seems essential to any form of process philosophy. Thus Hartshorne, so far as I can see, takes a better line here from the point of view of process philosophy. (For Hartshorne's trouble with this matter, see SYNTHESIS, 123 and 291. See also TWO PROCESS PHILOSOPHERS, 36–7.)

You may say that it is obvious that futurity and pastness are always relative. The battle of Hastings is future in relation to Caesar's crossing the Rubicon and past in relation to the battle of Waterloo. But this is not an adequate statement of our ordinary, common, non-relativistic view of time. For, according to this, one does not need to qualify the statement that something remembered lies in the past or something anticipated lies in the future, by an implicit reference to one's utterance as that in relation to which these events have these temporal properties. Rather, the remembered event and the anticipated event just are past and future, though of course the futurity and degree of pastness will be different a moment later.

This seems to be our normal common-sense idea of the matter. And it also seems to be the view required by process philosophy. But such a view is rejected by both Einstein's and Whitehead's relativity theory. Consequently, Hartshorne thought that neither relativity theory could be the absolute metaphysical truth. That Einstein's view worked well for science, he admitted, but he thought that the metaphysical truth must be otherwise. Exactly how this could be so was a continuing worry for him, but that it was so, he did not doubt.

So far as I can see, Whitehead, therefore, does not provide such a vision of an open future as does Hartshorne. Process philosophers should therefore prefer Hartshorne's view on this to Whitehead's.

Being as mathematically ignorant as I am, I say such things as this with great trepidation. But until I learn better, this is how this matter seems to me.

XII Process Theology

Perhaps the main field in which Whitehead and Hartshorne continue to be influential is in theology. For the challenge of their process theology to much of classical theology has had wide appeal. Whitehead is reported to have said: 'I consider Christian theology to be one of the great disasters of the human race' (DIALOGUES, 174). It should be emphasized that it was Christian *theology* to which he objected, not Christianity, or at any rate not Jesus as a teacher.

The features of the traditional theology of the religions of the book (Judaism, Christianity, Islam) from which process philosophers especially diverge are:

(1) The idea that God is absolutely omnipotent.

For, according to Whitehead and Hartshorne, God has to leave it to some extent to actual occasions what they do and thereby may mould the world in a way not the best in God's opinion. Nor is this because he voluntarily renounced his complete control of things so that humans could have the gift of freedom; rather, it is something which could not have been otherwise.

(2) The idea that God is unchanging.

We have seen that for both Whitehead and Hartshorne there is a contrast between an unchanging and necessary aspect to God and an aspect which is in constant change. (a) For Hartshorne the contrast is between the divine essence and the sequence of states in which this is re-actualized moment by moment. Each of these draws on the last set of experiences which have created themselves in the world, and sends out a transforming influence on its successors. (b) For Whitehead it is the contrast between God's 'primordial' and his 'consequent' nature. The former consists of what he always and unchangeably is; the latter is what he is in virtue of his commerce with the world of change.

In his primordial nature, God is aware of all eternal objects and their eternal relations one to another. These are all the characters which in principle could be actualized in existent things in the natural world of flux. In his consequent nature, God is aware of every actual occasion, once it has reached its terminal satisfaction. At that point, the occasion's process of concrescence is over and done with, but in its final determinate form, it enters the mind of God and is there for ever after, altering only in the sense that it becomes an element in a continually enlarging pattern, as more and more actual occasions similarly enter into it. (There does not seem to be any negative prehension in God.) This is what Whitehead calls the 'objective immortality' possessed by every actual occasion (and thus by the whole of what is past) when its phase of subjective immediacy is over.

Thus God does change on Whitehead's view. But since nothing is ever lost to him once it is there, he is not in flux, as are ordinary actual occasions. Whitehead refers to this as 'God's everlastingness', distinct both from his permanent primordial nature and from the perpetual 'perishing' character of actual occasions (as independent existents).

God, of course, does not merely register everything which happens, but plays an essential role in determining what will happen. For he is for ever influencing what each occasion makes of itself and passes on to subsequent occasions. (On this see more shortly.)

Whitehead thinks that this account of God shows how the cosmos (including God) satisfies the two great rival principles of philosophy: the notion of all things as in flux (Heraclitus *et al.*) and the notion of reality as static (Parmenides *et al.*). And these principles are not just descriptive, but refer to the two great rival values which, both in the natural and the human world, seem each to be unsatisfactory taken on its own.

The two great contrasts here 'are order as the condition for excellence, and order as stifling the freshness of living' (PR, 338/514). Cultures swing between these two values. This is evidenced in art. When a new style of art arrives, it brings a freshness with it which is a relief after the tedious work of artists who just go on doing the standard thing. And so that style of art becomes accepted as the norm. But in doing so, it gradually becomes ossified and tedious. Then a new style must come in with its own freshness, which will eventually ossify in its turn. And this is what Whitehead sees as the fate of all aspects of the life of a society (see PR, 340/516). Yet, as well as welcoming the new, we also hope that the old will not utterly cease, and are glad to realize that all things are preserved in God (see PR, 340/516).

There is a problem about Whitehead's God. God (he claims) is in a perpetual process of concrescence, as the data provided him by finite individuals, which he brings together and makes something novel out of, are constantly increased. But it is puzzling how this can be reconciled with his claim that God is no exception to his categorial scheme, and is structurally no different from finite actual occasions. For how can there be a process of concrescence which will never be completed, since concrescing is otherwise conceived as precisely the process through which an actual occasion gives itself a definite character (and does so, what is more, in solitude, unaffected by anything new once the concrescing has got going)? If there was supposed to be a terminal moment of time, still in the future, in which God will finally complete himself, the problem would be reduced, but not eliminated. But this seems not to be Whitehead's view; he seems to believe, rather, that time will never have a stop. So God as an actual entity is much less like an actual occasion than Whitehead allows. For Hartshorne, by contrast, the idea that time will go on for ever poses no similar problem, since each divine moment of experience comes to a conclusion just as do all finite ones.

A contrast between how Whitehead and Hartshorne see the entries of actual occasions into their objective immortality in God should be mentioned here. According to Whitehead, every actual occasion when its concrescing is over enters into God, but in doing so it loses its 'subjective immediacy' and acquires a wholly objective status. Hartshorne, in contrast, claims that God does include our individual subjective immediacy, though not as it first occurs.

I find Hartshorne's position somewhat baffling here. How can my subjective immediacy first not be an ingredient in God, and then subsequently be so? It must have changed in some way in entering into God, and this would seem to be precisely its loss of subjective immediacy. If it is said that it is subjectively immediate in God, just as it was when not within him, how do I know that my experience at the moment is presently in God or not? The question seems absurd. I am not objecting to the idea that our subjective immediacy may be an ingredient in the divine mind, for in fact

I think that it is. But this is not because first it was outside, and then inside. What seems absurd is that a change from being outside to inside God should make no difference to its felt quality.

Hartshorne, incidentally, regards himself as a 'panentheist'. A panentheist, as opposed to a pantheist, believes that the whole world is contained in God, but that there is more to God than there is in the world. Everything is inside God, once it has created itself, but it is reasonable to think that there is more to God than this quality of being a universal container, as he is for pantheism (at least as Hartshorne understands it). Whitehead, I believe, does not raise the question of whether he is or is not a panentheist. But if William Christian is right, he is not, since the cosmos as a whole is not, for him, really an individual at all. (See CHRISTIAN, 403–9.)

Both Whitehead and Hartshorne are liked by many because they emphasize creativity as the most essential feature of reality, holding that every actual occasion makes something at least a little novel out of the data it receives from the past and, in the case of Whitehead, with the aid of the appropriate eternal occasions which God presents it with.

Personally, I feel that, although there certainly is such a thing as creativity, exemplified in great music and art, process philosophers rather exaggerate the amount and degree of it that is around more generally. I am only too conscious in myself of thinking the same old thoughts, having the same old desires, and having the same old pleasures and pains. There is something in Dickens's linking particular remarks with particular people as things they say again and again. And the creativity ascribed even to the experiences which occur in what is normally thought of as inanimate is pretty slight.

XIII Whitehead's View of Religion

(A) Four Conceptions of God

Whitehead says that if we are to examine the nature of religion, we must not presuppose that it is always a good thing. It may be very bad, and it may be very good, whether from a doctrinal point of view or a moral point of view. And both in *Process and Reality* and in *Religion in the Making*, Whitehead gives a sketch of the development of religion. The earliest forms of religion, so he claims, had no rational basis, and were in fact for the most part rationalizations offered as providing a meaning for rituals which had originally been enjoyed for their own sake.

But when men rose above this primitive state, three main sorts of religion developed, which he classifies together as the 'rational religions'. (The only examples which he discusses are Buddhism and Christianity, with a side glance at Judaism, but I imagine that he is thinking of all the religions which are now called 'world religions'.) By this he means that they each have an intelligible doctrine as their basis. Although these religions bind their members together in a community, they also cater for the religious importance of solitude. For it is in our solitude that we escape most from the domination of our surroundings, and rational religions turn on beliefs which are similarly independent of mere local custom. (See RIM, 37.)

There are three conceptions of God which figure in rational religion:

1. The Eastern Asiatic concept of God as being some kind of ordering principle inherent in the world.
2. The Semitic concept of a highly personal God.
3. The pantheistic concept in which the world exists within God. (See RIM, 56–8.)

Each of these, according to Whitehead, was criticized unanswerably by Hume in his *Dialogues of Natural Religion.*

But there was a fourth, and better, conception of God in the teaching of Jesus, and at least in his earlier followers.

There is, however, in the Galilean origin of Christianity yet another suggestion which does not fit very well with any of the three main strands of thought. It does not emphasize the ruling Caesar, or the ruthless moralist, or the unmoved mover. It dwells upon the tender elements in the world, which slowly and in quietness operate by love; and it finds purpose in the present immediacy of a kingdom not of this world. Love neither rules, nor is it unmoved; also it is a little oblivious as to morals. It does not look to the future; for it finds its own reward in the immediate present. (PR, 343/520)

Such a God is to be reached 'through love and not through fear, with the help of John and not of Paul' (RIM, 63–4). This, at last, was an idea of God not repugnant to the modern mind.

This Christian tone in Whitehead's thought is combined, or so it seems to me, with a notion of God as a Nietzschean hero who does not care too much about sin or suffering, for his one great aim is intensity of feeling. For Whitehead often speaks of maximal intensity of experience as God's great aim, initially for the individual actual occasion which he seeks to influence, and via this for himself.[21] (See especially PR, 105/160.) And in doing so, he may rise above, or sink below, what we find most evil. (See next section.)

More attractive is Whitehead's remark:

The final principle of religion is that there is a wisdom in the nature of things, from which flow our direction of practice, and our possibility of the theoretical analysis of fact. It grounds this principle upon two sources of evidence, first upon our success in various special theoretical sciences, physical and others; and secondly upon our knowledge of a discernment of ordered relations, especially in aesthetic valuations, which stretches far beyond anything which has been expressed systematically in words. (RIM, 128)

And this view is associated with the idea that there is more to the world than the transitory. For everything of value is preserved in this system, as contributing 'its quality as an immortal fact to the order which informs the world' (RIM, 68).

But this makes God a highly impersonal reality. And it is doubtful how far this is Whitehead's own real view. For later he speaks of him as 'the great companion'.

As such an ideal companion, he is not all-powerful. For he leaves the different experiential centres in the world to follow the lure he holds out for them or to act in ways contrary to this. And because they are free to turn away from his guidance, there is much evil in the world. But God is always there making the best (one might say 'out of a bad job') and seeking to weave the evil in the world into a system which in its final upshot is good. (See RIM, 139.)

This is not perhaps far from a rather straightforward type of Unitarian Christianity. If one is expecting something more exciting and novel than this from Whitehead, one may be disappointed.

What needs to be added here is Whitehead's rather surprising claim in *Science and the Modern World* that the one end of religion is the worship of God.

Religion is the vision of something which stands beyond, behind, and within, the passing flux of immediate things.

The immediate reaction of human nature to the religious vision is worship. Religion has emerged into human experience mixed with the crudest fancies of barbaric imagination. Gradually, slowly, steadily the vision recurs in history, under nobler form and with clearer expression....

The vision claims nothing but worship; and worship is a surrender to the claim for assimilation, urged with the motive force of mutual love. The vision never overrules. It is always there, and it has the power of love presenting the one purpose whose fulfilment is eternal harmony. Such order as we find in nature is never force—it presents itself as the one harmonious adjustment of complex detail. Evil is the brute motive force of fragmentary purpose, disregarding the eternal vision. (SMW, 228)

(B) The Problem of Evil

This brings us to the problem of evil, as dealt with by Whitehead and also by Hartshorne.

Evil, triumphant in its enjoyment, is so far good in itself; but beyond itself it is evil in its character of a destructive agent among things greater than itself. In the summation of the more complete fact it has secured a descent towards nothingness, in contrast to the creativeness of what can without qualification be termed good. Evil is negative and destructive; what is good positive and creative. (RIM, 83)

So much for 'moral evil'. The fun (my example) which (Shakespeare's) Richard III found in being a villain is, so far as that goes, good in itself, but it clashes with the greater harmony which God is always seeking. As for physical evil or suffering, all Whitehead has to say on this here is that it is always aiming at its own elimination (which is by and large true enough). (See RIM, 82.)

Indeed, it seems to me that both Whitehead and Hartshorne pay insufficient attention to the problem of evil, and tend to give an over optimistic picture of human consciousness. Whitehead's essential position seems to be that 'The nature of evil is that the characters of things are mutually obstructive' (PR, 340/516). Thus evil is something not bad in itself, but simply, like dirt, matter in the wrong place. Every fresh actual occasion adds its bit to the creative advance of the universe. And it seems that this bit is never really bad in itself, only inapposite to the time at which it occurs. But eventually God will make it somehow contributory to the greater richness of the universe. (See PR, 223/341.)

A new actuality may occur in the wrong society, amid which its claims to efficacy act mainly as inhibitions. Then a weary task is set for creative function by an epoch of new creations to remove the inhibition. Insistence on birth at the wrong season is the trick of evil. In other words, the novel fact may throw back, inhibit, and delay. But the advance, when it does arrive will be richer in content, more fully conditioned and more stable. For in its objective efficacy an actual entity can only inhibit by reason of its alternative positive contribution. (PR, 223/341)

Thus Whitehead does not altogether celebrate the fact of time. In fact, he even runs it down to excess, in so far as he sees it as the main factor in the existence of evil. But this hardly lets God off the hook. For consider this. According to Whitehead, at every moment and place, there is an actual occasion absorbing data from its past and synthesizing it in conformity with its subjective aim into a harmonious totality. This applies to every moment of human consciousness. And where does it get its subjective aim from? Answer: from God, who feeds this moment of consciousness with awareness of the best eternal object for weaving something satisfactory out of its data. (And best, for God, it seems, means that which will most maximize intensity of feeling.) But what of the thoughts of those who crammed Jews or Gypsies into cattle trucks *en route* to the gas chambers? Did God really feed them with something serving this end? It may be said that he fed them with the best that their data allowed. But could he not have fed them with the decision to do everything they could to stop the activity in which they were engaged?

Did God perhaps offer them alternative subjective aims, suggesting the best, but allowing them to choose the worst? Or did he offer them just one, but without compelling them to adopt it? Yet it seems that they must have had some subjective aim if they were to finish creating themselves. Surely, not accepting the one offered cannot of itself be an aim. Or is the choice perhaps as to how effectively to pursue the offered aim?

In the following passage Whitehead gives the impression that God can make something good, from his own point of view, out of everything. However, this does seem to be qualified at the end by the suggestion that he only saves (as a permanent part of his consequent nature) what will be useful to his own satisfaction. But this sentence is said to be misleading by commentators, who hold that for Whitehead God preserves everything which has happened—that is, which has been experienced. This poses the problem of what God does with really evil thoughts. Or perhaps none really are evil. For Whitehead sometimes gives the impression that everyone is doing the best which they can in the circumstances. Thus, in one of his more Christian and less Nietzschean moods, he says:

The wisdom of subjective aim prehends every actuality for what it can be in such a perfected system—its sufferings, its sorrows, its failures, its triumphs, its immediacies of joy—woven by rightness of feeling into the harmony of the universal feeling, which is always immediate, always many, always one, always with novel advance, moving onward and never perishing. The revolts of destructive evil, purely self-regarding, are dismissed into their triviality of merely individual facts; and yet the good they did achieve in individual joy, in individual sorrow, in the introduction of needed contrast, is yet saved by its relation to the completed whole. The image—and it is but an image—the image under which this operative growth of God's nature is best conceived, is that of a tender care that nothing be lost.

The consequent nature of God is his judgment on the world. He saves the world as it passes into the immediacy of his own life. It is the judgment of a tenderness which loses nothing that can be saved.[22] It is also the judgment of a wisdom which uses what in the temporal world is mere wreckage. (PR, 346/524–5)

Whitehead might have taken over from Royce a more acceptable treatment of how evil can become good seen under God's eternal gaze. For Royce, as we have seen, evil is there in order that the greater good of its condemnation and defeat shall be realized. But I am not aware that Whitehead looks upon evil in this way. His position is perhaps rather a Benthamite or Nietzschean one, that the joy of a Hitler is good in itself, and even the pleasures of a torturer only bad in their consequences. This is a frightening subject. (See PR, 345–6/525–6.)

In a striking passage of *Process and Reality*, Whitehead assures us that the goal at which each actual occasion aims is an ideal presented to him by God, but that if the situation is a bad one, even God can only make the best of it, a best which may itself be bad.

This function of God is analogous to the remorseless working of things in Greek and in Buddhist thought. The initial aim is the best for that *impasse*. But if the best be bad, then the ruthlessness of God can be personified as Atè, the goddess of mischief. The chaff is burnt. What is inexorable in God, is valuation as an aim towards 'order'; and 'order' means 'society permissive of actualities with patterned intensity of feeling arising from adjusted contrasts.' (PR, 244/373)

In short, when Himmler thinks out speedier ways of exterminating Jews and Gypsies and hesitates for a moment between alternatives, God beckons him towards the one which will give both Himmler and God himself the more intense experience.

Indeed, there is something disturbing in the whole idea that intense experience for himself and us is what God primarily aims at. It is too like Nietzsche's view that what matters is a maximally vibrant way of living, rather than milksop piety. Of course, Whitehead more often stresses the values of compassionate attitudes, but there is no doubt that this dangerous element is present in his thought, somewhat disguised by the style of an English gentleman, which so appealed to his American admirers. (See DIALOGUES.) Another thought which strikes me on this matter is that terrible pain is, surely, among the intensest of feelings—so I wonder how far this enters into the divine goal.

Hartshorne takes a less terrifying view of the place of evil in the world. Mostly it arises as the unintended consequence of many agents each freely doing its own thing or from the decision of 'thinking agents' to do less than the best that they might, a decision which God could not prevent while still leaving them as free agents.

The tragedy of the world, I conclude, is the price of individuality. The greater the depth of individuality, the greater the possibilities for both good and evil. It is not simply a question of moral evil. The most innocent uses of freedom involve some risk of conflict and suffering. There are many decisions, and thus a composition of decisions, but this composition is itself no decision. It simply happens. It is chance or luck. If each of twenty children decides to shout, has any of them decided that there shall be the confused noise that ensues, preventing any of them from being properly heard? Every individual is fate for other individuals. Divine providence may be a sort of superfate, but its function is to set limits to the free interplay of lesser individuals, which otherwise would be pure chaos. Consider a committee with no chairman and no directives. This would indeed be chaos. Given a chairman and directives, there will still not be perfect order and harmony, and certainly not complete control of every detail according to any plan. (PERFECTION, 314; see also SYNTHESIS, 238)

This may seem fair enough if one can believe in that kind of freedom. But it hardly explains the sheer amount of both moral and natural evil which God is apparently prepared to put up with. Evil surely needs a more agonized treatment than either of our process philosophers offers us. (William James, if he was a process philosopher, did much better; but then his God was 'finite' in a sense in which neither Whitehead's nor Hartshorne's is.)

Somewhat connected with the problem of evil is the question (which may be meaningless, but still deserves to be asked): Is there anything which one can specify in a general kind of way as being the ultimate point of things? For conventional Christianity it would seem to be so that the good or the forgiven shall enter into heavenly bliss in contemplation of God's perfection. And for some it will also include the punishment of the irredeemably wicked.

Neither of these would seem to be the ultimate point of the world either for Whitehead or for Hartshorne. It is rather that God should have as wonderful a time as possible, granted what inferior agents are doing. (For Hartshorne's view, see especially PERFECTION, ch. 9.)

The primordial appetitions which jointly constitute God's purpose are seeking intensity, and not preservation. Because they are primordial, there is nothing to preserve. He, in his primordial nature, is unmoved by love for this particular, or that particular; for in this foundational process of creativity, there are no preconstituted particulars. In the foundations of his being, God is indifferent alike to preservation and to novelty. He cares not whether an immediate occasion be old or new, so far as concerns derivation from its ancestry. His aim for it is depth of satisfaction as an intermediate step towards the fulfillment of his own being. His tenderness is directed towards each actual occasion, as it arises.

Thus God's purpose in the creative advance is the evocation of intensities. (PR, 105/160–1)

It is possible to find this aspect of God, as conceived by Whitehead, somewhat distasteful. Even if he is 'the great companion', it seems to be for what he can get out of the relationship. Is it not a bit greedy of God to pursue his own satisfaction so vigorously and to be so self-satisfied, in spite of all the evil in the world? All in all, there seems to be an element of somewhat facile optimism about the world in these process philosophers.

(C) Doctrinal Religion Requires Metaphysical Support

Whitehead's most set discussion of religion is in his short book (originally Lowell Lectures) called *Religion in the Making (1926)*. But actually it does not throw much light on what actual form of religious allegiances and practices his philosophy would especially favour. Essentially, religion for him, as we shall see in our next section, was a matter of private experience of an eternal aspect to reality sustaining the fleeting phenomena.

Still, he was not uninterested in religion of a more doctrinal kind. And one striking claim he makes in this connection goes right against the view (of Pascal and Kierkegaard *et al.*) that metaphysics is irrelevant to religion. For he tells us that a rational religion can only be based upon metaphysics.

Religion requires a metaphysical backing; for its authority is endangered by the intensity of the emotions which it generates.... Thus dispassionate criticism of religious belief is beyond all things necessary. The foundations of dogma must be laid in a rational metaphysics which criticizes meanings, and endeavours to express the most general concepts adequate for the all-inclusive universe. (RIM, 71)

Whitehead speaks of Buddhism and Christianity as being the great religions of the world. They provide the two great religious conceptions of civilized man. But they are somewhat in decay at present (RIM, 33). And this is largely because there is a third conception now, that of science, which troubles them both somewhat. If they are to continue as inspirations, they must make use of metaphysics, as already indicated, to find an acceptable form in which they may be preserved. Buddhism may be thought to be in a better position in this respect than Christianity, in that it is closely associated with a distinctive metaphysics. However, this makes it less flexible than Christianity, and therefore less capable of rational advance (see RIM, 40).

Moreover, Buddhism, although its ethics is akin to that of Christianity, lacks the power to stimulate 'active personality', and to that extent is deficient as compared with Christianity (see RIM, 125).

(D) Is Religion a Social or a Private Phenomenon?

Josiah Royce and William James clashed as to whether the religious life was mainly that lived in a community or something experienced in private. For James, religious institutions just preserved in a faded, second-hand form what was only really known to exceptional individuals who had mystical or near mystical experiences. For Royce that was quite wrong, for religion was much more a matter of how the individual found his salvation in a loyal life within a beloved community.

On this matter (he does not refer to this dispute) Whitehead is much closer to James in his treatment of religion in *Religion in the Making* and elsewhere. Probably his most famous remark on religion is his definition of it as 'what the individual does with his own solitariness' (RIM, 6). By this he means, I think, that it is the drinking in of the nature of reality and God as one abstracts oneself from the rush of daily business. And he tells us that 'This doctrine is the direct negation of the theory that religion is primarily a social fact.... [For] all collective emotions leave untouched the awful ultimate fact which is the human being alone with itself, for its own sake' (RIM, 5).

Another definition which he offers is that 'Religion is force of belief cleansing the inward parts' (RIM, 5).

However, he allows that religious people are usually those who belong formally to a religious faith with its own dogmas. And in this connection he says that 'A religion, on its doctrinal side, can thus be defined as a system of general truths which have the effect of transforming character when they are sincerely held and vividly apprehended' (RIM, 5). This strikes me as rather a good definition of religion. But it does not tell us how the system of truths which one might learn from his process philosophy might be expected to transform a person's character.

It is hard to sum up what seems to me a somewhat disjointed view of religion in his main work on the subject (*Religion in the Making*). But what is clear is that the individual, who accepts something along the lines of Whitehead's metaphysics and really experiences the world in the character which Whitehead ascribes to it, will look for guidance from what he feels to be the ideal which God is presently holding out to him. And he will find comfort in the fact that God is working to lead humanity, and reality in general, into paths of increasing goodness in every sense, and that though reality is fleeting, all that is valuable (and even the evil transmuted eventually into a harmonious whole) is eternally preserved in God.

XIV Proofs of God's Existence

(A) Whitehead's Approach

Whitehead does not offer much by way of proof of his positions. He simply declares how things are, qualifying this sometimes by saying 'according to the philosophy of organism'. He would like us to evaluate it, by grasping it as a whole and then seeing (if we do) that it is the most satisfactory general account of the world in which we live that is available.

Perhaps the nearest to a proof specifically of God's existence is that he must be there as the home of all the eternal objects. This is because what exists only as a possibility must be grounded in an actuality. God is that actuality in which the existence of all possibilities—that is, eternal objects—is grounded. For his knowledge of them is his primordial nature.

And if there were not such eternal objects—that is, all the possibilities which might be actualized by (in Whitehead's jargon, might ingress into) actual occasions as they arise—there would be no possibility of there being anything new (so far as what concretely exists goes) for them to pick as what they will actualize.

Hartshorne, as we have seen, rejected this idea of the realm of eternal objects. It is only very general categories, according to him, which are eternally there in God. Such a category might be colour. But specific shades of colour only enter into reality when some actual occasion manages to make something more precise out of the general category of colour. And this colour, until other actual occasions have created more determinate versions of it, will be as determinate a colour as there presently is.

I have chosen the example of colour because it allows of an easier statement of the principle than some other examples might do.

Personally, though there are certainly problems about the eternal objects, I am inclined to think Whitehead more convincing here.

(B) Hartshorne's Ontological Argument

Hartshorne is much more generous with proofs than Whitehead, especially in the matter of God's existence. Thus he develops an ontological argument for God's existence which may (I hope) be informally but, for present purposes, adequately expressed as follows.

1. By 'God' is meant the one and only individual which cannot conceivably be surpassed (or equalled) in excellence by any other individual.
2. God either necessarily exists or necessarily does not exist.
3. If it is possible that God exists, then he exists and necessarily so.
4. It is possible that God exists.
5. So God exists and necessarily so.

(1) is formulated to allow for the fact that God may be surpassed in excellence by himself in the future. Here Hartshorne challenges the traditional view that God is unchanging and thus, as he see it, takes Anselm's admirable argumentation (in *Proslogion*, II–IV) one stage further. I note too that Hartshorne argues that 'equalled' is unnecessary, since two equal beings could surpass each other. That is why there can only be one God.

(2) follows from the fact that an individual which might not have existed is inferior to any individual which must have existed.

(3) follows from the modal principle that what is possibly necessary is necessary.

(4) shows that neither God's existence nor his non-existence could be an empirical fact. Thus both 'empirical theism' and 'empirical atheism' are non-starters. Hartshorne, of course, gives reasons for thinking it possible.

Some further explanation of the argument is required if we are to grasp its relation to the event ontology of process philosophy. The divine essence of unsurpassability which is necessarily actualized is a highly generic universal which can be actualized only in specific determinate forms of it: for example, knowing everything pertains to the divine essence but can only be actualized as knowing that p, where p covers all truth, in particular all contingent truth. But the sum of contingent truth changes moment by moment as fresh things happen, so that p is always increasing its content.[23] For moment by moment the divine essence is actualized by the successive events which constitute the life of God, and each event actualizes the divine essence afresh and differently. Thus the divine essence is necessarily actualized at every moment, but the total character of its momentary instances changes.

But if there can be different instances of this essence at different moments, why, we may ask, not different ones at the same time? Hartshorne answers, roughly speaking, that then, as rival constituents of the universe (i.e. the whole of things), they might limit each other's powers and one surpass the other in excellence, which counts against the divine essence as specified. This presupposes that different events are *different* in a different sense according as to whether they occur at the same or at a different time, which on my view of time is false. Of course, Hartshorne quite properly develops his views in terms of his own process conception of time.

(C) God and the Past

Hartshorne has another argument for God's existence, of more interest to me personally. There could not be determinate truths about the past, he claims, unless the past somehow still exists. And the only way in which it could do so is through having entered into the mind of God and stayed there. I have expressed my doubts about this claim in section X (H) of this chapter.

God does not know precisely what will happen in the future. But this is not a limitation on his knowledge. For there is no precise truth about the future so long as it is future.

There is at least a verbal difference between Whitehead and Hartshorne on how actual occasions enter into God when they fall into the past. For Whitehead, actual occasions lose their 'subjective immediacy', whereas for Hartshorne they retain it.

Hartshorne, we saw, wants to reject any notion that our moments of finite consciousness are only *represented* in God. He wants to say, rather, that they *enter into God with their full subjective immediacy*. Whitehead, by contrast, sometimes indicates that they are only represented in God, though perhaps his more careful formulation would be that they themselves enter it, but in the objective 'perished' form. (See PR, 12–13/18–19.)

Frankly, I think Hartshorne's view on this incoherent, because the idea that events first have a separate existence, apart from God, and then enter into his mind, does not make sense. For what is not in God's mind cannot be identical with what later is in God's mind.

So I do not think that the fact that there is a determinate truth about the past can be explained in Hartshorne's manner, still less prove the existence of God as he conceives him. For the fact that an event, after its initial occurrence, enters into God and is there for ever after can only provide the foundation of truth about the past if the event, as it survives for ever after in God's mind, corresponds appropriately to the past event when it occurred before its entry into it. It may be said that it is metaphysically necessary that it should thus correspond. But if so, there still has to be some content to this. And surely there cannot be such a correspondence unless both sides of the correspondence somehow exist. So the past event as it was in its initial occurrence must have some kind of reality independently of the reality pertaining to its objectified version in God's mind. But in that case, what ultimately makes it true that the event occurred is not that there is an objectified version of it in God's mind, but that it is somehow there independently to be corresponded with. But how can past events be somehow still there to be corresponded with? Only, as it seems to me, if each event is eternally there in its own moment of time, and its pastness is only relative to later events. (See next chapter.)

XV Process Philosophy and Ethics

(a) Its Ethical Implications

Process philosophers are inclined to claim that their metaphysic gives a better account of our ethical situation and greater encouragement to behave unselfishly than do more traditional philosophical systems. The two things most relevant from this point of view are (a) the replacement of continuants (enduring substances) by momentary totalities of experience; (b) the real interpenetration of the experiences of different individuals—that is, of different streams of personal experience; (c) panpsychism, or psychicalism, as Hartshorne prefers to call it.

(b) Process Philosophy and Environmental Ethics

One ethical virtue sometimes claimed for process philosophy is that it offers a justification of concern for the environment. This has been argued in several books. (See GRANGE, and for a critique of the claim, PALMER.) The idea is that the notion of nature as dead, lifeless, and unconscious limits our concern with it, while process philosophers see it as throbbing pervasively with more or less valuable feelings.

I believe that there is some truth in this. However, it is a more complicated matter than some enthusiasts seem to recognize. This is because the objects, and features of nature which call forth our relatively disinterested concern, are never actual occasions or momentary experiences, but large units (nexuses) which we see as whole objects only by a kind of illusion—that is, if process philosophy is right. The fact that, if Whitehead is right, sensory qualities do to some extent reveal what is being felt 'out there' may alter the picture slightly, but only at the cost of a highly problematic claim. I have examined this matter elsewhere, and it had better not take up space here.[24]

But one thing must be mentioned in this connection: namely, Hartshorne's work on bird song, particularly in *Born to Sing*, which brings together ornithology and philosophy in a brilliant manner. (See also Alexander F. Skutch, 'Bird Song and Philosophy'.)

This was based on extensive field research on songbirds across the whole of the United States, and in Australia, Japan, and India, Nepal, England, Middle and South America, Jamaica, Uganda and Kenya, New Zealand, Fiji, the Philippines, Malaya, Hong Kong, and Taiwan, etc. Hartshorne drew up an order of merit as singers, based on marks from one to nine in six or more tests, such as degree of complexity and ability to learn songs from other birds or humans. He concluded that, though there was a practical purpose in the singing (staking out territory or attracting a mate), it was also elaborated out of pure aesthetic enjoyment, sometimes by a pair of birds together; moreover, that the details could be determined only by an element of free choice. Birds, he found, strikingly exemplify the qualities particularly cherished by process philosophy. He also arrived at an intriguing idea as to the length of the specious present for various bird species.

(c) Egoism and Altruism

As we saw above, Hartshorne criticizes any idea that egoism, however enlightened, is basic either psychologically or ethically. Logically, it is not basic, since there is no difference logically between working for one's own good and for that of others, since each is as truly something other than the momentary self at work. Nor, psychologically, is it so universal that altruism has to be taught only as a means to self-fulfilment.

For me it is virtually self-evident that neither individual nor national self-interest can be *the* principles of action for a truly rational animal. Not even sub-rational animals in fact derive all their other-regarding behaviour from self-concern; ... It is imagined experiences that chiefly motivate us, as Santayana knew; and imagination may, yet need not, be preoccupied with one's own future weal or woe [any more than anyone else's]. For metaphysics to canonize the former option is a sad but common misuse of speculative reason....

The basic motivation, however, is neither the appeal of a self for that same self; nor even the appeal of other selves for the own self. Rather, it is something more general and yet, in its instances, more specific or concrete: the appeal of life for life—thus my past or future life (or self) for my present life or self and also the appeal of your past or future life (or the lives of birds, or the cosmic life) for your or my present life, reality, or self. Apparently it was Buddha who discovered this centuries before Christ, if I may so speak, rediscovered it. (SYNTHESIS, pp. xix–xx)

This is an interesting passage. Though I agree with it to quite an extent, there are some qualifications which I would like to make.

I note first an objection likely to be made, but not by me. This is the doctrine of the 'selfish gene' as put forward most popularly by Richard Dawkins, though even this is supposed to lead to 'kin altruism'.

The strongest point which Hartshorne is making is that there is nothing especially rational about an egoistic concern with one's own future as compared with concern with the present and future of others. In either case the thought of the present moment is directed at experiences beyond the experience of which it is a part. That they come in the series constituting oneself rather than in a series constituting another individual is neither here nor there so far as rationality goes. And even to suppose that, rational or not, human motivation (I leave the motivations of other creatures aside here) is primarily selfish is not true.

But this is based partly on the statement that 'It is imagined experiences that chiefly motivate us', which is open to challenge. For it is surely present experience which mainly motivates us. It does not do so, indeed, if by motivation is meant pursuit of a goal. But if by motivation is meant what explains psychologically why people do what they do and intend what they intend, it is present and past experience of one's own which chiefly motivates us.

First, as regards present experience—that is, experience 'compresent' with the mental genesis of action—this is clearly a main motivator. It is present pain which motivates the struggle to remove its apparent cause, and it is the pleasurableness of present experiences which makes us seek to preserve and strengthen them. Even when we have an explicit goal, it is the pleasure of anticipating its achievement which is the basic cause of our action (so far as that can be explained in mental terms).

But what of past experience as a motivator? Well, that requires a comment on personal identity. For myself, I agree with Hartshorne and other process philosophers that my existence over time is to be identified with the occurrence of a series of moments of experience which follow on from one another in a special way. This special way is much of the time a matter of experiences in the series each flowing into the next or mentally taking over, on waking, from the stream of experience which preceded sleep (or other interruptions of consciousness).

465

Moreover, the activity initiated in a later stretch of experience is conditioned in its active character to an enormous extent by 'rewards' and 'punishments' felt in earlier stretches of experience, which, partly for that very reason, belong to the same enduring self. (This is roughly what Bertrand Russell called 'mnemic causation'.) *My* behaviour can be conditioned by *your* past experiences only to the extent that they have been communicated to me by social intercourse. Or if this is not quite so, that is certainly the most basic case. Direct influence of your experiences on mine by telepathy may or may not be a fact; but if so, it is my resultant experience which has the larger influence on me subsequently, rather than any direct participation in your experiences.

An even more obvious point requires mention. This is that there is a continuity of purpose from moment to moment in a single stream of personal experience, which holds only exceptionally between the moments pertaining to different streams. When I start a sentence, it will probably be in a later specious present that it finishes. The same applies to physical actions. The experience of doing any physical action whatever, whether it be walking somewhere or sawing a piece of wood, lasts over a series of momentary experiences, and yet there is a complete continuity of purpose. Each total experience takes off from where the previous one left off. A large part of personal identity consists in this continuity of next with next over a longer or shorter period of time, and even when one purpose fulfils itself, its later moments are probably starting to express another purpose which will be carried out in the same next to next fashion.

With some married couples, or other intimates living together, it does indeed quite often happen that one finishes what the other was saying. But this is not the normal thing, and would seem to require a different sort of explanation.

Finally, there are emotional links of a very special kind between one's past and one's present, and this can hardly be wished away, however altruistic one may be.

Perhaps all these factors may change one day, but at the moment they mark a definite distinction between one person's experiences and another's.

So while I agree that the rational basis of ethics lies in the fact that there is in reality no great difference of kind between the fact that you are or will be happy or unhappy under certain circumstances and the fact that I am or will be, and that it is a full recognition of this which is the motivator of genuinely altruistic attitudes, the basis of egoism as a dominating psychological fact is not quite so easily set aside by reflection on the true nature of personal identity. There is bound to be a contrast between the influence on us of actual pleasure and pain and the influence of what must always remain conceived or imagined pleasure or pain. And even if the kind of direct participation in the experiences of others in which Hartshorne believes plays a part in determining or influencing our behaviour, I think it is bound to be less than the effect of our own experiences on our action.

Such facts as these should check exaggerated claims that another's future and mine should, or even could count for me as quite the same. Moreover, even if egoism and altruism are ethically on a par so far as the logic of the matter goes, it seems unlikely that they will ever be so psychologically, and any ethical position must take account of this.

XVI Process Philosophy in General and Religion

(A) Goodbye to the Unchanging God

Process philosophers and process theologians believe that they have a concept of God which is both metaphysically truer and religiously more sustaining than more classical Christian characterizations of him.

The unchanging God of classical metaphysics can offer the believer no kind of real social contact or help in troubled times through petitionary prayer. In fact, religious persons (whatever verbal commitments they may have on such matters) conceive him much more as process philosophy does than as classical metaphysics does. For, according to classical metaphysics, God is altogether unchanging. But the God of process philosophy is, whether we know it or not, continually interacting with us. He knows exactly what each of us is feeling at every moment, and continually provides us with hints as to what we should do next. If we enter into conscious contact with him, then the hints may become more explicit. So the God of process philosophy can be seen as 'the great companion', as the God of classical metaphysics cannot be.[25] It is worth quoting again the following passage in this connection: 'God is the great companion—the fellow-sufferer who understands' (PR, 351/53).

It has been said that a truly living (theistic) religion must regard God as a genuine person with whom there can be a real living relationship. When this is questioned, it is

the whole matter of personal intercourse, love and friendship, which is really here at stake. It is not merely one of the doctrines of religion, but the central doctrine, the motive for all religious exercises, that God cares for every one of us individually, that he knows Jane Smith by name, and what she is earning a week, and how much of it she devotes to keeping her poor paralyzed old mother.[26]

The appeal of many religions is that they promise us a life after death (though some fear this, if they think that they have displeased God more than pleased him). Process theology does not offer this (though it is not inconsistent with its basic claims). Yet it does offer us so-called objective immortality, for every detail of our lives is present as stored for ever after (though not anticipated before) in the mind of God as a known fact. For Whitehead, however, it is there as having lost its 'subjective immediacy'. Hartshorne seems sometimes to be denying that it has lost this (see SYN-THESIS, 118), yet it is hard to know what this denial amounts to, for if it is always there as subjectively immediate feeling of its own existence, it would seem that for all I know my present experience of my own existence is really already in the past. So it seems to me that the doctrines of both philosophers amount to saying that God will always remember everything about me and my life. Thus, neither Heaven nor Hell nor any other realm of the dead exists for these philosophers. But one may feel that it is better to be recalled as among the better things which have existed than as among the worse, and this may provide some of the motivation to be good which the Last Judgement is supposed to provide.

This may be a fairly lowly form of religious belief. It has little to do with the splendours of mysticism or even the emotions of one who stands in awe at 'the starry sky above and the moral law below'. None the less, it has probably been in effect the religious outlook of most of those who have belonged to Christian churches over the ages. And, in spite of the great complication of its metaphysics and theology, it does seem to me that the God of process philosophy is probably the metaphysical system which can best endorse this simple form of religion. And there are, of course, ways in which the metaphysics may be significantly unified with a rich religious life of which it does not offer a universally acceptable treatment.

It should be remembered, however, that Whitehead invokes God not only as an object for religious emotion, but as required as an explanatory principle in a satisfactory metaphysics. Thus he is required for an adequate explanation of both the uniformity and the novelty characteristic of nature. (See PR, 207/315–16, 225/343–4.) The same is true of Hartshorne.

(B) God as Sensitive Parent

So I suspect that the special appeal of process theology is that it postulates a God with whom one can have a genuinely personal relationship, as most

Christians (and of course, not only Christians) probably think (truly or falsely) that they have.

According to the old view, as set forth by most theologians and philosophers, God influences all things, nothing influences him. For him there are no 'stimuli'; hence when he influences or stimulates the world, it is in a wholly different way from the ordinary way.... Our new philosophical doctrine is that even God's creativity is his higher form of emergent experiential synthesis, or response to stimuli. He influences us supremely because he is supremely open to our influence.... Like the sensitive parent, or ruler, he enjoys observing our feelings and thoughts, and responds to these with a perfection of appreciation to which no parent or ruler can attain. (SYNTHESIS, 12)

This has some analogy with the emphasis on God as suffering along with us on the part of certain recent theologians. (See SYNTHESIS, 263.) However, there is a pervasive optimism in both Hartshorne and Whitehead which makes the general tone of their philosophy rather different from this. It is to God as the great companion, there to comfort us in sorrow, share in our happiness, and encourage us to behave decently to others, that their metaphysics points. He is not simply an eternal summation of all that has or will happen (as absolute idealism may be charged with making him), or still worse an eternal abstract object remote from all human concerns (like Aristotle's God); still less is he the punitive boss of some traditions, but something more like the God of the Lord's Prayer.

XVII Conclusion

Personally, I am sympathetic to process philosophy, mainly for its panpsychism and approximation at least to the notion of the specious present. Thereby it combines the view which seems true to many of us that an unexperienced reality is impossible, with a quite realistic view of the vast physical cosmos. However, for reasons to do with both time and relations in general, I do not actually think that it can be true.

My reasons will become clearer in the next chapter, in which I present my own viewpoint. But in essentials they are that I don't see how streams of consciousness can form a cosmos without belonging to a cosmic mind or experience. And I mean 'belonging to', rather than merely 'being prehended by', and I mean as they initially exist, not just as they become. The second main reason is that, as I see it, there can be no determinate truth about the past unless both it and the future are absolutely determinate in character and eternally just there, as is the present, e.g. the moment at which the reader is reading this or I am typing it. And I find the view that there is not such a truth both incredible and upsetting. If I and those whom I love are quite forgotten, will it not even be true that we once existed?

Notes

1. I have discussed James's philosophy and theology in some detail in JAMES AND BRADLEY.
2. Among philosophical and theological followers writing today, one might mention John B. Cobb, jun., Lewis Ford, and David Ray Griffin.
3. It is quite understandable that when presented as Gifford Lectures in Edinburgh his audience shrank somewhat disastrously—it has been said (but perhaps not reliably) to the two professors who invited him (Kemp Smith and A. E. Taylor) (see LOWE, ii. 250). His terminology has to be learnt like a new technical language, though when this is done, it is not really as difficult as is sometimes made out.
4. I owe this information to Professor John Cobb, who very kindly answered an email query from me thus: 'He grew up as an Episcopalian, and always associated himself vaguely with that tradition. However, in Chicago and Atlanta, he and his wife attended Unitarians churches quite faithfully. When I asked him about this in Atlanta, once, he said the Unitarian church there was the only one that was integrated. I think that in fact he was theologically a Unitarian. Since many Unitarians today are nontheistic and nonChristian, I would say that he was definitely a theistic Unitarian and closer to those who call themselves Christian.'
5. For a study of the relationship between the philosophies of Bradley and Whitehead, see McHENRY.
6. For an interesting attempt to defend the traditional view of an unchanging God against objections similar to those raised by process philosophy see Peter Geach's 'God's Relation to the World', in his *Logic Matters*.
7. We shall see that while Hartshorne thinks that there is an absolute distinction between the past and future and thinks, therefore, that relativity theory is misleading on this matter, Whitehead, by contrast, believes that no two actual occasions have quite the same past. This so complicates things that I shall leave it till later. What he does not mean is that my past consists only of 'my' experiences.
8. The feelings within an actual occasion include both its prehension of earlier actual occasions and of the eternal objects, and other things such as 'propositions', which I shall largely ignore.
9. So there are two aspects to an occasion's prehension, or feeling, of an earlier occasion: what it is a feeling of (called its 'datum') and how it feels it (called its

'subjective form'). But it is none too easy, I find, to be clear about this distinction. Eternal objects are said to divide into objective ones and subjective ones. Presumably the datum is characterized by the former, and the subjective form by the latter. The eternal objects characterizing the datum include both mathematical forms and sensa. However, it seems that some eternal objects can play either role. For example, the colour red is said to be able to occur either as characterizing the datum or as characterizing the subjective form. Moreover, Whitehead sometimes gives the impression that it is always the subjective form, rather than the datum, which is inherited by subsequent actual occasions. This is something which I must leave unsettled. It is perhaps sufficient to grasp that an actual occasion includes prehensions of actual occasions in its past, and that each prehension of a past actual occasion chooses one specific eternal object as, so to speak, its representative. Yet the prehension is of the past occasion as a particular, not simply as something including the selected eternal object. It must also be grasped that the prehension of the past occasion with the aid of the selected eternal object has its own subjective form, which may be more or less novel in character.

10. Conceptual prehension of an eternal object is prehension of it other than via any actual occasion into which it has ingressed. Whitehead seems to have thought that it is only via God that this can be done, but he is not quite consistent on the matter.

11. It is also problematic how the occasion's subjective aim, which is said to guide the whole process of concrescence, fits here. It seems that the choice of alternatives is really a choice of subjective aim.

12. Sometimes Whitehead seems to say that there is no real process, just a structure which can best be explained as though it were a process. (See PR, 227/347.) Yet, for the most part he seems to think of it as really occurring in a process which is remarkably like a specious present.

13. The scholarly Whitehead uses 'nexus' for both singular and plural. In the interests of clarity I use 'nexuses' for the plural. Nexuses are contrasted with mere multiplicities (= roughly classes or sets).

14. For a full discussion of this point, I should need to discuss his theory of symbolic reference. See PR, Part II, ch. 8.

15. For Bradley, like Whitehead, 'consciousness' had a narrower extension than 'experience'. But it is certain that 'experience' implied for him something subjectively lived through. See Ch. 6, n. 11.

16. The following passage strongly suggests this position: 'It follows from the ontological principle . . . that the notion of a "common world" must find its exemplification in the constitution of each actual entity, taken by itself for analysis. For an actual entity cannot be a member of a "common world," except in the sense that the "common world" is a constituent in its own constitution' (PR, 148/224).

17. Although it must not be thought of as having proper parts each of which is in a different place.

471

18. God is certainly the ultimate unifier of the world for Whitehead. But White-head seems ambivalent as to whether all relations between occasions are mediated by God or not. Still, whether only via God or more immediately, occasions are related to each other and space, and it is these relations which constitute space and time.
19. I have found Donald Sherburne's account of Whitehead's position clearer than anything which I have found in Whitehead. See SHERBURNE, 110–14.
20. I believe that he first made this claim in his 'Whitehead's Idea of God', 545–6.
21. One Christian complainant has said that Whitehead's God is 'in fact, an aesthete of highly dubious moral character, not worthy of being called God'. This is from Victor Lowe's summary of the view of Stephen E. Ely in ELY.
22. This does rather suggest negative prehension, but if so, it is contrary to what I take to be his more official view.
23. Similarly, love of all creatures may be part of the essence of God, but what he loves does not follow from this, for what creatures exist is contingent, even if largely settled by God's free willing. This fits in neatly with the process view that events are more basic than enduring individuals.
24. See various articles of mine on environmental ethics listed in bibliography to Ch. 9.
25. However, we have seen that in Whitehead's work this conception jostles for position with other rather alarming Nietzschean conceptions of God. See the reference to ELY in n. 21.
26. This is a quotation from Paul Gilbert Hamerton's *Human Intercourse* (1884), 166. I first came across it in Bradley's *Essays on Truth and Reality*, 450. Neither Bradley nor Hamerton believed in such a God, but each thought that calling God a person amounted to little unless understood as implying this.

Chapter 9

Pantheistic Idealism

I Introductory

It is time that I spelt out something of my own metaphysical views and said something about their relation to religion.

My position is a form of absolute idealism, very close to that of F. H. Bradley, but owing a good deal also to the thought of Josiah Royce and in certain respects to the positions of Whitehead and Hartshorne. It might be better to call it 'pantheistic' rather than 'absolute' idealism to dissociate it even more firmly from any absurd reduction of Nature to the human experience of it. However, I shall mostly use the more traditional expression.

So what follows is a summary statement of my philosophical views. Please note that I shall sometimes speak of my own position simply as 'absolute idealism' while being well aware that neither in its general thrust nor in details would it command the assent of all those properly called 'absolute idealists'.

There is this much in common, however, to all forms of absolute idealism, that they all decisively reject any sort of materialism. No description couched purely in the language of natural science can do justice to what a human being, or indeed an animal, truly is. And it is only in so far as we see others not merely as physical things (in any ordinary sense of 'physical') that we are likely to 'love our neighbour as ourselves'. Not that many of us can claim really to do this, if 'neighbour' is taken in the sense indicated by the parable of the good Samaritan, but at least we can move further towards it on the basis of a non-physicalist conception of what each of us is. So in so far as a metaphysical position makes plain the falsehood of physicalism, it serves the cause of religion in the best sense.

II Self and Not-Self

Each of us, as we are at any one moment, is most essentially a momentary centre of experience or state of consciousness with the duration of a specious present. A normal momentary centre divides, though not precisely, into a self side and a not-self side. The self side is directed on to the not-self side as its immediate object, and may act upon it or use it to act upon other things. (States where there is no such division are abnormal so far as human beings go.)

At each such moment we are having the experience of perceiving and usually acting on some apparently external things, and are having certain thoughts, imaginings, and emotions. This is what we are best described as most essentially being at any particular moment from a viewpoint outside us, because it is what another would be trying to imagine if they tried to imagine what it is like being us at that particular moment. But from each person's own perspective, they are the self side of the totality rather than the whole of it.

The most obvious component of the not-self side is the perceptual field. The idea of separate such fields for different senses is mistaken. Once infancy is passed, there is a unified perceptual field[1] which contains material from all the senses, as unconsciously worked on by various levels of brain processing, and from our habits of conceptualization. The perceptual field is experienced as surrounding our body as we experience it (with the help of some sense of what is behind us). Together these constitute what may be called our somatico-perceptual field. Action as we normally experience it is a process going on within this field.

It is our body which is experienced, to a great extent, as the initial home of agency, which indeed it is. As agent, it belongs to the self side of the centre of consciousness, but it moves over to the not-self side if subjected to a certain sort of 'objectifying scrutiny'. This objectifying scrutiny occurs most readily when the body is the object of visual experience, but it can also occur when it is felt from within. Feelings and thoughts likewise may move over to the not-self side when we introspect them. Another way in which the felt body may be moved over to the not-self side is if its sensations are enjoyed contemplatively. Something similar is true also of our thoughts and feelings.

The not-self which falls within a momentary such centre may be called the present internal not-self, as opposed to the external not-self. The self aspect of a momentary centre acts upon its internal not-self, but produces results, of which it may have a more or less accurate conception, in what may be called the external not-self (phenomenal or noumenal, see below). This is the rest of that inconceivably vast total reality of which the momentary centre is a tiny part.

It should be noted that both self side and not-self side present themselves sometimes as good, sometimes as bad, and, in the case of the not-self side sometimes as beautiful or alluring, sometimes as ugly, repulsive, or whatever.

The dominant way in which we conceive *the physical world* is as an indefinitely larger totality of which each of our somatico-perceptual fields is a fragment. Which fragment of the world we experience changes as we give ourselves the experience of moving about in it. Thus, at each moment the actual somatico-perceptual field which we experience is imagined or conceived (in a more or less detailed way) as extending both externally and inwardly beyond what is actually experienced into regions with partially specified characters. This may be by way of symbols which characterize it in its supposed present, past, or future character. These symbols may be linguistic, they may be imaginational, or they may have some other character. But there is also a more general sense of there being more of the same (more space and time), which seems hardly to employ anything which could be called a 'symbol'. The public world, accessible to all normal persons, and which we all seem to move about in, is the common construction which we each participate in constituting on the basis of our own somatico-perceptual field, as perhaps corrected by others to keep it in line with the shared construction.

Something should be said here about animal consciousness. Surely any animal which interacts with us in a deliberate way must have a not-self and a larger 'external' world constructed on its basis which is identical-in-difference, to put it *à la* Hegel, with ours (as, indeed, ours are each with each other). In the street a dog interacts with me so as to avoid our bumping into each other in much the same way as does another human being. It is evident that on the basis of perceptual experience, different but not utterly so, the dog constructs a 'life world' which corresponds sufficiently to mine for this kind of interaction. And even when interaction with us is minimal, the fact that we see a creature interacting with things in our sight (such as a sea-gull picking at something with a view to eating it) shows that we live in a common world. But what of ants? Well, I should like to explore this fascinating topic, but had better pass on to other things.

The overall character of our conscious state, of what as conscious beings we are, changes from moment to moment. Thus the history of our conscious lives is, as it has been said since William James, a stream of such total moments of experience. We, as continuing to exist over time, are the one and the same thing which is supposed to be modified in this way from moment to moment while retaining a core of identity. This, as I see it, is a kind of essence which is actualized in each of these momentary conscious states. As actualized in a series of such moments of experience, we may call it 'an individual'.

This will be fleshed out more fully as we proceed. So much was necessary as background to the discussion which follows.

III The Nature of Metaphysical Truth

The metaphysician is in search of what may be called absolute truth about the nature of reality. This absolute truth may not be suitable for day-to-day handling of the world; it may not even be useful for most of science and technology. But if it is seriously in conflict with religion, then something is wrong on one side or the other.

The task of the metaphysician may be regarded as twofold. He wishes to have a conception of the world such that

(a) the content of this conception is peculiarly perspicuous to him,
(b) the world really is as that content specifies it as being.

This might be expressed in an old terminology by saying that he wants to produce in his mind ideas which are 'clear and distinct' and which are also 'true'.

I am not, of course, saying that the metaphysician's hope or purpose is to know everything about everything. It is his purpose only to know something of the general character of reality as it really is. It is also a task for the metaphysician to determine whether there are some things concerning which it is intrinsically impossible for a human being to know the absolute truth. And he should also be aware of the sorts of thing of whose nature he himself, as a result of his own limitations (rather than those of mankind in general), can at best only point in the general direction where he thinks that the truth must lie. (My own such limitations are considerable.)

So the metaphysician wants to have something of the real character of things in general made peculiarly perspicuous to him, and this means that something of that character must be at least adumbrated by what falls within his own consciousness. And this, I believe, must consist in imagining it (or actually experiencing it, of course, but I leave this to be understood).

I shall concentrate on what is imaginable, since so much of what I will speak of can only be imagined (not immediately experienced). But there are, doubtless, things which we can experience, but cannot imagine. Anyway, in what follows 'imagine' must usually be understood as meaning 'imagine or immediately experience' (immediate in the sense that it is an actual component of one's own flow of experience, not that it is unworked on by conceptual thought).

There is, however, a *via media* between what is imaginable and what is unimaginable. For some things are imaginable only *indirectly*. To explain this, a word on a fundamental division of relations into two kinds must be indicated. (Please note that throughout this chapter I shall speak only of two-place relations. This is for simplicity, not because I fail to recognize many-place relations.)

Relations between things divide into two kinds: ideal relations and real relations. Ideal relations consist in some contrast or affinity (including difference in the degree of some common generic characteristic) between the terms of the relation, or in what may be called (in a broad sense) mathematical relations, such as that between two flags one of which *contains one more star than* the other. Real relations are those which are not merely ideal, but are, rather, some concrete way in which things are together or apart from each other and perhaps interact with each other.

Two contrasting landscape paintings hanging in the same gallery change their real relations when one is moved elsewhere, but they do not change their ideal relations, e.g. the brighter colour of the sky in one than in the other. A study of an ancient Greek philosopher and an ancient Indian one may be concerned only with the ideal relations between their thought (how close their views of the world were), or it may hypothesize actual influence on them both of some earlier thinker or thinkers. The former concerns ideal relations between them, the latter real relations.

I can now explain what indirect imaginability is. Something is indirectly imaginable if and only if one can specify its character as that which stands in an ideal and imaginable relation to what is imaginable (directly or indirectly). A simple example is this. One can imagine a human being, or something quite like one, with four arms, with six arms, and so forth, but one can hardly imagine such a being with a hundred arms. Yet, in so far as *having two more arms than* is an imaginable ideal relation, one can specify the character of possessing a hundred arms by imaginable steps which, starting from the character of possessing two arms, lead on to that of possessing a hundred arms. I suggest that a four-dimensional space may be indirectly imaginable in a kindred way. (The four-dimensional shapes within it would relate to three-dimensional shapes as those do to two-dimensional ones.)[2] It is to be emphasized, however, that the fact that it is (indirectly) imaginable does not prove that there actually is, or even could be, such a thing.

Those whose supposedly most basic knowledge is of something which cannot be made similarly perspicuous to them are not, even if their statements can properly be regarded as true, in sight of the kind of truth sought by the *metaphysician*. For *his* desired truth is the essence of some aspect of reality actually revealed to him as a presence in his consciousness, or as specifiable in terms of what is thus present, rather than merely something to which he is appropriately related by non-iconic symbols. (It is not the thing thought of which needs to be in his mind, but only its essence—echoes of Thomism here.)

IV Everything which Exists is either an Experience or a Part of an Experience

Try to imagine something which is unexperienced. Since physical things are the most obvious candidates for things which can exist unexperienced, choose some physical scene which is supposed not to be revealed to any mind. Note that the instruction is not to imagine something without bothering as to whether it is experienced or not, but to imagine something where its being unexperienced is part of what you are imagining. This requires that anything within one's image which could not pertain to something unexperienced must be not merely ignored but positively (so to speak) denied of it.

It seems to me evident that one cannot do so. One's imagery will always include such features, and though these may be discounted in the sense that they are not used to specify what is being imagined, they are always too much there for the imagery to be used to specify the absence of such features. Contrast this with the case of imagining a decapitated man, where the absence of a head may be indicated by a positive lack, so to speak, of something in the image.

That one cannot do this is a first phase in the argument of many idealists. But in evaluating this claim, one must dissociate it from an entirely bogus reason for making it: namely, that what you imagine is experienced by you, and hence not something unexperienced. (This is an argument which many think Berkeley used, though I think this rests on a misunderstanding.) This is a bogus reason, because, though when you imagine something, it can be said plausibly (though doubtfully) that your imagining it is a way of experiencing it, none the less, the fact that you are imagining it is not, in relevant cases, part of what you are imagining. If it were, then you could not imagine an experience as that of someone else. But this is definitely false. If you have experienced a particular kind of sensation, and you think that someone else is having it now, you can imagine it as being experienced by him or her, and not by you. (When you see someone else being hit very hard, you can imagine, up to a point, the pain he is feeling, but you are neither having, nor imagining yourself, but him, as having, that pain.)

What is the difference between imagining an experience as being one's own and imagining it as someone else's? A brief answer is that in the latter case you imagine it as part of a totality including a perspective on the world from a position in space and time, and perhaps with emotional feelings about things, which could not be yours. The elements of what you imagine, though based on your own experience, make a totality which you can imagine but could not actually live through.

But, that bogus reason rejected, what is the correct reason for saying that you cannot imagine a physical thing or scene as unexperienced? First, an important point about imagination should be noted: namely, that what you imagine includes only those characteristics of the image which you use to 'describe' or 'characterize' what you are imagining. (Imagining something by a fuzzy image is not imagining the thing as fuzzy.) Thus, while you can certainly imagine a physical thing without bothering your head as to whether it is experienced or not, you cannot imagine it as positively, so to speak, unexperienced. For you cannot include in the content of what you are imagining anything implying the absence of features the presence of which in anything marks it as an experience or as experienced (as you can imagine a man without hair on his head, to vary the example).

Try to imagine a country scene of any sort you like. I suggest that it cannot be imagined as lacking colours which are either beautiful, pretty, boring, or something of that sort; moreover, the image of the scene, if it is being imagined visually, cannot be deprived of a character which marks it as seen from some more or less specific position; nor can it be imagined as without any organization into a pattern of individuated wholes. But all these features show that you are not imagining it as unperceived, however you characterize it verbally. For similar reasons, one cannot have a clear and distinct idea of a perceived thing or scene as just what it would remain when it is unperceived.

Is it possible to imagine a flower, say, as without colour? (Black, white, and grey, of course, count as colours in this connection.) Well, surely not visually, but perhaps you can do so through imagery pertaining to other senses. Thus purely tactile imagery may allow you to imagine the shapes and texture of its petals, leaves, and stem. Combined with olfactory imagery, this may enable you to imagine a flower as it presumably figures in the colourless world of a man born blind. But the imagery is still bound to be replete with qualities that it seems clear could not be found outwith all consciousness, the possession of which hence prevents its use as a basis for imagining anything as unexperienced. I refer to the roughness and smoothness of surfaces, which varies with how you stroke them, and which will have some specific hedonic character, as will all images of smell; nor will some Gestalt organization be absent.

But perhaps one can indirectly imagine something as positively lacking all such properties. Well, it seems to me impossible to treat the quality of being unexperienced as indirectly imaginable in this way. One can imagine a physical reality and remove, in imagination, more and more of the features which mark it as present in or to a mind, or mark them as present in an ever feebler degree. But I do not see that this reduction of marks of mentality can ever lead to something totally lacking in such signs.

But granted, it may be objected, that you cannot imagine a physical thing or scene as lacking features which it could have only within consciousness, does it follow that you cannot conceive of such a thing?

Well, I believe that conceiving something (without imagining it directly) in a metaphysically adequate form is a species of indirectly imagining it. For conceiving must be more than merely verbal for metaphysics, and the only possible relevant form of conception which is neither purely verbal nor imaginational is a very sensuously impoverished form of imagination in which everything more qualitative in character is discounted and only the abstract structures exemplified in one's imagery are taken account of in one's reasoning. I use the word 'impoverished' in a non-evaluative sense. For using impoverished imagery and discounting even what quality is left may be the best way of thinking about things when concern is with their structure, rather than with what qualitatively fills out that structure. Indeed, this is the only way in which mathematical thinking can go beyond merely operating on symbols of mathematical entities but with the entities themselves. However, the metaphysician is, or should be, seeking a *general* view of reality in *its full concreteness*, and must not screen out everything except the extremely abstract. So he cannot believe in the reality of any-thing which he cannot imagine either directly or indirectly.

This does not mean that one must at every moment engage in direct or indirect imagination of the kind of thing with which one is concerned metaphysically. It is only that one's metaphysical viewpoint must be inadequate if one cannot do this at all, ever.

Something else which suggests that a physical thing or scene cannot be imagined as unexperienced is that it seems impossible to imagine a thing external to your body as not figuring as an element in some scene (such as a 'view') which has its own vague limits, such as do our perceptual fields. Yet an unexperienced physical world would presumably have no articula-tion into any such vaguely defined units as these scenes.

But after all, you may still insist, conceiving or thinking of something is not the same as imagining it. But here I repeat that the metaphysician, if he is serious, wants to know what reality is truly like in an intimate way, which amounts to imagining it, if not directly, then indirectly.

I shall speak of conceiving of this metaphysically adequate kind as 'intuitively fulfilled' conception, an expression taken from Husserl. Intui-tive fulfilment is a matter of degree, since direct imagination is more fulfilled than indirect imagination. However, either is quite acceptable for the metaphysician, since he will certainly want to range beyond what he can imagine directly.

Now if, for any reason, the metaphysician decides that there are things of which none of us can conceive, in an intuitively fulfilled way, even so far as their general character goes, then he must take refuge in 'things in themselves' of whose real character we must remain ignorant. (See below.) I should add, briefly, that he will regard himself as referring to a particular thing outside his current experience if and only if he conceives it as in an imaginable relation to something falling within his experience or is ex-periencing what he believes somehow to be its unique 'tug' upon him. It should be noted, however, that the metaphysician is hardly concerned with particulars. It is the general character of reality as a whole[3] which concerns him, and this requires only the tug of reality beyond his own consciousness, not the tug of anything particular within total reality.

The demand for imaginability, direct or indirect, is not a case of special pleading on the part of one cast of mind, as some philosophers may suggest. For imagining thus answers to one of the most traditional ways of explicating what it is to know a thing's character: namely, that it is for the feature 'formally' existing in the thing to exist 'objectively' in the mind (which means existing as an object in the mind, hence rather 'subjectively' in the modern sense). What is more, it seems to me that many philosophers who have scorned what they have called the imagination have in fact rested their case on what is the same thing under another name. In particular, I think that those who have claimed that they could not form a clear and distinct idea of such-and-such have meant what I would call being unable to imagine it. Why has the mind–body problem, as it has presented itself since Descartes, been so striking? Surely because we cannot imagine any kind of totality including brain and mind (in the sense of consciousness), but can only imagine each separately. That people who use what is essentially the same method come to different results is, I suggest, because they are concentrating on different aspects of the matter in question.

It will be as well to meet a challenge which may come from those especially averse to anything which smacks of idealism. Consciousness, someone might say to me, is the key concept in your ontology. But is consciousness itself something which can be imagined?

The answer is that an individual consciousness is indeed unimaginable by someone who thinks of it as some kind of usually invisible blob in the public world. For a person's consciousness at any moment *is*, or rather *includes*, what may be called his personal version of what he is perceiving and doing in the public world—that is, the world as it presents itself to, and is conceived by, anyone suitably situated within it. Since it is a personal version of the public world, it is clearly not in the public world. But that does not mean that it is in principle unimaginable. For if I try to imagine your consciousness, what I must do is attempt to conjure up something of what your version of some bit of the public world (either as perceived or as imagined) must be, including what you are physically doing within it, and that is not a meaningless attempt. How far the attempt may succeed is another matter. But whether it succeeds or not, I know that there is a reality whose nature I am trying to imagine. Suppose someone goes into a room where people are playing pop music which he finds abominable. He may then quite reasonably attempt to hear it as they do, and thereby reach something which could be called his more or less adequate imagination of this aspect of their consciousness. Some painters, though not all, are certainly attempting to put something of *their personal version of some bit or aspect of the public world* into the public world where it will be available, to some extent, to others. The paintings of Van Gogh are surely an example of this.

Another forgivable source of misunderstanding is this. What I am describing is something essentially non-relational and must be distinguished from *consciousness of,* which is a relation between a subject and an object of which it is aware. *Relational consciousness* in this sense is something which goes on within *non-relational consciousness.* Typically, it holds between the self side of a whole of non-relational consciousness and the not-self side— and somewhat differently with something in the *external* not-self, aware-ness of which is mediated by the *internal* not-self. Maybe my terminology is unfortunate in inviting this confusion, but the most obvious alternative expression, 'experience', could be misleading in other ways. Though I make use of it myself as pretty well synonymous with 'consciousness', Bradley for one objected to those who used 'consciousness' as I am mainly doing here, preferring to speak of 'immediate experience'. (See Ch. 6, n. 11.) However, 'consciousness' is associated with such expressions as 'stream of consciousness' by philosophers whose views are akin to mine.

It may be said that things can be experienced which are themselves neither experiences nor parts of an experience. This may sound correct if we attend to nothing but the words as superficially understood. But in fact, I suggest, all things which you can be said genuinely to experience are, when experienced, a part of your experience. In our paradigm case of your perceiving a physical object, the object as perceived is part of your experience. For its exact nature as it presents itself to you is part of what would have to be imagined by anyone wishing to know what it was like for you to be perceiving it.

You cannot say that you have really experienced things which you merely think of or imagine, though the thought or image of them is certainly a part of your experience. Or if you can, it must be called a mediated experience, and my claim concerns unmediated experience.

So I conclude that nothing exists except experience. But since the mental and the physical seem to cover everything concrete which we have any reason to think exists, it suggests that the world, so far as we have any reason to believe in its existence, consists of innumerable streams of experience interacting with each other, and that these streams include both those which constitute the consciousness of human beings and animals and other, or largely other, streams of experience which are the reality which appears to us as the familiar physical world.

V The Case for Panpsychism

It follows from this that in attempting to give some general characteriza-tion of the nature of reality, the metaphysician ought to drop the notion of unexperienced physical reality out of the picture. He must form a view of the world in which there is no such thing. But since our prime example of unexperienced reality is unperceived physical nature, it seems that he must really give up the idea of postulating anything at all which is unexperienced. The only world of which he can conceive must be an idealist one in which everything is experienced.[4] And to me that seems to amount to saying that there is nothing except experiences and what is part of an experience.

But since each of us human beings find himself in the midst of a vast surrounding reality with which he must cope in order to survive, a reality normally described as the physical world must exist or must at least be the appearance of what does so. And since nothing exists except experience, the physical world, or what appears as such, must somehow be composed of experience.

Certainly it is pragmatically useful to believe in realities other than experience, and in that sense, it is pragmatically true that unexperienced things exist, but not literally true. And chief among these pragmatically true, but literally false, beliefs is the belief that physical reality can occur without being associated with any consciousness. (Continue to bear in mind that I use 'consciousness' as synonymous with 'experience'. Both words refer to reality which genuinely feels its own being.)

What view of unexperienced physical objects are we now forced to, granted that there can be no such thing? For we are apparently bound to believe in them for practical purposes, and the metaphysician must explain how this is so, granted that there are really no such things. Well, to me it seems that it is only a panpsychist view of the world which can cope with the two facts (1) that only experience exists and (2) that the physical world exists. For this says that the physical world certainly exists, but that it consists in innumerable interacting streams of experience.

It makes no real difference whether I say that the physical world is real but that what it really consists in is a vast system of interacting streams of experience, or whether I say that it is not real as it stands but is the appearance of something which is: namely, a vast system of interacting streams of experience. Perhaps the best compromise is to contrast the phenomenal physical world with the noumenal physical world, or the physical world as it figures in our 'life world' with the physical world as it is in itself. (The noumenal reality of a thing, in a sense roughly Immanuel Kant's, is what it is in itself, rather than for a human type observer.[5])

The only two things which may hold the metaphysician back from complete commitment to this, are, first, that he may believe that there are universals (something on the line of Platonic Forms) which can exist unexperienced; and secondly, he may be tempted to postulate unknowable things in themselves somewhat *à la* Kant.

However, I think it best to say that universals *are*—that is, possess *being*—but do not exist, and that what exist are the particular things which exemplify them. Then, no view about their being can threaten the idealist view that nothing does, or can, exist except the experienced. This will amount to saying that universals of their very nature can only be exemplified in experiences. Whether their *being* is independent of their ever being thus exemplified is a difficult question, which I shall leave aside for now.

As regards things in themselves, reminding ourselves firmly that they are not physical things, we may remark that there seems no need to invoke them if we can do without them. Moreover, the fact that we cannot conceive of anything unexperienced may be evidence that unexperienced reality is intrinsically impossible. (Our best evidence that something is intrinsically impossible seems always to be that, although we can home in on it verbally, we can form no real conception of it, and that this inability becomes more and more obvious the more adequate our conception of such a thing. But I grant that this alternative of unknown things in themselves as the source of our experience deserves a more thorough discussion than I can offer here. See my VINDICATION, 127–9.)

So the existence of all things commonly recognized as conscious, together with everything supposedly non-conscious in their environment, consists in the existence of innumerable streams of consciousness or experience interacting with each other.[6] And many or all of these streams include representations of what is around them which depict it as a world of physical things interacting in space and with all the essential properties pertaining to physical things as ordinarily conceived. And indeed, the most essential of these properties can even be ascribed to them by the panpsychist if these are to be understood as abstract structural properties as I specified them in the chapter on Spinoza.

All this is summed up neatly by Royce thus:

Where we see inorganic Nature seemingly dead, there is, in fact, conscious life just as surely as there is any Being present in Nature at all. (W&I 2, 240)

A word should be said here about how the brain is understood by panpsychism. It is well established that before our conscious perception of anything occurs, a number of distinct processing activities have gone on in the brain, each dealing with the results of different sensory inputs. However, according to panpsychism, these brain processes (together with those which undergird all our thoughts, feelings, and imaginings) are themselves, in their noumenal essence, streams of experience of which we have no immediate consciousness, since they are distinct from the stream of our personal consciousness: namely, the consciousness which in the case of human beings calls itself by the first-person pronoun and which in animals, like us, orientates what we regard as their voluntary behaviour. What the neurologist knows concerns the abstract structure of what is going on, rather than its concrete nature.

Whether these streams include some specially high-level ones of more or less personal experience, constituting subordinate personalities, subtly influencing but distinct from the dominant flow, I shall not enquire, important as the issue is. If so, they constitute at least part of what is referred to as our unconscious.

I am inclined to think, at any rate, that each neuron has its noumenal essence, its own distinct stream of experience. However, panpsychism leaves it open whether the only streams involved are those constituting the existence of the atoms, or something even smaller, which make up the brain. These are questions for a panpsychist neurologist, not for me. In any case, this system of streams finally produces that high-level stream which constitutes our personal consciousness. Similarly, I leave it open whether the flow of our personal consciousness (or that of our subordinate personalities) is the noumenal essence of some special kind of brain process which brain specialists may one day distinguish. I am inclined to think that it is, but I am also inclined to think that this brain process breaks the normal laws of nature. (Something about all this may be found in my VINDICATION, 153–61.)

VI The Absolute

All those streams of experience which appear to us as the physical world, together with any other streams of experience there may be, are included, so I now claim, within a single absolute all-embracing experience or consciousness which includes absolutely everything, itself apart, which exists. For it must include all experiences which there are, and besides experience, so I have argued, nothing exists at all. (This absolute experience contains all persisting subjects of experience—subjective individuals as I shall shortly be calling them—in the sense that it includes all those experiences the successions of which ultimately constitutes their existence.) This all-embracing consciousness may be called either 'the Absolute', the 'Eternal Consciousness' (T. H. Green's expression), or 'God'. As regards the last expression, some idealists, as we have seen, have identified it with God, holding that it is what the concept of 'God' in mature religion amounts to, while others, which share much the same concept of the Absolute, have thought it too different from what most people, however intellectually sophisticated, understand by the term to be thus labelled.

Perhaps the most obvious reason for believing that there is such an Eternal Consciousness, or Absolute, is this. We normally think of things primarily in terms of their positions in space and time. Space is the great container in which we think of everything as existing, and time is the process through which these contents of space change from moment to moment. (For more on time and space, see sections X and XIV.)

But since nothing exists except experiences, they must have some kind of togetherness with each other. (For they can hardly each exist in splendid isolation if there is a universe at all.) This, as I see it, implies that they are all contained together in some great whole. This cannot be space, since space is a construction made within streams of finite experience, not something which they can themselves be within. (See section XIV below.) But what kind of whole can contain all these experiences? I believe that it can only be an infinitely more comprehensive experience which we may call the Absolute, or the Eternal Consciousness.

Whether it may also be called 'God' I leave open, though I shall use the adjective 'divine' as applicable to it. I might add that I regard it as possible, even likely, that there is some central core to the Absolute, which perhaps merits the name of 'God' rather than does the Absolute as a whole. It may be that this core is that to which people most essentially relate in various sorts of religious experience. This core may be, so to speak, the great power source of the rest of the universe—that is to say, of the surrounding parts of the Absolute.

VII The Absolute (Continued)

All finite consciousness is a component in one divine eternal consciousness. This (I now argue more fundamentally) is because things can only be in real relations to each other if they belong together as components of some great larger whole. Since all consciousnesses, so I shall argue, are in direct or indirect real relations with each other, they must, somehow, all belong together in some whole.

This argument may be developed more elaborately after some further reflection on the nature of relations and the contrast between ideal and real relations.[7] If certain terms have only ideal relations of contrast or affinity in character, they must belong to utterly sundered universes. Things which belong to the same universe must have real relations to each other. If there are things which are not in real relations to each other, then they are surely not in the same universe. And what we are bound to mean by the universe must be a whole containing everything with which we are in any sort of real relation, however indirect. This issue will be considered more fully in the next section. For now I shall assume that there is just one universe. This may include many different spatial and temporal systems, but there must be real relations of some sort between everything within what we can now refer to as 'the universe'.

But what, more precisely, are real (that is, not merely ideal) relations? If we attempt to imagine, directly or indirectly, the holding of a real relation between two or more terms, I suggest that we will always find that it consists in thinking of a whole to the overall character of which each contributes its bit, as a part thereof, a whole, moreover, which is at least as much a genuine individual as they are.[8] (Think of discovering the spatial relation between the streets of a town. Is not this to grasp how each street helps to give the townscape the overall pattern which it possesses? And the town is surely at least as much an individual as each street is.) The one exception to this is the part–whole relation itself. To imagine this holding between terms is to imagine the part as making its own particular contribution to the character of the whole.

Such relations may be called holistic relations. (For simplicity, I shall mostly drop reference to the part–whole relation itself, since the extension of my claims to this should be obvious.)

Well, I certainly cannot imagine two or more terms as relating to each other in a real way (not merely an ideal way) without imagining them as each part of such a whole; nor, I suspect, can you. For real relations seem always to be matter of some kind of juxtaposition within some whole to which the terms of the relation belong (or of some way in which one thing can be a part of another).

But could not causal relations bind things together without there being any sort of spatio-temporal whole of which they are all parts? No, for causal relations can only be the fact that certain more basic real relations hold between things according to a law. Or if causation is understood in any other way, the same result follows. (See end of section XVII for a full statement of this point.)

The position which we have reached so far, then, is that the universe consists of innumerable streams of experience, interacting with each other, and such that some of them constitute the mental histories of conscious persons to whom the system appears as a physical world. But if they are to be in any kind of real relation to each other, so I am claiming, there must be some whole which they constitute together (in most cases along with other things), and which is at least as genuinely an individual as they are. What kind of whole could this be?

Ordinary thought sees no great difficulty here. For it thinks of your consciousness as somehow located in your body (perhaps more specifically your brain)[9] and mine in my body, and that the bodies each play their own little part in constituting a spatially extended world. But this will not do, once the metaphysical claims which I have been making are granted. For what each of our bodies really is, is a system of lower-level streams of consciousness, and the bodies are therefore related to each other only in the way in which streams of consciousness can be, and this cannot be by spatial relations as we ordinarily conceive or imagine them.

And it seems to me that the only genuine wholes to which experiences can belong are wholes which are themselves experiences. An individual's sensations relate to his conscious thought processes in virtue of the fact that they help to constitute together a single state of consciousness. Since our states of consciousness are themselves experiences, it seems inconceivable that there should be any whole within which they belong together, and which is at least as individual as they are, other than a 'vaster' experience, or state of consciousness. Such a whole may or may not include absolutely every experience which there is. But if it does not, then it must be related to other states of consciousness in, or constituting, the universe, in virtue of the fact that they jointly contribute to the constitution of a still 'vaster' state of consciousness. In this way a state of consciousness must eventually be reached which is so 'vast' that it includes everything else which there is—that is, all the experiences which make up the world, which is to say itself. How real or noumenal space is to be understood in the light of this will be discussed in section XIV.

There are undoubtedly difficulties in this idea. The universe is supposed to be what may loosely (rather than mathematically) be called an infinitely comprehensive experience which includes all finite states of consciousness in something like the same sense as one of our states of consciousness includes individual sensations. But a big difference (apart from the scale of things in question) is that our sensations include no sense of themselves as separate beings, as our total states of consciousness do. However, we are not entirely lacking in examples of different pieces of our personality held together in one consciousness, yet having their own sense of self. In any case, I do not see any alternative view, and it is not surprising that there are puzzling features to the all-embracing experience or consciousness which is the Absolute. It has been objected that the infinite consciousness can hardly include bits of itself which are as ignorant as we are. But they are only ignorant, and only mistaken, in so far as they lack the supplementations which are other parts of that same infinite consciousness. (For further details, see VINDICATION, esp. 253–63, and section XIV in Ch. 2 above.)

We thus reach the conclusion that there is one total cosmic consciousness which includes all other experiences—that is, includes everything else or everything whatever if we speak of it as including itself. Or at least it includes everything to which we can have even the remotest of real relations—that is, any relation which is more that a contrast or affinity in character.

VIII Are There, Maybe, Other Universes?

Is the idea of there being perhaps another universe to be taken seriously? Well, personally, I think it unlikely that there are other universes. I have no real proof of this, just an inclination to believe it. For the satisfaction of the Eternal Consciousness which is our universe would be incomplete if it did not have good reason to suppose itself all-inclusive. Besides, what would keep these different universes apart?

What I am calling *our universe* may very well include unrelated time systems and space systems, or spatio-temporal systems. They would be unrelated temporally or spatially—or in both ways—but would be united to form the overall consciousness of *this* universe in the largest sense—that is, in *this* Eternal Consciousness.

Perhaps it cannot be settled rationally whether there are other universes beside this one, each of which is included in a different Absolute. But if there are, they can be in no real relation to anything within this universe, or to this universe as a whole.[10] They are quite unknowable by us, and our concern can only be with the character of this universe. And there is something disturbing in demoting our Absolute in such a way.

Thus, in my opinion, everything in the universe is in some real relation to everything else, though this may be very indirect. We may take this as certain, if only because something to which you and I are not even very indirectly related by a real relation cannot be regarded as part of what you or I mean by the universe. But whether there may be quite other universes remains problematic.

IX Continuants

A really fundamental account of the world would conceive of it as consisting in all sorts of series of momentary experiences, all united in one single absolute consciousness. Thus events—and for pan-experientialism, that means experiential units—are more basic than continuants: that is, individuals which last over time. I am far from denying that there are really such things as continuants, only claiming that their existence and history must at the most ultimate level be analysed as facts about streams of experience.

An ordinary finite continuant is an essence (better called 'an individual essence') characterizing all, or most, of the individual moments of experience pertaining to the series of experiences which constitute its life, or 'life'. But each such moment has a total character of which the essence is just one pervasive constituent. And this (its total character) is largely the result of what occurred in earlier moments of the stream *either* as a result of its interaction with other streams *or* as a result of creative activity within the stream *or* as a combination of both *or* as a fresh input from its present external experiential environment.[11] These essences are in fact just what continuants—that is, individuals existing over time—are.[12] The continuants of most significance to us are what we have been calling 'subjective individuals', but of course in the life world there are any number of other sorts of continuants: trees, mountains, planets, tables, dolls, houses, etc.

But is a series or stream of experience itself an experience? If not, then we have an existent which is, apparently, not experienced. The answer is that each experience feels itself to be 'flowing' out of and 'flowing' into another experience in the stream. This can be true even if there is a break in the stream during sleep, etc.[13] But if there is no such experience, then their unity must consist in the special kind of influence which the earlier ones have on the later. But, like all relations (ideal relations possibly excepted), it is ultimately a matter of how the terms are united in the Absolute.

X The Illusion of Time and the Question of Novelty

From the point of view of each subjective individual at all like ourselves, there is, at every moment of its life, a sense of the contrast between its past, its future, and its present.

Its future, or its more immediate future, is that of which it is even now (freely at least as it seems to itself) joining with much else in determining the character, through thought, desire, and action; the much else includes the present state of its body and its environment, and the actions of other conscious beings. Its past, on the other hand, is that which can be affected by no action of its now, or in what it counts as its own future.

All this is true. But what *is not* true, however (according to the metaphysics advocated here), is that the present has taken over from the past, so that the past has dropped out of existence, and that it itself is in the very act of dropping out of existence as the future dawns. For really all these moments of experience are just eternally there as components of the Absolute. And the Absolute does not change. For what at any moment one individual regards as their past or future (if that future occurs) is all eternally (not always) just there in the Absolute, each with its feeling of its own transitoriness, but without that actually dropping out of existence, which is how finite individuals interpret that feeling.

Nevertheless, absolute idealism entirely accepts the fact affirmed by Whitehead, using an expression from Samuel Alexander, 'that every ultimate actuality embodies in its own essence what Alexander terms "a principle of unrest", namely its becoming' (PR, 28/42) with the exception of course, of the one all-comprising Absolute Experience.

The expression 'principle of unrest' is very appropriate—for a total experience normally has an itching to be on to the next thing. But the absolute idealist sees this itching as something which belongs to each moment of experience in its eternal character as a component in eternity. What is false is that what it itches to pass on to, and what is indeed its continuation, occurs because it, the initial experience, drops out of reality, or at any rate loses 'subjective immediacy'.

Phenomenal time is in a certain sense unreal. Or at least, it is noumenal time conceived inadequately. Noumenal time must be some kind of arrangement within the Absolute of the different moments of experience which it includes. One proposal (advocated, as we saw, by Josiah Royce, even if not in these very words) is that noumenal time is the order of events within what may be called *the frozen specious present* of the Absolute.[14]

But is not some fuller characterization of phenomenal time required? Basically, it is the conception of one great chunk of reality, called *the future*, as having no final character as yet, and indeed as not being fully real, standing in contrast with two other great chunks of reality: *the present*, which is just *this experience now*, as one says, and what a historian would describe as contemporary with it, and *the past*, which is the unalterable background which has issued in *this now*.

Much of this *is* true, inasmuch as it must be a real feature of noumenal time. Later events really are the result of earlier events, and it is really true that this present experience has flowed out from earlier events, and that whatever agency it contains is contributing to determining the character of events later than itself. But these relations of *flowing into* and *flowing out of*, and of *being a partial determinant of*, are eternal relations between events which themselves are just eternally there.

Time as ordinarily conceived is unreal. But what of scientific conceptions of time? Actually, when the issue is pushed, scientists do not entirely agree one with another. However, the view of time presented here seems to fit well with Einstein's general theory of relativity. But I sometimes wonder how far the extent to which this counts against the ordinary conception of time, and points to the unreality of time, as we ordinarily conceive it and respond to emotionally, is adequately appreciated. In any case, my argument for the unreality of time, as ordinarily conceived, is based not on scientific, but on metaphysical considerations. It is of course reassuring that it fits so well with relativity theory, though I shall not try to chart the connection. A fuller statement of our reasons for calling time unreal now follows. This elaborates further on what I said in the chapter on Bosanquet.

My claim about time is that in literal truth the future is as determinate as the past, and that all moments of time and their contents are just eternally there in their quasi-temporal relations to one another, but such that no such moment drops out of reality and is replaced by another, as it will do so again in its turn.[15]

This can be deduced from the surely true proposition that the past is determinate, in the sense that every proposition about the past is true or false (or adequate to some precise degree). To deny this is to make a nonsense of our sense that nothing can make it cease to be true that things were as they were. Certainly it need not be known to anyone now for it to be true that an event occurred; nor need there be any evidence for its having done so. ('Anti-realism' about the past is incredible.)

If a thought now about the past, or some possible thought or proposition about it is true, that must be because there is some reality which makes it true.[16] This must be some portion or the whole of the past in its own precise character, which must somehow be there in its totality with an absolutely definite filling. But what kind of reality can be credited to the events which go to make up the past and are the determinants of the truth or falsehood of all possible propositions about it—say, to the pain which King Harold felt when the arrow pierced his eye at the battle of Hastings? Do they belong to a special region of reality wherein events are just as they were when present except for their acquisition of a special quality of pastness? That is how we sometimes think of them, and it is a view advocated by some philosophers. Yet, if events have changed in one respect, in acquiring this quality, is it certain that they have not changed in other ways too? A past pain is presumably a pain, but is it perhaps less intense? But surely a past which might change does not supply that anchoring of historical truth that we were seeking. Yet an untransformed past cannot have any quality of pastness; it must eternally be a realm of events each as much a fleeting present from its own point of view as is the feeling you have now, and only past as viewed from a perspective belonging to a different time.

It may be suggested that although events change in becoming past, it is metaphysically impossible that they should change in other ways. But this very statement that they do not and cannot change only makes sense as reporting a relation which holds between them as now possessing the quality of pastness and their then state of presentness, and this statement can only say something if the events in their presentness belong in reality as possible objects of reference. If the only past is the past *qua* past, then it makes no sense to say that necessarily it has not changed. Thus the notion of events undergoing a state of change into pastness provides a useless answer to the question as to what it is that historical propositions must correspond to for them to be true; since, if we are to make sense of the idea that they have not changed in other respects, we must introduce the same events in an unchanged state of presentness, and the propositions can correspond with these directly. And we must make sense of this idea if we are to deny the suggestion that they might change in other ways too.

Hartshorne argues, as we have seen, that the past is preserved in God's total conscious awareness of it. But unless the events are still present, and objects of some more direct awareness on his part, God's awareness of them is a kind of memory, and even a necessarily infallible memory requires something to be infallible about. If it is infallible about events which have become past, we have the same difficulties.

One can escape these difficulties only by saying that every past event is present in its own being and past only from the perspective of other events. (If the event is an experience, it is eternally the experience it is with just that feeling of emergence from and passage into other events of experience which is part of its inherent nature. But something similar would have to be true of events which are not experiences, if there were such. They would have to have a kind of inherent quality of transitoriness.) Reality, in the fullest sense, eternally includes every past event with that precise feeling or quality of transitoriness which qualifies it.[17]

If all events prior to *this* moment belong with their very sense or quality of transitoriness to reality in this eternal fashion, the same must be true eternally of all events subsequent to this one. For if this present event is a future event from the point of view of events which in themselves are eternally present, then the line of events up till this one is an eternal procession of such inherently present and transitory events, and to deny that their successors, from the point of view of eternal truth, are events with just the same inherent presentness is to think that time undergoes some fundamental change of character at just this point. In this present moment we have the example of an event which is fleetingly present in its own being, and which is the future of other events in the very same case. We must conclude that the future beyond any present is itself eternally a present too. All events are just eternally there, with their sense of passage, their recollections, and anticipations, and the total reality which includes them all is not in transition at all, and hence eternal. And something of the same sort ought to be accepted about all events, whether they are experiences or not; that is, they must have a kind of inherent quality of transitoriness.

This eternalistic view of time does not imply, and should be carefully distinguished from, the thesis of determinism, according to which one could, in principle, deduce from a full enough description of what has happened up to a certain time, taken in conjunction with the basic laws of nature, any detail about the unfolding of events subsequently.

To see how determinism differs from our eternalism, and is not implied by it, imagine space at a single moment divided into two parts. (Some naïvety in this conception of space at an instant does not affect its illustrative value.) What lies on one side will certainly be as determinate as what lies on the other side of the divide. This does not mean that there is any formula, comparable to a law and not merely *ad hoc*, which would allow you to read off the patterns of objects present on one side of the divide from those of what is on the other. In just the same way, the statement that the filling of the future is determinate does not imply anything as to what could be read off about it from what at any time we call the past and the present. But it does imply that the past is as genuine a reality as what we (at any moment) regard as the present, and that from this it follows that the same is true of the future.

Process philosophers sometimes suggest that any view at all like this denies that there can be real novelty in the world. But this is misleading. It is true that the Eternal Consciousness contains everything which is past, present, and future from the perspective of any moment of experience within it. But it is not true that it allows for no novelty *sub specie temporis*.

Noumenally later time is always somewhat different from, and may be astonishly different from, noumenally earlier times. Thus, temporally speaking, there is constant novelty—in fact, novelty at every moment. And if one wants striking examples of novelty, they are not hard to find. Every great or even minor poet, painter, and composer brings not only fresh works into existence, but a fresh sort of work. How different French impressionism is from any previous painting style. How different, and in different ways, is much of the music of each of Stravinsky and Schoenberg, from any music prior to the twentieth century. How different is the TV-dominated world from the pre-TV world. And, of course, the same applies to the physical cosmos ever since (or before?) the big bang.

The suggestion touched on above is that the Eternal Consciousness experiences everything in a 'frozen' specious present. That is, it experiences time relations in something like the way we do within a specious present. But, since there is no further time for it to move into, it neither is nor seems to itself to be itself in time. But the experiences of subjective individuals together with that of the Eternal Consciousness establishes a definite time system. (There may, however, be more than one time series.) This should be worked out in detail in a manner consonant with the theory of relativity, but I could not do this myself.

A further complaint by Whitehead and other process philosophers about views of time akin to that advanced here is that the doctrine of an eternal absolute cannot explain how temporal process emerged from it.[18] But this is no problem for the theory here advocated. It is not that something disconnected from time produced time conceived according to McTaggart's A series. (See Ch. 5, sect. XI.) That sort of time is an illusion (though a well-founded one). Rather does the Eternal Consciousness timelessly include all those finite experiences which seem to themselves to be in time and which are, indeed, in a non-temporal relation which is isomorphic to it. Time, so far as it is real, is a matter of the order of events within the eternal specious present of the Eternal Consciousness, together with the feeling of transitoriness within each of the moments of finite consciousness which it eternally contains.[19]

XI Mind and Body, Self and Not-Self: Construction of the Physical World

A human self is, from its own point of view, for the most part, the self side of a subjective individual. Otherwise put, it is 'the lived body' interacting with the experienced not-self, and via that with the external not-self. Human selves are distinguished from other selves as being rational thinking agents. There are, indeed, other such individuals which are rational agents, though to a lesser extent (i.e. some animal selves). I shall not take time here to analyse 'rationality' beyond remarking that it requires the ability to learn and reason in great detail about one's phenomenal environment and what must be done within it to achieve complex satisfaction and greater chances of survival. Doubtless this can only be slight for a non-linguistic creature.

The dominant way in which we conceive the physical world, or so I have contended, is as an indefinitely larger totality of which each of our somatico-perceptual fields is a fragment. Thus, at each moment the actual somatico-perceptual field which we experience is imagined or conceived as extending beyond what is actually experienced into regions with partially specified characters. (There is not much difference between what is perceived and what is imagined in actual phenomenological character. Indeed, it is only with the aid of imagination that the field is experienced as encircling us.)

The physical world thus conceived cannot be real. Besides the difficulties of conceiving of an existence which does or even can exist unexperienced which we have advanced above, the fact that you are in a certain sense always at the centre of the somatico-perceptual field on the basis of which you construct presently the physical world, whereas I am in that sense at the centre of the somatico-perceptual field on the basis of which I presently construct the physical world, makes it impossible that they are parts of a single spatial whole. Thus we are rivals for being at the centre of the constructed world, and a world which has each of us (and each of many others) at the centre cannot be conceived. (As Sartre puts it somewhere, I seem to remember, your centrality drains away mine.)

This is much the same as saying that a physical thing or scene can be envisaged only as existing from a certain perspective, and yet there is no perspective which has a right to be given this privileged place. If it is said that this is a matter of imagination, not of conception, I repeat that the metaphysician is in search not just of symbols by which he can represent things to himself, but of an intuitive grasp or conception of what they are really like. What he cannot grasp intuitively cannot come into his account of what the world really is. He will not try to play down his ignorance of any number of things and facts; but equally, he will not claim to know that things exist of which he cannot achieve such intuitively fulfilled conception, such as physical things conceived as positively divorced from any form of consciousness.

And intuitive fulfilment must take the form, as argued for above, either of direct imagining or of indirect imagining (imagining as in an imaginable relation to what can be imagined directly).

XII Body and Soul

These reflections apply to every ordinary subjective individual's body. It, no more than any other physical thing, can be conceived as divorced from all consciousness. If I am so deeply asleep that I have no consciousness of it (I need hardly talk of death here, where the body is obviously on a level with all other physical things), it must have some kind of experienced existence none the less, or be made up of parts which do.

For we must bear in mind here that the fact that the physical world, as it really is, consists of streams of experience does not mean that for every physical thing there is a single stream of experience which is what its existence over time consists in. For in the case of most standard physical objects, their noumenal backing will consist in very many interacting streams which are sufficiently close in their relationship to seem to be (and in a sense to be) a single physical thing.

In some of these complex realities there is a 'dominating' subjective individual which can, much of the time, make certain of the individuals which it 'dominates' act as it wishes; that is, it has control, to some considerable extent, over what its body will do.

The dominating individual of a group of more lowly individuals may be called the soul of the whole, and as such we may think of it even, in Spinozist fashion, as the divine idea of that whole. But are there divine ideas of wholes which do not have a dominating individual? One is inclined to deny this, because such an individual would apparently be doing no work in the world, and something like epiphenomenalism would be true of it. And epiphenomenalism seems a rather peculiar position for an idealist, for whom nothing exists except experience, to adopt.

But I don't think that we should assume this. For may not God have ideas of what exists and is going on at many different levels? Nor need we expect the divine higher-level ideas to affect the behaviour of the lower-level ideas. It may be something like a pre-established harmony which holds between them. For, as I see it, the world is really something like a musical work, say a symphony (or even a passacaglia), though all heard by God within one specious present. Then the different levels of God's ideas may be like individual lines in a musical composition, which harmonize without what is going on at one level being the efficient cause of what is going on at other levels.[20] Thus there may be a divine idea of a lake even if it, or its noumenal counterpart, plays no part in *causally* determining (in a manner accessible to science) what the lake 'does'.

However this may be, I see no decisive reason for denying that human and animal minds are *among* the determinants of brain states and consequent physical behaviour (each of these, of course, at the noumenal level being complexes of lower-level experience).

XIII The Scientific World

Whatever may be the truth of this matter, the physical world as we ordinarily conceive it (our life world) certainly has a kind of genuine existence inasmuch as it is a compulsory posit on the part of beings like ourselves when not deep in metaphysical or even scientific thought.

The life world may be contrasted not only with the noumenal world, but also with the scientific world—that is, the world as conceived by science at its most successful.

There are two alternative ways in which we may explicate the scientific concept of the world. (1) We may think of it as an imagined extension (externally and internally) of the life world, allowing it only the kind of reality which we ascribe to the life world—in short, as a mental construct, rather than an independent reality. (2) Or it may be conceived more 'realistically' as the reality which science characterizes and explains in symbols which tell us only of its structure, not the concrete filling of that structure. In that case it is the noumenal world conceived only in terms of its structure.

Both the life world and the scientific world may be thought of as functioning as diagrams of the noumenal world. But the scientific description can latch on to the noumenal world, only if it is associated with indexical expressions whose use points to particular bits of it, this occurring in truth through our experienced contact with it, however ill conceived the nature of this contact may be.

It will seem bizarre to many scientifically minded persons to regard consciousness as somehow more basic than the physical, seeing that it is absolutely evident from neurophysiology that consciousness is the result of brain activity, and that our state of consciousness at any moment seems to be settled entirely by what is going on in our brain. Now it is not yet out of the question that our consciousness may have more independent life of its own than is allowed by this view, often thought to be the only possible one for educated persons. This is not to deny that the possibilities open to it are *largely* the result of what is occurring in the brain. But the objection turns on a failure to distinguish the constructed physical world, which is what the physical world is for us in our ordinary dealings with things, from the noumenal physical world which consists of a quite extraordinarily complex system of interacting streams of consciousness or experience, of which the scientific account of the brain only charts and diagrammatically pictures the abstract structure. For panpsychism, the brain, like all other physical things, is a system of interacting streams of experience, and our consciousness is something which arises out of this and probably acts back on it (or accompanies it in virtue of the pre-established harmony).

XIV What is Space?

1. It is a real problem how space is to be conceived on a panpsychic view of reality. Space as we ordinarily conceive it (so I have suggested) is a reality of which each of our perceptual fields is a fragment. The idea of such a space, properly thought through, is, as we have seen, incoherent. Yet somehow, we do all think in terms of such a single space as the container of all physical things. And this idea is sufficiently coherent to be a tool—indeed, an essential tool—for finding our way around reality. We do so by ignoring the differences between one perspective on it, except as a symbol of where we personally are, and treating it as one single thing. As such, it is one of the most basic features of what we may follow Husserl in calling 'the life world' (even though my account of it is not quite the same).

But even if, for ordinary purposes, we accept this notion of space un-critically, it can only be with great confusion that we think of it as containing subjective individuals, or their streams of consciousness. For these are not public, accessible objects, as physical objects are conceived as being. Moreover, they are themselves so perspectival that they can hardly be conceived as contained in something quite unperspectival as space is supposed to be. Nothing which you can imagine as out there in a common space is remotely like a subjective individual or its experiences. The best you can do is to think of it as some sort of invisible blob inside people. Yet there are no such blobs within the human or animal brain or body.

Yet somehow, both our ordinary idea of space and also the space or space-time of Einstein must be representations with some truth to them of how all the subjective individuals hang together—such things as gravity too, but that cannot be undertaken here.

2. Now the problem which troubles me is how a purely panpsychic world can be conceived as spatial. And the main problem will have been solved if one can explain how it might be conceived as stretched out in even the simplest kind of space which has ever been believed in, and that is clearly a Euclidean three-dimensional space. So let us see how Euclidean space as we partly perceive, and partly think of it, could provide us with a kind of diagram of a system of subjective individuals in causal and/or communicational relations to each other. If we can do this, we can leave it to more expert minds to work out how the same might be done for space conceived in some more sophisticated way, perhaps as an aspect of Einsteinian space-time.

Of the two process philosophers whom I have discussed at some length, Hartshorne, so far as I know, says very little about space, while Whitehead's account of space does not seem to me to answer the basic question. I realize that my saying this must sound terribly arrogant since Whitehead was both a mathematician and something of a scientist. I certainly expected to find in Whitehead a resolution of my puzzle about how distinct streams of experience or, putting it in terms of continuants, subjective individuals, can be in anything of which space, as we ordinarily or as scientists conceive it, can be regarded as a representation or appearance. Yet I fear that Whitehead's account has failed to illuminate me, and I must try my own highly amateur shot at the problem and find an account of it which at least I myself find satisfactory.

My suggestion, then, is that noumenal space is the structure of the lines of possible causal or communicational influence between different subjective individuals.[21] Such an individual is, at any one time, in the process of causally influencing both its own future and the future of other subjective individuals. And space as we ordinarily conceive it is a kind of diagram representing the structure of a system of such causal influences holding between subjective individuals.

As a first step we may say that the more direct the causal influence—that is to say, the fewer causal intermediaries between one such individual and another—the spatially nearer they will present themselves as being both in the life world and in the scientific world. And since a straight line is the shortest distance between two points, it would seem that a straight line is the shortest line of possible influence exerted by one subjective individual over another (shortest in the sense that it requires the least number of intermediate individuals for its transmission). Such a 'straight line' will be made of points only in the sense that there could in principle have been any number of intervening individuals between individuals which are in fact neighbours. Note that if two individuals communicate without intermediaries, there is a notional straight line between them.

But we are still a long way from seeing how the three-dimensional life world can serve as a diagram of how innumerable subjective individuals can relate causally or communicationally to each other.

However, it is not too difficult to see how a two-dimensional diagram could be used to chart various possible lines of causal influence between one individual and another. I drew diagrams of lines of communication between different units of the Hungarian Army when I was doing my national service in the Army, conveying such facts as that A communicated with each of B, C, and D, but these three communicated with each other only via A. Of course, what was being illustrated in these diagrams was not spatial relations but causal ones. But that is just what is needed for panpsychism, for which lines of possible causal influence between various individuals must somehow exemplify a structure of which the arrangement of things in the space of our life world can serve as a diagram. However, these diagrams were only two-dimensional, and what we require is some idea of a system of causal relations between subjective individuals which is better represented by a three-dimensional rather than a two-dimensional figure.

For an organization is possible for which a two-dimensional diagram is inadequate and for which a three-dimensional model would serve far better. Suppose we have nine individuals A, B, C, D, E, F, G, H, and Z. Z can communicate directly with all of the others, but each of these can communicate directly only with three of the others plus Z. This is a possible causal or communicational network. Now this could be helpfully modelled as a cube with Z inside and each of the others located at one of its corners. Then we stipulate that the ones at the corners can only communicate directly in a straight line along the edge of the cube. So far as I can see, this would be a three-dimensional representation of the described causal network, and would therefore give a rough idea of how our three-dimensional world might represent a system of subjective individuals interacting with each other causally.

But there are many complications to all this. For one thing, objects change their positions in space. Another is that there may be lines of influence such as telepathy which cannot be charted in the same spatial diagrams as chart the causal relations which are the reality behind standard space. And, most important of all, the world of individuals of experience will not be internally infinite. The volume occupied by a subjective individual (that is, the volume pertaining to a diagram which depicted the causal relations between it and other individuals) would be of some definite size, but there would be nothing else inside it. Moreover, it is quite possible that different subjective individuals occupy different-sized volumes (and there may be something about them, such as the lines of causal influence which pass through them, which gives them a phenomenal shape). A final problem is that adequate answers to how both space and time as an ideal science may conceive them are more intimately related than my fumblings on the matter have taken into account.

I have not worked all this out at all thoroughly, and am probably incapable of doing so, but I believe that it could be done by an appropriately intelligent human mind. I expected to find a solution to my difficulties in the work of Whitehead, but my efforts in the last chapter show that I have not done so.

To sum up my own problem and conclusion, all the subjective individuals which make up reality (apart from the all-containing Absolute itself) cannot be in a space at all akin to the immediately experienced space in which the objects of our immediate awareness are situated. Putting it in Whiteheadian terms, they cannot be in space as that is presented to us in perception in the mode of presentational immediacy, or even in that combined with the sense we have of our own bodily being, which Whitehead interprets as perception in the mode of causal efficacy. Nor again can they be in the space in which we mainly locate things in our ordinary daily thought—that is, the Husserlian life world, this, as I have suggested, being an imagined greater whole of which our somatico-perceptual fields at any moment are the fragments immediately present to our consciousness. That imagined spatial whole is a useful tool for thinking about the world for most ordinary purposes, but it is a pragmatic and ultimately incoherent fiction. For our somatico-perceptual fields cannot be pieces in some cosmic three-dimensional jigsaw which is spatial in the same qualitative way as they are.

At one level the Absolute (for an absolute idealist like myself) substitutes for space and time as the great container of all lesser centres of experience, and their successive experiences in time. However, there must be some more precise truth as to the real arrangement within the Absolute which we interpret on the basis of our somatico-perceptual experience as a matter of their spatial and temporal relations, understood in terms of our ordinary incoherent concept of space and time as a continuation of the space and time of our immediate experience. As regards their temporal relations,

I am not so worried. For these can be conceived as a matter of their positions in the eternal specious present in which the history or temporal unrolling of the cosmos and all that it contains is experienced by the cosmic consciousness. But space is much more problematic. However, I have done all I can to suggest what real space may be, though my account is certainly clumsy and inadequate.

A word must be said about 'scientific space'. For science conducted at a somewhat simple level, I believe that space is simply the space of the life world. However, at a more fundamental level, I believe that it is pretty well what I call 'real space', but regarded in a more abstract way. In short, it is really the structure of the possible lines of communication between different objects. These objects are not conceived in a panpsychist way, but science offers no other way of conceiving their concrete nature nor the concrete relations between them, since what it tells is about the abstract structure of this system of relations and the part of each individual within it. Or rather, it either does this or conceives them in terms which are elaborations of our life world and which must stand or fall with the reality of that, and which therefore fall on my account. (I have a strong sense of the impertinence of these suggestions from a non-scientist, but I am forced to think that something of this sort is so.)

XV Pleasure and Pain, Volition and Action, Beauty and Goodness

All subjective individuals operate in a manner which tends to preserve anything pleasurable in their present contents and to reduce or eliminate anything which is painful in them. 'Pleasure' and 'pain' and their cognates are used here in the broadest possible sense, especially 'pain', which covers any kind of feeling of unease or boredom. That is, each momentary experience acts so that what is pleasurable in its contents is, if possible, passed on to the next moment, and what is painful is, if possible, either not passed on to it or only in a weaker form. I believe this to be a necessary truth about consciousness, but not an analytic one turning on definitions of pleasure and pain. These are distinctive qualities of experience, but ones which necessarily have this effect on the streams of consciousness to which they belong.[22] Its sense of what will bring or sustain pleasure or pain may be partly genetic, partly learnt. The language of desire and belief is inappropriate here, however, because at this level it is merely a psychic mechanism, without any intentional acts being involved.

But a human subjective individual normally does have at each moment more or less pleasant or painful (in the largest possible sense) ideas of various things which it might be about to experience. In accordance with the principle just mentioned, it will do what is best calculated to sustain the pleasant ideas and eliminate or make less intense the painful ideas. Acting caused by ideas in this way is what we call 'voluntary action'. Thus thought-controlled voluntary action (as opposed to action of a more reflex character) is action caused by ideas which, as pleasurable, tend to keep themselves going, or as painful, tend to eliminate themselves.[23]

Action in its real noumenal character must consist in the self side of the experience of a feeling self-acting upon the not-self side. Then this internal not-self affects the external environing not-self. Thus the action becomes an event in the real noumenal world, and thereby also in the inter-subjective life world of other subjective individuals.

The most prominent part of the self side of an experience (that part of an experience which is likely to call itself 'I') is, as we have seen, 'the lived body'. What this phenomenologically embodied I (ego) does is to a considerable extent determined by the individual's past experience of pleasure and pain as ensuing from various courses of action, and it acts in that way which seems best calculated to continue with present pleasure or to terminate present pain. At a more sophisticated level, its actions are caused by pleasurable or unpleasurable ideas of future consequences of action. These are not typically ideas of pleasure and pain, but their power comes from their own degree of these qualities.

This process for a human self is intertwined with its self-caused experience of linguistic and other symbols, which help determine how it will act upon the immediate not-self. Moreover, its attention goes beyond its immediate not-self, for it always has a sense of the continuity of this with the external not-self, and represents its supposed character to itself partly by these symbols, and more fundamentally by predicating universals which it finds within itself of what lies beyond.

For to desire that something should come into, or continue in, existence is for the idea of its doing so in the future to be pleasurable (often as providing a relief to a present state of unease), while to wish it not to occur or exist is for the idea of it to be unpleasant. The hedonistic mechanism of consciousness therefore tends to produce the behaviour which is most likely to sustain its pleasanter ideas and eliminate the more unpleasant ones. But nothing can sustain an idea so well as an actual encounter with that of which it is the idea, or that which shows that it is in the offing. Similarly, nothing can so reduce the intensity of, or eliminate, that of which it has an unpleasant idea than its evident or evidenced absence from where it might be expected to be.[24]

The goal at which my (positive) desire aims will be something conceived as good, which comes to saying that it is presented as bathed in a certain pleasurable quality. (This pleasurable quality energizes as a quality of my idea, but is presented as characterizing its object.) However, it may or may not be bathed in this quality when it is eventually confronted as an actuality, rather than as an ideated object. Only if it is, will it really be good. And this is as much to say that it will only *really* be good if it is actually experienced as good, whether by me or by another, either on the self side or on the not-self side of his experience. If its realization consists in the fact that my view of the world forces me to postulate it as a reality, and as good, though in truth it will not be experienced by anyone, then it will not really be good in itself (though it may be good that I believe it to be so). For a good which can occur without being experienced is an illusion. Therefore, to aim at the realization of a good in the experience of oneself or another is to aim at something capable of being really good, while to aim at something which will not be experienced is to aim at something which cannot really be good. But it all goes to fill out my general picture of the world, and to have this picture may be good. Still, there is a special rationality to action directed at good things which will actually be experienced, as opposed to merely posited by our more or less compulsory normal mode of thinking.

Similar remarks apply, *mutatis mutandis*, to a negative goal. Its object is presented as bathed in gloom or unpleasantness. (This unpleasant quality also energizes as a quality of my idea, but is presented as characterizing its object.) If my attempt to prevent its occurrence fails, and if it is something actually experienced, then it is a real evil. If it exists only as a compulsory posit, then it is not a real evil, though it may be bad that we are all forced to posit it. If, on the contrary, it is prevented, then a real evil has been prevented if it would have been as bad as it was conceived to be. However, if what has been prevented is only its compulsory positing, then the badness which has been prevented is only the badness of our obligation to posit it.

The experienced goodness which is rationally aimed at may be subjective good (good pertaining to the self side of an experience) or objective good (good pertaining to the not-self side of an experience). Subjective good is no less a real fact than objective good. Similarly, *mutatis mutandis*, for rationally aimed-at elimination or prevention of something bad.

Real experienced goodness and badness are not confined to human experience. They are found in animal experience as truly as in ours, and they must be there also in the streams of experience which are the nou-menal reality of those parts of the world which we normally regard as non-conscious. But this latter noumenal reality is so hidden from us that we cannot take much account of the values realized there in our own projects, or even in our meditations. Who knows what experiences constituted the Big Bang?

What action aims at (I must insist) is in general neither the promotion or sustaining of pleasure nor the reduction or elimination of present unease or pain. What it aims at is that of which the motivating idea is a pleasur-able idea (or aims to avoid if the motivating idea is unpleasant). If I help my neighbour in distress, it is the alleviation of his distress which is my goal, not the removal of my own unpleasant idea of it. Aim and motivat-ing idea must be distinguished. There is no suggestion here that we are all hedonistic egotists.

Similarly, if I try to preserve or to create an object of beauty, the *cause* is the pleasant idea of it as a future possibility, but my *goal* is the existence of that object in the future. The idea of something as being a good thing or a bad thing is a pleasant or unpleasant idea, but the pleasure or pain is typically experienced as a quality of the object. And where we are not thinking of the object as itself conscious, we call the pleasurable light in which it is set not 'pleasure' or 'pain', but 'goodness or badness', or 'beauty' or 'ugliness'.

This objective pleasure, as we may call it, which may pertain to the not-self is a real feature of things which present themselves as good or beauti-ful.[25] When I look at a painting which presents itself as beautiful, this quality of beauty, which is a form of objective pleasure, is a real character-istic of what is presented, just as are the colours of its parts. Similarly, the view from atop a hill is a real feature of something real: namely, that bit of the not-self which is for me a fragment of the real physical world. But in so far as my 'life world' includes things which are not actually experienced, the idea of them as existing with their independent beauty is an illusion. (Or it is so unless the Absolute is to be thought of as experiencing them, which is by no means certain, since its experience of physical things unobserved by us may be only of their noumenal basis.) However, it is no more an illusion than are the colours and shapes which we attribute to the conceived thing. For the thing only exists with its colours, shape, and beauty when it is the object side of an experience. Similar things apply obviously to pain and ugliness. Thus the bits of the life world which are experienced are absolutely genuine realities with their own beauties or negative aesthetic qualities, while those which are not experienced are compulsory imaginative posits.

But if it is still asked whether a thing can be really beautiful when no one sees it, I answer thus. (a) Neither it nor its beauty, as we perceive them, are a real part of the filling of a mind-independent world; but this is equally true of all colours, shapes, and the very air we experience ourselves breathing. (b) It is obviously really there as a component in our consciousness when we see it, and likewise there in the minds of similar others when they see it. (c) It is a real part of the phenomenal world—that is, of the life world as that is compulsorily posited. Thus, it is real as a part of the construction which human minds make on the basis of their actual perceptual fields. (d) Its beauty may or may not be a sign that something especially valuable in its noumenal character is influencing us unconsciously. (e) I set aside in this section questions as to what the Absolute may experience independently of the experience of subjective individuals.

But does not an object's beauty differ from its colour, and still more from its shape, in that the latter is forced upon everyone with normal senses as it is not? Up to a point, yes, but I suspect that either people's sense organs are operating a bit differently or the beauty is something which all normal people could learn to appreciate.

Thus goodness and badness really belong only to experiences, whether on the self side or the not-self side. But since the conceived or imagined unexperienced part of the life world is conceived or imagined as containing many features, like colour and indeed visible shape, which can really exist only as characterizing components in a conscious individual's somatico-perceptual fields, there is no reason why it should not be further conceived as having things possessing unexperienced goodness and badness, beauty and ugliness, just like unexperienced shape and colour. But in this case, because of the special sway on conduct of ideas of what is good or bad, beautiful or ugly, it is more problematic to what extent we should try to transcend this way of thinking in our daily dealings with one another and the wider world. The answer to this is quite complicated. On the whole, I should say that it is to be recollected when we are thinking out ethical matters at a very foundational level, but that for most purposes it is unnecessary. For, after all, most of what we are likely to think of as good or bad, beautiful or ugly, are things which are sometimes going to be directly experienced, and so, if we want to make the experienced world as good and beautiful as can be, we need not constantly bear in mind that it exists only in so far as it is experienced. But our metaphysical position does not denude the real world of beauty and value. If by the real world we mean the life world, then it is absurd to think away value from it without thinking away shape and colour and sound. And if by the real world we mean the noumenal world, then it is full of all the real value and disvalue which there is. (After all, it includes all experienced somatico-perceptual fields.)

Another point worth reflecting on is that the thoughts and beliefs which we have about things which, although they do not actually exist, are posits which our experiences force us to make (chiefly various sorts of unexperienced physical things) and in many cases which we believe, not unreasonably, that we would have perceived if we had taken certain steps, may themselves be experientally either good or bad. This lends a kind of value, positive or negative, to things which do not in fact exist, but that it is good or bad that we are normally forced to think of as doing so.

XVI Our Relations to External Things

Our real relations with other subjective individuals are of three main kinds. First, there is a relation with the subjective individuals which are the noumenal reality of the ordinary physical world as we experience it in perception and action. The larger part of a comfortable human life consists in doing things, like getting out of bed, eating breakfast, typing letters, going for a walk, tidying up our rooms, gardening, cooking, washing, going to the lavatory, etc., etc. The noumenal reality of all this is that each of us (each human subjective individual) is interacting most immediately with the system of individuals which is the noumenal reality of his body, and via this with the subjective individuals which are the noumenal reality of his larger physical environment.

Secondly, there are our exchanges of ideas with other subjective individuals and our emotional effects upon each other (largely mediated by language, which is too big a subject for me to explore here). In this case we can be regarded as to some extent aware of the noumenal reality of what we are concerned to engage with: namely, the other person or persons by way of conversation or more physical mutual activities. Of course, all these exchanges involve activity of the first type—that is, ordinary physical engagement of our body with other physical things, including the bodies of others. Moreover, the two types of exchange are so intertwined that it is hardly possible to think of them separately. In some cases, such as sexual intercourse, the physical and mental relations are intimately bound up with each other.

The third type of exchange is with non-human animals. This is a frequent thing for some, such as farmers. For others of us, it is mainly a matter of relating to our pets, or less intimately to animals we encounter elsewhere, such as a horse to which we might give a bite of an apple as we pass his field.

In the second and third cases in so far as we have a sense of what the other is thinking or feeling, we are conscious of engaging with their dominant noumenal reality—that is, their consciousness (even though most of us are unlikely to use such a high-flown expression). In the first case the relation is different—we are concerned only with the physical world as a thing which we depend on in various ways, use in various ways, and may find beautiful or hideous. We are indeed engaging with the noumenal reality, but without conceiving it as such, being aware only of the life world which our interaction with it creates for us.

But do we have any awareness of non-human and non-animal nature not merely as a phenomenon, but as a system of self-experiencing noumena? Well, I believe that the normal barrier between human experience and the experience which is the noumenal reality behind so-called non-conscious bits of physical reality may sometimes partially break down, and this may be a liberating or peaceful experience on the human side. This may occur in states of a mystical or near mystical kind, which occur most readily in certain environments. Thus it is a proper aim to preserve places where people can enjoy this kind of experience. This may be outdoors in parts of nature, or it may be in places set aside for prayer or meditation. Maybe some animals sometimes similarly experience the inner being of their environment.

My account of these matters may repel some by its kinship to dualism, with its too sharp contrast between the mental and the physical. It is necessary to insist, then, that almost all the time we simply live in the life world which we share with others. This is a compulsory construction which we each make on the basis of our own somatico-perceptual and emotional experience. It is the shared phenomenal world of all humans and, to some extent, animals. Since it is a perfectly satisfactory basis for almost all human activity, and is the home of much beauty, it is not something which we should try to pass beyond, or continually interpret in terms of what we (those who think along at all similar lines to mine) take to be the metaphysical truth. However, it is important that it is a rich phenomenal or life world that we inhabit. We should not try to think of it in drily physical terms, or in terms of an ultimate physics. And we must always be aware that the human or animal other has a consciousness much like ours, and shares with us in the same compulsory construction of our common life world, though it is presented to them from a different spatial perspective, and to a greater or lesser extent in different emotional colours.

It is time to elaborate on my brief remark on the nature of causation and influence in section VII. This is important because causation has been said to be the cement of the universe, and it may be proposed that this offers an alternative account of the togetherness of things to their being included together within the Absolute.

Two accounts initially present themselves as the most plausible account of the causal relation as holding between events. On the first account (which was for the moment endorsed above), X causes Y means that it is an instance of a law that, granted an X-like event, there is bound to be a Y-like event in a relation R to it. R is typically thought of rather vaguely as 'will be followed by'. (This is rather a simplification: see Ch. 6, sect. IX.) But whatever R may be, it cannot be the relation of causation which is being explicated. For it is R which is the real relation, and it is this which must be given a non-holistic analysis, rather than causation, and my claim is that this will fail for every such R.

An alternative view is that causation is a real relation of necessitation. But if so, there must be a whole in which each term is influentially united with the other. Otherwise the influencing and the influenced are impossibly cut off from each other, much like Leibniz's monads.

The best absolute idealist conception of causality is, I suggest, that at the level of the noumenal, X causes Y consists in the fact that their relation is an instance of one of the basic principles in which it—that is, the universe—operates and is thereby experienced as smoothly necessary by the Absolute itself. This gives an explanation of the difference between a law and a mere universal truth, which it is difficult to find otherwise.[26] And it lies in the background of causation as understood by common sense or perhaps even by science.

XVII Two Sorts of Real Relation

A deeper account of all these different sorts of relation would take account of a distinction between two (at least putative) kinds of real relation. All real relations require some kind of juxtaposition within a more comprehensive whole. But how far their juxtaposition within such a whole affects their individual characters is problematic. The issue will become clearer if we draw a distinction between two types of real relations: internal real relations and external real relations.

A real internal relation is one each of whose terms has a character within its own boundaries which it could have only if it is in that relation to the other. From this it follows that it could not have the same position in the universe (as determined by its real relations to other things) but a different inherent character.[27]

A real relation which is external, by contrast, is such that the inherent nature of each of its terms gives no clue as to the distinctive inherent character of the other (beyond that they are capable of fitting together with each other as they might have done to many otherwise quite different things). Philosophers divide into those, like the generality of absolute idealists, who think that all real relations are internal, and those, logical atomists especially, who hold that no real relations are internal, and a third group who think that some real relations are external and others internal.

It is to be noted that the position of those who think that a thing's real relations put no restriction whatever on its inherent character is quite evidently wrong. If we think of spatial relations in the life world, it is obvious that the shape of a thing restricts the possible spatial relations in which it can stand to other things. Think of how the shape of a piece of a jigsaw limits how it can be fitted into the whole, along with other pieces. Similarly, emotions of mutual love between two persons can hardly hold unless the feelings of each have certain inherent characteristics. However, for the logical atomist and others of that ilk, each piece or each emotional state could have been just the same in its inherent character if it had had its place in a different suitable whole or situation. The internalist, on the other hand, thinks that there is no other position within the universe which it could have occupied, granted its inherent character; nor could that position have been occupied by anything else of an even slightly different character.

My own view is that all real relations are internal at the noumenal level, though this is doubtless false of the natural world of common sense. (Jigsaw pieces of a different colour could have occupied the same position in the whole.) The main reason why I think this is as follows. At the noumenal level, all real relations are a matter of some kind of juxtaposition within the absolute consciousness. Now our concept of this must be based on our awareness of our own consciousness, and within this relations of juxtaposition between its contents always affect the quality of each content within, so to speak, its own bounds. A letter seen as belonging to one word looks different from the same letter seen as belonging to another word, etc., etc.

Even if it were not true that all real relations at the noumenal level were internal, it is still essential to allow that some are, if we are to understand such things as love and hate. (Feelings like this belong to the noumenal as well as to the phenomenal world.) In these emotional relations there must be some equivalent of juxtaposition of a spatial or temporal kind, and there must be some inherent character in at least one of the terms which echoes or mirrors the inherent character of the other. But this is not enough, or so I believe. There must be a kind of emotional together-ness which is real, not a mere echoing or mirroring of one state of mind by the other. But in fact, I believe that all real relations are internal. It is in virtue of this, perhaps, that there is a case for saying that the emotional history of a place may resonate with our own emotions when we are there.

The claim that all real relations are internal entails that there could not be two exactly similar moments of consciousness occurring in different contexts. Thus, precisely similar experiences are impossible.

XVIII Absolute Idealism and Ethics

(A) The Case for Ethical Hedonism

We saw in section XVI that it is the pleasurable alone which is truly good, and the painful or unpleasurable (including even a mild feeling of unease) which alone is truly bad. I am speaking, of course, of what is good as a proper goal of endeavour, and bad as something the prevention of which is a proper goal of endeavour. Moral goodness or badness as a predicate of persons is something different; so, of course, is the sense of 'good' in the description of someone as a good violinist.

Pleasure and pain are by no means the only positive and negative goals of human endeavour. We pursue that of which the idea is pleasurable or, in the negative case, painful. And there is no limit to the variety of human goals. However, since our pleasurable or unpleasurable ideas of things bathe them in a kind of pleasurable glow or unpleasurable horribleness, nothing except pleasurable or unpleasurable experiences, whether our own or someone else's, really correspond to what we think of ourselves as pursuing or preventing. But it is important not to get caught up in the idea that pleasurableness and pain are a particular sort of sensation which is connected only contingently to the rest of an experience. They are determinables of which the determinates are infinitely diverse. Moreover, the precise form of every pleasure or pain is intrinsically connected with the precise character of the whole experience in which they occur and the behaviour which they promote.

It is important to note, too, that objective pleasure and pain are just as important as subjective pleasure and pain. A beautiful woman, painting, or view are pleasurable as objects of experience, not as subjective states. Moreover, the constructed life world includes unexperienced things, including beautiful or disgusting things, just as they do colours and shapes. And our compulsory beliefs about it may be pleasurable or unpleasurable. Thus the existence in the world, as we are *compelled* to conceive it, of good or beautiful things is itself a hedonic good, even though, or when, they are not experienced. Similarly, *mutatis mutandis*, with bad or ugly things. Further, there must be lots of pleasure and pain in the noumenal world as the panpsychist conceives it, although apart from the experiences of humans and animals we cannot know much about it.

I should emphasize that I use pleasure and pain, or unpleasure, in a very broad sense to refer to every experience which it feels good or bad for an individual of any sort to live through—that is, for its stream of consciousness to contain. It is here that moral goodness and badness come in. They are qualities of mind, types of experience, which we find attractive or repellent for the concern, or lack thereof, for other people which they show. Thus there is beauty and ugliness of character.[28]

It will be seen that these reflections point to something like qualitative utilitarianism as the most rational ethic. And if my account of the Absolute is acceptable, it reinforces this direction of thought.

(B) Ethics and the Absolute

If pleasure, of very various sorts, is the one thing which is inherently good, and pain, of very various sorts, the one thing which is inherently bad, and this is true whosoever or whatsoever experiences them, why are we not all active utilitarians? In large part, I suggest, because in one way or another we think of the experiences of others as somehow less real than our own. We would not, of course, assent to the verbal statement that this is so, but it is not believed with adequate intuitive fulfilment, and this is only partly because we are not in a position to know what the feelings of others are as well as we know our own. (See the quotation from Royce on p. 365.) The recognition that we all belong within one Absolute

Consciousness which is in a sense present in all of us may help to dissipate that illusion.

For there is a sense in which we are not just contained within the Absolute, but the Absolute exists in each of us. For the essence of the Absolute is intense consciousness, and something of that intense consciousness is present in each of us. Thus the same spiritual essence is present in every person and ultimately in everything. That is why we should have a loving, or at the least a benevolent, attitude to others so far as we can, because we are not fundamentally separate beings. Immorality stems from thinking that our own experiences are real in a sense in which the experiences of others are not, from which it follows that they do not have that real goodness and badness which ours often do. (This was Royce's earlier view of ethics.) To be ethical is not to make some great contrast between Thou and I, or us and them, but to realize that every Thou is an I as truly as oneself, and that we all share a common destiny in its main particulars. This should increase the bonding each of us feels to other sentient individuals.

Sometimes a sacrifice of our own best chance of happiness is demanded of us by the known unhappiness of others, now or to come, and avoidable by our sacrifice. If we take in the reality of others and have entered into the practice of a life of loving or at least benevolent relations with others, then we may be motivated to make an act of self-sacrifice.

However, some egotism is difficult to avoid, primarily because it is only the *conception* of pleasure and pain in others which can work on us (however vivid that conception), whereas we are continually under the influence of our own actual pleasure and pain.

(C) Utilitarianism, Absolute Idealism, and the Individual

A charge often laid against utilitarianism is that it fails to recognize the importance of individual persons, who are reduced simply to receptacles of pleasure and pain. This charge is not justified if our experiences are conceived realistically. For it is part of the very nature of almost our every experience that it is redolent of our past and future. Anyway, the utilitarianism which I advocate does not think in terms of a hedonistic calculus. It claims only that what fundamentally matters is the spread of happiness and the prevention of likely unhappiness. How different moments of happiness or unhappiness, whether of the same person or of another, are weighted comparatively is another matter, which I must pass over here, as this is not a treatise on ethics.

(D) Utilitarianism and Hedonism as Traditional Enemies

As opposed to calculative utilitarianism, I favour what may be called 'way of life utilitarianism'. It is not a good way of living to be constantly doing calculations as to what course of action will yield either you, or all sentient individuals affected by an action, the greatest balance of pleasure over pain. Better to adopt a way of living which is likely to be as happy moment by moment for all concerned (you and those affected by what you do) as circumstances allow. And happiness at a moment is the moment's overall hedonic character, not a sum of individual pleasures which it contains, while unhappiness is similarly a matter of the overall hedonic character of one's consciousness at such moments. But such is the intimate relation between one moment of experience and another that each owes much of its character to all earlier moments of one's life. Thus, while a happy life is not a mere generalization about one's moment by moment consciousness, it seems to me rubbish to say that one cannot ask whether someone is presently happy or unhappy. Of course, there are bitter-sweet moments where the two are so blended that it is hard to know how to describe them.

(E) Attitudes of Absolute Idealists to Utilitarianism

In associating absolute idealism with utilitarianism, I am well aware that these two are traditional enemies. No one was more scathing about hedonistic utilitarianism than F. H. Bradley. Bosanquet seriously suggested that to regard pain as an evil is probably mistaken. T. H. Green thought that it was the increase of virtue, rather than pleasure, and reduction of vice, rather than pain, which should be our own and society's aim.

Why have so many idealists taken a dim view of hedonistic accounts of value? There are several reasons. One is that pleasure was understood as something other than an experience which feels good and pain as something other than an experience which feels bad. Such idealists tended to think of pleasure as a series of momentary titillations, which had nothing to do with the general course of one's life and the development of one's character. But this is simply not true of those experiences which we feel most deeply as good. Doubtless they also thought that certain forms of suffering can deepen the character (which is true, though they can also worsen it), and that an ethic which was concerned with simply totting up the quantity attributed to momentary pleasures and deduction of a sum of momentary pains trivialized life. But none of this is contrary to the kind of hedonistic utilitarianism advocated here.

But perhaps we should not talk of 'pleasure', but of experiences which feel good as they are actually felt, and talk not of 'pain', but of experiences which feel bad as they are actually felt. We are then not so very far from Bradley's later position that the good is what satisfies desire, and evil, in the sense most relevant here, is 'failure to realize an end'. (See APPEARANCE, 175 and 356.) But I am too deep in utilitarian lore to change my terminology.

(F) Self-Realization

The goal of life, according to many idealist philosophers, is self-realization. This was particularly the case with F. H. Bradley (in *Ethical Studies*). And, despite my disclaimer above, it may be thought that my account so reduces the significance of persons that it is hardly compatible with regarding self-realization as our highest good. (Indeed, absolute idealism has been accused of the same failure to register the importance of individuals as utilitarianism, and sometimes with justice. Bosanquet is a case in point. However, this derives from a lack of imagination regarding the plight of individuals.)

For people can be happy only if they feel that they are achieving something in their life. This means that they must have some ideal of the kind of person that they would like to be. If self-realization is the process of becoming that kind of person, or moving towards doing so, then I certainly agree that it is of the first importance for human beings. For it is a main determinant of their happiness over time.

However, self-realization, if it is not to be at the cost of others, must not take on too competitive a form. There will always be more losers than winners in competitive situations. Therefore, there is much to be said for reducing the amount of competitiveness in a society unless this can be of a type which does not cause sadness for the losers. It is much better if people are concerned to improve themselves than to win in the races of life.

Of course, it will be said that vigorous competition is required if human life is to reach the summits. This must be allowed to some extent, but it is always better if one is competing with oneself, so to speak, rather than with others. Or, alternatively, the goal of competition and the personality of the victor must be such that the winner is the kind of person whose victory will be a victory for all, rather than something liable to promote envy more than anything else.

To this it will be objected that a competitive economy serves to give more people what they want than does any more socialistic alternative.

But even so, it is for the good of all that firms try to produce a good service rather than to overtake others. This issue in economics cannot be discussed here, however.

XIX The Problem of Evil for Absolute Idealism

We all know the problem of evil as it arises for Judaeo-Christian theism, and presumably for Islam too. There is much evil in the world, which God must be either unable or unwilling to prevent. In the first case he is not absolutely omnipotent, in the second case not perfectly good, yet it is part of what makes him God in the relevant sense that he has these two properties.

Evil is divided into natural evil and moral evil. By the first is meant suffering, especially that which arises from natural, rather than human, causes; by moral evil is meant wickedness. (It is unclear to me whether pain caused by human wickedness, as opposed to the wickedness itself, is to be classed as natural or moral evil.) I might say in passing that so far as moral evil goes, I believe that it always rests on narrowness of vision, which an understanding of the fact that all conscious beings matter just as much in and to themselves as one matters to oneself, should dispel— could we only keep our grasp of this fact a strong enough influence on how we live our lives. (A few people seem never to grasp it.)

The formally most promising theological solution to the problem of evil appeals to the high value of free will. This claims that it is such a great good that human beings should have free will that it was worth God's risking that they would misuse it. However, some of us find it hard to make sense of free will in a sense which will do this job. Other solutions to the problem usually take the form of supposing that what appears as evil is really good, or at least an essential contribution to a good which outweighs its badness.

The problem of evil does not arise in quite the same way for absolute idealistic pantheism. For, according to this, God is the universe, conceived as a conscious being, rather than its creator. But it surely still does have a very similar problem.

Reality as a whole (what we properly call the universe), so I have argued, is a total experience which includes all experiences which there are (and thus all experiential continuants, or feeling individuals, which there are), and thus everything.[29] Since this whole is eternal, and change pertains to it only as an eternal ordering of events within it, it cannot suffer from the dissatisfactions of finite individuals. For dissatisfaction can only belong to something striving in time. Thus there can be no striving on the part of the whole. It must therefore experience the totality of things as being good.

But if this is so, how can it contain so many terrible evils? For myself, I totally reject the idea that these are only apparently evil. On the contrary, they are really so, quite dreadfully so in too many cases.

But before contributing my mite, let us consider, or remind ourselves, how the absolute idealists, discussed in this book, all of whom seem to have thought of the scheme of things as a whole as supremely good, dealt with the problem of evil: G. W. F. Hegel, T. H. Green, F. H. Bradley, Bernard Bosanquet, and Josiah Royce.

Hegel thinks all evil 'a subordinate and vanquished nullity'[30] required by the dialectical process from Being to the Absolute Idea. It arises because the Absolute Idea, in order to move on from being the merely abstract Logical Idea to its actualization in the concrete worlds of Nature and of Spirit, must alienate itself from itself and lose its sense of what it truly is, and that it can regain its sense of this only through a process requiring suffering.

But was quite so much evil required along the way? Granted, it has been replied, that some evil is required, who can say how much? But one is inclined to echo something said by Dostoevsky, and hold that the torture of one child by psychopaths (such as the Moors murderers or Frederick West) is enough to make us doubt that this world is the best possible.

T. H. Green has little to say on the issue, but seems to have thought of evil as an inevitable temporary (or at least constantly decreasing) phase in the process by which the Eternal Consciousness brings itself into the temporal world through human minds.

Bradley treated the problem of evil somewhat lightly. He said that since he did not believe in a creator who planned the world as it is, his philosophy gives no purchase to the problem of evil. But in so far as he thought that the world was perfect, surely he does have a version of the problem. (APPEARANCE, ch. 17; see also his letter to William James of 21 Sept. 1897, in CORRESPONDENCE, 160–2. See Bibliography for Ch. 6.)

Bernard Bosanquet, as we saw, deals with the problem in some detail in his Gifford Lectures. His approach, on the whole, is to emphasize how the standard examples of evil are really examples of something good, when properly understood. In my chapter on his thought I have already taken a pretty negative stand against him on this, so I shall say no more here.

Of our five absolute idealists, it is Royce who faces the problem most head on, and gives an answer which has some force. His position, put simply, is that the greatest possible goods are those which consist in the conquest of evil, and that their actualization therefore required much evil. He thinks that we can verify this in the way in which we experience our own lives. We all (so Royce hopes his reader will agree) must realize that we are at our best, not when we are just smoothly decent in situations which hold out no temptation to behave badly, but when we resist some temptation arising from the morally inferior elements in our personality. This is an example of the general principle that the world is better for the efforts of those who have rid it (or even just tried to rid it) of such evils as slavery and tyranny. Well, as Royce argues his case, I cannot in the end accept it. I cannot believe that the horrors inflicted on Jews and Gypsies by the Nazis or on Kurds and others of his own people by Saddam Hussein are worth it as providing the good involved in their defeat. In short, I cannot bring myself to deny that the world would have been better without its torturers, torture, and the tortured.

So, avoiding the problematic word 'perfect', what can I say myself in support of the universe's essential goodness? I can only suggest that all this evil must somehow be intrinsically bound up with what is good in the world, and that it simply had to be there if there was to be a world of any worth. Take anything in the world which makes it valuable, and it will be true that this could not have occurred unless the rest of history, human, natural, and cosmic, were just as it has been and will be and is 'now'.

So my position is quite different from the view that all apparent evil is really good. There is real unmitigated evil in the world, and it would be better if it was not there. My suggestion, rather, is that for some inscrutable reason it had to be there, though as something to be gradually overcome (i.e. which will diminish in the 'later' phases of the 'C series').

Inscrutable as the reason for this may be, if, as I have suggested, all real relations are internal, then we can be sure that none of what is good in the world could have occurred unless all that is evil in it occurred too. But this does not preclude that there might have been quite similar goods instead. And we do not know why it is that the precise goods which do occur in our world had to occur, rather than something else like them not similarly linked to so much evil.

I would find this easier to understand if I thought reincarnation true, and that we are all on a path to some eventual salvation which requires much suffering along the way. But I doubt that this is a sufficient ground for believing in reincarnation, and I cannot with intellectual honesty say more than that I think it just possibly true.[31]

Be that as it may, I incline somewhat uneasily to the view that there was really no alternative to the cosmos and its history just as it has unfolded and will continue to do so: that for reasons largely beyond us, it was just bound to be that way; and that in spite of its being that way and containing so much that is vile, it is still on balance better than nothing, in fact, on balance very good.

Certainly, there is no denying that the amount of horrible wickedness in the world is appalling. Nothing can be said to palliate this. But if the character of the universe is such that it is better that it (the universe) exists than that it does not, one may still be glad that it exists despite all this horror and wickedness. And one can cherish the hope that somehow human decency will increase rather than decrease with time.

If it is true that the world is necessary in its every detail, then this goes some way to solving intellectually (if not emotionally) the problem of evil, and allowing us to think that the existence of the world is something with which the Absolute is somberly pleased and with which we have the right to be so too. The objection most likely to be taken to this is that necessity is a matter of the relation between concepts rather than something which can pertain to existing facts. But I am not convinced that this is true. In fact, the claim that nothing factual can be necessary may seem rather a strange view for those not set against it by the arguments of most philosophers since Hume.

Still, in so far as we can speak of the Absolute as *choosing* its world, I would say that, if we understood things well enough, we would see that the only choice was between this world and nothing, and that it is *in toto* a good deal better than nothing. Not that nothing was a real alternative.

Can we conclude anything about the significance of human history (and cosmic and natural history too)?

XX Is the World Improving?

Why have I said that evil is *sub specie temporis* likely to be something reducing over time? Well, McTaggart was surely right in arguing that the goodness of the universe requires that *sub specie temporis* it is getting better rather than worse. And if we believe in the Absolute, it is hard not to accept the view that everything temporal is moving towards 'One far off divine event to which the whole Creation moves'.[32]

Unless this was so, the Absolute could not experience itself as good, as it seems a necessary truth that it does. For where there is consciousness with no restless urge to get on to the next moment, there must be satisfaction. So the Cosmic Mind must basically find itself and the world with which it is identical as something which, as a whole, is good.

Now it is surely easier to understand how the Eternal Consciousness may be joyous if we suppose that *sub specie temporis* the world is moving towards a final state of overall joy. This cannot be proved, but seems likely. Not, I admit, that present auguries are too favourable, but there is a long time to go yet, and there are some promising signs. I am thinking of all the UN and charitable aid agencies, the assertion of human rights against governments and dictators, the taking more seriously of the rights of animals, and widespread environmental concern. There are, at the present time, powerful forces working against these, but there does seem to be a slow process of the moralization of humankind which may be winning in the long run.[33]

XXI Religion

Does Absolute Idealism Meet our Criteria of what a Religion Is?

I come finally to a summing up of the bearings of absolute idealism on religion. Clearly the religious outlook which follows from, or at least fits well with, the metaphysic which I support is not orthodoxly Christian. On the other hand, it seems to me that it supports Jesus's two great commandments (though perhaps more straightforwardly the second):

Love the Lord thy God with all thy might, etc.
Love your neighbour as yourself.

But even if it is not orthodoxly Christian, it is at any rate a religious perspective on the world. Not that the present author is himself at all adequate as a representative of such a religious outlook. But there are some people who enjoy a more vibrant personality than I do myself and feel things more deeply, who seem intuitively to have a view of the world which comes to much the same as the message of this metaphysic.

Certainly we are all part of the Eternal Consciousness, and emotions of religious devotion towards it are not inappropriate. But does absolute idealism provide the basis for a genuinely religious outlook on life, or is it just a philosopher's lifeless, even if true, theory?

In the first chapter I suggested five conditions which must be met by anything properly called a religion. I said also that what satisfied all five conditions was a community religion, and that what satisfied only the first four was a personal religion. I added that a personal religion may function for some people as their personal interpretation of a community religion.

The conditions were that a religion must be:

1. A belief system held to be true which affects the whole way in which those who seriously believe in it live their lives.

2. A belief system intrinsically associated with emotions which can be called 'religious'. (It is hard to say precisely which emotions count as such. However, they must be in some way 'cosmic': that is, directed at the nature of things in general, envisaged somehow as forming a spiritual whole not exhaustively describable in terms of purely empirical or scientific terms.)

3. A system of moral precepts which the belief system and the cosmic emotion encourage and help people to live by.

4. Furthermore, a life suffused by these beliefs, emotions, and moral precepts must offer some kind of salvation, whether this be expressed secularly as happiness of an enduring kind, or as some general sense of well-being—or some reward in terms of happiness in the life to come. More generally, it offers a way of being saved from something bad, whether this be despair or sin or whatever.

5. Some would hold that a religion must, in addition to the foregoing, be held in common by a larger or smaller number of people, normally with some ceremonies expressive of their beliefs and feelings, or even for its supposed supernatural effects. In short, some people think that the only real religions are community religions.

Outlooks which arise from, or are closely associated with, a metaphysical system like any discussed in this book are unlikely to constitute community religions, but it seems to me that they are quite capable of functioning as personal religions, and for some of their adherents as a personal interpretation of a community religion. (There have been followers of Whitehead and Hartshorne who felt at home with Methodism, while conceiving God and other religious realities in terms of process philosophy.) Thus a religious outlook specially associated with process philosophy (the philosophy of Whitehead and Hartshorne and their followers) might be called a personal form of Christianity or some denomination thereof. A personal religion may of course have many adherents, but inasmuch as it has no organizational aspect, it counts as a personal religion. Spinozism, I suggest, is a personal religion for an unknown number of persons.

God, as Spinoza put it, loves himself with an intellectual love, and our love for others and for the Absolute itself is a component of that love. And, as Spinoza says, we can be part of the intellectual love with which God loves himself. We do this by accepting and understanding our lot in life and responding to the needs of others and our own in the way which a clear understanding points us toward.

Absolute Idealism and Community Religions

But what attitude should an absolute idealist take to organized community religions? Surely he should be sympathetic to them so long as they promote ethically desirable behaviour. Some of their doctrines are likely to be nearer than others to the metaphysical truth, as he conceives it, but that is not the ground on which they should be judged (though it may make it more appropriate for him to belong to one rather than another). For to me it seems that the main role of a church or other organized religion is that it does or should fulfil the need which people have (in my opinion) to be committed to some moral ideal, in which they are sustained by belonging to a community which encourages and celebrates it. People rather sneer at the idea of wanting to be able to label oneself something, but in fact, if one does, that is an encouragement to live up to what this implies.

Worship and Prayer

Worship and prayer are likely to be the things which a Pascal or a Kierkegaard finds most lacking in a religion based on absolute idealism. As a public act, prayer can only hold as an element in a community religion. How far an absolute idealist may feel that he can belong to some faith community, interpreting its doctrines and practices in his own way, is rather a personal matter, into which I shall not enter. But we may well ask whether an absolute idealist can make much sense of prayer and worship as personal activities. The real question is whether absolute idealism is likely to encourage any sort of private prayer or worship.

If prayer means a period of fresh commitment to one's highest ideals, with the aid of feelings directed towards God, however conceived, I see no reason why it should not be practised by someone whose personal religion had its basis in absolute idealism. If it is petitionary prayer, asking for certain things to happen not within the individual's power in any ordinary way, I suspect that it would be rejected by most absolute idealists as inappropriate. But if it is a similar commitment to one's own self-improvement, it might well be recommended and practised. It is also worth remembering the saying 'Prayer changes people and people change things'.

There is one thing, however, somewhat related to petitionary prayer, and that is *grace*, conceived of as a special act of God to help a particular individual achieve something, especially morally. For the absolute idealist, the whole world system, in space, time, and the absolute consciousness, is one unified whole, which cannot be interrupted by such special acts to help one individual; therefore he cannot accept such a notion. He may even think that the doctrine is ethically dubious, since it is implied that it was an arbitrary decision on the part of God to show special favour to one particular person. But whether one would like it to be true or not, it is a belief incompatible with absolute idealism.[34]

Worship, again, is most naturally thought of as a public act on the part of a community. The whole concept of worship has been associated with the idea of God, requiring it of us if we are to benefit from his operations in the world, such as that of a good harvest. It seems to many of us that a God who longs to be praised is not a very ethically compelling one, and that there is no question, in any case, of the laws of nature being suspended for our benefit. But if it is a way of opening oneself to a sense of the glory of God, however conceived, then it can have a place in the religion of an absolute idealist. But granted that absolute idealism presents a view of the world which can properly be called 'religious', it is very much a personal matter whether one persuaded of its truth finds that he can interpret enough of the beliefs and practices of any particular community religion to belong to it and be spiritually refreshed and ethically assisted by it. Suitably modified for our own time, I think that Spinoza's view of the universal religion is especially helpful here.

Absolute Idealism and the Benefits of Religion

In Chapter 1, again, I suggested that religion may be expected to fulfil a respectable number of the eight roles which follow:

1. provide an eternal object of love, which also provides a sense of ultimate safety;
2. give the encouraging news that ultimately the good is more powerful than the bad or evil;

3. provide a degree of comfort when the world looks bleak;
4. rid us of the sense of cosmic loneliness, which some feel;
5. promise (or threaten) a life after death, and perhaps reunion with one's loved ones;
6. promote ethically desirable behaviour, giving it a stronger motivation than a moral outlook abstracted from any system of beliefs about the world can do;
7. make moral demands upon us, not all of which are easy;
8. give practical guidance as how to behave.

I have some inclination to add a ninth function of religion, though it is somewhat close to the third item above, and should perhaps even replace that. This is

9. reconciliation, by which I mean some way of coming to terms with the nature of things.

The first four conditions are, I believe met, at least for people of a certain temperament, by absolute idealism. And so may be each of the others with the rather likely exception of (5). But many will not have emotions describable as 'religious' unless they believe in a God of a more personal nature than an Eternal Consciousness or Absolute.

Still, all must admit that there is an inconceivably[35] great Whole of which we are all parts. And modern astronomy has increased our sense of its vastness (whether it is strictly infinite mathematically or not) and of the innumerable strange processes going on within it. And most of us do feel at times amazed awe at 'the starry heavens', as did Kant, however we feel about 'the moral law within'.

Yet the impressive magnitude of the physical universe seems rather bleak if there is no consciousness of, or within it, but the human and animal, or similar creatures on some remote planets. But if this physical vastness is the way in which an inconceivably rich unitary mind appears to certain little bits of itself, the bleakness is less, and the wonder more.

It may be asked, can absolute idealism provide any kind of comfort in life's sorrows, which is what people are often looking for in a religious belief? Well, we must bear in mind that the Absolute is an eternal *nunc stans*. That is to say, it is not something which changes over time, but something which experiences all times in one comprehensive grasp. I have suggested, after Royce, that we may conceive of it as eternally (not always) experiencing something somewhat like, though infinitely vaster than, our specious present. If so, there will be, for it, a contrast between the earlier and the later. This will be a relation of the same kind as we feel at every moment of our conscious lives when we are *immediately* aware of one sound or sight, or other presentation, coming before another. But the specious present of this Eternal Consciousness will not be transitory like ours, no sooner experienced than gone, but something just eternally there.

It is obviously extremely difficult for us to imagine or conceive such a thing with any clarity. Still, the idea is not altogether beyond our comprehension. The two ideas of an experience (a) including a *before* and *an after* as our specious presents do, but (b) neither being nor seeming to be on its way out of existence, even as it comes into existence, as our experiences are, does not seem to me incoherent. Indeed, I am inclined to think that it is something which compels belief if we are to solve real logical, or ontological, problems.

But why should we think of the Eternal Consciousness as essentially good? I have given my reason already. To find something bad is to be dissatisfied with it, and how can there be dissatisfaction at something with no straining to be rid of it? But an Eternal Consciousness, as absolute idealism conceives it, cannot wish that it could move on to something better. For the very idea of its having a future is incoherent, since although it includes all time, it is not in time itself. So I can only suppose that the Eternal Consciousness is eternally satisfied with itself—that is, finds itself essentially good. And this it could not be, as remarked in section XIX, unless, conceived as a process in time, history is a movement towards some kind of consummation which will justify all that came before.

And this surely does provide some comfort, if a rather austere one. Whether we ourselves are to share in it or not, the idea of such a divine consummation gives a point to the universe which straight atheism does not.

Absolute Idealism and the Question of an Afterlife

This leads to the question of life after death. Absolute idealism is certainly consistent with this, but does not require or prove it. For the absolute idealist will see no difficulty in principle with the idea of a stream of consciousness so related to that which pertains to the present life as to be properly counted by anyone concerned (and by the Absolute) as its continuation after death as this historical person. But absolute idealism seems, in its general principles, equally consistent with our complete cessation as temporal beings after our death. More specific reasons and evidence may indeed point us one way or the other, but I claim no knowledge of any such thing myself.

But what of something more like the eternal existence as *an essence in God's mind*, such as Spinoza claimed we possessed? (See E5p23.)

Spinoza seems to have thought of this personal essence as something which of itself implies nothing as to its fate during its period of temporal actualization. For, if I follow him correctly, although the essence in its eternal form of being, as a component of the divine mind, is conscious, its consciousness involves no suggestion of its belonging to ancient Rome, the Stone Age, the seventeenth century in the Netherlands, or the thirtieth century CE, or indeed on some other remote planet. But if each of us is the actualization of such an eternal essence, it must surely be somehow more historical than Spinoza conceives it as being. I find it hard to believe that my essence is so indifferent to the period of its temporal actualization that it might just as well have been actualized in the Stone Age as in a period starting in 1932. If I have an eternal essence, I suspect that it is more like a unified synopsis of my life experienced within God as a single individual. (This has some affinity with Royce's view concerning an eternal self.) This idea fits well with absolute idealism, and may be difficult to avoid. But all it means is that it is eternally true that there is an idea of me in the divine mind—how far this idea has an individual unitary consciousness of itself is questionable. Either way, its reality implies nothing about personal immortality or post-mortality as ordinarily conceived.

But is it inconsistent to contrast my eternal essence with my existence in time, as I am following Spinoza in doing, while yet raising the question as to whether I shall exist as a historical person after death? No, for time certainly exists, as a phenomenon well founded in the C series, and it is quite in order philosophically to speculate about where it may be leading any of us in what for us now is the future.[36]

That being so, it is quite legitimate for me to talk about the past and the future. Moreover, time is not entirely an illusion. For each moment of consciousness has its precise position in the C series, which is the reality which we experience as time. The illusion is that each moment feels itself to be in the process of dropping out of existence as the next ones come.

For there is a kind of *earlier* and *later* in the Absolute, while ordinary moments of finite consciousness experience themselves as being in a certain position in time which makes it quite reasonable to raise the question of whether I do or do not exist as a temporal being after my death.[37]

So absolute idealism leaves immortality (or at least a period of post-mortal existence) as a possibility, and it also leaves it as a possibility that there is an eternal version of myself within it, which, like the Absolute itself, experiences a temporal succession in an eternal kind of frozen specious present. Anyone who has grounds, empirical or a priori, which suggest that we do have some sort of immortality or eternal existence, can certainly fit this into an absolute idealist view of things, but the bare theory of absolute idealism cannot establish this as fact.

On the other hand, in so far as the temporal succession is something which is experienced as an eternal whole by the Absolute, I do have a kind of eternity. For each moment of my consciousness is eternally experienced by the Absolute as part of its total contents. That we are eternal in this sense may or may not be thought a blessing. If our life has been predominantly dreadful, it may be a sorrowful thought that it is eternally just there. But if we are glad that we have lived our lives, we may be glad that they are eternally a part of the absolute experience which is total reality. (This is somewhat similar to Nietzsche's *amor fati*.)

Whatever we conclude within the parameters laid down, it seems to me that absolute idealism has in its own way a certain religious character calculated to promote religious emotions. For it reassures us that somehow reality is not so fleeting or so bad as it often seems. But whether we will personally experience more of its real and perfect eternal being than we do here and now, is a matter which, so far as I am concerned, is an open question, though at this moment I incline to the negative. All this wonderful Nature seems rather wasted if it is there for us only as a preparation for another world. Reincarnation is another matter, for it allows that we may all be in progress to some omega point of ultimate perfection which will occur in a timeless version of this world, rather than in another, and in which nature as a whole may be 'saved' if we like to put it so.

Notes

1. It has been said that this unified perceptual field is something of a myth on the part of many philosophers and psychologists. It is true that when not thinking about them, objects may loom up at us without appearing as units within such a field, but in some vaguer way or even as complete units on their own. This is surely often true. None the less, when one addresses oneself to what one is experiencing, one surely sees everything as held within just such a whole, though not a steady whole. It need hardly be said that this field is often filled in by past associations, rather than by present sensory stimuli. I myself frequently see a cat instead of the cushion which I should be seeing. And when I very occasionally mistake one of my identical twin daughters for the other, she looks different from what she does when, as is usual, I am right.
2. For old-fashioned but fascinating efforts to make four-dimensional shapes almost imaginable, see HINTON and ABBOTT.

3. Someone may suggest that it is an unwarranted assumption that reality as a whole has any general character. Well, of course there may be radically different sorts of reality (as mind and matter for the dualist). But if that is so, the metaphysician's task will be to form a clear and distinct idea (by contrasting direct or indirect imaginings) of each sort of reality and of how they are or are not related.

4. However, the view of truth taken here is realist. It is idealist only in the sense that it is realistically and objectively true that nothing exists which is not experienced.

5. 'Noumenal' initially meant intelligible, as opposed to perceivable or imaginable. As I use it, it is simply the adjectival form of 'thing in itself', since no other convenient adjective is available.

6. Hartshorne points out that his view allows that there are unconscious things. For just as a cricket team may consist (down to a certain level) of conscious beings, and yet not be conscious itself, so may a thing entirely composed of conscious atoms still be unconscious itself. The reader will be able to see from Chapters 2–9 that my own position is more complex than this. It's all a matter of how sharply distinct from surrounding consciousness the mental aspect of a physical thing is, and this is a matter of degree.

7. My most detailed presentation of the theory of relations adumbrated here is in VINDICATION, chs. 5 and 6, and JAMES AND BRADLEY, Part II, ch. 3, §§5–9.

8. 'At least as much' will do for my argument, though when that whole is the Absolute (see below), it will surely be more of an individual.

9. I say 'perhaps' because it is not so clear that in the general run of thought one has the brain in mind more than just generally the head, or even some other parts of the body. I am dealing in phenomenology here, not science.

10. It may be said that things in other universes would be related to things in ours by the relation *having no real relation to each other*. If this were accepted, some reformulation of some of the things said here would be required; but I think it best to say that this is not properly referred to as a relation, whether real or ideal, at all. Whether they might have ideal relations with each other is another matter.

11. I am unsure whether Whitehead is right that a total experience cannot be affected by what is contemporary with it.

12. Note that when I speak of a stream of experience, I am speaking of something which can cross periods of unconsciousness, at least in those more personal streams which constitute the consciousness of humans. All that is required is a certain sort of continuity of the stream before a period of unconsciousness and after. This is mainly a matter of how the later stretch of the stream picks up purposes from the earlier stretch, and feels itself to be a continuation of it.

13. Although my overall position is Bradleyan, the reader will recognize the strong influence of William James here.

14. Noumenal time plays a similar role in this account to what the C series does in McTaggart's metaphysics.

15. This section is adapted from my VINDICATION, 30–3. The core argument derives from George Santayana, but was not associated by him with absolute idealism.

16. You may say that it is enough that there *was* such a reality. But how can what was be distinct from what was not if the past has become nothing and in no sense *is*?

17. Leemon McHenry has objected to my line of thought by arguing, in the spirit of process philosophy, that I am conceiving the past as determinate in the same way as is the present, and then arguing that the future is in itself determinate in the same way. But, he says, I am starting out from a misconception as to the present. For this is, as long as it is present, in the process of self-creation, and therefore not determinate, only becoming so when it is past. (THE PAST; W&B, 145–53; and in conversation.)

    There are certainly difficult questions here about the phenomenology of time, and in particular of the present, even if it is the specious present that is in question, rather than a supposed instantaneous present. But it does seem to me that the short stretch of time which constitutes the present (or does so as it seems to itself) is definite in character, even if this definiteness includes the way in which it is creating itself. In any case, the difficulty about how there can be a truth about the past if it has become nothing or somehow different from what it *was* remains, and it seems to me that this can be resolved only if its reality is the same as that of the present, and is simply eternally creating itself, if it is true that that is what the present does. It follows, by the argument given above, that the future is also eternally creating itself within the limit set by what other moments of experience are eternally doing. How they do so in accordance with one another is, of course, for an absolute idealist, because the Absolute is eternally a whole of self-creating moments.

18. Whitehead reminds us that mathematics at the time of ancient Greece was splendid in its treatment of spatial figures and numerals, but had not developed a mathematics which could cope with temporal process. This led to thinking of the real world (which alone could be precisely thought of) as a timeless absolute, so that the 'final outcome has been that philosophy and theology have been saddled with the problem of deriving the historical world of change from a changeless world of ultimate reality' (MODES, 81–2).

19. For a fuller statement, see JAMES AND BRADLEY, Part II, ch. 4, §3, also HARTSHORNE.

20. Perhaps I am influenced by Schopenhauer in saying this. I don't know.

21. A fundamental answer would have to deal in streams of experience rather than subjective individuals. It is not that there are not really such things as subjective individuals, but that their existence and history must at the most ultimate level be analysed as facts about streams of experience.

22. See my INTRINSIC VALUE; also FOUNDATIONS.

23. These ideas, it may be worth noting, are most often ideas of the life world rather than of the world in its noumenal nature, though perhaps the latter could be linked up in similar fashion with behaviour.

24. This does not imply that the self is always or even normally seeking pleasure or the avoidance of pain for itself. For what the self is directed at is the goodness or badness of that of which it has energizing pleasant or unpleasant ideas.

25. George Santayana, in *The Sense of Beauty*, described beauty as objectified pleasure. I call it 'objective', rather, because it may from the start be pleasurable aspects of the internal not-self.

26. See my VINDICATION, esp. 239–41, for a more complete statement.

27. What is here called an internal real relation was called a strongly holistic relation in VINDICATION.

28. Is it true, as Bentham said, that every pleasure is good in itself? Is the pleasure of a torturer good even if outweighed by the suffering of the victim and of the whole social system in which such a thing can occur? Unfortunately, I think that one must admit that every pleasure is in a certain way good—but in most cases of moral evil, it is so indissolubly mixed up with suffering for others that one cannot really isolate it and ascribe an individual value to it. (See FOUNDA-TIONS, 235–8.)

29. Whether it contains not only all actualized possibilities, but also a consciousness of all unactualized possibilities, is a real metaphysical problem, which I shall put aside here.

30. HEGEL HISTORY, 15.

31. It is sometimes said that Buddhism is inconsistent in believing in reincarnation while denying the existence of a substantial self which is more than a series of events. But reincarnation can properly be said to occur if, after someone's death, an individual is born whose mental states are related to his states of consciousness very much as they were to each other. For myself I do speak of a kind of personal essence present along the stream of experiences. In any case, there are relations which could hold between an individual now and one in the past which make it appropriate for the later person, if he recognized this, to regard that person as his own past self. This could happen between lives. But whether such reincarnation really does take place is a different matter.

32. Tennyson, *In Memoriam*, last two lines. Of course, for absolute idealism the universe was not exactly created, unless by itself. Whitehead, incidentally, explicitly criticizes Tennyson's idea of such an ultimate finale. See PR, 111/169.

33. Having just used the expression 'animal rights', a brief word here on this topic is called for. To have a (moral) right (so I suggest) is for there to be *something about* one in virtue of which moral agents have certain duties towards one, whether one is a moral agent oneself or not (as in the case of human babies). And the most important, even if not the only, relevant *something about* an individual is that they have a capacity to feel pleasure or pain something as true of animals as of humans. But what of the natural environment? Well, apart

from the need to conserve it for our practical, aesthetic and recreational needs, and even survival, we need the spiritual refreshment from the sense of oneness with the mysterious Whole to which we all always belong but which we feel more readily in some places than in others.

34. I have been told by my friend Stephen Medcalf that it was because it had no place for the notion of grace that T. S. Eliot turned against his youthful absolute idealism.

35. I use 'inconceivably' in a loose, popular sense.

36. In any case, I am in no worse a boat than was Kant, who thought that his noumenal essence was non-temporal, but postulated his temporal continuing move towards perfection after his death.

37. Also it may contain alternative time series in no temporal relation to that through which we ourselves live.

Chapter 10

Concluding Remarks

A metaphysical system could be religiously helpful to an individual in such ways as the following:

1. It might provide something like a religion for someone who accepted its truth.
2. It might fortify or enrich a religion to which the individual was already committed or inclined.
3. It might prompt certain emotions which are appropriate to the world as it is believed to be, and say something useful about how it is best to live in it.

In so far as a religion requires a community of believers, a metaphysical system could not provide this of itself. It would have to be provided, if at all, by some existing religious community whose doctrines could be interpreted in terms of it.[1]

Leaving aside the community aspect of religion, how far could any of the metaphysical systems examined in this book function as a religion for those who accepted them? Well, I said in my opening chapter that a religion may be defined as 'a truth to live by'. Of course, by 'a truth' I mean what is believed to be so by its adherents. And I explained the meaning of this by listing four criteria to be satisfied by a view of things which would come out as a religion on this definition. Especially important was the fact that it would profess to show that reality is some kind of spiritual whole, the nature of which cannot be adequately described in the language of science.

One great difference between science and metaphysics is that metaphysics seems to have no technological implications such as distinguishes our own time more and more from earlier times. The reason is that metaphysics deals with matters so pervasive that there is no question of altering them. It does, however, have practical implications inasmuch as a metaphysical picture of the world affects how those who accept it live their lives and what uses of technology they think the best. Certainly the ideal metaphysician will be one who is something of a scientist too, yet open to aspects of reality which science as such ignores. But this does not mean that the thought of those who are not scientists is worthless or bound to be false so far as it goes.

Yet it would be hopeless to advance a metaphysical system which was at loggerheads with the best science, and I hope that I have not done so in Chapter 9. Whitehead is the ideal metaphysician, in my opinion, inasmuch as he was equally at home in both science and metaphysics and could reasonably seek to synthesize them. Incidentally, I believe that Spinoza, of our philosophers, would have been most able to relate his ideas to the general theory of relativity, and that the process philosophy of Whitehead and Hartshorne harmonizes the best with quantum physics.

It would be tedious to work through all the metaphysical systems discussed and consider how far they satisfied or did not satisfy these criteria. I have had my say with reference to the version of absolute idealism which I support; as for the other systems investigated, my answer is given or implied in individual chapters. For myself, if we leave aside Kierkegaard, as one who deliberately did not offer a metaphysically based view of the world, it seems to me that acceptance of the philosophy of any of the others is calculated to influence deeply the way one feels about the world and the way one lives within it.

Matthew Arnold said that religion is 'morality touched by emotion' (and was much mocked by Bradley for doing so). I certainly agree with him that it is the ethical implications of a religion which matter most. But I would amplify his account by saying that it was a morality touched with emotion arising from some general idea of the character of reality.

Each of our philosophers shows, to the extent that his system is right, that a purely materialist conception of the world cannot be true. By 'materialism' here I mean the view that reality as a whole is physical or material through and through, meaning roughly that it consists entirely of what can be found within our public space and is observable by the senses with or without the aid of scientific instruments. And it is desirable that this should be shown, since materialism can give no account of how anything can be good or bad, or why what happens to conscious beings matters. Each of these philosophies has a notion of God, or the Absolute, and tells us that this is the reality with which we must (implicitly) be in tune if our lives are to be worth much.

My general conclusion is that each of our philosophers has something to say on religion, which, if accepted, should affect their reader's religious life, either by confirming him in his existing faith or by suggesting a new religious path.

Quite a number of Christians have found that some of these philosophies provide an intellectual backing to their faith, which they were coming to fear was lacking. While they might find themselves changing their minds on points of detail in their creed, they have found in these philosophies a stronger intellectual backing for their general outlook than they have found elsewhere. In the nineteenth century Hegel achieved this for many, and in more recent times Whitehead and Hartshorne have done so. T. H. Green did this for Robert Elsmere in the novel of that name, and I believe that he did it for many real people. That Hegel can do this for many people today I doubt, though I may well be wrong. Green's philosophy seems to me something that people might more reasonably believe today, as too the philosophies of Whitehead and Hartshorne.

So how far do each of the philosophical systems which we have examined offer 'a truth to live by'? Recall that our question is not whether such a system is true or not, or whether the emotions it encourages and supports are really right and good. The question is simply whether it is calculated to produce in someone who accepts it, emotions and behaviour which would seem of great value to him.

Descartes

Descartes doubtless believed in God and in the more essential doctrines of Christianity. However, his philosophical concern with God was as a guarantee that if we use our intelligence aright, we will not fall into error. Pascal was not far off in saying that the Cartesian God was remote from anything significantly Christian (or even religious).

Spinoza

Spinoza offers a highly individual set of beliefs to live by, and thence a religion. Its closest antecedent is Stoicism. At points it chimes with Christianity, and at others with Vedanta Hinduism; but as a whole it is unique. Its basic message is that the world is magnificent and to be enjoyed, and that we should not repine at our lot in it. We must accept our own slot in the world system, and do our best to live a positive life, with concern for others an important part of it.

Spinoza firmly rejected the personal and often irrational God of the Jews. He also rejected God as conceived in anything approximating to orthodox Christianity. His most basic claim is that the universe is a self-conscious mental and physical reality which is aware of itself as the home of everything. As such, he, or more properly *it*, rejoices in its own existence and powers. We can rejoice too if we realize that our lives are an essential part of a necessary cosmic process stemming from, and taking place within, a necessarily existing and perfect Whole. And the more we manage to understand the process and our part in it, the more we will rejoice, because the best part of ourselves, our reason, will be achieving its own special satisfaction, that of understanding things. I would add, on Spinoza's behalf, that if we use our intellect to think things out creatively, then, even if some of our conclusions are wrong, there will still be a rightness, and indeed truth, in the way in which we see the necessary implications of our starting-points. And at our best, we will be reconciled to fate, because we will recognize that everything which happens does so necessarily. This does seem to me a religion, or capable of being one.

Kant

I paid little attention to Kant. But if we were persuaded by him, we would try to live very morally committed lives and seek, in the faith, but not knowledge, that God is there to ensure that this is a fundamentally ethical universe.

Hegel

For a time Hegel provided many thinkers with what they thought was a philosophical interpretation and justification of Christianity.

For he presented a kind of 'justification of the ways of God (or the World Order) to Man'. For a convinced nineteenth-century Christian worried about his faith, Hegel offered a way of remaining committed to it, without perhaps offering anything which the faith, so far as believed in, had not offered already. For someone trying to base their thought and life on Hegel's teaching, not merely as a peculiar way of defending their native faith, it would offer a satisfaction somewhat similar to that offered by Spinoza, that of apparently understanding the ways of the world and one's place within it. One must, so it teaches, fulfil one's role in the world, accepting that it is all part of a great process in which ultimately everything makes sense. But the overall position is less persuasive to me, at any rate, than Spinoza's, while some of Kierkegaard's criticisms of it for its lifelessness are justified.

Kierkegaard

Kierkegaard provided a telling critique of Hegelian Christianity, and urged us to make a leap of faith and accept the paradoxes of Christianity in the hope of saving our own souls. We should not try to escape our own personal need for salvation, and for an answer to those of the great questions *which concern us personally*, by attempting to deaden our sense of our own situation through the contemplation of an abstract philosophical account of *reality as a whole*. Yet, the kind of Christianity he stands for is, to my mind, somewhat repellent.

T. H. Green

T. H. Green taught that the only satisfactory human life was one of earnest altruistic endeavour. Altruism, however, should be concerned with providing the opportunity for others to improve their own moral character, rather than with making their lives more comfortable. Christianity carries the right message, but has mixed it up with supernatural accompaniments which a mature mind must reject. We know that our personal endeavour after righteousness, and the encouragement of righteousness in others, is something which we do in the company of the great world spirit which is expressing itself in human history. And this gives us hope that the struggle is not in vain. Green's optimism was rather hasty, but not necessarily disproved by recent horrors as a fact about how things will work out in the long run.

Green comes across attractively as a person who lived out his philosophy. However, his extreme opposition to any hedonic motivation whatever is over-strained. But a certain grimness in his message is modified by his belief that moral character requires the basics of decent living conditions, a qualification of which his follower Bernard Bosanquet lost sight. Upon the whole, the upshot is the ideal which has been that of most Christians. In short, the God of this philosopher is very much, in effect, the God of Christianity.

Bosanquet

Bosanquet is so rich in ideas that he certainly merits the attention which we have given him, though it is hard to pin any single great idea upon him. His early papers and lectures showed great insight into the problems which religion was facing in his time, and still is. His later philosophy addresses a host of issues of religious significance from a point of view quite similar to that of F. H. Bradley (whose philosophy is discussed only briefly in this book). But, though to a great extent I follow Bradley myself, for me Bosanquet's more specific position is, as a whole, quite unattractive because of his Panglossism and his lack of compassion for those who suffer.

On the other hand, for one who could accept it, there is no doubt that his philosophy provides 'a truth to live by'. This is that ultimately everything is for the best, and that each of us has a contribution to make to the perfection of the Absolute. However, our contribution may be that of being something the suppression of which is good, or something more positive, achieved by the moral level or cultural level which we reach and help others to reach.

According to Bosanquet, the immanent purpose of the universe is twofold: (1) the creation of great souls; (2) the development of great social and cultural institutions and achievements. If we play our part in promoting these great ideals, we know that we are acting in accord with the basic nature of things. Bosanquet's engagement in social work had a harsh quality about it, stemming from the belief that its task was to raise the moral character of its clients, rather than reduce their misery.

Bosanquet and Bradley each put forward a viewpoint of real religious significance for anyone who can accept it. By and large, I do accept the philosophy of Bradley, though qualified by elements of Spinoza and the process philosophers. It seems to me that it shows that the world does have a point, and that it is up to us to identify ourselves with what we may hope will be cherished rather than mourned by the Absolute Consciousness.

Royce

Josiah Royce sought to show us initially that the distinction between selves is not ultimate, and that each of us is under the illusion, which we must seek to correct, that our own joy and suffering are more real than those of others. We should steep ourselves in a sense of the equal reality of the aspirations of others, and look for ways in which the aspirations of all conscious individuals can be satisfied harmoniously, encouraged by the fact that we are all parts of one great conscious whole which is working towards this end. Thus we should live in the spirit of the unity of all conscious beings, which is in fact the ultimate truth of things.

Later his message was, rather, that we can find our salvation only by finding 'causes' of which we can be devoted servants, and that in doing so we are participating in the great adventures of an absolute self.

Royce is of enduring significance for having provided what, certain assumptions made, is the best solution to the problem of evil from a theistic or pantheistic point of view. He also gives, in his earlier work, what is to my mind the best account of the rational basis of ethics. However, this is spoilt for me by some of the developments of his philosophy of loyalty.

Theologically I recommend him as having thought out how God is related to time more satisfactorily than any other thinker of whom I know.

Whitehead and Hartshorne

These two process philosophers stressed the creativity of which we are all capable, and claimed that all that we do, we do in close relationship with God. The goal is intensity of feeling, for ourselves and ultimately for the divine consciousness. The love of beauty is an all important value, but greater than that is love of the God who is operating within us by always pointing to the best currently open to us.

This process philosophy, so it seems to me, is a metaphysical version of the theism characterizing the belief of many workaday Christians. (It may also be developed in ways which can enrich the other great world faiths.) It certainly challenges traditional Christian theology, but in doing so gives it more relevance to Christian practice. On the other hand, there is a certain Nietzschean quality which is quietly present in Whitehead's thought: namely, that since intensity of experience is the greatest value, it may sometimes override what is commonly called 'morality'; this tugs in a somewhat contra-Christian direction.

Pantheistic Absolute Idealism

In Chapter 9 I offered my own development of absolute idealism, which is really a synthesis of Spinozism and Bradleyism. Its message is that our deeper feelings are our best clue to what reality is really like. It is something tragically beautiful, which enjoys itself as the unity of the experiences of all finite beings, and thereby as the unity of everything. This is something which we tap into in hearing great music or being moved by the beauty and sublimity of nature, and is experienced more fully by mystics. Ethically it is our task to do what we can to reduce the terrible suffering which is so endemic to human, and to some other, life forms, but which it gives us reason to hope is leading humanity and nature on to something more blessed. It can certainly operate as a personal religion, and may serve as a personal interpretation of some liberal form or derivative of Christianity or Hinduism.

Influence Outside the Study or Lecture Room

I have said a little in the text regarding how far the philosophy of each thinker related significantly to his life outside the study or lecture room. It seems to me that Spinoza and Green are the most impressive for having lived out their philosophy in all aspects of their lives. But none of our philosophers, so far as I know, did anything which is a bad advertisement for his philosophy.

I make no great claims for what absolute idealism pulled towards Spinozism has done for me as a person, since I fall far short of any relevant ideal. But it has helped me feel that what is beautiful is not mere surface appearance, but a manifestation of some deep significance at the heart of things, and that ethical striving is not in vain.

Mystical Experience

One rather surprising lack in the thought of these metaphysicians is that no attention is paid to any of those 'religious experiences' which for William James were the only evidence for the existence of the God in whom he believed. Several of these systems present a view of the world which fits well with the vision of things usually prompted by mystical experience. For the absolute idealism of Green, Bradley, Bosanquet, and Royce, the world is a spiritual unity, and our salvation must consist in living in harmony with it. Yet they hardly touch on the subject.

Even the most non-mystical of us have probably experienced at times a sense of a greater whole with which we can feel at one and thus be relieved for a time of our usual daily worries. Especially is this true when one is alone (humanly speaking) in some solitary place, perhaps with the sea lapping around a rock on which one is perched. And there are all the other grander spiritual experiences described by William James, *The Varieties of Religious Experience* and by Walter T. Stace in *Mysticism and Philosophy*.

Yet the philosophers studied in this book showed little sympathy with, or knowledge of, the ideas which such experiences have inspired in Indian thought, especially in Advaita Vedanta. This is partly because they felt that such a religion sapped the vital energies which they thought had led to humanity's greatest achievements. Royce was the only one among them who paid much attention to Advaita Vedanta-type thought. However, he was anxious to contrast his form of absolute idealism, for which little but blood, sweat, and tears were offered us in our temporal life, with this Eastern form of it, for which the ideal was to detach oneself in meditation from the normal worried busyness of human life. Hartshorne, from a different perspective, showed some interest in Buddhism.

However, it seems to me that while James was wrong to oppose the role of philosophical reasoning in establishing religious claims, he was certainly right that any philosophical characterization of religion should take account of mystical experience, whether as reported or known to him personally. And he himself admitted that prima facie absolute idealism seemed the obvious interpretation of their content, though he sought to interpret this pluralistically rather than monistically.

I cannot discuss this matter further, but merely note this failure to engage with mysticism on the part of philosophers whose systems might make good sense of the feeling that the barriers are breaking down, between oneself and what surrounds one, as also does pantheistic idealism.

The Value of Most of these Metaphysical Systems

Perhaps the greatest value of all these philosophies at their best is that they give an account of why we should be concerned with the welfare of others besides ourselves. Spinoza thought that it was because one could only live a satisfactory life in friendly co-operation with others, while at the higher levels of human development the intellectual love of God was something which men could encourage each others in enjoying. Green thought that one could only find that personal satisfaction, which is the goal of all human striving, by living a life of active altruism. Royce, at what I think his best, thought that selfishness and cruelty arise from necessary instincts when they are not accompanied by an adequate realization in imagination that the feelings of others are just as real as one's own, and later thought that it was only in joint membership of a beloved community that people could save themselves from misery, a beloved community which ultimately was that of all human beings and perhaps many other genuine individuals also. Whitehead and Hartshorne taught that selfishness arises from failing to realize that one's own future self and the future selves of others are largely on a par so far as the present ego's relation to them goes. Absolute idealism teaches that there is a common essence, that of consciousness as such, which is present in all people, all animals, and all nature, and it should be that essence in all its myriad finite forms, and its actualization in the great cosmic whole of all things, to which one's final devotion should be given.

But do these others include animals or even aspects of so-called inanimate nature? Here Spinoza fell down, in my opinion. This is partly because, noble as his thought was, he was too much committed to basing concern with others on our need of them in order to live satisfactorily ourselves. For while he shared with Royce the view that to realize fully that another is experiencing pleasure or pain is intrinsically calculated to give oneself pleasure and pain too, he did not use this as the basis of his moral views and regarded animals as outside our moral universe. Green similarly gave ethics a foundation which scarcely provides for the non-human (though apparently he himself felt especially close to God in the countryside). But in the case of the other thinkers at their best, there is much to suggest that our ethical concerns should not be confined to other human beings.

But how relevant is the metaphysics of any of these thinkers to their ethical ideals? The answer is that each metaphysic teaches us (so far as we accept it) to look on the world with eyes refreshed by a fuller grasp of its nature. Common to them all is the belief that there is an Eternal Mind which is the ultimate foundation of everything, and that our efforts to improve things will not ultimately be in vain.

For Spinoza we should see it as the scene of innumerable individuals each striving for their own perfection within a whole which is ultimately perfect; for Hegel, as the unfolding of the *Logos*; for Green as an eternal divinity actualizing itself slowly in time; for Bosanquet as the scene of the great values of civilization; for Royce as the gradual binding of human beings, and all other real individuals, into a great community which as a whole is loved by all; for pantheistic idealism as a great spiritual being living out its life in innumerable centres of experience and combining these all into one great experience; for Whitehead and Hartshorne as innumerable actual occasions striving to achieve more and more intense experiences under the guidance, and ultimately for the benefit, of God— who, can strike one, I fear, as rather greedy for excitement.

One cannot deduce detailed guidance from such general visions, but it is bound to make a difference as to how one interprets the world around one and one's own situation in it whether one shares in one of them. For me the truest vision is of a world of feeling beings each enjoying life as well it can, but often forced by a grim ANANKE into a state of misery, which, however, is in principle remediable by efforts to which we can each contribute, all united in a cosmic mind which guarantees a final worthwhileness to it all.

For everyone of good will the question arises: how much is it appropriate to seek happiness, or some supposedly higher value, for oneself, and how much for other people? These metaphysical systems spell out in different ways the fact that one is not the only pebble on the beach. But it is worth taking on board the view of Henry Sidgwick that there is a special rationality *both* in seeking to promote one's own happiness *and* in seeking to promote the happiness of conscious beings at large, and that neither of these is merely an implication of the other. For myself I am not sure that it is appropriate to seek to justify self-love before the bar of reason; it is simply an ultimate fact about what it is to be an individual, and if it is good that there are individuals, then their self-love is good. Hence it is so inevitable a part of human nature (and not only human) to have a special concern with one's own welfare that to preach an altruism which would disparage this concern is to teach a morality which few can be expected to live by. So it is highly desirable that it be shown, if it be true, that there need not be too much conflict here. And upon the whole it is true, as these metaphysicians have striven to show.

Positive feelings are more effective than negative warnings, as promoters of useful ethical endeavour and satisfactory self-realization, and each of these metaphysical systems offers an ultimately positive picture of the nature of reality. And in that way I think that they can function as a religion for whomsoever satisfies himself that they are true. They cannot all be completely true, but that does not affect the main point that each is religiously relevant as providing what it claims to be 'a truth to live by'.

Note

1. However, St Thomas Aquinas provides a metaphysical system in terms of which Roman Catholic thinkers have largely developed their views.

Bibliography

Abbreviations used in the text are given in square brackets.

Chapter 1

Barrow, J. D., and Tipler, F. J., *The Anthropic Cosmological Principle*. Oxford and New York: Oxford University Press, 1986. [BARROW AND TIPLER]

Caird, Edward, *The Evolution of Religion*, 3rd edn. Glasgow: J. MacLehose and Sons, 1899. [EVOLUTION]

Dawkins, Richard, *The Blind Watchmaker: Why the Evidence of Evolution Reveals a Universe without Design*. London: Longmans, 1986. [DAWKINS]

Descartes, René, *Meditations on First Philosophy*, 1641. (There are several translations of the Latin original, as well as various translations and, of course, French editions.)

Ely, S. E., *The Religious Availability of Whitehead's God*. Madison: University of Wisconsin Press, 1943. [ELY]

James, Susan, *Passion and Action: The Emotions in Seventeenth-Century Philosophy*. Oxford: Clarendon Press, 1997. [PASSIONS]

James, William, *The Varieties of Religious Experience*. London: Longmans Green and Co., 1902. [VRE]

Kierkegaard, Søren, *Concluding Unscientific Postscript to Philosophical Fragments*, trans. Howard V. Hong and Edna V. Hong. Princeton: Princeton University Press, 1992. [POSTSCRIPT]

Leslie, John, *Infinite Minds*. Oxford: Clarendon Press, 2001.

Macmurray, John, *The Self as Agent*. London: Faber & Faber Ltd., 1957. [THE SELF]

Mill, J. S., *Three Essays on Religion*. London: Longmans, Green, Reader and Dyer, 1874. [MILL]

Paley, William, *Natural Theology: Evidences of the Existence and Attributes of the Deity, Collected from the Appearances of Nature*. Charlottesville, Va.: Lincoln-Rembrandt, 1986 (first published 1802).

Pascal, Blaise, *Pensées*, trans. Honor Levi. Oxford: Oxford University Press, 1995 (Sellier arrangement). [PENSÉES]

Sell, Alan P., *Philosophical Idealism and Christian Belief*. Cardiff: University of Wales Press, 1995. [SELL]

Sprigge, T. L. S., 'Pantheism'. *The Monist*, 80/2 (April 1997), 191–217.

Whitehead, A. N., *Religion in the Making*. Cambridge: Cambridge University Press, 1930.

Chapter 2. Spinoza

1. Works of Baruch or Benedictus Spinoza

Spinoza Opera, 4 vols., ed. Carl Gebhardt. Heidelberg: Carl Winters, 1925 (GEBHARDT, volumes indicated in Roman numerals). (This is regarded as the best edition of the complete text.)

i: *Korte Verhandeling van God: Renati Des Cartes Principiorum*

ii: *Tractatus de Intellectus Emendatione* and *Ethica*.

iii: *Tractatus Theologico-Politicus* and *Tractatus Politicus*

iv: *Epistolae*

2. English translations of the Works of Spinoza mainly used

——, *Ethics Demonstrated in Geometric Order*. (There are quite a number of translations of the *Ethica* into English. References are as described in text.)

——, *Complete Works*, with translations by Samuel Shirley. Indianapolis: Hackett Publishing Co., 2002. [SHIRLEY]

——, *The Collected Works of Spinoza*, i, ed. and trans. Edwin Curley. Princeton: Princeton University Press, 1985. [CURLEY]

——, *The Ethics* and *Treatise on the Emendation of the Intellect*, trans. Samuel Shirley. Indianapolis and Cambridge: Hackett Publishing Co., 1992. [EMENDATION]

——, *The Letters*, trans. Samuel Shirley. Indianapolis and Cambridge: Hackett Publishing Co., 1995. (The numbering of the letters, as in my text and notes, is standard across editions.) [LETTERS]

——, *Tractatus Theologico-Politicus*, trans. Samuel Shirley. Brill Paperbacks, Leiden, etc.: E. J. Brill, 1991. [BRILL] [TTP] (Also in SHIRLEY.)

——, *Tractatus Politicus*. [TP] (In SHIRLEY.)

3. Biography

Nadler, Stephen, *Spinoza: A Life*. Cambridge: Cambridge University Press, 1999. [NADLER LIFE]

There are two short seventeenth-century biographies of Spinoza: (1) by an unreliable follower, (2) by a Lutheran clergyman (Colerus) who became interested in Spinoza when he moved into his old lodgings in The Hague.

(1) *The Oldest Biography of Spinoza*, ed. and trans. from the French by A. Wolf. London: G. Allen & Unwin, 1927. (Said to be by Jean Maximilien Lucas.)

(2) Colerus, Johann, *Korte, dog waaragtige Levens-beschrijving von Benedictus de Spinosa* (*Short Life of Benedict de Spinosa*). The Hague: Marinus Nijhoff, 1906. Repr. and trans. in POLLOCK.

4. Commentaries (used or cited)

Allison, Henry E., *Benedict de Spinoza: An Introduction*. New Haven: Yale University Press, 1987.

Bennett, Jonathan, *An Examination of Spinoza's Ethics*. Cambridge: Cambridge University Press, 1984. [BENNETT]

Curley, E. M., *Spinoza's Metaphysics: An Essay in Interpretation*. Cambridge, Mass.: Harvard University Press, 1969.

—— *Behind the Geometrical Method: A Reading of Spinoza's Ethics*. Princeton: Princeton University Press, 1988. [CURLEY 1988]

Donagan, Alan, *Spinoza*. New York and London: Harvester Wheatsheaf, 1988. [DONAGAN]

Garrett, Don, 'Spinoza's Necessitarianism'. In YOVEL 1991.

Grene, Marjorie (ed.), *Spinoza: A Collection of Critical Essays*. New York: Anchor Books, 1973.

Harris, Errol, *Is there an Esoteric Doctrine in the Tractatus Theologico-Politicus?* Medelingen vanwege Het Spinozahuis. Leiden: E. J. Brill, 1978. [HARRIS 1]

—— *The Substance of Spinoza*. Atlantic Heights, NJ: Humanities Press International, 1995. [HARRIS 2]

Hosler, John, *Leibniz's Moral Philosophy*. London: Duckworth, 1975. [HOSLER]

Lloyd, Genevieve, 'Spinoza's Environmental Ethics'. *Inquiry*, 32 (1980). [LLOYD 2]

—— , *Part of Nature: Self-Knowledge in Spinoza's Ethics*. Ithaca, NY: Cornell University Press, 1994. [LLOYD 1]

Matheron, Alexandre, *Le Christ et le salut des ignorants chez Spinoza*. Paris: Aubier-Montaigne, 1971. [MATHERON]

—— *Individu et Communauté chez Spinoza*. Paris: Les Éditions de Minuit, 1988.

Matthews, Freya, *The Ecological Self*. London: Routledge, 1991. [MATTHEWS]

Nadler, Stephen, *Spinoza's Heresy: Immortality and the Human Mind*. Oxford: Clarendon Press, 2001. [NADLER HERESY]

Naess, Arne, 'The Shallow and the Deep, Long-Range Ecology Movement, A Summary'. *Inquiry*, 16 (1973). [NAESS 1]

—— 'Spinoza and Ecology'. In Sigrid Hessing (ed.), *Speculum Spinozanum (1677–1977)*, Boston: Routledge and Kegan Paul, 1977. [NAESS 2]

Parkinson, G. H. R., *Spinoza's Theory of Knowledge*. Oxford: Clarendon Press, 1954. [PARKINSON]

Pollock, Sir Frederick, *Spinoza: His Life and Philosophy*, 2nd edn. London: Duckworth and Co., 1899. [POLLOCK]

Roth, Leon, *Spinoza*. London: George Allen and Unwin Ltd., 1929 and 1954. [ROTH]

Sprigge, T. L. S., *Theories of Existence*. Hamondsworth: Pelican Books, 1984.

—— *On the Significance of Spinoza's Determinism*. Medelingen vanwege het Spinozahuis, 58. Leiden: Brill, 1988.

—— 'Is Spinozism a Religion?' In *Studia Spinozana*, xi (1995).

Strauss, Leo, 'How to Study Spinoza's *Tractatus Theologico-Politicus*.' In *Persecution and the Art of Writing*, Chicago: University of Chicago Press, 1952. [STRAUSS]

Thomas, James, *Intuition and Reality: A Study of the Attributes of Substance in the Absolute Idealism of Spinoza*. Aldershot: Ashgate Publishing Ltd., 1999.

Yovel, Yirmiyahu, *Spinoza and Other Heretics*, i: *The Marrano of Reason*. Princeton: Princeton University Press, 1989. [YOVEL HERETICS]

—— (ed.), *God and Nature: Spinoza's Metaphysics*. Leiden, etc.: E. J. Brill, 1991. (Collection of papers by various hands.) [YOVEL 1991]

Ze'en, Levy, 'On Some Early Responses to Spinoza's Philosophy in Jewish Thought'. In *Studia Spinozana*, vi (1990). Of special interest to Jewish readers.

5. Other works referred to

Armstrong, David, *A Materialist Theory of the Mind*. London: Routledge & Kegan Paul, 1968.

Bradley, F. H., *Appearance and Reality*. Oxford: Clarendon Press, 1897. [BRADLEY]

Broad, C. D., *Scientific Thought*. London: Routledge & Kegan Paul, 1923. [BROAD]

Dennett, Daniel C., *Consciousness Explained*. Boston: Little, Brown and Company, 1991.

Damasio, Antonio, *Looking for Spinoza*. London: William Heinemann, 2003.

Hartshorne, Charles, *The Logic of Perfection*. Chicago: Open Court, 1962.

—— *Creative Synthesis and Philosophic Method*. London: SCM Press, 1970.

Leslie, John, *Infinite Minds*. Oxford: Clarendon Press, 2001. [LESLIE]

Sprigge, T. L. S., *The Vindication of Absolute Idealism*. Edinburgh: Edinburgh University Press, 1983.

—— *James and Bradley: American Truth and British Reality*. Chicago: Open Court, 1993.

—— 'Hartshorne on the Past'. In Lewis E. Hahn (ed.), *The Philosophy of Charles Hartshorne*, La Salle, Ill.: Open Court, 1991, 397–414.

—— 'The Unreality of Time'. *Proceedings of the Aristotelian Society*, 92 (1991/2), 1–19.

Whitehead, A. N., *Process and Reality*, first publ. 1929; corrected edn., New York: The Free Press, 1978.

Chapter 3. Hegel

1. Chief works of Kant in English translation

Critique of Pure Reason, trans. Norman Kemp Smith. London: Macmillan and Co., 1963.

Critique of Practical Reason and Other Works, trans. T. K. Abbott. London: Longmans, Green and Co., 1948.

Critique of Judgement, trans. James Creed Merideth. Oxford: Clarendon Press, 1952.

Religion within the Boundaries of Mere Reason, trans. Allen Wood *et al*. Cambridge: Cambridge University Press, 1998.

2. Chief works of Hegel in English translation

Early Theological Writings, trans. T. M. Knox. Philadelphia: University of Pennsylvania Press, 1948. [ETW] (This has a helpful introduction by Richard Kroner.)

'The Tübingen Essay' (1793), trans. H. S. Harris in his *Hegel's Development towards the Sunlight* (see below), 481–508.

The Phenomenology of Spirit, trans. A. V. Miller. Oxford: Oxford University Press, 1977. [PHENOMENOLOGY]

The Phenomenology of Mind, trans J. Baillie. London: Allen & Unwin, 1949. [PHENOMENOLOGY]

(The former translation of Hegel's *Phänomenologie des Geistes* is probably the more accurate, but the latter has some helpful editorial apparatus.)

Hegel's Introductory Lectures on Aesthetics, trans. Bernard Bosanquet, with introduction by Michael Inwood. Harmondsworth: Penguin, 1993. (References in roman numerals to very short sections.) This is Hegel's introduction to the next entry which is a translation of lectures given by Hegel in 1823, 1826, and 1828–9 and first published (posthumously) in German, in 1835. Bosanquet's translation was first published in 1886. [INTRODUCTORY AESTHETICS]

Hegel, Aesthetics: Lectures on Fine Art, trans. T. M. Knox, i. Oxford: Clarendon Press, 1975. [FINE ART]

The Philosophy of History, trans. J. Sibree. New York: Dover Publications, Inc., 1956. [HEGEL HISTORY]

Lectures on the Philosophy of Religion: One-Volume Edition, The Lectures of 1827, ed. Peter C. Hodgson, trans. R. F. Brown *et al.* Berkeley: University of California Press, 1988. [LECTURES 1827]

The Christian Religion: Lectures on the Philosophy of Religion, part III: *The Revelatory, Consummate, Absolute Religion*, ed. and trans. Peter C. Hodgson. Missonla, Mont.: Scholars Press, 1979. [THE CHRISTIAN RELIGION]

The Science of Logic, trans. A. V. Miller. London: Allen & Unwin, 1969. (1st edn. 1812–13; rev. edn. 1832). [GREATER LOGIC]

3. The Encyclopaedia

I *THE LOGIC OF HEGEL, translated from the Encyclopaedia of the Philosophical Sciences* by William Wallace, 1st edn. 1873; 2nd edn. 1892. Oxford: Oxford University Press. 2nd edn. rev. and augmented. Oxford: Clarendon Press, 1892 and 1968. [ENCYCLOPAEDIA I]

II *HEGEL'S PHILOSOPHY OF NATURE, being Part Two of the Encyclopaedia of the Philosophical Sciences* (1830) trans. from Nicolin and Pöggeler's edition, 1959, and from the Zusätze in Michelet's text, 1847, by A. V. Miller, with a foreword by J. N. Findlay. [ENCYCLOPAEDIA II]

HEGEL'S *PHILOSOPHY OF MIND, being Part Three of the Encyclopaedia of the Philosophical Sciences* (1830), trans. William Wallace together with the Zusätze of 1825, trans. A. V. Miller. Oxford: Clarendon Press, 1971. [ENCYCLOPAEDIA III]

Bibliography

4. Hegel in German

Enzyklopädie der philosophischen im Grundrisse. In Sämtliche Werke, vi, ed. Hermann Glockner. Stuttgart: Frommans Verlag, 1968– .

Theologische Jugendschriften *nach den Handschriften der Kgl. Bibliothek in Berlin*, ed. Herman Nohl. Tübingen: J. C. B. Mohr, [NOHL] 1907.

5. Biography

Pinkard, Terry, *Hegel: A Biography.* Washington: Georgetown University Press; Cambridge: Cambridge University Press, 2000. [PINKARD]

6. Commentaries and other references

Bradley, F. H., *Ethical Studies*, 2nd edn. Oxford: Clarendon Press, 1927.

—— *Appearance and Reality: A Metaphysical Essay.* Oxford: Clarendon Press, 1930 (1st edn. 1893; 2nd edn. 1897).

—— *The Principles of Logic*, 2 vols., 2nd edn. Oxford: Oxford University Press, 1883 and reprints. [BRADLEY LOGIC]

Findlay, J. N., *Hegel: A Re-Examination.* London: George Allen & Unwin Ltd., 1958. [FINDLAY]

Beiser, Frederick C. (ed.), *The Cambridge Companion to Hegel.* Cambridge: Cambridge University Press, 1993. [HEGEL COMPANION]

Green, T. H., *Collected Works.* London: Longmans, 1888.

Harris, H. S., *Hegel's Development towards the Sunlight, 1770–1801.* Oxford: Clarendon Press, 1972.

McTaggart, J. M. E., *A Commentary on Hegel's Logic.* Cambridge: Cambridge University Press, 1910.

Reardon, B. M. G., *Hegel's Philosophy of Religion.* London: Macmillan, 1977. [REARDON]

Reyburn, Hugh A., *The Ethical Theory of Hegel: A Study of the Philosophy of Right.* Oxford: Clarendon Press, 1921.

Richter, Melvin, *The Politics of Conscience: T. H. Green and his Age.* London: Weidenfeld & Nicolson, 1964. [RICHTER]

Royce, Josiah, *Lectures on Modern Idealism.* New Haven and London: Yale University Press, 1964 (first publ. 1919). [MODERN IDEALISM]

Seth, Andrew, *Man's Place in the Cosmos and Other Essays.* Edinburgh: Blackwood, 1897; 2nd rev. and enlarged edn. 1902). [SETH]

Sprigge, T. L. S., 'Personal and Impersonal Identity.' *Mind*, 97/385 (Jan. 1988), 29–49.

Stace, W. T., *The Philosophy of Hegel.* New York: Dover Publications Inc., 1955 (first published 1924 by Macmillan and Co. Inc.).

Taylor, Charles, *Hegel.* Cambridge: Cambridge University Press, 1975. [TAYLOR]

Williamson, Raymond Keith, *Introduction to Hegel's Philosophy of Religion.* Albany, NY: State University of New York Press, 1984. [WILLIAMSON]

Yerkes, James, *The Christology of Hegel*. Missoula, Mont.: Scholars Press, 1978. [YERKES]

Chapter 4. Kierkegaard

1. English translations of cited or used works of Kierkegaard

A Kierkegaard Anthology, ed. Robert Bretall. Oxford: Oxford University Press; London: Geoffrey Cumberledge, 1947.

A Kierkegaard Reader: Texts and Narratives, ed. Roger Poole and Henrik Stangerup. London: Fourth Estate, *c*.1989.

Christian Discourses, trans. W. Lowrie. Princeton: Princeton University Press, 1971. [CHRISTIAN DISCOURSES]

Concluding Unscientific Postscript to Philosophical Fragments by Johannes Climacus, ed. and trans. with introduction and notes by Howard V. Hong and Edna H. Hong, 2 vols. Princeton: Princeton University Press, 1992. [POSTSCRIPT]

Either/Or, A Fragment of Life, ed. Victor Eremita, ed. and trans. Alastair Hannay. Harmondsworth: Penguin Books, 1992.

Fear and Trembling: Dialectical Lyric by Johannes de Silentio, trans. with an introduction by Alastair Hannay. Harmondsworth: Penguin Books, 1985.

The Concept of Anxiety: A Simple Psychologically Orienting Deliberation on the Dogmatic Issue of Hereditary Sin, trans. R. Thomte and A. B. Anderson. Princeton: Princeton University Press, 1980; also trans. W. Lowrie as *The Concept of Dread*. Princeton: Princeton University Press, 1957.

Philosophical Fragments, by Johannes Climacus, ed. and trans. Howard V. Hong and Edna H. Hong. Princeton: Princeton University Press, 1985. [FRAGMENTS]

Philosophical Fragments, trans. David F. Swenson. Princeton: Princeton University Press, 1962. [FRAGMENTS SWENSON]

The Works of Love (1847), ed. and trans. Howard V. Hong and Edna H. Hong. Princeton: Princeton University Press, 1955; New York: Harper & Brothers, 1962. [LOVE]

Training in Christianity, trans. Walter Lowrie. Oxford: Oxford University Press, 1941. [TRAINING]

2. Commentaries on Kierkegaard

Elrod, John W., *Kierkegaard and Christendom*. Princeton: Princeton University Press, 1981. [ELROD]

Fabro, Cornelio, *Some of Kierkegaard's Main Theories*, ed. Marie Mikulova Thulstrup. Copenhagen: Reitzel, 1988.

Gouwens, David Jay, *Kierkegaard as Religious Thinker*. Cambridge: Cambridge University Press, 1996.

Hannay, Alastair, *Kierkegaard*. London: Routledge & Kegan Paul, 1982. [HANNAY]

—— *Kierkegaard: A Biography*. Cambridge: Cambridge University Press, 2001.

Hannay, Alastair, and Marino, Gordon D. (eds.), *The Cambridge Companion to Kierkegaard*. Cambridge and New York: Cambridge University Press, 1998.

Quin, Philip L., 'Kierkegaard's Christian Ethics'. In *Cambridge Companion to Kierkegaard*, 349–75.

Walker, Jeremy D. B., *Kierkegaard: The Descent into God*. Kingston, Ont.: McGill–Queen's University Press, 1985.

Westphal, Merold, 'Kierkegaard and Hegel'. In *Cambridge Companion to Kierkegaard*.

3. Other

Harris, H. S., (transl.) 'The Tübingen Essay of 1793'. In *idem, Hegel's Development towards the Sunlight* (see below), 481–508. [TÜBINGEN ESSAY]

Hegel, G. W. F., *The Christian Religion*, ed. and trans. Peter C. Hodgson. Missoula, Mont.: Scholars Press, 1979. [THE CHRISTIAN RELIGION]

Funk, F. W., *et al.*, *The Five Gospels*, trans. and ed. R.W. Funk, F. W. Hoover, and the Jesus Seminar. New York: Scribner, 1993.

Santayana, George, *The Realm of Essence*. London: Constable and Co., 1927. [ESSENCE]

—— *The Realm of Matter*. London: Constable and Co., 1930. [MATTER]

Spinoza, Baruch, *Treatise on the Emendation of the Intellect* (various editions and translations). [EMENDATION]

—— *The Letters*, trans. Samuel Shirley. Indianapolis and Cambridge: Hackett Publishing Co., 1995. [SPINOZA LETTERS]

Chapter 5. Green

1. Works of T. H. Green

Collected Works of T. H. Green, ed. with a new introduction by Peter Nicholson. [The first four volumes are reprints of *Works of Thomas Hill Green*, ed. R. L. Nettleship. London: Longmans, 1888.] [WORKS]. Vol. 4 consists of 'Prolegomena to Ethics' and is referenced in text as PROLEGOMENA followed by section number.

2. Commentaries

Carter, Matt, *T. H. Green and the Development of Ethical Socialism*. Exeter: Imprint Academic, 2003.

Dimova-Cookson, Maria, *T. H. Green's Moral and Political Philosophy*. Basingstoke: Palgrave, 2001.

Richter, Melvin, *The Politics of Conscience: T. H. Green and his Age*. London: Weidenfeld & Nicolson, 1964. [RICHTER]

Sell, Alan P., *Philosophical Idealism and Christian Belief*. Cardiff: University of Wales Press, 1995. (Besides T. H. Green himself, this book examines the relationship to Christianity of Edward Caird, J. R. Illingworth, Henry Jones, Andrew Seth (a.k.a. A. S. Pringle-Pattison), C. C. J. Webb, and A. E. Taylor. Highly informative, though it judges these philosophers negatively according to how far they are from orthodox Christianity.)

Sidgwick, Henry, *Lectures on the Ethics of T. H. Green, H. Spencer and J. Martineau.* London: Macmillan, 1902. [LECTURES]

Simhony, Avital, 'T. H. Green and Henry Sidgwick on the "Profoundest Problems of Ethics" '. In W. J. Mander (ed.), *Anglo-American Idealism, 1865–1927*, Westport, Conn., and London: Greenwood Press, 2000, 33–50.

Thomas, Geoffrey, *The Moral Philosophy of T. H. Green.* Oxford: Clarendon Press, 1987.

Tyler, Colin, 'The Much-Maligned and Misunderstood Eternal Consciousness', *Bradley Studies* 9/2 (Autumn 2003), 126–38.

Wempe, Ben, *Beyond Equality: A Study of T. H. Green's Theory of Positive Freedom.* Delft: Eburon, 1986. [WEMPE]

3. Other

Butler, Joseph, *Fifteen Sermons Preached at the Rolls Chapel.* London: 1726. Various modern editions. [BUTLER]

Caird, Edward, *The Evolution of Religion.* Glasgow: James Maclehose and Sons, 1893, and later editions. [EVOLUTION]

Caird, John, *An Introduction to the Philosophy of Religion.* Glasgow: James Maclehose and Sons, 1910 (first pub. 1880).

Holland, Henry Scott, *A Bundle of Memories.* London: Wells, Gardner, Darton, 1915.

Jones, Sir Henry, and Muirhead, John Henry, *The Life and Philosophy of Edward Caird.* Glasgow: Maclehose, Jackson, and Co., 1921.

McTaggart, J. M. E., *The Nature of Existence,* ii. Cambridge: Cambridge University Press, 1927. [MCTAGGART]

Nicholson, Peter, *The Political Philosophy of the British Idealists.* Cambridge: Cambridge University Press, 1990.

Peterson, William S., *Victorian Heretic: Mrs Humphry Ward's Robert Elsmere.* New York: Humanities Press; Leicester: Leicester University Press, 1976.

Sidgwick, Henry, *The Methods of Ethics,* 7th edn. London: Macmillan and Co., 1930 (1st edn. 1874). [METHODS]

Stirling, J. H., *The Secret of Hegel: Being the Hegelian System in Origin, Principle, Form, and Matter.* London: Longman, 1865.

Ward, Mrs Humphry, *Robert Elsmere,* 3 vols. London: Smith, Elder, 1888. (The most convenient modern edition is that of The World's Classics, Oxford: Oxford University Press, 1987.)

Chapter 6. Bosanquet

I. Writings Cited or Used by Bernard Bosanquet

'Our Right to Regard Evil as a Mystery'. *Mind,* 8 (1883), 419–21.

Bibliography

Knowledge and Reality: A Critique of Mr. F. H. Bradley's 'Principles of Logic'. London: Kegan Paul, Trench, and Co., 1885.

Essays and Addresses. London: Swan Sonnenschein and Co., Paternoster Square, 1889. [E&A]

The Civilization of Christendom and Other Studies. London: Swan Sonennschein and Co., Paternoster Square, 1893. [CIVILIZATION]

The Essentials of Logic. London: Macmillan and Co., 1895. [THE ESSENTIALS]

The Philosophical Theory of the State, 4th edn. London: Macmillan, 1923 (1st edn. 1899). [THE STATE]

Logic or the Morphology of Knowledge, 2nd edn. London: Oxford University Press, 1911 (1st edn. 1888). [LOGIC]

The Principle of Individuality and Value. London: Macmillan, 1912. [PIV]

The Value and Destiny of the Individual. London: Macmillan, 1913. [VDI]

Social and International Ideals: Being Studies in Patriotism. London: Macmillan, 1917.

The Meeting of Extremes in Contemporary Philosophy. London: Macmillan and Co., Ltd., 1921.

Some Suggestions in Ethics. London: Macmillan, 1918.

Implication and Linear Inference. London: Macmillan and Co., Ltd., 1920. Repr. New York: Klaus, 1968. [RR]

What Religion Is. London: Macmillan, 1920. [RELIGION]

'Life and Philosophy'. In J. H. Muirhead (ed.), *Contemporary British Philosophy*, London: Allen & Unwin, 1924. [LIFE AND PHILOSOPHY]

Science and Philosophy and Other Essays. London: G. Allen & Unwin, 1927.

A History of Aesthetic, 2nd edn. London: George Allen & Unwin, 1934.

(Ed. and contributor), *Aspects of the Social Problem*. London and New York: Macmillan and Co., 1895.

2. Writings By F. H. Bradley

The Principles of Logic, 2nd edn. rev. with comments and terminal essays, 2 vols. Oxford: Oxford University Press, 1922; corrected impression 1928 (1st edn. 1883).

Ethical Studies. Oxford: Oxford University Press, 1927 (1st edn. 1876). [ETHICAL STUDIES]

Appearance and Reality: A Metaphysical Essay. Oxford: Clarendon Press, 1930 (1st edn. 1893; 2nd edn. 1897). [APPEARANCE]

Collected Works of F. H. Bradley, iv: *Selected Correspondence 1872–1904;* v: Selected Correspondence 1905–1924. Bristol: Thoemmes Press, 1999. [BRADLEY LETTERS 4 and 5]

3. Commentaries, etc.

Bosanquet, Helen, *Bernard Bosanquet: A Short Account of his Life*. London: Macmillan and Co., 1924. [A SHORT ACCOUNT]

Carter, Matt, *T. H. Green and the Development of Ethical Socialism*. Exeter: Imprint Academic, 2003.

Hobhouse, L., *The Metaphysical Theory of the State: A Criticism*. London: George Allen & Unwin Ltd., 1918.

McBriar, A. M., *An Edwardian Mixed Doubles: The Bosanquets versus the Webbs: A Study in British Social Policy 1890–1929*. Oxford: Clarendon Press, 1987. [MIXED DOUBLES]

Muirhead, J. H. (ed.), *Bernard Bosanquet and his Friends*. London: George Allen & Unwin Ltd., 1935. [BOSANQUET AND FRIENDS]

Richter, Melvin, *The Politics of Conscience: T. H. Green and his Age*. London: Weidenfeld & Nicolson, 1964. [RICHTER]

Stock, Guy (ed.), *Appearance versus Reality: New Essays on Bradley's Metaphysics*. Oxford: Clarendon Press, 1998.

Sweet, William, *Idealism and Rights: The Social Ontology of Human Rights in the Political Thought of Bernard Bosanquet*. Lanham, Md.: University Press of America, c.1997. [SWEET]

—— 'Bernard Bosanquet and the Nature of Religious Belief'. In W. J. Mander (ed.), *Anglo-American Idealism, 1865–1927*, Westport, Conn., and London: Greenwood Press, 2000.

Tcheng, Houang Kia, *De l'Humanisme à l'Absolutisme: L'Évolution de la Pensée Religieuse du Neo-Hegelian Anglais, Bernard Bosanquet*. Paris: Libraire Philosophique J. Vrin, 1954. [TCHENG]

4. Other Works

Bixley, J. S., 'Whitehead's Philosophy of Religion', in SCHILPP.

Bosanquet, Helen, *The Standard of Life*. London: Macmillan and Co., 1906. [THE STANDARD]

—— *The Strength of the People: A Study in Social Economics*. London and New York: Macmillan, 1902. [STRENGTH]

—— *Bernard Bosanquet: A short Account of his Life*. London: Macmillan & Co., 1924. [SHORT ACCOUNT]

Findlay, J. N., *Hegel: A Re-Examination*. London: George Allen & Unwin Ltd., 1970 (1st published 1958).

Honderich, Ted, *Consciousness*. Edinburgh: Edinburgh University Press, 2004. [CONSCIOUSNESS]

James, William, *Pragmatism: A New Name for Some Old Ways of Thinking*. London: Longmans, Green and Co., 1937. [PRAGMATISM]

—— *The Meaning of Truth*. Cambridge, Mass.: Harvard University Press, 1975. [MEANING OF TRUTH]

Keats, John, *Letters of John Keats*. Oxford: Oxford University Press, 1954. [KEATS]

Mackey, James P., *Jesus: The Man and the Myth*. London: SCM Press, 1979. [MACKEY]

Moore, G. E., *Principia Ethica*. Cambridge: Cambridge University Press, 1903.

Phillips, D. Z., *Faith and Philosophical Iuquiry*. London: Routledge & Kegan Paul, 1970.

Royce, Josiah, *The Religious Aspect of Philosophy*. Gloucester, Mass.: Peter Smith, 1965 (1st published 1885).

—— *The Spirit of Modern Philosophy*. New York: Norton and Co., 1967 (1st published 1892).

—— *The World and the Individual*, 1st and 2nd ser. New York: Dover Publications Inc., 1959 (1st published 1899 and 1901).

Schrödinger, Erwin, *What is Life?* and *Mind and Matter*. Cambridge: Cambridge University Press, 1969. [SCHRÖDINGER]

Schweitzer, Albert, *The Quest of the Historical Jesus*. Baltimore and London: The Johns Hopkins University Press, 1998 (1st English edn. 1910).

Sprigge, T. L. S., *James and Bradley: British Reality and American Truth*. Chicago: Open Court, 1993. [JAMES AND BRADLEY]

—— *The Vindication of Absolute Idealism*. Edinburgh: Edinburgh University Press, 1983.

—— 'The Unreality of Time' (Presidential Address). *Proceedings of the Aristotelian Society*, 92 (1992 1/2), 1–19.

—— 'Hartshorne on the Past'. In Lewis E. Hahn (ed.), *The Philosophy of Charles Hartshorne*, Library of Living Philosophers, La Salle, Ill.: Open Court Press, 1991, 397–414.

Taylor, A. E., *The Elements of Metaphysics*. London: Methuen, 1903 and 1961.

Templeton, Douglas A., *The New Testament as True Fiction*. Sheffield: Sheffield Academic Press, 1999. [TEMPLETON]

Whitehead, A. N., *Adventures in Ideas*. Cambridge: Cambridge University Press, 1961 (1st publ. in 1933). [ADVENTURES]

Chapter 7. Royce

1A. Works of Josiah Royce

The Religious Aspect of Philosophy: A Critique of the Bases of Conduct and of Faith. Boston and New York: Houghton, Mifflin & Co., 1885. [RELIGIOUS ASPECT]

The Feud of Oakfield Creek: A Novel of California Life. Boston and New York: Houghton, Mifflin and Co., 1887.

The Spirit of Modern Philosophy: An Essay in the Form of Lectures. Boston and New York: Houghton, Mifflin and Co., 1892. [SPIRIT]

Studies of Good and Evil: A Series of Essays upon the Problems of Philosophy and of Life. New York: D. Appleton and Co. 1898. Reprinted in unaltered form in Hamden, Conn.: Archon Books, 1964.

The World and the Individual. New York: Macmillan. First Series: *The Four Historical Conceptions of Being*, 1899. [W&I 1]

The World and the Individual. New York: Macmillan. Second Series: *Nature, Man, and the Moral Order*, 1901. [W&I 2]

Race Questions, Provincialism and Other American Problems. New York: Macmillan Co., 1908. Reprinted in Freeport, NY: Books for Libraries Press, 1967.

The Philosophy of Loyalty. New York: Macmillan Co., 1908. Translated into French, Italian, and Spanish. [LOYALTY]

William James and Other Essays on the Philosophy of Life. New York: Macmillan Co., 1911.

The Sources of Religious Insight. New York: C. Scribner's Sons, 1912. (Lectures delivered at Lake Forest College.) [SOURCES]

The Problem of Christianity, with an introduction by John E. Smith. Chicago and London: University of Chicago Press, 1968. This is a reprint of *The Problem of Christianity,* 2 vols. New York: Macmillan Co., 1913. i: *The Christian Doctrine of Life;* ii: *The Real World and the Christian Ideas.* (Lectures delivered at the Lowell Institute in Boston, and at Manchester College, Oxford.) [POC]

Fugitive Essays, ed. Jacob Loewenberg. Cambridge, Mass.: Harvard University Press, 1920.

Lectures on Modern Idealism. New Haven and London: Yale University Press, 1964 (first publ. 1919).

The Letters of Josiah Royce, ed. with an introduction by John Clendenning. Chicago: University of Chicago Press, 1970.

1B. Joint Authorship

The Conception of God: A Philosophical Discussion Concerning the Nature of the Divine Idea as a Demonstrable Reality, by Josiah Royce, Joseph Le Conte, George Holmes Howison, and Sidney Edward Mezes. New York: Macmillan Co.; London: Macmillan & Co. Ltd., 1897. This is a reprint of a volume published in 1895 consisting of lectures given by Le Conte, Howison, Mezes, and Royce on a celebratory visit of Royce to his Alma Mater, but with a long supplementary essay by Royce entitled 'The Absolute and the Individual'. I particularly recommend the lecture by Mezes.

2. Biography of Royce

Clendenning, John, *The Life and Thought of Josiah Royce,* rev. expanded edn. Nashville: Vanderbilt University Press, 1998. [CLENDENNING]

3. Other

Evans, Gareth, *The Varieties of Reference,* ed. John McDowell. Oxford: Clarendon Press, 1982.

James, William, *The Principles of Psychology,* i. New York: Holt, 1890. [PRINCIPLES]

—— *The Varieties of Religious Experience.* New York and London: Longmans, Green, 1902 (and later editions).

—— *Pragmatism: A New Names for Some Old Ways of Thinking.* Longmans, Green and Co. Inc., 1907, and many subsequent impresssions. [PRAGMATISM]

James, William, *Essays in Radical Empiricism*. New York: Longmans, Green and Co., 1922. [ERE]

Kripke, Saul A., *Naming and Necessity*, rev. edn. Cambridge, Mass.: Harvard University Press, 1980.

McGinn, Colin, *Mental Content*. Oxford: Blackwell, 1989.

Perry, Ralph Barton, *The Thought and Character of William James*, 2 vols. Boston: Little, Brown and Company, 1935. [PERRY]

Pettit, Philipp, and McDowell, John (eds.), *Subject, Thought, and Context*. Oxford: Clarendon Press, 1986.

Schilpp, Paul Arthur (ed.), *The Philosophy of C. I. Lewis*, 1st edn. La Salle, Ill.: Open Court, 1968.

Sprigge, T. L. S., *James and Bradley: American Truth and British Reality*. Chicago: Open Court Press, 1993. [JAMES AND BRADLEY]

—— 'Hartshorne on the Past'. In Lewis E. Halan (ed.), *The Philosophy of Charles Hartshorne*, La Salle, Ill.: Open Court, 1991, 397–414.

—— 'The Unreality of Time'. *Proceedings of the Aristotehan Society*, 92 (1991/2), 1–19.

Woodfield, A. (ed.), *Thought and Object: Essays on Intentionality*. Oxford: Clarendon Press, 1982.

Chapter 8. Process Thought

1. The Library of Living Philosophers

These two volumes in this series include chapters by various authors about each philosopher.

The Philosophy of A. N. Whitehead, ed. P. A. Schilpp. New York: Tudor Publishing, 1948. [SCHILPP]

The Philosophy of Charles Hartshorne, ed. Lewis E. Hahn. La Salle, Ill.: Open Court, 1991. [HAHN]. This includes Hartshorne's replies to his critics.

2. Whitehead

Whitehead only arrived at the metaphysical views which are examined in my chapter late in life, after he settled in the USA in 1924 (at Harvard). Before that he published an enormous number of works on mathematics and the philosophy thereof and the philosophy of science. Especially notable of course is *Principia Mathematica*, written in collaboration with Bertrand Russell.

For his final metaphysical position the key works, with dates of first publication, are as follows.

Science and the Modern World. London: Collins, Fontana Books 1975 (1st published by Cambridge University Press in 1925). [SMW]

Religion in the Making. Cambridge: Cambridge University Press, 1926. [RIM]

Process and Reality: An Essay in Cosmology (corrected edition), ed. D. R. Griffin and D. W. Sherburne. New York: The Free Press, 1978. (This is a carefully proofread version of the original edition of the work which was published in 1929 by Cambridge University Press.) N.B. My references give the pagination of the earlier edition after that of the later one. [PR]

Adventures of Ideas. Cambridge: Cambridge University Press, 1961 (1st published in 1933).

Modes of Thought. Cambridge: Cambridge University Press, 1968 (1st published in 1938). [MODES]

See also:

Lowe, Victor, *Alfred North Whitehead: The Man and his Work*. Baltimore: Johns Hopkins University Press, 2 vols., 1985 and 1990. [LOWE]

Sherburne, Donald (ed.), *A Guide to Process and Reality*. Bloomington, Ind.: Indiana University Press, 1975 (1st published 1966).

Price, Lucien, *Dialogues of Alfred North Whitehead*. London: M. Reinhardt, [1954]. [DIALOGUES]

Sessions, William Lad, *et al.*, *Two Process Philosophers: Hartshorne's Encounter with Whitehead*, ed. Lewis S. Ford. Tallahassee, Fla.: American Academy of Religion, 1973. [TWO PROCESS PHILOSOPHERS]

3. Hartshorne

The most significant works of Charles Hartshorne for my purposes here are the following.

Man's Vision of God and the Logic of Theism. Chicago: Willet Clark and Company, 1941; Lincoln, Nebr.: University of Nebraska Press, 1968; New York.: Harper and Brothers.

'Whitehead's Idea of God'. In SCHILPP, 545–6.

The Divine Relativity: A Social Conception of God. New Haven: Yale University Press, 1948.

The Logic of Perfection. La Salle, Ill.: Open Court, 1965. [PERFECTION]

Anselm's Discovery. La Salle, Ill.: Open Court, 1965.

Creative Synthesis and Philosophic Method. London: SCM Press, 1970. [SYNTHESIS]

Born to Sing: An Interpretation and World Survey of Bird Song. Bloomington, Ind.: Indiana University Press, 1973. [BORN TO SING]

Aquinas to Whitehead: Seven Centuries of Metaphysics of Religion. Milwaukee: Marquette University Press, 1976.

Creativity in American Philosophy. Albany, NY: State University of New York Press, 1984.

4. Commentaries and Developments

Christian, William A., *An Interpretation of Whitehead's Metaphysics*. New Haven: Yale University Press, 1959. [CHRISTIAN]

Ely, Stephen Lee, *The Religious Availability of Whitehead's God: A Critical Analysis*. Madison: University of Wisconsin Press, 1942.

Ford, Lewis S., *The Emergence of Whitehead's Metaphysics, 1925–1929*. Albany, NY: State University of New York Press, 1984.

Grange, Joseph, *Nature: An Environmental Cosmology*. Albany, NY: State University of New York Press, 1997. [GRANGE]

Griffin, David, 'Hartshorne's Differences from Whitehead'. In TWO PROCESS PHILO-SOPHERS, 40–1.

McHenry, Leemon, *Whitehead and Bradley: A Comparative Analysis*. Albany, NY: State University of New York Press, 1992. [MCHENRY]

Palmer, Clare, *Environmental Ethics and Process Thinking*. Oxford: Clarendon Press, 1998. [PALMER]

Sessions, William Lad, *et al.,*: *Process Philosophers: Hartshorne's Encounter with White-head*. Tallahasee, Fla.: American Academy of Religion, 1973. [TWO PROCESS PHILO-SOPHERS]

Skutch, Alexander F., 'Bird Song and Philosophy'. In *The Philosophy of Charles Hartshorne*, 72–6.

5. William James

For what may be called the process philosophy of William James, see especially: *The Principles of Psychology*, 2 vols. London: Macmillan and Co., 1901 (1st published 1890).

A Pluralistic Universe. New York: Longmans, Green and Co., 1909.

Some Problems of Philosophy. New York: Longmans, Green and Co., 1911.

6. Recent Developments of Process Thought

Cobb, John B. jun., *A Christian Natural Theology: Based on the Thought of Alfred North Whitehead*. Philadelphia: Westminster Press, 1965.

Griffin, David Ray, *God, Power, and Evil: A Process Theodicy*. Philadelphia: Westminster Press, 1976.

—— *Unsnarling the World-Knot: Consciousness, Freedom, and the Mind–Body Problem*. Lanham, Md.: University Press of America, 1991.

7. Other References

Bradley, F. H., *Essays on Truth and Reality*. Oxford: Clarendon Press, 1968 (1st published in 1914). [ETR]

—— *Selected Correspondence, 1872–1904. Collected Works*, iv. Bristol: Thoemmes Press, 1999. [BRADLEY CORRESPONDENCE 4]

Geach, Peter, *Logic Matters*. Berkeley: University of California Press, 1980.

Hamerton, Paul Gilbert, *Human Intercourse*. London: Macmillan and Co., 1884.

Parfit, David, *Reasons and Persons*. Oxford: Clarendon Press, 1984. [PARFIT]

Royce, Josiah, *The World and the Individual*. New York: Macmillan, 1899. [W&I 1]

—— *Nature, Man, and the Moral Order*. New York: Macmillan, 1901. [W&I 2]

Sherburne, Donald (ed.), *A Key to Whitehead's Process and Reality.* Bloomington, Ind., and London: University of Indiana Press, 1975. [SHERBURNE]

Sprigge, T. L. S., *James and Bradley: American Truth and British Reality.* Chicago: Open Court, 1993. [JAMES AND BRADLEY]

Chapter 9.   Pantheistic Idealism

1. References

Abbott, Edwin A., *Flatland: A Romance of Many Dimensions*, 2nd edn. Harmondsworth: Penguin Books, 1998 (1st publ. 1884). [ABBOTT]

Hegel, G. W. F., *The Philosophy of History*, trans. J. Sibree. New York: Dover Publications, Inc., 1956. [HEGEL HISTORY]

Hinton, Charles H., *The Fourth Dimension.* London: S. Sonnenschein & Co. Ltd., 1904. [HINTON]

McHenry, Leemon, *Whitehead and Bradley: A Comparative Analysis.* Albany, NY: State University of New York Press, 1992. [W&B]

—— 'The Ontology of the Past: Whitehead and Santayana'. *Journal of Speculative Philosophy*, 14/3 (2000), 223–4. [THE PAST]

Sprigge, T. L. S., *The Vindication of Absolute Idealism.* Edinburgh: Edinburgh University Press, 1983. [VINDICATION]

—— 'The Unreality of Time'. *Proceedings of the Aristotelian Society*, 92 (1991/2), 1–19. [UNREALITY]

—— 'Is the Esse of Intrinsic Value Percipi? Pleasure, Pain and Value'. In A. O'Hear (ed.), *Philosophy*, Cambridge: Cambridge University Press, 2000, 119–40. [INTRINSIC VALUE]

—— 'Hartshorne on the Past'. In Lewis E. Hahn, ed., *The Philosophy of Charles Hartshorne*, Library of Living Philosophers, La Salle, Ill.: Open Court Press, 1991, 397–414. [HARTSHORNE]

—— *The Rational Foundations of Ethics.* London: Routledge & Kegan Paul, 1987. [FOUNDATIONS]

2. Absolute Idealism and the Environment

Limitations of space made it impossible for me to discuss the implications of pantheistic idealism for environmental ethics, so I append a list of my writings on these topics.

'Idealism, Humanism and the Environment'. In Paul Coates and Daniel D. Hutto (eds.), *Current Issues in Idealism*, Bristol: Thoemmes Press, 1996, 267–302.

'Respect for the Non-Human'. In T. D. J. Chappell (ed.), *The Philosophy of the Environment*, Edinburgh: Edinburgh University Press, 1997, 117–34.

'Non-Human Rights: An Idealist Perspective'. *Inquiry*, 27 (1984), 439–61.

Bibliography

'Are There Intrinsic Values in Nature?' *Journal for Applied Philosophy*, 4/1 (1987), 21–8. Repr. in Brenda Almond and Donald Hill (eds.), *Applied Philosophy: Morals and Metaphysics in Contemporary Debate*, London: Routledge, 1991, 37–44.

'Some Recent Positions in Environmental Philosophy Examined'. *Inquiry*, 34/1 (March 1991), 107–28.

'Pantheism'. *The Monist*, 80/2 (April 1997), 191–217.

Review of *Environmental Ethics and Process Thinking*, by Clare Palmer. *Environmental Ethics*, 22 (2000), 191–4.

Review of *Nature: An Environmental Cosmology*, by Joseph Grange, *Process Studies*, 29/3–4 (1998), 354–7.

I have also written quite a number of articles and pamphlets on animal rights, of which the most substantial are:

'Metaphysics, Physicalism and Animal Rights'. *Inquiry*, 22 (1979), 101–43.

'Vivisection, Morals, Medicine: Commentary from an Anti-Vivisectionist Philosopher'. *Journal of Medical Ethics*, 9/2 (June 1982), 98–101.

'The Ethics of Animal Use in Biomedicine'. In S. Garratini and D. W. van Bekkum (eds.), *The Importance of Animal Experimentation for Safety and Biomedical Research*, Dordrecht: Kluwer Academic Publishers, 1990, 17–28.

'Do Animals have Rights?'. Undated pamphlet published by *The St Andrew Animal Fund.*

'The Ethics of Animal Experimentation'. Undated pamphlet published by *Advocates for Animals.*

'Experimentation in Biomedical Research: A Critique'. In Raanon Gillon (ed.), *Principles of Health Care Ethics*, Chichester and New York: John Wiley and Sons, 1994, 1053–66.

3. Other

Bradley, F. H., *Collected Works*, ed. Carol A. Keene, iv: *Selected Correspondence, 1905–1925*. Bristol: Thoemmes Press, 1999.

Santayana, George, *The Sense of Beauty*. New York: Charles Scribner's Sons, 1896.

Whitehead, A. N., *Modes of Thought*. Cambridge: Cambridge University Press, 1968. [MODES]

—— *Process and Reality*, corrected edition, ed. D. R. Griffin and D. W. Sherburne. New York: Free Press, 1978. [PR]

Index

The Philosophy of George Berkeley

A FIFTEEN-VOLUME
FACSIMILE SERIES REPRODUCING
CLASSIC STUDIES AND INCLUDING
FOUR NEVER-BEFORE-PUBLISHED TITLES

EDITED BY
George Pitcher
Princeton University

A GARLAND SERIES